Modern Britain, 1750 to the Present

This wide-ranging introduction to the history of modern Britain extends from the eighteenth century to the present day. James Vernon's distinctive history is woven around an account of the rise, fall and reinvention of liberal ideas about how markets, governments and empires should work. It is a history that takes seriously the different experiences within the British Isles and the British Empire, and offers a global history of Britain. Instead of tracing how Britons made the modern world, Vernon shows how the world shaped the course of Britain's modern history. Richly illustrated with figures and maps, the book features textboxes (on particular people, places and sources), further reading guides, highlighted key terms and a glossary. A supplementary online package includes additional primary sources, discussion questions and further reading suggestions, including useful links. This textbook is an essential resource for introductory courses on the history of modern Britain.

James Vernon is Professor of History at the University of California, Berkeley. He is the author of *Politics and the People* (1993), *Hunger: A Modern History* (2007) and *Distant Strangers: How Britain Became Modern* (2014), and the editor of *Rereading the Constitution* (1996), *The Peculiarities of Liberal Modernity in Imperial Britain* (2011) and the 'Berkeley Series in British Studies' for the University of California Press. He is also on the editorial boards of *Social History*, *Twentieth Century British History* and *Journal of British Studies*.

The Cambridge History of Britain is an innovative new textbook series covering the whole of British history from the breakdown of Roman power to the present day. The series is aimed at first-year undergraduates and above and volumes in the series will serve both as indispensable works of synthesis and as original interpretations of Britain's past. Each volume will offer an accessible survey of political, social, cultural and economic history, charting the changing shape of Britain as a result of the gradual integration of the four kingdoms and Britain's increasing interaction and exchange with Europe and the wider world. Each volume will also feature boxes, illustrations, maps, timelines and guides to further reading as well as a companion website with further primary source and illustrative materials.

VOLUMES IN THE SERIES

I *Early Medieval Britain*

II *Medieval Britain, c.1000–1500*

III *Early Modern Britain: 1450–1750*

IV *Modern Britain: 1750 to the Present*

THE CAMBRIDGE HISTORY OF BRITAIN

Modern Britain
1750 to the Present

James Vernon

CAMBRIDGE
UNIVERSITY PRESS

CAMBRIDGE
UNIVERSITY PRESS

University Printing House, Cambridge CB2 8BS, United Kingdom

One Liberty Plaza, 20th Floor, New York, NY 10006, USA

477 Williamstown Road, Port Melbourne, VIC 3207, Australia

314–321, 3rd Floor, Plot 3, Splendor Forum, Jasola District Centre, New Delhi – 110025, India

79 Anson Road, #06–04/06, Singapore 079906

Cambridge University Press is part of the University of Cambridge.

It furthers the University's mission by disseminating knowledge in the pursuit of education, learning and research at the highest international levels of excellence.

www.cambridge.org
Information on this title: www.cambridge.org/9781107031333
10.1017/9781139381611

First published 2017
Reprinted 2018

Printed in the United Kingdom by TJ International Ltd. Padstow Cornwall

A catalogue record for this publication is available from the British Library.

Library of Congress Cataloging in Publication Data
Names: Vernon, James, author.
Title: Modern Britain : 1750 to the present / James Vernon.
Description: Cambridge, United Kingdom ; New York, NY : Cambridge University
Press, 2017. | Series: Cambridge history of Britain ; 4
Identifiers: LCCN 2016041645| ISBN 9781107031333 (hardback) | ISBN
9781107686007 (paperback)
Subjects: LCSH: Great Britain – History – 1714–1837. | Great
Britain – History – Victoria, 1837–1901. | Great Britain – History – 20th
century. | Great Britain – History – Elizabeth II, 1952– | BISAC: HISTORY /
Europe / Great Britain.
Classification: LCC DA470 .V37 2017 | DDC 941.082–dc23
LC record available at https://lccn.loc.gov/2016041645

ISBN 978-1-107-03133-3 Hardback
ISBN 978-1-107-68600-7 Paperback

Additional resources for this publication at www.cambridge.org/CHOB-vernon

To my teachers and students

Contents

Acknowledgements

This book has my name on the cover but it is really the product of my conversation with generations of scholars as well as my teachers, students and colleagues. I hope all of them will see their influence at work. Caroline Ritter, Katie Harper, Trevor Jackson and Sam Wetherell actually wrote some of the book. They checked facts, tidied my prose, found images and produced those textboxes with their initials at the end. Brandon Williams marshalled the images and permissions. Elizabeth Friend-Smith somehow convinced me to write the book and Rosemary Crawford helped me finish it. It all begins and ends with Ros. Our family, near and far, kept me in the present. I never could have imagined writing this book without those who taught me at school and university. Since then my students have been the inspiration and my teachers. Thank you all.

Figures

Maps

Tables

Graphs

Textboxes

Preface

There are countless histories of modern Britain but little agreement about what it is, when it was, where it happened, who was part of it, or how it should be told. These histories share similar titles but cover different periods of time, extend across different geographical areas and tell very different stories. This is as it should be. History is about debate and interpretation. What some have recently dubbed the 'History Wars' are a set of arguments about how the national past should be understood and taught. As countries become demographically and culturally more diverse, politicians frequently offer increasingly prescriptive versions of their national pasts. In 2015 the British prime minister David Cameron claimed that 'British values' of democracy, equality, tolerance and the rule of law were rooted in a national history that stretched back 800 years. Those seeking to become British citizens are tested on a similar version of this national history and it is often proposed that this is the history British school children should be taught through the National Curriculum.

Those who advocate such histories complain that in recent decades an emphasis on economic, social and cultural history has undermined the seamless and self-congratulatory chronological narrative of the past anchored in political history. Once economic, social and cultural historians insisted that the experience of ordinary Britons – women and men of all classes, as well as people of all colours and creeds – had to be included in the national history, the question was to what degree they would change it. Similarly, as historians began to recognize the different roles of Scotland, Ireland, Wales and England in Britain's history, as well as their entanglement with continental Europe, the British Empire, and the rest of the world, it became increasingly difficult to imagine the national past as an 'island story' that stopped on the shores of the British Isles.

While our knowledge of British history is broader and richer in many ways, it remains hampered by two critical absences. The first is any sustained account of Britain's economic history and its local and global footprint. At a historical moment when the changing forms, locations and injuries of capitalism are painfully evident, they have receded from view in accounts of our national past. The second is the lack of an organizing narrative that can explain not just what changed, but why it did so. The task of the historian is not just to detail many historical events and processes but to explain their causes and relationships to each other within an overarching narrative. Without such a narrative we are all prey to the whitewashed and triumphalist versions of the national history championed by politicians.

Building on these debates, the aims of this book can be summarized as follows:

- To structure the history of Britain since 1750 around an account of the rise, fall and reinvention of what I will call **liberal political economy**. Liberal political economy was a cluster of assumptions about how governments, populations and empires worked best in relationship to each other when markets were made to operate freely.
- To propose that this process in Britain had a global history. This liberal political economy was germinated within the British Empire and had a world system built around it, but events, processes and peoples far beyond the **British world** shaped the history of its rise, demise and reinvention. In this sense Britons did not make the modern world; the world helped to make modern Britain.
- To offer a clear account and explanation of change over time. Accordingly, the book is structured around five chronological sections, each (except the last) with three thematic chapters that move from politics to economy and society. Each chapter contains a timeline of key events and is set up to explain a key transformation that reshaped the lives of Britons and often many others across the Empire and globe.
- To provide an accessible yet challenging book that can be used to teach British history across the English-speaking world. Having taught in Britain and the United States of America, I have tried to write a book that is comprehensible to students in North America with no prior knowledge of British history, while also covering material and presenting arguments that will be unfamiliar to those taught in Britain and the so-called former British world. A glossary of highlighted key-terms is included at the end of the book. Each chapter also contains textboxes that focus on particular people and places that were part of the processes the chapter explores, as well as sources through which the budding historian might conduct research.
- To be teachable as a set text in British history courses that cover the modern period over a semester or an academic year. The thirteen chapters mostly have four sections that may be assigned as introductory readings for two or three lectures a week. The guides to further reading and the additional primary source materials as well as study questions curated on the website provide sufficient material to stretch those taking a year-long class.

⧉ Where is Britain?

This may seem like a strange question given that the British Isles are located in north-west Europe at the easterly edge of the Atlantic Ocean. The Atlantic reaches Britain's northern coastline that faces a distant Iceland, while its eastern coast encounters the North Sea and looks across to Norway, Denmark and the Netherlands. Britain's southern coast meets the slim English Channel where Belgium, France and Spain lie in the distance. Already in that description of its location we are forced to confront Britain's difficult national question.

Even though it is not uncommon for the English, like those who live in other countries, to interchangeably use the terms England, Britain and the UK (United Kingdom), each has its own history and politics. England is just one of **four nations** in what was called, after **Acts of Union** with Scotland (1707) and Ireland (1800), the United Kingdom of Great Britain and Ireland. England had claimed dominion over Cornwall (which some consider Britain's fifth nation) and Wales since at least the eleventh century, but the alliance with Scotland, as well as the effective conquest of Ireland, required the creation of a single unified nation-state as well as a new sense of British national identity.

This process of imperial integration involved negotiation, compromise and armed conflict. Thus while both Scotland and Ireland lost their own Parliaments, Scotland maintained a separate legal and educational system and gained its own **Church of Scotland**. Union and English domination also catalysed nationalist reactions in Scotland, Ireland, Wales and Cornwall. At some point nationalist groups in all these countries armed themselves to resist English rule, but war actually broke out in Scotland and Ireland. While the **Jacobite** rebellions in eighteenth-century Scotland were defeated, armed conflict in Ireland continued sporadically for over a century before the Irish Free State was established in southern Ireland. This deeply controversial division of the island of Ireland in 1922 meant that the United Kingdom now represented 'Great Britain and Northern Ireland' (see Map 0.1). It also left Irish republicans campaigning, sometimes militarily, for independence for all of Ireland. Always a fiction, the idea of a United Kingdom remains in question today. In the final decades of the twentieth century, nationalist calls for devolution and independence were rewarded with the creation in 1998 of National Assemblies in Wales and Northern Ireland and the Scottish Parliament, each of which moderates rule from London. While the prospect of full independence for Scotland was defeated in a referendum in 2014, the Scottish National Party remains committed to independence and currently forms the government of Scotland.

Britain was not just a composite nation-state. It was also an imperial state that restlessly expanded its areas of influence and territorial sovereignty throughout the eighteenth, nineteenth and twentieth centuries (see Map 0.2). Across the political spectrum there were those who characterized this as a natural and beneficial process. The emigration of Britons overseas, they believed, had created a British world or 'Greater Britain' of English-speaking peoples that helped civilize the world by entrenching institutions rooted in Anglo-Saxon legal and political traditions. Of course this pattern of British settlement in North America (in what became the United States and Canada), Australia, New Zealand and South Africa depended upon the conquest of indigenous peoples no less than did those colonies in the Caribbean, Asia, the Pacific, Africa or the Middle East that were the product of war, invasion or commercial control. At its zenith in 1919 Britons could claim that the sun never set on their empire. It stretched over a quarter of the globe and included 458 million people, almost a third of the world's population, spread across 13 million square miles.

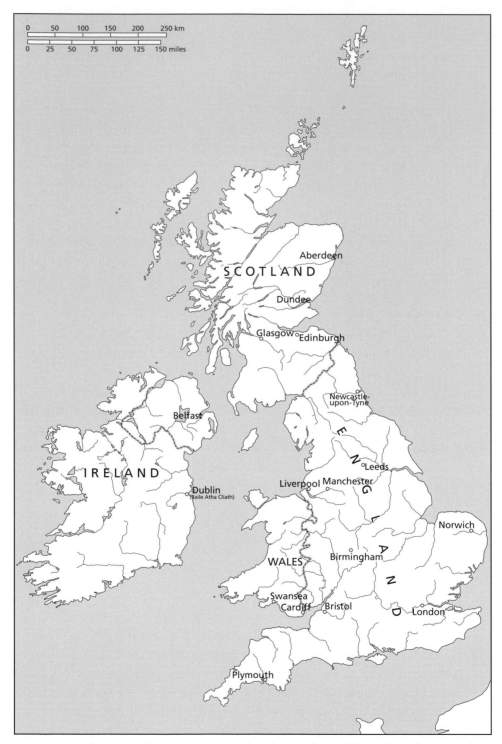

Map 0.1 Map of Britain as the United Kingdom of England, Wales, Scotland and Northern Ireland after 1922

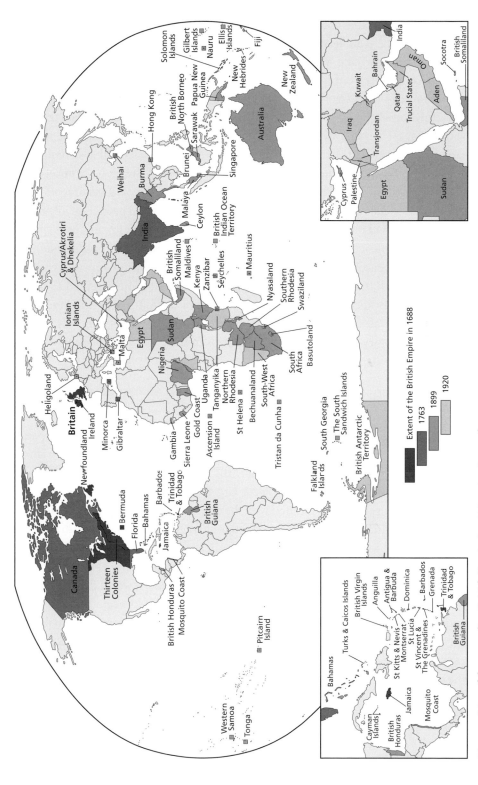

Map 0.2 Map of the expanding British Empire in 1688, 1763, 1899 and 1920

In Salman Rushdie's 1988 novel *The Satanic Verses* a character called Whisky Sisodia ruminates, 'The trouble with the English is that their history happened overseas, so they don't know what it means.' Remarkably, although racially diverse Britain was then made up of people from across its former colonies, and London remained the most cosmopolitan city in the world with over 250 languages spoken there, that still rang true. Certainly for far too long historians either forgot Britons' deep and varied relationships with Europe, their empire and the rest of the globe, or presumed that the relationship ran one way with all the influence emanating from Britain. Now that Britain no longer has an empire, and its role in Europe let alone the rest of the globe is uncertain, most historians acknowledge that Britain's economy, its systems of government, its understanding of social relations and of cultural hierarchies have all been indelibly marked by the world beyond its shores. Few any longer deny that British imperialism spread little but slavery, violence, disease, economic underdevelopment and political subjugation. Britain's emergence as the world superpower depended on these forms of exploitation. However, as a history of Britain since 1750, this book does not pretend to be either a history of the British Empire or a history of each of the four nations Ireland, Scotland, England and Wales. As these all demand books unto themselves, it is only their role in forging the history of Britain that I can address in the pages that follow.

When was Britain Modern?

Just as histories of modern Britain have different geographical foci, so they span wildly different periods of time. Invariably, especially in a series like this one, historians divide the world into distinct periods and eras – the ancient, the medieval, the early modern and the modern. These categories were largely the product of a European model of history and are generally associated with the end of the Roman Empire, the Renaissance and the French Revolution. Of course, the character and timing of these historical epochs, as well as their location in Europe, are always debated. When the modern age begins depends upon what you think distinguishes it from the early modern period. Historians pick moments to signal the arrival of the modern world depending on when they think the phenomena that best characterize its novelty were first present in the country they study. Historians of Britain variously identify its transition to the modern age with the establishment of a constitutional monarchy in the **Glorious Revolution** of 1688; its emergence as a global power in the **Seven Years' War** in 1763; the invention of the spinning jenny that revolutionized textile production and ushered in a new form of industrial capitalism from 1764; the consolidation of Britain's supremacy in Europe at the **Congress of Vienna** in 1814–15; the major reforms of its political system between 1829 and 1835; its hosting of the world's first major trade fair at the **Great Exhibition** of 1851; or the emergence of new technologies of communication and mass political movements from the 1870s. The chances are that if you are taking a class on modern British history it will have started at one of these dates.

This book begins in 1750, although its first three chapters look back to developments that mostly began in the late seventeenth century. There was little in 1750 that would seem familiar to us but many of the features of the world we inhabit today began to emerge from that date. And, critically, it was from the 1750s that a growing critique of the old order, of Britain's **ancien regime**, began to animate and give force to demands for a more liberalized political and economic order. The book ends at the present for it seeks to show that the Britain of today is a product of the imperial and global relationships that helped forge the rise, fall and reinvention of **liberal political economy**.

What is the History of Britain Since 1750?

Anyone teaching or writing a history of modern Britain has to decide not just when to begin, how far to reach geographically, but what story to tell. No single-volume history of modern Britain, especially if it ranges over almost three centuries like this one, can include everything. In any case History is not one damned thing after another, it is not about accumulating or remembering as many facts about the past as possible. The historian, whether writing a book or an exam, has to decide how to interpret the past and explain change over time with the available evidence. Although the historian has a duty to assess all the evidence of the past as objectively as possible, she also has to make interpretive choices, and that makes writing history a profoundly interpretive and, therefore, political, activity.

Most histories of modern Britain are surprisingly romantic accounts of how, despite the rapidity of its industrialization, **urbanization** and imperial expansion, Britain avoided major social conflict and revolution. In this story of Britain as a peaceable and stable kingdom, credit is usually given to its people's apparent predilection for tolerance and pluralism, or the adaptability of its institutions and ruling class. Until very recently this account even stretched to Britain's imperial history. The Empire was seen as almost accidentally acquired, an afterthought of emigration and established trading relationships, while decolonization was thought to be no less pragmatic and peaceful. In contrast my global history of the rise, fall and reinvention of **liberal political economy** in Britain is a largely tragic story. It demonstrates how political economies that promised emancipation and prosperity to Britons, colonial subjects and others across the globe, rarely delivered either, were frequently secured by violence, and have left us facing an ecological crisis. It traces how those who challenge the prevailing forms of political and economic organization invariably do so by appropriating its own terms of reference to highlight their contradictions and injustices in ways that mean the critics of the system often become incorporated within it. It is not all doom and gloom. Above all the book aims to be a hopeful history that reminds us that change can and does happen; even when all seems lost. It cherishes those who had the imagination and courage to think otherwise, those who challenged the varied and changing forms of inequity and subjugation that the rise, fall and reinvention of liberal political economy produced and depended upon.

What then do I mean by liberal political economy? Today, especially in the United States of America, to be liberal is to think of oneself as open-minded as well as socially and politically progressive. In Britain it is even still possible to be a Liberal; that is, to be a supporter of a political party (the Liberal Democrats) whose origins lay in the Liberal Party formally created in 1859. The liberal ideas of political and economic life that slowly emerged in the late eighteenth and early nineteenth centuries are very distant cousins to these contemporary politics. Never the preserve of any one political movement or party, liberal political economy was less a coherent ideology than a pattern of thought and set of assumptions about the relationship between political and economic life. To explain what these were, we have to understand how they emerged in the late eighteenth century, how they operated in the nineteenth, as well as how they were eventually challenged and reinvented in the twentieth century. The book is organized in five chronological sections that tell this story.

I
1750–1819: The Ends
of the Ancien Regime

1 The Imperial State

Introduction

The **four nations** of the British Isles were torn apart by civil wars, rebellions and revolution during the seventeenth century. These were bloody and brutal conflicts. In the so-called first **Civil War in England** (1642–46), 14 per cent of adult males died as a result of the conflict, a higher proportion of fatalities than in the First World War. Even this paled in comparison to England's invasion of Ireland (1649–53) under Thomas Cromwell when between 25 and 50 per cent of the Irish population perished. At the heart of these dreadful conflicts was a series of questions that struck at the very legitimacy of the state. Should a monarch or a parliament rule? Who had the authority to raise taxes and armies? Should the state have the right to prescribe the religious practice of its subjects, whether Catholic or Protestant? How could Scotland and Ireland resist the imperial ambitions of England? These questions were raised again in 1688, when a small group of Whigs in Parliament enacted a coup. That coup, later described as the **Glorious Revolution**, displaced the Catholic king, James Stuart (he was James II in England and Ireland, but James VII in Scotland), in favour of his Protestant daughter Mary and her Dutch husband William of Orange. In the tumultuous months between William and his army arriving at Torbay in November and the installation of William and Mary as monarchs first of England and Wales in February and then Scotland in May 1689, few were sanguine that peace had arrived at last, let alone that the legitimacy and stability of the state had finally been secured. **Tories** were worried that the authority of the monarchy had been eroded and that they would be left out in the cold by the new regime. Some even sympathized with the **Jacobites**, those eager to restore James to the throne, who remained particularly strong in Ireland and Scotland where war and rebellion continued to foment. The absolute power of monarchs across the rest of Europe, except the Netherlands, was unchallenged. The prospects for the survival of the revolutionary state were not promising.

And yet by 1819 the British state was the most powerful in the world. It had transformed itself into a United Kingdom with the Acts of Union with Scotland (1707) and Ireland (1800). It had fought an almost perpetual series of wars (for over half of the years between 1688 and 1815 Britain was engaged in major conflicts), culminating with the defeat of its major rivals to become the dominant power in Europe at the **Congress of Vienna** (1814–15). And it had successfully extended its imperial territories and ambitions in the Caribbean, North America, South Asia and the Pacific. So robust was the state that, despite widespread dearth and the spread of increasingly radical ideas propagated by the revolutions in America and France, it could arm 450,000 Volunteers to defend the country from threatened invasion by Napoleonic France in 1804, without fear of revolt. It had not of course all been plain sailing. The growing power of the state generated protests and rebellions within Britain as well as across the Empire, which were increasingly met with unparalleled coercion and violence.

In the midst of the English **Civil War** Thomas Hobbes's *The Leviathan* (1651) outlined the chaotic nature of social life in the absence of a strong state. He argued that people would consent to the rule of a sovereign power to avoid their lives being 'nasty, brutish and short'. As you can see in Figure 1.1 the frontispiece of the book depicted a

Figure 1.1 Frontispiece to Hobbes's Leviathan, 1651

monstrous sovereign rising above the landscape sword in hand with a quote from the Book of Job declaring 'There is no power on earth to be compared to him.' By 1819 the imperial British state had become a Leviathan. This chapter examines this remarkable transformation.

TIMELINE

1688–9	The 'Glorious' Revolution
1689	Bill of Rights and Act of Toleration
1689–97	Nine Years' War
1694	Bank of England established
1702–13	War of Spanish Succession
1707	Act of Union between Scotland and England
1715	Septennial Act
1756–63	Seven Years' War
1757	Battle of Plassey
1769	Arrest of John Wilkes MP
1773	Regulating Act (of East India Company)
1775–83	American War of Independence
1778	Impeachment of Warren Hastings
1780	Gordon Riots
1792	Friends of the People, London Corresponding Society, United Irishmen King's Proclamation Against Seditious Writings Association for Preserving Liberty and Property Against Republicans and Levellers
1795	Gagging Acts
1814–15	Congress of Vienna
1819	The Peterloo Massacre Six Acts

War and the Reach of the State

After the Revolution of 1688–9 the first job of the fledgling state was to survive. The post-revolutionary settlement sought to address the outstanding constitutional causes of the conflict with the Bill of Rights (1689) and the Acts of Toleration (1689) and Settlement (1701). The Bill of Rights helped establish a new type of constitutional monarchy unable to raise armies or taxes and unable to interfere in the conduct of law or parliamentary procedures and elections. Together with the Act of Settlement in 1701, it also enshrined the Protestant nature of the monarchy, barring Catholics from that office and ensuring that the throne would pass to Mary's heirs and then only to those of James's heirs who had married into the Protestant German House of Hanover. Parliament, not the hereditary principle of monarchy, determined the issue of succession – a truly revolutionary principle in a dynastic Europe ruled by monarchs who claimed (if rarely practised) absolute power. John Locke's *Two Treatises of Government* (1689) theorized that this new contract between Parliament and the monarchy endowed Englishmen with certain minimal rights and rested the legitimacy of government on their shoulders. The leading philosopher and political theorist of the age, Locke argued that the legitimacy of government resided in its ability to represent the people, with whom sovereignty lay. Finally, the Act of Toleration (1689) allowed freedom of worship to both Dissenting and non-conformist Protestants (those who chose not to join the congregation of the state's **Church of England**), but specifically excluded Catholics. All these groups remained barred from holding public office or being educated at the universities of Oxford and Cambridge.

This was a very English settlement. The Revolution was less than Glorious in Ireland and Scotland. In Ireland, where the Revolution effectively amounted to a military occupation, support for James was always yoked to a defence of Catholicism. Having initially fled to France, James quickly joined the armed resistance in Ireland, which was not finally defeated by William's troops until 1691. There followed a series of measures that ensured the so-called '**Ascendancy**' of the minority Protestant landowning class. Catholics were excluded from Parliament and public office (including the army) and were prevented from possessing firearms or buying and inheriting property. Over the following decades the Irish Parliament entrenched the interests of the Ascendancy, as well as that elite's peculiarly Anglo-Irish identity, as they sought to preserve and extend the government of Ireland independently of London.

In Scotland the **Jacobite** cause to restore the deposed James was especially strong in the Highlands where wars continued sporadically until 1694. Fuelled by French support, Jacobitism remained a potent force well into the eighteenth century, especially in the **Scottish Highlands** where the Risings of 1715 and 1745–6 were hatched. Even in England, chiefly in the northeast, there was support for the Jacobites among

Catholics and those who supported a restoration of the monarchy's authority over Parliament. However, while the Revolution had been militarily imposed upon Ireland, it had, despite the Jacobites, found important sources of support in Scotland, especially amongst Presbyterians. With the power and status of the Scottish Parliament heightened by the Revolution, it passed the Acts of Peace and War (1703) and Security (1704) to demonstrate its independence from both the monarch and Parliament south of the border. When the English Parliament responded by declaring all Scots south of the border as Aliens in 1705, the stage was set for negotiations that culminated in 1706 with the Scottish Parliament supporting the **Act of Union** between England and Scotland that came into effect the following year. To secure the votes £20,000 was sent north of the border and peerages and promotions liberally dispensed to supporters of Union. Yet Union also bought other advantages to Scotland. It provided the thriving tobacco and linen trades access to English colonial markets, while also enabling many Scots to build careers in the military and administrative service of the imperial state across the Empire. Eventually even the **Jacobite** clansmen of the Highlands formed regiments of the British army and became imperial warriors.

A Fiscal-Military Regime

Given the fragility of this peace, it was quickly apparent that the foundations of a new type of **fiscal-military state** had to be laid if the regime were to survive and secure itself against internal and external threats alike. The fiscal component of this state was a novel mode of debt-financing: the **national debt**. In recent decades our governments and international financial institutions have grown allergic to the idea of public borrowing, that is, a state borrowing money and going into debt in order to spend on things it otherwise could not afford. Yet without the invention of debt-financing in the late seventeenth century Britain would probably have remained an inconsequential and insecure state on the northwest fringes of Europe. There were three critical innovations that made debt-financing of the state possible. The first was the creation of the **Bank of England**. The Bank of England was formed in 1694, when the new state, effectively close to bankruptcy, and facing the prospect of imminent invasion by the French if its navy were not reinforced, needed to raise funds fast. In return for a loan of £1.2 million the government gave its creditors exclusive rights to form a bank with limited liability and to issue their own bank notes. As a debtor, the state now also had to prove to its creditors that it was fiscally competent, and so the second key feature of this new system was transparency and public accountability. The state of the state's finances was henceforward to be made available to, and vetted in, Parliament. Thus the post-revolutionary British state struck a Faustian bargain: in return for loans that would allow it to secure itself financially and militarily, it not only made itself dependent upon its creditors in the **City of London** but ensured that its future capacity for credit rested on a reputation for sound governance that was now a legitimate subject of public debate.

Although the state was now able to borrow money from the Bank of England, it still lacked the means to service the often prohibitive interest rates on those loans. It was the third key innovation – new techniques for collecting taxes – that made this possible. The state needed a reliable flow of tax revenues to service its debts. This was easier said than done, given that just decades before, attempts to raise taxes by the Stuart monarchy had helped to trigger the English **Civil War**. Yet before the **Revolution**, James II had created a more centralized and efficient system for collecting **excise duties**. Whereas other taxes were collected by local assessors paid on commission, the Board of Excise appointed salaried and centrally coordinated officers as collectors (there were over 2,000 by 1708). So effective was the system that after 1690 excise duties were extended to an increasing number of commodities and came to account for a growing percentage of taxation revenue – 29 per cent in 1710 and 52 per cent by 1795. Other taxes were also important to help the state service its loans. **Customs duties** steadily increased during the eighteenth century. By the 1780s some 400 customs officers were tracking the imports of around 1,200 goods on the London docks alone. Between 1690 and 1760 there were 800 Acts of Parliament regarding customs but from 1760 to 1830 there were an additional 1,300. In addition, taxes were raised on almost anything that moved and plenty that did not, from the sale of property to the number of windows, horses, dogs and women-servants on your property. Britain's tax revenue increased sixteenfold between 1660 and 1815 while its national income only tripled. Only the Dutch were taxed more heavily. Raising and collecting tax was critical to the new system of debt-financing constructed by the state around the Bank of England. Tax was the lifeblood that flowed through the veins of the Leviathan.

Chiefly this new fiscal system for raising monies was used to secure the state militarily against its dynastic and confessional rivals, as well as to extend its reach at home and abroad. The Bank of England's first loan was to rebuild a navy that over the following century became the most powerful in the world, projecting British power across the Atlantic, Indian and Pacific Oceans. During the first half of the eighteenth century the navy doubled its manpower and tonnage. It was an expensive and big business. By 1750 the navy's fleet amounted to a capital investment of almost £2.25 million (at least five times more that the fixed capital costs of the entire woollen industry and its 243 mills). Just maintaining that fleet cost half a million pounds a year. And this was just the cost of the ships. The major dockyards needed to build, repair and supply these ships were continually developed through the eighteenth century. By the 1770s they employed over 8,000 men; 2,000 men worked at each of the major docks of Portsmouth and Plymouth, dwarfing the size of any civilian enterprise. Given that the navy's yards also had to be supplied with wood, metal, guns, rope, sails and food, the **fiscal-military state** spawned an almost industrial complex.

Supplying the shipboard population was also a major exercise. By 1755 it had reached 40,000 men but four years later, at the height of the **Seven Years' War**, had almost doubled, making it the size of the two largest provincial cities of Bristol and Norwich *combined*. The navy was always short of men and relied heavily, especially at times of war, on the controversial practice of impressment, where men were involuntarily pressed into service by a press gang. At the start of the Seven Years' War up to half of naval seamen had been impressed, although half of those may have subsequently agreed to volunteer in return for a signing-on bonus or payment in advance. The navy had to recruit more men because as many of a quarter of seamen deserted every year, so intolerable were the conditions on board. Supplying ships with even a miserable level of supplies at sea was a colossal undertaking. The navy's shipboard population consumed almost 4 million pounds of flour and 11 million pounds of beef, over 4.5 million pounds of biscuits, and 2.5 million pounds of cheese.

Like the navy, the army grew exponentially during the eighteenth century: from an unprecedented 48,000 during the **Nine Years' War** (1689–97), 100,000 during the **War of the Spanish Succession (1702–13)**, 200,000 during the **American War of Independence** (1775–83), to 400,000 during the **Napoleonic Wars (1803–15)**. The further afield it went, and the more stretched its resources became over different continents and theatres of war, the more dependent it was upon local allies and mercenaries to help fight its battles. Twenty-five per cent of the army's budget went on hiring foreign troops up to the 1760s. Thus in 1757, when Britain was also fighting in Europe and North America, the decisive battle in the colonization of India at Plassey was fought with just 750 British soldiers employed by the **East India Company** and some 2,000 Indian sepoys. Overall the army and navy accounted for more than half of all government expenditure during the eighteenth century and reached over 70 per cent in the decade after the Revolution and during the Seven Years' War.

Building the Nation-State

All of this new fiscal capacity and military might was not just projected abroad. It was also used to secure the new nation-state of Britain. The construction of a new road system was critical here for it allowed troops to be sent to quell rebellions and created a new national network of transport and communication. The continuing **Jacobite** threat in Scotland was the initial catalyst. Between 1726 and 1750 military surveyors, engineers and soldiers laid 900 miles of paved road linking up the Highland forts of William and Augustus to Inverness as well as the lowland fortifications at Dumbarton and Stirling castles. The new techniques for planning and laying roads pioneered in Scotland found their way back to England, as **turnpike roads** proliferated from the 1750s to facilitate and capitalize on the movement of people and goods. As these roads remained regional in scale, it was the government's own **General Post Office** (GPO) that began prospecting a national network with standardized road surfaces that would allow its mail coaches to deliver a faster and more reliable service. It was only after the **Act of Union** with Ireland in 1800 that the **GPO** got its wish with the provision of two state-funded trunk roads that stretched 1,700 miles. One connected England to Wales and Wales to Ireland (via Holyhead); the other improved the Great North Road between London and Edinburgh. The rest of the 120,000-mile road network, 98 per cent of which was maintained by local **parishes** and turnpike trusts, only had to meet central standards – of smooth macadamized paving (named after McAdam, its engineer) mounded in the middle to assist drainage and set on a foundation of ten inches of gravel – after the Highways Act of 1835. The extension of the road network, the improved quality of road surfaces and stagecoach design slowly improved journey times and knit the nation more closely together. There was no shortage of stage coaches in the first half of the eighteenth century but their passengers endured long and gruelling journeys: by 1760, if the weather was kind, it still took two weeks to get from London to Edinburgh; whereas by the 1830s, 1,500 coaches left London each week and travelled around a national road network four to five times faster than had been possible in the 1750s.

The roads were essential to the business of the state, extending the reach of its eyes, ears and arms across the country. Soldiers, judges, tax collectors and mail coaches carrying government post travelled around the network, grasping control of the expanded and still unruly nation. Despite the terms of the Bill of Rights, the misleadingly titled Disbanding Act of 1699 legalized a peacetime standing army. This force, up to 15,000 strong, was highly mobile as it consisted primarily of horse regiments whose barracks were stationed strategically by trunk roads and scattered around the country. Intended to be conspicuously visible, it was hoped that their mere presence would prevent disorder, insurrection and smuggling along the coast that threatened to deprive the state of revenue. In a society that lacked any form of policing except occasionally by the most rudimentary work of local Watch Committees or **parish** constables, the army's crucial role in maintaining public order was formalized by the Riot Act of 1715. That Act enabled local mayors, magistrates or **Justices of the Peace** (JPs) to order the dispersal of twelve or more people considered 'unlawfully, riotously, and tumultuously assembled together'. Once a public proclamation had been read troops were allowed to intervene. And intervene they did to suppress any number of riots, whether over unpopular legislation, the price of food, insufficient wages or changes to working practices, the **enclosure** of common land, the introduction of tolls on **turnpike** roads, agitation for or against a candidate at an election, or a religious cause. In moments of political and economic crisis their resources were stretched. In 1757 twenty regiments were deployed to suppress riots across the country and in 1766 they intervened in no less that sixty-eight towns across twenty counties. In the **Gordon Riots** of 1780, when a march upon Parliament of 60,000 anti-Catholic protesters descended into looting and rioting that gripped the capital for five days, 12,000 troops were required to restore order. With no finely tuned techniques of crowd control, civilian (and occasionally military) injuries and casualties were common. The exemplary use of mounted charges and shots fired was supposed to act as a deterrent and disperse the rioters. It did not always work. In the Gordon Riots 285 people died when troops fired at those who refused to disperse.

The law also travelled by road as judges toured their circuits dispensing justice. The routine operation of the rule of law remained the preserve of local **Justices of the Peace**. They dispensed justice individually for minor misdemeanours in **Petty Sessions** but more serious crime was tried in front of four or more JPs at **Quarter Sessions**. Held four times a year in county towns (the capital of each county), they were opened by a ceremonial procession of the magistrates through the town to their court in full regalia. The symbolic display of the gravity and majesty of the law was at its height with the arrival of a High Court Judge at the local **Assize Court** held twice a year. With the country divided into six circuits, judges travelled their district to try cases referred to them by the Quarter Sessions, usually more complex or capital offences, in front of a jury. The ceremonial arrival of the circuit judge was a major occasion and its significance was heightened as the number of capital offences grew exponentially from 50 in 1688 to 200 by 1800 as Parliament sought to maintain the propertied order and the rule of law. Executions (by hanging or decapitation) were public and they were held frequently in London. By 1800 there were 200 a year in England and Wales alone (as opposed to just 3 a year in Scotland), and these were a fraction of those actually sentenced to death. The grisly spectacle of public executions was intended to have a salutary effect as a deterrent. At London's infamous Tyburn gallows (where Marble Arch now sits) vast crowds gathered to watch the condemned man transported there from Newgate Prison down Oxford Street to meet his death. It was not until 1783 that the gallows were relocated inside the walls of prisons. These symbolic displays of the rule of law, which the Bill of Rights had insisted would be independent from executive power, were vital to the projection of the state's authority and legitimacy.

Soldiers and judges were joined on the roads by those other equally important arms of the state, its tax collectors and mail coaches. The Board of Excise had divided the country into 886 'districts' and each collector was assigned a district and a series of tours around them consisting of 38-mile rural 'rides' and 6-mile urban 'walks' each day. They were busy men and the quality of the road network was essential to their work and thus to the fiscal reach of the state. Similarly, the **General Post Office**, founded in 1660 to provide a public service that would prevent the state from monopolizing the flow of information, actually served to extend the state's communicative reach. Alongside the post that the public had paid for in its mail coaches were 'franked' letters that allowed state officials and **MPs** to exchange information free of charge. While the system was notoriously corrupted by MPs selling their franks to others for profit, the volume of official mail increased dramatically in the eighteenth and early nineteenth centuries as the business of the state grew and with it the rapid transmission of information to and from London. In the 1760s it was estimated that the annual value of franked mail was £170,000, and by 1790 1.6 million franked letters circulated, a figure that reached 7.5 million in 1829. The creation of a road network along which soldiers, judges, taxmen and official correspondence could travel further and faster helped forge the nation-state.

A Composite State

In some ways, for all its growing fiscal and military power, the British state remained embedded in remarkably thin soil. For sure the number of state employees grew rapidly in the revenue-raising departments, from 2,500 in 1688 to 6,500 in 1755 and a staggering 20,000 by 1815. Although such figures were small in comparison to Britain's European rivals, they certainly seemed to indicate that a new type of Leviathan or government machine had been born – the early nineteenth-century radical **William Cobbett** described it simply as 'The Thing'. And yet, by 1797 84 per cent of government officials worked in the revenue departments. As most areas of civil government remained highly dispersed and localized, the number of state officials in other departments, while steadily increasing, certainly confounded the elaboration of a powerful bureaucratic system. There were some 150 in 1688, which quickly rose to 2,500 in 1755. Even at the end of the **Napoleonic Wars** key departments of state remained minimally staffed: the **Board of Trade** had just 20 officials, the **Home Office** 17 and the **Foreign Office** the relative riches of 30. Even the **Treasury** had only 82 staff in 1829.

The decentralized nature of the state was apparent at the multiple administrative levels of the nation, county, town and **parish**, each with their own ancient and overlapping jurisdictions. Ireland, or at least its Anglo-Irish landowners, boasted its own executive and Parliament in Dublin, while even after Union with England and Wales in 1707, Scotland had relative autonomy with regard to many civil matters. The rural counties were governed by a Lord Lieutenant, usually an aristocratic peer of the realm, who commanded the militia and appointed members of the local gentry to serve voluntarily as **Justices of the Peace**. They, in turn, in groups of four or more, ran the civil administration of the county at the **Quarter Sessions**, overseeing poor relief, highways, prisons and the suppression of 'nuisances' that were elastically defined. Although there had been 8,400 JPs in 1761, their numbers declined so steeply that, despite the introduction of stipendiary magistrates (who received a salary for their service) in 1792, there were just 4,500 by 1831, around a quarter of whom were members of the **clergy**. The basic unit of local government, however, remained the parish demarcated by the ecclesiastical boundaries of the Church. There were in excess of 10,000 parishes, each with its own set of churchwardens (normally local farmers or property owners), putatively elected by a meeting of parishioners in the church **vestry**, who appointed voluntary officials to oversee poor relief, road maintenance and the raising of the militia.

And, finally, some 200 towns boasted their own royal charter as corporations and thus their own system of government through a mayor, aldermen and councillors. Like parochial officials, how they were elected varied enormously depending on how broadly or narrowly the franchise had been set or developed over time. There were still further and even more arcane practices of local government. Their variety is less important than the way in which they were shaped around what was perceived as the natural social hierarchies that made the communities of county, **parish** and town cohere. Given the limited nature of the powers delegated to local government, Parliament was increasingly awash with private bills – 200 per session by the 1760s and trebling by 1789 – promoted by local inhabitants and sponsored by an MP, that advanced by promising 'improvements' like new **turnpike roads**, canals, bridges, harbours or **enclosure** of lands. In this way Parliament presented itself as responsive to local demands. The state was, in short, less evident for many in its new centralized fiscal-military forms than as a composite patchwork of local jurisdictions and responsibilities.

No Taxation Without Representation

The Revolution of 1688 had sought to legitimate the state by resolving the constitutional battles between Parliament and the monarchy that had plagued the seventeenth century by affording them joint sovereignty. Although there were those like John Locke who argued that Parliament owed its new authority to being a representative body of the people in whom ultimately sovereignty truly lay, the revolutionary settlement did nothing to alter how Parliament was elected or by whom. Indeed, while the structure of government in eighteenth-century Britain – with its constitutional monarchy, Parliament and electorate – looks familiar and modern, it was radically different to that which operates today.

The Structure of Politics

After the Revolution the monarchy remained a crucial force in government for much of the eighteenth century. It was the monarch who appointed government ministers to carry out their policies and to ensure Parliament would authorize the raising of taxes and the waging of wars that, especially before 1750, continued to have a strongly dynastic flavour. And it was the monarch and his or her ministers who set the wheels of patronage in motion, with the power to appoint government officials as well as positions in the armed services and **Anglican Church**. There were remarkably few occasions before 1750 when MPs flexed their muscles by voting down government measures – no minister was impeached, new taxes were rarely refused and, of course, a standing army had been allowed. Nonetheless, the growing scale of government business meant that, however competent, monarchs came increasingly to depend upon their ministers, whom they consulted individually and whose loyalty was expected to extend only to the king, not to their colleagues in what became known as the **Cabinet**. When some of those ministers became royal favourites, like Robert Walpole who exercised considerable influence over George I and George II, they became known (somewhat pejoratively) as the **prime minister**, and increasingly a single minister was held responsible for speaking for the government as a whole.

It would be wrong though to imagine that Parliament or ministers were simply royal lackeys. Parliament consisted of two chambers. The **House of Lords** was an unelected body that represented the aristocratic interest through those who inherited their position as lords. The **House of Commons** consisted of **members of Parliament (MPs)** who were elected by voters to represent specific **constituencies** around the country. Ministers had to court the support of different factions and parties in both Houses of Parliament, represented most clearly by the long-held ideological divisions between **Whigs** and **Tories**. First, there was the question of religion and the rights of those radical Protestants who were **Dissenters** from the **Anglican Church**. Second, there was the question of whether Parliament should override the hereditary principle of royal succession and thereby dilute the divine authority of the monarch as sovereign. On foreign policy, at issue was whether the revolutionary settlement would only be secured by expensive land wars with absolutist rivals in Europe or by a 'blue-water' policy that emphasized imperial expansion. These positions were increasingly tied to competing political economies, as Whigs emphasized the importance of trade and commerce, whereas for Tories land and its acquisition overseas was the source of wealth. Yet the competition between Whigs and Tories – who alternated in office between 1688 and 1714 before a long period of Whig oligarchy under Walpole until the accession of George III in 1760 – did not account for the loyalties of all MPs, many of whom saw such 'parties' as an anathema which divided the loyalties of the nation and prevented them from representing their own or local interests. There was no parliamentary organization that compelled members to vote as a party, just as party labels in the constituencies differed enormously and had various meanings. Members of Parliament (MPs) faced two, and sometimes three, ways of defining their loyalties: in relation to the governing ministers, to their **constituency** and to their own self-interested pursuit of patronage and power.

The Electoral System

MPs were elected by a system that had developed over centuries. Although much of that electoral system was created in the early fifteenth century, its significance rose in the seventeenth century as the role of Parliament became more prominent and the electorate increased in size. Elections remained a novelty during the seventeenth century. Before 1642 almost no **constituency** had contested elections; processes of selection, when local aristocrats selected candidates who were then returned unopposed, far outweighed those of election. The system seemed designed to avoid such contests. Outside of London and some of Wales, all constituencies returned two MPs, and as each elector had two votes they could split their loyalties between rival candidates. When elections did occur, uncertainty surrounded who could vote and how votes should be cast, while winning did not always mean having a majority of votes. However, after 1688, when elections were held with unprecedented regularity, the entire electoral system was slowly codified. As Whigs and Tories battled for control of Parliament, and rival local interests sought position and favour in the new state, no less than twelve elections were held between 1689 and 1715. The Septennial Act, limiting elections to every seven years, was passed in 1716 ostensibly to end the costly and often unruly 'rage of party' but also conveniently facilitating the 'supremacy' of the Whigs. Still, with only thirteen further elections between 1715 and 1802, there remained more than double the number of uncontested than contested **constituencies**.

After the **Act of Union** with Scotland in 1707, the distribution of **constituencies** and returning **MPs** reflected the unequal relations of power. There were 558 MPs elected by 314 constituencies, 245 of which were in England (primarily clustered in the south), with 45 in Scotland and 24 in Wales. There were two types of constituencies, the urban borough (known as a burgh in Scotland) and the rural county. In the counties residents who laid claim to freehold property worth 40 shillings a year could vote regardless of whether they owned the property or held it through leases, mortgages, offices or annuities. In contrast, the boroughs had four basic types of qualification, although each could have its own local peculiarities. There was the 'corporation' borough where only members of the corporation possessed the vote (and they in turn could be selected or elected); the 'burgage' borough where the vote was attached to specific properties rather than a person or group; the 'scot and lot' borough where all inhabitants that paid poor rates (and did not receive poor relief or alms) voted; and, finally, those where all 'freemen' of the borough were voters (the freedom of the town was variously in the gift of the corporation, inherited or attached to a specific occupation). In Scotland there was effectively no popular electorate as the burgh franchise rested with corporations who had one vote (so in a burgh constituency that included seven town corporations the final tally may have been five–two). These different qualifications produced electorates of wildly different sizes in the constituencies. There were less than 30 boroughs with an electorate of over 1,000, and more than half of them had less than 100 voters while some, that later became infamous as **'rotten' boroughs**, had just one or two. Despite these varieties, the franchise's link to property values meant that inflation ensured the size of the electorate as a whole steadily rose. In England and Wales the number of voters nearly doubled between 1689 and 1831 from 240,000 to 439,200, although given the faster rate of demographic growth, the proportion of the population enfranchised actually fell from 4.6 per cent to 3.2 per cent, or from 1 in 5 adult men to 1 in 7. Scotland's much smaller electorate rose faster, with a tenfold increase from under 500 in the 1770s to under 5,000 in 1831, when it still included only 1 in 100 adult men.

When contests were held, elections were boisterous and demotic affairs that engaged voters and non-voters alike. This was well captured by William Hogarth's 'The Humours of an Election' (Figures 1.2–1.5). Hogarth (1697–1764) was an influential painter and satirist of eighteenth-century life whose work helped establish the modern genre of the political cartoon, and influenced much book illustration during the nineteenth century. 'The Humours of an Election' was first published in the 1750s but it was reissued in the 1820s when very little about the nature of elections had changed. The first of these prints, 'The Election Entertainment', illustrates how prospective candidates were expected to 'treat' those whose support they sought, including those without the vote like women and children. In 'Canvassing for Votes' the Tory candidate eyes the admiring women on the balcony of the pub that is his campaign headquarters as a voter accepts a bribe and his supporters attack their rivals in the distance. Sitting members and prospective candidates had to actively canvass support to assess whether a contest was necessary or avoidable. If an MP had suitably 'nursed' the constituency – supporting local charities, advancing local causes and hiring 'campaign' workers – he hoped to avoid the expense of an election.

Figure 1.2 Hogarth's 'The Humours of an Election', 1755: 'An Election Entertainment'

Figure 1.3 'Canvassing for Votes'

Figure 1.4 'The Polling'

Figure 1.5 'Chairing the Member'

Once a contest was formally declared, weeks of campaigning – full of speeches, noisy processions, dinners and an endless stream of election literature – gave way to days of voting at the polls. Competing candidates went to enormous lengths to get out their voters (or to prevent the opposition from doing so), as Hogarth's 'The Polling' demonstrates with its procession of one-limbed, infirm and venereal-disease-ridden voters lined up on the steps of the '**hustings**', the purpose-built and centrally located platform upon which electors voted. All votes were publicly declared on the **hustings** where they were greeted with the approval or disapproval of the many non-voters gathered below. Everyone knew how you had voted, and, in case they missed it, poll books, recording how every elector had voted, were published after the election (see Textbox 1.1). 'Chairing the Member', Hogarth's last image, depicts the frequently disorderly scene after the final declaration of the poll when the triumphant candidate was 'chaired' around the constituency to celebrate his victory. Clearly, these were very different types of election to those we are used to today. Alcohol, corruption and violence were an endemic part of how support and votes were solicited and displayed. Striking too is the scale of participation, which included those without a vote. Indeed, the vote was not considered the property of an individual but a trust held on behalf of a broader community who had the right to hold electors accountable for their actions at the poll.

1.1 Source: Poll books

Poll books, a published record of how electors in a particular constituency cast their votes in an election contest, became increasingly common during the eighteenth century. They were first published after 1692 when an Act of Parliament required lists of electors and records of their votes to combat disputed results in county elections, but became ubiquitous as the number of constituencies holding election contests accelerated in the eighteenth and nineteenth centuries. They only ceased to be published after the **secret ballot** was introduced in 1872. Poll books consisted of a list of voters, their address or **parish** of residence, their occupation and a record of how they voted. Sometimes poll books also included a narrative of the election contest that reproduced many of the handbills, squibs, speeches and songs that were deployed by the rival candidates to woo supporters. When historians first discovered poll books in the 1960s they were primarily interested in using them to track voter behaviour over time, particularly to discern whether voting was structured by allegiance to a party or by occupational position. Much was made of whether voters chose to 'split' their two votes between opposing candidates, or whether they chose to 'lump' by casting a single vote for one candidate. Poll books have also been used to measure how rapidly the electorate was growing before and after the **Reform Act of 1832**, as well as what proportion of the population possessed the right to vote in each **constituency**. Since the 1980s historians have also used those poll books that contained the apparently ephemeral material produced during the campaigns to understand the culture of elections, their rich ceremonial forms, and the extent of participation in them by those who did not possess the vote. There are well over 2,000 poll books scattered in many local archives in Britain, although a disproportionate number exist in England and Wales. There are fine collections of them at the Guildhall Library and the Institute of Historical Research in London. Now many poll books, especially those published in the nineteenth century, are available on Google Books, online sites or databases such as http://electoralregisters.org.uk/pollbooks.htm.

Calls for 'Liberty'

After the Revolution the success of the **fiscal-military state** ensured that a delicate balance of powers between monarch, Parliament and electorate was maintained during the first half of the eighteenth century. That equilibrium was decisively unsettled during the 1760s. In the aftermath of the **Seven Years' War** critics in Britain and the American colonies highlighted the increasing powers of the state and asserted the claims of the people to greater representative power over it. It is ironic that the Seven Years' War proved a catalyst for the politics of reform, for Britain emerged victorious from that global conflagration as a growing power on the world stage. Essentially a war between Britain and France (and eventually Portugal and Spain) for control of imperial territories across the

Mediterranean, the Americas, the Caribbean, Asia and West Africa, it became entangled with conflicts between Prussia, Russia and the Holy Roman Empire in central Europe. By the end of the war the so-called **'First' British Empire** had been secured, with Minorca joining Gibraltar in the Mediterranean, Canada (including Quebec and Newfoundland) as well as Florida joining the thirteen North American colonies, and South Asia now under some degree of military control. This was a substantial victory for the nation and its new monarch George III who styled himself 'the Patriot King'.

And yet there were those – led by William Pitt, who had already resigned as **prime minister** over the reluctance of the king and his Scottish advisor Lord Bute to declare war on Spain in 1761 – who were critical of a peace settlement that required Britain to hand back its seizures of Cuba, the Philippines, Martinique and Grenada. The critics claimed that Bute, who was pushing through a very unpopular tax on cider to help cover the costs of war, had sold out to France. A torrent of abuse rained down upon him in the press and pamphlets. He was there portrayed as a Tory, a self-serving Scot, a **Jacobite**, a traitorous despot who had schemed and slept his way (with George's mother no less) to become the King's favourite. One of these critics was the flamboyant libertine MP John Wilkes. He pointedly used the forty-fifth issue of the *North Briton* periodical (thus invoking the Jacobite rebellion in Scotland in 1745) to lampoon Bute (who had already been forced to resign) and, more significantly, to criticize the King's speech at the opening of Parliament which announced 'Bute's Peace'. A general warrant for his arrest for seditious libel was issued and, because he was immune from the charge as an MP, he was expelled from the **House of Commons**. Fleeing to France to avoid arrest, Wilkes became a *cause célèbre* who had exposed the tyrannical nature of the king and his ministers.

Over the next decade Wilkes came to theatrically personify the cause of 'liberty', the rights of the people to ensure the state represented their interests through freedom of election, freedom of the press and the right to publish parliamentary debates. Returning from Paris in 1768 he stood for election in London's largest **constituency** of Middlesex and swept to victory with shouts of 'Wilkes and Liberty' and the number '45' daubed everywhere. Typically, Wilkes presented himself for arrest on the old charges, for which he was tried, imprisoned and again stripped of his seat, re-elected unopposed by the Middlesex electors, promptly disqualified by the Commons, again re-elected unopposed in Middlesex, again disqualified, and finally re-elected again but with the Commons declaring his beaten opponent victorious. It was a remarkable confrontation that placed the issues of representation and freedom of election – whether the king and his ministers or the people controlled Parliament – at the centre of political debate. It led to the resignation of another prime minister, the Duke of Grafton, and even more significantly generated an unprecedented 27 petitions, with 55,000 signatures, from across England in support of Wilkes during 1769. The first national movement for reform had been born and with it came a new political culture. Wilkes's image and the number '45' pro-liferated on prints, badges, mugs, buttons and plates, while pubs and children were named after him, toasts raised to him and gifts sent to him. Although Wilkes mobi-lized the support of tradesmen, shopkeepers and artisans who identified with him as a man of the people, the variety of clubs, lodges and associations that pledged their support to his cause defied easy social categorization. These supporters repre-sented a new movement for reform that wished to restore the constitutional rights of freeborn Englishmen which, they believed, had been eroded since 1688 – one group of supporters was pointedly called the Society for the Supporters of the Bill of Rights. Wilkes was not done when he was released from prison in 1770. He con-tinued to push for the publication of parliamentary debates (a right secured in 1771) and was re-elected to Parliament in 1774.

It was the increasingly rebellious American colonists that took up the broader cri-tique of the unrepresentative nature of the state. Wilkes was an icon for many in the American colonies. The Boston Sons of Liberty, which included John Hancock and Samuel Adams among its members, sent him a 45 pound turtle on his imprisonment in 1768; while the Charleston Club met at 7.45 and drank forty-five toasts to celebrate his release from prison in 1770. They shared Wilkes's rejection of the state's use of arbitrary powers against the representative will of the people, for after the **Seven Years' War** the American colonies were subjected to a new and more interventionist type of imperial rule by the Crown and its ministers in Parliament. After those long and costly wars across several continents, the British government sought not only a tighter political and legal grip upon its newly extended colonial territories but also to increase trade with, and revenue from, them.

During the 1760s a series of measures to increase duties upon the thirteen American colonies met with protest, to which Britain responded by imposing new forms of polit-ical, legal and military control. This pattern was quickly established with the passage of American Revenue and Currency Acts in 1764 as well as the Stamp Act in 1765 which effectively sought to tighten the regulation of imports, to establish pounds sterling as the only legal paper currency and to extend the taxes on all printed paper that applied in Britain. In short, the American colonies were being fiscally and commercially incorpo-rated into the imperial state without regard for their own legislatures. Protests spread, with many 'Sons of Liberty' associations springing up in towns and cities while nine of the thirteen colonial legislatures sent delegates to a Congress in New York whose very existence called into question the representative authority of the British Parliament. While the Stamp and Revenue Acts were then rescinded in the conciliatory Declaratory Act of 1766, Parliament still asserted its supreme authority and the binding nature of its legislation in the colonies. It was a ham-fisted compromise. Within a year the infa-mous Townshend Act sought to subject the colonies to the same import duties on key commodities as applied in Britain, prompting further protests, including a damaging boycott of British goods.

Although new taxes were invariably the trigger for these protests, at issue was the question of local autonomy in an increasingly centralized imperial system and therefore whether the right to government resided in Britain's parliamentary monarchy or in the colonies' own representative legislatures. At the centre of the commercial economy of the Atlantic world – linking North America to the Caribbean, the west coast of Africa and Britain – Boston was especially defensive of its liberties and watchful of the encroachments of the imperial state. The increasing military presence there, designed to enforce the new duties and regulations regarding trade in the thriving port, itself became a target of protest, culminating in the infamous Boston Massacre when five people were killed following a riotous protest at the garrison in 1770. Two years later, the British government made the Massachusetts governor and judiciary *de facto* Crown appointments by affording them salaries. Finally, the following year, when British-government-approved tea from the **East India Company** was dumped into Boston Harbour, the response from London was uncompromising. Massachusetts was subjected to a new Governor's Council appointed from London while the governor was afforded the power to appoint all judges. These so-called 'Intolerable Acts' catalysed the formation of an armed militia in Massachusetts drawing British troops into an escalating conflict that quickly spread to the other colonies and produced the **Declaration of Independence** in 1776.

Not all Americans were revolutionaries and not all revolutionaries were republicans, many were reluctant to embrace independence and not just those who continued to declare their loyalty to the Crown. Even so, the Declaration effectively translated both suspicion and hatred of the increasingly interventionist nature of British rule into a radical set of democratic principles of representation that placed sovereignty solely with the people, holding that 'all men are created equal, that they are endowed by their Creator with certain unalienable Rights, that among these are Life, Liberty and the pursuit of Happiness.' Many Sons of Liberty in the thirteen colonies had, like Wilkes, looked back to the Bill of Rights for the founding principles of representative government, yet by asserting its basis in the natural rights of man the Declaration radically exceeded it. In practice, of course, not all men were considered equal, most notably slaves. The British did their best to exploit that myopia, enlisting some 10,000 slaves to the loyalist cause, especially in the southern states, by the promise of freedom from bondage. Together with an estimated 500,000 **loyalists** (about a fifth of the white population), Britain spent six years failing to regain military, political and economic control of the thirteen colonies, during which time it was also sucked into conflicts with its European rivals the French, Dutch and Spanish in the Caribbean, Mediterranean and South Asia. Twenty years after emerging victorious from the **Seven Years' War**, Britain was again counting the huge costs of war, which this time included a humiliating defeat by the rebel army of its former colonial subjects in America and the flight of some 100,000 loyalists to Canada. It marked not only the end of the **'First' British Empire** but also a deepening and broadening radical critique of the imperial state at home and abroad.

While most Britons supported the war against the American colonies, there was sympathy for the American critique of the increasingly oligarchic nature of the state and for their attempt to reclaim the rights of freeborn Englishmen. Petitions for peace were sent to the king and the **House of Commons** debated the withdrawal of troops in 1778. Moreover, a new generation of the reform movement coalesced around figures like Major John Cartwright, the Reverend Christopher Wyvill and Thomas Paine that, despite their substantial differences, drew inspiration from the American Revolution. Paine, a former excise officer living in Philadelphia, set the ideological tone. At the beginning of 1776, he justified the revolt in America by arguing in *Common Sense* that only independence would rescue her people from the tyranny produced by the hereditary influence of the monarchy and aristocracy upon the British constitution. For Paine the state could only be legitimate if it took the form of a republic and gave all men the vote. Back in Britain the Dissenting minister Richard Price's *Observations on the Nature of Civil Liberty* (1776) hailed the revolution as beginning 'a new era in the history of mankind' and sold a remarkable 60,000 copies within a few months. Cartwright, whose naval career had not matched his elevation as a major in the militia, also published a radical pamphlet, *Take Your Choice!*, calling for **universal male suffrage** in 1776. In it he combined arguments for the restoration of the freeborn liberties of Englishman, which included **annual parliaments** (under an ancient constitution that stretched back to before the Norman Conquest of 1066), with calls for a **secret ballot**, equal member **constituencies** and the assertion, echoing Paine, that 'All are by nature free; all are by nature equal.' Readers were left in no doubt of the choice to be taken. The book's frontispiece compared a sturdy representative system based upon natural and civil rights with a distinctly precarious system of royal despotism. The argument that all men had a natural right and a historical claim to representation was a radical extension of Wilkes's claims, and would drive movements for reform down to 1918 when all men finally got the vote.

Not all reformers were so radical. Three years later Wyvill rallied the gentry in Yorkshire in protest against the excessive taxation necessitated by the ruinous cost of the wars in American and Europe. While Wyvill believed that government could only be made cheaper and more efficient if Parliament were made more representative, his programme did not include a broadening of the franchise but the replacement of **rotten boroughs** with more county members and triennial elections. It was the organization of his movement that held radical promise. In the first few months of 1780 he coordinated the collection of thirty-eight petitions (twenty-six from counties) from around the country in support of his demands and then held a meeting of their delegates at a convention in London. Like the Continental Congress of the American colonies, this body effectively formed an alternative parliament that was by inference more representative than the **House of Commons**. It was not a coincidence that by April Cartwright and his supporters had formed the Society for Constitutional Information that planned explicitly to create a permanent and radically alternative parliament elected by local bodies through a universal male franchise. It was, however, Wyvill's petitioning movement that got most traction. It pushed the Commons to declare that the 'influence of the crown has increased, is increasing and ought to be diminished'. It also helped secure some significant 'economical' reforms in 1782 that reduced both the size of the Civil List (the money afforded the monarchy by Parliament) and the number of government appointments and pensions. Further petitioning campaigns generated motions for reform in the House of Commons that won the support of over 140 MPs on three occasions. Even if many had been scared by the radicalism of Cartwright and the violent demotic will evident in the **Gordon Riots**, the issue of reform had been placed on the political agenda. The expense and unrepresentative nature of a state that placed an ever-growing tax burden upon its people could no longer be ignored.

 ## Old Corruption and the Colonial Question

The first volume of Gibbon's monumental history of the *Decline and Fall of the Roman Empire* was published in the year of the American Revolution. The sixth and final volume was released twelve years later in 1788 as Britons marked the centenary of the **Glorious Revolution** and eagerly followed the impeachment trial of Warren Hastings, the Governor-General of India. Gibbon's account of the implosion of the Roman Empire placed great emphasis on how the corruption of the imperial court and its nobles had eroded the authority of government, its ability to collect taxes and the effectiveness of its military. The parallels were striking and they helped make *Decline and Fall* one of the first best-selling history books.

The Scandal of Empire

After the loss of the American colonies the fate of the British Empire was increasingly seen to lie in South Asia with the **East India Company (EIC)**. Formed in 1600, the EIC was a **joint-stock company** afforded rights to trade in Asia by royal charter. After the Revolution, when it finally secured a complete monopoly on trade in the region, the EIC became an increasingly important component of the British state, providing it with lines of credit, tax revenue on its trade, and a military presence in South Asia to contain the trading and territorial ambitions of its European rivals, the French, Dutch and Portuguese. Indeed, the defeat of the Nawab of Bengal (the governor of Bengal, who remained loyal to the Mughal emperor) and French troops at the Battle of Plassey in 1757 during the **Seven Years' War** effectively gave the EIC military command in the region. By 1765, when Robert Clive, the hero of that campaign, secured from the emperor the right (known as the *diwani*) to tax the people of Bengal, ostensibly in return for military protection and the rule of law, the EIC had become a *de facto* sovereign ruler beyond jurisdiction of Crown or Parliament. With EIC officials like Clive amassing vast fortunes from personal trade in South Asia and returning to Britain, where they were called '**nabobs**', to buy country estates and seats as MPs, the influence of the company seemed to run to the very heart of government. Already busy consolidating its imperial control over the North American colonies, the British state moved quickly to re-establish its grip on the company state. First, in 1769 the EIC was compelled to provide an annual income of £400,000 to the British government and its dividend to shareholders was limited to 12.5 per cent of its profit while the rest was loaned to the state. Second, when the scale of company misrule was made apparent by the famine that killed a third of Bengal's population in 1770 and devastated the *diwani* revenue, the Regulating Act of 1773 subjected the Company to new political controls from London with the parliamentary appointment of a Governor-General, a Governing Council and a Supreme Court, controls further tightened by the India Act of 1784.

Nonetheless, when Warren Hastings, the first Governor-General appointed by London in 1773, was impeached in 1788, it remained the Company's government of India, its influence in Parliament and the personal enrichment of its officers that was really on trial. It was Edmund Burke, the Whig MP whose sympathies for the rebellious American colonies and support for economic reforms at home were well noted, who led the campaign against Hastings. Describing him as the 'captain general of iniquity' Burke outlined the profligacy, corruption and violence of Hastings' rule and its corrosive effect on Indian society. Burke was not opposed to imperialism but he thought that India should be governed in accord with its own customs and not by novel and foreign systems arrogantly devised by ambitious and greedy men with an eye on their future lives back in Britain. Although the trial, which dragged on for seven years, ended with the acquittal of Hastings, it had important and contradictory legacies. It reanimated critique of the wasteful and corrupt distribution of government offices, pensions and parliamentary seats at home that placed a heavier tax burden upon the people. Burke laid down a theory of rule as founded upon precedent moulded around the historical development of society, which he would develop further two years later in response to the revolution in France. London's control over the EIC was tightened by the appointment of the economic reformer Cornwallis to succeed Hastings as Governor-General, but while Cornwallis rooted out waste (mainly by dismissing Indian officials for corruption) and corruption (by placing officials on fixed salaries, not commissions), he also imposed a new and alien administrative system with the **Permanent Settlement** in 1793. Inspired by French physiocratic ideas as well as the historical model of the

English gentry, the Permanent Settlement consolidated the reorientation of Company revenue from trade to land by turning the *zamindars*, who had previously collected the *diwani*, effectively into a new class of landholders and fixing the levels of tax upon their land in perpetuity.

Remembering the Glorious Revolution

The high drama of the Hastings impeachment trial took place during the centenary celebrations for the Revolution of 1688–9. Revolution societies sprang up across the country to commemorate the event with dinners, toasts and tokens. Reformers used the centenary to bemoan what they saw as the Revolution's unfulfilled promises of representative government and civil rights for **Dissenters**. In Scotland petitions supporting the reform of the burghs gathered momentum during 1788 and 1789. The campaign to repeal the **Test and Corporations Acts** – which barred Dissenters from a university education, public office or a seat in Parliament – came to a head in 1787 when the leading Whig MP Charles James Fox moved its repeal in Parliament, an effort he repeated in 1789 and 1790. It was fitting then that, shortly after the outbreak of the French Revolution in 1789 and before the defeat of Fox's final effort at repeal, the leading reformer and Dissenting minister Richard Price delivered a sermon, later published as *Discourse on the Love of Our Country*, celebrating the **Glorious Revolution**. It had, he argued, established the people's right to representative government over the tyrannical rule of a royal sovereign and thereby ensured Britons had not become 'a base people, groaning under the infamy and misery of popery and slavery'. And yet it was, he concluded, 'an imperfect work' that had neither extended the right to representation nor religious liberty fully enough, in marked contrast to the revolution in France.

The notoriety of Price's pamphlet was assured by the eviscerating response to it by Edmund Burke. Despite Burke's impeccable **Whig** credentials, *Reflections on the Revolution in France* (1790) insisted that the Glorious Revolution was no innovation for it had only restored 'that ancient constitution of government which is our only security for law and liberty'. For Burke, history was not to be dispensed with by embracing novel theories. The principles of government were rooted in their historical evolution that bound together 'those who are living, those who are dead, and those who are to be born'.

While for Price and Burke the meaning of the Revolution of 1688 became defined in relation to the French Revolution, Thomas Paine's *The Rights of Man* (1791) responded to Burke by insisting that the future should not be governed by the past, let alone by the imperfect revolutionary settlement of 1688. Paine celebrated the revolutions in America and France for entirely dispensing with monarchs and asserting the natural and equal rights of all men to be represented. His critique of the hereditary principle of government appeared to challenge the very basis of rule by the propertied. Not content with asserting the radical case for representative government, Paine published a second installment of *The Rights of Man* in 1792 that laid out an agenda for far-reaching social reforms. A properly representative government, he argued, would redirect taxation so that instead of supporting aristocratic corruption and war it would sustain education for all and provide welfare to the sick, the elderly and children. Informed by enlightened intellectual debates and the revolutionary ferment in France, Paine's work was part of a remarkable proliferation of radical thinking in the 1790s that pushed his ideas still further. Mary Wollstonecraft's *Vindication of the Rights of Woman* (1792) dared to imagine women's equality with men and their right to education, while some in radical circles even contemplated extending women's legal, religious and political rights. Thomas Spence's *The Real Rights of Man* (1793) proposed that in every **parish** the land be returned to the people who had a natural right to it, not least because they had once held it in common. The debate that had begun around the meaning of the Revolution of 1688, and had rehearsed the familiar themes of a corrupt, wasteful and unrepresentative state, now contemplated a thorough reordering of the status quo.

Emboldened by these ideas, the reform movement was re-energized. There were reputedly 50,000 copies of Paine's *The Rights of Man* in circulation within three months of its publication when Burke's *Reflections*, published the previous year, had still only sold 19,000. The revived Society for Constitutional Information, the Friends of the People in Scotland, and the newly formed London Corresponding Society widely distributed or cheaply sold Paine's text. Founded in 1792, the London Corresponding Society heralded the advent of a more plebeian type of reform movement with a weekly subscription of a penny and a pledge that 'the number of our members be unlimited'. Informed by Paine's work and led by the Scottish shoemaker Thomas Hardy, its membership included small tradesmen, skilled artisans and working men. Within a year 6,000 people had signed a petition in support of its resolutions for reform that included distinctly Paine-ite demands for education and support for the sick and poor, as well as expressions of sympathy for the revolution in France.

Finally, into this mix came the United Irishmen. Formed in 1791 by the Protestant lawyer Theobald Wolfe Tone, the United Irishmen pledged 'to obtain an equal, full and adequate representation of all the people of Ireland' irrespective of their religion. With their own newspaper *The Northern Star* the United Irishmen also sought to build alliances with other groups, both Protestant and Catholic, concerned with removing civil disabilities and reducing Ireland's subordination to rule from London. This cocktail of reforming organizations that included **Dissenters**, Catholics, republicans, radical reformers and working men was alarming enough to many and not just those in government. To them the security of the state, the authority of the monarchy, the position of the Anglican church and even the entire social order seemed at risk.

The Counter-Revolution

Local groups pledging their support for 'Church and King' began to form in 1790 and 1791, when the house of the **Dissenter** Joseph Priestley, as well as a number of Baptist and Unitarian chapels, were attacked and destroyed in Birmingham. When Paine and his publisher were charged with sedition following the King's Proclamation Against Seditious Writings in May 1792, it unleashed a wave of **loyalist** meetings at which Paine was often burnt in effigy. Developments in France – where the proclamation of the republic in August 1792 was followed in January by the execution of the king and a declaration of war against Britain a week or so later – further alarmed **loyalists** and produced fresh tides of patriotic fervour. Within six months of its formation in November 1792 the Association for Preserving Liberty and Property Against Republicans and Levellers had over 2,000 local groups affiliated to it. This loyalist counter-revolution was partly whipped up by the formidable publicity machine of the government. It funded newspapers – like *The Sun* (1792), the *True Briton* (1793) and later *The Anti-Jacobin* (1797) – and hired printmakers to refute the radical case and demonize its leaders. Just four days after a London Corresponding Society meeting at Copenhagen Fields on 12 November 1795, James Gillray published a caricature of it (see Figure 1.6). The print portrays John Thelwall, renowned for his energetic oratory,

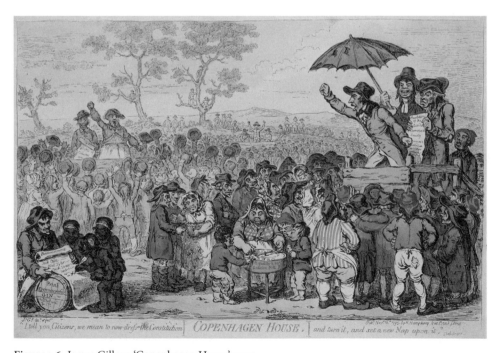

Figure 1.6 James Gillray, 'Copenhagen House', 1795

appealing to an audience of ragged working men, former slaves signing a petition, women selling their wares and, foregrounded in the centre, Fox and Pitt portrayed as children playing roulette. Loyalism was not just a state-sponsored affair, as can be seen by the Cheap Repository Tracts produced by Hannah More after 1795 (see Textbox 1.2 and Figure 1.7).

Figure 1.7 Hannah More, 1789

1.2 **Person: Hannah More (1745–1833)**

Hannah More was an evangelical writer and political activist who rose to prominence for her literary work and her use of the pen to oppose slavery and criticize the radical politics of the French Revolution. More grew up and continued to live in Bristol. She and her three sisters were raised under the tutelage of her father, a head teacher and former excise man, and her mother, the daughter of a farmer. A precocious literary talent who had published a verse drama about the appropriate forms of women's education at the age of seventeen,

her annual visits to London with her sisters soon established her as a member of the Blue Stocking Circle, an elite group of women in London's literary circles who promoted each other's work. More quickly became a prolific author of multiple plays, tracts on social and political issues, as well as speeches. While More agitated for women's education, she remained resolute about what she saw as unassailable differences between men and women. Despite her own career, More argued that women should never aspire to intellectual or political equality with men, and encouraged female students to pursue household skills such as sewing and knitting rather than more intellectual pursuits. An evangelical Anglican, she became a keen advocate for the anti-slavery movement during the 1780s, producing a poem titled 'Slavery' to publicize William Wilberforce's bill to abolish slavery in 1788. Increasingly, More's work preached the values of Christian virtues for all and the necessity of political loyalism among the working poor. Like her friend and contemporary Edmund Burke, for whose election as Bristol's MP in 1774 she successfully campaigned, More argued in favour of a static and hierarchically structured society, upheld by the active consent of the educated poor. To this end, between 1795 and 1817

More wrote and commissioned more than 200 'Cheap Repository Tracts' aimed at the literate poor and intended to counter a growing number of publications supporting the French Revolution such as Thomas Paine's 'Rights of Man'. The tracts wrote of the evils of political unrest and urged readers not to rise above their station in life, as well as condemning drunkenness, idleness and gambling. Within a year over 2 million of these tracts had been sold and were distributed as far afield as the United States, the West Indies and Sierra Leone. The final decades of her life were spent dealing with the loss of her sisters and her own failing health. She died in Bristol's Clifton district and was buried alongside her sisters in the village church at Wrington outside of the city. (S.W.)

'Pitt's Terror'

Yet the abuse and violence radicals received at the hands of **loyalists** was nothing compared to the repressive force of the state. An unparalleled network of government spies was assembled and they quickly fed back to London conspiracy theories of radical alliances with France and threats of armed insurgency. When the Scottish Friends of the People organized a national meeting of reformers at Edinburgh in October 1793 the government pounced. Its leaders were charged with sedition and quickly **transported** to Australia's Botany Bay for fourteen years (see Textbox 1.3 and Figure 1.8). Six months later, with rumours that another national meeting was planned, the government sought to chop off the head of the movement in England, arresting nineteen leading figures in the London Corresponding Society and Society for Constitutional Information for 'treasonable practices'. A week later **habeas corpus** (the right of detainees to a court hearing) was suspended in order to allow their continuing detention before a trial was eventually held in October for just three of them – Hardy, Thelwall and Tooke. The radicals skilfully used the occasion to put the imperial state on trial for its excessive expenditure on war with revolutionary France and its increasingly repressive use of emergency laws, as well as to advance their own case for its radical reform. Their acquittal was a major embarrassment for the government and a fillip to the reform movement. By 1795 the London Corresponding Society claimed a membership of around 10,000 spread across 90 branches. It was able to organize the largest ever demonstration in favour

Figure 1.8 The arrival of the first prisoners at Botany Bay

of reform when 100,000 people gathered at London's Copenhagen Fields. When the meeting ended some threw stones at the King's carriage as he went to open Parliament.

This affront to the king unleashed the final part of what a group of radicals in Norwich described as 'a system of terror, almost as hideous in its features, almost as gigantic in its stature, and infinitely more pernicious in its tendency, than France ever knew'. The so-called 'gagging acts' allowed magistrates to outlaw potentially seditious public meetings and expanded the definition of treason to include just about any act that threatened the authority of the king or Parliament. When widespread dearth

1.3 **Place: Botany Bay**

Botany Bay, the large bay where the Australian city of Sydney's airport and docks are now located, was where Captain James Cook first landed in Australia in 1770. Long the home of the Tharawal and Eora Aboriginal peoples, the British established a penal colony there in 1788 when Captain Arthur Phillip landed the First Fleet of eleven ships containing 850 convicts. Although the penal colony was soon moved to nearby Sydney Cove, it continued to be referred to in Britain as 'Botany Bay'. Those found guilty of a variety of different crimes in Britain had been exiled or forcibly transported for hundreds of years prior to the British settlement of Australia. The 1717 Transportation Act formalized and regulated the practice of penal **transportation**. Under the Act, criminals found guilty of crimes such as petty larceny were sentenced to seven or fourteen years of forced labour in the American colonies. After the American Revolution convicts were instead transported to Australia. Over 4,000 convicts landed at 'Botany Bay' in the first four years of the penal colony's existence. Many others did not survive the arduous eight-month journey.

Most of these prisoners were poor and illiterate, victims of laws that criminalized vagrancy; others were political prisoners (like those radical leaders transported during 'Pitt's Terror'), prisoners of war and the young children of convicts. Convicts were not imprisoned but compelled to work, and most of those who completed their sentence opted (or were forced by circumstance) to 'settle' in the Sydney area of the new colony that had been named New South Wales. There they faced violent attacks by the indigenous population, as well as frequent riots and rebellions in response to severe shortages of food and fresh water, and what was in effect the military rule of autocratic governors. The biggest victims of the Botany Bay colony were not the convicts themselves but the local Eora community of Aboriginal people, 70 per cent of whom were killed by smallpox brought by the first fleet of convicts. While the arrival of Lieutenant-Colonel Lachlan Macquarie as a reforming Governor-General in 1809 has been credited with stabilizing the new settler colony of New South Wales, penal transportation continued there until 1868. (S.W.)

gripped the country in 1799 and 1800 and government informers and spies fretted over fresh conspiracy theories, these measures were supplemented by **Combination Acts** that allowed magistrates to imprison for three months any working men who sought to organize together. The passage of these various repressive laws would have been inconceivable without the sense of a state of emergency. Some 300,000 **loyalists** joined up as Volunteers to defend king and country between 1794 and 1799 and during the invasion scare of 1804 their numbers reached a remarkable 450,000. It was loyalists determined to defend king and country, not radicals seeking a revolution, who succeeded in arming an unprecedented number of working men. The counter-revolution was complete.

Or almost, for as so often the bloodiest and most brutal episode was in Ireland. Disappointed by the partial reforms in 1793, when Catholics had been given the right to vote but not to sit in Parliament and London had reasserted its imperial control with a new Lord Lieutenant, the United Irishmen were preparing an armed rising. The plan was for Wolfe Tone to secure an invasion of French troops who would combine forces with Presbyterian Volunteers in the north and the secret societies of Catholic Defenders in the south. In December 1796 Tone set sail for Ireland with 15,000 French troops but bad weather prevented them from landing. Over the next two years the government in Ireland brutally snuffed out rebellions, suspended **habeas corpus**, and allowed its militia and troops to terrorize local populations. When Tone was finally captured, having belatedly returned in October 1798 with a token French force to aid renewed rebellions in the north and south, he used his court-martial hearing to eloquently repeat the case for a democratic, religiously equal and independent Ireland. He then chose to take his own life rather than face being hanged like a criminal. The rising, with its several rebellions and various reprisals, cost 12,000 Irish lives. The crushing military defeat of the rebels paved the way for the incorporation of Ireland into the United Kingdom with the **Act of Union** in 1800. Yet there were carrots as well as the stick. New peers were created, votes were purchased to the tune of £30,000, over £1 million was spent on compensating the disenfranchised boroughs, and **Catholic emancipation** was promised (although it was subsequently rescinded by George III at the cost of Pitt's resignation). All this was enough for the Irish Parliament to vote to dissolve itself in return for 100 seats in the **House of Commons** and 32 in the **House of Lords**.

Despite the kingdom being 'united', and a brief interlude in the war with Napoleon's France following the Treaty of Amiens in 1802, the imperial British state was still under threat. Although Nelson's defeat of the French and Spanish navies at the Battle of Trafalgar in 1805 effectively ended the threat of invasion, the war continued and even extended to North America in 1812 as the United States' ambition to colonize the Indian lands around the Great Lakes threatened upper Canada. Peace did not arrive until 1815 at the **Congress of Vienna**, following the defeat of Napoleon at the Battle of Waterloo (a bloodbath where 40,000 British and French troops died). In that peace treaty Britain secured new imperial territories like Trinidad, Ceylon and the Cape of Good Hope and finally established itself as the dominant power of Europe. The country, exhausted after twenty-two years of war, rejoiced with illuminations, bonfires and dinners.

The costs of war had been considerable. A quarter of a million men had died fighting for their country and over £1 billion had been spent. Britain was left with an unprecedented **national debt** of £745 million – over 250 per cent of GDP, still the highest ever – that required £50 million a year just to service the interest. As Britain's war machine was wound down and its bullion reserves built up to allow its currency to be pegged to gold, unemployment was rife. Moreover, following a series of bad harvests the **Corn Laws** were passed in 1815 to protect aristocratic landholders from a potential flood of cheap foreign grain that would have lowered their income as well as the cost of bread, the staple diet of the poor. For reformers this simply laid bare the ruinous expense, waste and corruption of an aristocratic state that feathered its own nest at the cost of an impoverished and unrepresented people.

From Pentrich to 'Peterloo'

Calls for radical reform were revived around a new generation of leaders and an increasingly withering critique of **Old Corruption**. While many of the humbler radical leaders of the 1790s had been forced to withdraw from politics, figures like Major Cartwright and Sir Francis Burdett had remained active but were gradually overshadowed by a new type of 'gentleman leader' in the form of **William Cobbett** and Henry 'Orator' Hunt. As affluent gentry farmers, Cobbett and Hunt promised to sacrifice their own social position to advance the rights of the people. A gifted writer, Cobbett had first taken up Wilkes's cause of publishing parliamentary debates before starting his own weekly newspaper *The Political Register* in 1802. When in 1817 he issued a cheap and unstamped edition of the *The Register* it quickly reached a circulation of 50,000. Like Thomas Wooler's more satirical *Black Dwarf* (1817–24), these newly assertive radical publications reached new readers and advanced a searing indictment of what had become known as 'Old Corruption' – the miseries of taxation and tyrannical violence rained down on the people to sustain the waste and corruption of an unrepresentative aristocratic state. During the 1790s there had been a little over a hundred prosecutions for seditious libel but in just four years between 1817 and 1821 there were 131 as radical writers and publishers got under the skin of the authorities with unnerving frequency thanks not just to their new scurrilous tone but the detail of their analysis. Nowhere was this better exemplified than in John Wade's *The Black Book: Corruption Unmasked!* published in 1820 with a subtitle that announced the comprehensiveness of its work – *Being an Account of Places, Pensions and Sinecures, The Revenues of the Clergy and Landed Aristocracy; The Salaries and Emoluments in Courts of Justice and the Police Department; the Expenditure of the Civil List … The Profits of the Bank of England. The Debt Revenue and Influence of the East India Company; The State of the Finances, Debt and Sinking Fund. To which is added, Correct Lists of both Houses of Parliament; showing their Family Connections, Parliamentary Influence, the Place and Pensions held by themselves or Relations … the whole forming a complete Exposition of the COST, INFLUENCE, PATRONAGE AND CORRUPTION OF THE BRITISH GOVERNMENT.* The Old Corruption at the heart of the unrepresentative state had no place to hide.

This critique resonated with many in the manufacturing districts of Scotland, the northwest of England and the Midlands, which alongside London became the new heartland of the reform movement. For some of the labouring poor insurrection was the answer. In December 1816, 10,000 people gathered for a reform meeting at London's

Spa Fields after which a group of Spenceans looted a gun shop and sought to seize the **Bank of England** and Tower of London. Four months later thousands of textile workers in Manchester determined to march to London wrapped in blankets to keep warm. By June hundreds of labourers joined a 'Rising' in Pentrich, Derbyshire, led by an unemployed stocking-maker. Partly thanks to the spies that had infiltrated radical circles, most infamously W.J. Richards, known as 'Oliver the Spy', these insurrections were met by the full force of the state: troops were mobilized, leaders were arrested and imprisoned, transported or executed. **William Cobbett** astutely accused the authorities of using spies 'not to prevent, but to produce those acts' so that they could generate a state of emergency that justified the suspension of **habeus corpus** (again) and the reintroduction of the 'gagging acts'. If the protests at Spa Fields, Manchester and Pentrich remained largely isolated affairs, a mass reform movement gathered momentum alongside them. A meeting of seventy radical leaders in January 1817 began a petitioning campaign that produced 700 petitions from 350 localities in its first year and 1,570 petitions during 1818. When motions for modest reforms were contemptuously defeated in Parliament, reformers resolved to convene a more representative anti-parliament with delegates elected by local assemblies. However, when in August 1819 50,000 gathered to hear Henry Hunt at Manchester's St Peter's Fields exhort them to do just that, the local magistrates sent in the cavalry who, drawing their swords, mercilessly killed 14 men and 4 women and injured a further 650, including over 150 women. It was a harrowing scene, reproduced in Figure 1.9.

Figure 1.9 The Peterloo Massacre, 1819

This horrific event appalled many. It powerfully dramatized the violence the state would deploy to suppress the case for reform and what many believed to be the ancient rights to freedom of speech and assembly. While the Home Secretary, Lord Sidmouth, praised the magistracy for preserving the peace, Henry Hunt and other leaders were arrested and imprisoned. So too was James Wroe, the editor of the *Manchester Observer*, who had published a harrowing account of the event comparing its carnage to the Battle of Waterloo, describing it as '**The Peterloo Massacre**'. Almost as soon as Parliament returned, an unparalleled series of repressive emergency measures were introduced that, once again, winded the reform movement. The notorious **Six Acts** effectively made any reform meeting 'an overt act of treasonable conspiracy', muzzled the radical press with stamp duties and definitions of blasphemy and seditious libel, and gave the magistracy sweeping powers to prevent any meeting of over fifty people, to prohibit military-style training and to inspect any property for arms. At no time had the British state claimed for itself and exercised greater powers.

Conclusion

After its fragile genesis in 1688, the state developed a formidable fiscal-military appara-tus that not only allowed it to secure itself but to extend its rule over the home nations of Scotland and Ireland as well imperial territories across several continents. Its foreign rivals, its colonial subjects in America and the reform movement at home all sought to challenge its increasing power and the centralization of its authority in London. The long eighteenth century that had begun with a supposedly **Glorious Revolution** ended with a counter-revolution that demonstrated the full violent force of the new Leviathan.

FURTHER READING

The past four decades have seen a great revival of work on what historians often describe as the 'long eighteenth century'. When that century is taken to begin and end depends upon one's view of it. Those preoccupied with the nature of the eighteenth-century state and its structures of government cannot agree whether it is best characterized as an ancien regime or as taking new and precociously modern forms.

Lewis Namier's classic work *The Structure of Politics at the Accession of George III* (London, 1929), written as fascism and communism spread across Europe after World War One, cast a long shadow. He portrayed England's political system as dominated by the patronage and power of the landed classes. Politics, he argued, had nothing to do with ideology and everything to do with competition for places and status. In contrast, J.C.D.C. Clark's *English Society, 1688–1832* (Cambridge, 1985) argued that ideology was what made the English state an ancien regime. It was the Anglican religion that tied together the central pillars of what he described as a 'confessional' or 'theocratic' state – monarchy, Church and aristocracy – that was not so different from those states on the continent of Europe ruled by absolute monarchs.

Others argued that the ancien regime worked to produce the future rather than to reproduce the past. No less than Namier and Clark, E.P. Thompson's *Whigs and Hunters: The Origin of the Black Acts* (1975) portrayed the eighteenth-century state as dominated by the landed classes. Yet Thompson highlighted how they passed and practised draconian laws dispossessing and criminalizing the poor and their common rights in order to create a new understanding of the sanctity of private property. Similarly, Linda Colley's *Britons: The Forging of a Nation, 1707–1837* (New Haven, 1992) argued that the new British nation-state created by the Acts of Union with Scotland and Ireland was tied together by a rabid anti-Catholicism that was propagated through an expanding print culture. The vitality and popular reach of eighteenth-century elections and political culture, despite their apparently archaic forms, are well addressed in Frank O'Gorman's *Voters, Patrons, and Parties: The Unreformed Electoral System of Hanoverian England 1734–1832* (Oxford, 1989) and Kathleen Wilson's *The Sense of the People: Politics, Culture and Imperialism in England, 1715–1785* (Cambridge, 1995).

An emphasis upon the novel elements and modern nature of the post-1688 state has also been a feature of recent work. John Brewer's *Sinews of Power: War, Money and the English State, 1688–1783* (Cambridge, Mass., 1990) started the trend by highlighting the centrality of debt-financing and taxation to the military success and imperial expansion of the English state. Steve Pincus's *1688: The First Modern Revolution* (New Haven, 2009) recovers how central ideological debates over political economy were to the Revolution of 1688 and its aftermath. For a complementary if contrasting view of the complex and composite nature of the British state, see Joanna Innes, *Inferior Politics: Social Problems and Social Policy in Eighteenth-Century Britain* (Oxford, 2009), David Eastwood's *Governing Rural England: Tradition and Transformation in Local Government 1780–1840* (Oxford, 1994), Julian Hoppit (ed.), *Parliaments, Nations and Identities in Britain and Ireland, 1660–1850* (Manchester, 2003) and D.W. Hayton and Clyve Jones (eds.), *Parliament, Politics and Policy in Britain and Ireland, c.1680–1832* (Oxford, 2014). Philip Stern's *The Company State: Corporate Sovereignty and the Early Modern Foundations of the British Empire in India* (Oxford, 2012) reminds us that the composite nature of the British state extended abroad as it subcontracted the business of governing India to a company that pioneered new innovations in the art of government.

Indeed, it is no longer possible to ignore the role imperial expansion played in forging Britain's own forms of government and political culture. The push to centralize and maximize imperial revenues after the **Seven Years' War** and differing responses to it is nicely detailed in C.A. Bayly's *Imperial Meridian: The British Empire and the World, 1780–1830* (London, 1989) and P.J. Marshall's *The Making and Unmaking of Empires: Britain, India and America, 1750–1783* (Oxford, 2007). Differing accounts of the revolt of the American colonies and its consequences for Britons are provided by H.T. Dickinson (ed.), *Britain and the American Revolution, 1760–1783* (London, 1998), and Eliga Gould's *The Persistence of Empire: British Political Culture in the Age of the American Revolution* (Chapel Hill, 2002). The political effects of the American Revolution across the Atlantic world are explored in Andrew O'Shaughnessy, *An Empire Divided: The American Revolution and the British Caribbean* (Philadelphia, 2000), and Vincent Morley's *Irish Opinion and the American Revolution, 1760–1783* (Cambridge, 2007). Stern's *Company State* and Nicholas Dirks's *The Scandal of Empire: India and the Creation of Imperial*

Britain (Cambridge, Mass., 2008) outline the attempts to rein in the autonomy of the **East India Company** and the reverberations of the impeachment trial of its first Governor-General.

The rise of the reform movement at home, its critique of **Old Corruption** and the counter-revolution against it after the French Revolution have generated a huge literature. Classic works that remain hard to beat include E.P. Thompson's *The Making of the English Working Class* (London, 1963), John Brewer's *Party Ideology and Popular Politics at the Accession of George III* (Cambridge, 1976), Iain McCalman's *Radical Underworld: Prophets, Revolutionaries and Pornographers in London, 1795–1840* (Cambridge, 1988), James Epstein's *Radical Expression: Political Language, Ritual and Symbol in England, 1790–1850* (Oxford, 1994) and Mark Philp (ed.), *The French Revolution and British Popular Politics* (Cambridge, 1991). The role of women and the gendering of these political formations is well covered in Anna Clark's *The Struggle for the Breeches: Gender and the Making of the British Working Class* (London, 1995), K. Gleadle and S. Richardson (eds.), *Women in British Politics: The Power of Petticoats* (Basingstoke, 2000) and Elaine Chalus, *Elite Women in English Political Life c.1754–1790* (Oxford, 2005).

2 An Enlightened Civil Society?

Introduction

The critique of the British state and the growth of political movements dedicated to its reform did not come out of thin air. They were made possible by the emergence, from Locke to Wollstonecraft, of new 'Enlightened' ideas about the nature of government and the rights of men and women. These ideas reached unprecedented numbers of people through the spread of print culture and new forms of association. This was, in turn, part of a broader set of developments known as the **Enlightenment** that produced a proliferation of new and competing ideas, critical of received wisdom and inherited structures of authority, that extended far beyond politics and were discussed by more and more people in an increasing variety of forms and venues. While the state placed real limits upon what it was possible to publish or say, it nonetheless presided over a dramatic expansion of both the content and form of public debate. This was a remarkable transformation given that during the seventeenth century society had been literally torn apart in the **Civil War** and Revolution by debates over the nature of religious and political authority. The central question of this chapter is, then, how did society become civil enough that sectarian and political debate became relatively normal, despite occasional outbreaks of large-scale violence like the **Gordon Riots** and the **Peterloo Massacre**? Measured in terms of the proliferation of public debate, and appeals to a public as the legitimate basis of support for a position, as well as the numbers and types of voluntary associations, Britain's civil society was the first to emerge from the **ancien regimes** of Europe.

And yet we should not rush to celebrate an apparent British genius for pluralism, voluntarism and civility. As we saw in Chapter 1, it was what reformers characterized as the unrepresentative and tyrannical nature of the British state – and the continuing dominance of it by the monarchy, aristocracy and Anglican Church – that often helped catalyse debate. In portraying Britain as an ancien regime, reformers were influenced by Enlightened ideas that emanated primarily from the continent of Europe and were informed by imperial encounters further afield. Not all forms of Enlightenment were necessarily radical, even though they commonly included the belief that scientific experimentation and reasoned debate, not the dogmatic application of theology or custom, were the way to understand and organize the world. Certainly those ideas could be used to challenge the authority of the established Protestant churches in Britain, as well as the hereditary nature of its social and political elite. Yet they were also used to expand the field of human knowledge and intellectual life for its own sake. Indeed, Enlightenment and civility did not necessarily mean emancipation. With them came a new a set of expectations about how to act in the world, what could or could not be said or done, and by whom, as women, the poor and colonial subjects of different races were considered too irrational to be part of civil society. Moreover, at the advent of the nineteenth century Britain's ancien regime remained arguably the most secure in Europe and the yoke of custom still lay heavy on its people.

TIMELINE

1687	Aphra Behn's *Love-Letters Between a Nobleman and his Sister*
1688	Gregory King's study of the 'Condition of England'
1700	Mary Astell's *Reflections on Marriage*
1711–14	*The Spectator*
1719	Daniel Defoe's *Robinson Crusoe*
1725	Henry Bourne's *Antiquitates Vulgares*
1739	551 coffee houses in London
1751	Society of Antiquaries
1759–60	Joseph Massie's study of 'Social Structure and Income'
1759	British Museum William Hogarth's 'The Cockpit'
1760s	Society for the Reformation of Manners
1764	Birmingham's Lunar Society
1768	Captain James Cook's First Voyage to South Seas Royal Academy of Arts
1779	Cook's death on Hawaii
1785	Sunday School Society
1787	George III's 'Proclamation for the Encouragement of Piety and Virtue' Committee for the Abolition of the African Slave Trade
1791	Methodists break from Anglican Church
1795	London Missionary Society
1799	Religious Tract Society
1802	Society for the Suppression of Vice
1824	Society for the Prevention of Cruelty to Animals

The Social Order

Society in eighteenth-century Britain was highly structured around a hierarchy of finely graded ranks and orders, stations and degrees, sorts and classes. When the tax official and statistician Gregory King investigated the 'state and condition of England' in 1696 he detailed no less than twenty social groups differentiated by various 'ranks, degrees, titles and qualifications'. Little had changed when Joseph Massie conducted a similar study of Britain's social structure over sixty years later (see Textbox 2.1). It was less the variety of these forms of social distinction – which combined political offices, economic occupations and social ranks – than their seemingly unchanging and hierarchical order that made Britain resemble a society structured by caste more than class.

The Natural Order of Things

For many Britons this hierarchy was considered the natural order of things and some even believed it reflected a divinely ordained 'chain of being' that had created a perfectly calibrated and mutually supporting division of rights, duties and labour across society. Whatever position one had been assigned by birth was considered fitting for one's abilities and, whether rich or poor, it was one's duty to obediently perform that role. In the acerbic words of the Tory man of letters Samuel Johnson, the British were naturally schooled in subordination by 'the fixed, invariable, external rules of distinction of rank, which create no jealousy, since they are held to be accidental' because they were products of history or nature. Needless to say, such views, endlessly propounded from the pulpits and pens of those well placed in this social order, legitimized a vastly unequal distribution of wealth and power.

As accidents of birth determined the life chances of Britons, so social groups tended to reproduce themselves. The aristocracy and gentry, whose wealth and power stemmed from their holdings of land, strictly regulated rights of inheritance through the laws of primogeniture and entail. These laws ensured that estates were not only left entirely to the eldest son but that he in turn was legally bound to do the same. Other sons, besides being left lump sums or annuities, were lined up for posts in the military, the church, the court or as a government official – hence the radical critique of aristocratic **Old Corruption**. Similarly, politics became an increasingly dynastic affair: in 1754 over half of MPs had followed in the footsteps of their fathers and over two thirds had some broader family connection to the House of Commons. The same was largely true of the professions, where a third of the **clergy** had followed their fathers, while the closed nature of the emerging legal and medical professions also served to allow them to reproduce themselves through families. In the world of business, merchants hired relatives as agents or clerks in their counting-houses and marriage was a vital way for raising and investing capital in an enterprise. As the marriage of women was also an essential mechanism for maintaining social status, daughters came with dowries designed to find them a husband who could secure their position in life. The trade in daughters on the marriage market reflected the utterly subordinate position of women in eighteenth-century society, which was again considered a natural and God-given state of affairs. No wonder that Mary Astell, often described as the first British feminist, asked in *Some Reflections Upon Marriage* (1700): 'If all men are born free, how is it that all women are born slaves?' Astell urged women to educate themselves so they could at least face their husbands as intellectual equals, but even with an education women had no legal rights as wives, for marriage ensured husbands exclusive ownership of property and custody of children. The strictly hierarchical nature of family life, with men ruling as patriarchs over women and children whose duty it was to obey, reflected that of society as a whole.

In society as a whole, no less than in the family, it was a system that entrenched a powerful oligarchy and remarkable inequalities of wealth. At the apex of this social structure stood a few hundred aristocratic families, bedecked with hereditary titles (as dukes, earls, marquesses, viscounts and barons), seats in the House of Lords and estates that by 1800 accounted for a quarter of all landed property in Britain (to say nothing of their sometimes extensive colonial holdings). The wealth generated by the rental income on these estates was often invested in London's burgeoning financial markets where it provided loans to the state, radiated around the world and provided total incomes of up to £30,000 a year. Their influence spread across the royal court, the military and the diplomatic service (where their sons were given posts), through the **House of Commons** (where their landed interest helped them influence the election of as many as a third of MPs) and as ministers (who remained almost exclusively aristocratic). By the end of the eighteenth century there was no other aristocracy in Europe as powerful, rich or entrenched. The local face of the ruling class was less the aristocracy than the landowning gentry. The gentry included at most 20,000 families, ranging from the titled peerage (dukes, marquesses, earl, viscounts and barons) and considerable incomes of as much as £2,000, to the vast majority of gentlemen, squires and Scottish lairds on a comparatively modest £300. This group, which was intricately involved in the local operation of the law, the church and politics, was so conscious of the fine gradations and relative status of their position that published guides to them – like those of Debrett and Burke – proliferated in the late eighteenth and early nineteenth centuries.

This was the social world inhabited by Jane Austen and captured in the portrait paintings of Thomas Gainsborough. Look at how in Figure 2.1 Gainsborough's portrait of the Andrews family worked to reproduce the social order. The Andrews were a gentry family of considerable resources thanks to their extensive land holdings, investment in shipping and trade and their loans to lesser members of the gentry. Robert Andrews was educated at Oxford and moved between his London residence in Mayfair's Grosvenor

Figure 2.1 Gainsborough's 'Mr and Mrs Andrews', 1748–9

Square and his country estate in Suffolk. His wife, Frances, grew up on a neighbouring estate which was sold to Andrews when he married Frances. She was married at sixteen years of age, and the estate was reputedly sold to Andrews as part of the dowry to help her father, whose textile business had fallen on hard times. The painting juxtaposes the oak and church as symbols of continuity with the tidy rows of corn innovatively laid by seed drill.

Below the gentry were families who also owned (or rented for life) their own property and sought the status of gentlemen. There were in excess of 10,000 merchants and some 80,000 manufacturers whose businesses could be considerable and generated incomes of between £40 and £600 a year. The budding professional classes (**clergy**, lawyers and increasingly medics and teachers) numbered over 20,000 and had incomes between £50 and £100. Some 350,000 freeholders and farmers (the vast majority of whom were tenants of the aristocracy and gentry) had incomes that stretched between £40 and £150 a year. Finally, there were 180,000 shopkeepers, publicans and tradesmen earning between £40 and £400. Altogether these groups accounted for little more than a quarter of the population. Those without property were fixed at the bottom of the social hierarchy where there was no less strict a pecking order of rank and status. At the top were the families of artisans, some 220,000 in number, themselves divided by their own hierarchies of status between masters, journeymen and apprentices. Distributed across a bewildering number of crafts and trades (by 1747 there were 350 recorded in London alone, where directories where needed to list them), from clockmakers to cutlers, chain makers to carpenters, their annual incomes rarely exceeded £25. Below them lay close to 60 per cent of the population, who lived precariously in conditions of want and misery, rarely earning more than £10 a year: from unskilled urban labourers, farm workers on annual contracts, seamen and fishermen, domestic servants, seasonal workers, soldiers and sailors, to paupers, vagrants and beggars.

The caste-like nature of this carefully observed social hierarchy should not be exaggerated. While it was clearly the case that membership of a status group was fixed at birth and that certain occupations were close to hereditary positions, there were no legal or religious barriers to social mobility. Indeed, there were notorious cases of individuals – like the explorer Captain Cook, the naval hero Admiral Nelson and the landscape architect Capability Brown – rising from humble positions to secure fame, fortune and social prestige as gentlemen. Social mobility may have been possible but it was extremely limited; the elite may have been open but in practice it carefully policed its entrance. Even when prosperous manufacturers and merchants purchased estates, built stately homes to become country gentlemen and married their daughters well, it could take generations before they fully acquired the requisite status as members of the gentry. At both the top and the bottom of the social scale the British jealously guarded their place on the social hierarchy against those on the rise, only welcoming as equals those who had fallen from greater heights.

God's Establishment

Entrenched within this social system, and in many ways providing a justification for its hierarchies and inequities, were the national churches. Although the churches of Scotland and Ireland had vast holdings of landed wealth, these paled in comparison to the **Church of England**. As the established Church of what some historians have described as a confessional state, the Church of England was very much part of the Establishment. Its wealth was immense and second only to the monarchy. It owned nearly a million acres of land as well as 16,000 churches, 30 cathedrals and 10,000 rectories and parsonages. The total value of these holdings is unknown but it was estimated (excluding the rectories) to be close to £35 million. The church's annual income from these holdings and from tithes (a local tax all parishioners paid to provide salaries for their rectors) was over £7 million. In addition, church rates, like tithes, were payable (by all parishioners irrespective of whether they were Anglicans) to the churchwarden for defraying the expenses of the local church and its officials.

The Anglican Church was not just phenomenally wealthy, it was insinuated into the very social and political structures of the **ancien regime**. The Church's leading figures, its bishops, were appointed by the Crown, and sat in the House of Lords alongside the peerage whose incomes they emulated (the Archbishop of York received £5,000 a year in 1750). The **Test and Corporations Acts** ensured that Anglicans had exclusive access to government and military posts as well as a university education at Oxford and Cambridge. In Ireland Roman Catholics could not attend university until Trinity College, Dublin, was opened to them in 1793. The invariably Oxbridge-educated **clergy** were beholden to the local gentry whose landed influence ensured that they dominated the church vestries responsible for appointing rectors and vicars. Many were afforded multiple appointments so that they were able to pool the income – from tithes and from farming the rectory's glebe lands – of several **parishes**. As many as a quarter of parishes had no resident rector and in some areas the rate of absenteeism was much higher; it reached 70 per cent in Devon by 1780. In Wales the church was so grievously out of touch with its congregation that no bishops and few clergy could even speak Welsh. Not surprisingly, when parsons did actually manage to preach from their pulpits on a Sunday in a language their flocks could understand, their message was one of obedience to God and deference to the social elite that had installed them. Similarly, the Patronage Act of 1711 gave the Scottish nobility (even if they were not members of the Church) powers to appoint the local parish ministers in the **Church of Scotland**. Although this was a restoration of the system that had operated before the **Act of Union**, it remained highly controversial with the Church and helped animate the breakaway of a new secession church in 1733. Even the physical layout of the national churches and their graveyards carefully observed and reinforced social hierarchy, with landowners always ensured their own pews (often in privately owned, upholstered and heated boxes) and burial sites closer to God.

Unsurprisingly, given these conditions, Anglican churches were rarely well attended, let alone places of great religious enthusiasm. The gentry perpetually bemoaned the receding grip of the Anglican Church upon society and for good reason. Only 10 per cent of the population in England and Wales took communion at Easter in 1801. That was partly a consequence of the desperate shortage of churches in growing cities (like Manchester where a single church served a population of 20,000 in 1750). The countryside was also losing communicants (25 per cent for 30 parishes in Oxford between 1738 and 1802). Nonetheless, the Anglican Church continued to structure the lives of most Britons. It ritually marked out, and provided the only official record of, the key rites of passage in people's lives: birth, death and marriage. And social life remained structured by the customary calendar of holidays and festivities presided over by the Church: New Year's Day, Twelfth Night, Plough Monday, Candlemas, Shrovetide, Lady Day, Palm Sunday, Easter, May Day Whitsun, Midsummer, Harvest Festival, Halloween, Guy Fawkes Night and Christmas. Even **wakes week** – the local, annual, week-long holiday – was held at the time of the saint's day after which the **parish** church was named. In these ways the Anglican Church was not just a vital part of the **ancien regime**'s social structure, it was insinuated into the very traditional fabric of social life in England. As we'll see, those **Dissenters** that refused its communion and community remained excluded from the offices of the state, universities and the life of what we might call 'Established Society'.

Religion and the Age of Reason

Perhaps unsurprisingly, then, critique of the **ancien regime** was animated as much by those **Dissenters** excluded from it and the evangelical revival within the Anglican Church as by the forward march of reason. In many ways religious debate and association proved the most important midwife of civil society.

Evangelical Revival

It would be wrong to caricature the Anglican Church as an entirely moribund institution for after the 1730s it was energized by an evangelical revival that emphasized the importance of a more direct, informal and heartfelt relationship with God mediated through preaching, prayer and music. It was an evangelical method of worship and piety developed by Oxford undergraduates in the 1730s that most energized Anglicanism, at least until the movement's break from the Church in 1791. At first Methodism had greatest resonance in those places and among those people most estranged from Anglicanism, namely the labouring poor in Cornwall, Wales and Ireland (it had less success in Scotland), as well as the industrializing urban centres in the northwest of England. Critical to that success was the work of charismatic preachers. In Wales the lay preachers Howell Harris and Daniel Rowland generated around 400 evangelical societies by 1750. George Whitefield and John Wesley quickly overshadowed these two. Travelling vast distances in regular circuits across the British Isles and beyond it to the North American colonies, they preached to large crowds in open-air meetings. The enthusiasm of these meetings – the drama of the sermons, the congregation's heartfelt expressions of belief with tears, shouts of exclamation and joyful singing – signalled an intense religious experience unlike anything offered in an Anglican church. This atmosphere produced the great flowering of hymns in the second half of the eighteenth century, many of which are still sung in Protestant churches across much of the world today. John Wesley's brother Charles wrote over 2,000 hymns, including the Christmas carol 'Hark the Herald Angels Sing' in 1739, but it was the captain of a slave ship, John Newton, who best captured the evangelical spirit with his hymn 'Amazing Grace' in the early 1770s.

Amazing Grace! How sweet the sound
That saved a wretch like me!
I once was lost, but now am found;
Was blind, but now I see.

'Twas grace that taught my heart to fear,
And grace my fears relieved;
How precious did that grace appear
The hour I first believed!

Despite theological disputes between those who believed in predestination (Harris and Whitefield) or free will (Rowland and Wesley), Methodism promised hope and terror in equal measure. The possibility of being born again and finding salvation through a more intimate and expressive relationship with God was only possible once one had acknowledged the ubiquity of sin and its grip upon one's heart and soul unless constant vigilance was maintained. Only around 80,000 people would have identified themselves as Methodists by the 1790s. Nonetheless, the movement's regular circuits of preaching, the publication of sermons, hymnals and journals, its own chapels, societies and annual conferences, had created a vibrant associational culture. Methodism also catalysed an intense debate among Anglicans, many of whom were appalled by the fervour of its practices and the humbleness of its adherents. Anglican disdain only worsened when Methodists broke from the **Church of England** and splintered into a plethora of rival groups, where healings and prophecies were not unknown, to say nothing of the often key role of women preachers.

As the evangelical revival within Anglicanism promoted charitable works, it encouraged forms of civic engagement that had often preceded it. The poor were always the object of this work. Long before the evangelical revival, the number of charitable schools established to teach the labouring poor had grown significantly in the early eighteenth century. By 1716 there were over 1,200 providing a rudimentary education to around 30,000 children. Hospitals were also established by charitable subscriptions in increasing numbers, and not just in London. Between 1735 and 1783 no less than 24 provincial hospitals were endowed. Similarly, between 1723 and 1773 some 2,000 workhouses were built to serve a single or several parishes. All this endeavour paled in comparison to the movements for moral reform and Sunday schools that gathered momentum from the 1780s. The increasing moral fervour of evangelism was evident when the head of the Church of England, George III, issued a 'Proclamation for the Encouragement of Piety and Virtue, and for the Preventing and Punishing of Vice, Profaneness and Immorality' in 1787, and the following year a Society was established by the evangelical Anglican William Wilberforce (soon to be feted for his role campaigning against the slave trade) to carry it into effect. It joined the revived Society for the Reformation of Manners (first established in 1690 but revived in 1757) and the Society of Universal Good Will (1786), and was soon accompanied by the London Missionary Society (1795), the Religious Tract Society (1799), the Anglican Church Missionary Society (1799), Wilberforce's Society for the Suppression of Vice (1802) and the enormously successful British And Foreign Bible Society (1804), which, within twenty years, had issued over 4 million bibles in 140 languages from Welsh to Hindi.

Similarly, moral reform, the movement to provide the otherwise uneducated children of the labouring poor with basic skills of reading and (sometimes) writing through Sunday schools, was not the preserve of Anglicanism. The Sunday School Society founded in 1785 was explicitly non-denominational, but each new Sunday school was always affiliated to a particular church or chapel. By 1821 there were 8,236 established, under half of which were affiliated to the Church of England, with almost 750,000 pupils enrolled. While the evangelical revival created new forms of association and civic engagement, and was occasionally informed by Enlightened currents of thought and practice, the attempt to energize the Anglican Church hardly represented a critical assault upon the **ancien regime**. Even so, the caricature of Methodism and Sunday schools as merely instilling devotion, obedience and a fatalistic acceptance of one's God-given position in society remains an unhelpful caricature.

Dissenters

It was through the tradition of Dissent that religion more obviously served as the midwife of a civil society critical of the **ancien regime**. Although the Act of Toleration provided **Dissenters** with liberty of conscience in 1689, the **Test and Corporations Acts** ensured that their civil rights to participate fully in public life remained severely circumscribed. Regardless of their theological differences, Dissenting groups – like the Quakers, Baptists, Congregationalists and Presbyterians – generally believed that God, not the monarchy or their bishops, was the sole head of the church and that he could be encountered directly by individuals through the study of Scripture without reliance upon external authorities like a priest. This demystification and democratization of faith meant that new creeds and self-governing sects could proliferate around charismatic preachers in a particular locality. Some dissipated as quickly as they had appeared, others endured. In the 1760s a coalminer named Dan Taylor built his own evangelical Baptist meeting-house in Hebden Bridge, reputedly by digging and carrying rocks from the Yorkshire moors. By 1770 he had started the Baptist New Connexion and over the following years he travelled 25,000 miles delivering 20,000 sermons. When he died in 1817 the New Connexion boasted some seventy affiliated chapels as well as an Academy begun in 1798. In this way the practice of Dissent generated a growing network of chapels, meeting-rooms, burial places, academies and Sunday schools which were in turn served by increasing volumes of published sermons, pamphlets, biographies of preachers, conversion stories and histories of each sect.

Unlike the established national church, Dissent was more receptive to the strains of Enlightened thought that sought to transform religion into a rational exercise devoid of the inertia of tradition, the grip of superstition or the drama of emotion. Education was critical here. **Dissenters** were fortunate enough to be excluded from the intellectual backwater that was Oxbridge where the Anglican **clergy** in waiting pored over the classics and were maintained in a state of blissful ignorance of the ideas of their own time emanating from Locke, Newton, Hume and Smith, let alone Voltaire, Rousseau and Kant. 'I bless God that I was born a Dissenter … and I was not educated at Oxford or Cambridge' declared the reformer Joseph Priestley. Although there was no confessional test for admission to the ancient Scottish universities of Edinburgh, Glasgow, Aberdeen and St Andrews, the higher education of Dissenters in England was received at their own academies, around thirty-five of which were established after 1689. Some of these academies were renowned for their emphasis on maths and science as well as a progressively open spirit of inquiry. 'Your Universities resemble pools of stagnant water,' wrote Priestley to the Anglican prime minister William Pitt in 1787, whereas 'ours are like rivers, which, taking their natural course, fertilize a whole country'. There can be little question that an education that encouraged debate, the exploration of new ideas and an appeal to reason as the sole authority of truth, helped radicalize Dissenters like Priestley from the 1770s. While some turned to the rational comprehension of God through Unitarianism and Deism (in 1774 Priestley helped establish Britain's first Unitarian congregation), many more became increasingly critical not just of the exclusion of Dissenters from public offices but the whole **ancien regime** with its irrational systems and monopolies of wealth and power based on faith and birth. It was no accident that some of the key radical voices of Britain's late Enlightenment either came from (Thomas Paine, Thomas Spence, William Godwin), inhabited (Richard Price, Joseph Priestley) or embraced (Mary Wollstonecraft) the tradition of Dissent.

A British Enlightenment?

Until relatively recently the term British Enlightenment was considered an oxymoron. The Enlightenment was considered to be the preserve of continental intellectuals who, by insisting that the world should only be understood and organized by the practice of reason, opened up the possibility of Europe's emancipation from the inherited structures of rule and authority, as well as the bondage of superstition and custom. Britons were considered too anti-intellectual to theorize; they were doers not thinkers, except perhaps north of the border where a Scottish Enlightenment could be discerned around the ancient universities. It was always a nonsensical view because the Enlightenment took many forms across the continent and was as much about practising inquiry and debate in clubs, societies and on the printed page as it was about producing abstract theories and learned treatises. Even in the realm of ideas Britain hardly had a shabby record. There was a clear genealogy of Enlightened thought stretching from Robert Boyle, Isaac Newton, Thomas Hobbes and John Locke in the late seventeenth century through to David Hume, **Adam Smith**, Jeremy Bentham, Thomas Paine and Mary Wollstonecraft in the eighteenth century. Nonetheless, some still insist that there was a more empirical and practical bent to the Enlightenment in Britain with its commitment to 'improvement' and the reform of social, political and economic life (see Textbox 2.1). However, the belief that the world could be progressively improved once the natural laws that governed its operation had been discovered by the practice of reason, scientific observation and experimentation was hardly unique to Britain, as the reforming energies of Europe's so-called Enlightened monarchs – Catherine II in Russia, Charles III in Spain, Joseph II of Austria, Louis XVI of France – demonstrate. Whether grounded in empirical research or abstract theory, the Enlightenment created a new order of things through the practice of human reason that did not so much displace God as make it possible to understand the world without reference to a divine force.

2.1 Source: Joseph Massie, 'Estimate of the Social Structure and Income in England and Wales, 1759–1760'

The idea of calculating the size of the population and the extent of national wealth was a product of the early British Enlightenment. In the late seventeenth century, figures like William Petty (1623–87) and Gregory King (1648–1712) developed statistical techniques for analysing demographic and economic trends that became known as political arithmetic. In 1688 King was the first to estimate the total population and wealth of England and Wales. Although contemporaries were aware that social and economic life was rapidly changing, it was not until 1760 that the political arithmetician named Joseph Massie sought to update King's estimates. Little is known about Massie but it is likely that he was a merchant with interests in the slave-driven West Indian sugar trade and that he wrote pamphlets supporting William Pitt during and after the **Seven Years' War**. It was probably this work that gained him access to papers of the Treasury Board, the Navy Office and the Excise Commissioners for his study. Published as a broadsheet, Massie's 'Estimate' used King's as a model, but revised the number of families in the various income brackets. Like King, Massie's estimates counted households or families, instead of individuals. Yet where King had carefully distinguished between the

number of families who were temporal lords, spiritual lords, baronets, knights, esquires and gentlemen, Massie was only interested in the differences of income within these categories. More importantly, Massie's estimates also indicate the structure of the total national income in the mid eighteenth century. For example, compared to King's classification of 'artisans and handycrafts', Massie categorized 'master manufacturers' as a group that was separate from 'manufacturers and Labourers', recognizing that by that time the manufacturer had become a character of some importance, distinguishable from the everyday artisan. Decades before the introduction of a national census, Massie's estimates reflected the growing interest in knowing demographic facts about society and provided contemporaries with information that could be used to debate economic and political questions. As a source Massie's Estimate is as useful for telling us about the forms of knowledge used to understand social and economic change as it is in detailing those changes. By 1764 his catalogue of books and pamphlets on trade, commerce and population stretched to 2,400 titles – a sign itself of the burgeoning interest in what would soon become known as political economy. (C.R.)

The Enlightenment was inescapably a transnational phenomenon. Its ideas, like the people who generated and the publications that articulated those ideas, moved across national borders. Many of the leading exponents of Enlightenment thought on the continent, like French and Swiss philosophers Voltaire and Rousseau, visited Britain, as did Benjamin Franklin, and the traffic was not all one way. **Adam Smith** visited Paris and Geneva where he met, among others, Voltaire, Franklin, and the French political economist Francois Quesnay. Thomas Paine lived in America and France as well as Britain and his work drew upon the intellectual culture of all three countries. Mary Wollstonecraft's *Vindication of the Rights of Woman* was an explicit engagement and refutation of Rousseau's theories that the education of women should be limited and confined to a preparation for the duties of wifehood.

Enlightened ideas did not just travel across Europe and America; they were shaped by the discovery of New Worlds in the Americas, Africa and the South Pacific as well as an increasing fascination with the cultures of the rival Chinese, Mughal and Ottoman empires. That discovery itself was an Enlightened enterprise is nicely illustrated by the career of Captain James Cook who became famous for his three voyages to the South Seas, beginning with the first in 1768 and ending in 1779 when he was killed in Hawaii. Cook's 'discovery' of Australia, New Zealand and the Pacific islands not only helped advance the science of navigation and cartography but also generated a wealth of new botanical knowledge as well as ethnographic observations of their indigenous peoples. The discovery of other cultures could take many forms, from accounts of travels in exotic distant lands (famously parodied by Jonathan Swift's *Gulliver's Travels* in 1726) to the study and translation of foreign languages and religious texts (the Koran was translated in 1734). Indeed, the forward march of reason and civility in Europe was increasingly understood in relation to other peoples. It was widely assumed that those peoples and races deemed more primitive were simply less advanced along the developmental path prescribed by the natural laws that governed the world. Particularly influential here was the work of figures like Hume, Smith, Adam Ferguson and John Millar in Scotland – where the study of philosophy, history and political economy were closely related – which mapped out the progressive development of societies along four discrete stages of civilization: the hunter-gatherer, the pastoral, the agricultural and the commercial. 'The great Map of Mankind', Edmund Burke declared, 'is unrolled at once and there is no state or gradation of barbarism, and no mode of refinement which we have not at the same moment under our view.' Regardless of how closely one adhered to such a view, eighteenth-century Britons were enthralled by encounter with different peoples and cultures. When indigenous people from the New World travelled to Britain they became objects of intense fascination. In the 1770s the Pacific islander known as Omai entranced high and low society alike: he had an audience with the king, met the leading scientists and artists of the day, and was the subject of pamphlets, plays, songs and ballads. Eighteenth-century Britons advanced their rational knowledge of

Figure 2.2 Omai with Joseph Banks and Dr Daniel Solander, 1775–6, by William Parry

the world and a conceited sense of their own advanced stage of civility through such encounters.

A Civil and Clubbable People

Omai's visit reminds us that the Enlightenment's propagation of reason as the ordering principle of the world rested on a new culture of public debate germinated in a myriad of new associations, institutions and forms of print culture.

Clubs and Societies

Institutions promoting intellectual inquiry multiplied from the middle of the eighteenth century. The Royal Society, founded in 1660, had long been at the centre of scientific discussion and included Isaac Newton and Joseph Banks (the botanist on Cook's first voyage and Omai's patron) among its presidents. The Society of Antiquaries received a royal charter in 1751, the British Museum was founded in 1759 and the Royal Academy of Arts was established in 1768. Based in London, these learned societies, with their royal charters of approval, remained the preserve of gentlemen and often had the air of an aristocratic club. The British Museum was located in the Montagu family's London mansion and its collections were based upon a series of aristocratic libraries. There was a quite different air to the Society for the Encouragement of Arts, Manufactures and Commerce established in 1754 and Birmingham's Lunar Society in 1764. Here the worlds of philosophical inquiry, scientific experimentation and the commercial arts of manufacturing fused in unprecedented ways. The Lunar Society was a veritable powerhouse of Enlightened polymaths; it included the natural philosopher, botanist, Deist and anti-slavery supporter Erasmus Darwin (grandfather of Charles); Joseph Priestley the reformer, philosopher, Unitarian, and chemist; Josiah Wedgwood who transformed the industrial production of pottery, became a Unitarian, supported parliamentary reform and whose eldest daughter married Erasmus Darwin's son; James Watt the mechanical engineer who, together with his business partner and fellow member of the Lunar Society, Matthew Boulton, improved the steam engine and made it commercially viable. Although its politics and geographical and social location were very different to the learned societies of London, the Lunar Society was in its own way – with the close religious, business and family connections of its members – just as exclusive.

The culture of Enlightenment, the spread of its ideas and the practice of debate, radiated out more broadly through coffee houses and newspapers. The first coffee house opened in Oxford in 1650 as an informal setting for the leading undergraduates to discuss points of common interest; by 1739 there were no fewer than 551 in London, most of which simply charged a penny for admission. Unlike the coffee house today, with its wireless network and customers barricaded behind computer screens, the first coffee houses were hubs of conversation. They were places where men met to exchange gossip, news, ideas, commodities, bets and even professional services. Many of them became associated with particular types of activity and became the foundation of new businesses, clubs or associations. Both Lloyd's of London (the global insurance market) and London's Stock Exchange grew out of coffee houses. They were also places where people came to read the burgeoning number of newspapers, journals, pamphlets and novels. Neither a private reception room, nor simply a commercial space, the coffee house was a place where people met, read and engaged in such heated argument that Ned Ward wrote a satire comparing this society to a mob. And yet, as we can see in Figure 2.3, the frontispiece to his work portrays a coffee house with a well-dressed clientele consuming the relative luxuries of coffee and tobacco in a room adorned with landscape paintings. This was very much a man's world. The only woman, dressed in a white shawl, stands behind the counter where she keeps a watchful eye on the boys who serve the customers. A product of this manly world of

Figure 2.3 Ned Ward, 'The CoffeeHous Mob', 1710

coffee houses, the fashionable periodical *The Spectator* (1711–14) carefully observed their social life and reproduced it in print. Despite a modest print run of just 3,000, its authors Joseph Addison and Richard Steele (Whig MPs and men of letters) claimed that it was read by 60,000 thanks to subscriptions by coffee houses where it was consumed by multiple readers.

An Urban Renaissance

This new culture of enquiry, association and sociability was primarily an urban phenomenon. London and Edinburgh led the way (respectively boasting twenty and twelve moral reform societies in 1700), and by 1714 over fifty towns in England and Wales had at least one religious society. While the number of clubs and associations grew slowly in the first half of the eighteenth century, their numbers rose precipitously from the 1740s, when there were less than 500 of them across the English-speaking world. Compare this to over 6,500 in existence by 1800. By 1750 London, with three quarters of a million people, had 66 different types of association and a total number of around 1,000; whereas Bristol, with 50,000 inhabitants, had a dozen or so different types of association; and even Northampton, with a population of just 5,000, had a total of three, including a Masonic lodge and a philosophical society. By 1800 London had close to 3,000 clubs and societies. Clubs and societies were created for all manner of purposes. Some, like bell-ringing or floristry societies, involved local or regional competition to perform the best peal of bells or grow the best tulip. Even the soberest of activities, like ringing bells, almost invariably occasioned drinking and festivity. Club life was rarely just improving or limited to the higher echelons of society – it was fun and demotic as well. The phenomenal growth of clubs and associational life also forged connections between localities as their organizations developed regional, national and even imperial profiles. The Freemasons led the way here with the national Grand Lodge (formed in England in 1717, Ireland in 1725 and Scotland in 1736) having affiliated local branches or lodges scattered across the country and the empire. Already by 1740 they had 180 lodges in Britain and 14 across North America, the Caribbean and South Asia, while between 1752 and 1816 a further 39 lodges were formed overseas. By 1807 there were 142 lodges in London, a further 388 across England, Wales and Scotland, and a staggering 669 in Ireland.

The physical shape of towns and cities changed to accommodate all this sociability. In the second half of the eighteenth century an urban renaissance transformed even modest-sized towns like Northampton. The construction of assembly rooms, theatres, concert rooms and Masonic lodges attracted the local gentry and professional classes. There was a profoundly regional character to the associational life of this urban renaissance. Each town developed its own unique attractions and societies in relation to those offered elsewhere in the catchment area, as surrounding towns competed to improve themselves and to attract local civil society. This was no less true of the growing number of seaside resorts and spa towns. As the clean air, salt water and even occasional sunshine of the coast were associated with good health, a number of resorts developed to attract those members of polite society looking for recreation and renewed vitality. In the south of England Margate, Weymouth and Brighton competed for this clientele, while Scarborough and Southport did the same on the eastern and western coasts in the north. Spa towns were also part of the fashionable circuit of recreations. Bath

2.2 Place: Bath

Bath's emergence as a fashionable resort city was an eighteenth-century phenomenon. Located on a bend of the River Avon in Somerset, Bath had originally been settled by the Romans, who were attracted to the site's mineral springs. The settlement lasted, but by the end of the seventeenth century, Bath was still a small medieval walled city with a residential population of around 3,000. A century later that number had grown almost twelvefold. The rapid change was a reflection of the growing affluence of the English gentry and a new urban culture of sociability. Those who flocked to Bath between the London winter season and summers on their country estates joined the town's inhabitants. If at first visitors went to Bath to take its waters, which were thought to ease pain and restore reason, they were also increasingly attracted by its social life and entertainments. After the refurbishment of the Roman Baths and the Pump Room at the beginning of the eighteenth century, a series of grand buildings was constructed in classic Georgian style such as Queen's Square, the Assembly Rooms, King's Circus and the Royal Crescent. The architects behind most of this construction were John Woods father and son, whose carefully regulated designs anticipated the town planning movement of the late nineteenth and early twentieth centuries. As Bath developed as a resort it became celebrated as a place where successful members of the urban merchant and professional classes mixed with landed and titled families, as well as a meeting place for the sexes. Once a retreat for the sick, Bath turned into a resort city for the healthy. Its success made it a model for subsequent resort towns in Britain, such as Tunbridge Wells, Epsom and Buxton. Partially due to the competition, and partially because of the changing structures of population and society, Bath did not sustain its position as a fashionable resort into the Victorian period. It was not until the second half of the twentieth century that its Georgian architecture made it popular with visiting tourists from around the world. (C.R.)

paved the way in the late seventeenth century but it truly flourished in the eighteenth century when it attracted genteel society in growing numbers, including famously Jane Austen whose family lived there between 1801 and 1805 (see Textbox 2.2). For those unable to travel to Bath there were plenty of alternatives like Tunbridge Wells, Epsom, Cheltenham, Buxton and Matlock.

These new spaces of sociability, visited at very specific times of the year according to the calendar of fashionable society, both enlivened the rhythms of life on provincial country estates and offered a chance of escape from the metropolitan gaze. They were supplemented as places to be seen, to meet, or to court by pleasure gardens. With their formal gardens, promenades, ponds, menageries, orchestras, dances, balls, fireworks and masquerades, pleasure gardens multiplied across London and spread (often using the same names of a Vauxhall or Ranelagh) as far afield as Dublin, Edinburgh, Bath, Bristol, Norwich, Birmingham, Liverpool and Manchester. Although entrance was by subscription or ticket, maintaining social exclusivity or establishing polite behaviour was not always easy as they became social laboratories where new styles and types of behaviour were experimented with. They famously spawned the world of the Macaroni, the young male fashion victims renowned for the excesses of their dress and a purported lack of moral fibre. So dissolute were the stories that surrounded Cuper's Gardens in London (next to Waterloo Bridge where the National Theatre now stands) that it was closed down in 1752. This was, after all, the age of a resurgent moral reform movement determined to ensure that the new forms of sociability would not propagate sin and erode the civility of society.

Print Culture

Newspapers also flourished in this world of association and debate, especially after the expiration of pre-publication censorship in 1695. By 1709 London alone boasted nineteen newspapers, including the first ever daily, *The Daily Courant*, and by 1820 there were no less than fifty-two titles published in London. Newspapers also began to proliferate in the provinces. The first provincial papers began publishing in Norwich (1701) and Bristol (1702) and there were thirty-five by 1760 and a hundred by 1820. London papers were also distributed in increasing numbers across the country: thus compared to the million plus circulated in this way in 1763 there were over 4.5 million by 1790. Compared to the 2.5 million newspapers sold in 1700, there were nearly 17 million newspapers sold a century later and this does not come close to telling us the size of their actual circulation for many were read aloud in company or shared in reading rooms and coffee houses (it was estimated that every London newspaper was read by thirty people in the 1820s).

Although the appetite for news appeared insatiable, we should not assume that Britain had simply become a reading nation. Illiteracy rates remained remarkably high and changed very little in the second half of the eighteenth century. Despite regional and occupational variations, roughly 40 per cent of men and 60 per cent of women remained illiterate. While educational grammars were produced and sold in ever greater numbers (Thomas Dyche's *Guide to the English Tongue* sold 500,000 copies over the century), those lower down the social order were only likely to encounter the printed word through listening to others read. The number of books in print nonetheless doubled over the course of the eighteenth century from 21,000 to 56,000. The biggest increase occurring after 1774 when a ruling of the House of Lords that publishers could not keep the works of authors in perpetual copyright significantly lowered the price of cheap books to as little as 6 pence. Among the proliferating forms of print was a new genre.

The novel, a work of fiction that centred upon the interior lives of the individuals that were the leading characters of the story as well as the portrayal of recognizable social types, came of age in Britain between the publication of Aphra Behn's *Love-Letters Between a Nobleman and his Sister* (1687), Daniel Defoe's *Robinson Crusoe* (1719) and Samuel Richardson's *Pamela* (1740). Although novels had tiny print runs, they quickly established a reading public who were consuming thousands of new titles by the end of the century. Despite their association with the imagination, novels were very much a product of the culture of Enlightenment. They circulated alongside a huge variety of learned and religious publications through private and commercial lending libraries that numbered almost 600 by the 1790s. Moreover, in its early epistolary and satirical forms, the novel was often highly didactic, providing readers with instructive moral lessons and a chance to observe social life by imaginatively inhabiting the predicaments, dilemmas and feelings of their characters. Nonetheless the novel was gradually coded as feminine as women turned to reading and writing them in increasing numbers. Despite the renown of novelists like Aphra Behn (1640–1689), Frances Burney (1752–1840) and Jane Austen (1775–1817) today, they represented just the tip of the iceberg. Despite the many impediments to women becoming authors (between 1740 and 1760 the total of women's novels published each year was never higher than four), by the 1810s they were producing more novels than men. It was surely no coincidence that, as Jane Austen remarks in *Northanger Abbey* (1818), 'there seems almost a general wish of decrying the capacity and undervaluing the labour of the novelist, and of slighting the performances which have only genius, wit, and taste to recommend them'.

In many ways the novel was the intellectual refuge of women routinely barred from participating in the Enlightened republic of letters. Just as the progressive development of reason and civility was measured in relation to the primitive state of other nations and races, so their possession was denied to those in Britain – particularly women, children and the labouring classes – considered incapable of rational thought and deliberation. It was commonly thought that women were captives of biology whose reproductive functions ensured they remained irrational and inferior to men. Consequently, the daughters and wives of gentlemen received a rudimentary education from a governess intended to develop their personal charms and ensure they had enough grace and too little learning to contradict the opinions of their husbands. This was the view famously elaborated by Rousseau in *Emile* (1757–61) to which Wollstonecraft's *Vindication* responded. Here Enlightenment ideas about who could practise reason converged with evangelically informed notions of women as moral guardians of the home and children. Whereas Rousseau believed that their lack of rational faculties made it necessary for men to guide the moral sentiments of women, the prescriptive literature influenced by evangelical thought insisted that the private arena of the home ensured that women and children remained insulated from the corrosive moral environment of the public world of commerce, politics and sociability. This ideology of **separate spheres** for men and women was always more of an ideal than a reality even for the genteel women to whom it was alone intended to apply. Some women, invariably those whose fathers allowed them access to the learning of their libraries, participated in Enlightened discussions either by publishing, like Catherine Macaulay and Mary Wollstonecraft, or through private correspondence and conversation. And a significant group of men in the more radical circles of the late Enlightenment, like the members of the Lunar Society, embraced the cause of women's rights to education, legal personality and even political representation. The Enlightenment legacy for women was thus distinctly doubled-edged: it both subjugated them and held out the promise of future emancipation.

The emergence of Romanticism in the late eighteenth century was both an escalation of the imaginative cult of sentiment and a reaction against the rationalist strictures of the Enlightenment. Romanticism took many forms but was united by a belief that reason alone could not comprehend the human condition or the sublime qualities of the natural world. Rational explanation seemed insufficient to understand the intensity of emotions that many felt emanated from the primal depths of the soul and were expressive of a spiritual state. The lyrical poetry of figures like William Blake, Samuel Taylor Coleridge, William Wordsworth, Lord Byron and Percy Bysshe Shelley set out to explore the sublime nature of the world and the depths of human emotion inspired variously by radical politics, opium addiction, sexual adventure and the landscape. Gothic novels that summoned up an imagined medieval world full of castles, ghosts and horror became hugely popular, while visions and visionaries proliferated around the edges of evangelical religion. During the 1790s Joanna Southcott, a farmer's daughter from Ottery St Mary in Devon who wrote and prophesied while entranced by the Holy Spirit, began to attract a small following of admirers which grew exponentially to tens of thousands when she declared she would soon give birth to the Son of God in 1802. It was from this world beyond the grasp of reason that *Frankenstein* arose. Published in 1818, this classic gothic horror novel portrayed the tragic and monstrous consequence of a scientist's attempt to create life. Its author Mary Shelley, the daughter of Enlightenment free-thinkers Mary Wollstonecraft and William Godwin, wrote the book after she had eloped with Percy Bysshe Shelley (who was already married) and while they were staying with Lord Byron in Geneva. Just as Mary Shelley's personal history fused together Enlightenment and Romanticism, so the monster she had Dr Frankenstein create represented the possibilities and dangers of a belief in the omnipotent power and progressive force of reason and science.

Anti-Slavery Campaigns

Perhaps nowhere do we more clearly see the new kind of civil society forged by evangelical concerns with moral reform, new rationalist understandings of the world, and a culture of debate and association, than in the anti-slavery campaigns. In the last three decades of the eighteenth century the anti-slavery movement generated an unprecedented number of petitions in support of abolition from every county in England (and from much of Scotland and Wales) and they were signed by a greater number of people across the social spectrum than ever before. As it was a campaign that repeatedly broke all the records and has a strong claim for being the first mass movement, it is worth asking how this was achieved. In part it was made possible by many of the things we have already touched upon: the increasing circulation of newspapers, the availability of printed materials through circulating libraries, the growing habit of association in clubs and societies. Enlightened ideas certainly also played a part. Slavery, insisted **Adam Smith** in 1776, was part of the corrupt and inefficient world of a mercantile economy that prevented the wealth of nations multiplying through the free circulation of trade and labour. In contrast, those gripped by the revivalist spirit of evangelicalism saw the loss of the American colonies as God's vengeance for Britain's sinful dependence upon a system of slavery that kept slaves from salvation because they were not free to choose between worshipping God or falling into sin. This was the lesson the Anglican Granville Sharp drew from the American Revolution in his *Law of Retribution, or A Serious Warning to Great Britain and Her Colonies, founded upon Examples of God's Temporal Vengeance Against Tyrants, Slave-Holders and Oppressors* (1776). Sharp and his fellow evangelicals, Thomas Clarkson and William Wilberforce, believed the slave trade was a dreadful stain on Britain's moral conscience and a test of faith that could only be met by abolition. Others took a more pragmatic stance and hoped that embracing the abolitionist cause would enable Britain to win over slaves to the **loyalist** side in the revolutionary wars in North America. Promising slaves their freedom in this way allowed Britain to defuse the critique of the tyranny of British rule and instead present the British empire as a guardian of, and force for, liberty.

Seven years after the American Revolution there were an estimated 10,000 former slaves made free by their support of the loyalist cause living in Britain's major transatlantic port towns of London, Bristol, Cardiff and Liverpool. Sharp, who in 1772 successfully secured a legal ruling that slave-owners had no jurisdiction over refugee slaves in England, turned his attention to this group, forming the Committee for the Relief of the Black Poor in 1785. Sharp aimed to establish a free black state in Africa for all emancipated or refugee slaves – a dream finally realized in 1808 when Sierra Leone formally became a British colony. Yet, despite a Quaker petition in 1783, it was the Committee for the Abolition of the African Slave Trade (1787) that created the national structure capable of creating and sustaining a mass campaign. The Committee, headquartered in London, quickly established a network of local agents and 'country committees' across the country whose job was to disseminate printed materials and galvanize support. Leading figures in the campaign, like Thomas Clarkson, would tour the country committees whipping up enthusiasm speech-by-speech, meeting-after-meeting, and feed information back to the London headquarters. A key part of this associational effort was the organization of petitions. Manchester led the way with a petition in 1787 that collected 11,000 signatures. In just three months of 1788, 103 petitions in favour of abolition were sent to Parliament, with just 30 per cent of the signatures coming from elite groups. Armed with this indication of the popular will, the following year William Wilberforce presented the first bill for abolition to the **House of Commons**. The petitioning effort of 1788 seemed trivial in 1792 when a staggering 519 petitions (the largest number ever collected in a parliamentary session, let alone on a single issue) from

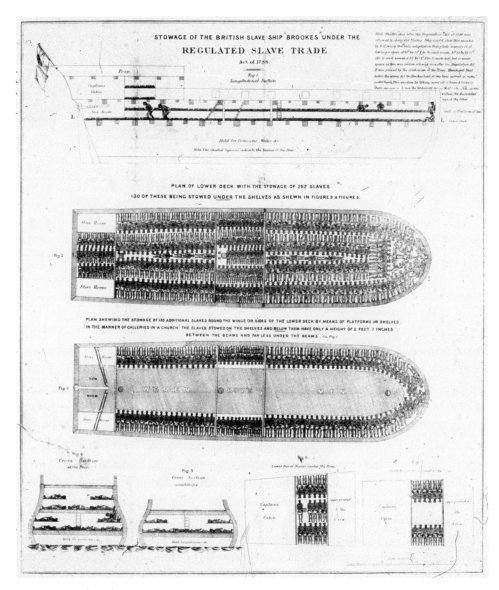

Figure 2.4 A slave ship

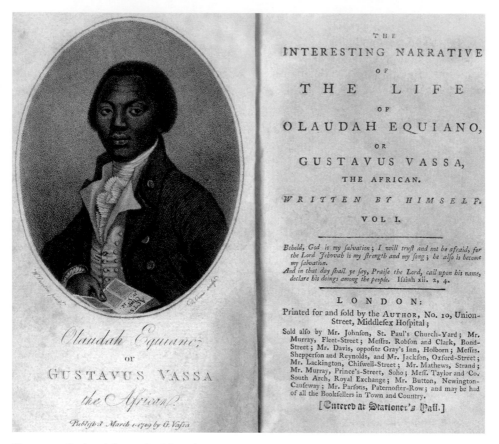

Figure 2.5 Equiano's *Interesting Narrative*, 1789

across the country were presented to Parliament. Defeat was grasped from jaws of victory as the Commons voted overwhelmingly (230 to 85) for what it insisted had to be 'gradual' abolition, only for the progress of the bill to be checked in the House of Lords where many still had considerable interests in the slave plantations of the Caribbean. The loyalist counter-revolution of the 1790s flattened even the fervour of abolitionism and was so brutally extended to the suppression of slave insurrections – in Haiti (1791), Grenada and St Vincent (1794–5) and Jamaica (1795–6) – that 45,000 British troops, as well as many more slaves, lost their lives in the Caribbean during the 1790s.

The stalling of abolition after 1792 cannot detract from the remarkable success of the movement over the preceding five years. If some of that success can be ascribed to its innovative organizational structure, much more belonged to its novel forms of campaigning. As the British public had long viewed the slavery of Africans as natural and legitimate, the task of convincing them otherwise was Herculean. Abolitionists pioneered forms of publicity that allowed them to dramatically illustrate, often with

2.3 Person: Olaudah Equiano

Almost everything that is known about the first ten years of Olaudah Equiano's life comes from his celebrated autobiography, *The Interesting Narrative of the Life of Olaudah Equiano, or Gustavus Vassa, the African* (1789). In it he gave a personal narrative of the different slave experiences in the Atlantic slave trade. Born around 1745 in West Africa, Equiano was captured by slave-traders as a small child, and then endured the '**Middle Passage**' from Africa to the Americas, as well as the experience of plantation labour in the West Indies and Virginia. In 1754 Equiano was sold to a British officer in the Royal Navy. As a slave on a naval ship, Equiano was trained in seamanship and saw action in several battles of the **Seven Years' War**. Between his extensive travels, he spent time in London, where he learned to read and write and was baptised – it was this education and introduction to Christianity that determined the course of much of the rest of his life. By the mid 1760s Equiano had been sold again, and was working on the island of Montserrat in the Caribbean. His sailing skills and his education kept him out of the plantation fields, but did not keep him from witnessing the horrors that were inflicted upon his fellow slaves. In 1766 Equiano bought his own freedom for the price of £40, and soon moved back to Britain where he became part of the growing population of former slaves living in the metropole. It was then that he not only began to fully embrace Methodism and to understand his life as the result of Providence but also met leaders of the abolition movement such as Granville Sharp and James Ramsay. In 1783 he helped alert Granville Sharp to reports of the slave ship *Zong*, whose crew drowned 133 African slaves in order to claim insurance for them as ruined cargo. The case brought Equiano fully into the anti-slavery movement, and he spent much of 1787 and 1788 writing letters and petitions, which he signed 'on behalf of my African brethren'. But Equiano's most significant contribution as an African speaking out against slavery came with the writing, publication and promotion of his autobiography. *The Interesting Narrative* resonated with the growing reading public for as well as providing a firsthand account of the horrors of the Atlantic slave trade, it could also be read as a spiritual journey, a travel or adventure narrative, and a sentimental novel. In 1792 Equiano married Susanna Cullen with whom he had two daughters, Ann Mary and Joanna. When Equiano died on 31 March 1797 he had already lost Susanna and Ann Mary. Joanna inherited her father's considerable estate of almost £1,000. The success of *The Interesting Narrative* made Equinao not only relatively rich but something of an international celebrity. Yet by the late nineteenth century he had been largely forgotten. It was not until the 1960s that his work and life were rediscovered. (C.R.)

arresting visual images that would resonate with the illiterate, the humanity of slaves and the inhumanity of slavery. In 1787 Thomas Clarkson's friend, Josiah Wedgwood, the pottery manufacturer and member of the Lunar Society, produced a medallion with an image of a slave kneeling and pleading, manacled arms raised, 'Am I Not a Man and a Brother?' The medallion was hugely popular in Britain and America where

Benjamin Franklin, president of Pennsylvania's Abolition Society, declared it that it was as effective as 'the best written pamphlet' and the image was quickly reproduced on pipes, plates, tea pots, tokens, enamel boxes and in print. The following year, the Plymouth Anti-Slavery Society published the image of a congested slave ship shown in Figure 2.4, that also became iconic. As a result of Clarkson's prodigious research on the appalling conditions aboard slave-trading ships, the Regulated Slave Trade Act had limited the numbers of slaves that ships could hold in 1788. Taking the example of the Liverpool-registered ship the *Brookes*, which had previously been reputed to carry as many as 600 slaves, the image graphically represented the new limit of 454 prescribed by the Act as no less appalling and inhumane. These images, like much of the literature produced by the anti-slavery movement, often tended to reduce slaves to either an individuated innocent child or an abstract mass. It was not until 1789 that the publication of *The Interesting Narrative of the Life of Olaudah Equiano, or Gustavas Vassa, the African, Written by Himself* (see Figure 2.5) provided slaves with a voice and a personality, albeit one that in recounting his conversion to Christianity made it happily conform to the prejudices of many evangelical abolitionists (see Textbox 2.3). Equiano's book, which he promoted on tours around the country, made him something of a celebrity. The book became an international bestseller, and by the time of Equiano's death in 1797 there were eight English editions as well as American, Dutch, Russian and French versions.

These startlingly novel forms of political communication mobilized Britons in unprecedented numbers and pushed many, especially women unable to sign petitions, to find inventive ways of entering civil society and expressing their views. Thus, when William Fox's pamphlet calling for a consumer boycott of sugar produced by slaves hit a nerve in 1791, it quickly ran to 25 editions and sold 70,000 copies, and gained the support of a reputed 300,000 consumers, chiefly women, who felt their purchase of West Indian sugar made them and their families complicit in slavery. It was not, however, until Napoleon's support for slavery allowed abolitionists to associate their campaign with the patriotic cause, that Parliament first outlawed slave-trading with French territories in 1806 and then extended the ban everywhere else the following year. The abolition of the trade by Britain did not end either the slave trade or the existence of slavery in the British Empire. At least 800,000 slaves continued to exist in the British West Indies and the brutal suppression of slave rebellions continued apace, infamously in Barbados (1816) and Demerara (1823), the latter catalysing Wilberforce and Thomas Buxton to establish the Anti-Slavery Society in 1823. As we will see in the next chapter, slavery remained a central feature of Britain's imperial economy and remained common in many of its African colonies for a century after the Slavery Abolition Act in 1833. That Britons came to think of themselves as living in an empire without slavery was a testament to the effectiveness of the anti-slavery movements of the late eighteenth and early nineteenth centuries.

The Yoke of Custom

The vast majority of Britons were remarkably unaffected by the evangelical revival and the Enlightenment. Popular culture remained a world apart. Its organizing principle was not reason, or the soul, but custom. Custom represented the inherited pattern of past practice, or at least a claim that certain 'traditions' stretched back to time out of mind, and was used to legitimate their continued existence. In that sense custom was not unlike what Enlightened men and women came to describe as a right: it was a claim to something being legitimate and natural, except that rather than being based on general principles it was rooted in the authority of the past. The past was the guide to how the present and future should be organized. In that sense the customary nature of popular culture was not far removed from the practices that decided who got to inherit wealth or to vote, and, as we shall see in the next chapter, it decided who had access to or use of common lands, and shaped the working conditions for many. Custom, handed down by word of mouth, and grounded in the collective memory of local populations, had no formal means of organization and varied from region to region.

Reforming Custom

During the eighteenth century enlightened scholars began to study customary culture in the hope of systematizing it and identifying which customs should be lost with the forward march of reason and progress. A deeply religious man who later published a liturgical manual, Henry Bourne set the tone with his laboriously titled *Antiquitates Vulgares: or, The Antiquities of the Common People … With proper reflection upon each of them: shewing which may be retain'd and which ought to be laid aside*. First published in 1725, it was expanded and revised by John Brand as *Observations on Popular Antiquities* in 1777 and then again by Henry Ellis in 1813 with the new and telling subtitle: *Chiefly illustrating the origin of our Vulgar Customs, Ceremonies and Superstitions*. Like Francis Grose's rival volume, *A Classical Dictionary of the Vulgar Tongue* (1785), these works were infused with the growing fervour of the moral reform movement intent on cleansing the country of its sinful ways. They represented popular customs as dangerous survivals from a heathen past. These customs, they suggested, were largely unchanged and remained grounded in superstition, ignorance and vulgarity, licensing unruly, cruel, immoral and criminal activities. Most of our knowledge of this customary popular culture comes through those intent on recording it so as to be better able to understand and reform it.

The litany of their grievances was legion. Chief among them was the charge of cruelty to animals. A whole series of customary sports like cock- or dog-fighting, or the baiting of bears, badgers and bulls (by bull terrier dogs named and bred for the purpose) were the first targets of moral reformers, who managed to have a number of parliamentary bills for their abolition debated in 1800, 1802, 1809 and 1810. It took almost another half-century for dog- and cock-fighting to be made illegal in 1849, bull- and bear-baiting having been outlawed in 1835 thanks to the campaigns of the Society for the Prevention of Cruelty to Animals (1824). Despite the invention of the term 'blood sports' to describe them in the early twentieth century, shooting and fox-hunting, with their strong connections to aristocratic estates, remained insulated from these campaigns until the twenty-first century when, in 2002, a mass campaign filled the streets of London with 400,000 protestors. Fox-hunting was finally banned in 2004 despite the best efforts of the House of Lords who rejected the legislation three times.

Ironically, many of the customs that appeared to reformers most morally dissolute were those that enforced strong communal codes of proper conduct. Wife-sales are a good example. Reformers were horrified that the custom, which allowed men to auction and sell their wives by parading them on a halter like cattle at market, undermined the sanctity and holy sacrament of marriage. Yet there is evidence that, in an age when divorce required an Act of Parliament only affordable to a select few, wife-sales were a highly ritualized form of separation that was often consensual with the wife purchased by her lover. Similarly, while many considered the custom of playing so-called 'rough music' (by banging pans and other resonant objects) a vulgar 'nuisance', it was commonly used as a form of censure against those like wife-beaters who had violated a communal norm. The same was true of Plough Monday, which marked the first Monday after the twelfth day of Christmas, when labourers returned to work in the fields. Groups of men, decorated with ribbons and white shirts, would drag a plough through the village, sometimes preceded by a band and accompanied by a boy dressed as an old maid and someone playing the fool, collecting money to allow them to drown their sorrows for having to return to work. Those who refused to donate had their garden or dunghill unceremoniously ploughed to the tune of rough music.

Next to cruelty, immorality and the ubiquity of alcohol in the moral reformer's critique of popular culture was its propensity for profligate behaviour that often resulted in unruly disorder. Fair days were always a source of some consternation. Every locality had its own fair at a particular time of the year, and whatever its specific traditions, it always signalled a time of festivity when social conventions were momentarily cast aside and the world was turned upside down. Thus during his *Tour Through England and Wales* (1727), Daniel Defoe was perturbed that at Charlton's Horn Fair the 'mob indeed at that time take all kinds of liberties, and the women are especially impudent for that day; as if it was a day that justified the giving of themselves a lease to all manner of indecency and immodesty, without any reproach'. Rather than study the origin of this custom, Defoe thought it should be 'suppressed as a nuisance and offence to all sober people'. In fairs across the country women chased men, boys subjected adults to threats of violence or humiliation in return for gifts, and the poor ridiculed and mocked the propertied, often fuelled by liberal quantities of alcohol and accompanied by rough music. Travelling showmen were also increasingly a part of fair days and would travel in circuits across the country offering a host of amusements and side stalls, from menageries of wild animals to boxing matches and freak shows. This type of licentious and boisterous behaviour was a common feature of most customary holidays throughout the year. Unruliness also marked local civic events or royal celebrations, where it often formed the price the propertied elites had to pay for the participation of those lower down the social scale whom they viewed with contempt. Indeed, one of the disturbing things about Hogarth's portrayal of a cock-fight in Figure 2.6 – where cruelty, alcohol and a lack of order are all abundant – was the promiscuous mix of men from all social ranks who jostle for position and exchange bets while the cocks fight for their lives.

Figure 2.6 Hogarth's 'The Cock-pit', 1759

The Magical World of Almanacs

The apparent lack of respect and morality signified by these vulgar customs was often seen to be the consequence of their roots in an almost pagan culture (or worse still, pre-Reformation Catholicism) full of magic and superstition. In fact, historians now take for granted that neither the Reformation nor the Enlightenment led to a decline of magic as a way of understanding and inhabiting the world. For many people across the social spectrum, astrology, superstition and the supernatural remained vital to the practice of everyday life. Fishermen and farmers often made decisions about when to plant or sail based upon astrological charts or the occurrence or good or bad omens.

Almanacs, which organized the calendar year around customary holidays, astrological charts and prophecies, were the most popular form of printed publication (including the Bible) and were increasingly published in miniature form so they could be carried in a pocket. As many as 400,000 of them were sold every year by the late seventeenth century, and such was their popularity after 1775 when the monopoly of their publication by the Stationers' Company was broken (even so they were publishing twenty-five titles in 1801) that they were subjected to new stamp duties in 1797. By the 1820s many different forms of almanac were produced by publishers with axes to grind and profits to make – from the radical publisher William Hone's *The Everyday Book* (1826) to the Society for the Diffusion of Useful Knowledge's thoroughly Christianized *British Almanac* (1828) shorn of all impious magic and superstition. Five years after the 1834 repeal of the stamp duty, the iconic *Old Moore's* almanac alone sold 517,000 copies and it was estimated that total sales of the genre topped 1.4 million. Even though almanacs became increasingly eclectic in form and included metrological and tidal charts, tables of weights and measures, as well as historical events, astrological predictions, prophecies and folk cures remained a staple of the genre. Magical thinking also continued to thrive in fortune-telling 'Books of Fate', which became almost as popular as almanacs in the early nineteenth century. For most of the population, and not just those living in more isolated rural conditions, magic and superstition remained more important than Enlightened thought to understanding the world. And yet through the almanac they did so by means of the very print culture that had been such an important vehicle of the Reformation and Enlightenment.

Conclusion

The titles of the two volumes of the New Oxford History of England covering this period characterize its people schizophrenically as 'Polite and Commercial' as well as 'Mad, Bad and Dangerous'. This nicely illustrates how historians are divided about how best to make sense of Britain during the eighteenth century: was it an intransigent

ancien regime founded upon the archaic authority of the monarchy, Church and aristocracy, or a precociously modern country that embraced an increasingly pluralistic and Enlightened civil society? However, this question, like the titles of the New Oxford History of England, presents us with a false dichotomy between two caricatures. Just as with Britain's great rival France, it was the very entrenched nature of the ancien regime that helped generate new forms of association and sociability as well as an Enlightened critique of its monopoly of power and authority. Religion as much as reason was the midwife of this new type of civil society: time and time again it was Dissenting critics of the Anglican Church's privileged position within the state, or its own evangelical members seeking to stir its moribund ministers and congregations, that pioneered new forms of thought and organization. Indeed, rational and moral reformers agreed that the customary culture that infused so much of everyday life for so many threatened the progress of reason and morality. As almanacs remind us, although custom was rooted in the authority of the past, and continued to manifest itself in practices that were increasingly thought to be irrational and immoral, it also bent to the winds of change and assumed no less central a place in the increasingly pluralistic civil society that emerged in eighteenth-century Britain. As Britons were able to debate and organize in unparalleled ways, so they provided each other with new conventions of behaviour and forms of rule. The ancien regime was certainly challenged and changed by these new strains of thought and patterns of association but it remained no less entrenched.

FURTHER READING

The Oxford Histories of England that encapsulate the contrasting ways of viewing the eighteenth century are Paul Langford's *A Polite and Commercial People: England, 1727–1783* (Oxford, 1998) and Boyd Hilton's *A Mad, Bad and Dangerous People? England, 1783–1846* (Oxford, 2006). For contrasting views on Scotland, see R.A. Houston and I.D. Whyte (eds.), *Scottish Society, 1500–1800* (Cambridge, 1989), and Christopher A. Whatley's *Scottish Society 1707–1830* (Manchester, 2000). These accounts should be complemented by H. Barker and E. Chalus (eds.), *Gender in Eighteenth-Century England* (London, 1997), and Kathleen Wilson (ed.), *A New Imperial History: Culture, Identity and Modernity in Britain and the Empire 1660–1840* (Cambridge, 2004).

The continuing hold, if changing forms, of England's landed aristocracy has been the focus of a good deal of work. See especially G.E. Mingay, *English Landed Society in the Eighteenth Century* (London, 1963); John Canon, *Aristocratic Century: The Peerage of Eighteenth-Century England* (Cambridge, 1984); J.V. Beckett, *The Aristocracy in England 1660–1914* (Oxford, 1986); Lawrence and Jeanne Stone, *An Open Elite? England 1540–1880* (Oxford, 1986). On Wales, see Philip Jenkins, *The Making of a Ruling Class: The Glamorgan Gentry, 1640–1790* (Cambridge, 1983); David Howell, *Patriarchs and Parasites: The Gentry of Southwest Wales in the Eighteenth Century* (Cardiff, 1986). On the gentry and its highly gendered forms, see Amanda Vickery, *The Gentleman's Daughter: Women's Lives in Georgian England* (New Haven, 1998); Katharine Glover, *Elite Women and Polite Society in Eighteenth-Century Scotland* (Woodbridge, 2011); Katie Barclay, *Love, Intimacy and Power: Marriage and Patriarchy in Scotland, 1650–1850* (Manchester, 2011).

It has only been in recent decades that historians have begun to explore the social worlds of the professional and middling sorts. On the professional classes, see Penelope Corfield, *Power and the Professions in Britain 1700–1850* (London, 2012). On merchants and the middling sorts, see L. Davidoff and C. Hall, *Family Fortunes: Men and Women of the English Middle Class, 1780–1850* (London, 1987); David Hancock, *Citizens of the World: London Merchants and the Integration of the British Atlantic Community* (Cambridge, 1995); and Margaret Hunt, *The Middling Sort: Commerce, Gender and the Family in England, 1680–1870* (Berkeley, 1996). John Styles's *The Dress of the People: Everyday Fashion in Eighteenth-Century England* (New Haven, 2007) provides a fascinating account of the material culture of these middling sorts and those struggling to become part of them.

The grim lives of the labouring poor have been well chronicled. The rural poor is well covered by K.D.M. Snell, *Annals of the Labouring Poor: Social Change and Agrarian England, 1660–1900* (Cambridge, 1987), and David Howell, *The Rural Poor in Eighteenth-Century Wales* (Cardiff, 2000). In Scotland the clearances of the Highlands and Lowlands dominate the story: their full horror is apparent in T.M. Devine (ed.), *Clearance and Improvement: Land, Power and People in Scotland, 1700–1900* (Scotland, 2010). Tim Hitchcock has done the most in recent years to recover the history of the urban poor: see his *Chronicling Poverty: The Voices and Strategies of the English Poor 1640–1840* (Basingstoke, 1997) and *Down and Out in Eighteenth-Century London* (London, 2004). Norma Myers has done a good job in *Reconstructing the Black Past: Blacks in Britain 1780–1830* (London, 1996).

Much of this literature is concerned with establishing whether the social order was characterized by stability or instability, continuity or change. There has been much debate about whether it is possible to understand the cleavages of eighteenth-century society in terms of class categories that emerged later: see E.P. Thompson, 'Eighteenth-Century English Society: Class Struggle without Class?', *Social History*, 3/2 (1978), 133–66; Penelope Corfield, 'Class by Name and Number in Eighteenth-Century Britain', in P. Corfield (ed.), *Language, Class and History* (Oxford, 1991), 101–30. In recent years, it has been the gendered nature of the entire social order that has most preoccupied historians. A good entry point to those discussions is Hannah Barker and Elaine Chalus (eds.), *Women's History, 1700–1850: An Introduction* (London, 2005).

Religion was at the centre of the eighteenth-century social order in each of Britain's **four nations**. David Hempton's *The Church in the Long Eighteenth Century* (London, 2011) provides the best and broadest overview of all the varieties of Christianity. The hegemony of the **Anglican Church** in England is gamely asserted in Jonathan Clark's *English Society, 1688–1832: Ideology, Social Structure, and Political Practice During the Ancien Regime* (Cambridge, 1985). In marked contrast, Brent Sirota's *The Christian Monitors: The Church of England and the Age of Benevolence, 1680–1830* (New Haven, 2014) sees the **Anglican Church** as the seedbed of the evangelical revival and its propagation of civil society.

The best accounts of the traditions of Dissent and the growth of Methodism are Michael R. Watts, *The Dissenters: From the Reformation to the French Revolution* (Oxford, 1978); and David Hempton's *The Religion of the People: Methodism and Popular Religion, c.1750–1900* (London, 1996). David Jones's *Glorious Work in the World: Welsh Methodism and the International Evangelical Revival, 1735–1750* (Cardiff, 2004) reminds us of the importance of Wales in the history of Methodism. That religion continued to help propagate civil society, especially in radical circles, is evident from Deborah Valenze, *Prophetic Sons and Daughters: Female Preaching and Popular Religion in Industrial England* (Princeton, 1985), and James Bradley, *Religion, Revolution and English Radicalism: Nonconformity in Eighteenth-Century Politics and Society* (Cambridge, 1990).

The best synthetic account of the Enlightenment in Britain is Roy Porter's *The Creation of the Modern World: The Untold Story of the British Enlightenment* (New York, 2001). The ambivalent place of women in the British Enlightenment is the subject of Karen O'Brien's *Women and Enlightenment in Eighteenth-Century Britain* (Cambridge, 2009). The Scottishness of many strands of Enlightened thought is captured in Alexander Broadie (ed.), *The Cambridge Companion to the Scottish Enlightenment* (Cambridge, 2003), and Richard Sher, *The Enlightenment and the Book: Scottish Authors and their Publishers in Eighteenth-Century Britain* (Chicago, 2006), while its highly gendered nature is illustrated by Rosalind Carr's *Gender and Enlightenment Culture in Eighteenth-Century Scotland* (Edinburgh, 2014).

The diverse, bustling and not always orderly social locations of Enlightened thought and public debate have been recuperated in recent years. Peter Borsay, *The English Urban Renaissance: Culture and Society in the Provincial Town, 1660–1770* (Oxford, 1989), Rosemary Sweer, *The English Town, 1680–1840* (New York, 1999), and Bob Harris and Charles McKean's *The Scottish Town in the Age of Enlightenment, 1740–1820* (Edinburgh, 2014) reminds us that the world did not stop at or revolve around London and Edinburgh. The classic account of the growth of public debate in Britain is Jürgen Habermas, *The Structural Transformation of the Public Sphere* (Boston, 1991). Peter Clark's *British Clubs and Societies 1580–1800* (Oxford, 2002) is the most comprehensive in its mapping of the growth of associational culture. Brian Cowan's *The Social Life of Coffee: The Emergence of the Coffeehouse* (New Haven, 2005) provides the best account of the coffee house as a new and commercialized site of public exchange and debate. The proliferation of print culture is best explored through Richard D. Altink, *The English Common Reader: A Social History of the Mass Reading Public* (n.p., n.d.); Hannah Barker, *Newspapers, Politics and English Society, 1695–1855* (London, 1999); James Raven, *The Business of Books: Booksellers and the English Book Trade, 1450–1800* (New Haven, 2007); William St. Clair, *The Reading Nation in the Romantic Period* (Cambridge, 2007).

The ways in which the anti-slavery movement built upon these new associational and print cultures is evident in J.R. Oldfield, *Popular Politics and British Anti-Slavery: The Mobilization of Public Opinion Against the Slave Trade, 1787–1807* (London, 1998). Clare Midgely's *Women Against Slavery: The British Campaigns, 1780–1870* (London, 1995) remains the definitive account of the ways in which women energized the movement, while Christopher L. Brown's *Moral Capital: Foundations of British Abolitionism* (Chapel Hill, 2006) recovers the importance of the American Revolution to the growth of abolitionism in Britain.

A number of historians have established the centrality of custom as the organizing principle of social life for most Britons, and the contempt for it and them by reformers championing the practice of reason or moral improvement. The classic statements are provided by Bob Bushaway, *By Rite: Custom, Ceremony and Community in England, 1700–1880* (London, 1982); Edward Thompson, *Customs in Common: Studies in Traditional Popular Culture* (London, 1993); Ronald Hutton, *Rise and Fall of Merry England: The Ritual Year, 1400–1700* (Oxford, 1994). For a useful selection of primary sources that portray the intersection and increasing antagonism between 'polite' and 'vulgar' forms of popular culture, see John Mullan and Christopher Reid (eds.), *Eighteenth-Century Popular Culture: A Selection* (Oxford, 2000).

3 An Imperial Economy and the Great Transformation

Introduction

The economic and social transformation of Britain between 1750 and 1819 was profound. Changes in the financial, agricultural, commercial and manufacturing sectors led to the dramatic growth and integration of the British economy and consolidated its expanding imperial and global reach. As Britain's population grew at unprecedented speeds, and settled as never before in towns and cities, British society was transformed. All of this seemed to set Britain apart from the rest of the world. In 1750 other countries, especially the Netherlands and early Qing China, could boast equally vibrant economies and urbanizing populations. Yet by 1819 Britain had begun to sustain levels of economic and population growth that made it slowly diverge from its rivals and become arguably the first industrial and urban society in the world. These changes generated an intense debate among contemporaries about how they should be understood and managed. From the late seventeenth century, rival theories of what would later be called 'political economy' developed, positing that wealth was generated either by monopolizing and protecting markets or by setting them free. The **mercantilist** view of political economy – which animated imperial acquisition of territory, the practice of slavery, monopoly trading practices and protectionist policies – was still dominant in 1750. Yet by 1819 it was under sustained pressure from critics like **Adam Smith** who believed that **free trade** in open markets was the basis of the wealth of nations. This chapter, then, asks why and how this great transformation occurred and what were its consequences for Britons as well as all those implicated in Britain's new global economic order.

Historians used to capture the speed and scale of this great transformation by referring to it primarily as *the* **Industrial Revolution**. Conceived as the product of a peculiarly British genius of invention and lasting just six decades – between the invention of the spinning jenny in 1764 and the passage of the **New Poor Law** in 1834 – the Industrial Revolution was often portrayed as nasty, brutish and short. So influential was it thought to be that Eric Hobsbawm, one of the finest historians of the twentieth century, believed it ushered in 'the most fundamental transformation of human life in the history of the world recorded in written document'. Economists were no less beguiled and studied it to discover the seemingly secret recipe that made economies 'take off' so that less developed nations could catch up. To this day historians remain bitterly divided about what caused the Industrial Revolution, how you measure the rates of economic growth it generated, and what effect it had on the standard of living for Britons, their imperial subjects, the environment and the lot of mankind generally. Despite these debates the Industrial Revolution no longer dominates our accounts of Britain's great transformation. That broader process is now seen as being nested in earlier financial, agricultural and commercial revolutions that often had a global character.

As important as the industrialization of the manufacturing sector may have been for increasing productivity and economic growth, it was largely confined to the textile industries that were concentrated in the Midlands and northwest of England as well as around Glasgow, Dundee and the Scottish Borders. The very existence of these industries was dependent upon the new global traffic of finance, commerce and agriculture that had emerged during the eighteenth century.

TIMELINE

1651–63	Navigation Acts
1694	Bank of England
1696	*Lloyd's News* Great Recoinage
1697	Garraway's *The Course of Exchange and Other Things*
1711	South Sea Company
1720	South Sea Bubble crash
1764	Hargreaves invents spinning jenny
1769	James Watt's patented steam engine
1772	The stock market
1773	London Clearing House
1774	Lloyd's
1776	*The Wealth of Nations*
1797	Bank of England issues paper notes
1795	Speenhamland revision of Poor Laws
1798	*Essay on the Principles of Population* (1798–1826)
1811	Luddites
1807	Abolition of slave trade
1815	Corn Laws

1816	Great Recoinage
1824	Imperial weights and measures
1833	Abolition of slavery
1846	Abolition of Corn Laws and sugar duties
1849	Abolition of Navigation Acts

Mercantilist Monopoly Capitalism

In 1776 when **Adam Smith**'s *The Wealth of Nations* famously championed the benefits of a commercial society organized around free markets, he was criticizing, not describing, the world that produced the Industrial Revolution. For that world was still dominated by a mercantilist system that had informed geopolitical competition between Europe's rival imperial powers since the sixteenth century. Mercantilist political economy combined what we would now think of as geopolitical competition with the management of economic life. As mercantilists believed that trade was limited by a zero-sum supply of land, labour and bullion, they advocated monopolizing as much as possible to secure the state from its rivals. This system of monopoly or war capitalism fuelled the pillage of European expansion across the world in the quest for gold, silver, slaves, tax revenue from land and raw materials (see Map 3.1). It also encouraged the protection and control of domestic trade by **tariffs**. Smith may have associated **mercantilism** with the **ancien regime** but it was a dynamic and innovative system. It pioneered new ways of accounting for the balance of trade and what was eventually called national income (see Textbox 2.1). It also drove efforts to increase the productivity and efficiency of land and labour, albeit with often catastrophic human and environmental consequences.

An Imperial Economy

The development of Britain's imperial economy was largely a consequence of mercantilist ideas. The quest for new territory and markets not only helped drive the colonization of the West Indies and North America but also propelled imperial expansion in South Asia, the South Pacific and southern and western Africa after the loss of the American colonies in 1776 (see Map 3.2). Although by no means a uniform process, there were familiar patterns. When 'New Worlds' were 'discovered', royal charters were granted to **joint-stock companies** – such as the Levant Company (1580), the **East India Company** (1599), the Hudson's Bay Company (1670), The Royal African Company

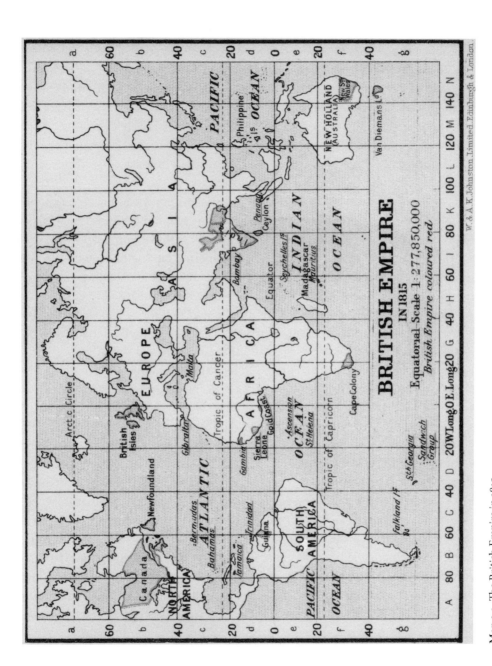

Map 3.1   The British Empire in 1815

(1672) and the South Sea Company (1711) – in return for monopoly rights to trade in that region. Generally, these companies were charged with the import of raw materials not otherwise available in Britain, like sugar, tobacco, tea, spices and, of course, slaves. These companies did not exhaust Britain's overseas trade, for a vibrant merchant culture, albeit often operating under monopoly controls, had developed in Europe and the the Atlantic world during the seventeenth and early eighteenth centuries. The triangular trade of the Atlantic world best exemplified the practice of mercantilist principles. First, tobacco, sugar and eventually cotton were imported from the slave plantations of the Caribbean and American colonies. These raw materials were then refined in Britain and made into tobacco products, rum and finished cottons before being exported to the continent of Europe or the west coast of Africa, where slaves were picked up and shipped back to the Caribbean and American colonies.

The web of mercantilist control of this imperial economy was impressive but hardly failsafe. Passed in the middle of the seventeenth century, the **Navigation Acts** sought to prevent England's colonies from trading directly with her European rivals. They did so by requiring that all colonial goods be transported on English ships while insisting that all trade conducted in the colonies with foreign merchants (that is, from outside the Empire) had to pass through British ports, where it was subjected to **customs duties**. An elaborate schedule of tariffs was imposed not just on foreign goods (to ensure they could not compete with any domestic rival) but also on all inter-colonial trade. By 1787 it took twenty-seven volumes to record all these tariffs and duties. It was left to the luckless Customs Board, created in 1671 to replace the farming of collection services, to enforce them. They did a decent job of it: by 1816 customs revenue accounted for 40 per cent of total government revenue. As these tariffs were deeply unpopular in both Britain and her colonies, smuggling and privateering were rife. In times of peace the Navy was enlisted alongside customs officers, who were granted increased powers throughout the eighteenth century, to police this illicit trade. They could not prevent it. Contraband shipping and trade continued across the Empire and along the remoter stretches of the British coast until the duties and tariffs disappeared in the nineteenth century.

Despite its imperfect grip on controls of trade, the mercantilist system decisively shaped the imperial British economy throughout the eighteenth century. Trade with Europe, which provided 30 per cent of imports in 1750, lessened in importance as war and overseas expansion dramatically increased the scale of colonial trade. The colonies already accounted for almost a quarter of all exports and half of all imports in the 1730s. The phenomenal growth of colonial trade was largely responsible for the doubling of overseas trade between 1700 and 1760, by which time Britain had begun importing food from its colonies. Combined exports to North America and the West Indies increased by 2,300 per cent during the eighteenth century. In the closed circuits of Britain's mercantile economy, slave-produced sugar and tobacco were initially dominant but cotton quickly became king.

Despite considerable opposition from the powerful woollen, silk and linen producers in Britain, cotton was mainly imported in the form of finished calicoes from India and Egypt. But with the supply of slave-produced raw cotton from the Caribbean and American colonies accelerating in the 1750s, cotton manufacturers proliferated near the ports of Liverpool, Manchester and Glasgow where they finished calicoes and exported them to colonial markets in the Atlantic world, chiefly Africa. Between 1750 and 1770 cotton exports increased tenfold, and 90 per cent of them went to these colonial markets. Even after independence the United States remained not just the chief supplier of raw cotton but the destination of two thirds of Britain's finished cotton goods, which by 1830 accounted for 50 per cent of all exports. But imports from the colonies were also a critical part of the re-export trade, which accounted for 40 per cent of total exports by the 1750s. Between 30 and 50 per cent of colonial sugar and tobacco was re-exported to European markets. A century after the passage of the first Navigation Act, British and colonial ships represented 80 per cent of all those docking in Britain's ports. The amount of tonnage they carried doubled between 1700 and 1770, when it stood at 593,962, but then it quadrupled between 1770 and 1820, when it reached 2,439,029. Britain's major ports – London, Bristol, Cardiff, Liverpool, Glasgow and Dundee – thrived (see Textbox 3.1).

3.1 Place: Liverpool Docks

In the early seventeenth century the small town of Liverpool on the northwest coast of England was a relative backwater in the shadow of the nearby ancient town of Chester. As Britain's nascent settlements in Virginia and New England developed, Liverpool became an alternative port to London, Bristol and Southampton. In 1699 the city saw its first slave ship leave its makeshift port, arriving in Barbados almost a year later with 220 African slaves destined for the island's sugar plantations. By the end of the eighteenth century Liverpool had become a major hub for the Atlantic slave trade, the slave cargo transported in ships that set sail from Liverpool accounted for approximately 80 per cent of Britain's entire transatlantic slave trade. These ships left Liverpool with goods such as guns, earthenware pots and textiles that were exchanged for slaves in West Africa, who were then sold in the Caribbean and North America. Between 1750 and 1807, it has been estimated, a third of Liverpool's shipping activity was related to the slave trade. Under the control of the town's corporation between 1709 and 1825 a sophisticated complex of docks emerged in the city to service this trade (Figure 3.1). The world's first 'wet dock', a space that allowed ships to be serviced efficiently while remaining afloat, opened in 1715, and a century later the total area of wet docks extended across 46 acres and included over 2 miles of waterfront quays. After the slave trade was abolished in 1807, Liverpool continued to be a major port city, a hub for transatlantic trade and a place where Irish refugees and a small number of freed slaves would settle. From the 1830s the docks were extended and reorganized around a series of colossal brick buildings and warehouses so that by 1857 there were over 15 miles of waterside quays. As the docks adapted to the growing size of ships powered by steam from the 1880s, they grew in size once again, stretching to 26 miles of quays by 1908. These docks thrived until the middle of the twentieth century, when a combination of war damage and technological change left them increasingly obsolete, and plunged the city into crisis. In 1988 the Albert Dock, first constructed in 1845, reopened as a waterside tourist attraction featuring a complex of museums, restaurants and television studios. (S.W.)

Figure 3.1 Liverpool Docks, *c.* 1885

Capitalism and Slavery

No less than colonialism, slavery was at the centre of the mercantilist system. Eric Williams, the first Prime Minister of Trinidad and Tobago, was wrong to argue in *Capitalism and Slavery* (1944) that the profits from slavery financed the **Industrial Revolution** – they were far more important than that. Britain dominated the slave trade in the eighteenth century, during which time, by the most conservative estimate, 40 per cent of the 6 million slaves transported from West Africa to the Caribbean and Americas went on British ships – 1.3 million of them between just 1777 and 1807.

Liverpool alone was sending fifty-three slave ships a year in the early 1750s. The ports of Bristol, Liverpool and London grew rich on the trade. They built the ships that worked the triangular trade: exporting guns, rum and finished textiles to pay for the slaves that were transported and sold in the Caribbean and American colonies to pro-duce produce sugar, cotton, tobacco and coffee that were then shipped back to Britain. Two thirds of Britain's sugar imports came through London in 1790, when the value of London's West Indies trade reached £3–4 million per annum, accounting for a third of the city's total trade. Even in the late eighteenth century, when the scale of its involve-ment with slavery had significantly declined, as much as 40 per cent of Bristol's income came from its connections with the slave economy.

Those slaves who survived the **Middle Passage** across the Atlantic faced inhuman conditions and high mortality rates. Slave plantations were laboratories not just for unspeakable forms of human cruelty but for new ways of organizing labour and cal-culating its productivity that would be partially replicated in Britain's new textile mills and manufacturing factories. Slave-drivers worked like foremen and overseers: they oversaw the division of labour between men, women and children, enforced long eighteen-hour shifts, disciplined the recalcitrant, and often kept careful accounts of the plantation as well as the levels of productivity of each slave for absentee owners. The coffee, tobacco, sugar and cotton produced by slaves fuelled new levels of con-sumer demand back in Britain, which in turn catalysed the manufacturing of cups, pipes, spoons and clothes. Large plantations required capital investment that was readily supplied by British investors eager for healthy returns. The City of London funnelled £37 million to the West Indies in the 1770s alone. The bitter fruits of slavery spread far beyond the port towns: they funded political careers, the construction of country estates, canals and cotton mills, the endowments of Oxbridge colleges, the liquidity of banks, the growth of marine insurance, mortgages and annuities, and so on. Many Britons had a stake in slavery (see Textbox 3.2). When slaves were finally emancipated in 1833, almost half of the £20 million awarded in compensation to slave-owners stayed in Britain where it was distributed to 3,000 absentee owners scat-tered across the country – the aristocracy and gentry, **clergy** and military, and women as well as men.

Agricultural 'Improvement'

Land and labour were not of course only found overseas. Landed wealth and the improvement of agriculture in Britain was a vital part of the mercantile system. Monopoly capitalism found no greater expression than in the concentration of land among the aristocracy and gentry. It has been estimated they owned up to 75 per cent of land in England and Wales by 1790, with small freeholders and the Church respec-tively claiming the remaining 15 per cent and 10 per cent. Similarly, only 2.5 per cent of Scots owned any land or property in 1770. Unlike many of its European neighbours and rivals, Britain no longer had a peasantry with claims to the land. By all accounts the landed classes' grip upon the land had grown tighter in the preceding century as they bought up small freeholders (who in the 1690s owned twice as much land) and enclosed previously common lands. The new rural social order ushered in by the quest for 'improvement' entrenched monopoly ownership, reduced most farmers to positions as tenants with limited leases, and ensured the landless rural poor were entirely dependent on the sale of their labour.

Enclosure was a vital part of agricultural improvement. Open fields and common or uninhabited lands (known in Scotland as 'commonties') had long provided the rural poor with access to materials (stone, peat, turf, wood), land to graze animals, grow crops and catch wildfowl, or rivers to fish. Enclosure sought to eradicate these practices by claiming these lands as the exclusive, private property of an individual – a claim made manifest by the construction of fences and ditches. Enclosure was not an invention of the eighteenth century but it accelerated from the 1760s as Acts of Enclosure were increasingly authorized by Parliament and enforced by the law. Whereas parliamentary Acts had enclosed less than 450,000 acres in England and Wales during the first half of the eighteenth century, 7 million acres were enclosed between 1760 and 1815. That was also the period when enclosure and the division of commonties among adjacent property holders in Scotland also gathered steam. Together with the forcible and sometimes violent evictions of tenant cottars and crofters to 'improve' large estates, they formed part of the clearances of both the Lowlands and Highlands that continued down to the 1820s. Once common land was enclosed as private property, landowners used the law to punish those who continued to try to harvest their customary rights. By codifying property rights and boundaries, enclosure also made it easier for turnpike trusts and joint-stock companies to negotiate with landowners over the construction of toll roads and canals – both of which boomed in the second half of the eighteenth century and represented a classically mercantile type of monopoly ownership of transportation networks. In England and Wales there were 150 turnpike trusts running toll roads during the 1750s but by 1825 there were a 1,000, operating 18,000 miles of road. Scotland also saw a massive investment of between £2 and 3 million in the development of roads and bridges by turnpike trusts between 1790 and 1815. In effect, enclosure represented a process of internal colonization or land grabs that consolidated the monopoly of land by the aptly named landed classes.

The growing pace of enclosure in the second half of the eighteenth century was largely driven by the increasing profitability of agriculture and by attempts to 'improve' the productivity of land. As agricultural improvement predated enclosure and the concentration of ownership, it cannot be credited solely to large enlightened landowners. New ways of 'husbanding' the land were already apparent in the first half of the eighteenth century. In the 1730s a lawyer and gentleman farmer, Jethro Tull, pioneered new forms of tilling the soil and sowing seeds in rows behind a horse-drawn hoe. Many farmers became interested in the quality of their soil and began experimenting with crop rotations (such as the Norfolk system of wheat, roots, barley and clover) and the use of turnips and manure to revitalize it. Improved drainage with the cutting of dykes, trenches and new systems of under-drainage with clay pipes, turned wetlands and meadows into farmable fields. These techniques, often developed by experimental practice and rooted in local networks and ecologies, were slowly disseminated and popularized by books like William Ellis's *Modern Husbandry or Practice of Farming* (1731) and Arthur Young's *The Farmer's Calendar* (1771).

Livestock breeding also became fashionable. Farmers sought to raise cattle, pigs and sheep that developed quickly and reached greater sizes and weights. New strains of dogs, horses and oxen better equipped for working their land were also bred. In the quest for bigger yields or hardier constitutions, selective breeding extended to crop varieties as well. It was a trend that extended to cultivable garden plants, which numbered in their hundreds in the late seventeenth century but reached 18,000 by 1839. New hand-tools and ploughing equipment proliferated. By the end of the eighteenth century agricultural shows, where livestock and giant vegetables competed for prizes alongside the demonstration of new equipment and techniques, were an annual feature of market and county towns. These shows were often sponsored by local agricultural societies devoted to improvement, like the one established at Peterborough in 1797 with the fourth Earl Fitzwilliam as its president. In 1810 there were fifty-nine of these societies, although the English Agricultural Society (whose motto was 'Practice with Science') only received a royal charter in 1840.

These new ways of improving land to make it more productive had significant consequences in the century after 1750. Between 10 and 15 million acres of previously uncultivated land were bought into production as woodlands and forests were cleared and marshes and fens were drained (by the 1840s uncultivated land even became known as 'wasteland'). Agricultural output doubled although the size of the agricultural workforce only marginally increased. By 1850 Britain had the smallest percentage of agricultural workers of any country, at just 22 per cent of the total workforce, and the largest proportion of urban inhabitants to feed. Yet if landowners sought to increase the productivity of land and labour, they also sought protection from foreign trade. Indeed, the continuing grip of mercantile ideas was strikingly apparent in 1804 and 1815 when parliaments dominated by the landed classes passed **Corn Laws** to protect the price of wheat (and, it was argued, the wages of agricultural workers) from cheaper European grain that it had not been possible to import during the **Napoleonic Wars**. Given that the high price of wheat restricted the labouring poor's capacity to buy their staple food, bread, the Corn Laws were hugely unpopular and armed troops were forced to defend Parliament when it passed the legislation in 1815.

Finance and Gentlemanly Capitalists

Just as **mercantilism** helped seed this revolution in agricultural production, so it also contributed to a financial revolution that established the City of London at the centre of the world's capital markets by 1750. Mercantilists had long believed that the supply of money in the form of coins, made possible by the possession of gold and silver bullion, determined prices and provided a measure of the total wealth generated by land, labour and trade. Yet it was not the stockpiling of bullion that made the City of London a global financial force. In fact, despite myriad efforts, the Royal Mint, charged with the production of coin, failed to ensure that there was enough silver and gold in circulation to facilitate everyday commercial transactions. As gold and silver coins were so clipped and worn that they rarely weighed their proper value, many employers and tradesmen issued their own token coins as cash. To counteract the shortage of bullion, a range of new financial instruments and forms of credit were created by merchants, the City of London and banks. The City also became a thriving centre for trading in shares of the growing number of joint-stock companies granted trading monopolies by Parliament. In addition, new financial services like maritime insurance proliferated as the volume of trade on British ships rose thanks to the **Navigation Acts**. Much of the investment in these stocks, instruments and services were from 'gentlemanly capitalists' whose surplus capital came from the increasing profitability of their landed estates and overseas investments, including, of course, in plantation slavery. Investors were not scared away by the dramatic crash that burst the speculative **South Sea Bubble** in 1720, although it unleashed a series of denunciations of the moral and social bases of finance capitalism. Such was the continuing scale of trade in financial services that by the 1770s its previously informal locations and practices were slowly formalized. The stock market and Lloyd's insurance moved out of the world of coffee houses and into purpose-built structures in 1772 and 1774, while thirty-one private merchant banks – built on the fortunes of families like the Barings, Warburgs and Rothschilds – created their own Clearing House in 1773. The City of London had taken its recognizably modern form by the late eighteenth century and it had done so largely on the back of mercantilist monopoly capitalism.

The Population Question

Yet despite the increasing national wealth generated by the protection of the mercantile system, many feared Britain's population was growing at such an alarming rate that destitution and calamity were inevitable. The Rev. **Thomas Malthus** became the chief exponent of this view in 1798 when his *An Essay on the Principle of Population* argued that population growth would always outstrip man's capacity to generate food, given the finite quantity of land. 'The power of population', he wrote, 'is indefinitely greater than the power in the earth to produce subsistence for man.' At one level this was a surprising argument for unlike France, which had been plagued by no less than sixteen famines during the eighteenth century, Britain's last famine had been in Scotland at the end of the previous century. Nonetheless, Malthus wrote in the immediate aftermath of the great dearth of 1794–6, and he attributed the swelling ranks of the poor to the fact that Britain now had more people than jobs or food to sustain them.

Certainly, the population of Britain and its constituent nations grew consistently during the eighteenth century (see Table 3.1). That growth accelerated markedly from 1770 and reached its peak in 1826, the very year Malthus published the final edition of his *Essay*. Malthus explained such rapid growth by blaming the poor for being unable or unwilling to prevent their sinful desire to procreate. The inevitable consequence of this failure, he contended, was the 'positive checks' provided by famine and disease that would naturally restore an equilibrium with the land's resources. While Malthus correctly identified that populations had risen and fallen cyclically in the past, Britain ironically became the exception to his rule as he was writing. Its population grew so much faster than its European rivals that although it represented just 5.7 per cent of Europe's land mass, its proportion of Europe's population rose from 7.6 per cent in 1680 to 11.7 per cent in 1860. Only the population of the United States of America grew at a faster rate, from an estimated 2.5 million in 1776 to 12.9 million in 1830. Much of that growth was endogenous not exogenous, that is to say, it came by dint of slavery, immigration and the imperial expansion of its territories westwards.

Many believed that the solution to rapid population growth and escalating levels of poverty was the imperial conquest and settlement of territory overseas. Throughout the eighteenth century Britons were dispersed across the Empire. At the end of the seventeenth century some 350,000 migrants had already left England for North America and the Caribbean in search of a new life, greater prosperity or religious freedom. In the five decades after Union they were joined by 30,000 Scots, many of them from the professional and business classes of the Lowlands. As the total numbers of emigrants from Britain accelerated during the eighteenth century, reaching 750,000 by its close,

Table 3.1 Population of the United Kingdom (millions)

	Eng & Wales	Scotland	Ireland	Total
1701	5.47			5.47
1751	6.47	1.27	3.12	10.9
1801	8.89	1.6	5.1	15.6
1851	17.93	2.89	6.55	27.4

their profile changed decisively as convicts (until 1776) and **indentured servants** or labourers predominated. Schemes of voluntary and forced emigration proliferated at the turn of the nineteenth century as tenant farmers and rural labourers were driven from the land. In the two years of 1800 and 1824, 20,000 and 24,000 Britons left the Isles. At this time, Canada became the focus of attempts to resettle the poor and to encourage the settlement of others who could help ensure the loyalty of its inhabitants to the British government. The abolition of the slave trade in 1807 generated a series of schemes to replace slaves with indentured labourers from Britain before turning on an industrial scale to those from South Asia and China after the abolition of slavery itself in 1833. Thus in Trinidad indentured labourers were first taken from the cleared **Scottish Highlands** as well as from prostitutes on the streets of London. Criminals and political offenders were less likely to be executed as deportation and forced penal labour were extended to Australia in 1786 (see Textbox 1.3).

These were tiny numbers that hardly solved the conundrum of how to adequately feed a population whose exponential growth **Malthus** feared would soon outstrip the capacity of British agriculturalists to feed it. The increasingly urban character of that population exacerbated this problem. Throughout the eighteenth century the vast majority of Britons lived in the countryside or in hundreds of small towns that rarely exceeded a thousand inhabitants. In 1700 there were just 31 cities of 5,000 or more inhabitants; by 1750 this had risen to 107 and by 1800 to 236. The number of people living in these cities rose accordingly: in 1700 just short of a million, by 1750 it had doubled to 1.8 million and by 1800 had done so again, reaching 3.8 million or almost a quarter of the total population. **Urbanization** was by no means confined to England and Wales. Scotland had the seventh largest urban population in Europe in 1750, but by 1800 it had become the fourth largest and by 1850 only England and Wales were more urbanized. Indeed, by 1850, as we will see in Chapter 5, Britain had become the first society in the world with half of its population living in cities of 5,000 or more. London consistently accounted for over 10 per cent of the entire country's population. While Paris and Constantinople were an equivalent size in 1750, by 1800 London had outgrown them both and was the first European city to boast a million inhabitants. Although London and Dublin were the only cities in Britain with a population of more than 100,000 in 1801, nine others joined them by 1851. Cities like Manchester, Birmingham and Glasgow grew even faster than London: in 1750 they had just 18,000, 24,000 and 32,000 inhabitants respectively; by 1800 they had 90,000, 74,000 and 44,000; by 1850, 303,000, 233,000 and 177,000. Dublin's population grew less quickly, from 90,000 in 1750 to 258,000 in 1850, but it was still three times the size of Belfast.

Migration to cities was largely regional and the preserve of the young, with the exception of London which drew people of all ages from across the country. As Britain's population grew at unprecedented rates, it became younger and more mobile. In 1851 when 60 per cent of the population were under twenty-four years of age, two thirds of those aged between twenty and twenty-four were urban migrants. The quest for work and marriage had long driven the young from their **parish** of settlement but for much of the eighteenth century that movement remained largely local, seasonal and circular. Increasingly, after 1750, those who moved to cities did not return to the countryside. By 1851 only half of those living in London over twenty years of age had been born there, while a third of Lancashire's inhabitants came from other counties, with the Irish alone accounting for over 10 per cent of the total. More than half of the inhabitants of industrializing cities like Glasgow and Manchester were born elsewhere, with the Irish accounting for 18 per cent of their respective populations.

Mortality rates in these burgeoning and rapidly built cities were dreadful. Housing was poor, heating a luxury of the rich, the air foul, the water contaminated, and the streets were crowded with animals, open sewers and trash. In London during the first half of the eighteenth century burial rates exceeded baptisms from between 25 per cent to 44 per cent as smallpox, measles and tuberculosis devoured its cold and overcrowded inhabitants. As many as 27,000 Londoners died in 1710 alone. London's population only grew because it was constantly replenished by an endless stream of migrants. Yet from the 1750s mortality rates in London declined and were even out-paced by baptisms by the 1790s. Given the paucity of the data we have, why and how this happened remains unclear and much debated. It is clear that contemporaries were concerned enough about the vile conditions of their cities to form urban Improvement Commissions to provide better lighting and paving and voluntary hospitals to improve the health of urban dwellers. Infant mortality, which was already much lower in Britain than on the continent of Europe, also improved as a consequence of cleaner streets, as well as improved child-rearing and health care. While in 1776, 60 per cent of urban growth was accounted for by migration and 40 per cent by natural growth, by 1851 those proportions had been reversed. Nonetheless there remained an urban penalty: in 1841 the death rate in the four largest cities was 27.3 per 1,000 compared to 26 per 1,000 for urban areas generally and 20.4 per 1,000 for all of England and Wales.

What, then, allowed Britain to break the Malthusian trap and sustain rapid popu-lation growth? Clearly falling mortality, within and beyond cities, was an important component, but as we shall again see in Chapter 5, the most dramatic improvement in mortality rates came in the nineteenth century as a consequence of smallpox inocula-tion and the improvement of water supply and sewerage. Life expectancy did lengthen but only slowly. At the beginning of the eighteenth century it stood at thirty-four years of age in England and thirty in Scotland; a century later it had risen to between for-ty-one and forty-two years in both places, where it remained until the 1850s. Fifty was a venerable age if you were lucky enough to make it. Before the mid nineteenth century the falling mortality rate was eclipsed by a rising birth rate. Indeed, it has been esti-mated that in England between 1750 and 1830 births outstripped deaths by two to one, making the rise in fertility account for two thirds of population growth. Simply put, this was possible because women married earlier and had more children. In 1750 women first married aged 25 but they did so at 23.2 by 1830. The younger age of marriage meant women began reproducing earlier and therefore had more children (illegitimacy rates and premarital conceptions also rose and accounted for half of all first births), 6.5 in 1850 as opposed to 5.5 in 1700. Although the evidence is spottier in Scotland, the trends were similar. Explaining Britain's population growth can therefore be boiled down to the simple equation that more children were being born and more were surviving and living longer. Whether people married earlier and had more children because standards of living were rising or to increase the earning potential of the family is much debated. We'll return to this question at the end of the chapter, but it is clear that **Malthus** was wrong, for the evidence suggests that people were not consumed by lust but were making prudential decisions about how many children they should have.

Mercantilist ideas and practices structured the organization of economic life across the British Empire during the long eighteenth century. Yet by 1819 this conception of the economy as a zero-sum game – a competition between states for finite resources (land, labour and trade) to support their populations – had begun to make less sense. Trade grew despite the loss of the American colonies, and an expanding and urbanizing population was fed by increasingly productive uses of the land. By the early nineteenth century two pillars of mercantilism – slavery and protection – were subject to increasing criticism, and calls for their abolition and reform grew louder. As we will see in Chapter 6, it took several decades to dismantle the system: first came the abolition of the slave trade (1807) and slavery (1833), then between 1811 and 1821 the pegging of Britain's currency to the **Gold Standard**, and finally the repeal of the **Corn Laws** and sugar duties (1846) and the **Navigation Acts** (1849). Until then the state was central to the orchestration of the mercantile system, and it was that system that helped forge not just the agricultural and financial revolutions but, as we shall now see, the Industrial Revolution as well.

Commerce and Manufacturing the Wealth of Nations

Adam Smith's critique of mercantilist monopoly capitalism was driven by his championing of an alternative, and altogether less gloomy, political economy. Far from being constrained by the finitude of the world's resources, he argued, *The Wealth of Nations* would be potentially limitless if trade were set free. Smith argued that markets worked best when left to operate freely, unhampered by mercantile monopolies and restrictions, in what he considered to be their natural state. Competition ensured an efficient division of labour that produced cheaper goods that were then available to more people. Rejecting the popular view that men's desire for luxury and wealth was sinful and selfish, he suggested it catalysed trade and motivated economic growth that would eventually benefit all. Not only would wealth be widely (if not evenly) distributed by an 'invisible hand' but as people would increasingly engage in transactions with strangers they wanted to impress, their moral conduct would improve. In the hands of Smith and **Malthus**, the new enlightened science of political economy continued to rely heavily on moral theory and ideas of divine Providence.

Manufacturing a New Division of Labour

Smith's ideal commercial society depended upon the withdrawal of the state from economic life but also, no less importantly, a division of labour and the instigation of new forms of production that could drive down the cost of goods and stimulate demand for them. At the start of *The Wealth of Nations* he turns to the example of the 'very trifling manufacture' of pin-making to illustrate the enormous gains in productivity made possible by the division of labour. Whereas one worker could make around 20 pins a day fashioning the whole product, ten men could make 48,000 a day when the manufacturing process was broken down into eighteen distinct operations so that one 'man draws out the wire, another straights it, a third cuts it, a fourth points it, a fifth grinds it at the top for receiving the head' and so on. Smith believed that not only would men find their natural position within this division of labour but that the massive increase in productivity it enabled was also made possible by the invention of new machinery – itself the product of a broader division of labour across society (for some invented and others made) that entrenched and justified social hierarchy.

The division of labour and the unleashing of the productive power of workers by mechanization was central to industrialization and it has placed the textile industry front and centre of our accounts. Textile production dramatically accelerated in the second half of the eighteenth century. Yorkshire produced 50,000 pieces of its characteristic light worsted wool before the 1760s but by the 1800s was generating 400,000 pieces. But cotton was king. Its production increased 6,000 per cent between 1760 and 1820. New technologies were vital to this transformation. While every British schoolchild used to be taught that Britain industrialized first because of the inventions of its brilliant engineers – John Kay's **flying shuttle** in 1733, James Hargreaves's spinning jenny in 1764, Richard Arkwright's water-powered spinning machine in 1768, Samuel Crompton's spinning mule in 1779 – we now know that most new mechanized forms of textile production developed slowly and were endlessly adapted in local settings, often by skilled workmen operating or overseeing the machines. The problem of improving cotton production unleashed an unprecedented level of industrial creativity that was made possible by a culture of enlightened experimentation.

At the heart of the problem were the different paces in which cotton could be spun into thread and woven into cloth. Keeping the pace of spinning and weaving in lockstep required constant innovation to avoid bottlenecks in the production process. At first most cotton cloth was produced by small domestic workshops that were family enterprises in the countryside: typically, children first 'carded' or flattened the raw cotton, women then spun it on a wheel to produce a thread which was then woven on a handloom by a man to produce finished cloth. As handlooms became faster with the widespread adoption of the flying shuttle in the 1760s, the spinning wheel could not keep up. Thus the spinning jenny made it possible to spin several threads at the same time on a moveable frame, a process accelerated by powering the wheel with water to further stretch the thread on rollers, and finally the combination of both techniques on the spinning mule, which became steam-driven by the 1790s. Although still prevalent in 1800, by 1838 water had effectively been displaced by steam as a source of power for these machines, accounting for just a quarter of the total. Handloom weavers were gradually and painfully displaced by power-looms, which grew in number from just 2,400 in 1813 to 224,000 in 1850. The mechanization of cotton production vastly increased output and reduced labour costs: in the early 1700s more than 1,100 hours of labour were required to produce a single kilogram of yarn but, by 1825, the same quantity was produced in just three hours at 1/370th of the labour cost. The centralization and mechanization of production meant that a country that had long had very high labour costs could suddenly produce textiles at a fraction of the costs of their largest international rivals like those in South Asia.

3.2 Person: Samuel Greg, 1758–1854

Samuel Greg was one of the first to mechanize the spinning of cotton in the late eighteenth century. Born in Belfast, his father, whose name he shared, was a wealthy merchant and shipowner, while his mother, Elizabeth, was the daughter of Samuel Hyde, a Lancashire merchant and landowner. As his parents' second son, Greg was sent to live with his mother's childless brothers at the age of eight to ensure the succession of their trade in linens across North America and Europe. Privately educated at the elite Harrow School, Greg became a partner of the firm in 1780 and inherited the business in 1782. By 1784 Greg diversified the business by building a cotton-spinning mill at Quarry Bank Mill on the outskirts of Manchester. The mill initially harnessed the energy of a nearby fast-flowing river to turn an Arkwright-style waterwheel, which in turn powered the spinning machinery by way of a belt. By 1810 Quarry Bank Mill was powered by a Boulton and Watt steam engine. Greg's mill kept labour costs low by employing 'apprenticed' children from local orphanages between the ages of ten and twelve. In 1790 he built a house to accommodate these children, whom he also provided with rudimentary education after their shifts at the mill. This small and initially rural enterprise had global roots that spanned the eighteenth-century British Empire. Despite his use of water and steam power, many of Greg's production techniques mirrored those of cotton-spinners in South

Asia, who were also his biggest rivals. Greg's raw cotton came from Jamaica and Brazil and was sourced and imported by merchant family members in the nearby port of Liverpool. Throughout his career Greg himself was the owner of a large slave plantation in Dominica, the Hillsborough Estate. When slavery was abolished in 1834, the family business was boosted by a compensation payment by the state totalling nearly £3,000. In 1789 Greg married Hannah Lightbody, the daughter of a prominent Liverpool Unitarian merchant with financial ties to the West Indies. They had thirteen children, seven daughters and six sons (one of whom died). Although Greg had been raised as a Scottish Presbyterian in Belfast, his own children became Unitarians like their mother and the family became part of the elite circle of wealthy non-conformist families in Manchester. When Greg retired from the business in 1832, having been attacked by a stag on the grounds of Quarry Bank Mill, it was the biggest coarse spinning and weaving enterprise in the country – exporting cloth to parts of Europe, North America and Russia. The lives of Greg and his family show how early industrial entrepreneurs were dependent on a century of prior British imperial expansion, and on the capital, trade networks and contacts provided by Atlantic slavery. (S.W.)

The greater productive power of mills had a dramatic effect on the experience of labour. As power looms had a voracious appetite, they were fed by the intensification of slave plantation labour that harvested raw cotton in the Caribbean and United States. The mechanization of production within mills or factories transformed the experience of labour and developed what was described as a new 'manufacturing system' (see Textbox 3.2). The old domestic form of production was part of a system of '**putting-out**' where merchant masters deposited the raw cotton and paid by piece-rate for the finished cloth while the weavers owned their own equipment, organized the division of labour within the family and worked their own hours. St Monday, the customary practice of taking Monday off to extend the weekend, was widely observed, as was a plethora of religious and political holidays. Moreover, at the start of the week the pace of work tended to be slow but accelerated mid-week to ensure jobs were completed by its end. Increasingly from the 1780s cotton masters centralized production in mills where they could gain greater control over workers – essentially imposing flat rates of pay for longer and more regular hours on new machines. Arkwright's mill at Cromford in Derbyshire employed 300 men by 1781; by 1841 the average size of the workforce in Lancashire's 975 mills was 193 (although 25 employed more than 1,000). The vast majority of these workers were women and children, for the divisions of labour within household forms of production were largely transferred to the factory setting. The big difference was that the master was no longer the male head of household but a foreman who imposed a new type of industrial discipline: regulating the length of breaks for meals, docking the pay of those who were late to work, and ensuring that workers were focused on production. Josiah Wedgewood, member of the Lunar Society and the producer of the famed anti-slavery medallion, was at the forefront of developing these new forms of factory discipline in his pottery works. Accidents, injuries and corporal punishment were common. The working day lengthened to fourteen hours and after the introduction of gas lighting in 1805 some of the larger mills introduced shift work and operated twenty-four hours a day for six days of the week. It has been estimated that the output of a mill with a workforce of 750 operatives was the equivalent of 200,000 domestic spinners and weavers! This intensification of labour was not confined to textile mills or other sectors like pottery that embraced new forms of factory organization: between 1750 and 1830 working hours rose generally by around 20 per cent. More work, not just its reorganization or mechanization, contributed to rising levels of production that signified the Industrial Revolution.

A Fossil-Fuelled Revolution

New forms of energy and power were also vital to rising levels of industrial output and productivity. Simply put, the eighteenth century witnessed a decisive shift from an **organically powered economy** – where heat energy came from wood and mechanical energy from water and wind as well as animal and human muscle – to one fuelled by coal. This turn to coal dramatically transformed the amount of power it was possible to generate for industrial production and decisively displaced organic forms of energy. In 1700, 2.6 million tons of coal were mined in England and Wales, accounting for 61 per cent of the total amount of energy consumed; by 1800 that had risen to 15 million tons of coal and 80 per cent of total energy consumption; and by 1850, 74 million tons of coal were produced, representing 92 per cent of all energy used. Put another way, the amount of energy provided by coal in 1800 alone was the equivalent of that which could be generated by 11 million acres of woodland (roughly a wood one third the size of England). No wonder that Britons became dependent upon – one might even say addicted to – fossil fuels. And happily for them they lived in a country blessed with rich and easily accessible mineral deposits. The largest coal deposits on the continent were in Belgium, France and Germany but these paled in comparison: in 1800 their *combined* output represented less than 20 per cent of that of England and Wales. China had plenty of coal but it lay deep and very far from the economically most advanced region of the Yangzi Delta. In 1800 Britain produced 80 per cent of the world's coal.

Abundant and accessible, British coal was cheap. The problem of transporting it, mining it deeper and harnessing its productive power lay at the heart of British industrialization. Coalfields were confined to southern Wales, the northwest and northeast of England and the Clyde Valley in Scotland. Rivers and coastal waterways allowed it to be shipped around the edges of the country (and particularly to London) but it could only be transported inland in small quantities by packhorses. It was the desire to transport coal from his mines in Worsley to Manchester that animated the Duke of

Bridgewater to build the first canal, which was subsequently named after him, between 1759 and 1761. The cost of coal in Manchester quickly fell by 75 per cent, reducing the cost of manufactured goods and making Bridgewater a fortune. Bridgewater spent the next fifteen years building the iconic Manchester to Liverpool canal. Not all the one thousand miles of canal that had been built by 1790 connected Britain's coalfields to its industrial regions and coastal ports, but until the advent of the railway it was the chief means of transporting coal.

The problem of mining coal, or rather of pumping water out of mines, led to the invention of the steam engine and the unleashing of coal's mechanical power. In the late seventeenth and early eighteenth centuries, two Thomases, Savery and Newcomen, developed coal-fired engines to pump water out of mines. These machines devoured almost as much coal as they enabled to be mined until James Watt refined the design by adding a separate condensing cylinder that increased their efficiency fivefold in 1769. Watt formed a partnership with Matthew Boulton to mass-produce these pumps in his Soho works at Birmingham and by the 1790s more than a thousand of their pumps were being used in Britain's coal mines. This, not simply innovation in the form of textile production, was the birth of the industrial age and heralded in the words of Fredrich Engels 'the victory of machine-work over hand-work'. Further refined, Watt and Boulton's steam engine became widely adopted and used for the milling of flour, sugar and stone, in cotton and paper mills, as well as for blast furnaces in iron production. Together with the replacement of charcoal with coke, as well as the use of new techniques of rolling and puddling, iron production accelerated fast (68,300 tons in 1788 to 244,000 in 1806 and 677,000 tons in 1828), further fuelling the demand for coal. Coal, iron and the steam engine in turn would beget the railway; the first tracks of the Stockton and Darlington Railway were created to carry coal in 1825. Within twenty years coal and iron production had tripled, the steel industry had been created and rail enabled it all to be transported to open up the export markets that would define the next phase of industrialization down to the 1880s.

A Great Transformation?

Of course, not all workers were transformed into wage-labourers in factories, and many forms of manufacturing remained unmechanized. In some areas, like the metal trades in Sheffield and Birmingham (famous for the production of cutlery, guns and toys), machines were adopted within small workshop settings without any centralization of production. In these workshops old working practices and the sense of the autonomy of workers within a craft or trade were fiercely protected. Thus St Monday was widely observed in many of Birmingham's workshops down to the mid nineteenth century. Handcraft and human power remained predominant in many forms of manufacturing like those that produced shoes, cabinets, buttons, clothes, sweets and boats, as well as the building and mining industries. Even in 1820 much of the country remained predominantly rural and had little contact with, or knowledge of, the industrializing regions, even though many people may have worn its cotton or used its dishware.

Some historians have wondered what all the fuss is about and questioned how revolutionary these early forms of industrialization were. At issue here is not the novelty of industrialization but its timing and effects. It has been suggested that longer working weeks and improvements in productivity had been occurring since the late seventeenth century, stimulated by the growing demands of an expanding population. Others have contended that, as the innovations of mechanization and factory production remained largely limited to textiles, productivity gains and growth rates were less dramatic than once believed. Graph 3.1 shows three competing estimates of English gross domestic product (that is, total output) per person between 1700 and 1860, adjusted for inflation. Deane and Cole provided the first and most dramatic estimate in the 1960s, showing a steep climb from a low start in the classic period of the Industrial Revolution between 1780 and 1830. In the 1980s this was challenged by Crafts and Harley who suggested that productivity rates had been considerably higher in the first half of the eighteenth century than previously believed and grew much less rapidly between 1780 and 1830. Most recently Gregory Clark has suggested that earlier productivity was even higher and that growth rates remained essentially flat (or even marginally declining) between 1740 and 1800 before accelerating to a higher level in the 1830s.

These debates are important for while they flatten out the diverse sectors of the economy, and neglect the profoundly different human and regional experiences, they locate more precisely when Britain's economy 'took off' and therefore help us identify what may have caused it to do so. The earlier estimates of Deane and Cole suggested industrialization was rapid enough after 1780 to earn the title 'Revolution', whereas the later

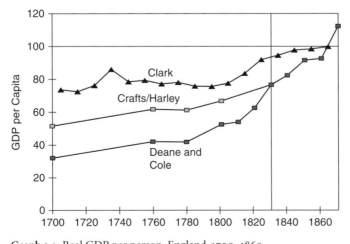

Graph 3.1 Real GDP per person, England, 1700–1869

figures of Crafts and Harley suggest that there was a long and continuous pattern of growth from 1700, while for Clark nothing really happened until the 1820s. Whatever the pace of this change, all can agree that Britain's economy grew at historically unprecedented levels by 1820, that it did indeed 'take off'. Rather like explaining the growth of Britain's population, however, we do not need to have a single explanation of that take-off – there was no one trigger or cause. Britain's imperial economy grew because the British state developed a mercantilist grip upon it, while new ideas and new ways of organizing labour transformed methods of production in agriculture and industry, some of which were fuelled by the availability of coal and financed by the surplus capital generated by landed income, slavery and the dramatic profits generated by trade and manufacturing. Industrialization before the 1820s may have been limited to specific areas and sectors but it was the product of a much broader, greater transformation of the economy that stretched across much of the globe.

Social and Environmental Consequences

Just as historians are divided about the causes and intensity of industrialization, so they have rarely agreed about its consequences. Unsurprisingly this debate revolves around how one views industrial capitalism, what its social and environmental effects were, and the responses of contemporaries to it. Generally speaking, 'optimists' point to rising wages and improvements in standards of living; while 'pessimists' highlight the negative impacts upon industrial workers, their opposition to new forms of labour, and the degradation of the environment more broadly. In part this is also an argument about method and how best to measure the effects of industrialization, with one side favouring aggregate data on production and wages, and the other emphasizing a human scale and different local, regional and occupational experiences.

Standards of Living

At the heart of this debate are attempts to establish whether the fruits of rising output and the increasing productivity of labour were reaped solely by employers in profit or trickled down to workers in the form of rising wages. Economic historians have spent decades trying to discover whether, adjusted for inflation, wages increased, stagnated or decreased. This is far from an exact science. We do know that despite rising output, prices of leading commodities rose from the 1760s and at an accelerating pace during the wars with revolutionary France between 1790 and 1815, before falling in the 1820s. There were local and regional price variations which in turn shaped differing wage levels. In the 1760s a carpenter in Exeter was paid 2 shillings a day, more than the rate of 1 shilling 11 pence available in Manchester. Similarly, in the 1790s an agricultural worker in Buckinghamshire was paid almost three shillings less per day than one in Northumberland who received 10 shillings 3 pence in the 1790s. These regional differentials shifted over time.

Moreover, many workers still did not become wage-labourers. Some were paid by piece-rate or received non-monetary forms of remuneration (like rent-free housing) or entitlement (dockers were allowed to gather and consume or sell anything spilt or 'dropped' when unloaded). Given the great shortage of officially minted coins until the Great Recoinage of 1816 (made possible partly by Matthew Boulton's new steam-driven Royal Mint at his Soho works), even wage-labourers were likely to paid by employer's tokens that were not universally recognized and might enable them to receive discounts for some goods or force them to pay higher prices for others. Finally, some employers, especially those whose cash flow was poor, paid workers partly in 'truck' through goods. Effectively this was a system by which employers obtained credit from their own workforce by using the money that would have been their wages to buy goods that were then distributed to workers at prices over which they had little control. The widespread use of credit was not confined to employers, for the shortage and unreliability of coin meant credit was essential for the exchange of many goods and services. Given that wages and prices were mediated by a variety of forms of credit, kind and entitlement, the transition from an economy of obligation to a cash economy was slow and still incomplete by the 1820s.

All of this makes the reconstruction of a national index of real wages complex and fraught. The general consensus now is that in real terms wages remained essentially static until the early nineteenth century and only began significantly improving after the 1820s as prices fell. In prosperous London it took a bricklayer until at least 1820 to have the same spending power as he had enjoyed in 1750. Similarly, per capita consumption levels which had been rising from 1750 dipped after 1770 and only began to recover after 1815. Even if wages and consumption did momentarily rise, they did so on the back of longer working weeks and days.

Despite all the difficulties with these calculations of wages and their purchasing power, their biggest shortcoming is the assumption that the consumption of more goods necessarily benefits mankind and redeems industrial capitalism. In contrast, those 'pessimists' who have focused on the social experience of industrialization point to its often catastrophic human consequences, highlighting, in the words of the historian E.P. Thompson, 'intensified exploitation, greater insecurity, and increasing human misery'. If plantations were the first factories, albeit ones that did not use wage-labour, there is no greater icon of industrialism's debasing of the human condition than slavery. Slaves were conceived less as human beings than as commodities to be bought, sold and worked to death. While this represented the operation of a nascent industrial capitalism *in extremis*, it was not a coincidence that in the 1830s the movement for **factory reform** equated the working conditions of factory workers with slavery. The initial leader of that movement, Richard Oastler, an evangelical Tory and a fierce opponent of slavery, argued that the children working in Bradford's textile factories were treated worse than slaves.

This was not the first time that children had proved the lightning rods of the new manufacturing system. As early as 1784 an epidemic at one of Sir Robert Peel's mills in Manchester killed many of the pauper children sent to work there by the local magistrates, who then (briefly) insisted on cutting off this cheap supply of labour unless their hours of work were limited. It was Peel, another evangelical Tory and father of the future prime minister, who introduced the first **Factory Acts** in 1802 and 1819 to limit the hours of pauper children. With no powers of inspection and little will to enforce it, these were ineffective measures that left all other children untouched. Nonetheless, like slaves, children became emblems of the dehumanizing effects of the new systems of industrial manufacturing (see Textbox 3.3). Of course, children and women had long been central to household forms of production and the generation of a so-called 'family wage' but only under the paternal supervision of their husbands and fathers. What alarmed some contemporaries most were not the dangerous conditions, the deafening noise and long hours of work in mills, but the demoralizing effects of the disintegration of the family and its natural structures of paternal authority.

 3.3 Source: *A Memoir of Robert Blincoe, An Orphan Boy; Sent from the Workhouse of St Pancras, London at Seven Years of Age, to Endure the Horrors of a Cotton-Mill, Through His Infancy and Youth with a Minute Detail of his Sufferings*

Robert Blincoe (c.1792–1860) was an orphan who grew up in a workhouse in London without knowing either of his parents. At six years old he began working as a chimney sweep before being apprenticed for fourteen years to a cotton-spinning firm near Nottingham along with eighty other children from the workhouse. In 1828, without his knowledge, Blincoe became the subject of this famous memoir, written by the Bolton-based journalist John Brown after holding a series of conversations with Blincoe. First published in serial form by the radical publisher Richard Carlile in his newspaper *The Lion* in 1828, it was republished by Carlile in *The Poor Man's Advocate* as well as in pamphlet form in 1832. Blincoe's early life was used to capture the appalling experiences of a child labourer at the dawn of the Industrial Revolution. Working fourteen hours a day, six days a week, he was charged with the dangerous job of picking loose cotton waste from underneath the spinning frames (in which he lost half a finger), and was routinely beaten by overseers. In one instance he describes being apprehended after trying to escape from work and likens his experience to that of African slaves. While the factual accuracy of Blincoe's story remains murky, the experiences described in the memoir were typical of child-labourers in the early nineteenth century. As a newspaper serial, and later a political pamphlet, the memoir sought to sensationalize and politicize the issue of child labour, furthering demands for the regulation of factories. It was intended to appeal to the same educated and often evangelical constituency that had campaigned for the abolition of slavery in the West Indies. The memoir was usually published with a portrait of Blincoe, showing him with crooked legs from a childhood spent collecting cotton waste from the factory floor and missing his left forefinger. (S.W.)

The restructuring of production, especially in the textile industries, left workers and previously proud independent tradesmen little choice but to become replaceable units of production as factory 'hands' or 'operatives'. Handloom weavers, like wool combers and calico printers, remain the exemplary case. Their numbers peaked at 250,000 in the 1820s when they were earning as much as 23 shillings a week, but just 25 years later there were only 43,000 earning just over 6 shillings 3 pence despite rising prices. The collapse of agricultural wages, especially in southern England, where family incomes fell as much as 30 per cent during the same period, provided a steady stream of urban migrants and factory hands.

The trade clubs and societies that had emerged over the preceding centuries to regulate apprenticeships, help members find work, and provide benefits when they fell sick or died, were primarily regional in orientation and not organizationally equipped to resist or temper the pressures of industrialization. What capacity they had was further limited by the counter-revolutionary legislation of the 1790s. The Friendly Society Act of 1793, together with the **Combination Acts** of 1799 and 1800, stripped trade societies of their ability to mobilize collectively, whether politically or economically (to hold meetings, to correspond with members, to hold strikes), while encouraging their forms of mutual aid (to support those who were sick or out of work or to pay for funerals). The Combination Acts were not repealed until 1824. Unsurprisingly the following year the first strike to gain national attention was the attempt by Bradford's newly formed Combers and Weavers Union to secure handloom piece-rates for power-woven cloth. Thereafter unionization spread quickly. If workers had been largely powerless to negotiate better pay or conditions before the repeal of the Combination Acts, they had certainly not meekly embraced the mechanization and restructuring of their labour. Throughout the second half of the eighteenth century workers, especially skilled craftsmen, pressured masters and employers with a repertoire that stretched from threatening letters, attacks on individuals and machine breaking. Nowhere was this clearer than in the **Luddite** rebellions of 1811–13. In the midst of the escalating prices exacerbated by the American blockade during the War of 1812 and Parliament's failure to address their petitions, textile workers in the East Midlands, Yorkshire and

Lancashire attacked and burnt down mills, smashed stocking-frames and intimidated mill-owners with threatening letters signed anonymously by 'Ned' or 'General Ludd'. Similarly, in 1830–31, across southern and eastern England, agricultural workers issued threatening proclamations, burnt hayricks and smashed the threshing machines that deprived them of winter work, in the name of a mythical '**Captain Swing**'.

Although the Luddites are now routinely associated with all those who refuse technological advance, they, like the Swing rioters and those who rioted over the installation of toll roads or the **enclosure** of common land, were not seeking to restore a traditional or lost golden age. Instead, they sought to ensure workers were not rendered powerless operatives by machines and factories. They gave voice to an alternative understanding of economic life as inseparable from its broader social context, where labour and life could not be reduced to economistic calculations of profit and loss. The same was also true of the food riots that continued to punctuate social life into the early nineteenth century. Food rioters were not just animated by hunger; they viewed the market as necessarily bound by social responsibilities. They strategically targeted the mills, merchants or magistrates they believed had failed to ensure that grain was sold locally at fair and affordable prices. It was, they insisted, the security and well-being of the community, not the profit principle, that should govern the operation of the market.

Friendly societies were another sign of this alternative moral economy. Like trade societies and clubs, friendly societies, whose membership cut across the social spectrum, provided benefits to members who found themselves out of work or sick, or to their widows when they died. As their numbers proliferated from the late eighteenth century (almost fifty were founded during the 1780s as opposed to just eight during the 1750s), especially in the industrializing north, some political economists and reformers viewed them as savings clubs or insurance societies for individuals. This was to miss the point. They were societies of friends who acted as one to secure all in their community, a community that spent lavish sums celebrating in ceremonial gatherings and performing in public parades and festivals. If, like food riots and machine-breaking, such behaviour seemed irrational to political economists, it made total sense to those who believed that markets and economic life should always be structured by people's social relations and moral obligations to each other. These were not remnants of a lost or dying past; they were practical and humane solutions to the challenges of industrial capitalism.

In effecting a dramatic transfer of wealth from labour to capital, industrialization highlighted the growing gap between the interests of employers and employees. It did not necessarily usher in a society structured by an understanding of class and class conflict. The historian E.P. Thompson suggested it was those workers whose crafts had been displaced or superseded by industrialization – like 'the poor stockinger, the **Luddite** cropper, "obsolete" handloom weaver', not the new factory hands and operatives – that helped make the English working class. Certainly there was a growing antagonism between workers and their employers produced by the immiseration of some and the alienation of others by industrial labour. Yet in the absence of any form of labour organization that transcended the interests of a particular region or craft, to say nothing of a political movement that spoke clearly and unambiguously in a language of class struggle that targeted employers not the aristocratic **ancien regime**, the making of a working class would have to wait until later in the nineteenth century.

Environmental Degradation

The planet was no less irrevocably altered than human life by industrialization, even if its environmental consequences have often been overlooked. All that we now know to be endangering our very existence on earth – deforestation, polluted waterways, industrial waste, the depletion of fossil fuels, acid rain and greenhouse gasses – were a product of Britain's economic transformation in the late eighteenth and early nineteenth centuries.

Britain may have been at the centre of that transformation but, as we have already seen, it depended upon satellite economic systems across the globe to produce its raw materials in what effectively became mono-crop environments. Plantation systems bent to the production of tobacco, cotton, sugar and tea fundamentally changed the previously diverse ecosystems of the West Indies, the southern United States of America and the Punjab in India. This not only changed their landscapes; it also reduced their own food supplies and exposed them to the problem of famine as never before. Although nothing as dramatic happened in Britain, its rural environment was also transformed by **enclosure** and the intensification of agricultural production. Indeed, it was in the second half of the eighteenth century that the British countryside assumed a form recognizable today to anyone either flying over it or walking through it. Enclosure accelerated the deforestation of Britain that had been occurring for centuries as woodlands were cleared and claimed for arable or pasture fields. As common lands were privatized, fields increased in size and miles and miles of new hedges and ditches demarcated their boundaries. In the century after 1750, 200,000 miles of new hedges were planted, the same amount as in the previous 500 years. As these hedgerows were designed to grow fast and keep people out, they were invariably made by planting hawthorn bushes; the diverse hedgerows that had sustained a rich wildlife in their foliage became increasingly rare. Indeed, animals like rabbits, hares, foxes and badgers that threatened crops or stock were culled in increasing numbers. We have already seen how selective breeding was used to genetically engineer not only bigger and better stock and crop yields but also the horses and oxen that worked the fields. The same was true of the pheasants reared to be shot for sport and many breeds of dogs – like the short terrier bred by the hunting enthusiast John 'Jack' Russell in 1819.

This engineering of the natural world was also apparent in the gardens and sur-rounding countryside of many aristocratic estates. Whereas agricultural improvement had sought to master and tame nature to harness its productive potential, a new gener-ation of landscape architects like 'Capability' Brown (1716–1783) and Humphry Repton (1752–1818) created a new aesthetic vision of the countryside. The once fashionable French garden style – of straight lines, clipped box hedges and calculated displays of ornaments – was replaced by what became a quintessentially 'English' style. Here the landscape was literally staged to appear as natural as possible even though it required the creation of a careful balance of rolling meadow, lakes, trees, shrubs and the odd neo-classical building or folly. Wildlife was only allowed access to this landscape to beautify it or to provide sport: concealed ditches excluded deer and cattle, hedges were grown that would not prevent foxhunting, and pheasants were bred for annual shoots. In the hands of romantic artists like John Constable (1776–1837), these highly manufactured landscapes quickly became celebrated as representing an essentially English rural idyll.

If the rural landscape was engineered to perfect nature, there was no design to Britain's rapidly growing and industrializing cities. Governed by archaic manorial or **parish** authorities, there was no planning, regulation or constraint to their growth. Builders scrambled to construct housing as quickly, cheaply and densely as possible. Cold and damp houses crowded into courts and alleys with little light, no clean water and open sewers. These were the slum conditions that greeted rural migrants who came in search of work and many others who still struggled to support families in the new industrial occupations. As we have seen, mortality rates soared and churchyards bulged with corpses they could not contain. Manchester, the shock city of industriali-zation, with its smoking chimneys and rivers blackened with pollution, was the poster child of this degraded urban environment. When the French commentator Alexis de Tocqueville visited the city in 1835 he was shocked and bewildered by the squalor of industrial progress: "From this foul drain the greatest stream of human industry flows out to fertilize the whole world. From this filthy sewer pure gold flows. Here humanity attains its most complete development and its most brutish; here civilization works its miracles, and civilized man is turned back almost into a savage." It would not be until the second half of the nineteenth century that the quality of the urban environment substantially improved with spectacular feats of engineering that required the flooding of rural valleys to supply clean water and the laying of complex sewer systems.

Long before reservoirs were dreamt of, Britain's waterways were transformed by the imperatives of agricultural and industrial production. The drainage of wetlands and marshes to claim more productive land, as well as the growing importance attached to the good drainage of farmland, meant that streams and rivers were slowly silted up. As water levels rose, flooding was a constant danger on low ground and higher, stronger bridges were required for crossing rivers with the increasingly heavy loads. There was a great boom in iron bridges before the advent of the railway, beginning with Abraham

View of the Iron Bridge over the River Severn, near Coalbrook dale, Shropshire.
Published by Alexr. Hogg No. 16, in Pater-noster Row.

Figure 3.2 The Iron Bridge at Coalbrookdale, Shropshire, c.1800

Darby's Iron Bridge at Coalbrookdale in 1779 – the first in the world. Used to transport the products of local coal and clay mines, as well as the iron from Darby's foundry, the novelty of this bridge made it a frequent subject of paintings like the one in Figure 3.2. These paintings often celebrated man's capacity not just to master the natural world but to enhance its beauty. This bridge became so famous that a hotel was opened nearby to accommodate those who came to view it.

Only iron bridges were strong enough to support a structure capable of facilitating the flow of sailboats (and eventually barges) below it that were so essential to Britain's coastal and inland waterway traffic. Downstream, silted rivers meant that coastal harbours, the very hubs of this traffic, required constant draining or dredging if their docks, warehouses and boatyards were to remain functional. If silt flowed from the agricultural landscape, so Britain's rivers hosted the increasing and alarming quantities of sewage that flowed from its cities. Urban sewer systems were a product of the second half of the nineteenth century and until that time most human and animal effluent (a small portion of this 'night soil' was recycled as manure to farmers) drained directly from streets. The estimated 200,000 cesspools that existed in London flowed in to tributaries of the Thames. By the 1850s an incredible 260 tons of raw sewage flowed into the Thames each day. Alongside silt and sewage, Britain's waterways were increasingly awash with industrial effluent. Water was critical to many early industrial processes. John Roebuck established his sulphuric acid works on the Forth in 1749 to access its sea salt as well as its water. Arkwright's textile mill at Cromford required the water-power generated by the Derwent Valley, just as Greg's mill at Quarry Bank siphoned water from the River Bolin (see Textbox 3.2). As textiles required bleaching and dyeing, vast quantities of chemicals like chlorine were washed away in streams and rivers. Manchester's three rivers were so polluted 'with waste dye-stuffs' that a Prussian official in 1814 thought they 'resemble[d] a dyer's vat'. In short, Britain's waterways began to be polluted on an unprecedented scale.

The attempt to master and tame nature to increase its productive potential had unforeseen and damaging consequences whose effects we are still living with today. Nowhere is the scale of this more apparent than in the shift away from a renewable and **organically powered economy** to one fuelled by non-renewable mineral deposits in the form of coal. The world-historical significance of this shift should not be underestimated: the solar energy system that had sustained life forms on earth for millennia was effectively displaced within a century. Contemporaries, particularly in towns and cities where large numbers of domestic coal fires were joined by the bilious fumes of industrial chimneys, were primarily concerned with the problem of air pollution which meant the sun made even rarer appearances. Approaching Manchester in 1814, that same Prussian official observed that the 'cloud of coal vapour may be observed from afar. The houses are blackened by it' (see Figure 3.3). And so were its inhabitants' lungs. Respiratory diseases like tuberculosis were common although there is no way of telling how much they were aggravated by smog and lack of sunlight. Rain, not uncommon in Britain, may have temporarily cleared the atmosphere but it was increasingly acidic and dropped its reddish sulfuric deposits across the surrounding hinterlands.

Figure 3.3 Manchester from Kersal Moor, *c.* 1852

Not surprisingly it was a Brit, Robert Angus Smith, who invented the term acid rain in 1859 when he found that the air in British cities was so acidic that litmus paper exposed to it reddened in ten minutes. Given the inefficiency of the second generation of steam engines produced by Watt and Boulton, as well as the humble open domestic fireplace (in which 80 per cent of the heat was lost up the chimney), the seemingly insatiable desire for coal was remarkably wasteful. Given the abundance of cheap coal in Britain, waste and inefficiency even of a non-renewable source hardly seemed to matter – even as late as 1905 Britain remained the world's largest consumer of coal. Here was probably the greatest catastrophe of Britain's industrialization and its most toxic legacy to the world: the idea that the demands of industry and the consumption of its goods were potentially limitless and must always be met. It turns out that **Malthus** was right and **Adam Smith** was wrong: the world's resources are finite and the vision of boundless economic growth now threatens its very existence.

Conclusion

The Industrial Revolution may have been nasty and brutish but it was decidedly not short. In fact, it was the last in a series of other revolutionary changes to the economy – in agriculture, finance and commerce – that had developed since the late seventeenth century. These changes created the conditions, both locally and globally, for the development of new techniques of manufacturing that vastly increased productivity levels and propelled Britain to unprecedented and sustained levels of economic growth. This great transformation was not the product of economic liberalization but of the very **mercantile** system and monopoly capitalism that **Adam Smith** so fervently denounced in his *Wealth of Nations*. Mercantilist policies enabled the British state, and the financiers and merchants who were its clients, to develop an imperial economy that sought to monopolize as much of the globe's land, labour and trade as possible. By the late eighteenth century the tentacles of this system crossed much of the globe but it was firmly rooted in the Atlantic triangular trade and the re-exporting of its bounty to the continent of Europe, the Ottoman lands and South and East Asia. Together with improvements in agricultural productivity, this system supported a population that was breaking what **Thomas Malthus** considered to be the laws of population growth, namely it continued to grow rapidly without exhausting the world's capacity to feed it. Yet given the grinding poverty in which most lived, this surge of people did only a little to fuel demand for what had become the basic necessities of life – bread, sugar, cloth and coal. Instead, it was the export business that drove the technical innovations, mechanization and new ways of organizing labour for the industrial manufacturing of textiles. Limited geographically to the northwest of England and to a relatively small section of the workforce, its influence was nonetheless outsized. What Britain gained in terms of its accelerating levels of growth was offset by the deleterious effects of forms of production that immiserated those whose handcrafts were displaced and alienated those who were made the wage-labouring operatives of machines in mills. By the end of the eighteenth century these machines were driven by steam engines fuelled by coal. This creation of an industrial economy powered by non-renewable fuels would soon make Britain the richest country in the world but it would have catastrophic environmental consequences for the entire world. Even as early as 1819 the great transformation of Britain's imperial economy and rapidly growing population had made it diverge from the rest of the world. From this position of strength its global pre-eminence was to be extended still further in the following century.

FURTHER READING

The literature on the great transformation is vast and it is easy to quickly get lost in the weeds. Three classic works remain essential starting points: Arnold Toynbee's *Lectures on the Industrial Revolution in England* (London, 1887), Eric Williams's *Capitalism and Slavery* (London, 1944) and Karl Polanyi's *The Great Transformation* (London, 1945). M.J. Daunton's *Progress and Poverty: An Economic and Social History of Britain 1700–1850* (Oxford, 1995) provides a good and recent general overview.

In recent decades historians have endeavoured to create a more nuanced understanding of **mercantilism** than that originally presented by its chief critic **Adam Smith**. D.C. Coleman's important edited collection, *Revisions in Mercantilism* (London, 1969), emphasized the limits of Britain's mercantilist policies and their failure to ever construct a closed imperial system. Steve Pincus's *1688: The First Modern Revolution* (New Haven, 2009) usefully reminds us that the debate over mercantilism and its alternatives stretched deep into the seventeenth century and increasingly mapped onto the ideological divisions of Whigs and Tories either side of 1688. His essay 'Rethinking Mercantilism: Political Economy, The British Economy, the British Empire, and the Atlantic World in the Seventeenth and Eighteenth Centuries', *William and Mary Quarterly*, 69/1 (2012), 3–34, rightly insists that the debate about mercantilism and its alternatives spread across the British Empire. The most recent edition to this revisionist literature is Philip J. Stern and Carl Wennerlind (eds.), *Mercantilism Reimagined: Political Economy in Early Modern Britain and its Empire* (Oxford, 2014).

The imperial nature of Britain's economy in the long eighteenth century is now well established. A good general account that places it in a global context is R. Findlay and Kevin H. O'Rourke, *Power and Plenty: Trade, War, and the World Economy in the Second Millennium* (Princeton, 2007), while E.J. Hobsbawm, *Industry and Empire* (London, 1968), remains an important statement. Sven Beckert's *Empire of Cotton: A New History of Global Capitalism* (London, 2014) provides still further reinforcement. Of the joint-stock chartered companies, the **East India Company** has received most attention: see H.V. Bowen, *The Business of Empire: The East India Company and Imperial Britain, 1756–1833* (Cambridge, 2005), and Philip J. Stern,

The Company State: Corporate Sovereignty and the Early Modern Foundations of the British Empire in India (Oxford, 2011). The imperial culture of merchants based in London is well reconstructed in David Hancock, *Citizens of the World: London Merchants and the Integration of the British Atlantic Community, 1735–1785* (Cambridge, 1995), and Nuala Zahedieh, *The Capital and the Colonies* (Cambridge, 2010).

Viewed from the other sides of the Atlantic, slavery and piracy come into sharper focus: see Marcus Rediker, *Villains of All Nations: Atlantic Pirates in the Golden Age* (London, 2004), Philip D. Curtin, *The Rise and Fall of the Plantation Complex: Essays in Atlantic History* (Cambridge, 1990), and Trevor Burnard, *Planters, Merchants, and Slaves: Plantation Societies in British America, 1650–1820* (Chicago, 2015). On the full oceanic reach of the slave trade, see James Walvin, *Crossings: Africa, the Americas and the Atlantic Slave Trade* (London, 2013). On the extent of slave-ownership, and its influence over many spheres of life in Britain, see Catherine Hall et al. (eds.), *Legacies of British Slave-Ownership: Colonial Slavery and the Formation of Victorian Britain* (Cambridge, 2014).

The most definitive account of the agricultural revolution in England is by Mark Overton, *Agricultural Revolution in England: The Transformation of the Agrarian Economy, 1500–1850* (Cambridge, 1996). His emphasis on the *longue durée* of that transformation is at odds with the shorter and later periodization of J.D. Chambers and G.E. Mingay's *The Agricultural Revolution, 1750–1880* (London, 1966). Joan Thirsk (ed.), *The English Rural Landscape* (Oxford, 2000), and B.A. Holderness and Michael Turner, *Land, Labour and Agriculture, 1700–1920* (London, 1991), are also helpful. There is nothing to compare to T.M. Devine's magisterial *The Transformation of Rural Scotland: Social Change and the Agrarian Economy, 1660–1815* (Edinburgh, 1994). While there is less material on the demography of Scotland and Ireland, the best account of population trends in Britain at this time is Roger Schofield, 'British Population Change, 1700–1871', in R. Floud and D. McCloskey (eds.), *The Economic History of Britain Since 1700*, vol. I (Cambridge, 1981), 60–95. The literature on **urbanization** is surprisingly sparse but fear not: Peter Clark (ed.), *The Cambridge Urban History of Britain*, vol. II: *1540–1840* (Cambridge, 1995), and Lynn Hollen Lees and Paul Hohenberg, *The Making of Urban Europe, 1000–1994* (Cambridge, Mass., 1995), provide great overviews.

Only in recent decades, as the financial sector has grown increasingly important in our own lives, have historians paid much attention to its role in the great transformation. P.J. Cain and A.G. Hopkins, 'Gentlemanly Capitalism and British Overseas Expansion: The Old Colonial System, 1688–1850', *Economic History Review*, 39 (1986), is the best point of departure. The financial revolution in the City of London is explored in P.G.M. Dickson, *The Financial Revolution in England: A Study in the Development of Public Credit, 1688–1756* (London, 1967), while the debates it occasioned are the subject of Carl Wennerlind's *Casualties of Credit: The English Financial Revolution, 1620–1720* (Cambridge, Mass., 2011). These accounts are placed in broader imperial and global context by Giovanni Arrighi, *The Long Twentieth Century: Money, Power and the Origins of Our Times* (London, 1994).

Finally, we come to the commercial and industrial revolutions. Kenneth Pomeranz's *The Great Divergence: China, Europe and the Making of the Modern World Economy* (Princeton, 2001) argues that Britain was able to become the first industrial nation because it had rich and conveniently located coal deposits. The centrality of coal, and the shift from organic- to mineral-powered forms of production, is echoed in E.A. Wrigley, *Energy and the English Industrial*

Revolution (Cambridge, 2010). Joel Mokyr provides a trenchant case that Enlightenment culture and technology transfer among a skilled workforce drove innovation in *The Enlightened Economy: An Economic History of Britain 1700–1850* (New Haven, 2009). Robert C. Allen's *The British Industrial Revolution in Global Perspective* (Cambridge, 2009) argues that it was the high price of labour, not the availability of coal or Enlightened experimentation, that propelled technological innovation to reduce labour costs. Prasannan Parthasarathi's *Why Europe Grew Rich and Asia Did Not: Global Economic Divergence 1600–1850* (Cambridge, 2011) has more to say about the role of the state. Jan de Vries, *The Industrious Revolution: Consumer Behavior and the Household Economy, 1650 to the Present* (Cambridge, 2008), and Maxine Berg's *Luxury and Pleasure in Eighteenth-Century England* (Oxford, 2007) are the most definitive statements that consumption and the demand for goods preceded and drove innovations in manufacturing. For the debate about the timing and measurement of economic growth, see P. Deane and W.A. Cole, *British Economic Growth, 1688–1959* (Cambridge, 1962), N.F.R. Crafts, *British Economic Growth During the Industrial Revolution* (Oxford, 1985), and Gregory Clark, *A Farewell to Alms: A Brief Economic History of the World* (Princeton, 2007).

The effects of industrialization are no less contentious than its causes. For powerful statements of the pessimists' case, see E.P. Thompson, *The Making of the English Working Class* (London, 1963); E.J. Hobsbawm, *Industry and Empire* (London, 1968); and, most recently, M. Berg and P. Hudson, 'Rehabilitating the Industrial Revolution', *Economic History Review*, 45/1 (1992), 24–50; and Jane Humphries, *Childhood and Child Labour in the British Industrial Revolution* (Cambridge, 2010). The most recent optimistic assessments, using respectively anthropometric and cultural measures, are R. Floud, K. Wachter and A. Gregory, *Height, Health and History: Nutritional Status in the United Kingdom, 1750–1980* (Cambridge, 1990), and Emma Griffiths, *Liberty's Dawn: A People's History of the Industrial Revolution* (Oxford, 2014). We are still waiting for a good environmental history of the great transformation in Britain and its global footprint. In the meantime B.W. Clapp, *An Environmental History of Britain Since the Industrial Revolution* (London, 1994), and Peter Thorsheim's *Inventing Pollution: Coal Smoke and Culture in Britain Since 1800* (Athens, Ohio, 2006) are our guides. However, Fredrik Jonsson's *Enlightenment Frontier; The Scottish Highlands and the Origins of Environmentalism* (New Haven, 2013) is a splendid account of competing views of the environment and its 'improvement'.

II

1819–1885: Becoming Liberal and Global

4 A Liberal Revolution in Government

Introduction

We have seen that by 1819 Britain's **ancien regime** – dominated by the monarchy, the aristocracy and the established **Anglican Church** – extended its imperial territories and emerged as the strongest state in Europe. The expanding commercial reach of its Empire and a new fiscal-military apparatus allowed the new Leviathan of the British state to wage a hugely expensive series of wars against its rivals while violently securing itself against its reforming critics, whether in colonial Boston or on the bloody fields of Peterloo. By the 1880s Britons, if not their colonial subjects, were governed by a fundamentally different type of state, one still recognizable in the Anglo-American world today. The principles of efficiency and meritocracy displaced those of custom and birth that had characterized **Old Corruption**. Government was to be cheap and no longer dependent upon debt-financing or excessive taxation. As the business of government became dissociated from the narrow interests of the monarchy, aristocracy and **clergy**, it was elevated to an Enlightenment science whose rationale and practice appeared to be based upon natural laws that were beyond question. This transformation has been described as a **'revolution in government'**, one that is often associated with a new 'age of reform' of Britain's political and economic structures. The question then is how, why and when did this happen?

At the heart of this revolution in government was the doctrine of *laissez-faire*. This French phrase meaning 'leave alone' in fact expressed the attempts of **Adam Smith** and his followers to reimagine the relationship between the state and economic life. Whereas Britain's **ancien regime** had sought a tight mercantilist control of economic life, proponents of *laissez-faire* believed that the state should not interfere with the economy or disturb what they believed were the natural rhythms of markets. They believed that the effectiveness of the state should no longer be measured by how much power and control it could exercise, or how many taxes it could raise. Instead, it would be assessed by how successfully it freed markets (so that their supposedly natural forms could maximize the wealth of the nation), as well as how cheaply and efficiently it could operate. Like markets, it was argued, the industry and moral character of respectable families and individuals were best realized when they were left alone by the state to govern themselves. Indeed, a new gospel of **self-help** developed that insisted, in the words of its most famous exponent Samuel Smiles, 'Whatever is done for men or classes, to a certain extent takes away the stimulus and necessity of doing for themselves; and where men are subjected to over-guidance and over-government, the inevitable tendency is to render them comparatively helpless.' Practising self-help depended upon a plethora of new guides to character and conduct that insinuated themselves into the everyday lives of Britons. The revolution in government was not just about the development of a new and modern type of state; it was about creating a new type of person who could govern themselves.

The doctrine of *laissez-faire* should not be equated with what we would now call small government or the minimal state. It actually unleashed an unprecedented degree of state power and intervention. Making markets free demanded that the state develop new capacities and responsibilities. While the boundaries of state power were drawn around a market economy, they were extended to enable new ways of governing the rapidly expanding population and shaping what contemporaries referred to as 'the condition of England' or **'the social question'**. New forms of intervention and increasingly centralized structures of government addressed population groups – criminals, vagrants, paupers, the insane, the unsanitary, the uneducated – that were considered incapable of self-help. New types of institution – prisons, workhouses, asylums and schools – were built in remarkably similar styles to house these groups and, where possible, reform their moral character. Moreover, social problems associated with these groups – poverty, crime and insanitary conditions – were seen as legitimate arenas of state intervention. These problems were understood to be unrelated to the market economy, which was absolved of all responsibility for them.

The state also grew in size and scope as it expanded its imperial reach overseas. Indeed, many of the new techniques of governing, such as a professional cadre of disinterested administrators, were first germinated in the colonies before being introduced in Britain. However, the traffic was by no means one-way. The imperial state frequently sought to tighten its control over the colonies, not least to ensure a flow of tax revenue and to forge a stronger imperial economy. Despite these mutually constitutive relationships, there is no question that colonial subjects were ruled differently than Britons, just as white settlers in places like Australia, Canada, New Zealand and southern Africa were ruled differently to the indigenous peoples of those territories. Hardening attitudes to racial difference justified an intensification of the colonial states' capacity to intervene in colonial populations and territories in ways that would have been inconceivable back in Britain with its supposedly more civilized subjects. The consolidation and expansion of colonial territory was achieved by an almost continual series of so-called 'small' and often 'dirty' colonial wars against such disparate peoples as Afghans, Zulus and Chinese.

Why then characterize this revolution in government as 'liberal' if the *laissez-faire* state grew in size and repressive capacity? We must begin by shedding our own understandings of the term and its association with either progressive politics in the United States or the history of the Liberal Democrat party in the United Kingdom. Instead, the **liberalism** I will refer to emerged out of the Enlightened critiques of Old Corruption and Britain's ancien regime in the eighteenth century. During the nineteenth century that liberalism coalesced around a belief that *laissez-faire*, **free trade**, cheap and representative forms of government, religious freedom, the rule of law (and its independence from executive authority), meritocracy and individual self-improvement would bring prosperity and civilization to all who *deserved* it. It was not just colonial subjects who were considered undeserving of these freedoms and excluded from their benefits. Many in Britain were also thought to lack the capacity for self-improvement and self-government. These liberal beliefs were not the preserve of any one social group or political party. They became the common sense of the age. Even if they were not accepted, or not accepted in their entirety, by everyone, they became enshrined in the institutions and practices of government that shaped the daily lives of Britons and served to distinguish them from their colonial subjects. And for some, this liberal revolution in government was what prevented the revolutions that convulsed much of continental Europe in 1848 from happening in Britain.

TIMELINE

1791	Ordnance Survey (India 1817, Ireland 1824, Scotland 1843)
1801	Census
1806	East India Company College at Haileybury
1807	Abolition of the slave trade
1813	Repeal of the Statute of Artificers
1815	Corn Laws End of the Napoleonic Wars
1818, 1824	Church Building Acts
1821	Pound on the gold standard
1823	Reform of the Masters and Servants Acts
1824	Imperial weights and measures
1828	Repeal of the Test and Corporation Acts
1829	Catholic emancipation Metropolitan Police Act
1832	Parliamentary Reform Act
1833	Abolition of slavery
1834	Royal Statistical Society

1834	New Poor Law (Ireland 1838)
1835	Municipal Corporations Act
1836	General Registrar Office
1839	Rural Constabulary Act
1840	Penny Post
1841	Ordnance Survey Act
1842	*Report on the Sanitary Conditions of the Labouring Population*
1844	Bank Act and Companies Act
1845	Museums Act
1846	Repeal of the Corn Laws and sugar duties
1848	Public Health Act
1849	Repeal of the Navigation Acts
1850	Libraries Act
1852	State opening of new Houses of Parliament
1853	Ordnance Survey maps all of England and Wales (Ireland 1846, Scotland 1882)
1853–4	Northcote-Trevelyan Report
1855	Repeal of the stamp duties on newspapers
1856	Police Act (Scotland 1857)
1859	Samuel Smiles, *Self-Help*
1861	Mrs Beeton, *Book of Household Management*
1866	Sanitation Act
1869	National Criminal Record
1870	Education Act Open competition civil service
1871	Abolition of University Tests Acts
1872	Public Health Act Education Act (Scotland)

1877	Queen Victoria made Empress of India
1880	Definition of Time Act
1884	Greenwich Mean Time
1885	Scottish Office

The New Science of Government

As we saw in Chapter 1, the frontispiece to Hobbes's *Leviathan* personified the state in the figure of the sovereign, sword and pastoral staff in hand, rising formidably above his territory. The **'revolution in government'** that took shape in the aftermath of the **Napoleonic Wars** created a new type of state, one characterized not by the personal authority of the monarch, but by the development of new anonymous and impersonal, bureaucratic, systems. Central to this transformation was an understanding of government as a science, not as an art exercised by a person. The science of government depended upon the acquisition and analysis of data to determine the most rational and efficient ways of organizing the state. This was not a new idea in the nineteenth century, nor was it unique to Britain. Europe's Enlightened absolute monarchs, like Britain's **ancien regime**, had experimented with these ideas but it was the American and French revolutionary states that pressed them furthest in the final decades of the eighteenth century. In Britain it was war, not revolution, that catalysed a new science of government, albeit one that was experimental, piecemeal and pragmatic in application as it was engrafted around the ancien regime's structures of rule. This much is clear in the state's attempts to systematically map the territories and count the population it sought dominion over through the **Ordnance Survey** and the Census.

Mapping the State

As the name suggests, the Ordnance Survey was a military endeavour to survey the landscape for security and defence of the realm. The idea of an Ordnance Survey was first hatched in the wake of the **Jacobite** revolt of 1745, when military surveyors started using techniques of triangulation to map the rebellious **Scottish Highlands**. In 1791, under threat of invasion from revolutionary France, it was extended to the southern coastal regions of England. Similarly, the origins of the Great Trigonometric Survey of

India lay in the attempts to map the breadth of the peninsula of India after the defeat of the Tipu Sultan in the Fourth Mysore War in 1799. Despite the increasing precision of trigonometric surveying, it was laborious and required the mobilization of huge resources by the state. By the end of the **Napoleonic Wars**, two thirds of England and Wales still remained off the grid of the Ordnance Survey. It was not until 1853 that all of England and Wales was mapped. The Ordnance Surveys of Ireland and Scotland began in 1824 and 1843 and did not conclude until 1846 and 1882 respectively. The Great Trigonometric Survey of India was finally completed in 1866 when it confirmed that the Himalayas were the highest mountain range in the world, and named its highest point after one of the key architects of the project, George Everest.

These maps provided the state with more than simply a bird's-eye view of the territories it governed. They literally enabled administrators to visualize the nation or colonial state as a bounded, unified, geographical entity. The Ordnance Survey also provided the state with unprecedented power. An 1841 Act gave surveyors the legal right to enter any private property, powers to collect, codify and fix place and street names (often, of course, in standardized English), to number or name residences, to determine administrative and property boundaries and to make visible the interiors of public buildings. Local knowledge and understanding of place gave way to a standardized national one – at least on the map. In Figure 4.1 we can see an Ordnance Survey map that covered the area in central Manchester where St Peter's Fields, infamous scene of the **Peterloo Massacre**, had once been. Created between 1848 and 1850, the map is scaled at 60 inches to a mile. It is detailed enough to reveal manholes, lampposts and the interiors of public buildings such as the churches, schools, museums, theatres and concert

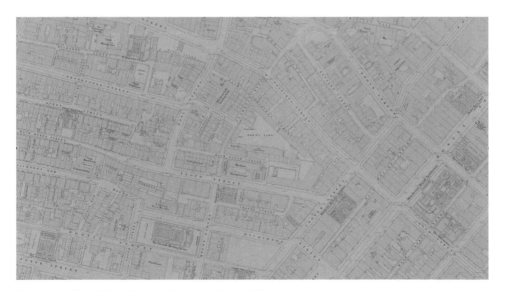

Figure 4.1 Central Manchester: Ordnance Survey Map, 1848–50

halls that, like the map, visually erase the memory of Peterloo. Just as contemporary GPS systems have taught us new ways of moving through and seeing space, so in the nineteenth century these maps taught not just state officials but ordinary people to use space differently, viewing it from above as homogeneous and proportional, as well as empty of people. By 1892 England and Wales were mapped on a scale large enough for officials to determine the size of people's doorsteps. The survey of Egypt, which began that year, took just a decade to complete and mapped the nation in such detail that it included the names of every landowner, however small their plot. If these maps enabled the imperial state to think and act in new ways, it also projected its size and strength in maps of the world that placed Britain at its centre and marked its extensive Empire in striking pink.

Counting and Managing People

States across the world had long conducted occasional population censuses for the purpose of raising taxes or armies, but the first modern censuses really began in 1791 in the young republics of France and America. Britain (or more accurately England, Wales and Scotland) followed suit a decade later in the midst of the **Napoleonic Wars** and in the shadow of **Malthus**'s apocalyptic warning that population growth threatened famine. Ireland's first census came twenty years later. What differentiated these censuses from their precursors was that they were systematic in approach and forensic in detail. Every ten years the population was to be counted on a single day, 10 March, and in unprecedented detail. Each household had its address and the number, sex and occupation of its members recorded by local parochial officers, who were directed by district supervisors, who in turn reported to a central office. Previously, the **Anglican Church** had collected the only vital statistics about the population in local **parish** registers of births, deaths and marriages. There were no records of **Dissenters** and Catholics baptised, married or buried in their own chapels and churches. In Scotland, learned individuals had set out to count the population, the first successful attempt, in 1755, being that of the minister Alexander Webster, who sent out questionnaires for his fellow ministers to survey their parishes. In Ireland, similar estimates were made by individuals and, once in 1731, the Irish House of Lords used local **clergy**, though populations could be estimated by returns on the Hearth Tax. A **General Registrar's Office** (GRO) was created for England and Wales in 1836 to rectify the situation and make the state, not the church, responsible for collecting this information. Although it was not legally compulsory to register a birth, death or marriage with the state until as late as 1875, non-Anglicans could finally register these life events. By 1841, when the General Registrar's Office had also taken responsibility for the conduct and analysis of the Census, the state had entirely secularized and centralized the collection of vital statistics (see Textbox 4.1).

The newly inquisitive state developed a vast machinery of data collection and management. The General Registrar's Office divided the nation into 626 districts, each with its own registrar. Within a year they had returned a million entries that were centrally stored in fireproof iron boxes. This paled in comparison to its operation of the Census in 1841, when 35,000 local enumerators were appointed to record, for the first time, the names and details of each household member. The operation was extended even further when General Registrar's Offices were created for Scotland and Ireland in 1855 and 1863. The first Census in India began in 1865, just eight years after the imposition of direct colonial rule. By 1881 half a million people were involved in collecting the names, age, sex, occupation, residence, place of birth, caste and religion of every person in India.

The state was not just inquisitive about the population. From the 1830s, as statistical societies were established across the country (the **Royal Statistical Society** was established in 1834), the state began gathering and analysing statistical data with increasing fervour. The **Board of Trade** had fitfully collected data on trade during the eighteenth century, but in 1832 it became the first government ministry to create its own statistical department and consistently monitor trade flows. That same year the reform of the electoral system created a new **Electoral Register** that monitored the size of the electorate. The **New Poor Law** of 1834 produced new mechanisms for the collection and analysis of data on the scale of poverty across the country. The reporting of some fifty types of indicted crimes had begun in 1805, but by 1834 almost all crimes were covered, and by the 1850s they were annually published in the *Judicial Statistics of England and Wales*. The systematic collection and central analysis of these statistics helped produce a different type of empirically minded administrative state with the capacity to think and act in new ways. For the first time the state could identify patterns of trade, poverty, mortality and crime so that it could govern them more effectively and measure how successfully it did so. Government was becoming a science.

Experts and the Invention of the Civil Service

The Enlightenment was clearly important in germinating this understanding of government and the technical capacities of the state to deliver it. Jeremy Bentham, the Enlightenment philosopher and political theorist, argued that only rational forms of organization could generate efficient government. Bentham also insisted that the test for any form of government was not how ancient or even how representative it was, but how useful it was in delivering happiness to the greatest number of individuals. It was an argument that neither defenders of the **ancien regime**, nor radicals and advocates of local self-government, warmed to. Yet in the hands of his acolyte **Edwin Chadwick**, Bentham's ideas converged with statistical methods to develop an increasingly influential machinery of government. That machinery worked as

4.1 Source: The Census

The Census is a vital source for historians in myriad ways. Its aggregate data are how we know about the growth of populations nationally, the size of cities and rates of **urbanization**, flows of migration within and beyond the nation, as well as the changing demographic of local areas or composition of households. It is also the key source for people interested in tracing their family history and genealogy, which is why the censuses conducted between 1841 and 1911 are now available online. Censuses, then, allow historians to understand large macro as well as small micro trends of social life. All of this is made possible because censuses record a vast amount of information. Although the first four Censuses were simple head counts that did not record names, they quickly became more complex. After 1851 they tell us the names, age, sex, marital status, relationship to head of household, place of birth and occupation of every individual. As well as yielding these personal details, they also tell us what it was important for the state to see or to count. Therefore, like every source, we have to remember that it is partial and must be read with care. The 1881 Census (Figure 4.2), for instance, statistically erased much of the work married women did by ignoring not just housework (like all Censuses), but part-time needlework, laundry work and seasonal agricultural work. It chose to make visible for the first time various forms of mental and physical disability, which it categorized as 'deaf and dumb', blind, 'imbecile or idiot' or a 'lunatic'. Nonetheless, the Census remains one of the richest sources historians have. Through it every single individual has a history.

follows. An empirical investigation of social life would statistically identify problems that required extended study by those with expert knowledge of the issues. Invariably, these experts would then solve the problem by forming new centralized governmental structures, like the General Registrar's Office with their own local administrative districts that were dependent neither on the old structures of government in counties, boroughs and parishes nor on their personnel. Instead, the business of government was to be conducted by experts in Whitehall whose regulations were imposed across the country by an army of inspectors who checked that a trained cadre of local officials was following instructions.

Chadwick's career helps to exemplify this method. A lawyer by training, it was his later work as Bentham's assistant and growing interest in social questions that qualified him to be appointed a member of the government committee devised to reform the Poor Law in 1832. Two years later the recommendations of that committee resulted in a **New Poor Law**, and Chadwick served as Secretary to the new centralized Poor Law Commission charged with managing it. This Commission administered the New Poor Law not through parishes, as in the old system, but through new local units of government known as unions. The unions then had to file 'Returns' that kept the

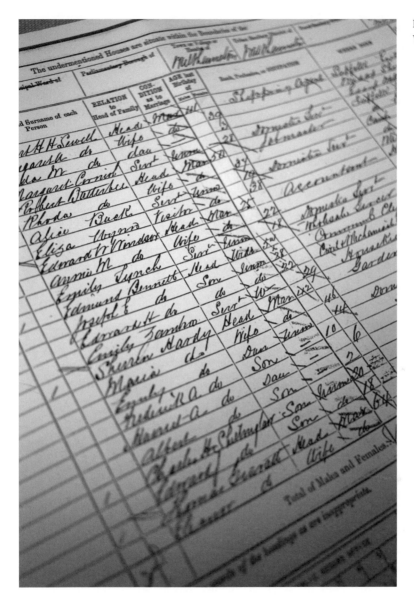

Figure 4.2 Census, Walthamstow, 1881

Commission informed as to the numbers of paupers in each area, while a network of inspectors ensured that central rules and regulations were being properly implemented locally. Similarly, the publication of Chadwick's *Report on the Sanitary Conditions of the Labouring Population* in 1842 was instrumental in the development of the **Public Health Act** six years later. That Act created a General Board of Health upon which Chadwick also sat as a commissioner, overseeing the operation of new local sanitary boards with the help again of a team of inspectors.

Working in this way, government was now to be disinterested, scientific and eventually even meritocratic. As we have seen, the **East India Company**'s administrative class felt the full force of this critique during Burke's attempts to impeach Governor Hastings. Although the East India Company did not stop recruiting its officials through the old patronage networks, it reformed its administrative service by establishing training colleges at Fort William (1800) and Haileybury (1806). Students at the East India Company College in Haileybury were taught subjects like law, political economy (**Thomas Malthus** taught there until 1834), maths, philosophy and classics that were thought to prepare them as an administrative class, while at Fort William in Calcutta they were trained in 'oriental' languages. More remarkably, students were streamed into different levels of service depending upon their success in exams. By 1829, the East India Company offered competitive entrance exams so that merit – not birth or connection – determined who could join what it now called its 'civil service'. These exams, which were conducted in London, were only opened to Indians in 1852. No such system existed in Britain, where officials continued to be appointed by political allies and patrons, and were frequently suspected of advancing their own venal self-interest.

Not surprisingly then, it was an old India hand, Charles Trevelyan, trained at Haileybury and Fort William, who played a crucial role in importing the East India Company model to Britain. The **Northcote-Trevelyan Report** he co-authored in 1854 argued that the administrative service of the British state needed root-and-branch reform. It proposed that officials could only become efficient and work disinterestedly in service to the public when they were recruited by open competition, afforded anonymity and given permanent appointments supported by adequate salaries and pensions. It also proposed creating an elite group of administrative generalists capable of the critical thought needed to implement policies and preside over the more routine and mechanical work of clerks and those with specialist expert knowledge. The following year, a new Civil Service Commission was created to slowly implement these reforms and try to establish the idea of an independent and disinterested civil service.

The new civil service quickly resembled a caste system. At its top were the elite 'upper division' civil servants. As disinterested thought, independence of character and the capacity to honourably maintain the secrets of the state were identified as traits that were the preserve of a gentlemanly liberal arts education, this elite was invariably the product of a select group of private schools and Oxbridge (Oxford or Cambridge University). As late as 1914, there were just 450 members of this 'upper division' and 78 per cent of them were Oxbridge graduates, where 60 per cent of them had studied classics. Below this elite group of gentlemanly governors came the specialists with expert or technical knowledge – inspectors, engineers, surveyors, statisticians, actuaries, veterinarians, chemists, medics, meteorologists and so on. And last in the new carefully constructed hierarchy of the civil service came the lower-division clerks tasked with the so-called 'mechanical' work of copying and drafting that was so important to the flow of information through government departments. By 1871 there were 2,000 of these workers, paid a uniform rate of 10 pence an hour, and by 1875 they were supplemented by a new category of 'boy' clerk who was routinely released at age twenty. There was growing concern that as this group lacked the generous salary, career structure and social prestige of the higher classes, they would leak the secrets of the state to an increasingly predatory press. Yet it was not until 1911 that the Official Secrets Act was finally introduced to bolster the culture of honourable secrecy that was so central to the ethos of the reformed civil service.

Propelled by a new science of government that demanded reform and, as we shall see in Chapter 6, a more representative and responsive political system, the numbers of civil servants rose dramatically. While at the close of the eighteenth century the British state had employed over 16,000 people, by 1821 that figure had risen to 27,000, by 1851 39,000 and by 1871 53,000. As impressive as this growth was, the size of the British state still paled in comparison to the French state, which in 1851 had 122,000 civil servants (not including the military and state-paid members of the **clergy**), and 265,000 in 1871. In unified Germany, by the end of the nineteenth century the traditional judicial and administrative core of the civil service alone numbered 400,000, rising to 1.2 million if military administration, railways and the post are included. All told, between 1882 and 1895, Germany went from 1.265 million government workers to 1.855 million. Tsarist Russia had over 61,000 civil servants in 1847, 71,000 in 1850 and 82,000 in 1856 (a small number for its imperial population, but enormous given the relatively small number of Russians who were not serfs). Yet the British state was an imperial one. The **East India Company** alone was a vast bureaucratic machine. The approximately 800 senior servants it employed overseas were just the tip of the iceberg: in London alone it employed 1,730 people in 1785 as clerks or as workers in its London warehouses and wharves. There appear to be no good estimates for the number of clerical support staff and other employees it retained in India. The same was true of the Colonial Service formed in 1837, which never included the Indian civil service, but which nonetheless had a thousand overseas appointments in 1900.

This army of civil servants was kept busy by communication systems that enabled a burgeoning amount of information to flow from the centre to the localities and back again. The Royal Mail, enhanced by the incorporation of Ireland into the service, the introduction of a flat-rate **Penny Post** in 1840, and the growth of the railway network, remained a critical mode of communication for officials. From 1845, though, the **General Post Office** also became the home of a telegraph system that allowed officials to send and receive messages across the United Kingdom in minutes, not days, and across the Empire in hours, not weeks or months. The tentacles of cable spread from Britain to Ireland in 1852, to North America and India in the 1860s, to Hong Kong (1871), New Zealand (1876) and eastern and southern Africa (1879). No other system of communication became so vital to the business of government for the imperial state. By 1880 the General Post Office was the largest branch of the state and employed over 50,000 people. The humble British Post Office, with its network of offices around the country and postboxes in every neighbourhood, enabled officials to communicate faster over distance than ever before. In doing so it bound together the nation and its Empire as a single area of governance.

The standardization of time is a good illustration of this flattening effect. Before simultaneous telegraphic transmission across distance was possible, many localities operated on their own time system. Famously, the clock on Bristol's Corn Exchange, built in the 1740s, had two minute hands: one for London and the other for Bristol time. As telegraph cables followed railway lines, rail companies were the first to synchronize their timetables around London time. Yet remote rural areas were untouched by this process and remained so even after the Definition of Time Act of 1880 legislated a standardized national time, and after the world's time system was calibrated around London's Greenwich Mean Time in 1884.

The **'revolution in government'** was not, then, about reducing the size or role of the state. It was about changing the way it operated and how it claimed legitimacy and authority. A new science of government inspired a bureaucratic machinery that rendered power more rational and efficient, as well as impersonal and disinterested. In this form, state power was to slowly extend over an increasing range of economic and social life.

The Local, Colonial and Charismatic State

This new machinery of government did not extend uniformly across either Britain or its Empire. There were limits to its capacity to extend its reach. It also faced the opposition of those defending other visions of government as best mediated either through personal relations and patronage networks, or through local forms of self-government. This meant that the **'revolution in government'** created new structures that were often layered on top of, or alongside, earlier ones. For example, if we take just England and Wales, after 1834 the **New Poor Law** unions removed the care of the poor from the responsibility of the **parish**, but parishes continued to levy rates for maintaining churches and roads. In 1830, a single parish could already come under the multiple jurisdictions of the parish **vestry**, the manorial Court Leet, **Justices of the Peace** and the county **Quarter Sessions**, but by 1870 these had been supplemented (and sometimes replaced) by Poor Law unions, municipal corporations (town councils) as well as school and sanitary boards.

Nor did the theocratic nature of the **ancien regime** melt away like snow in the bright light of the new science of government. Although the repeal of the **Test and Corporations Acts** in 1828 and **Catholic emancipation** in 1829 finally allowed non-Anglicans to hold public office, the entrenched nature of the Anglican state remained palpable. The Church Building Acts of 1818 and 1824 provided £1.5 million of public funds for the construction of new churches in an attempt to compete with the proliferation of non-Anglican places of worship (of the 48,894 built between 1770 and 1830, just 5 per cent or 2,292 were Anglican). A further 2,000 new Anglican churches were built between 1831 and 1851 and by 1918 just under 4,000 had been completed. Non-Anglicans were still forced to pay rates for the maintenance of the **parish** church they never attended until these were made voluntary in 1853 and eventually abolished in 1868. The universities of Oxford and Cambridge remarkably remained closed to non-Anglicans until 1871, at which point they threw caution to the wind and also began to admit women! Significantly, however, when the state began to fund elementary education in 1833 it did so by supporting Anglican 'church schools'. Although in 1870 a new system of National Education created state elementary schools managed by locally elected boards (not parishes), church schools, albeit now of all denominations, continued to receive funds. The Church of Scotland retained greater power for longer, leading some to suggest that until the late nineteenth century Scotland is best characterized as a parish state. It was only after the Church of Scotland was effectively broken in two by 'the Disruption' of 1843, when 40 per cent of its Kirk left to join the rival Free Church, that the church lost control of administering poor relief in 1845 and then education in 1872. It was perhaps not until the creation of the Scottish Office, as the branch of the British state with oversight of the various forms of burgh, board and parish government in Scotland, that power was eventually centralized in London.

Suspicion of the centralization of power meant that much of the legislation inspired by the revolution in government was introduced later (and often differently) in Scotland and Ireland. Even in England and Wales it was usually adoptive, meaning it was only implemented if localities chose to do so – at least to begin with. Some brief examples: the **Municipal Corporations Act** of 1835, the result of a commission investigating the problem of urban government, reformed 178 previously incorporated towns (albeit leaving a hundred others unreformed) by insisting all had to have elected town councils, and it also allowed other towns and cities to become incorporated. By 1851 only eighteen towns had chosen to become incorporated, although a further forty-four did so by 1881. Similarly, under the Municipal Corporations Act towns that were incorporated were enabled to establish police forces, as were counties by the Rural Constabulary Act four years later. Nonetheless, by 1848 13 per cent of the 191 incorporated boroughs in England and Wales still lacked a police force, as did 41 per cent of counties in 1853. It was not until the **Police Act** of 1856 (and the following year for Scotland) that it became compulsory for all towns and counties to have a police force, and an inspectorate was developed to ensure the efficiency of each local force. And, finally, while the **Public Health Act** of 1848 enabled towns to establish local boards of health if 10 per cent of their inhabitants petitioned for one, and denied the choice to those towns whose mortality rate exceeded 23 per 1,000, by 1875 all local authorities (even those in Scotland that were not covered by the 1848 Act) were charged to do so.

This pattern of passing adoptive legislation and then eventually making it compulsory when localities failed to take advantage of it was a typical pattern. Even when new forms of government were mandated, they were not always strictly enforced. A good example here is the **New Poor Law**, which, as we have seen, required Poor Law unions to construct workhouses and instructed them to only provide relief to those incarcerated within them. By no means were all Poor Law unions either able or willing to enforce the new regime: 40 per cent of them failed to build a Workhouse by 1860, and as late as the 1890s 76 per cent of those receiving poor relief were doing so in their own homes, not as inmates of a workhouse. There were, then, real constraints upon and limits to the hold of the revolution in government over Britain.

Not so in the colonies. Without the constraints of representative structures, and with a good deal of racial disdain for their inhabitants, imperial administrators enchanted by the science of government were wont to use colonies as laboratories and impose new systems of rule on populations at will. Land and tax reforms were imposed upon India and Ireland that were unimaginable back in England and Wales or even Scotland. Similarly, the Criminal Tribes Act of 1871 drew upon the nascent European science of race to designate certain castes and tribes in northern India as 'addicted' to crime. This judgement was then used to allow police to practise forms of surveillance as well as to restrict the mobility of or even arrest those considered dangerous in ways that would have been impossible in Britain. While some of the machinery for the revolution of government, like a reformed civil service, were imported from India, it was generally believed that other forms of rule were more appropriate elsewhere. Thus, while the Irish Poor Law was belatedly introduced in 1838, the closest India ever got to one was the creation of famine camps for the distribution of relief in return for work after 1883. Similarly, outside of Dublin (whose sewers were built in the 1850s and 1860s) Ireland was not afforded public health measures until after 1878. In India, preventive medicine was largely limited to military hygiene until the 1860s, after which it developed in fits and starts. It was not until the 1890s that a series of plague epidemics and the development of 'tropical medicine' catalysed systematic sanitation efforts directed by the state.

At least during this period, however systematic it hoped to be, much colonial government remained remarkably attenuated and dependent upon military force and the local 'man on the spot'. They key figure here was the **District Officer**, who had a good deal of autonomy. This was hardly surprising given that even by the late nineteenth century there were little more than a thousand civil servants in British India governing over 300 million people with a myriad of languages. Chiefly responsible for collecting taxes and maintaining law and order in districts that could extend to 4,000 square miles, it was his training that ensured the District Officer did not line his own pockets or go 'native'.

Yet given that the **East India Company** in the first half of the nineteenth century has been well characterized as a 'garrison state', the District Officer had a vast military apparatus to call upon if needed. Thirty-five per cent of the East India Company's revenue went to support its military which consisted of 20,000 Indian sepoys alone.

The limited resources and logistical challenges of governing vast and distant territories meant that even more 'indirect' forms of rule were developed that ceded authority to a local indigenous figure. Alliances with hundreds of princely rulers were vital to the East India Company's conquest of India, and when these princes' positions were secured after the imposition of direct rule in 1858, they governed almost a third of the country. Although advised by members of the Indian civil service, they were left to rule as they saw fit and were excused from taxation in return for their support of the Indian army. A similar system was used to colonize Africa. In the Cape Colony the British governor afforded Xhosa chiefs jurisdiction over their own customary affairs, but appointed agents or commissioners, like a District Officer, to oversee the operation of British law, which was imposed for cases of murder, witchcraft and theft.

In the colonies, then, the science of government was always combined with more personal forms of rule that often relied upon symbolic shows of force. Just like the tour of High Court judges around the **Assizes** in the eighteenth century, the appearance of a District Officer and his retinue in a remote region was as much to 'show the flag' as to collect taxes and dispense justice. Indeed, the more bureaucratic the machinery of government became in the nineteenth century, the more the ceremonial display of power proliferated. Whitehall may have become the belly of the bureaucratic beast, but it also became the ceremonial centre of the imperial state. Fittingly for the site of the old royal court, it was there that the monarchy, slowly denuded of its executive authority, was provided with new ritualized displays of power. Queen Victoria began the state opening of Parliament in 1852 and on the occasion of her jubilee in 1877 was made Empress of India (see Figure 4.3). To mark the occasion, a great Imperial Assembly, or Durbar, was held in Delhi by Lord Curzon, the Governor-General of India. No wonder that Walter Bagehot, the editor of *The Economist* and an astute observer of politics, reflected in 1867 that the English constitution coupled what he characterized as its 'efficient' parts that got the business of government done with the almost mystical aura that surrounded its 'dignified' parts like the monarchy.

Cheap Government

Though its presence was by no means universal, the massive expansion of government poses the question of how Britons came to trust the new powers of the state. After all, they had railed against the excessive taxation that had supported the corrupt offices and pensions of an unrepresentative **ancien regime** and serviced its **national debt**. In contrast, whatever its size, the new science of government legitimated itself by claiming

Figure 4.3 Queen Victoria as the Empress of India, 1887

to be cheap as well as efficient and meritocratic. In addition, a new generation of economically liberal Tories clustered around figures like William Huskisson, who became president of the **Board of Trade** in 1823 and reformed the **Navigation Acts**, and Robert Peel, who became Home Secretary in 1822 and prime minister in 1834–5 and 1841–6, when he repealed the **Corn Laws** and sugar duties. In the wake of the **Napoleonic Wars** they sought to put Britain on the **gold standard** and introduce austerity measures that would instil a new ethic of fiscal discipline that met the approval of those who thought debt was sinful.

Cheap government and the reduction of the tax burden became one of the centrepieces of the new statecraft. Tax revenue peaked at 23 per cent of GNP in 1810, but by the 1830s had fallen to below 15 per cent and reached its lowest at 8 per cent in 1880. The revenue from **excise taxes** fell sharply in the first half of the nineteenth century, while the number and form of **customs duties** were radically reduced and simplified. Whereas in 1800 there were over 1,500 different customs duties, by the 1890s only four commodities (albeit the ones most central to the pleasures of most people – tobacco, wine, foreign spirits and tea) accounted for 95 per cent of customs revenue. Yet, government did not really become cheap, and nor did the tax burden considerably lessen. Between 1850 and 1890 the expenditure of central government grew at an average rate of 1.5 per cent, but was outpaced by that of local government at 2.9 per cent. Local taxation through rates became a vital way of funding the new machinery of government, which, as we have seen, was often constructed around new local jurisdictions: town councils, Poor Law unions, sanitary boards and boards of education, or parochial boards in Scotland. If taxation through local rates appeared to provide greater accountability, the introduction of income tax in 1846 helped depoliticize taxation further by collecting much of it at source through uniform schedules and rates of assessment. So uncontentious was this new mechanism that just 361 surveyors and inspectors were employed by the new Inland Revenue to oversee the system. Compare that to over 2,000 excise officials a century or so earlier. It was not, then, that government became cheap but that its techniques for raising revenue became less corrupt as they were rendered transparent and accountable.

Finally, the state and its forms of taxation were also seen as more legitimate because they were no longer oriented around war with European dynastic rivals. Instead, the state's activities seemed focused upon the domestic **social question** of the condition of England, and it was this area that so much local taxation addressed. In fact, of course, the British state remained a belligerent one, eager to expand its imperial territories. Between the **Congress of Vienna** in 1814–15 and the outbreak of the First World War a century later, the British state was almost perpetually at war with someone somewhere in the world. The genius of the British imperial state in this period was that Britain's colonial subjects were made to pay for the costs of these 'small' colonial wars. The Indian army was critical here, for it was widely deployed in the subcontinent as well as across the Mediterranean, the Middle East, Africa and East and Southeast Asia. By the late nineteenth century, two thirds of the 325,000 men who made up the armed forces of the Empire, including a sizeable British contingent funded by the infamous '**Home Charges**', were supported by Indian taxpayers. Cheap government was possible in Britain because the imperial ambitions of the state came at the expense of its colonies.

Making a Market Economy

In the economic realm, the new science of government was informed by the work of political economists like **Adam Smith** and David Ricardo. Despite their differences, they shared a critique of the **ancien regime**'s mercantilist systems for protecting trade and labour, and imagined a new role for the state in economic life. As Smith and his followers argued that only the natural rhythms of markets could maximize the wealth of nations, the job of the state was to adopt a policy of **laissez-faire** and leave the market alone. Yet here was a paradox. Removing the mercantilist system of controls that shackled markets, preventing them from becoming natural self-regulating systems, required massive state intervention. In effect, more government was needed to make markets free from government.

By 1849, the central pillars of the mercantilist economy – slavery, monopoly trading companies, the **Corn Laws**, the sugar duties and the **Navigation Acts** – had all been repealed. In their place, a new set of financial and legal infrastructures was created to enshrine a new era of liberalized labour markets and **free trade**. Politically there was broad agreement in Westminster about the imposition of these policies. They were first introduced by economically 'liberal Tories' like the future prime minister Robert Peel as Britain emerged from the **Napoleonic Wars**, accelerated by the reforming Whig governments of the 1830s and then consolidated by the newly branded Conservative Party in the 1840s.

Making Labour and Trade 'Free'

The mercantilist system depended upon myriad forms of unfree labour. Alongside slavery there was the widespread use of **indentured servitude** in the American colonies, where contracts bound workers to employers for specific lengths of service and conditions of labour. In Britain the Statute of Artificers (1563) and the Settlement and Poor Laws (1662) regulated wage rates, enforced the seven-year terms of apprentices to their masters and restricted the mobility of workers. In early modern Scotland, similar laws restricting mobility existed, though less effectively enforced than in England. Certain Scottish labourers – namely coal and salt workers – were restricted in their mobility, and specific burghs could enact further restrictions during harvests. The labouring poor of Ireland were mostly rural farm tenants, living under conditions shaped by absentee English landlords, Catholic disenfranchisement and the draconian Act of Settlement for Ireland imposed by Oliver Cromwell in 1652. Although some elements of this system were already in decline by the late eighteenth century, it was transformed by a series of liberalizing reforms that sought to make labour a commodity that could be freely bought and sold in an open market. This began with the abolition of the slave trade in 1807 and continued with the repeal of the Statute of Artificers in 1813, the reform of the Masters and Servants Acts in 1823, the abolition of slavery in 1833 and the reform of the Poor Laws in 1834. From that point on, in Britain at least, labour was a commodity like any other. Employers were free to set the terms of employment and workers were free to seek work where they could.

The state legally enforced the freedom of this labour market, and defined the terms of freedom. Under the revised Masters and Servants Acts of 1823, an average of 10,000 workers were imprisoned every year between 1857 and 1875 for breach of contract, while many more received fines or had their wages abated by the courts. The capacity of workers to defend their interests was prohibited by the Unlawful Societies Act and **Combination Acts** of 1799 and 1800 which outlawed unions and collective action. Although these laws were briefly relaxed in 1824, locally courts continued to prosecute those who formed unions. Thus, infamously, in 1834 a group of farm workers in Dorset were transported to the penal colony of Australia for having sworn a secret oath of allegiance to their union. They became known as the 'Tolpuddle Martyrs'.

The punitive approach to workers ushered in by this new legal regime was fuelled by two beliefs. First, that only the disciplines of a labour market, forced open by the state, would make workers industrious and adequately punish the slothful. Second, the widespread acceptance of Ricardo's wage-fund theory, which posited that as there was a finite amount of capital, not only would higher wages reduce profits, invest-ment and growth, workers also competed against each other so wage increases for some would penalize others. It was not until John Stuart Mill's *Principles of Political Economy* (1869) challenged this theory that trade unions were legally recognized by the state in 1871.

There were other limits to the freedom of the labour market. The state itself used forced labour in its prisons and penal colonies, while after 1834 the **New Poor Law** made paupers work for their relief and paid them less than they would receive had they been 'free' labour. Moreover, the imperial state created an elaborate legal infrastructure for the use of varied forms of bonded and **indentured labour** to replace the 'stock' of slave labour that was abolished in 1833. It is estimated that some 4 million Indians, Chinese, Malays and Sinhalese were sent across the world as unfree labourers between the 1830s and the Great War. If labour was everywhere reduced to a commodity, the professed freedom of the labour market at home continued to be dependent upon a variety of unfree forms of labour long after the abolition of slavery.

The liberalization of trade also began as Britain emerged from the **Napoleonic Wars**. Initially that process was overshadowed by the controversial passage of the **Corn Laws** in 1815, seemingly a mercantilist measure par excellence. The Corn Laws were designed less to raise tax revenue than to discourage Britain's rapidly growing population from becoming dependent upon imported wheat for bread – the staple of their diet. The Act only allowed wheat to be imported when its price in Britain had reached 80 shillings a quarter and then it was allowed in with no duties. Elsewhere, at the same time, the old monopolies and protections of the mercantilist system began to tumble. In 1813 the **East India Company** lost its monopoly of trade in South and Southeast Asia, while the port of London lost its exclusive rights to shipping from the East Indies. Thereafter these markets were open to private merchants and the provincial ports of Liverpool, Bristol and Glasgow. A decade later, with the economically liberal Tory William Huskisson at the **Board of Trade**, the **Navigation Acts**, that other great centrepiece of the mercantilist system, were relaxed. The Reciprocity of Duties Act of 1823 lifted restrictions on foreign shipping wherever reciprocal agreements could be made that allowed Britain's merchant navy access to new markets and ports. In the following two years Huskisson also dramatically reduced the number of commodities subject to protectionist duties and reduced the scale on those that remained. Even the Corn Laws were revised in 1828 when the 80 shilling ceiling for imported wheat was replaced with a sliding scale of duties. Such was the determination of the state to make markets free that having taken away the monopoly rights of the **East India Company** to Chinese trade in 1833, it began the **Opium Wars** (1839–42, 1856–60) with that country to impose its vision of **free trade**. The Corn Laws and the Navigation Acts were not finally repealed until 1846 and 1849, and while the former took a great deal of agitation by the **Anti-Corn Law League** to achieve, the state's efforts to create more liberalized markets had been evident since the 1810s.

Forging a Fiscal System

The work of the state in crafting this new economic system was not simply destructive. It was not just about removing mercantilist obstacles so markets could be restored to their supposedly natural state of freedom and self-regulation. The state also created a new fiscal and legal infrastructure that would properly regulate flows of cash, capital and trade. For in reality, markets were never left to regulate themselves.

Take the fiscal system. Throughout the eighteenth century, the cash economy overseen by the Royal Mint and the **Bank of England** was in perpetual crisis. In the late seventeenth century John Locke and Isaac Newton hoped to design a system in which the Bank of England would keep bullion reserves that allowed all cash in circulation (whatever its form) to be 'convertible' to gold or silver. Yet a shortage of gold and silver led to such a serious shortage of coin that forgery was rife and most coins were light, meaning they did not weigh their stated value. Many everyday transactions had to be conducted by credit, various forms of paper money, or the alternative currency of tradesmen's tokens. Such was the shortage of bullion during the wars with revolutionary France that convertibility to bullion was lost in 1797 and the Bank of England issued paper money. As the pound sterling depreciated against other countries and prices rose, figures like David Ricardo, **Malthus**, Huskisson and Peel successfully argued for a return to convertibility by 1811. Taking advantage of a new steam-powered Royal Mint invented by Matthew Boulton (with James Watt, the inventor of the steam engine; see Chapter 3) that made coins impossible to counterfeit, the Great Recoinage of 1816 restored gold coins to their proper weight and used copper and silver for coins of lesser value. By 1821, as the bullion reserves of the Bank of England had been fully restored, the **gold standard** was finally established, and thus the value of sterling was fortified against other currencies.

Yet the new fiscal discipline – which, it was hoped, would end speculative frenzies by reducing the amount of cash in circulation – required further reforms. As privately owned and joint-stock provincial banks were still able to issue their own notes, the Bank Acts of 1826, 1833 and 1844 slowly tightened the Bank of England's control of the banking system and gave it a monopoly on issuing new notes, so long as they did not exceed their reserves of bullion. Here the stability of the new market economy was ironically engineered by the state through a joint-stock monopoly in the form of the Bank of England.

Joint-stock companies, which proliferated in the speculative bubbles of the first half of the nineteenth century, were also subjected to new forms of regulation. Indeed, the modern form of corporate capitalism was a product of the legal regimes laid down by the Victorian state with the **Companies Act** of 1844, the introduction of limited liability in 1855 and two further Companies Acts in 1856 and 1862. This legislation transferred the privileges and corporate form once afforded by the state to joint-stock companies, intended to serve the public interest, to private commercial enterprises whose shares were publicly traded. It made it easier to form joint-stock companies, but it also created a formal process of registration and sought to protect investors by making those corporations and their accounts more legible, while limiting the personal liabilities of shareholders. Effectively, as corporations were given their own legal personality, their owners, the shareholders, were no longer held responsible for its actions. In effect, shareholders were allowed to benefit from corporate success but were insulated from failure. Ironically, even the corporation had been transformed into a private enterprise by the state when it was no longer deemed appropriate for government to 'interfere' in the business of a company.

If the fiscal system and company law seem rarefied realms of state action in making the market economy, consider its work standardizing and regulating the weights and measures used for most commercial exchanges. For centuries, weights and measures had been based on locally or regionally specific standards (thus a gallon could be measured differently in Aberdeen than in Liverpool), or differed from trade to trade (thus a pound of Cornish tin was not the same as a pound of Jamaican sugar). A succession of parliamentary inquiries in 1750, 1790, 1814, 1816 and 1820 sought the standardization that was finally achieved with the **Imperial Weights and Measures Act** of 1824. This Act reduced the units of measurement to just three (yard, pound and gallon) and created a single standard policed by a new inspectorate whose powers were repeatedly extended in 1835, 1847, 1855, 1858 and 1878. By 1878, when the **Board of Trade** had sole jurisdiction for the regulation of weights, measures *and* coins, it controlled an inspectorate empowered to enter any premise or examine the equipment of anyone, anywhere, selling goods. Here, the state projected a new understanding of the market as a uniform space stretching across all of its territories in order to facilitate trade across the newly United Kingdom and its Empire (India adopted the imperial standard in 1870). Just as importantly, the state represented itself as a neutral and fair arbiter in those commercial transactions. Quite literally the state made the new forms of the market economy possible while positing the market as a self-regulating sphere that it would leave alone.

Governing the Social

Nowhere was the full reach of the newly inquisitive and assertive state more evident than in addressing what contemporaries called the **social question**. The social question was the problem of what to do about the deteriorating conditions of the rapidly expanding population. Of particular concern were the swelling ranks of the poor, many of whom were increasingly congregating in cities where criminality and disease were rife. It was no accident that the **revolution in government** was made possible in part by the state developing new ways of counting its population and the numbers of paupers and crimes, as well as rates and patterns of mortality. The doctrine of *laissez-faire* meant that the state not only had to leave the market economy it had created alone, but had to absolve it of responsibility for causing, let alone solving, the problems posed by the social question. Instead, problems of poverty, crime and sanitation were blamed on those who suffered them. These groups were not only seen as having failed to meet the disciplines of the new market society; their endurance of horrible conditions marked them out as a race apart that was not fully human. It became the responsibility of the state to unleash new forms of discipline upon these problematic populations. Like the market, they could not learn to be free, or to enjoy the fruits of liberal government, without an unprecedented degree of state intervention. In short, the logic of colonial government was evident in Britain even if the severity of its forms overseas was unmatched at home.

Crime and Security

The foundations of a new system of policing were laid in 1748, when the London magistrate Henry Fielding employed detectives known as the Bow Street Runners to catch criminals while disregarding the parochial boundaries that hindered the work of **parish** constables and watchmen. But it was when Robert Peel, as Home Secretary, created the Irish Constabulary in 1822, that we can mark the arrival of a state prepared to take unprecedented steps to maintain social order. Subsuming all local police forces into four provincial forces, whose Inspector-Generals were directly appointed by the British state's government in Dublin Castle, it was made a unitary force in 1836, by which time Ireland had three times more police per capita than England and Wales. In many ways the Irish Constabulary provided the blueprint for Peel's subsequent establishment of London's Metropolitan Police Force in 1829, an innovation that earnt the British police the nickname of 'bobbies' after their founder. The Irish Constabulary and Metropolitan Police Force created a new professional structure for policing as a career, complete with a code of behaviour and decent salaries, to attract officers of sound moral character who would be incorruptible. In some ways this anticipated the reforms that created the civil service, and was certainly designed to overcome widespread suspicion of the police as simply the eyes, ears and arms of an increasingly strong and centralized state. Due to this suspicion, together with concerns over the cost of policing to ratepayers, when policing spread to the provinces after the Burgh Police Act of 1833 in Scotland, and the **Municipal Corporations Act** of 1835 and the Rural Constabulary Act of 1839 in England and Wales, it did so slowly and under the local control of towns and counties.

In marked contrast, recognizing that the security of London was central to the survival of the state, the Metropolitan Police Force was placed under the direct control of the **Home Office**. Its job was certainly to police what statistics showed was a surge of crime in the capital, but its officers were also deployed around the country to help maintain order where local forces were deemed wanting. Over 2,000 officers were used in this way between 1830 and 1838. That the security of the state, not just crime, was their concern was evident when, at the height of the **Chartist** movement for the reform of Parliament in 1839–42, the Home Office took control of policing in its urban hotbeds of Birmingham, Bolton and Manchester. The size of the Force was unparalleled. It was established with a little under 3,000 officers, had 5,500 by 1851 (a quarter of all policemen in England and Wales) and surged in size to over 13,000 by 1885. Even so, at times of crisis their numbers were supplemented by the use of local inhabitants volunteering as special constables as well as by troops. In 1848, when revolutions swept the continent of Europe, the Home Secretary prohibited the Chartists from marching to Parliament to present a petition and stationed over 8,000 troops on London's streets to enforce the ban.

It was not until the 1850s that a national police force truly developed. The **Police Act** of 1856 (in Scotland 1857) made it compulsory for localities to have a police force and subjected them to a centralized system of inspection and regulation by the Home Office, which rewarded the most efficient with grants. The central coordination of local policing was encouraged by the creation of the National Criminal Record in 1869. This enabled local forces to share information on crimes and criminals almost instantly through the telegraph system. By then, policing was routinely informed by an understanding that society included a set of 'criminal classes'. The collective character of this group was defined by their own personal failings and flawed moral character, thought to have nothing to do with the broader social and economic conditions in which they lived. In fact, most crimes appear to have been opportunistic, with the number of 'habitual' offenders as low as 4,000 in the 1870s. Yet because the emerging market economy was not seen as a cause of crime, rising crime rates justified and required the full force of the state.

The restructuring of prisons serves to illustrate this well. New theories of punishment and crime prevention developed in the late eighteenth century that favoured penal reform over exemplary executions or **transportation** to penal colonies. Instead of exacting revenge upon the body of the offender, emphasis was placed upon their mental discipline and moral reform. It was again Robert Peel as Home Secretary who oversaw the recalibration of criminal sentences to reflect these ideas, as well as the centralization and reform of the prison service with the Gaols Act of 1823. Over the course of the nineteenth century, a convict prison system replaced floating hulks, an extensive local prison system, and transportation to penal colonies, a practice which finally trickled away in 1869. Systems for classifying different types of prisoner, the use of hard labour, silent regimes, and fierce discipline including flogging, as well as the introduction of solitary confinement for the most recalcitrant of inmates, became features of the new model prisons like Pentonville (1842), Dartmoor (1852), Brixton (1853), Strangeways in Salford (1869) and Barlinnie Prison near Glasgow (1882) that are still in use today. These prisons had similar designs, with high enclosed walls that ensured prisoners could not see or be seen outside. Many also shared some of the features imagined by Bentham in his **Panopticon** – a central point around which corridors, blocks and cells were organized so that guards and prisoners could be observed at all times (see Figure 4.4). A centralized system of inspection, introduced in 1835 and extended in 1844, sought to ensure that prisons and the prison service conformed to centrally coordinated and uniform standards. More than 15 million people served prison sentences between 1837 and 1901.

Poverty and Sanitation

Nothing better illustrates the **'revolution in government'** and the determination of the new state it crafted to address the **social question** than the **New Poor Law**. It was introduced first in England and Wales in 1834, then in Ireland in 1838, and finally in Scotland in 1845. In each country commissions of inquiry were established in which experts, like Chadwick in England, disinterestedly identified a problem to be solved, namely the growing number of poor people as well as the haphazard nature and escalating cost of their relief. The old system of relief, they argued, administered through

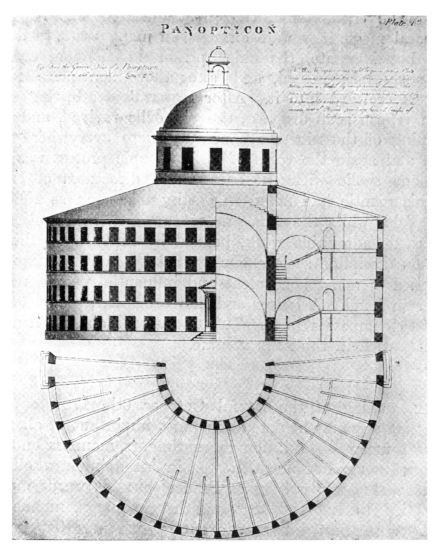

Figure 4.4 Bentham's Panopticon, 1796

the ecclesiastical structure of local parishes, was part of the problem. In providing relief 'out of doors' – that is, to workers in their own homes – and by sometimes using it to supplement low wages, it made the poor more dependent and less industrious. Like the criminal classes, the poor were now understood as a distinct group and a particular type of person – the pauper – whose failed moral character made them the architects of their own misery. Now poverty was neither considered to be a consequence of the rhythms of economic life, nor was it seen as an appropriate object of Christian charity. Understood instead as a social problem the task of the New Poor Law was to take the administration of its relief out of the hands of the Church by creating a new civil structure of Poor Law unions (or parochial boards in Scotland) overseen by inspectors and a central Commission that could institute a new punitive regime of poor relief. Only such governmental intervention could transform the moral character of the poor so that they could become industrious and independent and be able to support themselves with wages set by the free labour market. One reason the New Poor Law was not introduced in Scotland until 1845 was that evangelical religious leaders, like the influential Malthusian political economist and minister of the **Church of Scotland** Thomas Chalmers, continued to insist that the churches should be central to the delivery of relief and the moral salvation of the poor.

Across the United Kingdom the ambitions of the New Poor Law to make poor relief a deterrent manifested themselves with similar policies. First, poor relief was set at lower rates and made 'less eligible' than the wages available on the labour market, which they were no longer allowed to supplement. Second, poor relief could not be received 'out of doors', but required incarceration in workhouses which were busily built by the New Poor Law unions and parochial boards, the vast majority conforming in general principle to the Panopticon design. Third, workhouses lived up to their name, for their inhabitants were made to work for their relief, often doing hard but menial labour designed to teach them the value of industry. Men would grind rocks and bones for fertilizer (at least until 1845 when a scandal at the Andover workhouse revealed that hungry inmates were eating flesh and sucking marrow from the bones), while women were put to needlework and made to clean. Fourth, families were broken up on admission and segregated into discrete groups divided by age and sex: those under fourteen, the able-bodied between fourteen and sixty, and those over sixty. Fifth, discipline was strictly enforced by a master and a matron who oversaw all elements of life in the workhouse. Personal possessions were confiscated, inmates were made to wear common uniforms, swearing and fighting were prohibited, prayers and Anglican worship compulsory. Meals, which were notoriously inadequate, were taken away from the disorderly and disobedient. It was a remarkable extension of state power into the intimate lives of certain populations.

The same could be said of the state's attempt, once again under the direction of **Edwin Chadwick**, to transform the sanitary conditions of the growing urban population. Just as crime and poverty had been designated social questions unconnected to, let alone caused by, the emergent market economy, so Chadwick considered sanitation to be a matter of urban design and personal morality. As he put it in his initial 1842 *Report on Sanitary Conditions*, 'the removal of noxious physical circumstances, and the promotion of civic, household, and personal cleanliness, are necessary to the improvement of the moral condition of the population'. Addressing the slum conditions of Britain's cities required the creation of a new structure of government and the provision of a new sanitary infrastructure, as well as the development of new standards of sociability that equated health and sanitation with civility. Thus, the

1848 **Public Health Act** allowed localities in England and Wales to create new local boards of health and appoint a medical officer, as well as inspectors, to oversee what, after a flurry of further legislation, became a widening circle of sanitary regulation. In Scotland and Ireland sanitary reform remained more limited. In Scotland it was covered by various Police Acts until the Public Health (Scotland) Act was passed in 1867. The same was true in Ireland where limited sanitary measures were enabled by the Towns Improvement Act of 1854, until the Public Health (Ireland) Act of 1878. By 1875 local boards of health in England and Wales were charged with ensuring the provision of underground drains and sewers, reservoirs and fresh water, public urinals and toilets, discrete burial places and public parks (see Textbox 4.2), licensing abattoirs and lodging houses, the widening and lighting of streets, smoke and noise abatement, the vaccination of children and the vaginal inspection of prostitutes.

4.2 Place: Queen's Park, Glasgow

Opened in 1862, Glasgow's Queen's Park comprises 150 acres of carefully sculptured hills, woods and lakes. Named after Mary Queen of Scots who had been defeated in the Battle of Langside near the site, the land was bought by Glasgow Corporation in 1857. It was designed by Joseph Paxton, the famous architect whose 'Crystal Palace' building had served as the centrepiece of the 1851 **Great Exhibition**. Paxton was a key figure in the development of urban parks and designed one of the first ones in Liverpool's Birkenhead which was opened in 1847. Most were the results of philanthropy and public subscription, although the Public Health Act of 1875 enabled local authorities to raise funds for parks and maintain them at public expense. Victorian urban parks were a response to the overcrowding, pollution, germs and noise of cities that had rapidly urbanized. Paxton hoped that Queen's Park would help bring order, civility and health to a city whose population had grown from 78,000 to almost 400,000 and suffered several deadly outbreaks of cholera in the first half of the century. Paxton's designs usually sought to screen the city from view, using shrubs and trees to create screened walkways, rather than to create open vistas, but as Queen's Park was set on a hill overlooking Glasgow's Southside, Paxton placed one of his trademark glasshouses at its highest point. As Victorian urban parks proliferated across Britain and its Empire in the second half of the nineteenth century, they became sites for the conspicuous display of civility. At a time when few had access to clean running water, fountains were a common feature, as were statues of city worthies and promenades where inhabitants could exercise in their Sunday best on the weekends and enjoy the flowers and shrubs. London's Victoria Park (1845) bedded 200,000 flowers each year. Many parks were gated and fenced so that they could be better policed. As Glasgow became a leading site for socialist protest in the twentieth century, Queen's Park became a focal point for working-class agitation, hosting the city's annual May Day parade. More recently the park has hosted Scottish independence rallies and live music concerts. (S.W.)

The state had insinuated itself into the very structures of the urban environment, as well as the bodies of its subjects. To be an unsanitary town or person, marked by dirt and disease, was to invite the intervention of the state.

The new science of government, then, enabled the massive extension of state power to forge a free market economy as well as to address what it deemed a quite separate set of social questions. The state reached into new areas of everyday life, took new forms and administrative shapes, and in doing so belied the **laissez-faire** approach that was supposed to characterize it.

Religion, Moral Reform and the Family

It should be clear from the moralized language of character that infused so much of the new science of government – disinterested, independent, industrious, civilized – that its presence was not found only in the new institutional forms of the state. Government was everywhere in Victorian Britain not just because the state had wound itself into the lineaments of everyday life, but because it was ceded to those who were considered capable of governing themselves. If those populations considered to be social problems experienced the full force and reach of the state, those who demonstrated their industry, independence and civility were left alone and given the responsibility of their own self-improvement and moral government. Being free from the intervention of the state depended upon a different sort of government that required one to follow the rules of freedom.

Religion had long been a key conduit for learning and practising the art of moral government. And yet, despite the evangelical revival and the proliferation of new places of worship in the first half of the nineteenth century, there was widespread concern that the burgeoning population, especially in cities, was escaping the influence of organized religion. To test these fears, the 1851 Census included a count of how many people attended church on a particular Sunday. It discovered that an alarming 60 per cent of the population did not attend any place of worship. Worse still, half of those who did not were Anglicans, and the highest rate of non-attendance was among the labouring poor in cities, where it peaked at 80 per cent. Clearly, religion could no longer be expected to provide the moral compass for the urban working classes whose morals many commentators felt were most in need of government.

If the question of moral government now exceeded religion, the language of moral reform and self-improvement became something like a new type of secular religion. The high priest of this new gospel was Samuel Smiles, the writer of *Self-Help* (1859), aimed at respectable working men, which quickly acquired canonical status, selling 20,000 copies in its first year. Smiles believed that government by the state undermined the capacity of individuals to govern themselves, for it destroyed the independence which he believed was the cornerstone of developing a strong moral character.

He offered a hodgepodge of advice about the qualities required to acquire moral character (application, perseverance, industry, energy, fiscal responsibility and courage) as well as stories about the exemplary lives of self-made men who rose from humble ranks to fame and fortune. Above all, the key to improving one's moral character was the development of good habits through liturgical practice and participation in new forms of **rational recreation**.

A plethora of new institutions and leisure practices promoting rational forms of recreation facilitated the ceaseless work of self-improvement. The purpose of leisure was not to pursue pleasure but to do the intellectual and moral work necessary to recreate and improve oneself. In this climate the **temperance movement** promoting abstinence from alcohol made rapid advances in Britain from the 1830s and soon spread to the United States of America. In 1834, the British and Foreign Temperance Society measured itself at over 85,000 members in England. The United Kingdom Alliance, which agitated for prohibition after 1853, saw 620,000 attendees at its 1873 meetings nationwide. In 1869 and 1872, Permissive Bills put before Parliament which would allow localities to outlaw the buying and selling of alcohol for themselves, gathered 800,000 and 1.4 million signatures respectively. Moral reformers, as well as working men convinced that alcohol was an aristocratic plot to keep them in a state of ignorance and bondage, promoted sober environments such as purpose-built temperance halls, which unlike pubs were characterized by order, discipline and a culture of inquiry. For many working men, taking the pledge of abstinence was almost like a conversion experience of being born again. If taking the pledge enabled them to use their recreation to forge a new and improved version of themselves, staying sober was a test of their capacity for self-government, and a demonstration of the strength of their moral character.

As literacy and the acquisition of knowledge were likewise increasingly equated with self-discipline, self-improvement and civility, new cultural institutions designed to propagate these qualities proliferated. The first Mechanics' Institutes, designed to educate working men in the evenings after work, opened in Scotland in the 1820s and quickly spread south of the border, numbering over 700 by 1850. The introduction of the **Penny Post** in 1840 – allowing a flat rate for delivery of letters across the country – and the final repeal of the stamp duties on newspapers in 1855, which radicals had long described as a tax on knowledge, encouraged the dramatic growth of letter-writing and newspaper-reading. The Museums Act of 1845 and the Public Library Act of 1850 allowed local ratepayers to vote for establishing public libraries and museums. If these were expressly designed to help working people have access to knowledge and culture, they also inculcated new standards of conduct. A hush descended upon these new cathedrals of learning just as it had previously upon places of worship. The silence and ordered discipline (which for libraries included a system of classification named after its American creator Melvil Dewey in 1876) of these institutions illustrated the self-discipline, rational control and self-improvement of those who used and visited them. We would be hard pressed to suggest that something called 'the state' taught us all to be quiet in libraries, and yet it is evident that a diffuse form of government was at work.

As forms of self-government, the practices of self-improvement and the language of character were highly gendered and rooted in the patriarchal structures of the family. As husbands and fathers, men were supposed to rule their own household and its inhabitants. It was their responsibility to maintain the family's independence by supporting it financially, as well as to maintain its public reputation by conducting themselves respectably at work and in the local community. If they were able to do so, the household remained a private realm free from the interference of agencies of the state or moral reformers. In these respectable households the family home became a private refuge from the world at large, shielded behind fences and hedges as well as shutters and curtains of thick fabrics. Indeed, the greater the privacy a family could afford the greater its respectability. In the homes of the poor, abutting the street and frequently shared with other families and lodgers, respectability and privacy were rare commodities. Even in these precarious conditions men were still the kings of their own castles; they were the first to be fed and set the rules of the household.

In respectable and independent households men could afford for their wives to stay at home. In these households the job of women was to care for their male master, manage the household and raise children. Many had the help of servants in doing so, although, as the immense popularity of *Mrs Beeton's Book of Household Management* (1861) demonstrated, affording this was a continuous struggle that required constant vigilance (see Textbox 4.3). If all domestic work was done by servants, an annual income of £500 per annum was needed. but even the lower middle classes, earning around £150 per annum as teachers, shopkeepers or clerks, could still afford a cook and a maid or two. Published two years after Smiles's *Self-Help*, Beeton's book advised women on how to run their households in ways that would protect and enhance the family's respectability (see Figure 4.5).

4.3 Person: Mrs Beeton (1836–1865)

Isabella Beaton was born Isabella Mayson in 1836 to a lower middle-class London family. The eldest of three children, her father died when she was small, and her mother remarried a wealthier man with five children of his own. Her mother and stepfather added thirteen more children to the brood, making Isabella the eldest of twenty-one children. They spent much of their time on their maternal grandmother's estate, and Isabella acted as an assistant householder to her grandmother. It is perhaps no surprise, then, that she thought of herself as an expert on extreme household management. When she left home and married Samuel Beeton in 1856, she worked alongside him in his publishing business, writing for the monthly *English Woman's Domestic Magazine*. She wrote her own book, *Mrs Beeton's Book of Household Management*, in 1861, which sold over 60,000 copies in its first year of publication, and nearly 2 million by 1868. Beeton embodied many of the contradictions of Victorian class and gender expectations. The espousal of a so-called traditional family household depended on the tireless devotion of Beeton to her public work as a writer, journalist and editor, working in partnership with her husband in the publishing business. Middle-class femininity, as read in *Household Management*, did not simply exist, but had to be constructed, and Victorian domesticity was as modern an invention as the market economy. As a final testament to the difficulty and fragility of women's lives as mothers, Beeton died from infection after childbirth at the age of twenty-eight. (K.H.)

Figure 4.5 Mrs Beeton, 1859

The epigraph of the first chapter, taken from the Bible's Proverbs, outlined the key qualities respectable women must possess: 'Strength, and honour are her clothing; and she shall rejoice in time to come. She openeth her mouth with wisdom; and in her tongue is the law of kindness. She looketh well to the ways of her household; and eateth not the bread of idleness. Her children arise up, and call her blessed; her husband also, and he praiseth her.' If, as Smiles had insisted, 'the nation comes from the nursery', Beeton made sure women knew how to run the households in which children were raised. All the rituals of family life that continue to be the hallmarks of family households considered respectable and well run – eating together, evening entertainments (reading and games), observing religious celebrations, weekend walks, annual holidays – are a product of this regime. The purpose of the respectable, private household was to create an environment that would allow men to recuperate from their physically and morally exhausting toil in the public world, as well as to raise and protect children. Where once children had been seen as miniature adults who could work, drink alcohol and have sex (before 1875 the age of consent was just twelve), in these households childhood was reconceived as a time of innocence and purity that needed the protection and safety of the private, domestic world. Naturally, those households that could not afford for women to stay at home and protect children as innocents were deemed unrespectable and subject to the unwelcome attentions of moral reformers and agencies of the state.

As the **revolution in government** transformed the nature and reach of the state, those who wished to be let alone by it had to demonstrate the appropriate forms of self-government. In an environment where only problematic social groups felt the full force of the state, it was imperative to maintain one's reputation as independent and respectable. This required constant vigilance and liturgical practice. If statecraft had been rendered a science by the 'revolution in government', governing the self became an art that transformed everyday life even in the most private of realms like the family household.

Conclusion

In an 1891 essay outlining the historical basis of socialism, the social reformer and political theorist Sidney Webb detailed how extensive the powers of the state had become in the era of so-called liberal government and *laissez-faire*:

Besides our international relations and the army, navy, police and the courts of justice, the community now carries on for itself, in some part or another of these islands, the post office, telegraphs, carriage of small commodities, coinage, surveys, the regulation of the currency and note issue, the provision of weights and measures, the making, sweeping, lighting, and repairing of streets, roads, and bridges, life insurance, the grant of annuities, shipbuilding, stock-broking, banking, farming, and money-lending. It provides for many thousands of us from birth to burial – midwifery, nursery, education, board and lodging, vaccination, medical attendance, medicine, public worship, amusements, and interment. It furnishes and maintains its own museums, parks, art galleries, libraries, concert halls, roads, streets, bridges, markets, slaughter-houses, fire-engines, light-houses, pilots, ferries, surf-boats, steam-tugs, life-boats, cemeteries, public baths, wash houses, pounds, harbors, piers, wharves, hospitals, dispensaries, gas-works, water-works, tramways, telegraph cables, allotments, cow meadows, artisans' dwellings, schools, churches, and reading-rooms. It carries on and publishes its own researches in geology, meteorology, statistics, zoology, geography, and even theology. In our Colonies the English Government further allows and encourages the communities to provide for themselves railways, canals, pawn broking, theaters, forestry, cinchona farms, irrigation, leper villages, casinos, bathing establishments, and immigration, and to deal in ballast, guano, quinine, opium, salt, and what not.

Very little of this vast infrastructure had existed at the end of the **Napoleonic Wars**, when most Britons across the political spectrum remained deeply suspicious of the state. When historians finally awoke to the way in which the rhetoric of *laissez-faire* belied a remarkable growth of state capacity and power, they largely saw it as a consequence of the state becoming more representative, more secure, more efficient and cheaper. That is to say, they largely repeated the story that the Victorian advocates of the **revolution in government** told themselves, blithely ignoring the colonial state.

Instead, this chapter has suggested that Britons came to trust the state when it was no longer considered synonymous with the **ancien regime** and the interests of the monarchy, aristocracy and **Anglican Church**. Central to that transformation was the development of a new science and machinery of government that appeared disinterested and beyond politics. This enabled the new and savage powers of the state to occupy the minds and bodies of its subjects in both Britain and its Empire. The science of government was of course infused with politics nonetheless. It was a liberal politics that sought to secure the state and its rule of law and order, to dismantle mercantilist controls and create a market economy, and to discipline those groups who failed to support themselves or threatened the health and security of the population. Although *laissez-faire* was a fiction, those well versed in the new arts of self-government, those who demonstrated that they were civil subjects able to ensure their own independence and respectability, were let alone.

FURTHER READING

The classic debate on the Victorian **revolution in government** took place during the 1950s as historians argued about the origins of the **welfare state** that was developing at that time. Samuel Finer's *The Life and Times of Sir Edwin Chadwick* (London, 1952) and Eric Stokes's *The English Utilitarians and India* (Oxford, 1959) argued that Bentham's ideas and disciples were critical to the emergence of the new science of government. In contrast, in a widely influential essay, 'The Nineteenth-Century Revolution in Government', *Historical Journal*, 1 (1958), 52–67,

Oliver MacDonagh suggested that the new approach and mechanisms of government were a pragmatic response to new economic and social conditions that were well publicized in print by those who thought them intolerable and demanded remedies. MacDonagh's work inspired a generation of scholarship in this vein usefully summarized in Roy MacLeod (ed.), *Government and Expertise: Specialists, Administrators and Professionals, 1860–1919* (Cambridge, 1988).

Since the 1980s the unravelling of the welfare state has led historians to revisit the idea of *laissez-faire* government. Good introductory accounts can be found in Eric Evans, *The Forging of the Modern State: Early Industrial Britain, 1783–1870* (London, 1983), and Peter Mandler (ed.), *Liberty and Authority in Victorian Britain* (Oxford, 2006).

Although the conventional focus of that work is political history, it has recently been enriched by those interested in economic affairs. In *Trusting Leviathan: The Politics of Taxation in Britain, 1799–1914* (Cambridge, 2001), Martin Daunton explores when and how Britons came to accept being taxed by the state. Paul Johnson's *Making the Market: The Victorian Origins of Corporate Capitalism* (Cambridge, 2010) as well as Mark Freeman, Robin Pearson and James Taylor's *Shareholder Democracies? Corporate Governance in Britain and Ireland before 1850* (Chicago, 2012) examine how the state intervened to create a legal framework that posited the market economy as a self-regulating sphere.

Social and cultural historians, especially those influenced by the late work of Michel Foucault, have shifted our attention away from the state as a thing towards broader relations of power and government. Patrick Joyce's *The Rule of Freedom: Liberalism and the Modern City* (London, 2003) explores how liberal forms of government were embedded in the urban fabric and everyday life of city-dwellers. It is an approach that has gained particular traction around the treatment of public health and new forms of expertise. See, for examples, Mary Poovey's *Making a Social Body: British Cultural Formation, 1830–1864* (Chicago, 1995); Christopher Hamlin's *Public Health and Social Justice in the Age of Chadwick: Britain 1804–1854* (Cambridge, 1998); Chris Otter's *The Victorian Eye: A Political History of Light and Vision in Britain, 1800–1910* (Chicago, 2008), and Tom Crook, *Governing Systems: Modernity and the Making of Public Health in England, 1830-1910* (Berkeley, 2016).

The gendered nature of liberal government and its structuring of family and social life around **separate spheres** has been explored by feminist scholars. The key texts here are Leonore Davidoff and Catherine Hall, *Family Fortunes: Men and Women of the English Middle Class, 1780–1850* (London, 1987), Mary Poovey, *Uneven Developments: The Ideological Work of Gender in Mid-Victorian England* (Chicago, 1988), Judith Walkowitz, *Prostitution and Victorian Society: Women, Class, and the State* (Cambridge, 1980), and Anna Clark, *The Struggle for the Breeches: Gender and the Making of the British Working Class* (London, 1995). John Tosh's *A Man's Place: Masculinity and the Middle Class Home in Victorian England* (New Haven, 1999) explores the burdens of patriarchy for men.

Recent work in the field of British imperialism and postcolonial studies has shown how the governance of empire informed the development of the British state. Notable texts in this area include those which explicitly discuss the role of empire in the metropole: Catherine Hall, *Civilizing Subjects: Metropole and Colony in the English Imagination, 1830–1867* (Oxford, 2002), and Richard Price, *Making Empire: Colonial Encounters and the Creation of Imperial Rule in Nineteenth-Century Africa* (Cambridge, 2008). Texts that re-imagine the divide between the liberal British state and the illiberal imperial state include Bernard Semmel, *The Rise of*

Free Trade Imperialism: Classical Political Economy, the Empire of Free Trade and Imperialism 1750–1850 (Cambridge, 1970), Uday Mehta's article 'Liberal Strategies of Exclusion', *Politics and Society*, 18/4 (1990), 427–54, Gyan Prakash, *Another Reason: Science and the Imagination of Modern India* (Princeton, 1999), Karuna Mantena, *Alibis of Empire: Henry Maine and the Ends of Liberal Imperialism* (Princeton, 2010), Timothy Mitchell, *Rule of Experts: Egypt, Techno-politics, and Modernity* (Berkeley, 2002).

Lauren Goodlad's *Victorian Literature and the Victorian State: Character and Governance in a Liberal Society* (Baltimore, 2003) and David Vincent's *The Culture of Secrecy: Britain 1832–1998* (Oxford, 1998) explore how the language of character shaped the creation of a new governing class in the civil service.

Max Weber's *Politics as a Vocation* (1919) famously argued that the modern state replaced the charismatic authority of monarchs with impersonal and bureaucratic forms of power. It is not a view shared by David Cannadine. The themes of his classic essay on the British monarchy, 'The Context, Performance, and Meaning of Ritual: The British Monarchy and the "Invention of Tradition," c. 1820–1977', in Hobsbawm and Ranger (eds.), *The Invention of Tradition* (Cambridge, 1983), are developed further and given an imperial gloss in *Ornamentalism: How the British Saw the Empire* (Oxford, 2001).

Finally, there are those who pay close attention to the persistent localism of Britain's nation-state. The classic account remains Sidney and Beatrice Webb's *English Local Government: The Parish and the County* (London, 1906) and its most recent elaboration by David Eastwood, *Government and Community in the English Provinces, 1700–1870* (Basingstoke, 1997).

5 An Empire of Free Trade?

Introduction

In 1876, Walter Bagehot, the much respected editor of *The Economist*, reflected on the influence of **Adam Smith**'s *Wealth of Nations*, written a century earlier. In 1776 its publication marked a major critique of Britain's mercantilist political economy, an almost utopian plea for an era of **free trade** that appeared distant and remote. Yet a century later, Bagehot remarked,

the whole commercial policy of the country is not so much founded on it as in instinct with it. Ideas which are paradoxes everywhere else in the world are accepted axioms here as results of it. No other form of political philosophy has ever had one thousandth part of the influence on us; its teachings have settled down into the common sense of the nation, and have become irreversible.

How then did Smith's once-reviled argument that only free trade could ensure the wealth of nations become accepted as a self-evident truth and part of the natural order of things? It is an especially perplexing transformation given that, as Bagehot acknowledged, it was clearly a 'political philosophy' not a simple piece of economic policy, and outside of Britain was neither believed nor practised.

Although Bagehot insisted that the 'life of almost everyone in England – perhaps of everyone – is … better in consequence of it', that was, and remains, a matter of great debate. It is beyond question that Britain's embrace of free trade during the nineteenth century helped forge, for the first time, a global economic system. Within this system, Britain took full advantage of its early innovations in industrial manufacturing by exporting finished goods to its Empire and the world in return for natural resources and raw materials. This flow of trade created an increasingly globalized economy that was tied together by British shipping and communication networks, as well as British capital. Secured by the **gold standard**, the pound sterling became the global currency whose value other currencies were pegged to. As London's capital markets flourished, the stock market boomed. Overseas investment opened up foreign markets by providing railways and sufficient development for the import of British goods. Britain became not just the workshop of the world, but its transport hub and financial centre.

Just as the global economy was shaped around Britain's commitment to the free flow of trade and capital, so the country itself was transformed by it. Britain experienced a second wave of industrialization from the 1830s, fuelled by coal, the production of iron and steel, and the growth of railways and steam-powered shipping that allowed its goods to be transported around the world. As the population continued to grow at a rapid rate, it was slowly redistributed from rural to urban areas and from agricultural to industrial forms of production. In the second half of the nineteenth century Britain became the first society in the world to have a predominantly urban population. The number and size of towns and cities grew exponentially. The inhabitants were increasingly fed on foods imported from across the world – beef from Argentina, wheat from the United States, tea from India and China, lamb from the Antipodes and sugar still from the West Indies. Socially and economically the Britain Bagehot observed in 1876 was almost unrecognizable compared to that of 1819. It is those changes, and the key role free trade had in generating them, that this chapter explores.

TIMELINE

1823	Relaxation of Navigation Acts
1824	Imperial weights and measures
1828	Reduction of Corn Laws
1830	Liverpool–Manchester Railway
1832	Harriet Martineau, *Illustrations of Political Economy*
1833	Abolition of slavery End of East India Company's remaining monopolies
1838	Anti-Corn Law League
1839–42	First Opium War
1841	Friedrich List, *National System of Political Economy*
1843	*The Economist*
1844	Bank Act and Companies Act
1845	Artisans' and Labourers' Dwellings Act
1845	Engels, *The Condition of the Working Class in England* (in German)
1846–50	Great Famine in Ireland
1846	Repeal of the Corn Laws and sugar duties
1848	Sir Charles Trevelyan, *The Irish Crisis*
1849	Repeal of the Navigation Acts
1851	The Great Exhibition

1853–6	Crimean War
1853	Completion of Woodhead Tunnel
1856–60	Second Opium War
1858	End of the East India Company
1860	Cobden–Chevalier Treaty
1861–5	The Cotton Famine
1865	W.S. Jevons, *The Coal Question*
1871	50 per cent of Britons live in towns with over 10,000 people
1873–96	The Great Depression
1876	Bagehot's 'Postulates of English Political Economy'
1888	English translation of Marx's *On the Question of Free Trade*

The Gospel of Free Trade

Although political economy was represented as an Enlightened science, it remained infused with providential forms of explanation and a highly moralized sensibility that resonated with evangelical currents of thought. While the fiscal discipline imposed by the **gold standard**, and cheap government, spoke to an ethos of personal restraint and national rectitude, **free trade** became a gospel that for many evoked a new moral vision of the world. If for Smith free trade had been a stick for beating the mercantilist **ancien regime**, those who picked it up in the nineteenth century radicalized the cause and looked to construct a new world upon it.

That world was to be free of imperialism, war and want. As commerce depended upon cooperation between strangers for their mutual benefit, they believed the era of free trade would spread civility, peace and understanding as well as prosperity. In such a world, colonies were a remnant of an archaic mercantilist view of capturing finite markets and territory. In this world of peace and understanding, prosperity would favour those who were found most morally deserving of it. The distributive hand of the market was thought to reward industry and those of sound moral character. It would also punish sloth and sin, so that poverty and bankruptcy were seen as punishments, indelible evidence of a personal moral failure. The liberal political economy of free trade and cheap government took shape in what one historian has described as 'the Age of Atonement'. It was indelibly marked by evangelical structures of thought and feeling. Free trade was a gospel that authorized the idea of a free market as part of God's divine plan. It legitimated the deeply unequal social order it created at home as well as the uneven division of labour it produced around the world.

The messianic beliefs surrounding free trade were slow to fade. That was even the case in the late nineteenth century, when political economy was slowly reborn as the field of economics, with historical and quantitative approaches to the economy replacing Bagehot's 'political philosophy'. Although the rest of the world sought to protect their developing national economies behind protectionist tariffs following the onset of the **Great Depression** in the 1870s, Britain remained firmly committed to the doctrine of free trade and the maintenance of the gold standard. Long after they were economically viable policies, they were sustained by the moral and political vision with which they were established. Indeed, it was not until 1931 that they were abandoned.

The Manchester School

So who was responsible for evangelizing the gospel of **free trade**? Although many, like Harriet Martineau in her *Illustrations of Political Economy* (1832), had sought to popularize the ideas of Smith, it was the **Anti-Corn Law League**, founded in 1838 by the mill owners Richard Cobden and John Bright, that made free trade a popular appeal. They endowed free trade with a moral charge, and built a political movement around it. Cobden and Bright were deeply connected to the cotton industry in and around Manchester and supported parliamentary reform. Bright, a Quaker, was also conspicuous in local campaigns against the church rates and in favour of temperance. As the name suggests, the League targeted the **Corn Laws** as illustrative of an unrepresentative Parliament which defended the interests of the landed aristocracy by protecting the price of corn at the expense of consumers. Manchester became the headquarters of the League, and by the 1840s the cause of free trade was dubbed by the future Conservative prime minister Benjamin Disraeli the '**Manchester school**' of political economy. The name stuck and the League, as well as the cause, became closely associated with the merchants and manufacturers of that city. It is certainly true that the League was strongly supported by manufacturers and merchants, especially in the centres of the cotton and wool trade, Manchester and Leeds. The League, and the broader case of free trade, were also popular in Scotland – and not just amongst the merchants and manufacturers of the booming cities. For the genius of the League was to yoke the cause of free trade to that of the consumer. The Corn Laws, they argued, inflated the price of the people's bread, their staple food, so that the poor grew hungry while the landed classes grew rich. Nowhere was this more apparent than in their representation of the big and little loaf that adorned so much of their publicity material, including, as we can see in Figure 5.1, their membership cards. This Anti-Corn Law League membership card belonged to Betty Howarth from Accrington who was the 16,271st member of the League. It makes sense that the League's message would resonate with women as managers of the household budget. Although there is little evidence that women of the labouring poor were involved in the League, it is not surprising that Harriet Martineau donated the proceeds of her novel *Dawn Island* (1845) to it.

The success of the League owed much to innovative organization methods to spread its message. At the peak of its support in 1842 and 1843 the League boasted 316 local associations. The local associations raised funds to support a national headquarters that employed fifteen full-time lecturers and a staff of twenty, who distributed a million pamphlets per week and produced the weekly *Anti-Corn Law Circular*. As well as mobilizing public opinion, the League sought to maximize the number of 'Abolitionist' MPs who supported the repeal of the Corn Laws. They were the first group to develop a nationally conceived electoral strategy that targeted winning specific constituencies. Taking advantage of the **Penny Post**, the league mailed 300,000 letters a week directly to specifically selected voters in these constituencies. This was an unprecedented and formidable political machine and it left an indelible mark on Manchester as a city (see Textbox 5.1 and Figure 5.2).

Figure 5.1 The Big and Little Loaf

5.1 Place: Free Trade Hall, Manchester

The Free Trade Hall on Peter Street in Manchester was weighted with symbolism right from its construction (1853–6). It was built upon the site of the **Peterloo Massacre**. It was built by public subscription to commemorate the repeal of the **Corn Laws**, on land provided by Anti-Corn Law activist Richard Cobden. After its erection, the Hall was used for public meetings, bazaars and speeches and, after 1858, musical concerts. With Manchester being the seat of the textile industry, the Free Trade Hall saw numerous meetings regarding the American Civil War and its impact on cotton imports during the 1860s. Despite the hardship faced in the city during the ensuing **Cotton Famine**, textile workers met at the Hall in 1862 to support the Union in the fight to abolish slavery. A similar meeting was held in 1863, by the Union and Emancipation Society, in which the speaker chastised the American southern states for not agitating hard enough for **free trade**, and the North for being too protectionist, therefore causing the Civil War. In 1904, Winston Churchill notably delivered a speech defending free trade (long after most nations in the world had abandoned it and returned to tariffs). In 1905, the **Women's Social and Political Union** held an impromptu meeting outside the hall, in protest at not having their questions answered by the Liberal MP speaking inside. The Hall was home to the Hallé Orchestra after 1858, until it was damaged by bombs during the Blitz. It reopened as a concert hall in 1951, and both Bob Dylan and the Sex Pistols performed there.

And it bore remarkable fruit. Even though Robert Peel had been an economically liberal Tory for decades, the League helped ensure that as prime minister in the 1840s he dismantled the final pillars of the ancien regime's mercantile system, including its symbolic centrepiece the Corn Laws. This was all the more remarkable because Peel's newly rebranded Conservative Party was associated with the interests of the landed classes. Yet his budgets of 1842 and 1845 lowered tariff rates on the Corn Laws, removed or reduced **customs duties** on over a thousand other commodities, and offset the loss of revenue by introducing an income tax on those who earned more than £150 a year. Although the so-called **Manchester school** clearly influenced Peel, he claimed the developing famine in Ireland, and the need to import cheap foreign food to ease the crisis, finally convinced him to repeal the Corn Laws in 1846. So contentious was the repeal that 231 of 343 Conservative MPs voted against the measure.

It was not just the self-interested landed classes who rejected the Manchester school's political economy of **free trade**. The Tory man of letters and biting satirist Thomas Carlyle famously derided political economy as a 'dismal science'. Defending slavery in *The Occasional Discourse on the Negro Question* (1849), he rejected the idea that it was possible to 'find the secrets of this Universe in "supply and demand" and reducing the

Figure 5.2 Free Trade Hall, Manchester, *c.*1890s

duty of human governors to that of letting men alone'. While Carlyle typically hinged his argument upon the perverse racialized logic that black men had to be compelled to work, others shared his suspicion of the 'laws' of political economy. Echoing Carlyle, Tory paternalists also wished to maintain what they saw as an organic social system that placed a burden of responsibility upon those atop its natural hierarchy towards those at its bottom. These so-called 'One Nation Tories' believed that the political economy of free trade and *laissez-faire* disrupted this organic unity and produced a society polarized between two nations – variously construed as rich and poor, north and south, urban and rural. Peel's chief critic within his own party, the future prime minister Benjamin Disraeli, published a novel, *Sybil, or The Two Nations*, in 1845 warning of the dire conditions of the labouring poor, and the need for the ruling classes to address them. Disraeli's politics, though infused with a romantic paternalism, resonated among more radical Tory critics of the punitive regimes of the factory and workhouse. Thus Richard Oastler took up the case of **factory reform** to protect children and women from the dehumanizing system of 'Yorkshire slavery' in textile mills. Oastler was an anti-slavery campaigner, and yet he was also a protectionist and an opponent of **Catholic emancipation**. Tory radicals like the brilliant orator Rev. J.R. Stephens, who campaigned for factory reform, opposed the **New Poor Law** and frequently spoke at Chartist meetings in the northwest, gave this politics a more demotic edge.

Stephens was hugely popular with the labouring classes, who were radicalized by these campaigns, and it was they who formed the basis of the Chartist movement in the late 1830s. As we shall see in Chapter 6, **Chartism** focused its demands upon the suffrage question and the reform of Parliament to represent the interests of all men. Although many Chartists concurred with the **Anti-Corn Law League**'s analysis of the aristocratic nature of the state, they remained sceptical of a movement that prioritized issues of trade over democratic reforms of government. They pointed out that according to the wage theory of the liberal political economist David Ricardo, cheaper bread would only lower wages and not improve the lot of working people. In so far as Chartism addressed political economy, it was primarily to address the question of public finances. Their argument, first elaborated by **William Cobbett** and John Fielden in the 1820s, was that the state orchestrated a financial system – through the **national debt**, the banking system and taxation – that conspired to impoverish the productive classes, namely the labouring poor, and bankrupt the nation. Marx and Engels's critique of liberal political economy only began to register in the 1880s with the gradual translation of their work, including *On the Question of Free Trade* in 1888, and the formation of the Social Democratic Federation (SDF). Yet if Marx saw free trade as a necessary phase in the history of capitalism (one representing the triumph of the industrial bourgeoisie) that would lead to its overthrow, the SDF simply advocated the abandonment of free trade in order to protect British jobs in the face of rising unemployment.

What united all these domestic critics of free trade was their insistence that the laws of liberal political economy were not universally true but instead grounded in history and politics. In many ways this view was more cogently expressed by those living in countries whose economies were configured as satellites to Britain's empire of free trade. As the German Friedrich List argued in his *National System of Political Economy* (1841), free trade made sense for Britain. Her early industrialization meant she could flood overseas markets with cheap finished goods. This was the imperialism of free trade. Free trade promised freedom and prosperity but delivered the subordination and under-development of economies that were made satellites to Britain's. To counter this, List argued that developing economies with infant industries needed tariffs to protect them from the imperialism of Britain's freely traded cheaper goods. Those who in the 1860s turned to historical models of economic analysis echoed this critique that free trade was only ideally suited to Britain because of its historically unique comparative economic advantage over its rivals. Not surprisingly, Britain's colonial critics of free trade in Ireland and India were at the forefront of this endeavour, as was Arnold Toynbee, the Oxford historian who popularized the term 'the industrial revolution' in his posthumously published *Lectures on the Industrial Revolution in England* (1884).

Cobden and Bright were blind to this imperialism of free trade. They were often staunch critics of British imperialism, even though they were prone to accept the existing terms of colonial government. At his most radical, Bright insisted that the Empire, and British India in particular, worked as a 'gigantic system of outdoor relief for the aristocracy of Great Britain'. Although they believed trade alone would civilize other nations, they were critical of the use of force to compel other countries to open their markets. They opposed the **Opium War** of 1839–42, when the **East India Company** forced China to export tea in return for Indian opium, and established the treaty ports of Hong Kong, Canton and Shanghai as gateways to China's markets. Their opposition to the Crimean War (1853–6) and the Second Opium War that began in 1856 was reputed to have lost both men their parliamentary seats in the election of 1857. Yet both men believed that Britain had a key role in bringing civility and prosperity to the world through an informal empire of free trade, one held together by commercial exchange rather than formal structures of rule. Free trade would afford Britain the commercial benefits of an empire without the prohibitive costs of territorial war and colonial government. If that created unequal relationships, in which the rest of the world would grow what Britain would manufacture and finance, then so be it.

Famine and the Great Exhibition

Nowhere were the unequal relationships and effects of the empire of **free trade** more evident than in the juxtaposition of the **Great Famine** in Ireland and the staging of the world's first trade fair at the **Great Exhibition** in London. Indeed, the scale of the demographic catastrophe that was the Great Famine only became fully apparent when the census returns of 1851 came in, just as the Great Exhibition was opening in Hyde Park to celebrate the new peace and prosperity ushered in by an era of free trade. Historians argue about how to count the casualties of the Irish famine, but we know that when the famine broke in 1845 Ireland's rapidly growing population had reached 8.5 million (it had been 8.2 million in 1841) and that by 1851 it had fallen to 6.6 million. In excess of a million people were killed by the famine and over 2 million fled Ireland's fatal shores in the decade between 1845 and 1855, half of whom emigrated to the United States. The potato blight that triggered the famine in Ireland also wracked the **Scottish Highlands** from 1846, killing many of the young and old and reducing a third of the population to famine relief by 1848. The Great Exhibition may have been intended to celebrate Britain's position as the richest nation on earth, but despite the Acts of Union, millions of its inhabitants in Ireland, and tens of thousands in Scotland, still starved.

Peel used the developing famine to justify repealing the **Corn Laws** but all this did was render Ireland a laboratory for an experiment with the **Manchester school**'s liberal political economy. Charles Trevelyan, who we have already seen was a key architect of the independent civil service, was placed in charge of this experiment and helpfully wrote up the preliminary results in *The Irish Crisis* (1848). Trevelyan shared many Britons' sense that the Irish people were problematic on several counts: they remained predominantly Catholic in a Protestant nation-state, and their continuing poverty seemed to affirm that they were uncivilized 'Celts' whom the forward march of history had evaded. Put another way, as *The Times* wrote in 1843, the Irish lacked all the qualities that had made Britons great: 'Ireland and the Irish have in great measure themselves to thank for their poverty … It is by industry, toil, perseverance, economy, prudence, by self-denial and self-dependence, that a state becomes mighty and its people happy.' The backwardness of the Irish economy was, then, blamed on the lazy and primitive nature of its people. There was no recognition that under British rule Ireland had been starved of capital investment in infrastructure like railways and flooded with cheap textiles that destroyed the cottage production of cottons and linens. Moreover, as agricultural production was restructured around export markets, Ireland's rapidly growing and predominantly rural population were rendered increasingly dependent upon potatoes. This recipe for disaster was complete when a fungal blight devastated the potato crop.

Trevelyan saw this disaster as an opportunity to save Ireland from itself with a sharp dose of liberal political economy. The potato blight was, he wrote, 'a direct stroke of an all-wise and all-merciful providence' that would provide 'the sharp but effectual remedy by which the cure is likely to be effected'. Making the most of this opportunity required that far from enacting a policy of *laissez-faire*, the British state had to actively impose free trade, restructure patterns of land use to make agriculture more productive and teach the Irish the disciplines of the market and the virtues of industry. Thus free trade did indeed bring cheap food to Ireland but in the form of Indian maize that people in Ireland neither liked nor knew how to cook. Meanwhile, so the principle of free trade was not violated, the export of Irish grain continued apace, albeit under armed guard to protect it from a population facing mass starvation. Landlords eager to restructure their estates around high-yield exported crops evicted half a million tenants, mainly smallhold farmers or labourers who were unable to feed themselves, let alone pay their rents. Needless to say, their customary rights as tenants were not protected by the state.

Finally, Trevelyan experimented with various forms of relief designed to keep people alive and yet prevent them from becoming dependent on the colonial state. None were to be supported by taxpayers on the mainland, for Ireland had to be taught to how to support itself. Public works schemes where men were paid below market rates soon had to be supplemented by soup kitchens to feed the women and children whom their wages could not support. Finally, the Irish Poor Law, introduced in 1838, was revised to allow the provision of outdoor relief in the form of food for two months, in return for gruelling menial labour like stone-breaking. Like the **New Poor Law** on the mainland, it was designed to deter people from claiming relief. Even so, by 1848 close to 1.5 million people were receiving outdoor relief and almost a million more were housed in the new workhouses built over the previous decade. In the **Scottish Highlands** famine was subjected to a similar political economy of relief. The government's initial provision of grain at controlled prices was coupled with loans to landowners to set up relief work on their estates under the Drainage and Public Works Act. Yet from 1847 the vast majority of relief was raised by and channelled through the voluntary sector and

Free Church of Scotland in the form of a Central Board of Management for Highland Relief. Influenced by Trevelyan, they introduced a no less bureaucratic destitution test that provided the most desperate with meagre rations of relief in exchange for public works. In Trevelyan's hands the British state developed a new approach that conformed to the principles of liberal political economy. It intervened to open markets and make trade free, while also providing carefully calibrated and punitive forms of relief to populations it had reduced to famine. This approach would be developed further from the 1880s in India, that other land reduced to famine by British rule.

Mainland Britons were unnerved by the spectre of starvation across the Irish Sea. The famine in Ireland was the first to be extensively covered by the press. The reading public, which stretched across and beyond the empire, devoured their grisly reports. The now familiar tropes of famine reporting emerged at this moment (see Textbox 5.2). The suffering of men whose job was to support their families was largely passed over to emphasize the plight of innocent women and children (see Figure 5.3). Newspapers asked their readers to contribute to humanitarian relief funds to relieve those whose suffering they reported – the first such funds came from British residents in Calcutta who raised £14,000 in a few months. In this sense, the history of humanitarianism should not be seen as developing in opposition to liberal political economy, but rather as a compensation for its unequal consequences.

Even some of the most ardent advocates of an evangelically informed political economy, like Scotland's Thomas Chalmers, began to wonder whether the laws of liberal political economy applied to Ireland. **John Mitchel**, the Protestant Irish nationalist, needed little convincing. In a series of articles published in *The Nation* and *The United Irishman* between 1846 and 1848, Mitchel articulated a devastating critique of Britain's policy that was later republished in *The Last Conquest of Ireland (Perhaps)* (1861). 'The Almighty indeed sent the potato blight', he wrote, 'but the English created the famine.' Imposing the laws of liberal political economy in Ireland was, he declared, tantamount to the systematic murder of its people. In 1847 he published a pamphlet with an impassioned plea for a specifically *Irish Political Economy*, one that would not force Ireland's industry and agriculture into a futile competition with mainland Britain. Deported to Bermuda for sedition in 1848, Mitchel escaped to the United States where he defended the South and its system of slavery on similar grounds in the run-up to the Civil War.

That there was an alternative to the gospel of free trade and liberal political economy seemed unimaginable to the organizers of the **Great Exhibition** in 1851. As Figure 5.4 shows, the world's first trade fair was opened amidst much pomp and circumstance, and a throng of 2,500 visitors, by Queen Victoria on 1 May. Both the building, the world's first construction of glass and steel known as the Crystal Palace, and its architect Joseph Paxton, the seventh son of a humble farming family, epitomized the spirit of optimism and the belief in the progress and prosperity promised by free trade. The Great Exhibition was a celebration of, and a monument to, the prosperity and civility

BRIDGET O'DONNEL AND CHILDREN.

Figure 5.3 Bridget O'Donnel and children, 1849

5.2 Source: 'The Condition of Ireland: Illustrations of the New Poor Law', *The Illustrated London News,* 1849–50

On 15 December 1849 *The Illustrated London News* began a series of seven weekly reports on the operation of Ireland's New Poor Law in an area of County Clare which had been ravaged by famine. Launched in 1842, *The Illustrated London News* was the world's first illustrated weekly newspaper, and a decade later it boasted a circulation of 150,000. Its reporting on the condition of Ireland by an unnamed correspondent shows how important it is to read news reports carefully and critically. The correspondent goes out of his way to emphasize his firsthand experience of suffering to establish the authority of his reports, even in some of his 'sketches' ventriloquizing the words of those he interviews. At one level the Irish are consistently portrayed as a subhuman race apart. The homeless of the region, it was reported, had less hope than 'the savages of New South Wales or the Brazils'. At best they made do with makeshift shelters called 'Scalps' (more or less a hole in the ground) which 'resemble, though not quite so large, one of the ant-hills of the African forests'. At the same time, the writer expresses great sympathy for the Irish, and concurs with **John Mitchel** that the ravages of famine were caused by 'vicious legislation' in the name of political economy. The land had been misused, and the **New Poor Law**, inflected with the same principles of liberal political economy that led Ireland to ruin, was not only aggravating poverty, but leading to the very idleness that it was meant to prevent. The writer observes: 'The doubly melancholy spectacle of a strong man asking for work as the means of getting food; and of the fertile earth wooing his labours, in order to yield up to him its rich but latent stores: yet it lies idle and unfruitful.' In also highlighting the innocent plight of women and children, like Bridget O'Donnel and her emaciated children, these articles helped establish one of the most common features in word and image of what became the genre of famine reporting.

spread by Britain's empire of free trade: 14,000 exhibitors from across the world displayed 100,000 exhibits that included raw materials, machinery, manufactured goods and fine arts. Seemingly everything the world had to offer was there – from musical and scientific instruments, lace and linens, fine jewels and wax flowers, furniture and pottery, hydraulic machines and lathes. Yet, if the bountiful world of free trade was on display, it was a world made to revolve around Britain and its Empire, which claimed half of the total exhibition space. The empire of free trade's new international division of labour was neatly staged. Raw materials from across the Empire and around the world came to Britain to be transformed into manufactured goods through new forms of skilled labour and mechanized production. Truly it appeared Britain had become the workshop of the world; it made what the world grew.

When the Great Exhibition closed on 1 October, 6 million people had visited this new cathedral of free trade, close to quarter of the total population of the United Kingdom. The Congregationalist minister, Rev. George Clayton, was so inspired by his visit that he delivered

Figure 5.4 Queen Victoria opens the Great Exhibition, 1851

no less than three sermons about it at his chapel on York Street in London's Walworth. Having warned his flock of the dangers and duties posed by the Great Exhibition in his first two sermons, the third celebrated it as a 'Monument to National Greatness', a 'Stimulus to Diligence and Industry' as well as 'Healthful and Honorable Emulation'. It was also, he insisted, an indication not just of the 'Amelioration' and 'Evangelization' of the world, but a humble example of 'the incomparable brightness and inconceivable splendour' of heaven. It is unlikely that many left the Great Exhibition with Clayton's evangelical fervour. Yet the 4.5 million people who bought the cheapest one-shilling tickets encountered a world of goods and a social world that they would not have seen before. The Crystal Palace encouraged a particular model of sociability. No dogs or smoking were allowed and public bathrooms and restrooms, complete with flushing toilets, were provided. While refreshments of filtered water and baked buns were sold, the Austrian and Saxony Courts distributed free samples of cologne and chocolate. This was an environment in which the civility and self-improvement of visitors was as much on display as the world of free trade, strengthening the association between respectability and liberal political economy.

Of course, like Smith's *The Wealth of Nations*, the Great Exhibition was a promissory note. Carefully planned over the course of four turbulent years wracked by famine in Ireland, economic turmoil, and revolution across the continent of Europe, it represented the world advocates of free trade and liberal political economy wanted to inaugurate. Although there were 300 local committees involved in the organizing, they predominantly came from the manufacturing regions of England and Scotland where the **Anti-Corn Law League** had been strongest. Those at whose expense the triumph of free trade took place – Ireland, the agricultural sector and the world of labour – were conspicuously under-represented. Henry Vincent, one of the **Chartist** leaders sympathetic to the idea of the Great Exhibition, had tried and failed to get working-class representation on its organizing Royal Commission. In their place came frequent rhetorical gestures to 'the dignity of labour' that the satirical magazine *Punch*, started a decade earlier, pilloried in Figure 5.5. Here the well-fed figure of Punch tries to interest a discerning gentleman in the emaciated and distinctly undignified speci-mens of labour – a needlewoman, a seventy-five-year-old male labourer, a distressed shoemaker and a sweater – in display cases. The promise of the Great Exhibition's Machinery Court to summon a world in which mechanization would transform the productivity of labour remained a chimera. If Britain was the workshop of the world, the old worlds of labour, depending upon the skill of the hand and the power of the human body, remained vital to it. The Crystal Palace contained 300,000 panes of glass that were hand-blown and transported from Birmingham on canals in barges pulled by

SPECIMENS FROM MR. PUNCH'S INDUSTRIAL EXHIBITION OF 1850.
(TO BE IMPROVED IN 1851).

Figure 5.5 The Dignity of Labour at the Great Exhibition

men and donkeys. Even though the manufacturers of this glass employed 1,200 men, factories of this size remained rare, as small (and often domestic) workshops predominated in most trades.

Liberal political economy did not usher in an era of free trade as the Great Exhibition would have had its visitors believe. The reduction of both the number of commodities subject to customs and the size of those tariffs that had begun in the 1820s continued with William Gladstone as president of the **Board of Trade** under Peel's administration in the 1840s, but there remained 400 goods on which customs were paid after the repeal of the **Corn Laws**. Fittingly, it was Cobden who, negotiating a trade agreement with France known as the **Cobden–Chevalier Treaty** in 1860, reduced that number to just 48. In fact, for all the rhetoric of free-traders about the moral urgency of unilateral action by Britain, reciprocal or bilateral deals like that brokered by Cobden and Chevalier were more common. When the Liberal Gladstone became prime minister and appointed Bright as president of the Board of Trade in 1868, it appeared that an era of free trade was finally possible. Within the space of a few years, the **Great Depression** of 1873–96 saw a collapse of prices in global markets and led to a return of protectionist policies among Britain's major trading rivals: the United States, Germany and France.

Few would have agreed with **Chartist** Julian Harney that the Crystal Palace displayed the 'plunder, wrung from the people of all lands, by their conquerors, the men of blood, privilege and capital'. Yet his critique captured the way in which the gospel of **free trade**, the product of a particular politics in Britain, became the common sense of the nation. At the same time, it created a new division of labour across the Empire and the globe that for many nations necessitated a return to trade barriers and protection.

An Industrial and Global Economy

For all its wishful thinking, the **Great Exhibition** did accurately stage how Britain's deeply unequal trading relations allowed it to become the workshop of the world. From the 1840s to the 1870s Britain dominated world trade. The pound sterling, with its value secured by the **gold standard**, became the global currency to which others pegged the value of their own currencies. By the 1870s Britain's emerging rivals – the United States, Germany and France – had joined the gold standard. With just 2 per cent of the world's population, Britain produced 40 per cent of the world's manufactured goods and accounted for 25 per cent of the world's trade. The volume of British exports increased exponentially: on an index in which 1880 represents 100, it stood at just 7 in 1820, and then rose to 18 in 1840, 55 in 1860. Most of these exports were still destined for the old European or colonial markets, which pretty consistently accounted for around 70 per cent of them between 1820 and 1900. However, they also made their way to those parts of the Americas, Asia and Africa that were not part of the British Empire.

Britain, however, became not just the workshop of the world, but its distributor and financier too. Transported on steam-powered ships and on overseas railways designed by British engineers and financed by British capital, the reach of British trade extended. Indeed, the world seemed to have shrunk so rapidly that in 1873 Jules Verne's character Phileas Fogg wagered he could travel around it in just eighty days from London. Britain continued to rule the waves after the repeal of the **Navigation Acts** thanks to the development of steam-powered ships. By the 1860s, steamship lines extended across the Mediterranean and Atlantic, and by the 1890s traversed the Indian and Pacific Oceans, as we can see from Map 5.1. By 1900 British ships carried 50 per cent of the world's trade and one third of its total tonnage. Britain's telegraph network followed its shipping lines. By 1908, 56 per cent of the almost 300,000 miles of international submarine cables were British-owned. British capital flowed through these telegraph cables for they enabled investments to be made on the other side of the world at almost real-time prices. Between 1850 and 1914, British capital flooded overseas in the successful quest for lucrative investments that extended far beyond its colonies (see Map 5.2). By 1914 British capital accounted for 44 per cent of investment around the world.

In short, between the 1850s and the 1870s Britain built a new global economic order with London at the centre. Never before had the global economy been so interconnected. This became painfully evident with two successive crises: the **Cotton Famine** of 1861–5, caused by Britain's inability to import cotton from the American South during the American Civil War; and the Euro-American financial crisis that led to the first **Great Depression** of 1873–96. These two crises led to a reconfiguration of that global economic order that would decisively shape the development of Britain's still-industrializing economy.

King Cotton

Textiles, and especially cotton, remained vital to the emergence of Britain as the workshop of the world and depended upon a grossly uneven distribution of labour and wealth. Cotton production increased 5 per cent a year in the first half of the nineteenth century. Seven million spindles were at work in Britain in 1820, and their numbers had increased almost sixfold by 1850. With exports growing at 6.3 per cent each year, manufactured cotton goods accounted for half of all Britain's exports between 1815 and 1840. Even though that proportion dropped to around 35 per cent from 1870, cotton remained the nation's largest export until the outbreak of the Second World War in 1939! While cotton experienced a relative decline as a percentage of total exports, the value of exported cotton continued to rise: in 1815 it amounted to £20.6 million, £30.1 million by 1851, peaking for several decades at £80.1 million in 1872, and rose again in the first decade of the twentieth century to reach £127.2 million in 1913. By the 1850s the flood of

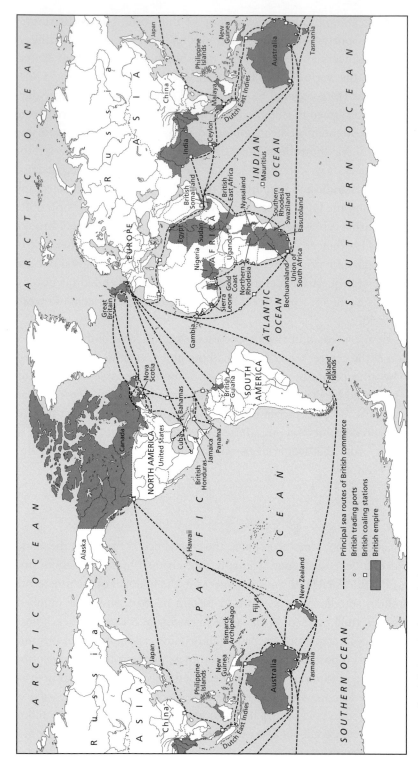

Map 5.1 The global reach of Britain's shipping lines in 1892

Map 5.2   The flow of Britain's overseas investments to 1914

cotton cheaply harvested by slaves in the United States, cheaply mass-manufactured on British spindles, and exported around the world had devastated the once thriving cotton manufacturers in the Ottoman lands, South Asia and China.

Having been the first to mechanize and centralize production in the late eighteenth century, cotton mills continued to increase in size and develop new forms of labour discipline, cost accounting and management systems. If these mills proved the prototype of the modern industrial factory, they did so on a different scale. In 1841 only 21 mills in Lancashire, the heart of the textile district, employed more than 1,000 people each, and these were very much the exception; the average mill had less than 200 employees. From the 1870s a new generation of joint-stock companies built larger and more capital-intensive mills. Whereas mills in the 1820s typically had around 350 spinning mules powered by engines with as little as 48 horsepower, by the 1860s they had 1,200 spinning mules driven by 700 horsepower, and by 1910 the new mills could have 100,000 spindles powered by electricity or massive 1,500 horsepower engines.

Mechanization did not reduce the number of mill workers but it did help change their composition. As we can see from Table 5.3, only agriculture and domestic service employed more people in Britain than the cotton industry throughout the nineteenth century. Women remained a central part of the workforce in cotton mills, as did children until the introduction of compulsory elementary education in 1880. Children accounted for a third of all mill workers in the 1830s. A succession of **Factory Acts** sought to ensure that only those over nine years old worked the maximum of ten hours a day but enforcement was notoriously patchy. As late as 1860, 10 per cent of Lancashire's mill workers were children. In 1851 men outnumbered women in textile mills, but a combination of increasing mechanization and the quest for cheaper labour meant that a decade later this was no longer true. Mills were notoriously appalling places to work. Their ever-larger size, the increasing power of their machines, as well as the need to keep temperatures and humidity high to prevent threads from fraying, made them deafening, dusty and dangerous.

Textile mills had a voracious appetite for cotton that could be turned to cloth. It was sourced from parts of the world where labour was enslaved or cheap and working conditions made those of Lancashire's mills look positively luxurious. At first, cotton harvested by slaves in the southern United States enabled the growth of Britain's textile sector. From 1815 to 1859, Britain imported around 75 per cent of the cotton harvested by slaves in the American South. Such was the demand for American cotton in Britain that more than a million slaves experienced a second **Middle Passage** from the upper to the deep South to produce it. By 1860, 80 per cent of the imported raw cotton in Britain came from the United States. For all the rhetoric of abolitionists, and the continuing efforts of anti-slavery campaigners, few Britons or exponents of free trade questioned the dependence of the textile industry on slavery abroad. It was the American Civil War

(1861–5) that threw this system into crisis. The Confederate southern states refused to export raw cotton in the hope of winning Britain's support, which was followed by the blockade imposed by the northern Union. These events generated a '**Cotton Famine**' in Lancashire. As supplies dried up and the price of raw cotton escalated, thousands of cotton operatives were laid off or placed on short time. By the end of 1862 half a million workers were receiving relief. The small mill-town of Stalybridge, with a population of under 25,000, had 7,000 operatives out of work by 1863. The Cotton Famine dramatically illustrated both the uneven division of labour and the growing interdependence of an emergent global economy.

The loss of American slavery and the bitter fruit of its cotton harvest catalysed the development of alternative cotton sources. There were British schemes to start cotton cultivation in Argentina, but these paled in comparison to the development of production in Egypt and India. During the American Civil War, British capital invested heavily in Egyptian cotton and production escalated accordingly. The average annual yield of cotton in Egypt was 23,035 tons between 1850 and 1859, 65 per cent of which was exported to Britain. In the following decade the average annual output of cotton rose to 76,562 tons, and by 1880 that figure had reached 119,773, 75 per cent of which was headed for Britain. As the price of cotton rose, more cultivated land was turned over to the thirsty crop of cotton, depriving food crops of land and water. New technologies like steam-powered ploughs, packing-presses and gin factories intensified production, while the Alexandria to Cairo railway line ensured that all this Egyptian cotton could be readily available for export. The production of Indian cotton was also decisively reshaped. Despite increasing competition from the finished cotton goods manufactured in British mills, the weavers and spinners of western India still used the majority of the raw cotton grown in its eastern regions. During the 1860s that cotton harvest was quickly redirected to the mills of Lancashire. Whereas 563,000 bales of cotton were imported from India in 1860, by 1866 this was 1,866,610. As early as 1862 Indian cotton effectively replaced that from the United States, accounting for 1,069,000 of a total 1,133,000 imported bales. To paraphrase Gandhi's later characterization of the relationship between the mills of Bengal and Lancashire: Indian pennies were paid to those who harvested and shipped the cotton so that British workers could be paid shillings to turn cotton into cloth, which was sold back to only the richest of Indians who could afford it.

The Rise of Heavy Industry

Just as textiles had inaugurated the first phase of industrialization in the late eighteenth and early nineteenth centuries, the new heavy industries of coal, iron and steel – as well as their progenies, steam-powered railways and ships – ushered in the next phase from the 1840s.

Coal was the king of this industrial age. Already by 1850 the 64 million tons of coal mined accounted for 92 per cent of Britain's total energy consumption. Coal fuelled steam-powered forms of industrial production that, measured in terms of horsepower, became increasingly efficient. In 1850 steam engines generating 300,000 horsepower were widely used, but by 1870 they had been replaced by ones producing 977,000 horsepower, itself a fraction of the 9.65 million horsepower engines used across British industry by 1907. Such was Britain's total dependence upon coal for steam-powered production that its leading economist, W.S. Jevons, published *The Coal Question* in 1865. He warned that coal stocks could be exhausted within fifty or a hundred years, and along with them, 'England's manufacturing and commercial greatness'. And yet, less than twenty years later total coal output had increased to 163 million tons and did not reach its peak of 287 million tons until 1913. Not only was the growing domestic demand for coal met, but coal was also increasingly exported to fuel the attempts of other countries to industrialize. Coal exports grew from 3.8 per cent in 1840, to 15.3 per cent in 1887, to 20.4 per cent in 1903, when they represented 10 per cent of total exports. In the 1860s Britain was producing 50 per cent of the world's coal.

Coal production remained remarkably dispersed and unmechanized. Miners worked coal seams with a pick and axe, and the coal they harvested had to be pushed in carts before it could be lifted from the shaft by steam-engines and sorted by hand. Mining remained a difficult and dangerous job even besides the frequent accidents and disasters that killed and maimed many, and for which there was no insurance or compensation until 1897. About a thousand miners were killed every year by accidents between the 1850s and 1880s, to say nothing of those who died early of various lung diseases. Even though mechanized coal-cutters were available from the 1880s, and underground haulage improved as electricity began to replace steam-power, these innovations accounted for just 1 per cent of total output in 1900. With few productivity gains, the number of miners grew rapidly from 230,000 in 1854 to almost 540,000 twenty years later, and doubled again to a million in 1914. Remarkably, given the total dependence of the country upon coal for both domestic heating and industrial production, it was only after the 1880s that miners began to unionize and flex their industrial muscle. After that, their story became crucial to the rise of the labour movement in Britain.

Coal was critical to the production of another staple industry: iron and steel. Innovation in both the capacity and efficiency of furnaces helped to propel the production of iron and steel and keep their price low. The growth of iron and steel production between 1850 and 1880 was spectacular: iron production rose from 2,250,000 to 7,873,000 tons, while steel increased even more dramatically from 49,000 tons to 1,316,000 tons. Already by the 1860s Britain was producing 53 per cent of the world's iron and was the largest producer of steel. The growth of exports in iron and steel was phenomenal: in 1830 it stood at 118,000 tons, by 1850 it had shot up to 783,000 tons, and 3,793,000 by 1880. Thereafter, exports began to slowly shrink as first the United States and then Germany began producing more iron and steel thanks in part to their adoption of new technologies and production processes. The iron and steel industry was vital to the mechanization of industrial production at home and abroad. It provided the materials that allowed engineers to develop not only the machines that would transform manufacturing, but also the railways and ships that transported products around the world.

Perhaps nothing characterizes Britain's industrial age more than the railway. The iconic opening of the Liverpool–Manchester Railway in 1830 ushered in a remarkable flurry of investment and construction that, as is evident in Map 5.3, two decades later had expanded into a rail network spread over 6,000 miles (see Table 5.1). At the height of this frenzy of development, the railways consumed vast quantities of British capital, labour and iron. Thus, between 1845 and 1850 railways accounted for almost half of domestic investments, consumed close to 20 per cent of Britain's iron output and employed around 4 per cent of its working men. Along with those who operated the trains and track, building the network – cutting embankments, laying bridges, tunnels and viaducts, and building stations – required vast reservoirs of labour. Carpenters, joiners, bricklayers, stonemasons, carters, hod carriers, bankers, tunnellers, as well as the unskilled general labourers known as 'navvies', were all put to work. Infamously poorly paid for long gruelling days, the railway 'navvy' worked on short-term contracts and lived in shanty constructions along the lines he built. Those who worked on the Woodhead Tunnel, carved under the hills of the Peak District between Manchester and Sheffield between 1839 and 1852, were perpetually soaked by water, suffocated by dust and fumes, and plagued with injuries. Over fifty died in its construction, twenty-eight from a cholera outbreak. The great marvels created by the railway engineers were built on the sweat and lives of men like these, badly treated and long forgotten.

If nothing quite replicated the rail mania of the late 1840s, by the 1870s the size of the network had doubled again, reaching into once remote regions like Cornwall, Wales and the **Scottish Highlands**. In 1873, 439 million people and 187.8 million tons of freight were transported by rail, the vast majority by the 28 companies that controlled 80 per cent of the network. That network tied together the country and shrank

Table 5.1 The railway

	Track (thousands of miles)	Passengers (millions)	Freight (millions of tons)
1850	6,084	67.4	
1873	13,981	439.0	187.8
1910	20,015	1,295.5	507.9

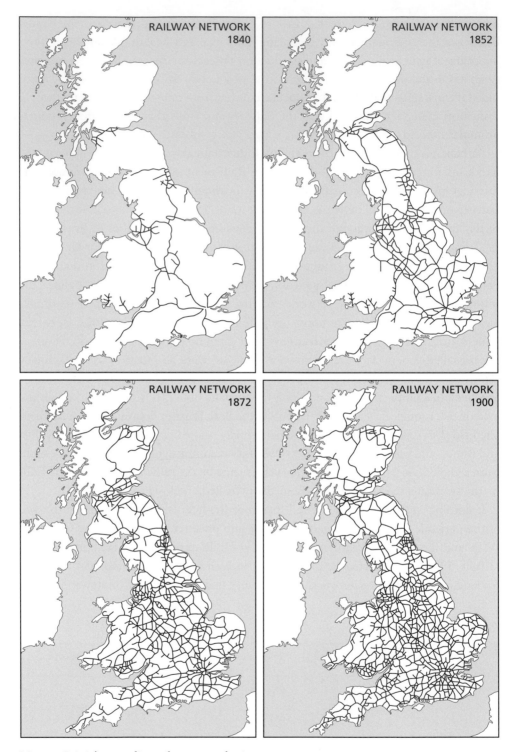

Map 5.3 Britain's expanding railway network, 1840–1900

time and distance in unprecedented ways. In 1750 it had taken eighty hours to travel from London to Manchester by stagecoach; a century later a train could get you there in less than eight. Trade was no longer confined to local and regional circuits or coastal routes. Rail opened up the hinterlands of Britain to new markets overseas. The value of British exports doubled between 1840 and 1859.

Such was the importance of rail for facilitating trade, and such were the potential profits on investments, that British capital, expertise and manpower flooded overseas to develop railways elsewhere (see Textbox 5.3 and Figure 5.6). The export of iron rails, trains and rolling stock quickly followed. The iron web of rail spun around Britain was reproduced across much of the world. The railways of the United States, Argentina, Canada and Russia, to name just a few outside Britain's colonial territories, were largely financed, engineered and equipped by Britons. Overseas railways enabled the transportation of raw materials and foods across great land masses so that they could be imported by Britain and its manufacturers: cotton from the Egyptian delta, corn from the American Midwest, beef from the Argentine pampas, wool from southern Australia, gold from the South African goldfields, timber from the Baltic and Canada, as well as flax from the Russian Steppes.

In India, spurred on by the Great Revolt of 1857 (known in Britain as the Mutiny) and the imposition of direct rule from London, the colonial state did not wait for private enterprise. On the promise of a 5 per cent return, £100 million of British capital had been invested in Indian railways by 1870, and a further £100 million by 1914. More track was laid in the single year of 1858–9 than existed previously; by 1865 the network included 3,514 miles of track and by the turn of the twentieth century it had grown to 25,102 miles and was on its way to becoming the third largest in the world. It was a network that not only facilitated the drain of raw materials from India for British trade, but enabled the rapid deployment of military power to quell future unrest.

The passage of goods and materials on this increasingly global web of rail was connected to Britain by its merchant navy, which still largely ruled the waves. Despite the challenge of the American fleet, the **Navigation Acts** ensured that when British ships set sail in 1840 they carried 29.5 per cent of the world's tonnage. That pre-eminent position was extended with the introduction of steam power and the use of lighter and more durable steel hulls from the 1850s. Steamships represented just 5 per cent of the total fleet in 1850, but by 1874 they accounted for 33 per cent and reached parity with sail in 1903. Yet the tonnage carried by steam, not to mention its greater speed and reach, quickly outpaced that of sail. In 1853 just 250,000 of the 4 million tons of freight was carried by steam, whereas by 1913 just 847,000 of a total of 12 million tons was carried by sail. The tipping point, when the tonnage of steamships exceeded that of sail, came in 1883. By 1890 British ships carried 35.8 per cent of world tonnage. By then, as we can see from Map 5.1, those ships traversed the globe, thanks in part to the opening of the Suez Canal in 1869, which brought Australasia 3,000 miles closer to Britain. The names of British companies and lines – Alfred Holt's Blue Funnel line to

5.3 Person: Sandford Fleming (1827–1915)

Sandford Fleming was an engineer and geographer whose life and career were closely bound up with Britain's imperial expansion in the second half of the nineteenth century. Born at Kirkcaldy in Scotland, Fleming emigrated to Canada in 1845 at the age of eighteen, having studied as a surveyor. He arrived during a formative moment in the history of this vast colony, a period of westward expansion. From the 1820s onwards a number of large joint-stock companies had been building forts and trading outposts that stretched to Canada's Pacific coast. These outposts were formed into a series of autonomous colonies such as British Columbia and Alberta, many of which remained separate from Canada's Confederation in 1867 as a Dominion of the British Empire. Fleming became intricately involved in this process of colonial expansion. By the time he married Ann Jean Hall in 1855, the eldest daughter of an MP and sheriff of Peterborough county in Ontario, Fleming was chief engineer of the Northern Railway. As chief railway engineer for Nova Scotia, he completed the construction of the line from Truro to Pictou under budget and on time between 1864 and 1867. As an early advocate for the construction of a transcontinental railroad, one that would stretch thousands of miles to connect the Atlantic and Pacific oceans and encourage peripheral territories such as British Columbia to join the federation, Fleming was appointed its chief engineer in 1871. His arduous journey across the Rocky Mountains searching for a route was highly publicized as a heroic excursion. When the whole line had been surveyed and 600 miles of the railway constructed, the government handed the project over to a private company, the Canadian Pacific Railway of which Fleming became a director, and in 1883 he crossed the continent on its completed line. During this time Fleming's ambitions moved from the continental to the global. His attempt to create and manage a vast railway network left him interested in finding ways to standardize time-keeping in different parts of the world. Fleming devised a global means of standardizing time across the planet, a system that would be linked to the Greenwich meridian in London. His system, which he called 'Cosmic Time', laid the basis for the twenty-four 'time zones' that presently divide the globe. A deeply religious man, who published books of prayer and service, he and his wife had six children.

East Asia, Cunard to North America, P&O to India and Australasia – were renowned across the world. Shipping was Britain's largest so-called invisible export. It outstripped all the other services sold to other countries, earning even more than the interests *and* dividends from overseas investments until the 1870s.

Finance Capital and Overseas Investments

This second phase of industrialization generated vast profits and a huge surplus of capital. Already by the 1840s, it is estimated that that surplus stood at around £60 million,

Figure 5.6 Sandford Fleming (left) watches Donald Smith driving the last spike of Canada's
Transcontinental Railway, 1885

something close to twice the capital value of the entire cotton industry. As more capital-intensive enterprises, chiefly railways, developed, they generated new opportunities
for investment. Huge speculative frenzies like the 'railway mania' of the 1840s were
invariably followed by 'crashes' and then liquidity crises for the banking system. Boom
and bust was the natural cycle of Victorian capitalism. As we saw in the previous chapter, this encouraged the state to pass a series of Bank Acts and Company Acts between
the 1820s and 1860s in the quest to stabilize the financial system. The liquidity of banks
slowly improved as the smaller private ones went out of business and were consumed
or replaced by larger joint-stock enterprises. There were 327 private banks in 1850,
but just 51 remained by 1900. These banks primarily held the savings of their customers on deposit and invested them in the City's financial markets. They may have
offered short-term loans to businesses, but generally stayed away from making long-
term investments. Even in this age of economic transformation, the vast majority of
British businesses were small private partnerships, often family affairs, with low levels
of capitalization. Most manufacturers employed around twenty people in the 1860s,
and by 1900 this figure had only risen to thirty. When they needed capital investment

they typically turned to family, friends and the marriage market, to find new partners to invest. Partners shared the company's profits and shouldered its losses – bankruptcy was always a real and present danger.

The Companies Acts of 1844 and 1856 made it easier for firms to go public and float shares on the stock market to raise capital, not least by limiting the liabilities of shareholders. Yet remarkably, few companies went public. Less than a thousand had done so by 1856 and by 1868 there were just 2,900 registered public companies. Even by 1885 they represented under 10 per cent of companies and remained clustered around cotton combines, iron and steel, shipping and breweries. Unsurprisingly, then, shares in manufacturing and commercial companies represented a tiny fraction of the securities traded on the stock market. They accounted for less than 2 per cent in 1853 and despite growing in the final quarter of the century remained under 8 per cent on the eve of the Great War.

Despite its minimal relevance to most British businesses, the stock market grew exponentially up to the 1880s. The origins of the stock market lay in the coffee houses of the City of London after the **Glorious Revolution**, but its modern metropolitan form was established in 1801. Provincial stock exchanges also proliferated. Dublin created the first in 1799, but their numbers grew so rapidly after the opening of the Manchester and Liverpool exchanges in 1836 that every major city boasted one by the 1880s. In 1801 London's stock market had 500 members trading in securities amounting to £456 million; by 1851 it had 906 members trading in £1.2 billion; and by 1913 over 5,500 members traded in £11.2 billion. Between 1853 and 1913, the lowest price of purchasing shares fell from over £50 in the 1840s to £1 in the 1880s. Even though the number of those owning these stocks quadrupled between 1870 and 1914, it remained limited to probably no more than 250,000 people. The gentlemanly world of finance capitalism, once so vital to **mercantilism** and the **ancien regime**, embraced the liberalization of trade around the **gold standard** for it facilitated the movement of capital overseas.

Initially, the phenomenal growth of the stock market was based around the development of capital-intensive businesses like rail and banking, as well as municipal utilities like water and gas. Increasingly, however, it owed much to investments in governments, railways and large utilities overseas. Overseas railways alone accounted for 40 per cent of Britain's investments abroad in the final quarter of the nineteenth century. Telegraph networks that enabled almost real-time trades across continents aided this development. When the London and New York stock exchanges were connected by telegraph in 1866 the length of a trade was reduced from sixteen days to twenty minutes. In the 1840s, Britons invested less than £200 million abroad, or less than 10 per cent of all traded securities. A combination of low rates of return on domestic government bonds and the volatility and uncertainty of investing in domestic enterprises (only 42 per cent of the joint-stock companies created between 1844 and 1868 survived) sent investors looking abroad for safer and higher rates of return. Table 5.2 shows how both the scale

Table 5.2 Overseas investments and earnings

	Investments (millions of pounds)	Earnings (%)
1850	264	9.4
1870	1,058	35.3
1900	2,000	103.6
1913	4,000	199.6

of overseas investments, and their rate of return, accelerated dramatically in the second half of the nineteenth century. As a percentage of gross national wealth, overseas assets doubled between 1859 and 1870 to 11.9 per cent, and continued to rise to 21.1 per cent in 1890 and 26.2 per cent in 1910. Like shipping, the invisible earnings of these overseas investments ensured a stable balance of payments and secured the strength of the pound as the global currency.

British capital was spread unevenly across the world, as the most receptive markets and the most lucrative returns changed over time. In the 1830s the vast majority, 66 per cent, of all overseas investments went to Europe. The newly independent and cash-strapped Latin American countries attracted the next largest share at 23 per cent; £30 million were invested in Argentina alone in 1826. By 1854 the balance of British investments flowed away from these regions to the rapidly industrializing economy of the United States, which now accounted for 25 per cent.

The Great Depression

The increasing interdependence of a global economy forged by the unparalleled reach of British manufacturing, transportation and finance was made painfully apparent by the financial crisis that ushered in the **Great Depression** of 1873 to 1896. The immediate trigger of the crisis was over-investment of European capital in rail stock, especially in the United States. On 9 May 1873 a crash on Vienna's stock exchange produced a chain reaction of bankruptcies and bank failures that in turn made Germany's booming banks withdraw their investments in American railways. By September, as the value of rail stocks collapsed, American banks began to dramatically fail. The New York Stock Exchange was closed on 20 September. The day after, nineteen banks went bankrupt. By 1875, $800 million of American rail bonds were in default. Such was the severity of the crisis that in 1873 even the **Bank of England** was forced to protect its reserves by raising its bank rate to 9 per cent. This was 7 per cent higher than it had been in the preceding decades, when the British economy boomed and capital was cheap and abundant.

The Great Depression was a global crisis, but its effects were manifested differently around the world. Britain did not experience the rash of bankruptcies and bank failures so prevalent in Germany and the United States, but neither did she see their quick recoveries. With larger companies investing in newer production technologies, German and American manufacturers began to outstrip their British rivals. In 1870 Britain boasted 32 per cent of the world's manufacturing capacity, almost the proportion of the United States and Germany *combined*. By 1910 that figure had halved to less than 15 per cent, smaller than Germany's 15.9 per cent and the 35.3 per cent claimed by the United States. As global production and supply increased and commodity prices fell, governments introduced tariffs to protect their manufacturers. Russia did so in 1874, Germany in 1879, and the United States extended its tariffs in 1875. In 1892 France introduced tariffs that ended the Cobden–Chevalier Treaty of 1860. Despite losing these markets, Britain kept faith in the gospel of free trade and as a consequence became increasingly dependent upon exploiting and extending its imperial resources to keep up.

In the quest for new unprotected markets, British investments were steadily redirected from Europe to the Empire. During the 1870s, 33 per cent of overseas investments went to the Empire. Two thirds of these imperial investments went to India alone. By the 1880s, 47 per cent of British investments went to the Empire, with 30 per cent bound for developing economies in the white settler colonies and a further 20 per cent to Latin America (where Britain's economic influence rendered Argentina, Chile and Uruguay almost informal colonies). The dependence of the British economy upon the Empire was strikingly apparent. Nowhere was the new form of economic imperialism more apparent than in Egypt. By 1880 Britain received 80 per cent of Egypt's exports, supplied almost half of its imports, and held a third of its debt. As the global crisis sent the Ottoman Empire's finances crashing, Britain first sought to protect its Egyptian trade and investments by taking Dual Control with France in 1879, and then annexed the country in 1882. Imperialism rescued the British economy. The prosperity of its workers, manufacturers and financiers became even more dependent upon the subjugation of others.

If British workers were insulated from the global shock, they were not immune. As demand contracted and prices fell, unemployment and the numbers working short-time rose. By the mid 1880s even the most privileged of British workers, skilled labourers who were members of trade unions, had an unemployment rate of 7.5 per cent. As we will see in Chapter 9, new forms of trade unionism and labour politics emerged during the 1880s to articulate the discontent of working people as a class, rather than organizing around the limited interests of skilled craftsmen. And yet, as wages did not generally fall and the price of food fell, those left in work were sometimes better off during the Great Depression.

This was not true for those who worked in agriculture. In 1868 Britain produced 80 per cent of its own food, but by 1900 it imported 75 per cent of its cereals and 40 per cent of its meat. The land of roast beef imported 68,000 cattle and 230,000 sheep in 1851, but by 1880 those figures had jumped to 700,000 and nearly 13 million. With a flood of cheaper foreign grain and meat imported from the Americas, agricultural output fell from around £250 million in 1871 to £165 million in 1878. Even though it briefly rallied back to £190 million in the early 1880s, farms continued to go bankrupt in unprecedented numbers (700 farms in 1881 alone). Between 1870 and 1911, 2.5 million acres fell out of agricultural production. Those agricultural labourers still in work saw their wages stagnate or fall. Seven and a half million of those who lived in the countryside flocked to the cities or emigrated in search of work. In 1841 more people worked in agriculture than in any other sector, but by 1881 there were more domestic servants than farm workers, and by 1911 transport, construction and engineering, as well as domestic service, were larger occupations (see Table 5.3). Put differently, agricultural labourers represented 20 per cent of the workforce in 1871 but just 8 per cent by 1914.

The Great Depression changed not just the structure of Britain's economy but its society as well. For the first time Britain became a predominantly urban nation, setting the scene for the gradual erosion of the power of the landed classes. Where mercantilists had once seen land as the source of all wealth, it accounted for just a quarter of national wealth by 1878 and a mere 8 per cent by 1914. As land values fell by 50 per cent and rental incomes by 20 per cent between 1870 and 1914, the price of commercial property increased 300 per cent. These catastrophic trends were of greatest consequence for the small number of 7,400 families who owned half of the country in 1871. While Britain insisted on reforming land tenure in India and Ireland, land remained an aristocratic monopoly domestically, despite calls for reform by the likes of the Land Tenure Reform League, the Land Nationalisation Society and the various campaigns for rural workers to have 'Three Acres and a Cow'. So popular was the call of the American Henry George

Table 5.3 Main sectors of employment (thousands), 1841–1911

	1841	1881	1911
Agriculture	1,515	1,633	1,553
Domestic service	1,244	1,994	2,583
Transport/ communication	200	885	1,609
Building/construction	377	877	1,800
Mining	225	612	1,210
Metal industries	410	1,026	1,923
Textiles	883	1,299	1,302

for a land tax that his book *Progress and Poverty* sold 100,000 copies in four years. But with 80 per cent of MPs still connected to this landed interest, it would take another generation, the introduction of an estate tax and the death of many aristocratic young men in the Great War for the old political and economic power of the landed classes to be eroded. That was how, in the last quarter of the nineteenth century, Britain became a predominantly industrial and urban nation.

The World's First Urban Nation

At the dawn of the nineteenth century Britain remained a mainly rural society, with 80 per cent of its 15.6 million inhabitants living in the countryside. A century later those proportions had reversed. In 1901, 80 per cent of a population that had now reached 41.5 million lived in towns or cities. Precisely when the tipping point was reached and more Britons lived in urban rather than rural environments hangs on questions of definition. It was 1851 if urbanity is defined by towns of 2,500 people, and 1871 if that figure rises to 10,000, and 1901 if 50,000 is the measure of an urban area. Any which way, Britain was the first predominantly urban society in the world. **Urbanization** was not a simple consequence of industrialization. Many of those who migrated to towns and cities were not engaged in the new industrial sectors but in construction, domestic service, transport and retail. Indeed, the pace of urbanization only really accelerated in the final quarter of the nineteenth century with the collapse of British agriculture. In 1871 half of Britain's 31.5 million inhabitants remained rural. By 1911 that figure had fallen precipitously to just 25 per cent of 45 million – a loss of over 7.5 million people from the countryside (with the southeast of England, Scotland and Wales hit especially hard).

British cities continued to grow at a phenomenal rate. As we have seen, London was the first city in the modern world to have a million inhabitants, but it again doubled in size by 1841, and by 1881, with 4.7 million residents, it was the size of Paris, New York, Tokyo, Beijing and Mexico City *combined*. The pace of its growth hardly slackened until 1931 when there were 8.2 million Londoners. Throughout this period, London accounted for around 15 per cent of the population of England and Wales. No other city rivalled London in physical size, but plenty of others grew just as rapidly. Manchester was the real shock city of the nineteenth century, prompting Engels to capture the appalling conditions of its shanty-towns in *The Condition of the Working Class in England* (1845). Its population was just 75,000 in 1801 but by 1851 it reached 339,000, and 645,000 by 1901. Similar rates of growth were apparent in a host of other cities associated with new forms of industrial production like Glasgow, Dundee, Birmingham, Belfast, Swansea, Gateshead, Sheffield and Coventry. The same was true of commercial ports like Liverpool, Hull and Cardiff. Even the leisure towns populated by those who had made their fortunes and retired – places like Brighton and

Bournemouth – grew at break-neck speed. In 1811 only London had a population over 100,000, whereas a century later 35 per cent of the population lived in forty-one cities of that size. By 1900 a third of Scotland lived in Glasgow, Edinburgh, Dundee and Aberdeen.

Migration

Where did all these people come from? London was unusual. It served as a magnet for people across the country as well as the Empire. All roads led there, but the streets were not paved with gold. Many more found themselves living or working on them than making their fortunes. When the journalist Henry Mayhew sought to capture the character of London's streets in the 1840s he described 'the wandering tribes' of the labouring poor who populated them. London's population was especially fluid: many of its inhabitants were 'comers and goers', temporary residents who came to the city either when work was slack elsewhere or for the gentry's 'season' of festivities. In 1851 less than half of London's population had been born there. Even permanent residents were often transient figures, frequently moving in the quest for accommodation that was cheaper, better or closer to work. In the 1840s over half of the families in the London parishes of Westminster and St George-in-the-East had lived in their homes for less than a year. A study of Bethnal Green in the 1880s similarly found 40 per cent of its inhabitants had moved within a year. The image of settled communities where everybody knew each other is a nostalgic fiction.

Other towns and cities tended to draw migrants from their surrounding hinterland and counties. Only in the second half of the nineteenth century did the rail network extend the circle of urban migration. The exception was those fleeing from Ireland during and after the famine. The size of the Irish population on the mainland almost doubled in size between 1841 and 1861 when it reached over 800,000. The majority found their way to major urban centres like London, Manchester, Birmingham, Liverpool and Glasgow. Scots too headed south of the border in large but unrecorded numbers. What we do know is that, again like the post-Famine Irish, Scots also emigrated abroad en masse. Ten thousand a year left Scotland in the quarter-century before the gold rushes in California, British Columbia and Australia of the 1840s and 1850s, and those numbers doubled over the next quarter-century. A combination of the clearances and famine ensured that the Highlands lost a third of its population between 1841 and 1861. In the famine years alone, 17,000 emigrated to Canada and Australia, often with the assistance of landlords. Yet even the Lowlands haemorrhaged people, and did so from thriving towns and cities as much as from the countryside as professional people and skilled artisans joined those in search of cheap and fertile land for a more prosperous life overseas. The vast majority of emigration from Britain was to its so-called 'white settler' colonies and the United States of America. Between 1815 and 1850 over 2.7

million head out to this **British world**, but between 1851 and 1881 they were joined by almost 6.5 million more Brits (over 65 per cent of whom headed to the United States).

Back in Britain itself, cities were growing not just by the tide of migration but as a result of their own endogenous growth. The number of Britons continued to grow exponentially after the 1820s. By 1851 the population (including famine-hollowed Ireland) was 27.4 million, and by 1901 it reached 41.5 million. As the rural population remained essentially static until its decline from the 1870s, it was towns and cities that accounted for the dramatic growth. Just in the decade between 1871 and 1881, Britain's urban population rose by just shy of 20 per cent.

Cities became emblems of Britain's wealth, power and modernity. The urban landscape that Britons still inhabit was in large part crafted in the Victorian age. By the 1880s many towns and cities introduced gaslights and widened main streets, built town halls and police stations, laid squares and parks, and boasted exchanges, railway stations, libraries, art galleries, theatres, as well as even cathedrals and the first department stores.

Human and Environmental Costs

Yet behind this veneer of grandeur and civility lay a human and environmental morass. The population may have grown rapidly in cities, but it also died at alarming rates. Infant mortality rates were horribly high and life expectancy strikingly short for urban dwellers. A male baby born in Liverpool in 1861 could expect an average of twenty-six years of life, half that of those living in rural areas or small towns. Similarly, the mortality rate in Scotland's four biggest cities was almost double that of Orkney and Shetland. Infant mortality rates in London dropped quite dramatically the further out you lived. In the 1860s the infant mortality rate at Temple was 190 per 1,000 births, whereas just 18 miles away it dropped to 130 and was just 100 a further 25 miles out. In the first half of the nineteenth century, epidemics of smallpox, typhus, influenza and cholera could quickly decimate the densely crowded urban populations. A cholera outbreak in the winter of 1848–9 killed almost 15,000 Londoners. With inhabitants dropping like flies, the church graveyards of cities were full and overflowing. As bodies were buried on top of other bodies, the dead continued to defy burial. The appearance of bones, putrefied flesh and noxious fumes in crowded graveyards obsessed sanitary reformers like **Edwin Chadwick** whose *Report on the Sanitary Conditions of the Labouring Population* constantly returned to the unhealthy presence of the dead among the living.

Victorian cities were deeply unwholesome places. Until the second half of the century, city streets were awash with animal and human excrement. It has been estimated that London's human inhabitants generated as much as 320,000 tons of faeces and 2.25 million gallons of urine in the 1840s. To this was added veritable mountains of animal waste. Leaving aside dogs, cats and rodents, London's horses alone were producing almost 120,000 tons of manure *every* day at mid century. London's annual supply of meat – 220,000 cattle and 1.5 million sheep by the 1850s – were driven through the city's streets to Spitalfields markets, generating another 50,000 tons of shit. These disoriented animals were then butchered at the abattoirs surrounding Spitalfields. The streets filled with the sounds of their dying squeals as well as the blood from their carcasses. Sanitary reformers managed to get the driving of live animals stopped in 1855, so that by 1868 Spitalfields was reopened as a market for already slaughtered meat. Much of that meat came from a giant new abattoir built down the Thames at Deptford. Removed from the sight and smell of Londoners, within a decade the Deptford abattoir was killing 100,000 imported livestock every year.

With no running water or sewers, animal and human waste sat in cesspools, drained into streams and seeped onto the streets. By the 1850s, London was generating half a million gallons of waste every day. Not even the river Thames could always cope with this tsunami of effluent, as was apparent when it backed up in 1858 and caused 'the Great Stink'. After the passage of the **Public Health Act** of 1848 the sanitary movement was largely successful in transforming the urban environment. Four years after its creation in 1855, the Metropolitan Board of Works had built 450 miles of main sewers in London that connected to an additional 13,000 miles of smaller local sewers. Using gravity and hydraulic pumping stations, this sewerage system flushed the effluent further down the Thames estuary some eight miles from Charing Cross. These sewers also contained pipes for fresh water that was sourced from a new network of reservoirs built in and around the capital between the 1830s and 1880s. Even before the medic John Snow decisively showed that the cholera outbreak of 1854 could be traced to contaminated water at London's Broad Street pump, cities had been seeking fresh and running supplies of water. Six reservoirs had been built in Edinburgh by 1850 – but in the following half-century there were no less than 140 water-supply dams built in Britain. One of the largest, Thirlmere in Cumbria, served Manchester from 1894 via a 95-mile aqueduct. Cities reshaped the rural environment no less than the urban one (see Textbox 8.2). Valleys were flooded and people displaced to serve cities' unquenchable thirst for fresh water.

Although we now associate the Victorian city with the large suburban villas that still adorn streets in Britain, the majority of housing was appallingly overcrowded. The well-to-do flocked to new suburbs that were a respectable distance from, and generally upwind of, the slums that housed most city-dwellers. The grand villas of Headingly in Leeds and Victoria Park in Manchester were developed from the 1820s and 1830s, just as London's gentry classes flocked to the squares and gardens of Belgravia. By the 1880s, rail, trams and the London Underground, developed from the 1860s, allowed the respectable classes to reside in still more distant suburbs, like London's Bedford Park Estate, built to much acclaim in the 1870s. The new suburban villas were replete with bedrooms for each member of the family, separate rooms for dining and entertaining, servants' quarters in the cellars or attics, kitchen and upstairs bathroom with running water, flushable water closets and toilets, as well as no doubt the paper lavatory roll, invented in 1879. The houses of the well-to-do provided light, ventilation, sanitary conditions, space and privacy. Their inhabitants were, after all, fleeing the stench, foul air and what they believed was a deadly miasma of the slums that housed the lower orders.

Built quickly and cheaply, with profit rather than health or comfort in mind, slum housing was packed into courts, alleys and streets. The misery of these slums was well captured by Gustave Doré in the 1870s in his portrayal of the neighbourhood that Charles Dickens had two decades earlier described as 'Devil's Acre' in London's Westminster (see Figure 5.7). Their unventilated earthen cellars were sometimes used as cesspools, but the very poor also lived in them. Damp, cold and overcrowded, most dwellings were occupied by several families, with as many as sixteen to a room, along

Figure 5.7 'Devil's Acre', Westminster, London slum, 1872

with a veritable horde of vermin and bugs. In the 1830s a third of Liverpool's inhabitants lived in cellars. Between 1840 and 1900, 120,000 slums were cleared to make way for railway lines in London, but they were soon replaced by equally densely packed and inadequate constructions. Although philanthropists began to provide 'model dwellings' for artisans from the 1840s, these were usually tenements, which by the end of the century housed less than 3 per cent of Londoners. The Artisans' and Labourers' Dwellings Act of 1875 ensured that local authorities enforced minimal standards of construction and sanitation but did little to increase housing stock. Nor could it compel them to transform the sanitary conditions of the slums. In the late 1860s, 94 per cent of houses in Middlesbrough had only privies, usually connected to ash pits that frequently overflowed and whose contents seeped into the surrounding soil. When Manchester replaced 25,000 privies with self-contained pail closets that could be regularly emptied by the council, it was estimated that each year 3 million gallons of urine and feces were kept from the city's drains and rivers. Still only 15 per cent of Manchester's 67,000 houses had a water closet. Running water and flushable toilets were a twentieth-century experience for many. In 1901, 11,000 houses in Hull still had their excrement removed 'through dwelling rooms to the removing cart'. Even on the eve of World War Two a third of the British population lacked access to piped water.

The pace of **urbanization** in Britain was unparalleled. Vast numbers of people flocked to cities in search of work, settled there and reproduced. It was a trend that accelerated in the final quarter of the nineteenth century as the agricultural sector was hit hard by the **Great Depression**. And yet, as the world's first urban nation, Britain's towns and cities were Janus-faced. They were the sites not just of great new buildings that displayed the new wealth and power of those cities, but of new infrastructures such as roads, lighting and sewers that promised to engineer a higher form of civilization. Yet the vast majority of their inhabitants lived, and often worked, in intolerable conditions that sent them to early and overpopulated graves. No wonder so many Britons chose to emigrate abroad.

Conclusion

If the nineteenth century was the British century, it was in large measure due to the global economic system it forged through the doctrine of free trade. Elevated to the status of a gospel, that doctrine presented political economy in starkly moral terms. Its advocates believed that free trade would bring peace, prosperity and civility to Britain and the rest of the world. Free trade, they insisted, would reward those with industrious and moral characters and discipline the rest. It was a doctrine that legitimated gross disparities of wealth at home and abroad. In Britain it created two nations, those who possessed capital and those who could only sell their labour. It also forged a global economy upon a deeply uneven division of labour where the rest of the world grew and consumed what Britain made. The structural inequity of this system was made possible by what is sometimes referred to by economic historians as the 'comparative advantage' of Britain's early industrialization. In the eighteenth century Britain's early innovations in manufacturing, as well the growing reach of its shipping and finance, were enabled by slavery and colonial trade. In the nineteenth century, the second wave of coal-powered industrialization allowed Britain to become the workshop of the world and export its goods to overseas markets opened up by British gunboats, capital, steamships and railways. The economies of many countries, not just those that were formally colonized, were locked into a new subordinate relationship with Britain. This was the imperialism of free trade.

The Great Depression decisively changed the imperial structure of the global economy forged by Britain in the final quarter of the century. As rival economies like Germany and the United States adopted protectionist policies and began to match Britain's manufacturing capacity, the Empire became the destination of last resort for British goods and capital. Moreover, as agricultural prices fell during the Great Depression, fuelled by increases in global production as well as cheaper, faster and refrigerated shipping, Britain became a net food importer. The promise of free trade to produce cheap food had finally arrived, but it came at the cost of many of Britain's farmers going out of business. Only then did Britain's countryside experience depopulation. While many left to find work or farm overseas, especially in the white settler colonies, most moved to towns and cities. Since 1801 the pace of urbanization had been rapid due to migration and population growth, yet it was not until 1870 that more Britons lived in towns and cities than in the countryside, and by 1900 80 per cent did. Britain became an industrial and urban nation in the last quarter of the nineteenth century. Yet the vast majority of its population lived and worked in dire conditions that meant few lived into their fifties. The British century may have impoverished and subjugated many overseas but neither was it a triumph for its own people.

FURTHER READING

Economic history has fallen out of fashion and has become increasingly technical. By far the best general guide to the questions and themes of this chapter remains E.J. Hobsbawm, *Industry and Empire* (London, 1968). The political and social history is exhaustively covered in the more parochial K. Theodore Hoppen, *The Mid-Victorian Generation, 1846–1886* (Oxford, 1998).

Britain's embrace of free trade under the gold standard as the chief characteristic of the emergent liberal political economy has attracted much attention. The central place of imperialism and the continuing traction of mercantilist thought are addressed in Bernard Semmel, *The Rise of Free Trade Imperialism: Classical Political Economy, the Empire of Free Trade and Imperialism, 1750–1850* (Cambridge, 1970). Boyd Hilton's *Corn, Cash and Commerce: The Economic*

Policies of the Tory Governments, 1815–1830 (Oxford, 1977) remains the definitive guide to the liberal Tory administrations that established the gold standard and slowly liberalized trade. His *The Age of Atonement: The Influence of Evangelicalism on Social and Economic Thought, 1795–1865* (Oxford, 1988) traces the importance of evangelical culture to these economic debates. Paul Pickering and Alex Tyrell's *The People's Bread: A History of the Anti-Corn Law League* (London, 2000) tells you all that you need to know about that organization. For accounts of the subsequent grip of free trade upon the souls, politics and economic lives of Britons, see A.C. Howe, *Free Trade and Liberal England, 1846–1946* (Oxford, 1997), and Frank Trentmann, *Free Trade Nation: Consumption, Civil Society and Commerce in Modern Britain* (Oxford, 2008). Marc-William Palen's *The 'Conspiracy' of Free Trade: The Anglo-American Struggle Over Empire and Economic Globalization 1846–1896* (Cambridge, 2016) recovers the deepening transatlantic arguments over the imperialism of free trade. The calls for economic nationalism in the face of Britain's imperialism of free trade were also evident in Ireland's and India's anti-colonial movements, as told by James Vernon's *Hunger: A Modern History* (Cambridge, Mass., 2007) and Manu Goswami's *Producing India: From Colonial Economy to National Space* (Chicago, 2004).

The Great Exhibition has a number of books devoted to it. Jeffrey Auerbach's *The Great Exhibition of 1851: A Nation on Display* (New Haven, 1999) is the place to start, but questions about the Exhibition's framing of Empire and the global division of labour are best explored in Lara Kriegel, *Grand Designs: Labor, Empire and the Museum in Victorian Culture* (Durham, NC, 2007), and Paul Young, *Globalization and the Great Exhibition: The Victorian New World Order* (Basingstoke, 2009). Of the many books on the Famine in Ireland, I would suggest three: Cormac O'Grada, *Black '47 and Beyond: The Great Irish Famine in History, Economy and Memory* (Princeton, 1999), James Donnelly, *The Great Irish Potato Famine* (Thrupp, 2001), and David P. Nally, *Human Encumbrances: Political Violence and the Great Irish Famine* (Notre Dame, 2011). On the famine in the Scottish Highlands, see T.M. Devine, *The Great Highland Famine* (Edinburgh, 1988).

It is hard to beat Sven Beckert, *Empire of Cotton: A Global History* (London, 2014), or Ronald Findlay and Kevin O'Rourke, *Power and Plenty: Trade, War and the World Economy in the Second Millennium* (Princeton, 2007), as accounts of how Britain's embrace of free trade, enabled by American slavery, quickly produced a new global order. For complementary accounts of the growing importance of the gold standard and British capital in global trade, see Barry Eichengreen, *Globalizing Capital: A History of the International Monetary System* (Princeton, 1996), and P. Cain and A.G. Hopkins, 'Gentlemanly Capitalism and British Expansion Overseas II: New Imperialism, 1850–1945', *Economic History Review*, 40/1 (1987), 1–26. The centrality of emigration, trade, improved transportation and finance to the expanding British world is explored by James Belich, *Replenishing the Earth: The Settler Revolution and the Rise of the Anglo-World, 1783–1939* (Oxford, 2009); Gary Magee and Andrew Thompson (eds.), *Empire and Globalisation: Networks of People, Goods and Capital in the British World, c.1850–1914* (Cambridge, 2010); Marjory Harper and Stephen Constantine, *Migration and Empire* (Oxford, 2010). Chris Otter's 'Liberty and Ecology: Resources, Markets, and the British Contribution to the Global Environmental Crisis', in S. Gunn and J. Vernon (eds.), *The Peculiarities of Liberal Modernity in Imperial Britain* (Berkeley, 2011), is a bracing reminder of how the British world system of free trade re-engineered the global environment.

The most up-to-date general histories of the accelerating industrialization of the British economy are R. Floud and D. McCloskey (eds.), *The Economic History of Britain since 1700*, 2 vols., 2nd edn (Cambridge, 1994), and E.A. Wrigley, *Continuity, Chance and Change: The Character of the Industrial Revolution in England* (Cambridge, 1988). For the dramatic impact of railways upon Britain, see Wolfgang Schivelbusch, *The Railway Journey: The Industrialization of Time and Space in the Nineteenth Century* (Munich, 1977), and Christian Wolmar, *Fire and Steam: A New History of the Railways in Britain* (London, 2007). Raphael Samuel's 'Workshop of the World: Steam Power and Hand Technology in Mid-Victorian Britain', *History Workshop*, 3 (1977), 6–72, remains the best, and most lyrical, account of the persistence of hand technology in the age of manufacture. Sonia Rose's *Limited Livelihoods: Gender and Class in Nineteenth-Century England* (London, 1992) and Carolyn Steedman's *Labours Lost: Domestic Service and the Making of Modern England* (Cambridge, 2009) reminds us how women's labour is so often erased by the focus on heavy industries.

The best general accounts of urbanization in Britain are found in Martin Daunton, 'Introduction', in Martin Daunton (ed.),*Cambridge Urban History of Britain,* vol. III: *1840–1950* (Cambridge, 2000), 1–58, and Simon Gunn, 'Urbanization', in Chris Williams (ed.), *A Companion to Nineteenth-Century Britain* (Blackwell, 2004). Tristram Hunt, *Building Jerusalem: The Rise and Fall of the Victorian City* (London, 2004), and A.S. Wohl, *Endangered Lives: Public Health in Victorian Britain* (London, 1983), provide as good a picture of the hopes and fears, pleasures and miseries, of urban life. Harriet Ritvo's *The Dawn of Green: Manchester, Thirlmere, and Modern Environmentalism* (Chicago, 2009) and James Winter's *Secure from Rash Assault: Sustaining the Victorian Environment* (Berkeley, 1999) remind us that cities reshaped the environment.

6 Practising Democracy

Introduction

After the **Peterloo Massacre** in 1819, few would have imagined that Britain, let alone some of its settler colonies, would have the system of representative politics they did in 1885. Although in Britain it would take until 1918 for all men to be able to vote, in Australia and New Zealand they had been doing so since late 1854 and 1879 respectively. Despite lagging behind its precocious colonies, representative politics in Britain were beginning to resemble what we would today call a democratic system. There were regular elections, votes were cast by **secret ballot**, the treating of voters by candidates and much else had been outlawed as corrupt; the geographical distribution and number of MPs had been made to better correspond to centres of population; political parties had developed national organizations to compete for votes and newspapers provided national coverage of politics. Much also remained radically different from what we consider the democratic forms of politics today. As at Peterloo, a good deal of political activity continued to happen outdoors, on the streets or in mass meetings. Speeches at those meetings were not amplified and could go on for hours. Meetings and campaigns were often unruly and violent affairs. Many continued to believe that those with the vote should use it to represent a broader community (like the family, or a trade) that included non-voters, rather than just their own individual opinions. Nonetheless, if any veterans of Peterloo had still been alive in 1885 they would have had cause to reflect upon the remarkable transformation of British politics.

Politicians in Britain, especially those who belong to the parties that sought to prevent most Britons getting to vote, still like to boast about the nation's history of democracy. When they do so, the expansion of the electorate by the **Reform Acts of 1832, 1867 and 1884** occupy almost as mythical a place as the **Magna Carta** of 1215 or the **Glorious Revolution** of 1688. Britons, we are told, not only invented democracy but introduced it in such measured terms that they were able to avoid the revolutions that swept the continents of Europe and Latin America in the middle of the nineteenth century. Their parliamentary system was so perfected that Westminster became the mother of – and model for – all colonial Parliaments. This story is conceited and wrong. It emphasizes the genius of the ruling class rather than the long struggle by the British people for basic civil rights, like freedom of speech and assembly, and the vote. It is a story that equates possession of the vote and the size of the electorate with 'democracy' as it is understood today in the Anglo-American world. It is an insular national story that neglects to account for the divergent paths of Britain's colonies and the influence of other countries on Britain. It also conveniently forgets that while civil rights and the vote were grudgingly given to some Britons, they were systematically denied to most of those colonized and denied sovereignty by Britain. It is a story that no historian has believed in for a long time.

So how do we explain the transformation of British politics? Certainly the electoral reforms that reshaped who got to vote (at every level, whether for the **parish**, the municipality or Parliament) between 1818 and 1885 are an important part of the story of British democracy. Passed by Whig, Tory, Liberal and Conservative governments, the aim of many of these reforms was broadly liberal. They were less concerned to increase the number of voters, let alone to usher in 'democracy', than to create a particular type of voter. That voter had to be what was called a 'fit and proper person' – that is to say, a man who was able to make informed decisions 'independently', and to be beyond the influence of anything other than his own conscience. These liberal reforms placed the propertied, male individual, and the representation of his opinion, at the centre of a new conception of politics. What were once seen as legitimate elements of the representative process were outlawed as 'corrupt practices' that perverted the truly representative nature of politics. As it was increasingly the opinions of individuals, rather than the interests of a group, that mattered, both the influence of the aristocracy and the unruliness of 'the mob' or 'crowd' were considered illegitimate.

Those excluded from this new system in Britain were left to champion the force of numbers and collective mobilization, most famously in the shape of **Chartism**. Print culture, especially printed petitions and a press made cheaper by lower taxes and cheaper production methods, allowed such movements to connect disparate local groups into national movements. Without question, these processes meant that greater numbers of people became politically active around a larger number of issues than ever before, but the forms of their activity were increasingly channelled (not always successfully) to conform to new political practices. The number of voluntary groups, which would today be called pressure groups or NGOs (non-governmental organizations), seeking a place in civil society and a voice in the new political process grew exponentially. With increasingly elaborate nationwide organizational structures, they campaigned to win the hearts and minds of the population rather than the votes of the electorate. Once legalized, **friendly societies** and trade unions proliferated to address the social and economic issues that they believed the new forms of politics left largely unaddressed.

TIMELINE

1818	Sturges Bournes Act
1819	Peterloo Massacre and the Six Acts
1824	Repeal of the Combination Acts

1828	Repeal of Test and Corporations Acts
1829	Catholic emancipation Birmingham Political Union
1831	National Union of Working Classes and Others 'Captain Swing' disturbances
1832	The Reform Act Electoral Register
1835	Municipal Reform Act
1836	Reduction of stamp duties
1839	First Chartist petition
1840	National Charter Association
1842	Second Chartist petition
1848	Third Chartist petition and meeting at Kennington Common
1851	Harriet Taylor's *Enfranchisement of Women*
1852	New Houses of Parliament
1853	Corrupt Practices Act Repeal of Stamp Acts
1857	Matrimonial Causes Act
1858	Last Chartist Convention *The English Woman's Journal* Removal of Jewish Disabilities
1860	Liberal Registration Association
1861	Repeal of paper duties
1864	International Working Man's Association
1865	Reform League
1867	Second Reform Act
1868	Abolition of church rates
1868	Trades Union Congress

1869	Labour Representation Committee
1870	Married Women's Property Act Conservative Central Office
1871	Disestablishment of Irish Church
1872	Secret Ballot Act Agricultural Labourers' Union
1879	Irish Land League
1881	Coercion Act (Ireland)
1881	Irish Land Act
1882	Married Women's Property Act
1883	Corrupt Practices Act
1884	Third Reform Act
1885	Redistribution of Seats Act

The Mass Platform and the Politics of the Excluded

Peterloo did not crush the hopes of those who pushed for the radical reforms required to make the electoral system more representative of 'the people'. Yet due to the Six Acts, the imprisonment of radical leaders and the austerity policies designed to get Britain on the **gold standard**, the reform movement did not recover steam until the late 1820s. When it did remerge in the form of **Political Unions**, it did so as a broad coalition not solely concerned with the suffrage question but with a host of other issues like the abolition of slavery, **factory reform**, **free trade**, currency reform, the repeal of stamp duties on newspapers as well as the removal of Irish tithes and civil disabilities against **Dissenters**. The first Political Union was established at Birmingham in 1829 by Thomas Attwood, a free trader and currency reformer, who shared much of the radical **William Cobbett**'s analysis of the ruinous fiscal policies imposed by a corrupt and aristocratic oligarchy. Over the next two years around 120 Political Unions were formed around the country, although many were clustered in the growing towns and cities of the Midlands and north of England that, like Birmingham, lacked any parliamentary representation. With a limited membership of just 18,000, they nonetheless organized countless meetings for reform and generated 3,000 petitions that generally called for all adult men to have the vote, annual elections and a **secret ballot**. The motto of the Birmingham Political Union, 'Peace, Law and Order', sought both to keep together a disparate alliance that included all faiths, as well as the urban middle classes and the labouring poor, and to allay the concerns of those who believed any reform of Parliament was dangerous.

The radical and more demotic edge to the reform movement lay elsewhere. Henry Hunt, the veteran of Peterloo, was elected as an MP in 1830 for the borough of Preston where, unusually, all householders had the vote. It was a platform that enabled him to speak for 'the people' in the **House of Commons** and push the case for **universal male suffrage**. Disenchanted by the moderate proposals of the **Political Unions** and fuelled by the ideas of Paine and Owen circulated in Henry Hethrington's *Poor Man's Guardian*, London's radical artisans formed the **National Union of Working Classes and Others**. Its founding constitution in 1831 included a Declaration of the Rights of Man and the insistence 'to obtain for every working man, unrestricted by unjust and partial laws, the full value of his labour, and the free disposal of the produce of his labour'. Cobbett also continued to agitate, not least through his still widely read newspaper *The Political Register*. In 1831 Cobbett successfully defended himself against a charge of seditious libel for an article supporting the widespread rioting that convulsed the countryside between August 1830 and December 1831. Evoking the mythical **'Captain Swing'** in anonymous letters, like those signed by 'General Ludd' two decades earlier, agricultural labourers destroyed the threshing machines they believed were destroying their livelihoods. Clustered, but not confined, to the south and east of England, Cobbett described some 1,400 incidents as amounting to a 'Rural War'. It was certainly one the authorities took seriously: 19 people were executed, 481 transported and over 700 imprisoned. Even without France's July Revolution in 1830, the landed classes' fear of revolutionary ferment was real and their backlash ferocious.

There is no question that the **Reform Act of 1832**, which will be discussed in the next section, would not have happened without these agitations and movements for reform. Indeed, the limited scope of the Act was designed to release the pressure for reform, constrain its extent, and break apart the fragile alliance of the reform movement. By abolishing the worst abuses of the old electoral system, enfranchising not just the previously unrepresented towns and cities but those whom its framers believed were the respectable and propertied 'middle classes', the Reform Act sought to consolidate landed power. In doing so, it specifically excluded the artisans and labouring poor who made up the vast majority of the population. They were considered too vulgar, ignorant and unruly to be part of even a reformed political nation. A new tripartite understanding of class difference was entrenched within the political system. The Whig government of the first reformed Parliament dramatically illustrated the price the labouring classes paid for not getting the vote in 1832. The failure to enforce a ten-hour day in the **Factory Act** of 1833 or to abolish stamp duties on newspapers in 1836, the introduction of a punitive **New Poor Law** in 1834, as well as the creation of new police forces under the Municipal Reform and Rural Constabulary Acts of 1835 and 1839, outraged many who still believed only universal manhood suffrage would render Parliament truly representative of the people.

The Chartist Challenge

By 1838 these various campaigns had coalesced in the **Chartist movement**. The six demands of the 'People's Charter' that gave the movement its name had long been standard banners of radical reform. They were: **universal male suffrage**, annual elections, a **secret ballot**, constituencies of equal size, and the abolition of all property qualifications for, and payment of, MPs. These demands reflected the widespread belief that the economic and social conditions of working people would not improve until they were properly represented in Parliament. Although, like earlier reform movements, the precise flavour and composition of Chartism varied considerably from region to region and locale to locale, its aim was to generate mass support around its platform through meetings and petitions. In 1838 alone, hundreds of thousands gathered at 'monster meetings': 200,000 at Birmingham's Holloway Head and 300,000 at Manchester's Kersal Moor, and perhaps 500,000 at Hartshead Moor between Leeds, Huddersfield and Bradford. While many Chartists believed that the moral force of their arguments and the breadth of their support would win the day, there were those who believed that only the use of physical force could ensure victory. Adopted in 1839, the Chartist motto, 'Peaceably if we can, forcibly if we must', reflected this tactical uncertainty, as well as the distance of Chartism from the Birmingham Political Union formed just a decade earlier. In reality, though, the number of times Chartists armed and used physical force, as they did in the Newport Uprising of 1839, was small and always occasioned a brutally violent response from the state (see Textbox 6.1 and Figure 6.1).

A striking feature of Chartism was the incessant agitation of a new generation of radical leaders, chief among them Feargus O'Connor. During the Chartist agitation of 1839, before rail travel became common, O'Connor traveled 1,500 miles and spoke at 22 public meetings – often for several hours – in a single month. In the 14 months between June 1838 and August 1839 he was on the road for 123 days and gave just under 150 speeches. By this time O'Connor's newspaper, *The Northern Star*, was selling 40,000 copies and claimed a readership of 300,000. Its format – which combined reporting on the local activities of Chartist groups, national politics, letters and poems from its readers as well as sensational crime stories – proved very effective at connecting the dots of the movement with a national mass platform. In Scotland the Chartist newspaper *The True Scotsman* did similar work. By 1839 the first national petition collected 1.3 million signatures, a considerably greater number than those able to vote in elections after 1832. The failure of petitions and mass meetings to sustain Chartism catalysed the creation of the National Charter Association in 1840. The hope was that this would provide Chartists with a stable and sustainable organization as well as one

Figure 6.1 The Newport Rising, 4 November 1839

that could model itself as an alternative and more representative Parliament. The National Charter Association was funded by a quarterly subscription of 2 pence and membership cards were issued to men and women alike. Local branches were formed and encouraged to send delegates to an annual convention that set policy and strategy. By the late 1840s over a thousand localities had sent delegates. Yet petitions and mass meetings remained critical for demonstrating the moral force of Chartism. By 1842 the second national petition collected an unprecedented 3.3 million signatures that covered 6 miles of paper (see Figure 6.2). In Scotland, where ideas of moral force remained deeply informed by a religious spirit, Chartist churches were established to overcome the hostility towards Chartism of the Church of Scotland. At least twenty were established by 1841.

Although Chartism reached the height of its support in 1842, it arguably offered the greatest revolutionary threat in 1848. While revolutions unfolded on the continent of Europe and the horrors of the Irish Famine fuelled that country's nationalist critique, the Chartists held a giant demonstration of 150,000 people after its National Convention in April on London's Kennington Common (now the Oval cricket ground). As we can see in Figure 6.3 the magnitude of the event was captured in the very first photograph taken of a political demonstration. The plan was to march to Parliament to present another petition – this one with 2 million signatures – but the government was so alarmed by the size and timing of the protest that it banned the march and deployed 8,000 troops and police and 85,000 volunteer special constables on the streets of the

6.1 Place: The Westgate Hotel, Newport, Wales

The Westgate Hotel in Newport, Wales, was the scene of one of the largest armed rebellions against the state in nineteenth-century Britain. On 4 November 1839 between 1,000 and 5,000 Chartists marched on the city of Newport, assembling in a small square outside the hotel, where they believed that a handful of their fellow activists had been imprisoned. Newport was on the southern fringe of a major coalfield, and since the beginning of the century the town's docks had become a conduit for transporting vast quantities of coal and iron ore to other parts of industrializing Britain. As a result the city's population grew sevenfold between 1801 and 1831. The events in Newport were born out of frustration with the government's rejection of the first Chartist petition a few months earlier, as well as the recent arrest of the Chartist leader Henry Vincent, who toured Wales in the 1830s recruiting people to the movement. The Chartists arrived at the Westgate Hotel armed with bludgeons and homemade firearms, as rumours circulated among the authorities that they planned to seize control of the city. Many of the protesters had arrived from Welsh coalfields the evening before, and once the scale of the demonstration became clear, the town's mayor called on 500 special constables to defend the city. An attempt by the protestors to enter the hotel led to a pitched gun battle lasting half an hour, during which more than 20 Chartists were killed (the exact number is unclear). After the uprising more than 200 Chartists were arrested, including their leader John Frost, who became the last person in Britain sentenced to be drawn and quartered (a sentence that was later overturned). The square outside the Westgate was renamed John Frost Square in the twentieth century and in 1978 a large mural was commissioned in Newport commemorating the uprising. (S.W.)

Figure 6.2 Presenting the Chartist petition in 1842

Figure 6.3 Chartists at Kennington Common, 1848

capital. While the day passed peaceably, the rejection of the petition, as in 1839 and 1842, sparked a flurry of violent protests across the country over the summer. Some Chartist leaders were in contact with liberal nationalist activists in Ireland, France and Italy, and closely followed the revolutions in those places as well as in Vienna, parts of Poland and the German states, Spain and Hungary. Whereas in the aftermath of 1842 the state had indiscriminately arrested 15,000 people, in 1848 it surgically cut off the head of the movement, arresting just over 150 Chartist leaders in London, Liverpool, Manchester, York, Bradford, Ashton and Edinburgh. Most were imprisoned for two years, some with hard labour, and only those arrested after the Irish Confederate uprising were transported. The British state had not only survived the Chartist challenge but shown itself to be the strongest and most secure in Europe.

Chartism was never again a mass movement but it did not disappear in 1848. A classic combination of repression and reform broke the movement apart. The repeal of the **Corn Laws** in 1846, the passing of the ten-hour day with the **Factory Act** of 1847, the **Public Health Act** in 1848 and the repeal of the Stamp Acts in 1855 helped disarm some elements of the Chartist critique. Those who believed that a liberal political economy of cheap government and **free trade** could finally end **Old Corruption** drifted away from the movement. The Chartist Land Plan, designed by O'Connor to provide plots and votes to working men, was wound up in 1850 and two years later *The Northern Star* ceased publication. The last Chartist petition in 1851 collected under 12,000 signatures. Yet the National Convention continued to meet down to 1858 and was not officially wound up until 1860. The Chartist Julian Harney's unequivocally named newspaper *The Red Republican* published the first English translation of Karl Marx and Fredrich Engels's *The Communist Manifesto* in 1850. *The People's Paper*, owned and edited by another Chartist leader, Ernest Jones, continued to advocate **universal male suffrage** and to expose the coercive and illiberal nature of the state at home and abroad. Marx occasionally wrote for the paper. During the 1850s and 1860s, radical politics fractured. Attention turned overseas with campaigns in support of liberal nationalists like Kossouth and Garibaldi, the North in the American Civil War and socialist internationalism. Yet, domestically, despite the defeat of Reform Bills in 1859 and 1860, the energies of radicalism lay in movements for secularism, cooperation, republicanism and opposing compulsory vaccination.

Reform Movements After Chartism

It was the International Working Man's Association, founded in 1864 and influenced by Marx, that regathered radical politics around the suffrage question through a new **Reform League** in 1865. The Reform League led the agitation for a **Second Reform Act**. It grew immensely in size after the **House of Commons** rejected a reform bill proposed by the new Liberal government, which excluded those considered neither respectable or independent enough to vote, namely the unskilled labouring poor and those chillingly compared to sewage as the 'residuum'. By 1866 the Reform League boasted some 600 branches across the country, although its strength remained in the capital. MPs who supported reform, like John Bright, spoke to vast crowds at their demonstrations. So perturbed was the government by the size of support in London that it sought, unsuccessfully, to prevent the use of 'royal parks' like Hyde Park for public meetings. These events unfolded in a feverish environment marked, as we shall see in Chapter 7, by the brutal suppression of both the Morant Bay rebellion in Jamaica and growing Fenian agitation in Ireland. The debates about who was civilized, respectable and independent enough to vote were influenced by these colonial events. One of the leading opponents of reform, the Liberal MP Robert Lowe, had sharpened his opposition to an extended franchise as an MP in Australia during the 1840s.

The same was true with the **Reform Act of 1884**, which responded to the growing radicalization of agricultural labourers in the wake of the **Great Depression**. As we will see in Chapter 7, the collapse of agricultural prices and land values left tenant farmers and agricultural workers especially vulnerable to evictions by landlords facing falling revenues and rising debts. The **Irish Land League**, established in 1879, was one response to this crisis. Echoing the Tenant's Right League of the 1850s, The Land League's calls for fair rents, fixity of tenure and free sale for tenants culminated in boycotts of landlords and rent strikes. The groundswell of support for the Land League in the countryside helped propel its president, Charles Stewart Parnell, and the Home Rule League to win 63 seats in the 1880 election (over half of Ireland's total 103 MPs). Unsurprisingly, after the 1884 Reform Act Parnell's new Irish Parliamentary Party, purged of many of its Protestant landowning MPs, increased their number of seats to 85 at the 1885 election. 'The Land War' in Ireland was echoed on the mainland. When a sheriff tried to use a force of 50 Glaswegian policemen to serve summonses for eviction to a number of crofters in the Braes region of the Isle of Skye in April 1882, it unleashed a wave of protests across the Highlands and Islands as well as the forma-tion of a Highland Land Law Reform Association League modelled on the Irish Land League. At the election of 1885 the Crofters' Party decisively defeated both Liberal and Conservative MPs in the Highlands. In England and Wales, Joseph Arch established an **Agricultural Labourers' Union** in 1872 to push for higher wages, emigration schemes and the enfranchisement of rural workers. Within two years it claimed over a tenth of agricultural workers as members. A long strike in 1874 ended in devastating defeat and the collapse of the Union's membership, and thereafter it focused on campaigning for the vote. The reform that came in 1884 effectively extended the householder and lodger qualifications of the boroughs to the country, and for the first time included Ireland on the same terms as the rest of the United Kingdom.

All of these movements for reform were dominated by men who campaigned for universal suffrage only for males. Women were, however, part of their mass platform: they helped organize, they attended meetings and they signed petitions. At the height of its support **Chartism** boasted 150 separate women's organizations. Despite the pres-ence of women, these reform movements were resolutely masculine in orientation. They claimed the vote in order to secure a breadwinner's wage that could support wives and daughters at home. Female domesticity was the proof of male respectability and independence.

Until the formation of the **National Union of Women's Suffrage Societies** in 1887, the voices in support of women voting came from rarefied circles, not a mass platform. Harriet Taylor, fresh from marrying John Stuart Mill (see Textbox 6.2 and Figure 6.4), published *The Enfranchisement of Women* in 1851. Soon afterwards, a group of elite women launched *The English Woman's Journal* in 1858 and established a committee room and library at London's Langham Place. This **Langham Place Circle**, as it became known, focused less on the suffrage question than on securing women's basic legal and civil rights to own property, get divorced, as well as have access to universities and the medical profession. The campaigns of these groups were remarkably successful. The **Matrimonial Causes Act** of 1857 ensured that divorce cases no longer had to be held in Parliament, although the legal expenses involved in proving adultery, bigamy, cruelty or desertion were so onerous that few could afford it. Moreover, the Act reinforced the double standard by ensuring that even those women who could afford to do so

6.2 Person: John Stuart Mill (1806–1873)

John Stuart Mill was born in 1806, the the eldest son of the Scottish non-conformist, Benthamite reformer, historian and administrator of British India, James Mill. James obsessively and deliberately applied his own philosophical beliefs about the infinite mutability of the young mind and assumed the task of educating his nine children himself. As a young man John Stuart Mill met many of the intellectual luminaries of his age, such as David Ricardo, Jean-Baptiste Say and Auguste Comte. At the age of seventeen he was appointed as an administrator of the British East India Company, a position he held until the Company was abolished in 1858 and one that did not prevent him from regularly publishing essays and books on questions of philosophy, political economy and literature. In 1826 Mill suffered a nervous breakdown that many have read as indicative of the complex relationship he had with his father and his Benthamite training. Upon recovering, he fell in love with Harriet Taylor in 1830, although she was married and had two children. They courted each other in public and private until Harriet's husband died in 1849. They married in 1851, the same year as Taylor published *The Enfranchisement of Women*. Taylor deeply influenced Mill's work. After Taylor's death in 1858, Mill threw himself into political activism, becoming a Liberal MP in 1865 and campaigning for women's suffrage. Mill embodied the complexity and changing contours of liberal thought. Although he had advocated for the **secret ballot** in the 1830s, he argued against it in the 1850s, insisting that voting should be seen as a trust rather than a right. Having initially embraced Ricardo's wage-fund theory – that, as capital was finite, wages would always be limited by the size of the working population – he renounced it in 1869. A fierce advocate for civil rights and representative forms of government, he nonetheless defended colonialism on the grounds that not all were ready for its responsibilities, while also insisting during the Governor Eyre controversy following the Morant Bay rebellion that colonial rule had to uphold the rule of law. Mill died a wealthy man with an estate valued at £14,000, of which £6,000 was bequeathed to women's education. (K.H.)

could not divorce men for adultery. The ancient universities of Oxford and Cambridge and Edinburgh began to open their exams to women in the 1860s and eventually to establish separate women's colleges from the 1870s (Girton College, Cambridge, was the first in 1869). In 1873 Elizabeth Garret Anderson became the first woman doctor to be recognized by the British Medical Association. Scotland's ancient universities were a little slower to follow, despite the formation of Ladies' Educational Associations in the late 1860s, with Edinburgh, Glasgow, Aberdeen and St Andrews admitting women only from 1892. The **Married Women's Property Acts** of 1870 and 1882 gave women a separate legal personality from their husbands, enabling them to inherit and own property as well as to earn income from it. In 1884 the law that allowed wives to be imprisoned for refusing to have sex with their husbands was revoked.

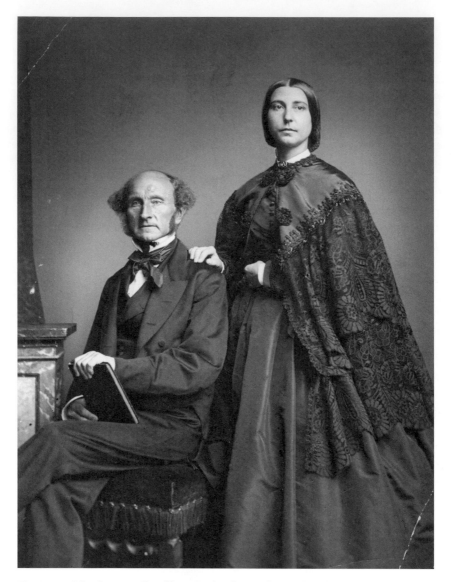

Figure 6.4 John Stuart Mill and his step-daughter Helen Taylor, 1860

These campaigns went a long way to establish that women were not the property of men and should share their rights to education and employment. Yet the issue of women's suffrage remained such anathema that when a group of women organized a petition for it during the debates surrounding electoral reform in 1866 they collected just 1,499 signatures (60 with Scottish addresses). When the **Reform Act of 1867** reaffirmed the exclusion of women from the vote, it catalysed the creation of the National Society for Women's Suffrage in 1868 and the Irish Women's Suffrage Society in 1872. It was, however, the Married Women's Property Act of 1870 that first enabled women to vote as propertied individuals in the school board elections that were inaugurated with the introduction of national elementary education in 1870. After that, as we shall see in Chapter 9, the number of women voting at local elections slowly grew.

Dissenters and non-conformists were heavily represented in most reform movements. Yet, unlike the mass movement for **Catholic emancipation** in Ireland, the removal of civil disabilities for Jews and those Protestants outside the Anglican Church were not achieved by large-scale protests. The Repeal of the **Test and Corporation Acts** and Catholic emancipation in 1828 and 1829 opened up public offices to non-Anglicans but hardly heralded an end of the Anglican establishment. Non-Anglicans continued to have to pay church rates to maintain the local church until this was made voluntary in 1853 and eventually abolished in 1868. From 1833 the state provided funds for Anglican schools, although that funding was extended to Methodist and Catholic Schools in 1847, and Jewish ones from 1853. Jewish disabilities to public office were finally removed in 1858, as were the remaining barriers for non-conformists to teach or study at Oxford or Cambridge in 1871. Only in 1888, eight years after the election of the radical MP and atheist Charles Bradlaugh, was the necessity of MPs swearing a religious oath rescinded. Unlike Ireland, where the Protestant Irish Church was disestablished in 1871 (as was the Anglican Church in Wales from 1920), Anglicanism remained the authorized state religion whose bishops continued to sit in the House of Lords. Indeed, the state continued to provide funds to support the Anglican Church across its Empire.

Reforming the Electoral System

Although the 'Great' **Reform Act of 1832** was often identified as the key turning point, it was the restructuring of **parish** voting by the **Sturges Bourne Act** in 1818 that both started and set the tenor of electoral reform. Most Britons' experience of politics began in the parish with meetings at the church **vestry**. Based upon customary practices that varied from place to place, meetings of most parish vestries were open to either all rate-payers or to all householders, women as well as men. With the rising tide of disaffection after the **Napoleonic Wars**, the demotic potential of these vestries worried the Tory government. As the only form of urban government in the newer and rapidly expanding towns and cities, as well as possessing responsibility for administering the growing bill for poor relief, they were of especial concern. The Sturges Bourne Act therefore introduced a new sliding scale of voting at parish meetings so that the more property one owned the more votes one possessed, regardless of where one actually lived. Those who did not pay rates were excluded from even attending parish meetings. Property, not residence, became the principle of representation; or, more accurately, the principle of excluding many from the electorate.

Propertied and Male

The Great **Reform Act**, passed in 1832 by a Whig government in the hope of dividing and thus taking the wind out of the sails of the reform movement, was a similar con-juring act. Passed separately but to the same effect in Scotland and Ireland, the Reform Act standardized the right to vote around property. The myriad forms of inherited and customary rights to vote that, as we saw in Chapter 1, had previously character-ized the electoral system were eradicated. They were replaced by a uniform property qualification, albeit one that differed between the urban 'borough' and rural 'county' constituencies. In the boroughs, householders who either owned or rented a property worth £10 a year qualified to vote. In the counties the franchise was primarily con-solidated around those whose freehold property was worth 40 shillings a year, but it was also granted to those who leased or rented properties of £50 per year and those whose copyhold tenure was worth £10 a year. Just as significantly, the right to vote was restricted to 'male persons only' for the first time (in Scotland, where married women could possess property, some men qualified to vote as husbands of propertied women!). Although there is little evidence that women ever voted in large numbers at parliamentary elections, they were not specifically excluded until 1832. Although the size of Britain's electorate increased from around 516,000 to about 813,000, a good deal of that increase was accounted for by the 'ancient right' voters who were grand-fathered into the new system. Their qualifications were eradicated in 1832 but they continued to vote until they died. In some constituencies this meant that the initial growth of the electorate after 1832 was checked and even declined in the following decades. The most significant change came in Scotland, where the electorate went from around 4,500 to 64,447 overnight, a growth of 1,400 per cent, whereas the Irish electorate rose modestly from from 49,000 to 92,142 in 1832. Voters in England and Wales represented almost 81 per cent of Britain's total electorate, with Scotland's voters accounting for 7.9 per cent and Ireland's 11.4 per cent.

The Reform Act also sought to redistribute the number of voters, and the MPs they elected, more evenly across the country. Before 1832 the majority of MPs were returned from the south of England, often from underpopulated areas, in constitu-encies with less than a hundred electors. The Reform Act abolished 56 of the most infamous **rotten or pocket boroughs** whose often diminutive electorates returned 111 of the 558 MPs in the **House of Commons** before 1832. Thirty other constit-uencies were reduced to electing one, not two, MPs. In total the seats of 144 MPs were removed. These seats were redistributed among 63 new borough seats created in the growing urban areas of the Midlands and northern England as well as 26 rural counties (which generally were the larger old counties split in half and given two additional MPs). The total number of MPs from England dropped by 17, 8 of which went to Scotland, 5 to Ireland and 4 to Wales. If geographical redistribution changed the electoral of map of Britain, it did not create constituencies of similar size in which each vote had the same representational power. There remained 35 constituencies with fewer than 300 voters, while Liverpool's electorate was 11,000 strong. Indeed, the number of MPs elected by boroughs actually fell from 465 to 399 whereas the number of those returned by the counties rose from 188 to 253. This was designed to preserve the 'influence' of the landed aristocracy in the rural counties and the older and smaller boroughs, and to prevent their clout from being overwhelmed by the growing middle classes from the urban areas of the industrializing north. In 1833 the British electorate represented just 7 per cent of the adult population: one in five adult men got to vote in England and Wales, as opposed to one in eight in Scotland, and a wretched one in 20 in Ireland. The conservative framing of the Reform Act protected as much as it displaced the **ancien regime**. No wonder the **Chartist** movement developed to push for further reforms, including giving all adult men the vote and equalizing the size of constituencies.

The Reform Act conformed to the principle that only men of property should vote, first established by the **Sturges Bourne Act**. It was a principle that was further consolidated in the **New Poor Law** of 1834 and the **Municipal Corporations Act** of 1835, and subsequently in the Second and Third **Reform Acts** of 1867 and 1884. Unlike in Scotland where the Burgh Act of 1833 enabled all householders to vote, the Municipal Corporations Act of two years later removed customary rights of voting from those in old incorporated towns and provided a uniform entitlement to all male ratepayers. Similarly, only male ratepayers could vote in elections for the Boards of Guardians, who ran the Poor Law Unions after 1834. Yet, as with the provisions of the Sturges Bourne Act, they did so on a sliding scale according to the rateable value of their property (and absentee ratepayers were allowed to vote by proxy).

Ironically it was Britain's colonies that pushed for a more demotic franchise, albeit to establish firmer hierarchies of gender and racial difference. The exception, as normal, was Ireland. In the wake of the catastrophe of the Irish Famine, wide disparities of property valuation and stricter registration requirements, the county electorate in Ireland shrank from about 75,000 to around 27,000. The Irish Franchise Act of 1850 sought both to create a better registration process around a uniform propertied qualification for male voters and to increase the size of the electorate. It did so by reducing the propertied qualification from £10 to £8 in the boroughs and £12 in the counties, while also opening the franchise to those who occupied rather than owned those properties. Although the electorate tripled in size overnight, this still allowed only 10 per cent of adult males in Ireland to vote. It was a different story in Britain's white settler colonies of Australia, New Zealand, Canada and the Cape where, as earlier in the American and

Caribbean colonies, the suffrage question was intimately related to claims of sovereignty and racial superiority.

The Atlantic territories in North America and the Caribbean colonized in the seventeenth century had been afforded limited self-government through a system that was designed to mirror Britain's own representative system. They generally had a Governor-General appointed by the Crown, a Legislative Council whose members were selected by the Governor-General, and a House of Assembly with representatives elected by a small number of white, male, propertied and often specifically Protestant voters. In addition, many of these colonies had a system of local **parish** government in which male householders had a vote. After the **American War of Independence** this system of partial self-government fell out of favour in London. It was only gradually reintroduced to the Australian colonies from 1850, New Zealand in 1852 and the Cape Colony in 1854. Nova Scotia, which had an elected Assembly from 1758, was the first colony to decouple the franchise from a limited property qualification: in 1851 the vote was extended to all white men who had paid taxes in the previous year, and three years later **universal male suffrage** was introduced. Given that indigenous men as well as white men on poor relief or employed by the colony were denied the vote, it was not quite universal! Nonetheless, this was the most inclusive franchise of not just all the Canadian colonies, but of the entire British colonial world. It lasted just nine years. By 1863 restrictive property qualifications were reimposed, and this was the norm across the other colonies that became part of the Confederation in 1867. It took almost twenty years for Canada to establish a uniform propertied franchise across its provinces in 1885 and it was one that continued to exclude women and, with some partial exceptions, indigenous peoples.

In the Australian colonies property qualifications that limited the number of white male voters were dispensed with shortly after the creation of representative Parliaments in 1850. Southern Australia led the way in 1856, followed quickly by Victoria and New South Wales in 1857 and 1858, while in Queensland and Western Australia it did not happen until 1872 and 1893. Giving the vote to all of Australia's white men emphasized that their independence and industry gave them a stake in the colony, and helped to cast off the country's old associations with the penal colony. Yet it also distinguished them from Aboriginal men, who were deemed unable to claim sovereignty over their land, let alone to be fit and proper persons to vote in a new and alien system of government.

In these settler societies the suffrage – and its demotic reach – became inseparable from asserting the importance of masculinity in assuming sovereignty of a land that had been colonized from indigenous populations. Indigenous claims to land and citizenship were less easily ignored or erased in New Zealand and the Cape. White settlement in New Zealand catalysed a series of deadly Musket Wars between Maori tribes that stretched from 1807 to 1842. The Treaty of Waitangi, signed in 1840, helped facilitate the end of these conflicts by ostensibly guaranteeing Maori possession of their lands in exchange for becoming subjects of the British sovereign. Yet the disputed nature of sovereignty, together with land grabs by the New Zealand Company and Church Missionary

Society, fuelled the first armed conflicts between Maori and British settlers between 1842 and 1846. In this context the New Zealand Constitution Act of 1852 afforded self-government through an electorate that was determined by property qualification. Maori communal ownership of land excluded all but 100 of them, who possessed property as individuals, from this franchise. Maori were also afforded four reserved seats on the legislative council appointed by the Governor-General. After another series of wars between Maori and settlers that culminated with 18,000 British troops on the islands in the 1860s, Maori were given separate 'communal' electorates and four reserved seats from a total of sixty-one in the parliament of 1867 (see Textbox 6.3). Little more than a decade later in 1879, all adult white male New Zealanders were enfranchised. If disputed

6.3 Source: Maori Representation Act, 1867

In the mid nineteenth century New Zealand witnessed a demographic upheaval triggered by mass settler migration and indigenous depopulation as a result of disease and war. In 1840 the white (Pakeha) settler population of New Zealand numbered just 2,000, with a Maori population estimated to be 100,000. By 1881, the Maori population had decreased to 46,750 set against a Pakeha population of 487,280. This reversal of the position of the Maori population was reflected in their disavowal in the Government of New Zealand Act of 1852 which, in applying a property qualification to individual voters, effectively excluded Maori from the franchise. It was only in 1867 when the Maori population had been decimated and militarily defeated that the Maori Representation Act awarded **universal male suffrage** to Maori over twenty-one years of age to elect four reserved seats out of a total of sixty-one in Parliament 'for the better protection of the interests of Her Majesty's Subjects of the Native race'. (For the text of the Maori Representation Act, see www.enzs.auckland.ac.nz/document.php?wid=810&action=null.) The Act, which variously uses the term native, Aboriginal and Maori, specified that 'half-castes' were also included

in the measure, which it emphasized was introduced as a temporary experimental measure for five years (it was made permanent in 1876). Yet the text of the Act tells us remarkably little about how Maori men were to be polled, other than stipulating that they would be so within four geographically defined provinces that did not necessarily correspond to prior forms of indigenous authority. Thus until 1948, there was no fixed electoral roll for Maori voters, due, it was alleged, to illiteracy, language barriers and the transient, non-propertied nature of Maori communities. Most interestingly, perhaps, Maori voters were not awarded a **secret ballot** until 1938, sixty-eight years later than Pakeha voters. The Maori community were not yet deemed capable of becoming liberal political subjects. The Act, published in Wellington under the authority of the New Zealand government, is a reminder that legislation rarely betrays why it was passed or how it operated in practice. In fact, it occludes the role that Maori themselves played in a complex process of negotiation and contestation which has continued around claims to sovereignty, citizenship and separate electorates to this day. (S.W.)

treaties and war were the backdrop for the calibration of suffrage and sovereignty in New Zealand, the Cape Colony provided a still different picture. When the Cape established a system of representative government in 1853, it did so with a franchise that was effectively colour-blind. Black Africans and 'coloureds' who met the relatively low property qualification (which included communal lands) were given the right to vote, a right upheld in 1874 and 1878 when it was challenged by those representing British white settlers in the Eastern Cape.

Unlike the increasingly expansive, if racially marked, male franchises of Britain's settler colonies, the Second and Third **Reform Acts** of 1867 and 1884 were slow and less generous in their definition of which Britons were 'fit and proper persons' to vote. Passed by the Conservative Party in the hope of outflanking their Liberal rivals and restraining the extent of reform, the Second Reform Act reduced the thresholds of the value of property that qualified one to vote. The borough franchise was extended to all ratepayers as well as to lodgers paying at least £10 per year in rent. In the counties those occupying property rated at £12 per year (or £14 in Scotland) as well as those owning land worth £5 a year got the vote. Less than twenty years later, the Third Reform Act removed the county and borough divide, giving the vote to all ratepayers and lodgers occupying properties worth £10 a year wherever they lived.

The 1867 and 1884 Reform Acts had much greater consequences for the size of the electorate than the first Reform Act. Population growth and the inflation of property values meant that the electorate had grown to 1,310,000 on the eve of the Second Reform Act, but by 1868 it had almost doubled to 2,500,000. In England, Wales and Scotland, one in three adult males now possessed the vote, while in Ireland only one in six did. The Third Reform Act accelerated the trend, increasing the electorate to 5,600,000 so that it included two in three adult males in England and Wales, three in five in Scotland and one in two in Ireland. It is often forgotten that the greatest effects of these reforms in terms of the expansion of the number of voters were in Scotland (which had its own Reform Act in 1868) and Ireland. Still, more than 70 per cent of British adults remained disenfranchised in 1885. They were denied citizenship by qualifications that, besides gender, continued to link the vote to the value of property owned or occupied. By 1885, the list of countries, not including Britain's own colonies, that had abandoned such constraints and granted all men the vote was long: Switzerland (1848), Denmark (1849), Colombia (1853), Greece (1864), Spain (1869), USA (1870), Germany (1871) and France (1875).

The redistribution of MPs to lessen the huge discrepancies in the size of constituencies also continued. The English, Welsh and Scottish reforms of 1867 and 1868 got rid of 11 boroughs, reduced a further 35 to returning one MP and merged two Scottish counties. This made 53 seats available for redistribution: nine were awarded to new boroughs, one to the University of London, eight additional seats were given to existing ones (Birmingham and Manchester, for example, now elected three rather than two

MPs) and 25 additional seats were given to the counties. A special Act was introduced in 1885 that went still further, edging ever closer to creating single-member constituencies of similar sizes as the national norm. Whereas there had been 240 constituencies returning two MPs in 1832, by 1885 there were just 27. This was achieved by merging 103 boroughs with counties, reducing 39 boroughs to returning one MP and disenfranchising two boroughs, each of which had returned two MPs. Of the 138 seats this made available, an additional 40 went to London alone, a further 37 went to other existing boroughs and six new single-member boroughs were created. The counties received an extra 74 MPs – 66 of them in England and Wales – continuing the trend established in 1832 of maintaining or enhancing their electoral power. Advocates for more proportional forms of representation, or even constituencies with the same number of electors so that each vote would have the same weight wherever it was cast, did not succeed. In its distribution of seats, Britain's electoral system remained wedded to representing communities and places, not simply individuals. At the same time, some individuals – those considered the most 'fit and proper' – were awarded more electoral power than others. Such was the case with seats afforded to universities so that their students and graduates could vote twice: once in the **constituency** of their home residence and once in the university constituency. The same was true of business owners who could vote both where they owned a business and where their home was. By 1914 half a million people got to vote twice, while close to 60 per cent of Britons still did not get to vote at all.

Despite these limitations, the various Reform Acts did create new classes of voters. As the allegiance of voters could not be taken for granted, election contests became more frequent affairs. The Reform Acts did not change the frequency of general elections (as opposed to by-elections, usually caused by the death of a sitting MP), which since the Septennial Act of 1716 occurred every seven years. Yet, gradually, parliaments were dissolved and elections held more frequently: by 1867 general elections were held on average every five years, and that fell to four by 1884. It was only in 1911 that the maximum length of a parliament between elections was reduced to five years. Before 1832 it was actually unusual for a **constituency** to have a contest when a general election was called. This was especially the case outside England. In the election of 1830, only 239 Scots got to cast their vote and not a single Welsh elector. Even in England and Wales only half of the constituencies had contested elections between 1832 and 1867. As the electorate increased, so did competition for the loyalties of new voters. After 1867, 70 per cent of constituencies had contests and after 1884 that increased to 80 per cent. Such was the gathering frequency that their growing political and cultural importance was reflected in a host of novels that sought to capture their atmosphere. Perhaps the most iconic were Charles Dickens's *Pickwick Papers* (1837), George Elliot's *Felix Holt* (1866) and Anthony Trollope's *Ralph the Heir* (1871) – a thinly veiled account of his own unsuccessful campaign to get elected as MP for Beverley in 1868.

A New Electoral Culture

These novels recognized that the changing culture of elections was just as significant as the expansion and redistribution of the electorate. The electoral reforms that were introduced between 1818 and 1885 did not just constrain the numbers able to vote but determined how elections should be conducted and understood. Traditionally elections had been about candidates as well as voters and non-voters alike, deploying 'influence' to manage the balance of 'interests'. Although few had the vote, those who did were entrusted to use it in such a way as to virtually represent the interests of those who could not vote. While many continued to uphold this view of elections, increasingly the reform of the electoral process at the **parish**, municipal and parliamentary levels prioritized opinion over influence, and the representation of individuals not interests. Those without the vote were deliberately excluded from elections where voters acted as individuals, answerable only to their own conscience. Novelists from Dickens to Trollope therefore invariably focused on those elements of elections that were coming to be understood as illegitimate, namely unruliness, violence and 'corrupt practices'.

Electors were now expected to consider the vote as their own to use as they alone saw fit. Great efforts were made to insulate them from the 'undue influences' that became defined as 'corruption', regardless of whether they emanated from the unruly 'crowd' or the generous patron. No less than six bills against corrupt practices were moved and defeated in Parliament between 1806 and 1842, showing how deeply entrenched the 'unreformed' electoral culture still was. The tide turned with the passage of the **Corrupt Practices Act** of 1854. Thereafter, election expenses were officially audited, albeit ineffectively, and small fines were introduced for bribery, treating and intimidation. A further Act in 1883 outlawed the employment of election workers, placed limits on election expenses and imposed harsher penalties upon candidates (not their agents), including imprisonment and exclusion from voting or holding public office for seven years. Trollope spent £400 trying to get elected in Beverley in 1868 and still came in at the bottom of the poll in a **constituency** that two years later was disenfranchised for wholesale corruption. Shorn of the ability to hire or treat voters or non-voters, the costs of fighting an election campaign fell. Official returns showed that candidates spent £1.8 million on the election campaign in 1880, a striking figure compared to the £750,000 spent during the 1895 election. Within the space of a generation, a new understanding of corruption had begun to transform how elections were conducted.

Elections, and the act of voting itself, were transformed in other ways to make them less rowdy affairs, in which the voter was protected from undue influences. The creation of the **Electoral Register** in 1832 ensured that electors' right to vote was tested in court before the election, not on the **hustings** during it. The length of the poll, reduced to eight days in 1828, was set at just sixteen hours over two days in 1832. Instead of one central hustings, like that in Figure 6.5, that attracted a large crowd who kept electors

SCENE AT THE HUSTINGS IN THE DAYS OF OPEN ELECTION.

Figure 6.5 The hustings: voting in public

accountable for their vote, a hustings now had to be built for every six hundred electors. Increasingly, the tradition of open voting in public was challenged. The **New Poor Law** and the **Municipal Corporations Act** introduced new ways of voting in private. Ballot cards were distributed to electors at home and were then either returned by hand, by post or were collected by paid agents. Privacy, not secrecy, was the issue: the illiterate needed help completing their ballots. The point was to take the act of voting off the streets where voters could be intimidated or influenced and unruly crowds could gather.

The introduction of the **secret ballot** was the apogee of this process of sanitizing elections for the individuated voter. It was first introduced for school board elections in 1870 and for municipal and parliamentary elections in 1872. Following the Australian model practised since 1856 and adopted by New Zealand in 1870, new private polling booths were designed which guaranteed both the secrecy of the vote and (eventually) the anonymity of the voter (see Figure 6.6). A new sanctity and decorum surrounded the act of voting. Polling places – one every four miles with one booth for every 150 electors – contained clear instructions that electors had to keep their vote secret and leave as soon as they had voted, while anyone found 'interfering' with voters would

Figure 6.6 The secret ballot at Westminster

be immediately removed. Some, including John Stuart Mill who believed that electors should be accountable, found these mandates unmanly and un-English. Although 35,000 voters declared themselves illiterate and had their ballots marked by a polling clerk (thus violating the secrecy of their vote) at the 1880 election, the secret ballot was here to stay. And with it came the disappearance of the poll book, the published record of who had voted for whom. Voters were no longer accountable to anyone but themselves.

Or such was the theory. In practice, the politics of influence retained a stubborn grip. Certainly factory owners in small towns, like landlords of rural estates, continued to march their voting employees to the poll and to treat them with parties, picnics, holidays and festivals. Yet the politics of influence was reshaped around the new contours of anti-corruption legislation. After 1883 the reputations of the party agents who assisted candidates to get elected rested upon their knowledge of electoral law and how to bend it. Denied the opportunity to 'hire' party workers, prospective candidates and sitting members alike still competed to 'nurse' **constituencies** by making charitable donations and supporting local events. The expense of competing for public office still required considerable personal resources. Between the 1830s and 1880s the vast majority of MPs continued to be members of the aristocracy and landed classes, with under a quarter of them being bankers, merchants or manufacturers. This began to change after 1883 but only at a glacial pace.

The Organization of Party Politics

The extension of the franchise and the development of a new electoral culture required new ways of mobilizing voters and winning and organizing their support. This was the work of the new political parties and the organizational machines they developed to compete for the loyalties of new voters. We have already seen that within Parliament the majority of MPs thought of themselves as Whigs and Tories and voted accordingly. Yet within local constituencies parliamentary parties had little reach and it was up to candidates to present, organize and fund their campaigns as they saw fit. Before 1867 parties had weak roots and were adapted to fit local political conditions. Many candidates even continued to insist that they were their own men who voted as they saw fit in the interests of their constituents, not of a parliamentary party. 'Independence' from party remained an electoral asset that even the most partisan tried to periodically claim, and candidates were as likely to present themselves according to the colour of their supporters as under a party label. And colours themselves had no uniformity across constituencies, even after the party organizations began to develop their grip upon constituencies. Thus, as late as 1927 the Conservative Party had no uniform colour, with some candidates using red and others blue.

Political parties began to extend themselves nationally (with the exception of Ireland) and entrench themselves locally after the Reform Acts of 1867 and 1884 created over 4 million new voters. The loyalties of this new electorate were uncertain and the traditional forms of influence were not only increasingly seen as 'corrupt' but could not be applied to such numbers. Party political organizations began to develop after 1867, then, to compete for the loyalties of voters. They did so by creating central organizations capable of mobilizing local associations in the constituencies. First, the Conservative Central Office (1870) and the Liberal Central Association (1874) – which were actually preceded by the Liberal Registration Association (1860) – began to coordinate and then direct party campaigning. Their influence only really began to be felt after the 1883 **Corrupt Practices Act** and was made manifest, as we'll see in Chapter 9, by the growth of a new cadre of professional party agents and centrally produced election literature. With their own professional organizations and journals specific to each party, agents became the central party's 'fixers' on the ground, responsible for getting voters registered and organizing the growing ranks of party volunteers.

Rhetorically at least, these central organizations were accountable to a mass membership organized through local **constituency** associations that were represented at an annual conference. The Conservative Party led the way with the creation of the National

Union of Conservative Associations in 1867 as an umbrella for local associations (but only forty-four had been formed by 1873). Established a decade later, the National Liberal Federation had just seventy-seven local associations by 1880. Both parties held an annual conference for representatives of the local associations, but the intention was to energize supporters rather than to listen to them – the Conservatives even celebrated their lack of a constitution. Party membership was an elastic term despite the best efforts of Birmingham's Liberal Party Association to borrow from American practices and throw it open to 'the caucus' at a subscription of 1 shilling a year in 1872. Almost everywhere else the entry bar was lower and party membership came simply by nomination or a pledge of support. Animated local associations with an active 'membership' only became important after the 1883 anti-corruption legislation made parties reliant on volunteers for their campaign work. Women were only allowed to be members of the new party organizations created to harness their energies. The Conservative **Primrose League** and the Women's Liberal Association were both founded in 1881 expressly for this purpose, although the latter did confound party leaders by advocating the expansion of the female franchise.

The slow tightening of central party discipline was also apparent in Parliament, whose procedures were slowly transformed by increasing demands that it become a more representative body. Parliamentary parties developed offices for '**party whips**' who were responsible for ensuring MPs followed the voting instructions of party leaders. Despite their name, party whips tended to use the powers of patronage, awarding jobs to loyalists rather than engaging in any physical coercion. The numbers of MPs who described themselves as 'Independent' or refused to toe any party line slowly diminished. In 1860 the proportion of parliamentary divisions in which more than nine tenths of MPs voted on the same side was just 6 per cent. Yet by 1871 it had risen to 35 per cent, by 1881 it was close to half and by 1891 it was more than three quarters. The increasing subordination of the MP to his (for there were no women MPs until 1918) party whip did not, however, entirely eliminate maverick MPs prepared to buck all discipline or promise of advancement. Although parties had not taken control of the political process, either in Parliament or 'out of doors' (as MPs referred to the country), by 1885 they were on their way to doing so.

As Parliament became more representative, its business, and the interest of the public in the activities of its members, grew substantially. There is no question that Parliament sought to restore its legitimacy not just by grudgingly expanding the electorate but also by busily addressing the issues the public demanded be heard. A key development here was the increasing transparency of the **House of Commons**, which made MPs more accountable to their constituents. Although Wilkes famously ensured that the Commons would be open to the press from 1771, it was only after certain seats in the chamber were reserved for them in 1803 that journalists reported regularly on Parliament. The following year, Cobbett published *Parliamentary Debates* as a supplement to his *Political Register* and by 1812 this enterprise, a close-to-verbatim report of debates, was taken over by his publisher Hansard. Hansard, still going today, made parliamentary reporting systematic and enabled newspapers across the country to report on events and debates in Parliament. As by 1836 many newspapers were reporting the division lists of how MPs had voted, Parliament began releasing its own lists. Radical MPs were increasingly held to account for their voting record and made to pledge they would vote in specific way on certain issues. When the House of Commons chamber reopened in 1852 after the fire of 1834, the new building included a specially designated 'Press Gallery'.

All of this made MPs more anxious to be seen and heard. In 1810, under 200 MPs made just 1,194 speeches, but by 1847 over 300 MPs made 5,332 speeches and by 1884 over 400 MPs made a staggering 21,160 speeches. Whereas MPs rarely asked ministers questions in the 1840s, by the 1880s there were over 3,000 per session: the beginning of **Prime Minister's Questions**. The increasing visibility of MPs was partly a consequence of the growing amount of government business that the Commons needed to debate. The number of public bills and division lists (the occasions when MPs voted) also increased dramatically. There were on average fewer than 150 public bills each session between 1802 and 1811, but there were close to 250 in the sessions between 1877 and 1886, and this rose again to 350 between 1887 and 1896. Similarly, the number of divisions per session reached 300 by 1881, up from under 200 twenty years earlier. Such was the weight of business that Parliament was compelled to refine its rules and procedures. Thus the Commons stopped having a debate on every petition it received in 1849. As most of the procedural changes, particularly once they accelerated in the 1870s and 1880s, were designed to make the Commons more efficient, they tended to thwart debate and bolster the ability of governments to push through legislative programmes. No less than the reform of the electorate, the reform of parliamentary procedure entrenched a new model of how representative politics was to be conducted.

The Press and Pressure Groups

The development of a new structure and culture for the conduct of representative politics was not simply about the suffrage question and the reform of Parliament. As we saw in Chapter 2, the growth of civil society in the eighteenth century was sustained by the proliferation of newspapers and campaigning groups. Yet, in terms of both quantity and quality, the nascent civil society that had emerged before Peterloo was a shadow compared to what had taken shape by 1885. Newspapers were an essential component, without which reform movements could not have spread their message to constituents and enabled them to read about the activities, or inactivities, of their MPs. They created the sense of an expanded public engaged in political discussion that far exceeded the numbers able to vote. They also enabled this public discussion to take ever more diverse forms as a plurality of groups broadened the subjects which politics addressed. These groups, often focused on a single issue, sought not just to put pressure on Parliament to address their campaigns but to educate and reform the public as well. Once known as 'pressure groups', we would now describe them as NGOs, or non-governmental organizations.

Newspapers and the Public

In the wake of Peterloo the state continued its old tactics for containing and preventing the development of an informed reading public with competing points of view. Although the expansion of treason law in 1795 to include conspiring against the government (and not just imagining the King's death) was made permanent in 1817, it was little used after 1820. Instead, the laws of sedition and blasphemy, tightened by the Six Acts in the wake of Peterloo, were used more frequently to censor the press. Radical journalists and newspaper proprietors from Cobbett and O'Connor to Jones and Bradlaugh continued to be prosecuted under them down to the 1870s. And this, of course, paled in comparison to the situation in Ireland where a new Treason and Felony Act was introduced in 1848 that muzzled the press by enabling the prosecution and deportation of the leaders of the Young Ireland movement like **John Mitchel**. It was also used against the Fenians, or Irish Revolutionary Brotherhood, in the 1860s. If on the mainland the censorship of the press through the laws of sedition and blasphemy tended to be confined to those moments when the state felt most imperilled, the use of stamp, paper and advertising duties continued to keep newspapers out of the hands of the labouring poor. The stamp duties on newspapers had already been increased to 4 pence in 1815, but the Six Acts extended them to those journals that had previously avoided the tax by publishing opinions rather than news. This made the cost of most at least 6 pence, a prohibitive expense to most working people, who earned less than 10 pence a week. Styling these duties as 'taxes on knowledge', radical proprietors and publishers rebelliously issued unstamped newspapers, the so-called **'pauper press'**. This unleashed a game of cat and mouse in which the unstamped newspapers pushed the boundaries of the state's tolerance and then were met with fines, arrests and prosecutions. In this 'war of the unstamped', when one paper was forced to close, another one invariably began.

Cheap, rebellious and irreverent, the unstamped press widened the circle of the newspaper-reading public as well as the boundaries of what it was possible to say. By 1835 the two largest unstamped papers – *The Poor Man's Guardian* and *The Police Gazette* – sold more copies than *The Times*. All told, the six most popular unstamped papers were estimated to have a circulation of 200,000. Yet, because a single copy normally circulated through more than one set of hands and was often read aloud to those who could not read, it is hard to estimate the size of their audience. Indeed, given that thirty people read every London newspaper in the 1820s, circulation figures must remain rough and ready. Nonetheless, at the dawn of the nineteenth century 17 million stamped papers were sold in a year, a number that almost doubled to 33 million by 1835. This was the year before the Whig government of the first reformed Parliament sought to ameliorate those it had excluded from the vote in 1832 by reducing stamp and paper duties to just 1 penny. Within two years the sales of stamped newspapers had risen to 53 million. Within thirty years the number of newspapers officially in circulation had grown threefold. Yet the repeal of the last stamp and paper duties in 1853 and 1861, along with the development of new printing technologies, did not immediately unleash a genuinely popular press. *The Times* clung on to its reputation as the paper of record for the governing classes and sold less than 70,000 copies a day for 3 pence each in the 1870s. *The Daily Telegraph*, the most popular metropolitan paper at that time, had a circulation of just 190,000. It was the Sunday papers, like *The News of the World* and *Reynold's News*, that reached the largest audience and were most widely read by the working classes. Sold for a penny, *Reynold's News* published a heady concoction of radical politics, mysteries and sensationalist news that reached a circulation of 350,000 a week by the 1870s.

The local or provincial press, as newspapers published outside London were called, grew steadily between 1760 and 1854 from 35 to 289. Some, like the *Manchester Guardian* and *Leeds Mercury*, as well as *The Scotsman* in Edinburgh, acquired national reputations. These provincial papers reflected the still profoundly local nature of civil society; they carried detailed reports of the activities of local clubs, societies and philanthropic associations as well as meetings by political organizations and official bodies like vestries, courts and town councils. They had a distinct voice and a steadfastly local angle that refused to reproduce the contents of the London papers. After the repeal of the Stamp Act their numbers rapidly escalated. By 1864 the aggregate circulation figures for the provincial press were almost twice as large as the metropolitan press. In 1877 there were 938 provincial papers and Mancunians alone could read 23 local papers. Whereas the *Manchester Guardian* sold 9,000 copies (each of which reputedly reached between fifty and eighty readers) in the 1840s, by the 1870s its circulation had risen to 40,000.

The size and reach of the press were not all that changed; so did the nature of journalism itself. While the loyalist and radical press had always worn their politics on their sleeve, by the mid nineteenth century many newspapers sought to prove the respectability of the press as 'the Fourth Estate' by separating the objectivity of news reporting from editorial perspective. Thus in the 1860s, although Oldham's two newspapers, the *Chronicle* and *Standard*, had close relationships with the local Liberal and Conservative Parties, they reported news in much the same way. From the 1870s this view began to be challenged by a new style of journalism that did not just report news but made it by its own investigative reporting and campaigns.

A young editor of *The Northern Echo*, W.T. Stead, did more than most to develop this '**New Journalism**' by taking up the cause of the 'atrocities' against Bulgaria's Christian population in 1876 by an Ottoman Empire facing widespread insurrection. Such was the resonance of the story, and the political opportunity it offered given Conservative prime minister Benjamin Disraeli's support for the Ottomans, that Gladstone made 'the Bulgarian Horrors' a key part of his famous campaign for election in Midlothian that took him back to office as prime minister in 1880. Stead's technique, soon widely replicated by other New Journalists from the 1880s, was to sensationally expose a problem by intimate stories of an individual, or his own personal encounters, and connect his readers to the suffering of others. Thus his exposé of the slavery of London's child prostitutes for *The Pall Mall Gazette* (the paper he now edited) in 1885 focused on Stead's own heroic rescue of thirteen-year-old Lily who had been sold as a virgin by her drunken parents. It turned out that Stead had not only botched important parts of the story like the girl's name and the consent of her father to the sale, but had also bought the girl himself to secure the story. Yet, and this was always the point for Stead, he had got the nation's attention, and the following year the **Criminal Law Amendment Act** raised the age of consent from twelve to sixteen. New Journalists like Stead changed the politics of reporting. Newspapers were no longer just to inform the public; they now also created publics that were concerned with particular issues or reports.

NGOs and the Politics of Pressure

Single-issue movements and organizations did as much as anything to carve out new political cultures in the nineteenth century. Although we saw their presence in the eighteenth century with the moral purity and anti-slavery campaigns, their number and size grew rapidly after the **Napoleonic Wars**. As they could rise and fall as quickly as the tides of enthusiasm they generated, some were more like movements than organizations. This was the case with the campaigns against the **New Poor Law**, or in the intermittent mobilizations for **factory reform**. Few were like the **Anti-Corn Law League**, which developed an organization and campaigning methods that became the aspiration and model of political parties thirty years later. In an age before opinion polls, these groups sought to educate and mobilize public opinion. Above all they demonstrated the pluralist nature of British civil society and its increasingly diverse range of voices, causes and publics. Although there remained real constraints about what could be said and how it could be articulated, this pluralism would have been hard to predict on the field of Peterloo in 1819 or even after the deportation of Chartist leaders in 1839 and Irish nationalists in 1848.

How then did these organizations and movements create and mobilize the public in support of their causes? They did so in myriad ways. They organized processions of their supporters through towns and held public meetings in which countless speeches were delivered. The more respectable and affluent the movement, the more likely these meetings were to be held indoors in purpose-built halls where tickets were required for admission so that opponents could not disrupt the event with heckles or counter-chants. The construction of the Free Trade Hall in Manchester on the site of Peterloo by the Anti-Corn Law League is a fine illustration of how these groups slowly reshaped the politics of pressure (see Textbox 5.1). As urban growth obliterated many of the open spaces that had long been used for public meetings, mass demonstrations continued to be coded as dangerous and unrespectable. The right of public assembly continued to be fiercely defended, though, in the **Reform League**'s demonstrations in London in the 1860s and again twenty years later when the Social Democratic Federation organized a meeting of the unemployed in Trafalgar Square that clashed with police in November 1887. The ensuing battle became known as 'Bloody Sunday' and it inspired W.T. Stead to establish a Law and Liberty League in support of its victims and the right of assembly.

Newspapers, and print culture more generally, were an indispensable part of the armoury of groups campaigning around specific issues. **Chartism** and the **Anti-Corn Law League** were unimaginable without the *Northern Star* and *Anti-Corn Law Circular*. Most Victorian pressure groups had a regularly published official organ: the National Temperance League circulated a *Temperance Record*, the National Society for Women's Suffrage had the *Women's Suffrage Journal*, and the campaign to repeal the **Contagious Diseases Acts** published the *Shield*. Yet while newspapers were effective at connecting local groups and generating a sense of a national movement, they remained prohibitively expensive despite the rapidly falling costs of production. Other forms of print could circulate as widely at a fraction of the cost. The numbers of pamphlets and tracts published were phenomenal. For example, the National Anti-Vivisection Society, which protested against animal testing, put out 8,672 books, pamphlets and leaflets in 1885 alone. Many sank with little trace, yet some were instant successes. Gladstone's *The Bulgarian Horrors and the Question of the East* sold more than 200,000 copies in three weeks after its publication in September 1874. Posters and handbills also proliferated, posted on walls and distributed on the streets. These ephemera could be produced quickly and reached a public whose literacy or access to newspapers and pamphlets remained limited.

And, finally, there were petitions, which remained arguably the most powerful demonstration of the weight of public opinion on particular issues throughout the nineteenth century. We have already seen how rapidly petitioning grew in the late eighteenth century, but once again this was dwarfed by the scale and frequency of petitioning in the nineteenth century. There was an average of 176 petitions a year between 1785 and 1790, but this grew to 899 (1811–15), then to 4,656 (1828–32) and peaked at 14,014 (1838–42). Even these figures obscure the intensity of petitioning activity in a single year like 1842, when the Chartist petition alone collected over 3 million signatures (almost one third of the adult population). After the exposure of fraudulent signatures on the Chartist petition of 1848, the size of petitions began to dwindle, but there were still significant peaks of petitioning activity in the 1860s, 1870s and 1890s. Thus, when Josephine Butler led a campaign by the Ladies' National Association against the treatment of prostitutes under a series of Contagious Diseases Acts in 1864, 1866 and 1868, it generated no less than 17,367 petitions between 1870 and 1885, even if in total they collected just 2.5 million signatures.

Friendly Societies and Trade Unions

Not all NGOs campaigned to change or defend specific policies of the state. The Temperance Society ended up advocating for local authorities to tighten licensing laws and even pushed for prohibition by the state. Yet initially it was more concerned with the salvation of individuals and a culture of sobriety that could help keep its members dry. Similarly, **friendly societies** – the largest and arguably the most important of all nineteenth-century NGOs – developed organizations that allowed their members to provide mutual financial and social support to each other. Although most of their members were working men, many friendly societies had a membership that stretched across the social spectrum. In the 1790s there were those who feared friendly societies were cover organizations for revolutionary plots, yet by the mid nineteenth century they were widely seen as a source of independence and hence respectability for working men. By 1850 there were 4 million members of friendly societies, or one half of the adult male population. Scattered across the country – though concentrated in the industrializing regions – and extending across the Empire, there were some 25,000 local friendly societies in Britain by mid century, increasingly many of them affiliated to national organizations like the Oddfellows or Manchester Unity. While they offered mutual protection from the hazards of life under industrial capitalism – accidents, sickness, old age and death – by the pooling of dues and voluntary contributions, they also offered a culture of conviviality. Fittingly, until they began to build their own halls, they often met in pubs and spent the evening toasting their friendship and eschewing the forbidden subjects of politics or religion.

At first, trade unions, navigating a complex legal terrain, were more concerned with representing the interests of their members in the workplace and providing forms of mutual support outside of it, than in engaging in the political process. Although unions were supposedly decriminalized after the repeal of the **Combination Acts** in 1824, both employers and the state remained fiercely hostile to them. Employers invoked the wage-fund theory to justify their inability to increase wages or improve conditions, while the state still worried that unions had secret revolutionary objectives, as was evident in the deportation of the Tolpuddle Martyrs in 1834 and the leaders of the Glasgow Cotton Spinners' Strike three years later. Like friendly societies, they often first emerged in local contexts around the grievances or the wish for mutual support of a specific craft. The first tentative attempt at national affiliation was by the Grand National Consolidated Trades Union, organized by the philanthropist and proto-socialist employer Robert Owen in 1830s. By the 1850s more modest national organizations, like the Amalgamated Society of Engineers, had greater success uniting skilled workers across a specific trade. By the 1860s it had 30,000 members across 300 branches and a London headquarters that handled subscriptions, benefits and representative decision-making. Yet, although trade unions boasted over 800,000 members by the end of the 1860s, they often competed with each other to maintain the hierarchies of status and wages within different trades for the skilled working men they represented.

The **Trades Union Congress** (TUC) and Labour Representation Committee (LRC), formed in 1868 and 1869, sought to overcome these sectional differences and demand that Parliament address the interests of labour more generally. The attempt of the TUC to build solidarity across unions had a faltering start, but by 1871 its third Congress drew representatives of 49 unions who represented 290,000 members. They were united in part by the limitations of the Trade Union Act passed that year. Following a contentious 1867 court ruling, the Act reaffirmed unions' legal status and the right to strike, but failed to decriminalize picketing. The need to lobby Parliament on behalf of the 'labour interest' was recognized by the formation of the TUC's Parliamentary Committee in 1872, while the LRC worked to get union-endorsed candidates elected as MPs. By 1874 the TUC's Congress attracted 153 unions representing 1.2 million members and the LRC got its first two MPs elected to the **House of Commons** (they had six by 1886). As MPs were not paid, working men could only get elected if they had financial support from a trade union. It was no coincidence, especially given the competition for the support of the newly enfranchised skilled working man between the Liberal and Conservative Parties, that between 1874 and 1880 a swath of legislation reduced the working day to ten hours, prohibited the employment of children under nine in mills (and under eight elsewhere), legalized picketing and took the first tentative steps towards making employers, not workers, liable for accidents and injuries at work. As we'll see in Chapter 9, a new generation of unionism, emboldened by the **Great Depression** and the collapse of the wage-fund theory after J.S. Mill's renunciation of it in 1869, would emerge in the late 1880s and successfully mobilize unskilled workers.

Conclusion

Without question, British politics and the representative political process were fundamentally transformed between 1818 and 1885. Rather than being 'politics without democracy' as one historian has claimed, this was the age in which a new, liberal understanding of politics and its democratic forms were first developed. As the British people mobilized in unprecedented numbers to claim what we now take to be basic civil rights – freedom of speech, freedom of the press, freedom of assembly, the right to vote – a state still dominated by the landed classes sought to contain, limit and channel the nature of reform. The repressive apparatus installed by the Six Acts after Peterloo did not meekly melt away in a haze of liberal reforms. Proprietors of unstamped newspapers, those guilty of sedition and 'conspiracy', as well as those going on strike, picketing or attending meetings in newly prohibited places, continued to be subjected to fines, imprisonment and even deportation until remarkably late. While the vote was begrudgingly granted to an increasing number of people, 70 per cent of Britons remained unenfranchised in 1884. Those propertied men considered fit and proper to vote did so in ways designed to protect them as individuals from what were now designated influence and corruption. If Parliament gradually became a more representative body, it was in part thanks to the proliferation of newspapers and NGOs that campaigned around specific issues. Yet, despite the proliferation of an increasingly diverse set of voices in the political process, the organizational forms of civil society began to mirror that of the new electoral culture and its subject. It was less unruly and oriented around men who possessed property and literacy. The liberal forms of representative politics that developed in Britain before 1885 were marked by a determination to discipline demos as much as to emancipate it.

 FURTHER READING

All debates among historians about how British politics was transformed between the first and last quarters of the nineteenth century returns to a central, haunting, question: why was Britain almost unique in Europe in avoiding a revolution? The old Whig view, first articulated by T.B. Macaulay in his *History of England* (1848) as the continent was convulsed by revolt, was that the growth of civil society after the **Glorious Revolution** and the reform of the electoral system had enabled Britain to secure political stability. For Macaulay, and for generations of subsequent historians, the rising middle class was vital in forging those developments. A socially more inclusive version of this story of British exceptionalism, that recognized the role of the labouring classes in the development of civil society and in generating pressure on Parliament for reform, developed in the 1970s. Good examples of this genre are Patricia Hollis's *Pressure from Without in Early Victorian England* (London,

1974) and Brian Harrison's *Peaceable Kingdom: Stability and Change in Modern Britain* (Oxford, 1982).

In contrast, while historians in the Tory tradition grudgingly acknowledge the growth of civil society and the growing pressure for reform, they emphasize the genius of the governing classes in defusing it through measured legislation. In these works, power lies at the parliamentary centre. The best example of this work remains Maurice Cowling's *1867: Disraeli, Gladstone and Revolution* (Cambridge, 1967) but Jonathan Clark's *English Society 1688–1832: Ideology, Social Structure and Political Practice During the Ancien Regime* (Cambridge, 1985) and Michael Bentley's aptly named *Politics Without Democracy 1815–1918: Perception and Preoccupation in British Government* (London, 1984) are good variations on this theme.

Those influenced by Anglo-Marxism tell a no less exceptionalist island story, yet one rooted in a tradition of radical protest generated by the working class. Here, reform movements episodically reach crescendos that threaten revolution until they are brutally repressed by the state seeking to disable protest and revolution. E.P. Thompson's magisterial *The Making of the English Working Classes* (London, 1963) remains the definitive text that extends to the reform agitations of 1829 to 1832. Other key statements include Eric Hobsbawm and George Rudé, *Captain Swing* (London, 1969); Dorothy Thompson, *The Chartists: Popular Politics in the Industrial Revolution* (New York, 1984); John Saville, *1848: The British State and the Chartist Movement* (Cambridge, 1987); R. Harrison, *Before the Socialists: Studies in Labour and Politics 1861–1881* (London, 1965); James Epstein, *Radical Expression: Political Language, Ritual and Symbol in England, 1790–1850* (Oxford, 1994); Malcolm Chase, *Chartism: A New History* (Manchester, 2007). For a revisionist emphasis on the capacity of reform, not repression, to disarm popular politics see Gareth Stedman Jones's *Languages of Class: Studies in English Working Class History, 1832–1982* (Cambridge, 1983) and Dror Wahrman's *Imagining the Middle Class: The Political Representation of Class in Britain, c.1780–1840* (Cambridge, 1995).

Feminist scholars have highlighted the ways in which the political process, including movements pressing for its radical reform, was inveterately male even when it included women. The key texts here are Catherine Hall, *White, Male and Middle Class: Explorations in Feminism and History* (Cambridge, 1992); Clare Midgley, *Women Against Slavery: The British Campaigns, 1780–1870* (London, 1992); Anna Clark, *The Struggle for the Breeches: Gender and the Making of the British Working Class* (London, 1995); Helen Rogers, *Women and the People: Authority, Authorship and the Radical Tradition in Nineteenth-Century England* (Aldershot, 2000); Kathryn Gleadle, *Borderline Citizens: Women, Gender, and Political Culture in Britain, 1815–1867* (Oxford, 2009).

The insularity and Englishness of so much of this literature is immediately apparent to those who look beyond England and Wales. K. Theodore Hoppen and Gordon Pentland provide the best accounts of the different dynamics and effects of electoral reform in Ireland and Scotland in their respective *Elections, Politics and Society in Ireland, 1832–1885* (Oxford, 1984) and *Radicalism, Reform and National Identity in Scotland 1820–1833* (Woodbridge, 2008); the latter places the 1832 Reform Act in its proper British context by showing the specific effects it had on Scotland. Catherine Hall, Keith McClelland and Jane Rendall's *Defining the Victorian Nation: Class, Race, Gender and the British Reform Act of 1867* (Cambridge, 2000) places the Second Reform Act in its broader imperial context; while Rob Saunders's *Democracy and the*

Vote in British Politics, 1848–1867 (Farnham, 2011) highlights the ways debates in Britain were shaped by an understanding of 'democracy' in France and the United States. I have learnt a great deal about the importance of settler colonialism to the questions of sovereignty and suffrage from Julie Evans (ed.), *Equal Subjects, Unequal Rights: Indigenous Peoples in British Settler Colonies* (Manchester, 2003), Lisa Ford, *Settler Sovereignty: Jurisdiction and Indigenous People in America and Australia* (Cambridge, Mass., 2011), Alan Lester and Zoe Laidlaw (eds.), *Indigenous Communities and Settler Colonialism: Land Holding, Loss and and Survival in an Interconnected World* (Basingstoke, 2015), and Leigh Boucher's forthcoming *Sovereignty, Suffrage and Settler Colonialism in the Nineteenth-Century British Empire*.

A greater interest in the culture of politics beyond Westminster has also enabled historians to reassess the celebratory accounts of electoral reform offered in Charles Seymour, *Electoral Reform in England and Wales: The Development and Operation of the Parliamentary Franchise 1832–1885* (New Haven, 1915), and Michael Brock, *The Great Reform Act* (London, 1973). Frank O'Gorman's *Voters, Patrons, and Parties: The Unreformed Electoral System of Hanoverian England 1734–1832* (Oxford, 1989) remains the definitive work demonstrating the vitality of the electoral system before 1832 and the limited impact of reforms to it. My own *Politics and the People: A Study in English Political Culture 1815–1867* (1993) charts the creation of a less unruly political culture around a new liberal subject of politics; this account is usefully qualified by Jon Lawrence's *Electing Our Masters: The Hustings in British Politics from Hogarth to Blair* (Oxford, 2009).

The literature on the press is less developed, but the best guides are Joel Wiener, *The War of the Unstamped: The Movement to Repeal the British Newspaper Tax, 1830–1836* (Ithca, NY, 1969); Joel Wiener (ed.), *Papers for the Millions: The New Journalism in Britain, 1850s to 1914* (New York, 1988); Lucy Brown, *Victorian News and Newspapers* (Oxford, 1985); and Mark Hampton, *Visions of the Press in Britain, 1850–1950* (Urbana, 2004).

III

1885–1931: The Crises of Liberalism

7 The British Imperium

Introduction

In 1883, John Seeley, the Professor of Modern History at the University of Cambridge, published a history of the British Empire. Within two years *The Expansion of England* had sold 80,000 copies. He chastised his fellow historians for not recognizing that much of 'the history of England is not in England but in the Americas and Asia' and yet denied there was any logic to imperial expansion. 'We seem, as it were,' he infamously declared, 'to have conquered and peopled half the world in a fit of absence of mind.' Just twenty years later, John Hobson decisively challenged this view of Britons as accidental imperialists in *Imperialism: A Study* (1902). Hobson had long been preoccupied with the inadequacies of classical liberal economics to either explain or remedy the unemployment and poverty caused by the **Great Depression**. When covering the **South African War** as a journalist for the *Manchester Guardian*, he became convinced that Britain's imperialism was a product of its economic problems at home. Far from being accidental, he argued, imperialism was a consequence of Euro-American economies competing with each other to find new markets for goods and capital that were either not in demand at home or offered too minimal a return on investment. Over the next two decades, Vladimir Lenin and John Maynard Keynes developed his interpretation in different ways to explain the outbreak of World War I and the deepening economic crises of the 1920s. The political and economic crisis of 1931 finally brought an end to Britain's dogged attachment to **free trade** and the **gold standard** and deepened the British economy's structural dependence upon the Empire. At that point, only the rarefied circle of imperial historians at Cambridge, where Seeley had left his stamp, could still believe that imperialism had no logic.

Seeley's *The Expansion of England* was timely; it was published just prior to a period of dramatic growth for the British Empire. As Britain competed with its rival European empires to claim African territories, it annexed 2.5 million square miles in the decade after the Congress of Berlin (1885). At the end of World War One, when the Treaty of Versailles assigned some of the former colonies of the defeated German and Ottoman empires to Britain in 1919, the British Empire reached its zenith. Stretching over a quarter of the globe, and including almost a third of the world's population, the British Empire contained 458 million people spread across 13 million square miles. This Age of Empire was not then, as Seeley would have it, a solely British story. It was global in scale as imperial rivals competed for markets, geopolitical influence, and, as we will see Chapter 8, to advance the civility and racial health of their nation. The First World War, the world's first truly global conflict, was a consequence of this competition. It was fought with all the resources available to modern imperial states: new industrial technologies, emergency powers and an unprecedented power to allow populations to live or die. It was a deadly combination in which 10 million soldiers (and an estimated

7 million civilians) lost their lives. Around a million of these casualties were from across the British Empire, three quarters of them from Britain itself.

Without question, the First World War mobilized the support of many colonial subjects who fought, died and provided logistical support to defend the British Empire. It also accelerated colonial nationalist movements and critiques of Britain's imperial political economy that had been propagated in Ireland, the Caribbean and India during the second half of the nineteenth century. The Great Depression intensified the extraction of wealth and resources from Britain's colonies and the global division of labour upon which the imperialism of free trade depended. In light of this, Irish and Indian nationalists highlighted the fundamental contradictions that underwrote Britons' beliefs in the liberal nature of their Empire. They argued that despite being promised civilization, prosperity and the rule of law, Britain's colonies had been reduced to poverty and famine and subjected to increasingly racialized forms of state violence and emergency rule. As we will see in Chapter 9, it was a critique that resonated in Britain, where members of the labour and women's suffrage movements also highlighted the illiberal ways in which the state met their protests before and after the Great War. In 1919, when the contributions of colonial soldiers in defending the motherland resulted in neither the embrace of the Wilsonian rhetoric of self-determination nor imperial reform, an unprecedented wave of revolts spread across the British Empire. These revolts were quickly neutralized by the tried and tested combination of brutal repression and grudging reform. Yet, thereafter, imperialism had to be reinvented and justified in new ways both to embrace the opportunities of the new internationalism and to meet the challenges posed by colonial nationalists.

When Seeley published *The Expansion of England* in 1883, it appeared that the British Empire had been acquired effortlessly under a liberal political economy that had made Britain a world hegemon. By 1931, Britain had not only abandoned the central elements of the liberal political economy – free trade, the gold standard and cheap government – that had seemingly tied together an Empire now so large the sun never set on it; it had also been displaced by its former colony the United States as the world's superpower. This chapter explores how and why that happened.

TIMELINE

1857	Great Revolt (India)
1858	Irish Republican Brotherhood Direct rule over India
1865	Morant Bay Rebellion
1867	Canada gains Dominion status

1870	First Land Act (Ireland)
1871	Formal colonization of the Gold Coast
1873	Irish Home Rule Party
1878–80	Second Afghan War
1880	Formal colonization of Kenya
1881	Second Land Act (Ireland)
1882	Formal colonization of Egypt
1883	John Seeley, *The Expansion of England* Famine Code in India
1885	Berlin Conference on the Congo Indian National Congress
1886	First Home Rule for Ireland Bill defeated Chamber of Commerce of the Empire established
1890	Formal colonization of Uganda
1892	Dadabhai Naoroji elected first Indian MP in Britain
1893	Second Home Rule for Ireland Bill defeated
1899	Formal colonization of Sudan
1899–1902	South African (Boer) War
1901	Dabadhai Naoroji, *Poverty and Un-British Rule in India* Australia gains Dominion status
1902	J.A. Hobson, *Imperialism: A Study*
1906	Indian National Congress supports home rule for India
1907	New Zealand and Newfoundland gain Dominion status
1910	South Africa gains Dominion status
1912	Third Home Rule for Ireland Bill
1914	Declaration of the First World War Defence of the Realm Act (DORA) Aliens Registration Act

1915	Ministry of Munitions Gallipoli Internment of aliens
1916	Battle of the Somme Easter Rising in Ireland Introduction of conscription
1917	Food rationing Imperial War Graves Commission Russian Revolution
1919	Amritsar Massacre Treaty of Versailles Ottoman mandates and former German colonies annexed Government of India Act/Montagu-Chelmsford reforms
1919–21	Anglo-Irish War
1920	League of Nations Government of Ireland Act
1921	Anglo-Irish Treaty
1922	Egypt gains nominal independence
1923	Southern Rhodesia declares independence
1924	British Empire Exhibition
1925	Return to gold standard
1926	General Strike Balfour Declaration
1929	Wall Street Crash
1931	National Government End of gold standard Introduction of General Tariff Statute of Westminster

The 'New Imperialism'

A combination of the **Great Depression** and the consolidation of the nation-states of Germany, Italy, the United States and the Meiji Restoration in Japan spawned a new era of imperial competition in a quest for new resources and territories. This competition was global in scale. The rules of the game were effectively set at the **Berlin Conference** in 1884 and 1885, when the chief European imperial powers – and the Ottoman Empire and the United States – equated the occupation of territory with legitimate claims to sovereignty.

In Central Asia, Britain's so-called 'Great Game' with Russia began with the struggle for control over Afghanistan in the 1830s. The Second Afghan War of 1878–1880 reignited tensions, which continued through the 1890s over tsarist ambitions in Tibet, China and Mongolia. When Russia was defeated by Japan over control of Korea and Manchuria in the war of 1904–5, an Anglo-Russian Convention in 1907 refocused the attention of both powers on Germany's intensifying interests in the fragile Ottoman Empire. They were particularly concerned with Germany's construction of a railway from 1903 that was to connect Berlin to Baghdad through what is now Turkey, Syria and Iraq.

Asia was no less an imperial battlefield. China and Siam were slowly picked apart. While Japan successfully went to war to annex Korea and Taiwan in 1895, during the 1880s and 1890s Germany, France, Russia and Britain all claimed trading privileges in different informal spheres of imperial influence – Russia in Manchuria, Britain in the Yangtze Valley and the northeastern Weihaiwei coast, and France in the Guangzhou Bay. France, which had already defeated Spain to tighten its imperial grip on Vietnam in the 1850s and 1860s, slowly extended what became known as French Indo-China by annexing Cambodia and Laos from Siam. Britain meanwhile also eroded Siamese territory and influence by colonizing Burma, Malaya, Singapore, North Borneo and Brunei, while the Netherlands retained their long-standing colony of the Dutch East Indies (Indonesia). The expansion of the United States did not stop in Texas, New Mexico and California at the end of the Mexican-American War in the 1840s, or with the purchase of Alaska from Russia in 1867. It continued with the Spanish-American War in 1898 when Puerto Rico, Guam and the Philippines joined Hawaii as part of America's overseas empire (see Map 7.1).

And then there was the so-called '**Scramble for Africa**' as European nations – chiefly Britain, Germany, France, Italy and Portugal – moved quickly in the final decades of the nineteenth century to divide up that continent (see Map 7.2). While there had been an earlier European presence in Africa, it had largely taken shape 'informally' through trade, missionary work, and explorations like that undertaken by David Livingstone and Henry Stanley, rather than by war and formal conquest. In 1870 only 10 per cent of the continent had been formally colonized; by 1914 only 10 per cent remained uncolonized. The pattern was set by Belgium's brutal colonization of the Congo. Belgium's King Leopold hired Henry Stanley to negotiate treaties with local chiefs along the Congo in the 1860s and 1870s. In 1885, with the blessing of the **Berlin Conference**, King Leopold established the **Congo Free State**, complete with its rich rubber and ivory reserves, as his personal possession.

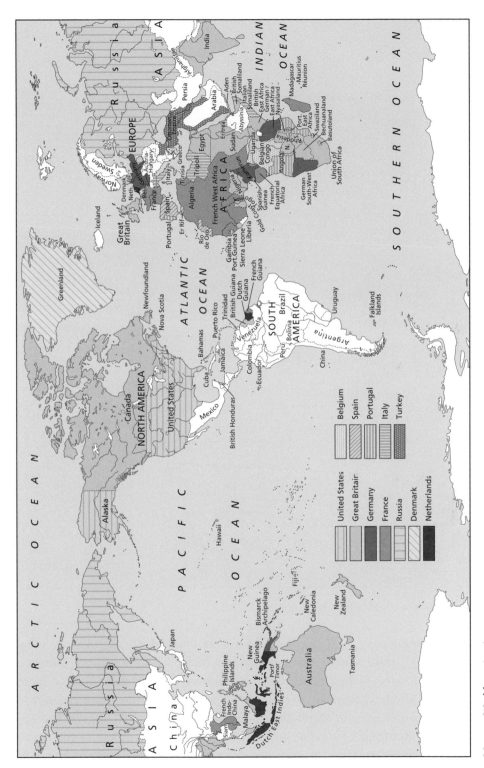

Map 7.1 World empires in 1902

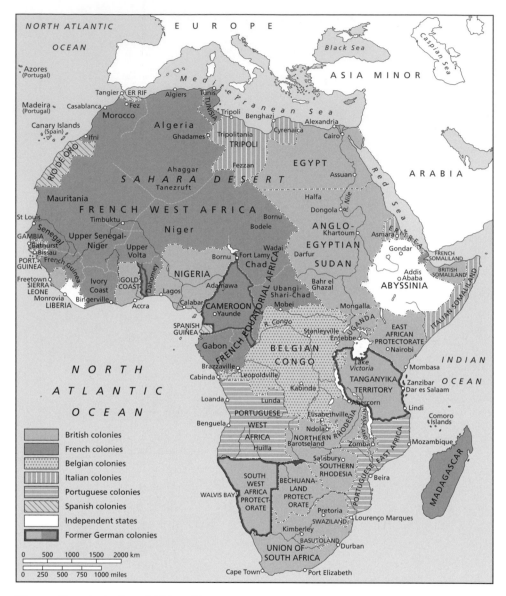

Map 7.2 The colonization of Africa, 1884–1912

Leopold's ambitions to expand the colony were checked on all sides. By 1889, Cecil Rhodes's British South African Company had pushed northwards through Matabeleland to south of the Zambezi River, establishing what was to become Northern and Southern Rhodesia. Similarly, in 1884 and 1885 German explorers and traders, like Carl Peters and his German Colonization Society, successfully sought imperial charters and **protectorates** from Chancellor Bismarck to create the colonies of German East (Tanganyika) and West Africa (Cameroon) that nestled up to the Belgian Congo. So too did the new Portugese territories of Angola and Mozambique, colonized in 1891. With a foothold in Algeria from the 1830s, France quickly extended its colonial possessions in the north and west with French Equatorial Africa in 1884 and French West Africa in 1889 as well as Madagascar in the east. Meanwhile, Britain steadily claimed much of the rest of central-eastern Africa, colonizing Kenya (1880), Somaliland (1884), Sudan (1899), Uganda (1890), as well as territories in the west and north from the Gold Coast (1871), Egypt (1882) and Nigeria (1886). Britain also consolidated its hold upon southern Africa. Expanding from the Cape Colony, Britain pushed the Dutch 'Boer' Afrikaners north into the Orange Free State and Transvaal, while also defeating the Zulus to extend its territorial control of Natal. Britain's ambition to secure the gold-rich resources of Transvaal catalysed the South African or Boer War of 1899–1902, which incorporated the Orange Free State and Transvaal into the British Empire as self-governing colonies.

An Imperial Economy

That this competition between empires across the world was shaped, but not determined, by the **Great Depression** is well illustrated by the British case. As we saw in Chapter 5, British trade and investment was increasingly reoriented towards its colonies in the final decades of the nineteenth century. Exports to the colonies increased from 30 to 35 per cent of total exports between 1870 and 1914, and continued to rise after the Great War, reaching 41 per cent by 1938. The vast majority of those exports went not to the new colonial territories but to the white settler colonies that became Dominions in the early twentieth century: Canada, Australia, New Zealand and South Africa. By the 1930s, they alone accounted for a quarter of all British exports. Although imports from the Empire remained at around 25 per cent of the total between the 1850s and 1914, their value rose prodigiously, from £39,240,000 in 1857 to £172,640,000 in 1914. Raw materials were imported from across the British Empire. The smallest value of imports came from the West Indies and British Africa, with just £2,900,000 and £5,800,000 respectively. Then came South Africa, British Asia (meaning Malaya, Burma and Hong Kong) and Canada with £10,700,000, £22,700,000 and £27,300,000 respectively. India and Ceylon, as well as Australia and New Zealand, exported the most to Britain, with total values of £44,800,000 and £56,300,000. Food (including tea and coffee), cotton, timber, rubber and gold accounted for the vast majority of these imports. By 1913, Britain imported 87 per cent of its tea, 80 per cent of its wool, 57 per cent of its rubber, 35 per cent of its grain, and 25 per cent of its meat from the colonies. These commodities fuelled the British economy and its people, but they were also often re-exported: 30 per cent of imperial imports were re-exported in 1913, half of the total of Britain's re-export business. In one way, when Joseph Chamberlain (then Colonial Secretary) first called for the abandonment of **free trade** in favour of an imperial tariff system in 1903, he was describing a trans-colonial system of trade that was already well established.

As the Great Depression deflated commodity prices, squeezed profits and lowered rates of return on British securities, British capital flooded overseas in search of higher yields. Britain's overseas investments increased from £770 million in 1870 to £4,107 million in 1914, and the earnings on them rose from 35.3 to 199.6 per cent in the same period. As a percentage of gross national wealth, overseas assets already represented 11.9 per cent in 1870, but they reached 21.1 per cent in 1890 and 26.2 per cent in 1910. Between the 1880s and 1914, over 47 per cent of British investments went to the Empire. By 1914, only 21 per cent of British investments went to the United States, and 5 per cent to Europe. India, which had accounted for 20 per cent of British investment in 1870, was receiving just 9 per cent in 1914, compared to 37 per cent for the the the new British Dominions. The growing dependence of the British economy on the Empire for trade, as well as for the invisible earnings on overseas investments that made up the balance of payments between its exports and imports, may have been first established during the Great Depression but it had deepened by 1914.

It is no coincidence that new organizations, like the Chambers of Commerce of the Empire (1886), were formed to better integrate the imperial economy. As we will see in Chapter 8, from the 1880s many Britons pushed for new forms of imperial federation that would not only create stronger economic, political and cultural ties to bind the Empire together, but would aid its commercial development. In the Dominions these social, cultural and political ties were strong enough to prolong the attachment and dependence of those economies to Britain. And, of course, the increasing numbers of Britons who emigrated to the Dominions between 1870 and 1914 also helped cement this sense of a Greater Britain.

Elsewhere, in the so-called 'dependent' colonies, the increasingly economically extractive character of imperialism after the Great Depression was more evident and less consensual. India provides a good example. From the 1870s massive investment in infrastructure projects like railways and irrigation schemes helped develop its economy and provided Britain with wheat, raw cotton, jute and tea, the value of its exports rising from 329 million rupees in 1860 to 2,490 million rupees in 1913. As many of those exports also went to European and American markets (often at favourable tariff rates unavailable to British goods), they helped Britain overcome its balance of payments deficits with those parts of the world. Moreover, as other export markets were closed off to Britain behind tariffs, India was forced to trade freely with Britain, importing its iron and steel as well as a quarter of its cotton textiles by 1914. By 1913 Britain's trade surplus with India financed two thirds of her balance of payments deficit! Although British investments in India steadily declined between 1870 and 1914, the scale of India's public debt serviced in the City of London rose from 7 to 60 per cent between 1858 and 1914. Britain insisted the government of India take on public borrowing to finance the

Home Charges required to maintain British troops and officials in India, as well as the infrastructure projects designed to better integrate the Indian economy with its metropolitan counterpart. All of this was made worse by the fact that, at Britain's insistence, India's currency was pegged to silver and its value fell rapidly from the 1870s. India was only allowed to join the **gold standard** in 1899 to be better able to pay its debt. This systematic subordination of India to service the British economy became a key target of anti-colonial critique.

Colonial Critiques of the Imperium

From the 1880s colonial nationalism was increasingly engaged with economic questions. Since the Famine, Irish nationalism – in the form of the Irish Republican Brotherhood (1858) and the Home Rule Party (1873) – was preoccupied with securing Ireland's political representation or independence. As we saw in Chapter 6, the Great Depression re-energized a nationalist critique of the Anglo-Irish monopoly on land that left some 800 families, many of them living outside of Ireland, owning half of Ireland. The collapse of agricultural prices and land values left many of these landlords overleveraged by mortgages on their estates, just as it left their tenant farmers unable to pay the rents that serviced those loans. Landlords and their estate managers were neither hesitant nor restrained in evicting those who fell behind or refused to pay their rent. When families sought to avoid eviction by occupying the dwelling, a battering ram was sometimes used to knock down a wall. The resulting crisis quickly became known as the Land War.

Ironically it was an Anglo-Irish Protestant landowner, Charles Stewart Parnell, who became the leader of the **Irish Land League** formed in 1879 to represent the plight of tenant farmers with appeals to retake the 'people's land'. With over 500 branches and a membership that peaked at 200,000 members, the Land League organized mass meetings, rent strikes and, when legal means failed, protested forced evictions with attacks on landlords' properties and cattle. They also organized boycotts of estate managers and those who took on the tenancy from evicted families. The police recorded 2,600 of these 'outrages' in 1880 alone. Indeed, the term 'boycott' comes from one community refusing to serve and socially isolating an estate manager called Captain Charles Boycott who, on behalf of his absentee landlord in County Mayo, evicted tenants after refusing to reduce their rents by 25 per cent. The Land League also campaigned for the three F's – fair rents, fixity of tenure and free sale – that Gladstone's first Land Act of 1870 had failed to deliver. By 1881 the second Land Act, again passed by Gladstone's Liberal Party, partially conceded those rights and, ironically, threatened to do what was not possible on the mainland: end the aristocratic monopoly on land. A Coercion Act, allowing anyone suspected of crime or conspiracy to be imprisoned without trial, accompanied it. One of the first to be arrested was Charles Stewart Parnell along with

his fellow leaders of the Land League. The Irish Land League helped catalyse the formation of a Highland Land Law Reform Association in Scotland, where Gaelic-speaking
tenant 'crofters' also organized rent strikes and campaigned to end evictions and the
removal of their grazing rights by gaming and trespass laws. An expeditionary force
of troops was dispatched to Skye for the first time since the Jacobite Rising of 1745 and
a government commission was established in 1883 under Lord Napier to investigate
the grievances of the crofters. Three years later, after the Crofters' Party had won some
notable seats at the 1885 election, the Crofters' Holding Act introduced some of the recommendations of the Napier Commission, providing crofters with security of tenure
and fair rentals.

In India an emergent nationalist movement also took shape around economic issues
from the 1870s. A key figure here was the Parsi cotton trader Dadabhai Naoroji, who
became the first leader of the **Indian National Congress** in 1886. For two decades
before that, Naoroji had argued that colonial rule was draining India of its wealth and
reducing its people to poverty and famine. This was, he insisted, decidedly 'un-British'.
India was not only denied free trade in order to service Britain's economy with a massive
surplus of exports, but she was forced to pay for the extravagance of colonial officials
and the ambitions of her generals through the **Home Charges**. Naoroji estimated that
about a quarter of India's wealth, between £200 million and £300 million, was drained
by Britain every year. While the colonial government published an annual Moral and
Material Progress Report to demonstrate how its rule delivered prosperity and civility,
Naoroji and his colleagues argued that 80 per cent of India's population lived in grinding poverty on an income of just 20 rupees, considerably below the 34 rupees required
for subsistence. Worse still, even by official estimates, 15 million Indians, almost half
the population of England and Wales, were killed by famine in the forty years following
direct rule from London in 1858.

Naoroji's analysis caught on in Britain. His ardent belief in free trade and his equation of the Home Charges with **Old Corruption** played well in radical and Liberal
circles. In 1892 he was elected as the first Indian MP, representing Finsbury in London
for the Liberal Party. Henry Hyndman, the leader of the Marxist-influenced Social
Democratic Federation, was a long-term admirer whose book *The Ruin of India by
British Rule* (1907) almost precisely echoed Naoroji's own *Poverty and Un-British Rule
in India* (1901). He was even a participant at the first meeting of the Second International
alliance of labour and socialist movements held in Paris in 1889. Yet many of his allies
in India did not share his belief that India's salvation lay with free trade or changing
opinions in Britain. Radicalized by the partition of Bengal in 1905, the Indian National
Congress finally demanded home rule, while the ***swadeshi*** movement was launched to
urge a boycott of all British goods in favour of only indigenous products. *Swadeshi* was
an explicitly economic form of nationalism that sought to redress 'the drain' identified
by Naoroji. By the early twentieth century, then, colonial nationalists had exposed the

economically exploitative nature of imperialism and the emptiness of its promise of prosperity.

A Liberal Empire and its States of Emergency

The dramatic nature of imperial expansion in the four decades before 1919 also put renewed strain upon the idea that Britain's Empire was liberal. Without a credible promise of prosperity, the colonial project was under more pressure to deliver the rule of law that would ultimately prepare the colonized for political representation once they had become civilized subjects. Colonial revolts and nationalist movements undermined such claims and highlighted the violence of the imperial state and its frequent recourse to coercive emergency measures that suspended that same rule of law.

The Political Structures of Colonialism

By the 1880s, the British Empire consisted of three very different types of polity – the **self-governing colony**, the **protectorate** and the **Crown colony** – with contrasting forms of rule. As we have seen, the limited system of self-government, where parliaments or assemblies were subordinate to a governor appointed by the Crown, was first deployed in the North American and Caribbean colonies and was then introduced to Nova Scotia, Canada, Australia, New Zealand and the Cape between 1846 and 1854. As we saw in Chapter 6, for the most part, with the important exceptions of New Zealand and the Cape, this form of self-government meant the rule of white male voters over indigenous peoples. White rule was not necessarily British rule. The Canadian and Australian constitutions effectively declared their autonomy from Britain in 1867 and 1901, while the Imperial Conference of 1907 granted a similar 'Dominion' status to New Zealand and Newfoundland. South Africa also adopted Dominion status in 1910, when its four self-governing colonies of Natal, Cape Colony, Transvaal and Orange Free State formed the Union of South Africa.

In contrast, protectorates offered indigenous peoples 'protection' as a dominion of the British Crown while retaining sovereign control of their territories with their own legal and political systems. In practice, protectorates provided Britain with a type of 'indirect rule' established by treaties with local rulers who usually consolidated their own power over rivals by becoming de facto client governors. In these protectorates Britain effectively created heads of state – variously titled as sultans, sheikhs, kings or chiefs – that resembled the British monarchy. British officials were always in place to advise these local rulers and to ensure that the British rule of law was administered to Britons, or to others when it was considered necessary. When **Lord Lugard**, the governor of Nigeria, celebrated this system by writing *The Dual Mandate* in 1922, it was effectively coming to an end.

As a general trend, protectorates usually gave way to more direct forms of rule when those installed as monarchical figures sought to claim real sovereign power or proved unyielding to British influence. This was true when Bechuanaland in 1885, Zululand in 1887, Gambia in 1888, North Borneo in 1906, Kenya in 1920 and Northern Rhodesia in 1924 became 'Crown colonies' or were annexed to colonies. The **Crown colony**, first created in 1815, allowed direct rule from London and the imposition of British laws and the institutions (like courts and militia) to enforce them. Their numbers proliferated as the pace of colonization accelerated. The new Caribbean colonies, annexed during the **Napoleonic Wars**, were made Crown colonies, as were the Falkland Islands (1832), Hong Kong (1843), Vancouver Island (1849), the Windward Islands (1855), the Cayman Islands (1859), British Honduras or Belize (1862), Straits Settlement (1867), Fiji (1874), the Gold Coast (1874), British New Guinea (1888) and Asante (1901).

Outside of the white settler colonies that were formally recognized as self-governing Dominions in 1907, the trend was towards greater, not lesser, control from London. Jamaica was a case in point. A colony since the seventeenth century, Jamaica had an elected House of Assembly that retained a veto over all money bills, including the governor's salary. Originally limited, by property qualifications, to the English settlers who became planters, the Assembly's electorate was far from representative. Just before its abolition in 1865, its 49 members were elected by an electorate of under 2,000 of Jamaica's population of over 400,000. Nonetheless, a system of local government through **parish** vestries enfranchised all freeholders and gave them responsibility for the maintenance of schools and roads as well as the Church.

By the 1860s worsening economic conditions had led to rising tensions between the old 'plantocracy' and the now free but desperately poor black populations, who petitioned the Queen requesting the right to cultivate unused Crown lands. In October 1865 the trial of a black man imprisoned for trespassing on an abandoned plantation was disrupted and those held responsible for the protest were arrested. A few days later, demonstrators sought to gather at the Court House in Morant Bay but were met by a local militia force who promptly shot seven of them. Fearful of further reprisals, Governor Eyre declared martial law and deployed government troops to unleash a fearful crackdown. The government murdered 439 black Jamaicans, destroyed around 1,000 houses, flogged 600 men and women (some pregnant) in public, and executed the 354 men considered 'ringleaders', many with no trial. The brutality and legality of Eyre's action were hotly debated in Britain. A committee that included John Stuart Mill (see Textbox 6.2) and Charles Darwin was formed to bring criminal charges against Eyre for murder. Thomas Carlyle formed a rival group – supported by Charles Dickens and John Ruskin – to defend him on the grounds that he was upholding, not violating, the rule of law. Needless to say, Eyre never faced trial, but Jamaica promptly lost its Assembly and by December had become a Crown colony ruled directly from London.

India was a peculiar amalgam that nicely encapsulates the varieties of British rule. The Great Revolt of 1857, still known in Britain as the 'Mutiny', ended the outsourcing of rule to the **East India Company**. In its place came direct rule from London through an appointed Governor-General and unelected Legislative Council that consisted primarily of his provincial governors. Nonetheless, the government of much of India continued to be conducted 'indirectly' through alliances with local leaders in the so-called 'princely states'. These were afforded considerable autonomy in return for their military loyalty and tax revenue. Outside of these princely states, Indians were slowly and grudgingly afforded limited local and provincial responsibilities. From 1882, local ratepayers were given the chance to elect municipal commissioners. Votes were distributed on a sliding scale (that ensured the 3 per cent of residents who were British had 20 per cent of the votes) and elected just two thirds of the commissioners. The rest were appointed either by the provincial governor or 'commercial interests' (in Calcutta the Bengal Chamber of Commerce, the Calcutta Trades Association and the Port Commission all had nominated seats). Only in 1909, in response to the growing influence of the **Indian National Congress** and the *swadeshi* movement, were Indians finally allowed to elect members to provincial Legislative Councils. Here too, forms of selection offset the influence of elections. Elected members took their seats alongside those appointed by the government of India or nominated by various commercial interests and religious communities. Whereas in the colonies that became Dominions, men (and women in New Zealand and Australia from 1893 and 1902) were granted the right to vote as individuals, in India, like New Zealand, indigenous populations were only granted it as representatives of different communal group and interests.

The Illiberal Empire

The imperative of imperial expansion and consolidation ensured that British colonies had no uniform political structure or common set of institutions. Yet despite this variety all were supposed to deliver the rule of law. It was the rule of law that made Britain's Empire liberal and enabled it to have a civilizing influence upon its subjects. Or such was the theory. In practice, as was the case in India during the Revolt and Jamaica during the Morant Bay Rebellion, the legality of rule was always in question, for the rule of law was frequently suspended to enable the violent suppression of protests and revolts. It should already be apparent from the repression of reform movements in Britain between 1792 and 1794, Peterloo and the Six Acts of 1819, and during the Chartist protests that culminated in 1848, that the declaration of states of emergency to unleash the coercive powers of the state was not confined to the colonies. What was different about their use in colonial contexts was the severity of the violence deployed. It was inconceivable that Chartists would have been flogged in public like those who rebelled in Morant Bay, or that Henry Hunt or the Chartist Feargus O'Connor would have been publicly executed, let alone by being blown apart with a cannonball like the leaders of the Revolt in India (see Figure 7.1). As we will see in the following chapter, the violence of colonial rule was in part made possible by the hardening of theories of racial difference. Simply put, the lives of people of colour (including here the poor Irish), especially those who questioned the civility and legality of British rule, were considered of little value. What value they possessed for the colonial state was in being used as exemplary figures of punishment to deter others from questioning its legitimacy.

Only occasionally, as with Eyre's brutal suppression of the Morant Bay Rebellion, did Britons become aware that what they imagined to be a liberal and civilizing empire was in fact predicated upon the violence of colonial rule. Another such occasion was the war in South Africa between 1899 and 1902. There had been decades of escalating tension between the predominantly rural population of white Afrikaners – known as 'Boers' – who had settled in Transvaal and Orange Free State, and the British population based in Cape Colony. The discovery of the gold and diamond fields in Transvaal and the political and economic ambitions of Cecil Rhodes, president of Cape Colony and head of the British South African Company, only aggravated the situation. War broke out when the British prime minister, the Conservative and arch-imperialist Lord Salisbury, supported Rhodes's desire to annex the Afrikaner states. As a

Figure 7.1 The execution of Indian sepoys, 1857

journalist covering the war, Hobson analysed both its economic causes and Salisbury's use of it to whip up a patriotic fervour (what a popular song framed as '**jingoism**') at home. Thus, much public attention was focused on the heroic suffering and fortitude of those Britons placed under siege at Ladysmith, Mafeking and Kimberly by Afrikaners attempting to starve them into submission before the arrival of relieving British troops.

The **South African War** was another dirty colonial war. While Afrikaner soldiers initially outnumbered British troops by three to one, by the end of the war Britain had mobilized 450,000 men to defeat under 90,000 Afrikaners. They were commanded by Lord Kitchener who in 1898 had taken revenge for Britain's military defeat and the death of General Gordon in Khartoum fourteen years earlier by killing and wounding 26,000 of the Mahdiyya's Dervish Army at the infamous Battle of Omdurman at a cost of just 46 British soldiers. Frustrated by his inability to contain the guerrilla fighting of his opponents, Kitchener developed a system of no less than 34 camps to concentrate those civilians suspected of assisting the enemy as well as those left homeless by Britain's own scorched-earth tactics. Although they were presented as refugee camps to provide humanitarian assistance, their sanitary conditions and food supply were deeply inadequate. Within 14 months an estimated quarter of the Afrikaner population, 20,000 to 25,000 people, mainly women, children and elderly men, died of malnutrition and disease. In addition, a tenth of the black African population, 14,000 people contained in their own camps, also perished. It was Emily Hobhouse (see Textbox 8.1), who came from a well-connected Liberal and pacifist family, who broke the news of what she described as 'the cruel system' of camps in Britain, writing a report that detailed their appalling conditions. The leader of the Liberal Party, Henry Campbell Bannerman, quickly condemned what he described as 'the methods of barbarism' used by Britain in the South African War. The government immediately appointed the suffragist Millicent Fawcett to head a commission of investigation, and its report, issued after the cessation of war, corroborated Hobhouse's claims. The war not only cost the lives of 22,000 British troops and £222 million; it once again exposed the illiberalism of British imperialism.

This was not news in Ireland. Although the **New Imperialism** catalysed new analyses and critiques of the British Empire, it was the old metropolitan colony just across the Irish Sea that arguably did most to highlight the limits of Britain's **liberalism**. After the Land War, the campaign for home rule spearheaded by Parnell's Irish Parliamentary Party was hugely successful electorally, returning 85 of the 103 Irish MPs at the 1885 election. This convinced the Liberal prime minister William Gladstone to back a Home Rule Bill the following year. The Bill tore his party apart and was narrowly defeated by 343 to 313 votes as 93 Liberals, including even once-radical figures like Joseph Chamberlain and John Bright, voted against it. They did so for a variety of reasons: to defend the Union between Ireland and Britain; to prevent what they saw as the break-up of the British Empire; or because they thought the Irish incapable of self-government. Over the following decade, many of these Liberal Unionists, including Chamberlain, began to drift towards the Conservative Party. That process accelerated when, with the support of Irish MPs, Gladstone formed a minority government in 1892 and managed to get a second Home Rule Bill passed by the **House of Commons** with a majority of 34 votes, only to see it rejected by the unelected **House of Lords**. If this was liberal representative government at work, then to many it had ceased to function.

It was not until a Liberal government again became dependent upon the support of MPs from the Irish Parliamentary Party in 1910 that they were able to check the power of the House of Lords and broker a third Home Rule Bill. In 1912, a year after the Parliament Act trimmed the House of Lords' power of veto to just two years, a new Home Rule Bill was introduced. Like the preceding bill, it was a moderate

Figure 7.2 Roger Casement, 1900

proposal that sought to temper the powers of an Irish Parliament. The House of Commons, which would continue to have MPs from Ireland, retained control over all matters relating to Ireland's defence and taxation. Once again the Bill was passed by the House of Commons and rejected by the Lords, whose veto was set to expire in September 1914. Unionists in Ireland and the mainland quickly mobilized in opposition to what they considered the 'coercion' of Ulster, whose population were predominantly Anglo-Protestants fiercely hostile to Catholicism. Paramilitary groups were established to defend the Union by force and by 1913 they had clustered under the umbrella of the newly formed Ulster Volunteer Force. In response, Irish nationalists formed their own Irish Volunteer Force 'to secure and maintain the rights and liberties common to the whole people of Ireland'. Despite the escalation and militarization of these hostilities, when war broke out in August 1914, a month before the Lords veto on Home Rule was due to expire, it did so in Belgium and France instead of Ireland.

7.1 Person: Roger Casement (1864–1916)

Prior to becoming a martyr for the cause of Irish independence in the Easter Rising of 1916, Roger Casement worked for the very imperial system he would later die trying to destroy. He was born near Dublin into an Irish family with mixed Protestant and Roman Catholic lineages. Raised as a Protestant, he was secretly baptised as a Catholic by his mother on a trip to Rhyl in North Wales at the age of four. At nineteen he became a purser on a ship heading to the Congo. He spent the next twenty-odd years of his life in Africa, working, among other things, as a surveyor for the infamous Belgian King Leopold's Congo International Association from 1884 to 1889. In 1892 he became a British official working first in the Gulf of Guinea and then in Portuguese East Africa and Gabon. Back in the Congo in 1902, he reported the cruelty of Belgian colonialism there to London, for which he was awarded a CMG in 1905. His next series of consular posts was in Latin America (Brazil and Peru), where his work investigating various atrocities suffered by local populations earnt him a knighthood in 1911. All the while interested in the work of the Gaelic League, he slowly became more entangled in the Irish nationalist cause. Around the time of the Irish Home Rule Bill, in 1913, he became a leading member of the Irish Volunteer Force. At the outbreak of World War I, Casement flirted with the idea of a German–Irish military alliance that would free Ireland and defeat Britain, and he lived in Germany until 1916. He returned to Ireland in advance of the **Easter Rising**, attempting to arrange for a German submarine to supply rifles. The rendezvous failed, and Casement was arrested upon reaching shore. During his trial and leading up to his execution, British intelligence documents chronicling his homosexuality – taken from his own diaries – were released to the press in an attempt to negate his martyrdom. (K.H.)

Immediately, as the British state assumed unparalleled emergency powers with the **Defence of the Realm Act**, the enactment of Home Rule was suspended for the duration of World War I. The fragile unity of the nationalist movement, held together by the constitutionalist strategy of Irish Parliamentary Party leader John Redmond, broke apart. Redmond committed his party to the defence of the British Empire that he still wished Ireland to belong to; he was supported by 175,000 'National Volunteers' who joined the British army to fight alongside the division from Ulster. A smaller group, estimated to be less than 14,000 strong, retained the name of the Irish Volunteers and opposed the war effort with the support of the Irish Republican Brotherhood. Some within the organization, like its military director Patrick Pearse, wished to go further and lead an insurrection against the British while their attention and resources lay in fighting Germany on the Western Front in France. On Easter Monday of 1916, against the orders of Eoin MacNeill, the Volunteers' Chief of Staff, Pearse led what was supposed to be an armed revolt that would establish Ireland as a republic. Divisions within the movement and a lack of coordination left 1,200 men fighting British troops in Dublin for six days until they were bombed into submission while holed up in the General Post Office. The British government responded in a now-routine way. Martial law was declared, republican leaders, whether they were involved with the Volunteers and the Irish Republican Brotherhood or not, were rounded up and interned – some 3,400 in Ireland and a further 1,500 on the mainland. The fifteen leaders, including Roger Casement (see Textbox 7.1 and Figure 7.2), of what became known as the **Easter Rising**, were executed. The Rising and its repression were a defining moment for Irish nationalism. Thereafter, republicans willing to embrace a military strategy outflanked the old constitutionalist home rulers. Ireland was heading to its own war to rid itself of British rule.

An Imperial and Industrial War

World War I was a product of the competition between Europe's imperial powers that had been accelerating for decades. In the summer of 1914, the scramble for territories and markets beyond Europe gave way to a struggle for control of the Balkans – especially Serbia – between the Austro-Hungarian, German, Russian and Ottoman empires. When a Serbian nationalist assassinated the Austrian heir-apparent Archduke Franz Ferdinand on 28 June, Austria, with the backing of Germany, sought to tighten its grip on Serbia. Russia mobilized in support of its Serbians allies. Britain kept its distance from the conflict until its most feared rival, Germany, declared war on Russia on 1 August and two days later invaded Belgium with the intention of occupying France. No one anticipated that the war would last for more than four years, would be fought on an industrial and global scale, or would demand the unprecedented 'total' mobilization of states' resources as well as their subjects at home and abroad. During the 1920s and 1930s, Britons would come to refer to it as the 'Great War' to register the enormity of its impact upon their lives.

Defending the Motherland

World War I was not just a product of the new imperial age; it was fought on an imperial scale. Although it was the first major European conflagration in Europe to engage Britain since the **Napoleonic Wars**, Map 7.3 reminds us that it was also an imperial war fought in Africa, the Middle East and the Pacific as Britain attacked German colonies and the territories of the Ottoman Empire. Perhaps most significantly, it was a war fought with colonial troops and support workers by all the empires at war. Whereas France and Germany forcibly enlisted some of the colonial troops they deployed, Britain did not introduce conscription in any of its colonies, although only widespread hostility to its plans to do so in Ireland ensured this was so. It is one of the contradictory elements of this imperial war that, despite the growing critiques of colonialism, many colonial subjects volunteered to defend the mother country and its empire.

India's army, so long vital to the strategic defence of the British Empire in East Asia, Africa and the Middle East, provided the largest number of colonial soldiers. A remarkable 1.5 million men were recruited from India, of whom over 60,000 died, mostly fighting in Mesopotamia but also on the Western Front. The self-governing 'Dominions' of Australia, Canada, Newfoundland, New Zealand and South Africa contributed a further 1.3 million troops. They fought in all the theatres of war. Troops from Australia and New Zealand captured the German colonies of Samoa and New Guinea before the end of 1914; fought in Turkey, Egypt, Syria and Palestine; and fought on the Western Front like their counterparts from Canada and Newfoundland. South African troops led the assault against the colonies of German South Africa (for which some Afrikaners fought) and East Africa. We have already seen that many Irishmen, an estimated 200,000, joined the British or Allied armies and fought in France, Serbia, Greece, Palestine and Turkey. Although black colonial subjects from the Caribbean and Britain's African colonies also volunteered for military service, they were not allowed to fight against white Europeans on the Western Front. The British West Indies Regiment was sent to France to do the support work of digging trenches and loading ammunition rather than as combatants. This racialized division of labour was further apparent by the over 200,000 colonial subjects from China, Egypt, South Africa, the West Indies, Mauritius and Fiji who were recruited to work behind the Front on the supply lines. Britain did not just draw upon its colonial manpower; it ensured that its colonies paid for their own war effort and that some even made further financial contributions. India alone put £146 million into Britain's war chest between 1914 and 1920. Again, Britain

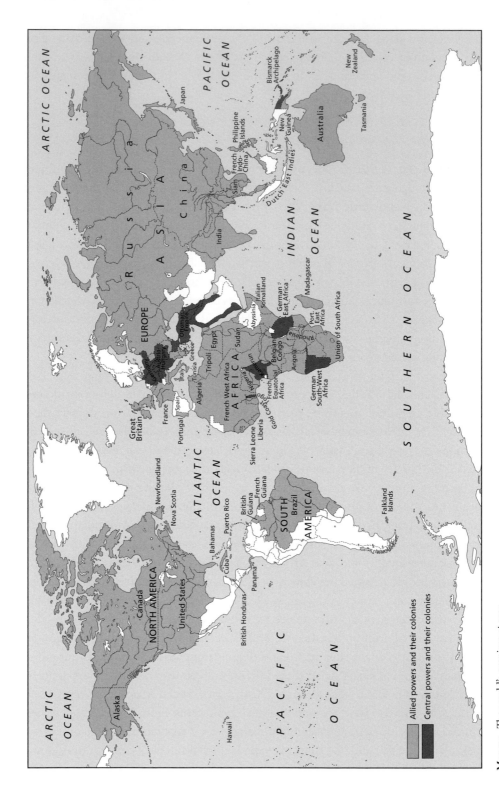

Map 7.3 The world's empires at war

Allied powers and their colonies

Central powers and their colonies

ARCTIC OCEAN

ARCTIC OCEAN

PACIFIC OCEAN

RUSSIA

EUROPE

China

Japan

Philippine Islands

French Indo-China

Siam

Dutch East Indies

India

Bismarck Archipelago

New Guinea

New Zealand

Australia

Tasmania

INDIAN OCEAN

Madagascar

Abyssinia

Italian Somaliland

German East Africa

Port. East Africa

Union of South Africa

Ottoman Empire

Austria-Hungary

Greece

Italy

Tunisia

Tripoli

Egypt

Sudan

AFRICA

Algeria

French West Africa

Sierra Leone

Liberia

Gold Coast

Nigeria

French Equatorial Africa

Belgian Congo

Angola

Rhodesia

German South-West Africa

Serbia

Great Britain

France

Spain

Portugal

ATLANTIC OCEAN

Newfoundland

Nova Scotia

Puerto Rico

Bahamas

Cuba

British Honduras

Panama

NORTH AMERICA

United States

Canada

Alaska

British Guiana

French Guiana

SOUTH AMERICA

Brazil

Falkland Islands

Hawaii

PACIFIC OCEAN

SOUTHERN OCEAN

was not unique here. The French, Germans, Ottomans, Russians and Americans all deployed colonial subjects to support their war efforts. The Great War really was an imperial war.

A State of Emergency at Home

The warring empires maximized not just their colonial manpower but all the emergency powers and industrialized military technologies they could muster. Almost immediately after Britain declared war, it passed the **Defence of the Realm Act** (DORA), giving the state unprecedented controls over its domestic population and resources. Civil liberties were an early casualty. On 8 August 1914, the same day that DORA was passed, an Aliens Restriction Act made it compulsory for all aliens over sixteen years of age to register with the police. Upon registering, they would possibly face internment if they were men or, if they were women and children, deportation. Just under 30,000 'enemy aliens' were deported within six months, the vast majority of whom – over 23,000 – had German ties. Another 32,000 men were interned during the war and often subjected to forced labour. In the patriotic zeal of the early months of the war, few noticed and still fewer cared about the civil liberties of aliens, especially after a German U-boat submarine sank the *Lusitania* ocean liner, killing almost 1,200 civilians in May 1915.

Much more contentious was the eventual introduction of conscription in January 1916. Britain's **ancien regime** had used press gangs and mercenaries to man its military with what the Duke of Wellington, the famous general of the **Napoleonic Wars**, had described as 'the scum of the earth.' A liberal Britain was to have, in contrast, a volunteer army. And, as we'll see in Chapter 8, young men volunteered in large numbers at the outbreak of the Great War: 3 million men enlisted between August 1914 and January 1916. As the pace of recruitment fell and the horrific scale of casualties became increasingly apparent in 1915, calls for conscription grew louder. Those who objected to the war on religious or political grounds formed the No-Conscription Fellowship in November 1914 without any expectation that conscription would become an issue. A year later they led the campaign against the Military Services Bill, which would introduce conscription. Pacifist groups opposed to the war, like the Independent Labour Party and the Quakers, supported them, but so too did those who rejected the compulsion of individuals by the state, like the *Manchester Guardian*. While a further 3 million were conscripted to fight before the war's end, 16,000 men refused to fight as 'conscientious objectors', although 3,400 of those served in the Non-Combatant Corps. Those who refused to serve in any capacity had their cases held before military tribunals: 6,000 of them – including the leaders of the No-Conscription Fellowship, Fenner Brockway and Clifford Allen – were arrested and imprisoned. Some went on hunger strike to protest their treatment in prison and 130 of them were force-fed. All were denied the right to vote as citizens in 1918. Conscription, and the punitive treatment of conscientious objectors, were a powerful demonstration that the liberal state had successfully claimed unprecedented powers over the lives of its subjects in the name of the emergency conditions of war.

The wartime state of emergency also removed the remaining tenets of liberal political economy. The **gold standard** and **free trade** were necessarily suspended in a world at war, while cheap government and **laissez-faire** were no longer viable given the demands of total war. Even the sanctity of private property was curtailed as **DORA** afforded the state control of privately owned railways, mines, shipyards, engineering and armament factories. Twelve new government departments, with responsibilities for new areas like munitions, food control, transport, information and health, were created to oversee this transformation. The size of the civil service doubled during the war, reaching 400,000 people by its end. With all these new responsibilities, cheap government and the **Treasury**'s control of government expenditure were no longer possible. The government spent just £184 million in 1913; by 1918 its gross expenditure stood at £2,696,200,000. Income tax was persistently raised to help pay for all of this, increasing by 500 per cent during the war. The wealthiest saw their income tax rise from 8 to 42 per cent, while estates worth over £2 million were taxed at 40 per cent. This was not enough. The **national debt**, so aggressively cut in the decades after the **Napoleonic Wars**, rose from £650 million in 1914 to £6.14 billion in 1919. Whereas once Britain had provided loans to foreign governments, it became heavily indebted to the United States and its merchant banks, who propped up the pound as it came under increasing pressure in 1916 and 1917; Britain owed America £1 billion in loans by 1919. Even by 1934, three years after Britain had ceased to make its repayments, she owed America £866 million. Without question, Britain's capacity to raise funds from the wealth of its own population, to drain more resources from its Empire, and to borrow from its allies helped ensure its eventual victory. Britain and its Empire spent a total of $23 billion, $4 billion more than Germany and only $2 billion less than the combined expenditure of the Central Powers.

The state literally took command of the war economy. Lloyd George's **Ministry of Munitions**, newly created in 1915, directed operations, albeit with a raft of businessmen providing advice. By the end of the war the staff in its headquarters numbered 25,000 – the size of the entire Civil Service a century earlier – and they supervised the production of over 3 million workers. Not only did the state become the nation's largest employer, it introduced large-scale factory production on a scale never before seen. The size of these factories was unprecedented. In November 1917 the government's Royal Arsenal munitions factory at Woolwich employed 28,000 women, 4,200 men and 6,500 boys. The introduction of electricity-powered plants, the use of machine-tools for standardized mass production, and new cost-accounting procedures transformed manufacturing. By 1918 this war machine had produced 170 million artillery shells,

4 million rifles, 250,000 machine guns, 52,000 planes and 25,000 big guns. Similarly, by the end of the war, the Ministry of Food had transformed the production, distribution and consumption of food. As the Great Depression and Britain's free trade regime had rendered the country dependent on imports for 77 per cent of its wheat and 40 per cent of its beef, its food supply was hugely vulnerable. At least 300,000 tons of merchant shipping were lost every month of 1916 to German U-boat attacks. By September of that year, despite endless injunctions for people to engage in voluntary rationing, prices had risen by 65 per cent and food shortages had generated lengthy queues as well as considerable unrest. In 1917 a Corn Production Act ensured that 3 million acres of land were converted from pasture to cereal production, exempted skilled agricultural labourers from conscription, and either requisitioned or recruited additional labour from 84,000 soldiers, 30,000 POWs and 16,000 members of the Women's Land Army. The following year, rationing for all basic commodities was finally introduced and 85 per cent of all civilian food was by then bought and sold by the state, which also controlled its price and its distribution. *Laissez-faire* was, it appeared, a thing of the past.

The state industrialized British manufacturing and agriculture on a new mass scale because the Great War was the first truly industrial war. Fought by competing global Empires with the new technologies and materials wrought during the second wave of industrialization in the last quarter of the nineteenth century, its lethal violence was unprecedented. New industrial, and industrially produced, technologies of murder transformed the conduct of war. Whereas the Napoleonic Wars were fought with muskets that had a range of 50 to 70 yards and were slow to reload, the Great War was fought with breech-loading rifles with ranges of over 500 yards. Some have suggested that the disparity between the rifle and the musket is greater than that between the musket and the bow and arrow. The industrial scale of slaughter, though, was the product of the machine gun. Its name says it all. First invented by an American during the Civil War in the 1860s and quickly deployed in Britain's colonial wars from the 1870s, by the time of the Great War the machine gun could fire 600 rounds a minute over a range of 4,000 yards. Produced in the huge armaments factories of Birmingham and London, at the start of the war there were just 1,000 used by the British army. By the war's end, 39,000 were deployed. Industrially manufactured and precision engineered, massive artillery guns (of up to 17 inches in diameter) launched barrages of shells with increasing frequency to produce a new type of blanket bombing that prepared the way for infantry advances. The British army had just 300 of these 'big guns' in 1914; it had 6,000 of them by 1918. Tanks and airplanes too, while not a major presence or purveyors of mass murder, were a further feature of the new industrial technology used during the Great War. So too were barbed wire, flamethrowers and mustard gas (as well as the ineffective masks used for protection against it). And even if animals still provided much of the transportation to and from the front lines, the numbers of cars, lorries and motorbikes used by British forces increased dramatically. They had just 334 lorries and

133 cars in 1914; by 1918 those figures had risen to 32,000 and 7,000 respectively. None of these technologies had been available before the second wave of industrialization, and all of them were industrially produced on a mass scale.

The Empire of the Dead

These industrial technologies, developed competitively between the warring empires, produced an unprecedented industrial scale of murder. The war killed over 16 million people and left a further 20 million wounded. Although, as with earlier wars, disease killed many, far more were murdered or wounded on the battlefield than in any previous conflict. The final tally provided by Britain's War Office in 1922 listed a total of 908,371 'soldiers' from its Empire who were killed in action, died of wounds or as prisoners of war, or were missing in action. The vast majority of these – 704,121 – were from Britain itself, but 64,449 Indians, 56,639 Canadians, 59,330 Australians, 16,711 New Zealanders and 7,121 South Africans also lost their lives. The numbers wounded were of course far larger: 1,663,435 Britons, 152,171 Australians, 149,732 Canadians, 69,214 Indians, 41,317 New Zealanders and 12,029 South Africans. Vast numbers of animals also died. It is estimated that a total of 8 million horses died during the Great War as they were used both in cavalry charges (especially by the British in East Africa and Palestine) and for the transportation of supplies. Just under half a million horses used by British forces were killed, and a further 2.5 million were wounded. In terms of military casualties, the Great War was the deadliest war in human history to date by some distance.

The mortality rates during particular campaigns and battles were staggering. Russia's 'Brusilov' offensive against the Central Powers in what is now Ukraine during two months of the summer of 1916 resulted in 1.6 million casualties. When the British, French and German armies fought the Battle of the Somme between 1 July and 18 November 1916, 1.2 million were killed, a third of whom were from the British army. At the end of the first day of fighting alone there were 20,000 dead and 60,000 casualties. Over half a million lost their lives at Gallipoli trying to secure the strategically vital Dardanelle Straits from Ottoman control in 1915, the vast majority from disease. During the Battle of Verdun between French and German troops, 7,000 horses were killed by artillery in one day. With competing empires using the same industrial technologies of murder across the world, there was almost no end to this roll call of horror and slaughter. Given the carnage, almost all these figures are estimates that are disputed and endlessly revised. Thus the British War Office figures have been revised upwards by the government's **Imperial War Graves Commission**, the body created in 1917 to deal with the war dead.

Just as the British state took command of its economy and population, so it took control of dealing with those who died defending it across much of the world. Such was the scale of casualties that the British army, pushed at first by the work of the Red Cross, were compelled to develop new systems for identifying corpses, burying them and keeping records of their location. French land was purchased to establish purpose-built cemeteries for the troops from the British Empire, each in a uniform style that specified the design and inscription of each headstone regardless of religion, class or colour. Wealthy families, once able to ship the bodies of their dead sons home or rely upon their fellow officers to personalize their graves, were no longer allowed to do so. Like the humblest of families, they too were denied the chance to design the headstone or craft its inscription. The state, not the family, let alone a church or chapel, now took care of the dead and decided where they were to be buried and how they were to be remembered. The creation of the Imperial War Graves Commission in 1917 sought to extend this treatment of the dead, and the uniformity of its forms of remembrance, across the Empire. By the end of the war, having hired Chinese workers to clean up battles sites and collect scattered remains, they had taken responsibility for 587,000 graves (many with no name) and identified a further 559,000 casualties as having no known grave. Once all the cemeteries had been built by 1927, there were 500 of them scattered across the Empire and they contained over 400,000 headstones and 400 Stones of Remembrance for the missing dead (see Textbox 7.2 and Figure 7.3).

The shadow of grief for these missing but remembered men was immense. Very quickly after the construction of these cemeteries, the pilgrimages of families, friends and comrades to visit loved ones spawned a veritable tourist industry complete with published guides to the battles, trenches and graves of the Western Front. The dead may have been left overseas but they haunted the spaces of the living long after the Great War. In 1919 a temporary cenotaph was constructed at the very heart of the imperial state in Whitehall to begin a Remembrance Day ceremony. From that day forward, across the British Empire, a minute's silence is held on the eleventh hour of the eleventh day of the eleventh month to commemorate those who lost their lives. The permanent cenotaph installed in the 1920s was designed by Edwin Luytens. Luytens, one of the in-house architects of the Imperial War Graves Commission since before the Armistice, probably did more than anyone to create an imperial architecture of remembrance. His War Memorial in Leicester's Victoria Park (1923) is almost identical to the India Gate built in New Delhi (1931), a city he designed much of. Yet almost every town of any size in Britain soon boasted its own more modest memorial. Mostly built by public donations, we know there are at least 60,000 such memorials across the country, which legislation in 1923 enabled local authorities to maintain. This figure does not include the many memorials placed within chapels and churches. In Glossop, a mill-town between Manchester and Sheffield with a population of around 20,000, while the names of the 309 of its inhabitants who died during the Great War were inscribed on a war memorial in the town square, it was supplemented by fourteen other memorials in the town's numerous chapels and churches.

7.2 Place: Imperial War Grave cemetery, Étaples, France

The largest Imperial War Grave cemetery in France was in Étaples, just south of Boulogne in France. Designed by Edwin Luytens in the 1920s, it was built on a site previously occupied by a complex of more than a dozen British army field hospitals that in 1917 received 40,000 wounded soldiers every month. Ten months after the Armistice, three hospitals and a convalescent home still remained. Along with the cemetery's stark, white and uniform gravestones that were so characteristic of the work of the Imperial War Graves Commission, the site featured a stone archway and cenotaph adorned by stone flags. This area of France saw troops from across the British Empire. The 10,771 dead buried here include soldiers from Australia, India, Canada, New Zealand and South Africa, 658 Germans and 73 unidentified bodies. Also among the war dead buried here are at least five women of the Women's Army Auxiliary Corps: Doris Mary Lurker, Mary Maria Matthews, Blanche Amelia Page, Edith Routledge and Emma Whittaker. The cemetery was reopened in World War Two as Allied military hospitals were briefly set up again at Étaples between January and May 1940.

Figure 7.3 Imperial war graves at Étaples, France

The state may have taken charge of the bodies of the dead and forged an imperial culture around their commemoration, but localities still sought to symbolically bring their dead home.

A New Internationalism?

The carnage of World War I sent shock waves around the globe. The product of a modern world made by industrial empires, it called into question the very idea that this modernity would entail the progressive development of civilization and prosperity. In a world changed by war, questions abounded in post-war Britain. Could Britain re-establish the central place of the British imperium and the imperialism of its liberal political economy of free trade, the **gold standard** and cheap government? How could the victorious empires divide up the former colonial territories of the German and Ottoman Empires and maintain a new balance of power that would finally silence the guns, ending the slaughter and the ruinous expense of war? Could Britain maintain its position as the dominant superpower of the world given its growing debt burden and dependence on American loans?

The reality was that despite the victory of the British Empire and her allies, Britain faced new and uncertain global conditions over which it had little control. The Bolshevik Revolution in Russia emboldened labour movements across the globe and terrified the aristocracies and monarchs of Europe. The fear that revolution could be contagious was exacerbated by the fact that millions of demobilized soldiers were returning home to look for work in an imperial and global economy still shattered by war. While no fan of revolution, **Woodrow Wilson**, the president of the newly ascendant American Empire that had largely avoided the expense of war and helped bankroll Britain's war effort, also wanted to craft the post-war world. Wilson believed that Europe's empires could only avoid war if they recognized the right of some nations to sovereignty and self-determination. As he did not consider people of colour yet ready for such a privilege, they would have to remain the custodians of empires like his own or those of France and Britain. The **League of Nations** emerged from the various peace conferences and treaties of 1919, to encourage new modes of international cooperation as well as to place former German and Ottoman colonies under the 'trusteeship' of the victorious empires as '**Mandates**'. The British Empire thus grew considerably in 1919, having acquired the British Cameroons, Togoland and Tanganyika in Africa; the Pacific Islands of Nauru and Samoa; and Iraq, Palestine and Transjordan in the Middle East.

A Family of Nations?

Nationalism and imperialism remained central features of the new internationalism of the post-war world. If the Empire had risen to Britain's defence during the war, the contributions of colonial troops, together with the Wilsonian rhetoric of self-determination, fuelled the fire of nationalism after the Armistice. In Canada a determination to keep French Canadians loyal after the imposition of conscription in 1917, a suspicion of Britain's imperial expansion into the Middle East, and unwillingness to shoulder the costs of war, fuelled calls for still greater independence from London. In South Africa, despite Smuts's best efforts, Afrikaner calls for a separate republic gathered steam through the National Party led by General Hertzog, while the white settlers in Southern Rhodesia voted to become a self-governing colony in 1923. The sacrifices of Australians and New Zealanders at Gallipoli were marked almost immediately by the creation of Anzac Day on 25 April 1916. **Anzac Day** was a decidedly national commemoration, one that celebrated Australians and New Zealanders as noble victims of a flawed British strategy. After the Armistice it pointedly remained the national day of remembrance in preference to 11 November. For Australians, Anzac Day quickly became associated with the idealized figure of the rugged, manly, bushman 'digger' and thus part of the national creation story. As we shall shortly see, the series of Imperial Conferences that followed the war in 1918, 1919, 1921 and 1923 sought to contain this wave of Dominion nationalism.

Yet beyond the Dominions colonial nationalism was less easily contained or accommodated in the post-war British imperium. In 1919, a series of riots, strikes, nationalist mobilizations, revolts and wars erupted across the British Empire. In Britain, as we shall see in Chapter 9, most men and some women who had helped defend the British Empire were rewarded with citizenship and the right to vote in 1918. In 1919, a series of riots broke out against people of colour mainly in the port towns of Liverpool, Cardiff, Glasgow, South Shields, London and Hull. Dismayed by the refusal to politically recognize their loyalty and service, encouraged yet abandoned by the Wilsonian rhetoric of self-determination, nationalist movements in Ireland, India, Egypt and Iraq erupted to press the case for independence or home rule. The politics of black internationalism also gathered steam. The Pan-African Congress, which first met in London in 1900, regathered in Paris during the peace conference of 1918 to emphasize their exclusion from those discussions. At the start of the war in 1914, Marcus Garvey established the Universal Negro Improvement Association and African Communities (Imperial) League in Jamaica. As unrest fermented across the Caribbean during the war, returning veterans of the West Indian regiment, as well as some returning from Britain where they had been targeted in the 1919 'race riots', joined a wave of protests and strikes in Belize, Jamaica, Grenada and British Honduras. And, finally, both Somalis and Afghans fought renewed wars against British rule. The Treaty of Versailles may have provided a peace settlement for Euro-America, but those colonial subjects across the world excluded from it protested en masse.

With its military no longer engaged in a global conflict, Britain was quick to redeploy forces to its rebellious colonies, where it either declared a state of emergency or war. Either way, anti-colonial protests were dealt with quickly and violently. In the wake of the Rising, the Irish republican party of Sinn Fein, led by Éamon de Valera, decisively defeated John Redmond's Irish Parliamentary Party, which remained wedded to home rule and loyalty to the British Empire at the election of 1918. Having won 73 of the 105 Irish seats in the 1918 election, Sinn Fein refused to legitimate British rule in Ireland by having their MPs go to Westminster. Instead, they made a unilateral declaration of independence in January 1919 and established their own Parliament in Ireland, known in Gaelic as the *Dáil Éireann*. War was effectively declared by both sides. An **Irish Republican Army (IRA)**, forged from the forces of the Irish Volunteers and Irish Republican Brotherhood after the catastrophe of the Rising, was established to protect the *Dail* and Ireland's self-declared sovereignty. By September, Winston Churchill, as Secretary of the War Office, had begun to dispatch volunteers, many demobilized soldiers, to supplement and militarize the forces of the Royal Irish Constabulary. Two years later almost 10,000 of these 'black and tans', known for their improvised uniform of khaki bottoms and dark green tops, had volunteered. They became infamous for their lack of discipline, violent attacks upon civilian populations, and burning and sacking of towns as 'reprisals' for IRA successes. This **Anglo-Irish War** lasted for two years of bitter fighting. With British forces outnumbering the IRA by five to one, the war was characterized by a pattern of guerrilla attacks by the IRA and fierce counter-insurgency responses by the British army and Royal Irish Constabulary. Of the 2,000 people who died, 750 of them were civilians. A further 4,400 IRA activists were arrested and imprisoned without trial.

In India the extension of wartime 'emergency measures' by the **Rowlatt Act** of March 1919 inflamed the nationalist movement, which rightly saw it as an attempt to contain its growing support. The Rowlatt Act was a blunt instrument of repressive force against what it considered sedition, not unlike the Six Acts. It extended the colonial government's power to imprison without trial those considered politically subversive; it authorized the continued incarceration of the Young Muslim leaders suspected of pan-Islamic sympathies with the defeated Ottoman Empire; and it tightened restrictions on the press. In sum, it effectively denied Indians freedom of speech. Gandhi, who had recently risen to prominence within the nationalist movement by leading grassroots mobilizations in western India and Bihar, led a campaign against it. Inevitably, that campaign quickly culminated in Gandhi's arrest and the intensification of protests that, in the Punjab especially, sometimes turned violent. Such was the case in the Sikh holy city of Amritsar in 1919, where Brigadier-General Reginald Dyer enforced martial law and banned all public meetings. When thousands gathered within a walled enclosure close to the city's Golden Temple to protest the ban, Dyer ordered 90 Indian and Gurkha troops to fire over 1,500 rounds of ammunition at the defenceless crowd for between 10 and 15 minutes. Although the official report suggested that 379 people were killed and a further 1,200 wounded, the number of casualties is thought to have been closer to 1,000. Although the governor of the Punjab hailed Dyer as a hero, his actions were widely condemned back in Britain where an official Committee of Inquiry forced his resignation. Like Governor Eyre before him, some rallied to his support, with *The Morning Post* raising £26,000 from public donations to support his retirement.

In the **House of Commons** Winston Churchill censured Dyer for his 'monstrous' actions but insisted the **Amritsar Massacre** was 'an event which stands in singular and sinister isolation'. Nothing could have been further from the truth as Churchill, who had sent the black and tans to Ireland, well knew. In 1919 he had already approved the use of tear gas against Kurds in Iraq, and the following year he was also instrumental in developing the system of 'air control' that was used to crush colonial revolts in Iraq and Somaliland. The RAF had already proved decisive in 1919 during the Third Anglo-Afghan War, fighting in the mountainous terrain around the Khyber Pass (where Dyer was sent after Amritsar). **Air control** consisted of using aerial bombardment as a way of fighting nomadic 'tribal' groups and destroying isolated settlements in vast and hostile territories where it was difficult to send ground troops. In Somaliland, since Kitchener's brutal victory at Omdurman in 1898, the British military had been unable to crush the Islamic state established by Mohammed Abdullah Hassan (whom Britons referred to as 'the Mad Mullah') in 1914. Yet within the first month of 1920, the use of twelve airplanes, together with a minimal ground force of Somaliland Camel Corps and the King's African Rifles, defeated Hassan's 'Dervish' army and destroyed their strongholds. Similarly, in Iraq, two squadrons from the RAF decisively changed the course of a revolt which had successfully spread along the Euphrates. In the space of a few months, the RAF dropped 97 tons of bombs and fired 183,861 rounds of ammunition. Saturation bombing had come of age. The distinction between military and civilian targets evaporated, for air control was intended to have a pacifying 'moral effect' that would prevent others from taking up arms. From Ireland to Iraq, British counter-insurgency techniques were developed to repress the widespread colonial revolts of 1919 and 1920.

Despite their violent repression, some colonial nationalists did successfully wring the concession of important (if inadequate) reforms from Britain's imperial state. The empire could not be preserved by force alone. The Government of India Act passed in June 1919, often known as the Montagu-Chelmsford reforms after its architects, failed to quell the unrest surrounding the Rowlatt Act, but it did extend the franchise (and its 'communal' divisions), the responsibilities of elected provincial councils, and increase Indian representation in the Central Legislature. Nonetheless, the Viceroy continued to take his orders solely from London and the provincial councils were denied responsibility for the key areas of finance and law and order. It was a long way from home rule. As was the 'independence' offered to Egypt in 1922 after three years of nationalist protests occasionally dampened down by martial law. Egypt got its own king and government, but Britain effectively kept control of the country's finances and foreign relations and also continued its military occupation.

In Ireland, the war catalysed a political process that resulted first in the partition of the country by the Government of Ireland Act in 1920, with the northern counties of Ulster given their own Parliament in June 1921. The following month a truce was declared with the IRA, and by December months of negotiation had produced the Anglo-Irish Treaty. The Treaty preserved partition in return for 'independence' as a Dominion within the British Empire. It did not satisfy republicans who wanted a united Ireland and to be no part of the British Empire. A civil war immediately broke out with many from Sinn Fein and the IRA refusing to accept the legitimacy of the new 'Irish Free State' and its government headed by Michael Collins and W.T. Cosgrove. Armed by the British, and declaring martial law, the Irish Free State quickly defeated the republican movement, executing 77 of its leaders and imprisoning 12,000 of its activists and supporters. In total it is estimated that between 2,000 and 5,000 people lost their lives in this brutish but short civil war.

The colonial revolts that followed World War I changed the shape of the British Empire. Even so, some continued to believe that it provided an exemplary model of international cooperation. The South African leader **Jan Smuts**, who had fought the British during the war of 1899–1902 before leading the campaign against the German army in East Africa during the Great War, was one such advocate. As a member of the Imperial War Cabinet, he spoke to Parliament in 1917, celebrating how the 'British commonwealth of nations' had come together to defend the British Empire during the Great War. Two Imperial Conferences were held in 1917 and 1918, and Smuts' ideas were influential in the formation of the **League of Nations** in 1920. It is no accident that the real work of binding together the Empire as a family of nations occurred in the 1920s, the golden age of Euro-American liberal internationalism, when it was hoped that a new set of international institutions and organizations would bring peace and prosperity after the misery of war. Two further Imperial Conferences were held in 1921 and 1923, the latter including the Irish Free State. The British Empire Exhibition in 1924, for which Wembley football stadium was constructed, sought to 'strengthen bonds that bind mother Country to her Sister States and Daughters'. Similarly, formed in 1926 by Leo Amory, the Secretary of State for the Dominions, the Empire Marketing Board sought to develop imperial economic integration by encouraging Britons to consume foods and raw materials from the colonies (see Textbox 7.3). Once the **Balfour Declaration** of 1926 and the **Statute of Westminster** of 1931 had finally conceded that the Dominions were not only 'autonomous communities … within the British Commonwealth of Nations' but had complete freedom from Westminster even in foreign policy, the structure of the Commonwealth was complete. This autonomy came at a price. As we shall see in Chapter 11, in return for political independence the Dominions were bound to Britain economically through a tariff system of imperial preference and the common currency provided by the **Sterling Area**. This would further entrench Britain's economic dependence upon trade with its Dominions, which

7.3 Source: 'One Family', Colonial Film Archive

A year after its creation, the Empire Marketing Board's chief civil servant Stephen Tallents, fresh from his management of public relations for the government during the General Strike, established a Film Unit under the leadership of the young, left-wing, Scot, John Grierson. The Unit quickly became renowned for its innovative work and the creation of a new type of documentary film. Directed by Walter Creighton in 1930, 'One Family' was perhaps the strangest and most extravagant of these films. The film depicts a young boy falling asleep in his geography class and dreaming of baking a Christmas pudding for the king. The boy travels around the Empire assembling ingredients – butter from New Zealand, eggs from Ireland, fruit from South Africa, raisins from Australia and even bread from Scotland. The 'Empire Pudding' was intended as symbol of the Empire's capacity to be self-sufficient and the complementary nature of the imperial economy. The film was screened at the Palace Theatre in London and proved a critical and commercial disaster, raising only £334 (not enough to even pay for the band hired to promote the premiere) and panned by one critic for being 'abysmally vomit-making'. Many of the films of the Empire Marketing Board are available to view at the British Film Institute and the British Empire and Commonwealth Museum. A full catalogue of these films, and those of the successor Colonial Film Unit, is available at http://colonialfilm .org.uk/node/40.

had been growing since the **Great Depression** in the 1870s. The British imperium had helped Britain win the war; its job now was to help it survive the peace.

The Economics of Peace

The economist John Maynard Keynes had warned in his *Economic Consequences of the Peace* (1919) that the politicians negotiating the Treaty of Versailles had their eyes set on the wrong prize. Preoccupied with political questions of how to reconcile imperialism with new international mechanisms and the rhetoric of self-determination and national sovereignty, they had neglected the structural economic pressures that had really led the world to war. If Britain's war economy had at first enabled it to mask its growing economic problems, the attempt to return to the pre-war policies of a liberal political economy left them harshly exposed.

First, the cost of the war, and the growing size of the **national debt** attracted a critique of state expenditure that focused, as we will see in Chapter 8, on the very modest programme of post-war social reconstruction to create 'a land fit for heroes'. Given the massive increase in government and taxation during the war, businesses (who had faced an excess-profit tax and a base rate corporation tax for the first time during the war), the wealthiest (who had been taxed at higher rates on their unearned incomes from land and investments), and those simply taxed on their salaries hoped for a return to the less onerous pre-war conditions. Instead, government spending on civil matters alone increased from £523 million to £590 million between 1920 and 1921 and taxation per head also continued to rise from £18 in 1919 to £24 in 1921. The calls for lower taxes and a return to cheap government were led by the Anti-Waste League, which was established in 1921 by the influential press baron Lord Rothermere, the owner of two popular newspapers, the *Daily Mirror* and *Daily Mail*. When the League quickly won three by-elections, the coalition government headed by Lloyd George created a Committee of National Expenditure, chaired by the businessman-turned-politician Eric Geddes, to explore how government spending could be reduced. The resulting '**Geddes Axe**' instituted a series of austerity measures that cut a total of £52 million, mainly from the defence budget but also from nascent social programmes.

The Geddes Axe was a political solution for a government caught between Conservatives pushing for lower taxes and less spending and the growing popularity of the Labour Party calling for more social programmes and higher taxes on the wealthiest. Its deflationary effect may have contained inflation but it did not restore cheap government. Public expenditure quickly began to grow again, even as the numbers of registered unemployed rose to the unprecedented level of 1.5 million in 1922.

With the economy in recession, the growing size of the **national debt** put pressure on the pound. This was especially the case in relation to the dollar. Britain was not only heavily indebted to the United States, whose GDP had surpassed that of the entire British Empire in 1916. The US dollar rose in value from its pre-war level of $4.87 to the pound to $3.40 by 1920. Although the weak value of the pound should have made Britain's exports more competitive, a brief rally of overseas trade between 1919 and 1921 gave way to a long slide. Between 1920 and 1925 the indexed average value of exports fell by almost half, from a post-war high of 245 to 126. The trade deficit between exports and imports worsened considerably. In 1913 it had stood at £146 million and, despite rallying to £183 million in 1922, it more than doubled to £393 million by 1925. The pound's sinking status and value also shook overseas investments, whose invisible earnings had long maintained Britain's balance of payments, which had already contracted by 20 per cent during the war. When the Conservative Party came to power in 1924, its new Chancellor of the Exchequer, Winston Churchill, believed that only a return to the **gold standard** could restore the prestige of the pound, redeem Britain's dire balance of payments and ensure the City of London, not Wall Street, remained the financial capital of the world. Ironically it required loans of $200 million from the United States Federal Reserve, and a further $100 million from J.P. Morgan, to enable Churchill to return the pound to the gold standard at its pre-war value against the US dollar.

If the gold standard had once helped make Britain the workshop of the world, it now accelerated the decline of its export industries. Whereas the value of domestic exports was £7.7 million in 1925, it more than halved by 1932 to £3.6 million. This veritable collapse of Britain's exports badly hit the staple industries that depended upon overseas markets. 4,318,000 tons of iron and steel had been exported in 1923, just 1,887,000 tons were in 1932. Cotton and coal were similar stories: 4,324 million yards of manufactured cotton goods were exported in 1923, but by 1931 1,790 million were; 79,459,000 tons of coal were exported in 1923, and just 38,899,000 by 1932. As overseas demand fell, employers reduced output, reduced their workforces and sought to restrain wages to protect their profits. Britain's 1.5 million coalminers produced 249.6 million tons of coal in 1922; by 1933 almost half the number of miners (789,100) produced 207.1 million tons. Likewise, in 1923, 7,441,000 tons of iron and 8,482,000 tons of steel were produced by around 121,000 workers; by 1931, fewer than 75,000 workers produced 3,773,000 tons of iron and 5,203,000 tons of steel. Unemployment, which had already reached unprecedented levels in 1922, with just 1.5 million of 11 million workers covered by social insurance, became endemic. Throughout the 1920s there were never less than a million, or 10 per cent of insured workers, unemployed and by 1931 their number had exceeded 2.5 million or 22 per cent of the insured. As uninsured workers – like married women, the self-employed, part-time workers or those in agriculture – were not counted, it is reasonable to inflate the official unemployment figures by at least 20 per cent. In many areas, particularly agriculture and coal mining, employers sought to defend their shrinking profits by reducing the wages and extending the hours of those employees they had not laid off. As we will see in Chapter 9, this fermented a new era of labour politics that culminated in the **General Strike** of 1926 and the organization of unemployed workers into **hunger marches** during the 1920s and 1930s.

Although the United States had displaced Britain as the economic hegemon of the world, its spectacular growth and speculative boom was bought to a sudden end by the Wall Street Crash in October 1929. The Great Depression was a global crisis. The sudden contraction of the world's most rapidly growing economy had disastrous consequences for a world already struggling to recover from the Great War. The entire post-war financial system collapsed like a pack of cards when the United States ceased its loans to Germany, which in turn stopped its reparations payments to France and Britain, which in turn defaulted on their loan held by American creditors. As governments raced to protect their national economies behind protectionist tariffs – including two of Britain's most important export markets, the United States and Canada – world trade dramatically shrank, its value collapsing by two thirds between 1929 and 1934. This was catastrophic for an ailing British economy. Within three years it was in ruins: the value of its exports and the production of iron and steel halved, while unemployment leapt from 10–15 per cent to 20–25 per cent, with almost 3 million out of work in 1932. Even the once impregnable **Bank of England** faced a run on its gold reserves in 1931.

So grave was the crisis that when the Labour government elected in 1929 could not agree on implementing a new set of austerity measures – including cuts to unemployment benefit – a **National Government**, representing all political parties, was formed in August 1931 with the leaders of the Labour and Conservative parties, Ramsay MacDonald and Stanley Baldwin, as prime minister and deputy prime minister. Within a month the National Government both modestly raised taxes and cut unemployment benefit as well as the salaries of all government employees by 10 per cent (the prospect of a larger 25 per cent cut had induced a mutiny among sailors at the naval base of Invergordon). This was not enough to reassure the financial markets, and the pound again came under such pressure that the National Government was forced to abandon the gold standard. In the ensuing election of October 1931 the National Government was returned to power with a larger majority of mainly Conservative MPs. It was then that Britain finally abandoned free trade and imposed a General Tariff of 10 per cent on all manufactured goods (but not on food or raw materials). Fittingly, it was Joseph Chamberlain's son Neville who, as Chancellor of the Exchequer, announced the policy. The imperialism of free trade, cheap government and the gold standard may have come to an end in 1931 but, as we will see in Chapter 10, a new imperial system was constructed in its place to sustain the social policies and economic prosperity that Britons increasingly came to see as their right.

Conclusion

Between the Berlin Congress on the Congo in 1884–1885 and the **Statute of Westminster** in 1931, the British Empire was transformed. Territorially, its expansion was so dramatic and stretched over so many hemispheres and continents that it truly did become the empire upon which the sun never set. That spectacular growth was neither an accident, nor a product of some innate British genius for ruling the world. It was driven by the reconfiguration of the global economy after the Great Depression and by the geopolitical competition between empires across the world for territory and markets. As its competitors sought to protect their economies behind tariffs, Britain became increasingly dependent on colonial trade and overseas investments. As the imperialism of free trade became ever more draining on the colonies, and colonial governments more forceful in their repression of dissent, the situation energized nationalist critiques of the illiberalism of British rule. Yet, when imperial competition across the globe culminated with the outbreak of World War I, colonial subjects rushed to defend the British Empire, in part to establish their readiness for self-government or independence. The violence and scale of this first industrial war between global empires were horrific.

Britain only emerged victorious from it having drawn upon all its imperial resources, suspended the liberal political economy that had tied together the British Empire, and accumulated a huge **national debt**. Despite Britain's best efforts to help shape the post-war world, the world was not the same and it transformed the British imperium. With its Empire buffeted by a rising tide of nationalist revolt and its economy unable to re-establish the dominance of its global trade and finance, Britain was finally forced to abandon its liberal political economy. By 1931, the structural dependence of the ailing British economy upon its colonies was plainly evident, not just in a protectionist trade policy and currency system that spanned the Empire, but in the gradual, grudging and often violent moves towards greater self-government in the colonies.

FURTHER READING

Almost all discussions of the **New Imperialism** are in some way a response to the J.A. Hobson's *Imperialism: A Study* (1902) with which we began this chapter. At the core of the debate is whether there was a political, economic or cultural logic to the sudden colonization of the world in the closing decades of the nineteenth century. True to the Cambridge school of imperial history established by Seeley, Ronald Robinson, John Gallagher and Alice Denny's enormously influential *Africa and the Victorians: The Official Mind of Imperialism* (London, 1961) argued that officials in Whitehall reluctantly drove colonization in order to protect Britain's strategic interests in the East. P.J. Cain and A.G. Hopkins, *British Imperialism: Innovation and Expansion 1688–1914* (London, 1993), argue that the financiers of the City of London, whose overseas investments were so important to the health of the British economy, pushed the New Imperialism in Britain. Others have suggested that it was the hardening of theories of racial difference that propelled a new culture of conquest. Edward Said's *Orientalism* (London, 1978) and *Culture and Imperialism* (London, 1993) were critical here. His work was extended by feminist scholars like Anne McClintock, whose *Imperial Leather: Race, Gender, and Sexuality in the Colonial Contest* (New York, 1995) demonstrated, as we'll see in the following chapter, the centrality of gender and sexuality to understandings of race. The influence of these approaches is evident in two fine collections of essays: F. Cooper and A. Stoler (eds.), *Tensions of Empire: Colonial Cultures in a Bourgeois World* (Berkeley, 1997), and Catherine Hall (ed.), *Cultures of Empire: Colonizers in Britain and the Empire in the Nineteenth and Twentieth Centuries* (Manchester, 2000).

When we place British imperialism in a broader European or global context, it appears less exceptional and particular. Eric Hobsbawm's compelling account of *The Age of Empire: 1875–1914* (London, 1987) sees it as firmly rooted in the newly globalized Euro-American economies from the 1870s. Most recently, Antoinette Burton and Tony Ballantyne, *Empires and the Reach of the Global* (Cambridge, 2014), show the ways in which the competing Japanese, Ottoman and British empires helped create this newly global economy and the cultural and political forms of resistance to imperialism.

In recent years historians have also paid increasing attention to the critical social, political, economic and cultural role of the white settler colonies in creating a British 'world' or

'Anglosphere'. The key work here is James Belich, *Replenishing the Earth: The Settler Revolution and the Rise of the Anglo-World, 1783–1939* (Oxford, 2009). John Darwin's *The Empire Project: The Rise and Fall of the British World-System, 1830–1970* (Cambridge, 2009) incorporates the Dominion story into a more conventional account of British imperialism.

The place of colonial revolts in generating increasingly racialized and hostile views of colonial subjects in the second half of the nineteenth century is discussed in Thomas Metcalf's *Ideologies of the Raj* (Cambridge, 1995). Their use to justify the suspension of the rule of law and the increasing violence of colonial government is the subject of Nasser Hussein's *The Jurisprudence of Emergency: Colonialism and the Rule of Law* (Ann Arbor, 2003). Manu Goswami's *Producing India: From Colonial Economy to National Space* (Chicago, 2004) does a terrific job at showing how colonial nationalism contested the political economy of empire in which it was forged.

Although histories of World War I are legion, historians of Britain tend to neglect its imperial and global dimensions. John Morrow, *The Great War: An Imperial History* (London, 2004), and Lawrence Sondhaus, *World War One: The Global Revolution* (Cambridge, 2011), broaden the geographical frame but are primarily oriented around its military history. Back in Britain, how the war catalysed the twentieth-century growth of the state is well covered in James Cronin's *The Politics of State Expansion: War, State and Society in Twentieth-Century Britain* (London, 1991). The fiscal dynamic of the war, and the politics of taxation it generated, are discussed in Martin Daunton's *Just Taxes: The Politics of Taxation in Britain, 1914–1979* (Cambridge, 2002). The internment of aliens and the imprisonment of conscientious objectors are the subjects of books by Panikos Panayi, *Prisoners of Britain: German Civilian and Combatant Internees during the First World War* (Manchester, 2012), John Rae, *Conscience and Politics: The British Government and the Conscientious Objector to Military Service, 1916–1919* (Oxford, 1970), and Felicity Goodall, *We Will Not Go to War: Conscientious Objection During the World Wars* (Stroud, 2010).

The reconfiguration of the British imperium after the war has attracted a growing amount of attention in recent years. Mark Mazower's *No Enchanted Place: The End of Empire and the Ideological Origins of the United Nations* (Princeton, 2009) traces the influence of Smuts and the British imperial model to the development of internationalism and the League of Nations. While Erez Manela's *The Wilsonian Moment: Self-Determination and the International Origins of Anticolonial Nationalism* (Oxford, 2007) underplays the prior history of colonial nationalism, it outlines the dashed hopes for self-determination felt by many, which helped fuel the anti-colonial revolts that followed Versailles in 1919. Adam Tooze's *The Deluge: The Great War and the Remaking of Global Order, 1916–1931* (London, 2014) shows Britain's gradual eclipse by the financial and industrial power of the rising American Empire and the reconfiguration of the global economic system after the Wall Street Crash. The domestic politics of the final abandonment of **free trade** and the **gold standard** is the culmination of Frank Trentmann's *Free Trade Nation: Commerce, Consumption and Civil Society in Modern Britain* (Oxford, 2008).

8   The Social Problem

Introduction

Twenty minutes before midnight on 14 April 1912, the largest ship ever built hit an iceberg off the coast of Newfoundland on its maiden voyage across the Atlantic. Within hours, the *Titanic* sank and over 1,500 people perished. The world was shocked by the catastrophe, but not just because of the horrific number of casualties. Built in Belfast, the size, power and opulence of the Titanic symbolized Britain's global pre-eminence as the richest and most powerful country in the world. If Britain's navy had ruled the waves when the song 'Rule Britannia' was penned in 1740, its merchant navy and shipping lines now commanded the world's oceans and connected the largest intercontinental empire the world had ever seen. What type of portent was the doomed voyage of the *Titanic*? If the largest ship in the world could sink, what unseen iceberg lay before Britain to threaten its Empire, wealth and global power?

There were certainly Britons who began to see icebergs on every horizon. The belief that **liberalism** and its political economy had made possible the progressive improvement of the world – ushering in a new era of prosperity, political reform and the expansion of a civilizing empire – began to erode in the final decades of the nineteenth century. Doubt was not endemic, and many continued to believe that Britain had found the keys to the future. Even so, it was very real for those concerned with the poverty and dreadful social conditions most Britons experienced despite living in the richest country on earth. A growing awareness of these social problems caused some Britons to believe that the nation's progress had given way to degeneration.

Poverty had neither gone away nor been dramatically worsened by the **Great Depression**, but it had become more visible and widely discussed. Although poverty is always with us, it only becomes visible at specific moments when it is viewed as problematic. This happened in the late nineteenth century for a variety of reasons. New forms of social investigation highlighted and scientifically measured the alarming extent of poverty. The promise of liberal political economy to deliver wealth to the nation was exposed as a fiction. Indeed, it was increasingly recognized that poverty could not be explained as a personal moral incapacity when market failures and economic crises, like the **Cotton Famine** and Great Depression, were clearly beyond the control of national governments, let alone individuals.

Worse still, new scientific ways of studying society demonstrated that poverty was not just a problem for the poor. The health, security and prosperity of all members of society, as well as the future of the Empire, were threatened by the blight of poverty. Modern social sciences, especially what would become sociology and anthropology, emerged from this work. Tasked with discovering the natural laws that governed the operation of society, investigators often drew on biological

Figure 8.1 The *Titanic*, 1912

models and metaphors to imagine how it could be engineered to evolve progressively. As we have seen in Chapter 4, the exponents of liberal political economy
triumphed by insisting that markets should be credited for producing wealth but
not blamed for generating poverty and abysmal social conditions. As it was claimed
that social problems were the responsibility of the poor themselves, liberal political
economy remained untarnished by them. By the dawn of the twentieth century,
the **social question** had taken centre stage and prompted cries for social reform at
home and abroad. The task of government increasingly became developing a society
that secured the racial health of the nation so that it could compete economically,
politically and militarily on a global stage with its imperial rivals. The First World
War was the consequence of this geopolitical competition, demonstrating Britain's
dependence upon its Empire and generating a new social contract between the
state and those citizens who fought to defend it. Few in 1885 would have imagined
that by 1931 the state would take responsibility for insulating British citizens, if not
imperial subjects, from what were now understood to be the failure of markets and
the liberal political economy that had made them free. This chapter is the story of
that transformation.

TIMELINE

1853	Social Science Association
1859	Charles Darwin, *The Origin of Species*
1861–5	Cotton Famine
1865	Commons Preservation Society
1866	James Greenwood, *A Night in the Workhouse*
1869	Charity Organization Society
1873	Herbert Spencer, *The Study of Sociology*
1883	Andrew Mearns, *The Bitter Cry of Outcast London* Social Democratic Federation Christian Boys' Brigade
1884	Imperial Federation League Fabian Society Toynbee Hall National Footpaths Preservation Society
1885	W.T. Stead, *The Maiden Tribute of Modern Babylon* Criminal Law Amendment Act Socialist League National Association for Supplying Female Medical Aid to the Women of India
1889	Christian Social Union
1890	William Booth, *In Darkest England and the Way Out*
1891–1903	Charles Booth, *Life and Labour of the People of London*
1891	British edition of Engels, *The Condition of the Working Class in England*
1893	Independent Labour Party
1894	First English translation of Richard von Krafft-Ebing's *Psycopathia Sexualis*
1895	London School of Economics Oscar Wilde's conviction National Trust for Places of Historical Interest and Natural Beauty

1897	Havelock Ellis, *Sexual Inversion* Workmen's Compensation Act
1898	Ebenezer Howard, *Tomorrow: A Peaceful Path to Real Reform*
1899	Rudyard Kipling, 'The White Man's Burden'
1901	Seebohm Rowntree, *Poverty* Immigration Restriction Act (Australia) Pacific Island Labourers Act (Australia)
1903	Tariff Reform League
1904	Sociological Society Inter-Departmental Committee on Physical Deterioration
1905	Aliens Act
1907	Notification of Births Act
1909	Empire Press Union 'The People's Budget' Old Age Pension
1910	Girl Guides
1911	National Insurance
1912	Sinking of the *Titanic* Havelock Ellis, *The Task of Social Hygiene*
1913	Mental Deficiency Act
1914–18	World War I
1915	Ministry of Munitions and Welfare Department Care of Mothers and Young Children Act
1916	Committee of Reconstruction
1917	Siegfried Sassoon, 'Finished with the War: A Soldier's Declaration'
1918	Industrial Fatigue Research Board

Wealth and Poverty

For some, the four decades before the Great War were a golden age of prosperity. Certainly, the enormous wealth of the world's richest nation was concentrated among very few: 90 per cent of Britain's wealth belonged to just 10 per cent of its population. Rather than fading into irrelevance, the aristocracy was yoked to a new plutocracy that included those who had made their fortunes from banking and industry. The Dukes of Westminster, Northumberland, Sutherland, Bedford and Portland remained the richest men in the world. In fact, despite dwindling returns from their landed estates, their wealth continued to grow, as they had long diversified their investments into business, finance and the marriage market. By 1896 a quarter of the peerage were registered as directors of companies. The ninth Duke of Marlborough (close friend and first cousin to Winston Churchill) married an American heiress, a Vanderbilt, to help restore the family estate at Bleinheim Palace outside of Oxford. He received a dowry of $2,500,000 worth of railway stock with a guarantee of 4 per cent annual dividend as well as an annual income of $100,000. In turn, the men of industry and finance built landed estates, sent their children to Eton and Oxbridge, and became peers of the realm. In 1873 the fifteen living members of the Crawshay family, who made their fortunes with iron and coal, possessed no less than eight country houses with a total of some 4,000 acres of land. Having purchased land from the ailing Marlborough estate, the Rothschild family built Waddesdon Manor in the style of a French chateau with an impressive collection of Renaissance art, and the obligatory English landscape gardens between 1874 and 1889. Evelyn Baring turned down the opportunity of going into the family banking business to take up a career as a colonial administrator in India and Egypt as Earl Cromer. There was no country in the world with such wealth, or with such a configuration of wealth, and yet the orthodoxy remained that eventually the benefits of immense personal wealth would trickle down through investments and expenditure.

The 'trickle-down' theory was supported by the fact that standards of living were finally beginning to improve for many. Measured in aggregate terms, standards of living were slowly rising as real wages grew at 1.58 per cent per year between 1881 and 1899 before falling to an annual growth rate of just 0.29 per cent until 1913. As this growth occurred, food prices fell, the size of families decreased, sanitary conditions improved and working hours were reduced, and the condition of the working classes slowly began to improve. Why, then, did contemporaries become so concerned about the scale and effects of poverty during this apparent *belle époque*?

The Rediscovery of Poverty

The answer is that poverty increasingly came to demonstrate the failures of liberal political economy. The reams of statistics, armies of inspectors, and new institutions and agencies for intervention that were designed to address the **social question** from the 1830s had inadvertently illustrated the irritating persistence of poverty. Even the state's own Poor Law returns for 1900 showed there were 577,000 people still receiving outdoor relief and a further 215,000 inhabitants of workhouses. The stubborn grip of poverty on Britain inspired many to investigate where it was to be found and why it remained such a prominent feature in the lives of many.

Some date the beginning of these attempts to document the lives of the poor to a series of articles written by Henry Mayhew and published by the *Morning Chronicle* during the late 1840s. Mayhew's concern for the swelling ranks of the poor was not novel, but his approach was. He identified characteristic 'types', interviewed them and sought to detail their lives. Decades later his work served as a model for those investigating the reach and depth of poverty still haunting the nation's capital. A new genre of writing emerged in a slew of publications that came thick and fast after James Greenwood's account, *A Night in the Workhouse*, in 1866: Andrew Mearns's *Bitter Cry of Outcast London* and George Sim's *How the Poor Live* in 1883; W.T. Stead's *The Maiden Tribute of Modern Babylon* in 1885; William Booth's *In Darkest England and the Way Out* in 1890; Robert Sherard's *The Cry of the Poor* and Charles Masterman's *The Heart of the Empire* in 1901; and Jack London's *The People of the Abyss*, published in 1903.

Like Mayhew's, this type of work was often first serialized in the **new journalism** of newspapers, where it sought to make news by sensationally grabbing the attention of readers before being published in book form. The *Pall Mall Gazette*, for example, was the vehicle for Greenwood, Mearns and, of course, its editor Stead. This work often combined disgust and fear of the poor with a visceral and magnetic attraction to the exploration of their world. Yet for all their emphasis on that world's darkness, dirt and danger, they created empathy for the poor by focusing on the suffering of specific individuals. Just as in the reporting of famine, these stories invariably focused on women and children. They could be more easily presented as innocent victims and their poverty blamed on their lazy, drunken and abusive husbands and fathers.

Mayhew in effect laid the groundwork for a tradition of social research that we would now call participant observation, where the credibility of the study depends on the researcher's ability to enter the world of its subjects. The closer they could get to the poor, and the greater their empathy with their subjects, the more they would learn from them and the better they would be able to get their readers to connect with their suffering. For Greenwood in London, that meant pretending to be one of the poor; for Stead, it was to be a libertine and sex trafficker. More often it meant finding someone else with a knowledge of the poor, like a charity or mission worker, to act as a local guide. Often the sensationalism of these investigative reports was aimed at compelling readers to donate relief funds to charities like George Sim's Referee Children's Free Breakfast and Dinner Fund or William Booth's Salvation Army. Invariably, the figure of the journalist, his heroic struggle to convey the truth to his readers and to relieve the distress or save the souls of his subjects, moved centre stage. If this work made poverty visible again and highlighted the inadequacies of the Poor Law, it usually promoted voluntary charitable and missionary work over calls for state intervention. The fear that the souls of the poor were being lost to the devil was a driving force for figures like Mearns, Secretary to the London Congregational Union, and William Booth, founder of the Salvation Army.

The Science of Social Investigation

Assessing the extent of poverty also motivated a very different form of social research. Rather than dwelling on the subjective experience of poverty and the need to provoke sympathy for it to entice charitable endeavour, a new form of social investigation sought to objectively measure its scale in ways that could facilitate intervention by the state. Those who conducted this research styled themselves as scientists of the social world. Where social explorers sought proximity to the poor, these social scientists sought an appropriate distance from where they could gain a disinterested perspective of the problem as a whole. As measuring the scale of poverty across the nation was impossible, they instead focused on particular places as case studies. Charles Booth's *Life and Labour of the People of London* alone took seventeen monumental volumes to measure poverty in the capital. The findings were published over twelve years between 1891 and 1903. Similarly, Seebohm Rowntree used his hometown of York, where his Quaker family ran a chocolate

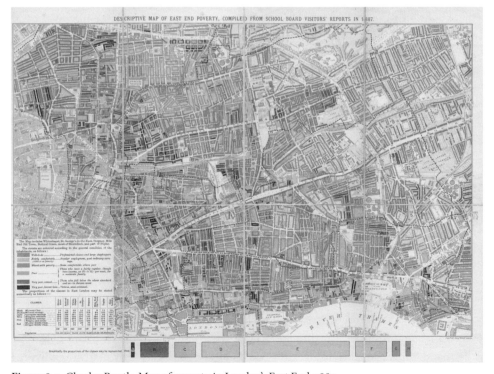

Figure 8.2 Charles Booth, Map of poverty in London's East End, 1889

8.1 Person: Emily Hobhouse (1860–1926)

Emily Hobhouse was born and raised in Cornwall where she was educated at home. Her father was archdeacon of Bodmin and her mother the daughter of a baronet. Emily was their fifth child and she lived with them and did charitable parish work until her father died. At that point she set sail for the United States and Mexico where she worked to improve the welfare of émigré Cornish miners. Returning to England after a failed engagement to an American businessman, she worked at the Women's Industrial Council as a social investigator and produced several reports on child labour. Her life's cause arrived, however, with the coming of the South African War. Opposed to the war and Britain's 'scorched-earth' offensive which included concentrating tens of thousands of women and children into vast outdoor refugee camps, she founded the Distress Fund for South African Women and Children. In 1900 she travelled to South Africa to oversee the charity's distribution of money. When she arrived she was struck by the number and the scale of the concentration camps that had emerged during the war, as well as the overcrowding, disease and high rates of mortality among the mostly female residents. She used vivid descriptions of these conditions to denounce the camps, both publicly and privately to her well-connected family friends in Parliament. These reports prompted an official government investigation, chaired by the suffrage campaigner Millicent Fawcett. In 1903 Hobhouse returned to South Africa, where she worked for four years establishing resettlement schemes and industrial schools. It was then that she became friends with Mohandas Gandhi. During the Great War she became active in the international women's movement for peace and investigated the plight of refugees, interned civilians and prisoners of war. After the war she became involved with raising money for the relief of enemy children and with the newly formed Save the Children Fund. On her death in 1926, her unpublished autobiography and her ashes were taken to South Africa, where she remains feted as a national hero. (S.W.)

factory, as the case study for *Poverty: A Study of Town Life* in 1901. Booth's and Rowntree's findings were remarkably similar. Booth estimated that 35 per cent of Londoners lived in poverty and Rowntree that 30 per cent of those who lived in York were poor. Never before had there been such a precise measurement of the scale of poverty.

The scientific manner of these studies gave credibility and authority to their findings. Booth and Rowntree did not get their own hands dirty by visiting the homes of the poor. Instead they enlisted young women whose social or philanthropic work afforded them experience of, and access to, the homes of the labouring poor. Booth's cousin Beatrice Potter, for example, worked on his study before she became a leading Fabian socialist with her husband Sydney Webb. The investigative work of women like Potter was sensitive and difficult, for they were tasked with attaining the intimate details of the lives and budgets of each household. Most families, and certainly many men within them, jealously guarded the knowledge of how much they earned and spent. As women

Figure 8.3 Emily Hobhouse, 1902

were generally those charged with balancing the household books, Booth and Rowntree believed that 'lady visitors' like Potter were more likely to be told their secrets. If tact and sensitivity were required, so was a fidelity to the forms of the study, the breakdown of each budget and the case notes on each household. These forms ensured that a universal standard measurement was applied to each household, allowing Booth and Rowntree to aggregate them for 'scientific' comparison. It would be too simple to suggest that these early studies of poverty positioned women as those who could empathize, and men as the ones who counted, but it was certainly Booth and Rowntree who were credited as authors and claimed as the founding practitioners of social science in Britain. Women investigators were largely excluded from the canon of the social sciences as they took professional shape around the London School of Economics (1895) and the Sociological Society (1904). There were, however, some notable exceptions. Married to Sydney Webb, Beatrice Potter unusually went on to co-author several books with him, co-found the London School of Economics, and sit on the Royal Commission on the Poor Laws from 1905. Her Fabian socialist colleague Maud Pember Reeves moved to Britain from New Zealand with her husband William, who was later appointed by the Webbs as Director of the LSE in 1908; Maud wrote a searing investigation into the lives of London's poor called *Round About a Pound a Week* (1913) and was later appointed director of the Women's Section of the Ministry of Food in 1917. Emily Hobhouse (see Textbox 8.1 and Figure 8.2) is another good example.

Booth and Rowntree scientifically measured the scale of poverty while also grading it by degree and type. In this act, the objectivity of science quickly became enmeshed with their personal disdain for the poor. As we can see from Figure 8.3, Booth identified seven distinct types of households within London, which he ordered in a social hierarchy ranging, in descending order, from the wealthy 'Upper-middle and Upper-classes' down to the 'vicious' and 'semi-criminal' 'Lowest class'. Each category was afforded its own colour so that every street in London was colour-coded to illustrate the locations of wealth and poverty in the capital. In this hierarchy, measures of income were never entirely separate from questions of morality. The lowest class was racialized as black, while the categories further up the social hierarchy were coded in progressively lighter colours. Rowntree divided the poor into two distinct groups: those in primary and those in secondary poverty. He ordered these categories around his Quaker sensibilities as much as by income. The 10 per cent who lived in primary 'poverty' simply lacked sufficient income to buy the minimum necessities to sustain a healthy and productive life. The 20 per cent in 'secondary' poverty had sufficient income to escape poverty but were sucked back into it by their own unwise expenditures on things, like meat and alcohol, that Rowntree disapproved of or thought unnecessary. Thus for all their scientific charts, graphs and maps, Booth's and Rowntree's work remained haunted by a moral scorn for their subjects.

If the ethnographic investigations of the lives of the poor allowed poverty to be rediscovered in the late nineteenth century, it was its quantification and measurement by Booth and Rowntree that made its scale visible for the first time. If the depth and breadth of poverty came to resemble for some an iceberg underneath the opulent ocean of the richest nation, the question remained what consequences it would have and what was to be done. Slowly the poor were being perceived as less of a problem for themselves and more one for society as a whole.

Degeneration and the Imperial Race

The depth and scale of poverty seemed to indicate that the forward march of liberal progress and self-improvement had been halted. Worse still, some feared that they denoted the very opposite of progress: the degeneration of society. Increasingly, social degeneration was conceived less in moral and cultural terms than in biological ones.

The Darwinian revolution is vital to understanding this distinction. It reflected the increasing salience of science as a basis of knowledge and its capacity to turn upside-down an understanding of the world. The culture of science was everywhere in mid-Victorian Britain, for it was only after the 1860s and 1870s that it even began to confine itself to the laboratory, professionalize and divide into discrete academic disciplines. Plants and animals from across the world filled botanical gardens and zoos, amateurs collected and studied everything they could from rocks to birds, and scientific displays and experiments were as likely to be staged in Mechanics' Institutes as the British Museum. Scientific debates about the nature of the world, the body and the mind infused popular culture. As many of those debates addressed the degree to which the natural world reflected a divine plan, or whether its laws of operation ensured it would develop in a progressive direction, they infused science with concepts from politics and literature.

Charles Darwin emerged from this world. An amateur botanist in the 1830s, he secured a position on a naval ship surveying the South American coast and became fascinated by the varieties of animal and plant species there. Influenced by **Malthus**'s view that the constraints of nature and its food supply shaped the rise and fall of populations, Darwin developed a theory of evolution by natural selection, positing that only species best suited to their environment would survive. As the environment and its food supply were constantly changing, random variations – such as the length of a bird's beak or the legs of a lizard – would determine the ability of a species to perpetuate and evolve or perish. Aware of the controversy that would inevitably surround his views, Darwin did not publish *The Origin of Species* until 1859. Even though scientists had for decades been challenging the biblical idea that God made the world in seven days, many held Darwin culpable for the death of divine explanations of the world. While some continued to believe that there could still be a divine plan to this self-regulating system, this was a stretch, given the role of chance and the bleak view of deathly competition in an uncertain world.

Eugenics and the Science of Race

By the time Darwin extended his theory of natural selection to the evolution of the human race in *The Descent of Man* (1871), the stage was set for its application to the social world. The polymath Herbert Spencer argued that the state should exit from both markets and the social world, as only then could the natural laws of evolution apply. Two years after the appearance of *The Descent of Man*, Spencer described society as a constantly evolving biological organism in *The Study of Sociology* (1873). But what became known as social Darwinism was primarily associated with the work of Darwin's cousin, Francis Galton, and the science of **eugenics**. Galton was interested not just in the physical variety of the human form – height, skull size and shape, even fingerprints – but the degree to which nature, not nurture (a phrase he invented), determined one's intelligence. He came to believe that it was possible to read from a person's physical characteristics their mental and even moral character. For instance, during the early 1880s, at the suggestion of Herbert Spencer, he developed a technique of composite photography that allowed him to posit that criminal types had a particular facial structure. By 1883 he had coined the term 'eugenics' to refer to a science that could perfect racial development either by encouraging the reproduction of healthy stock, by promoting social hygiene, or by preventing the 'multiplication of the unfit' (incarceration, sterilization and birth control were all promoted by Galton's followers). By 1904 Galton was promoting his work at the Sociological Society and was able to establish a Eugenics Laboratory at University College London, with his acolyte, the mathematician Karl Pearson, at its head. Eugenics may have originated in Britain but it was part of a transnational conversation that had particular resonance in the United States and Germany in the decades either side of the Great War.

While few were actively engaged in the scientific research of eugenics, its presentation of race, the population question and the laws of social development were widely influential. Individuals involved in the anti-slavery movement, like those who formed the Aborigines' Protection Society in 1837, combined universalist ideas of racial equality with a paternalist belief that the 'uncivilized tribes' needed guided development. The optimism of that universalism was quickly dispelled when a series of revolts across the colonies – most notably in India in 1857 and Jamaica in 1865, as well as the escalating Fenian campaigns in Ireland and mainland Britain between 1865 and 1867 – decisively hardened attitudes about racial difference. If other races had once been seen as backward but perfectible, racial differences and hierarchies were increasingly understood as immutable and unchanging. Colonial officials, most notably in India, developed ethnographic surveys both to delineate the racial composition of their subjects and to advance the science of race. Herbert Risley, an ethnographic researcher, used anthropometric measures to identify seven racial types in *The Tribes and Castes of Bengal* (1891). His methods can be seen in the understanding of caste and race he deployed for the Indian Census when he became its director in 1899.

If colonies were fertile laboratories for studying racial difference, so too were the metropolitan poor. As early as the 1840s, Mayhew's ethnographies of London's labouring poor referred to 'nomadic races' and 'wandering Tribes' in the metropolis. Reading moral character from their physical appearance, he wrote: 'There is a greater development of the animal than of the intellectual or moral nature of man, and ... they are all more or less distinguished for their high cheek-bones and protruding jaws – for their use of a slang language – for their lax ideas of property – for their general improvidence – their repugnance to continuous labour – their disregard of female honour – their love of cruelty – their pugnacity – and their utter want of religion.' This sense of the poor as a race apart, and the association of their neighbourhoods with Africa and the East, infused the literature of social observers and investigators. Just as Charles Booth represented the lowest class with black on his maps, so William Booth's *In Darkest England* compared the condition of the poor in East London, with 'its monotonous darkness, its malaria and its gloom, its dwarfish de-humanized inhabitants, the slavery to which they are subjected, their privations and their misery', to those of 'Darkest Africa'. The increasingly pessimistic view of other races across the empire was echoed by the racialization of the poor at home.

By the 1880s, old Malthusian fears of overpopulation gave way to related concerns about both the stagnation of national growth and the degeneration of the population's racial health. Simply put, declining fertility was disproportionately evident among the wealthier classes; thus it was feared that Britain's racial stock would be diluted by the 'unfit' and 'feeble' – but more rapidly reproducing – urban poor. 'Unfit' and 'feeble' denoted both the physical *and* moral inadequacies of the poor. If the poor were chiefly to blame for the degeneration of Britons as a superior, imperial race, they were not alone. The poor Jewish migrants who settled in East London from the 1870s, fleeing pogroms in Russia and eastern Europe, were also held responsible. Just like the increasing presence of Irish migrants on the mainland after the Famine, it was feared that this new 'alien invasion' generated still more overcrowding and insanitary conditions that would only further threaten the tenuous racial health of the poor white Anglo-Saxon.

The new figure of the 'homosexual' was added to this cocktail of racial degradation. Same-sex relations between men had always existed but during the nineteenth century they became increasingly vilified. Those who practised what was known as 'sodomy' or 'buggery' became the target of blackmailers and police. While a successful prosecution rested upon proof that anal sex had occurred, newspapers reported sodomy trials through a haze of euphemisms about 'nameless offences' and 'abominable crimes'. The **Criminal Law Amendment Act** of 1885 (introduced in the wake of Stead's exposure of sexual slavery in *The Maiden Tribute of Modern Babylon*) raised the age of consent to sixteen and enabled the prosecution of brothel keepers, but also broadened the criminalization of same-sex relations between men to any type of 'gross indecency'. Under this law, Oscar Wilde, bohemian aesthete and writer, was famously convicted in 1895 and sentenced to two years of hard labour. Ironically, this prosecution followed Wilde's own attempt to defend his character by charging the Marquess of Queensberry with libel for having called him a sodomite. The growing interest in establishing heterosexuality as the norm was also evident in the emergence of sexology to scientifically study what was taken to be sexual abnormality. Wilde's trial was sandwiched by the publication of the first English translation of Richard von Krafft-Ebing's *Psychopathia Sexualis* (the original had been published in 1886) and Havelock Ellis's *Sexual Inversion* in 1897, the first such study in Britain. These sexology case studies served to sediment a particular view of the types of people who engaged in 'abnormal' forms of sexual behaviour. Homosexual men were portrayed as effeminate and neurotic, precisely the image of 'the dandy' Wilde presented at his trial. Havelock Ellis may have sought to treat his subjects dispassionately and scientifically but his book *The Task of Social Hygiene* (1912) called for the cleansing of feeble-minded and degenerate types from the population by eugenic controls on reproduction.

An Imperial Race at War

Following Nazi Germany's sterilization of the unfit from 1933 and the extermination of Jews, homosexuals and gypsies during World War Two, eugenicist views are today seen as extremist. However, in the first three decades of the twentieth century eugenicist concerns about degeneration were widely held and crossed the political spectrum. It was commonplace that the social problem of poverty and the racial health of Britons were thought to be connected to the fate of the British Empire. Nowhere was this more evident than when, during the **South African War** (1899–1901), military doctors deemed three out of every five men who volunteered for military duty as physically unfit to serve. If the British Empire were to survive, let alone continue to grow in the era of new imperial competition, it would need a fitter, stronger, healthier and more productive imperial race to be reared at home. Imperial rivalry and expansion in the final quarter of the nineteenth century were marked by enhanced militarization. Britain was again almost perpetually at war. Even by the count of the War Office (which did not count seemingly 'small wars' where less than 4,000 British troops were deployed), there were fifteen major wars between 1857 and 1899.

Like that of its rivals, Britain's imperial expansion depended upon the deployment of new military technologies, like the machine guns unleashed in the wars against the Zulus and Ashanti in southern Africa during the 1870s, as well as the extension of its military infrastructure. As the territorial reach of the British Empire dramatically expanded, the British navy grew in size and reach. In 1875, just 20 of its 241 vessels were battleships and the navy's budget of £9.5 million supported 34,000 employees. By 1898, 52 of its 287 vessels were battleships and its budget and personnel had both increased almost threefold to £23.8 million and 97,000. By then, new naval bases had been established in Fiji, Weihaiwai, Mombassa, Zanzibar, the Seychelles, Alexandria, Cyprus and Lagos; and the numbers of ships in the Mediterranean, East and West Africa and China increased significantly. Similarly, the British army grew in size from 160,000 men in 1876 to 195,000 in 1898. As Map 8.1 shows, an increasing number of British troops were stationed across the Empire in the second half of the nineteenth century and colonial populations were taxed to support their 'defence'. Nonetheless, the British Empire remained dependent upon locally funded colonial forces to fight its wars and put down revolts. In India, ethnographers identified specific castes and tribes of '**martial races**' by assessing their loyalty and size. These groups – like the Sikhs in India, the Gurkhas in Nepal and the Dyaks in Borneo – were then recruited into colonial regiments. After the Revolt of 1857, the Empire massively invested in the strategically vital Indian army. By the late nineteenth century, two thirds of the 325,000 troops across the Empire were based in, and paid for, by India. Between 1867 and 1903, the Indian army was deployed in Burma, China, East Africa, Ethiopia, Egypt, Malaya, Malta, Somaliland, South Africa, Sudan and Tibet.

The White Man's Burden

Economic interest alone did not drive the geopolitical competition of imperialism. It cannot, for instance, explain why Europeans competed to claim the vast but economically worthless Antarctic territories by reaching the South Pole, as the Antarctic expeditions led by Norway's Roald Amundsen and Britain's Robert Scott did in 1912. Nor can it explain the widespread belief among Europeans that their empires each had a 'civilizing mission', exposing colonial subjects to Christianity and the European culture that they considered the most advanced in the world. Of course, an understanding that no other civilization could match Europe's, and that other races were more 'primitive' or 'backward' under the laws of historical development, fuelled this belief. The racism of the late nineteenth century was thus just as rooted in the knowledge generated by the humanities and emergent social sciences as it was in the biological sciences. There is perhaps no finer illustration of this in Britain than Rudyard Kipling's 1899 poem, 'The White Man's Burden: The United States and the Philippine Islands'. For Kipling, imperialism was a duty for all white men to spread health, industry and civility to 'sullen peoples', who were 'half-devil and half-child'.

Kipling published the poem to urge Americans to shoulder the burdens of imperialism in the Philippines, secured from Spain the previous year. For many Britons like him, the United States continued to be part of a broader Anglo world. In 1883, imperial historian John Seeley's *The Expansion of England* claimed that the United States was part of an Empire bound together by 'a homogeneous people, one in blood, language, religion and laws, but dispersed over a boundless space'. Indeed, the United States continued to be the most popular destination for those emigrating from Britain, attracting almost 14 million Britons in the century before the Great War. Seeley was not alone in reflecting upon how the migration of a further 7.2 million Britons between 1815 and 1914 to the white settler colonies of Canada, Australia and New Zealand, as well as the Cape and Natal in southern Africa, created an

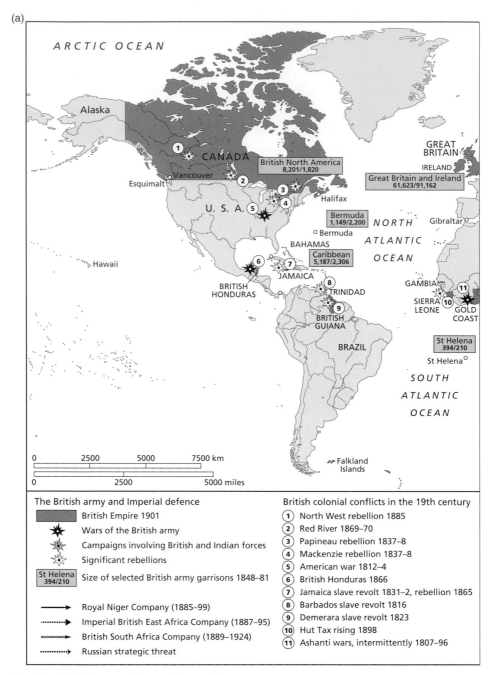

(a)

The British army and Imperial defence

- British Empire 1901
- Wars of the British army
- Campaigns involving British and Indian forces
- Significant rebellions
- St Helena 394/210 Size of selected British army garrisons 1848–81

- → Royal Niger Company (1885–99)
- ·····▸ Imperial British East Africa Company (1887–95)
- ⇒ British South Africa Company (1889–1924)
- ·····▸ Russian strategic threat

British colonial conflicts in the 19th century

1. North West rebellion 1885
2. Red River 1869–70
3. Papineau rebellion 1837–8
4. Mackenzie rebellion 1837–8
5. American war 1812–4
6. British Honduras 1866
7. Jamaica slave revolt 1831–2, rebellion 1865
8. Barbados slave revolt 1816
9. Demerara slave revolt 1823
10. Hut Tax rising 1898
11. Ashanti wars, intermittently 1807–96

Map 8.1 Colonial wars and imperial security

(b)

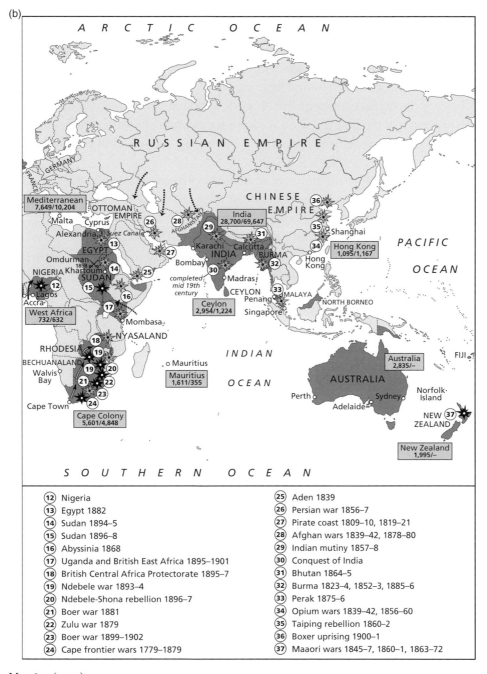

⑫ Nigeria	㉕ Aden 1839
⑬ Egypt 1882	㉖ Persian war 1856–7
⑭ Sudan 1894–5	㉗ Pirate coast 1809–10, 1819–21
⑮ Sudan 1896–8	㉘ Afghan wars 1839–42, 1878–80
⑯ Abyssinia 1868	㉙ Indian mutiny 1857–8
⑰ Uganda and British East Africa 1895–1901	㉚ Conquest of India
⑱ British Central Africa Protectorate 1895–7	㉛ Bhutan 1864–5
⑲ Ndebele war 1893–4	㉜ Burma 1823–4, 1852–3, 1885–6
⑳ Ndebele-Shona rebellion 1896–7	㉝ Perak 1875–6
㉑ Boer war 1881	㉞ Opium wars 1839–42, 1856–60
㉒ Zulu war 1879	㉟ Taiping rebellion 1860–2
㉓ Boer war 1899–1902	㊱ Boxer uprising 1900–1
㉔ Cape frontier wars 1779–1879	㊲ Maaori wars 1845–7, 1860–1, 1863–72

Map 8.1 (cont.)

expanded Anglosphere. What he neglected was that, as we saw in Chapter 7, Scots, Welsh and Irish were often disproportionately part of this exodus. It was very much a British world, not an Anglosphere. As early as 1868 the young Charles Dilke, a baronet and future Liberal MP who famously criticized the monarchy and declared himself a republican in 1871, found huge success with his travelogue *Greater Britain* celebrating the achievements of the 'English-speaking, white-inhabited, and self-governed' parts of the Empire. For Seeley and Dilke, and many other late Victorians, this English-speaking or British world was potentially the salvation of both Britain and the world.

For some, alarmed by the prospect of domestic Britain's moral and racial degeneration, the white settler colonies represented an improved or pristine version of the motherland. Certainly this was also the view from those colonies, which helped attract emigrants in increasing numbers: 1.7 million alone in the decade before 1914. The growing calls for a closer political union between Britain and those colonies were part of this hope that a transcontinental British world could strengthen the imperial race and broaden its international influence. An Imperial Federation League was created in 1884 expressly for that purpose. Although it had little success, irregular Imperial Conferences were convened from 1887 and an Empire Press Union formed in 1909 to facilitate the transmission of news within the British world. Finally, there were those like Joseph Chamberlain, who in 1903, just after the **South African War** that he had helped conduct as Colonial Secretary, established the Tariff Reform League to urge Britons to abandon **free trade** and create a system of tariffs that would protect British jobs and promote trade within the Empire.

Imperial Social Reform and National Efficiency

The increasing visibility of poverty in Britain was not the only impetus for social reform. In addition, Britons grew more aware of social problems' potential consequences for their ability to compete on the global stage. It did not go unnoticed that Britain's two principal rivals, Germany and the United States, were busily engaged in their own social reform programmes. In that sense, the new humanitarian concern for the poor was often closely connected to concerns about racial health and what was termed '**national efficiency**'. Nonetheless, increasing recognition of the depth and scale of poverty in the world's richest country slowly led to calls for the government to take a more active role in managing the inequities and social problems generated by liberalized markets and **free trade**. By the early twentieth century, various ideas were mooted across the political spectrum for how best the state could address poverty. While this represented a significant shift, it did not equate to a wholesale rejection of liberal political economy. Instead of asking how best the state could make markets work more efficiently, the question was how, in the best interests of society as a whole, it could secure social security for those left adrift by the market.

The Politics of Social Reform

It was, then, no coincidence that early forms of socialism, as well as political groups that oriented themselves around social questions, emerged in earnest from the 1880s. A new 'gas and water' or 'municipal' form of socialism was pioneered in Birmingham during the 1870s when its newly elected Liberal mayor Joseph Chamberlain purchased the rival companies providing the city with gas and water to lower prices and improve delivery. In the following decades, so-called municipal socialists used local taxation to improve social conditions through the construction of major infrastructure projects like the Elan Valley Reservoirs (see Textbox 8.2 and Figure 8.4). The first explicitly – if rather eccentric – socialist organization was the Social Democratic Federation (SDF, 1883). It was quickly joined by a host of other groups from the Fabian Society (1884), the Socialist League (1885), the Scottish Labour Party (1888), the Christian Social Union (1889) and the Independent Labour Party (1893).

At this point, in its various guises, with the notable exception of the Socialist Labour Party (1903), socialism was not much interested in revolution, the state control of markets or the collapse of industrial capitalism. Although it increasingly evoked the language of class struggle, its vision was of a cooperative, and broadly anti-industrial, social community. For some, like the Fabian and Christian Socialists, socialism was primarily about the battle of ideas to make government more socially efficient or ethical. Religion remained deeply engrained as the proliferation of socialist Sunday Schools and Labour Churches demonstrated (see Textbox 9.2). Five thousand people attended a service at the Labour Church at the conference convened by Keir Hardie to establish the Independent Labour Party (ILP) in 1893. Much socialist activity was the product of artists, intellectuals and the well-to-do (figures like William Morris, Sidney Webb, George Bernard Shaw and Henry Hyndman, the gentlemanly leader of the SDF). The exception was the ILP, which emerged out of labour struggles in the industrial town of Bradford with working men like Keir Hardie and Tom Mann as its leaders, and quickly gained support in the industrial north, South Wales and Clydeside. It sought the gradual amelioration of the social conditions of the unemployed and working poor through the ballot box, especially by winning local elections for school boards and poor law guardians (after property qualifications were removed in 1894). Many of these early forms of socialism remained deeply marked by radical critiques of the aristocratic monopolies of land, calls for the freedom of assembly and speech, as well as social conditions in which individuals could be morally and economically emancipated.

8.2 Place: Elan Valley Reservoirs, Wales

By the late nineteenth century, the continuing growth of Birmingham's population had created an environmental crisis. Despite the city pioneering 'gas and water' socialism, there remained a chronic shortage of clean water, placing intolerable strain on nearby rivers such as the Bourne and the Blythe that had traditionally sourced the city. Since the 1870s, when Joseph Chamberlain first floated the idea, Birmingham's city council had campaigned to get its water supply from mid Wales. Parliamentary permission to do so eventually came in 1892, followed by the compulsory purchase of 69 square miles of land in the Elan and Claerwen valleys. More than a hundred local residents were displaced as eighteen farms, a school, church and three manor houses were destroyed (only property owners received compensation). In their place the city built a colossal dam on the River Elan, creating a chain of five man-made reservoirs. The reservoirs were connected to Birmingham via a 73-mile pipeline that followed a very gentle downward gradient, falling 52 metres, allowing water to flow freely into the city. It was an enormous undertaking, requiring the labour of thousands of Irish navvies and taking more than ten years to complete. Prospective workers and their families were forced to spend a night in a nearby hostel, where they were de-loused and screened for infectious diseases, before being moved to Elan Village, a temporary settlement of wooden huts built for workers with its own school, library and pub. Children over eleven years of age were made to work and only men were allowed to drink at the pub. The water supply was officially opened by King Edward VII on 21 July 1904. (S.W.)

Nonetheless, socialism and the social problems associated with poverty challenged liberal political economy as the common sense of the age. The Conservative Party not only raised the issue of protection and tariff reform, but increasingly turned to issues of social reform. A Conservative government passed the **Workmen's Compensation Act** in 1897 that made accidents and injuries at work the liability of the employer, not the employee. In 1904 the Conservatives established the **Inter-Departmental Committee on Physical Deterioration** to explore the issue of racial degeneration, and in 1905 passed the **Aliens Act** to introduce the nation's first restrictions upon immigration in the name of protecting British workers from competition for jobs. Despite its commitment to **free trade**, civil rights and individualism, a '**New Liberalism**', reoriented around social questions, was developed by Liberal Party intellectuals like L.T. Hobhouse (Emily Hobhouse's brother) and Henry Massingham. At its centre was the recognition that poverty could no longer be seen as the sole responsibility of the poor. The increasingly conspicuous concentration of wealth and deteriorating social conditions, they argued, not only prevented many from escaping the trap of poverty but also threatened the health and prosperity of society as a whole. New Liberals thus argued

Figure 8.4 Elan Valley Resevoirs

that society had to provide a minimal level of assistance to those who were willing but unable to lift themselves out of poverty. Self-improvement now required the helping hand of the state.

National Efficiency and the New Liberal State

And that helping hand was readily extended when the Liberal Party returned to power after eleven years of opposition in 1906. Despite concluding that there was no reliable historical evidence of degeneration, the **Inter-Departmental Committee on Physical Deterioration** did not counsel complacency about the nation's racial health. The Committee recommendations, aimed especially at children who were seen as both blameless for their condition and redeemable in their health, were soon implemented. A suite of legislation provided school meals for the needy (1906), made the medical inspection of all schoolchildren compulsory (1907) and prohibited selling liquor to, or sleeping in the same bed with, children (1909). As rearing an imperial race began in the nursery, the school curriculum for girls included a growing emphasis on the domestic sciences necessary for keeping a healthy home. While lady philanthropists had long condescended to instruct the poorest mothers how to run their households and raise their children, the Board of Health now encouraged local authorities to appoint 'Health

Visitors' to do this work after the Notification of Births Act (1907). And, finally, the Mental Deficiency Act (1913) forcibly confined to state asylums (but did not sterilize, as Winston Churchill, one of its framers, had wished) those identified as 'feeble-minded' so they could not undermine the health of the imperial race. In the 1870s the state's right to insist upon compulsory vaccination and education was hotly debated. Four decades later, the state had largely assumed the task of social hygiene as its own, inserting itself into the previously private world of parenting with little contention.

Even more dramatic was the state's attempt to grapple with, and restructure its approach to, the problem of poverty. The first indication of this was the creation of a Royal Commission in 1905 to investigate the escalating expense (£12 million a year) of the Poor Law and its apparent ineffectiveness at redeeming the poor. There is no better illustration of the agonized nature of the move away from liberal political economy than the Commission's conflicted reports issued after four years of deliberation. The majority reaffirmed the central principle of the 1834 Act that poverty was the responsibility of individuals. Yet, a minority report, co-written by Beatrice Webb, insisted that poverty was the product of systemic problems that were beyond the control of individuals. Although the Poor Law was not abolished until 1948, a range of other measures designed to provide less punitive forms of relief to the poor and unemployed increasingly supplemented it between 1909 and 1931.

The foundation of that process was the **People's Budget** crafted by David Lloyd George as the New Liberal Chancellor of the Exchequer in 1909. Lloyd George's budget raised taxes centrally to fund two new welfare measures designed to relieve the pressure upon locally financed workhouses by enabling two of their largest populations, the aged and the unemployed, to escape its clutches. Alongside indirect sales taxes on alcohol and tobacco that appealed to the Liberal Party's temperance-supporting base, the People's Budget controversially extended income tax for the higher brackets as well as death duties (first introduced in 1894), and introduced a capital gains tax on the value of land when it was sold. Clearly aimed at the richest, these taxes were used to redistribute wealth, funding the introduction of an Old Age Pension (1909) and a partial system of National Insurance (1911) to provide security for the unemployed. The Old Age Pension provided 5 shillings a week to those over seventy years old and was quickly claimed by a million beneficiaries. National Insurance was a system of social security that protected around 2.25 million men in trades, like building and engineering, which had cyclical patterns of employment. Each year these men were eligible for a benefit of 7 shillings a week for up to five weeks after their first week of no pay. This benefit was paid for through contributions, of around 2 pence per week, from employers, employees and the state. This benefit was also supplemented by a national system of labour exchanges, established in 1909 by the combined efforts of Winston Churchill and William Beveridge, to help those out of work find jobs (and to test that those covered under National Insurance were actively looking for work).

A striking feature of the 'New Liberal' social reforms introduced in the decade before the Great War was not just their reliance upon the new cadre of social scientific experts like the Webbs, Beveridge and Rowntree, but the degree to which they drew upon similar developments elsewhere. Rowntree, for instance, whose study of poverty was deeply influenced by German and American nutritional scientists, gave evidence to the Inter-departmental Committee on Physical Deterioration. Having met Lloyd George in 1907, he helped him develop the plans for the Old Age Pension and, less successfully, following a study of Belgium, to address land reform. During the Great War, in Lloyd George's **Ministry of Munitions**, he established the relationship between welfare and productivity of workers in ways that helped consolidate the expanded role of the state in social policy. Similarly, Beveridge, who had been mentored by the Webbs, visited Germany to study the system of social insurance introduced by Bismarck in 1889 and also worked closely with Lloyd George in developing the National Insurance scheme. Indeed, different forms of social security developed across Euro-America at this time with Belgium and France following Germany in 1901 and 1905, and the Progressive Party in the United States campaigning for one from 1912. Not only were their administrative architects in conversation with each other, but politicians were acutely aware that rival imperial powers were passing similar legislation.

Although these reforms were authorized by social science and presented as essential if Britain were to remain internationally competitive, the **People's Budget** provoked a constitutional crisis. Lloyd George was smart enough to link the new forms of taxation not just to Old Age Pensions and National Insurance, but also to the rebuilding of Britain's navy, which had been outstripped by Germany's. Yet to many it appeared that his budget had decisively shifted away from a central tenet of liberal political economy – cheap government. Moreover, the aristocracy in the **House of Lords** saw it as an instrument of class war against their landed interests. In November 1909, six months after the budget's passage through the **House of Commons**, it was rejected by the Lords. Never before had the question of who governed Britain – the elected House of Commons or the unelected second chamber – been posed so sharply. Two months later an election was held to resolve the issue and the House of Lords finally passed the budget. Within eighteen months the Lords lost their right to veto over financial matters with the introduction of the Parliament Act. Effectively, taxation was thereafter linked to social policy, which in the following decades would become the chief and most rapidly expanding cost of government.

Social Reform Beyond the State

The issue of social reform not only generated an unprecedented extension of the role of the state and the reach of its taxation; numerous voluntary organizations were also concerned with improving the social, racial and moral conditions of Britons.

The **Charity Organization Society**, which also had a presence in Germany and the United States, sought to develop a more scientific approach to philanthropy to make certain that it was suitably spare and punitive so as not to render its recipients more dependent. Founded by Octavia Hill and Helen Bosanquet in 1869, it developed a system of detailed casework designed less to identify need than to note which households most deserved relief. Unsurprisingly, Bosanquet was Beatrice Webb's principal adversary on the Poor Law Commission and a major influence on the Majority Report defending its liberal principles. In contrast, from the 1880s several universities founded **Settlement Houses** in London to enable their students to live in communities with the poor so they could better understand poverty and seek to alleviate it more effectively. The first of these, Toynbee Hall in Whitechapel, was established in 1884 in honour of Oxford historian Arnold Toynbee. A fierce critic of industrialism, he had died the previous year and his posthumously published lectures popularized the term 'Industrial Revolution'. Toynbee Hall attracted figures like the Webbs and Beveridge and became a model for the widespread development of similar Settlement Houses across the United States, starting with Jane Addams's Hull House in Chicago five years later.

Many of those interested in social reform and racial health thought of the city as the problem. William Booth may have enlisted his Salvation Army to evangelize the ungodly urban poor in the Dantesque hell of darkest England, but as is evident from Figure 8.5, he envisioned their escape to new farm colonies in the countryside or to overseas colonies. As the **Great Depression** drove people from the countryside to the city, many thought that the creation of farm colonies would morally and physically regenerate the poor. To perform this role, the countryside itself had to be protected and preserved. The National Footpaths Preservation Society was established in 1884, eleven years before Octavia Hill helped to form the National Trust for Places of Historical Interest and Natural Beauty. Both of these organizations had their roots in the Commons Preservation Society (1865), an organization that brought together Hill, John Stuart Mill (see Textbox 6.2) and William Morris to defend common lands and open spaces from urban development. The question of how cities could be made hospitable and less corrosive to Britain's racial health preoccupied the late Victorians. It informed public health measures, gas and water municipal socialism, as well as the development of the idea of town planning. In 1898, Ebenezer Howard published a utopian plan for building what he described as '**garden cities**' under the title *Tomorrow: A Peaceful Path to Real Reform*. As we can see from Figure 8.6, garden cities would combine the best of the countryside and the city. They would bring order to nature while naturalizing the city. Slums would be a thing of the past, as the garden city would create socially mixed communities that would facilitate cooperative endeavours, and all would have equal access to the light, fresh air and recreational open spaces necessary

Figure 8.5 The Way Out of Darkest England, 1890

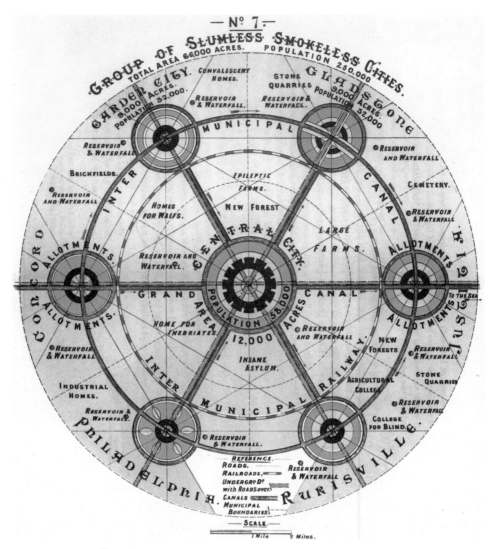

Figure 8.6 Howard's garden city, 1898

for health. Like Booth's Salvation Army, Howard's idea quickly spread across the world, taking root especially in the United States, as well as the broader British world where it influenced the construction of parts of Cape Town, Adelaide and Tel Aviv.

As with the development of social policy by the state, voluntary efforts to improve the nation's racial health also often focused on children. The production of muscular Christian boys became the defining ethos of private boarding schools for boys that proliferated from the 1860s and were immortalized in Thomas Hughes's novel *Tom Brown's Schooldays* (1857). Physical education, particularly the development of team games like rugby, football and cricket, was used to develop 'manliness'. Manliness was not confined to physical strength and endurance; it also consisted of an understanding of one's duty and the moral discipline necessary to sublimate the individual into a collective effort. By the turn of the twentieth century many of these schools had also formed cadet corps to better prepare young men to be leaders of men across the Empire. In 1908 these were formalized as the Officer Training Corps, an extension of the army funded by the War Office. By 1914, 20,000 schoolboys belonged to an OTC.

In many ways the youth movements that proliferated in the late nineteenth and early twentieth centuries sought to extend this training in imperial, Christian, manliness to the 95 per cent of boys who were not privately educated. The Christian Boys' Brigade was formed in 1883 and promoted 'the habits of Obedience, Reverence, Discipline, Self-Respect and all that tends towards a true Christian manliness'. By the early twentieth century it boasted over 2,000 companies across the British world. Yet it was the formation of the Boy Scouts in 1908 that quickly cast all rival groups in its shadow. Its founder, General Baden-Powell, the hero of the siege at Ladysmith during the **South African War**, was determined to better prepare young Britons for the challenges of imperial rule. Despite the creation of the Girl Guides in 1910, scouting was primarily intended to train boys for an imperial adventure. Its military disciplines and hierarchy were designed to instil the requisite qualities of duty, loyalty and manliness. By 1914 there were 150,000 Boy Scouts in troops across the British Empire (Gibraltar, Malta, Canada, Australia, New Zealand, South Africa and India), Europe and the Americas.

The Empire and the Social Question

The imperial and global reach of these organizations demonstrated that the question of whether social reform could improve racial health and **national efficiency** was by no means confined to Britain. The Empire was of course integral to this question. We have already seen how a new British world was created as the state and philanthropic groups sponsored emigration schemes to relocate those in distress and to help settle and whiten the colonies. Even though deportation as a criminal sentence was formally ended in 1868, orphans and pauper children continued to be shipped abroad by churches and philanthropic groups hoping to save them while ridding Britain of their presence. The apex of these efforts was between the 1870s and 1920s when 90,000 children were sent overseas.

The flow of Britons to populate the Anglosphere was largely uncontended in the so-called white settler colonies. Opportunity and optimism abounded in their rapidly growing and booming economies in the second half of the nineteenth century. Yet from the 1880s, as the **Great Depression** and imperial competition intensified across much of the globe, the mood began to darken and the issues of poverty, racial health and social reform rose to the surface. As the United States passed the Chinese Exclusion Act in 1882, falling wages and rising unemployment catalysed racist animosity towards

Asian and Polynesian migrants along Australia's northern and eastern coasts. In both countries, Asian migrants were accused of not only stealing jobs and land but threatening racial purity and health as well. The masthead of the radical and republican weekly newspaper *Bulletin* (which had a circulation of around 80,000) proclaimed 'Australia for the White Man' and the paper characteristically insisted in 1887 that 'no Nigger, no Chinaman, no lascar, no kanaka, no purveyor of cheap coloured labour is an Australian'. Ironically, it was the Australian bush, suitably cleansed of Aborigines, that was imagined as the new heart of white Australia. By 1901 the Immigration Restriction and Pacific Island Labourers Acts, which effectively excluded migration from Asia and deported many Pacific Island 'kanakas', instituted a 'White Australia' policy that was to endure until the second half of the twentieth century. Keeping Australia white was about keeping it British and ensuring that it did not develop a poor white problem. The same arguments were used by the British Brothers' League which was established in 1902 to combat the 'alien invasion' of 'destitute foreigners' who threatened to rob the returning **South African war** veterans of jobs and houses. 'England for the English' was their slogan, and they too agitated successfully, leading to the **Aliens Act** of 1905.

Needless to say, the racial health of the colonies was intricately connected to questions of gender and sexuality. Just as in Britain, the production of imperial men in the white settler colonies required a gendered division of labour and sexual economy. Until the second half of the nineteenth century, the empire was a man's world. Life on the frontier of imperial expansion was not just dangerous and militarized, it also entailed sexual relations with indigenous women. As women were increasingly encouraged to join their husbands on colonial service or to emigrate themselves, their job became to model the cleanliness, order and civility of British families. Maternalism and social hygiene took on a particular resonance in the colonies, especially those that were believed to propagate 'tropical diseases'. While mixed-race relationships between British men and their 'concubines' had once been a common feature of colonial life, they were viewed with increasing disapproval, as any progeny risked the dilution of Britain's racial stock. The idea of British women having sex with colonial subjects was inconceivable outside of a framework of rape and assault. Southern Rhodesia was the first colony to make this a capital offence in 1903. In fact, the status of white women in colonies like New Zealand and Australia was so heightened that they won the vote decades before their counterparts in Britain (in 1893 and 1902 respectively).

Imperial social reform further established the superiority of white women over their indigenous counterparts. British women had long been engaged in missionary and charitable work throughout the Empire (see Textbox 8.1). By the late nineteenth century, though, they were becoming an increasingly legitimate political voice campaigning for the education and protection of colonial women of colour, who were invariably portrayed as ignorant, unsanitary and oversexed. Across the Empire, but especially in

India, British women often led organized efforts to raise the age of consent and to abolish child marriage and female infanticide. They made their cases by portraying colonial women as helpless victims of backward customs and superstitions. British women were increasingly seen to have a special role in teaching female colonial subjects about social hygiene. After Lady Dufferin established the National Association for Supplying Female Medical Aid to the Women of India in 1885, its hospitals and dispensaries – which numbered sixty-five by 1893 – attracted many British women medics whose professional advancement at home remained restricted. The apogee of British women's involvement in imperial social reform came when Eleanor Rathbone, a leading feminist and one of the first women MPs, campaigned against the practice of clictoridectomy in Kenya and child marriage in India during the late 1920s and early 1930s.

Social reform was a profoundly imperial question. In Britain poverty was no longer seen as simply impacting the poor; it undermined the nation's racial health and **national efficiency** in ways that threatened the security of the Empire. Men and women had to be made capable of rearing an imperial race whose progeny could populate the British world and ensure its hegemony against its imperial rivals. Achieving this not only required the imperial state to take a more active role in the social lives of its subjects, but also relied on a plethora of voluntary agencies determined to make Britain and its Empire a beacon of moral and social hygiene.

The Great War's New Social Contract

Some of those in the thrall of **eugenics** believed that the first major continental war in Europe since 1815 would provide a suitable test of Britain's **national efficiency** and weed out its most inferior and degenerate racial stock. Of course, it did not work like that. By the end of 1914 Britain had lost close to 90,000 men – the exact size of its newly reformed professional army – trying to stop the German advance in Belgium and northern France. The rush of volunteers to replace them was immense. In little more than fifteen months from late 1914, some 2 million men enlisted to fight. Many were driven by a sense of their masculine and imperial duty awakened by reports of German 'atrocities' against 'neutral' Belgian women and children. Duty was also invoked in the iconic recruiting poster of Figure 8.7, where the Secretary for War, the hero of Sudan and South Africa, Lord Kitchener, declared that 'Your Country Needs You', and his pointed finger followed British men. Those yet to volunteer were shamed as unmanly cowards and presented with white feathers in public from women who sought to demonstrate their own patriotic citizenship by joining the **Order of the White Feather**. 'If he does not think that you and your country are worth fighting for', one of its posters read, 'do you think he is worthy of you?' As we can see from Figure 8.8 women in the East End of London flew their own flags warning men to 'serve

Figure 8.7 'Your Country Needs You'

Figure 8.8 The White Feather, *c.*1916

your country or wear this'. This sense that no less than the masculinity, patriotism and honour of British men were at stake had been deeply embedded over decades of imperial militarism.

Imperial Men in the Trenches

The reality of war bore almost no relation to its ideal. Perhaps only T.E. Lawrence, involved in the Arab Revolt against the Ottomans on the Eastern Front, conformed to the imperial romance of war as a manly adventure. And yet Lawrence was an ambivalent figure. Born out of wedlock, he was an unconventional, small and bookish man who adopted Arab dress – hardly the manly specimen of Edwardian militarism's imperial race. The cult that grew around 'Lawrence of Arabia', crafted by the hugely popular lecture tours of an American journalist in 1919 and Lawrence's own account of the war in *The Seven Pillars of Wisdom* (1922), was a post-war invention for a nation in dire need of a heroic version of the Great War. For, as we saw in the last chapter, the world's first industrial war was fought between competing empires with pre-industrial military strategies. The result was a veritable bloodbath, with soldiers dug into entrenched positions for months and years on end, engaging in wave after wave of deadly and unsuccessful attempts to break enemy lines. On Europe's Western Front, conditions in trenches that quickly turned to mud were horrendous. The noise of artillery barrages was deafening, and fear was endemic among soldiers. They expected to be killed at any moment by something or someone they would never see, or to spend days caught in the no-man's-land between enemy lines amidst the rotting flesh of the unrecovered dead. The horror and futility of a war seemingly without end, and the sense of powerlessness that overwhelmed troops fighting in these conditions, had a profound effect (see Textbox 8.3).

Far from proving the masculinity of the imperial race, the experience of fighting on the Western Front was frequently emasculating. Almost a third of the British Empire's troops, 1.64 million men, were wounded and rendered dependent upon the care of the tens of thousands of women who joined the Red Cross's Voluntary Aid Detachments as nurses. Of these men, at the end of the war 400,000 were considered worthy of state pensions to compensate the loss of earnings from their physical injuries. The number of men crippled and maimed was unprecedented, and although they catalysed new medical research in areas like orthopaedics, the long-term care of paraplegics or the blinded was left largely to charities. The mental scars of war were harder to assess and went uncompensated. It is impossible to estimate the number of men who suffered mental breakdowns as a consequence of the war, but it was significant enough for Dr Charles Myers to coin the term **'shell-shock'** in 1915. By the war's end, 80,000 men had been treated for shell-shock, even though many doctors and military men continued to believe that breakdowns were feigned by 'malingerers', or were the product of exhaustion or an effeminate excess of emotion. Mental breakdowns accounted for a third of all discharges from the army in 1917. First considered to be the consequence of physical damage to the nerves, a range of treatments like water cures and electro-convulsive therapy was used to restore men to their proper manly state. Eventually, as the varied manifestations of shell-shock were recognized as psychological trauma, a new 'talking cure' was developed that proved an important conduit for the spread of psychoanalytic practice in Britain.

Military discipline was required to keep some men at war. It alone cannot explain why British troops, unlike their French counterparts, did not revolt in mutiny. No question military discipline was harsh and reflected the disdain that many of the officer classes felt for soldiers who came from the working classes. Those guilty of minor misdemeanours were subject to field punishments like being tied to a fixed object for a period of time, and flogging was still used on Indian troops. The loyalty of troops rather than their lack of discipline was the real concern. Fifty thousand soldiers were subjected to court-martial for offences – like being absent without leave, insubordination or wounding oneself – that were thought to undermine the very structures of military authority. Three thousand men were sentenced to death by firing squad at these military trials, in which there was no jury and sometimes no witnesses called to their defence. A small proportion of these condemned men, 306 of them, were shot mainly for desertion or cowardice but also for charges such as quitting or sleeping at one's post. The seventeen-year-old Thomas Highgate was the first British soldier to be executed, in September 1914. The son of a farm labourer, he was undefended at his trial and was shot for desertion, having fled to a barn during the Battle of Mons. Almost a century later, in 2006, the 306 soldiers executed for desertion or cowardice were granted an official pardon by the British government.

The inhumanity of war was not immediately apparent on the Home Front despite the lengthening lists of casualties. Censorship constrained the capacity of journalists to provide accurate accounts of the experience of war, while soldiers' letters home to loved ones, or their conversations, if they were lucky enough to return on leave, mostly edited out the incomprehensible horrors they had witnessed. It was poetry that broke the silence. In July 1917 the Oxbridge-educated and much-decorated officer Siegfried Sassoon published an open letter to his commanding officer titled 'Finished with the War: A Soldier's Declaration' lamenting the 'unjust' politics of the war, the suffering of the troops and the 'callous complacency' of those at home who were oblivious to the agonies of war. Rather than being court-martialled, Sassoon was declared mentally unfit for service and dispatched to Craiglockhart War Hospital in Edinburgh, where he met Wilfred Owen, who was being treated for shell-shock. Although the poetry these two men produced in Edinburgh was only slowly published, it decisively shaped

8.3 Source: Wilfred Owen, 'Dulce et Decorum est'

Bent double, like old beggars under sacks,

Knock-kneed, coughing like hags, we cursed through sludge,
Till on the haunting flares we turned our backs,
And towards our distant rest began to trudge.
Men marched asleep. Many had lost their boots,
But limped on, blood-shod. All went lame; all blind;
Drunk with fatigue; deaf even to the hoots
Of gas-shells dropping softly behind.

Gas! GAS! Quick, boys! – An ecstasy of fumbling,
Fitting the clumsy helmets just in time,
But someone still was yelling out and stumbling
And flound'ring like a man in fire or lime. –
Dim through the misty panes and thick green light,
As under a green sea, I saw him drowning.

In all my dreams before my helpless sight,
He plunges at me, guttering, choking, drowning.

If in some smothering dreams, you too could pace
Behind the wagon that we flung him in,
And watch the white eyes writhing in his face,
His hanging face, like a devil's sick of sin;
If you could hear, at every jolt, the blood
Come gargling from the froth-corrupted lungs,
Obscene as cancer, bitter as the cud
Of vile, incurable sores on innocent tongues, –
My friend, you would not tell with such high zest
To children ardent for some desperate glory,
The old Lie: *Dulce et decorum est*
Pro patria mori.

Wilfred Owen's poem, 'Dolce et Decorum est', is perhaps the best known of the many poems written by young men fighting in the trenches of World War I. The poem tells the horrific story of a poison gas attack on a group of soldiers. Amidst a devastated landscape of 'sludge' and 'haunted flares' one soldier is unable to fit his mask in time and is struck down by the gas, 'choking, drowning … his hanging face, like a devil's sick of sin'. The poem's title is a reference to the line 'Dulce et decorum est pro patria mori' by the Roman poet Horace, meaning 'how sweet and honourable it is to die for one's country'. When Britain first joined the war in 1914, this line was used to spur on thousands of men who enthusiastically signed up to fight, not knowing the horrors that awaited them on the Western Front. The poem, written three years later, speaks to a broken and brutalized youth, disillusioned with what Owen called the 'old Lie' of nobly dying for your country. It also alludes to the **shell-shock** and long-term trauma suffered by those who fought, describing
how the image of the suffering soldier appeared in 'all my dreams before my helpless sight'. Owen himself was killed in November 1918, and exactly one week before the war ended. (S.W.)

an understanding of the war as brutal and futile. When Owen's 'Anthem for Doomed Youth' was published in 1920, it quickly became iconic not just of the lost generation of young men buried overseas, but of the end of allegiance to the liberal progress and civility they had been told it was their duty to defend with their lives (see Textbox 8.3). A decade letter, two veterans of the Great War published *1066 and All That!*, a searing parody of the triumphalist version of history still taught in British schools, civilization ending in 1918 when, they joked, History as a progressive series of battles 'came to a.'

As George Orwell later wrote, the idea of 'Progress had finally ended in the biggest massacre in history'.

State Welfare and its Workers

Rebuilding the imperial race would take more than a few prosthetic limbs. It would require a new social contract whose foundations were laid during the war itself. Just as the state took command of the wartime economy, as we saw in Chapter 7, so it took responsibility for those at home supporting its war effort. The newly created **Ministry of Munitions**, with Lloyd George at its head, was at the heart of this process. By 1916 it was responsible for a quarter of Britain's total workforce, with 1.6 million workers in its 'controlled industries' and a further 340,000 in its own National Factories. At the end of the war it supervised the work of over 3 million employees. About 700,000 of these were women working in armament factories, known as the 'munitionettes'. Their presence 'diluting' a male workforce, stretched thin by enlistment, was secured by agreement with the trade unions, in return for a no-strike clause as well as the maintenance of wage differentials between men and women workers. Having previously struggled for legal recognition of its activities, the labour movement now had the ear of government, which recognized its centrality to the war economy.

Yet it was the desire to increase the productivity of workers, not an attempt to satiate the demands of the labour movement, that made the **Ministry of Munitions** experiment with new forms of social welfare for its employees. Lloyd George turned to Rowntree in 1915 to establish his own laboratory within the Ministry in the shape of the Welfare Department. Rowntree was interested in how the worker's human motor could be made more efficient and less prone to 'industrial fatigue' and accidents by providing proper nutrition, ventilation and light, as well as closely regulated shifts and hours of labour. In the hands of Lloyd George and Rowntree, under pressure of war, American **scientific management** – or Taylorism – was given a decidedly different twist in Britain that emphasized social welfare. By 1917 the Ministry of Munitions had increased productivity by reducing hours of labour, had 840 industrial canteens feeding around 800,000 workers, had provided some crèches for childcare, and employed 800 welfare supervisors who oversaw the conditions in their factories. The growth of armament factories meant that new houses had to be built by the state to house workers. Constructed rapidly between February and December 1915 by the Ministry of Works, 'Well Hall Garden City' estate housed workers from the Royal Arsenal at Woolwich alongside a large number of temporary hutments. As its name suggests, the estate's design was heavily influenced by the **garden city** movement. When it was purchased by the Royal Arsenal Co-operative Society in 1925, its name was changed to 'Progress Estate'. There was also a special interest in the welfare of the often young and single women workers, less in their health or efficiency than in their morals. Although they were housed in single-sex hostels with firm rules for their behaviour, respectable women volunteered to form a Women's Police Service to provide additional oversight and instruction on moral and social hygiene. When the war ended, the legacy of these industrial-welfare initiatives were apparent in the formation of the Industrial Fatigue Research Board (1918), the Industrial Welfare Society (1919) and the National Institute of Industrial Psychology (1921), all of which sought to better understand how workers could be made fitter, healthier and more productive.

War was good for mothers and babies as well. The Board of Education passed the Care of Mothers and Young Children Act in 1915 to provide local authorities and voluntary groups with funds to establish health centres for giving advice and support to expectant and new mothers. There were almost 450 of these operating by 1917 and they provided milk at cost price to mothers and their children. The number of health visitors who provided 'help' to mothers in their homes more than doubled between 1914 and 1918, and the state sponsored the training of midwives from 1918. If these wartime social policies struggled to rid themselves of the old concerns with **national efficiency** and racial hygiene, they still forged a new social contract between the state and its citizens.

In 1916 the government formed a **Committee of Reconstruction** with a wide brief to consider social and economic policy, and enlisted experts like Rowntree and Beatrice Webb. The persistence of slums and the rising costs of rents squeezing working-class budgets made housing a key issue for raising a healthy race. The following year a separate committee, chaired by Liberal MP Tudor Walters, urged the construction of new publicly funded housing stock. The hope was not just that the slum-dweller would be eradicated with the slums, but that the new houses with baths, toilets, running water, electric light, gas cookers and gardens would civilize their inhabitants. As the war drew to a close, both King George V and Lloyd George declared that the construction of 'homes fit for heroes' would be a priority of government. Fittingly, it was the new Ministry of Health that developed the Housing and Town Planning Act of 1919, which provided local authorities with subsidies for the construction of 500,000 new homes. A raft of other social reforms was also introduced. For the first time those wounded in war were afforded pensions, 400,000 of them, with a special department in the new Ministry of Pensions responsible for calibrating the compensation for the loss of different parts of the body. The Education Act (1918) raised the age of compulsory schooling to fourteen, the Old Age Pensions Act (1919) increased the basic pension to 10 shillings and extended it to include those receiving poor relief, and in 1921 National Insurance was expanded to cover around 9 million more workers (from the original 2.25 million), with the benefits extended to 47 weeks from 15 weeks. As we saw in Chapter 7, expenditure on these new social programmes became the target of the campaign against government 'waste' and were ultimately slashed by the '**Geddes Axe**' in 1922. The post-war dreams of building a better society in the interests of all were left unrealized, like the projected new public housing stock of which only half has built. Even the basic safety net of social security extended in 1921 came under great pressure as the number of insured workers unemployed never fell below 10 per cent and rose to 22 per cent in the crisis of 1931. When Ramsay MacDonald asked his recently elected Labour government to introduce austerity measures that included a 20 per cent cut to unemployment benefit to help reduce the budget deficit and the mounting pressure on the pound, it split his party. It took the formation of an emergency cross-party National Government by MacDonald to introduce a 10 per cent cut. The new social contract imagined during the Great War may not have fully materialized but defending even its hollowed out form led to the collapse of the Labour government in 1931.

Conclusion

The social policies supported by the state in the decades either side of the Great War, let alone the range of voluntary agencies engaged in philanthropic social work, would have been unimaginable in the 1870s. The rediscovery of poverty from the 1880s gradually eroded the central assumption that liberal political economy would deliver prosperity and civility to all. Those concerned with the persistence of poverty developed new scientific ways of measuring its scale and effects. These early social scientists demonstrated that poverty not only held almost a third of the world's richest nation in its grasp, but threatened the racial health of society as a whole, the efficiency of the nation and the strength of the empire. The poor were no longer a danger merely to themselves. A plethora of social reformers created organizations designed to solve the problem of poverty and ensure Britons continued to be an imperial race. Social reform was an imperial endeavour that sought to strengthen Britain as a competitor for territory and markets with its rival imperial powers. The colonies were used to understand racial difference as well as to propagate – racially, politically and culturally – an English-speaking British world. In the decade before the First World War a self-consciously 'New Liberal' government introduced a range of measures designed to improve the racial health of the nation. When imperial competition finally descended into the global conflagration of the Great War, the British state's desire and capacity to increase the health and productivity of its population was greatly enhanced. Despite the retreat in social policy in the decade after the Armistice, the social problem had redefined the nature of liberal political economy and the relationship between the state and its citizens.

FURTHER READING

The best general surveys of the political and intellectual history of Britain in this period – José Harris, *Private Lives, Public Spirit: Britain 1870–1914* (London, 1995), and G.R. Searle, *A New England? Peace and War 1886–1918* (Oxford, 2004) – contain a good deal of discussion about how the social problems associated with poverty transformed liberal political economy and the state. Unlike my account, which emphasizes that this process was not complete until 1931, they see the Great War as the decisive turning point in part because they focus almost exclusively on Britain, not its place within the broader imperial and global context.

Despite the enormous disparities of wealth that deepened from the 1880s, the rich have attracted less attention than the poor. The best accounts remain F.M.L. Thompson, *English Landed Society in the Nineteenth Century* (London, 1963), and W.D. Rubenstein, *Men of Property: The Very Wealthy in Britain Since the Industrial Revolution* (London, 1981). The rediscovery of poverty and the racialization of the poor is excellently covered in different ways by Gareth Stedman Jones's *Outcast London* (Oxford, 1971), Judith Walkowitz, *City of Dreadful Delight: Narratives of Sexual Danger in Late Victorian London* (London, 1992), and Seth Koven, *Slumming: Sexual and Social Politics in Victorian London* (Princeton, 2004). They also touch on the emergence of the social sciences, a subject further developed in David Englander and Rosemary O'Day (eds.), *Retrieved Riches: Social Investigation in Britain, 1840–1914* (Aldershot, 1995), and James Vernon, *Hunger: A Modern History* (Cambridge, Mass., 2007). The transnational, or transatlantic, nature of the new social sciences and the politics they helped generate is nicely explored in Daniel Rodgers, *Atlantic Crossings: Social Politics in a Progressive Age* (Cambridge, Mass., 1998).

Some historians deny the centrality of racial thought to the nationalism and imperialism so prevalent in the decades leading up to the Great War. This is the view provided in Peter Mandler's *English National Character: The History of an Idea from Edmund Burke to Tony Blair* (New Haven, 2006) and David Cannadine's *Ornamentalism: How the British Saw their Empire* (London, 2001). It is not my view. The hardening of theories of racial difference at home is explored by Nancy Stepan, *The Idea of Race in Science: Great Britain 1800–1960* (Basingstoke, 1982), and Dan Stone, *Breeding Superman: Nietzsche, Race and Eugenics in Edwardian and Interwar Britain* (Liverpool, 2002). Their elaboration across the Empire, where the cultivation of whiteness was always understood in relation to other races, is addressed in Dane Kennedy, *Islands of White: Settler Society and Culture in Kenya and Southern Rhodesia, 1890–1939* (Durham, NC, 1987), and Tony Ballantyne, *Orientalism and Race: Ayrianism in the British Empire* (Basingstoke, 2001).

Ideas of gender and sexuality were not just inseparable from understandings of racial difference; they helped generate them in both the metropolitan and colonial contexts. On the gendering of race, see Antoinette Burton, *Burdens of History: British Feminists, Indian Women, and Imperial Culture, 1865–1915* (Chapel Hill, 1994); Mrinalini Sinha, *Colonial Masculinity: The 'Manly Englishman' and the 'Effeminate Bengali' in the Late Nineteenth Century* (Manchester, 1995); Philippa Levine, *Prostitution, Race and Politics: Policing Venereal Disease in the British Empire* (New York, 2003). On the production of imperial men, see J.A. Mangan, *'Manufactured' Masculinity: Making Imperial Manliness, Morality and Militarism* (London, 2013). The pioneering book by Jeffrey Weeks, *Sex, Politics and Society: The Regulation of Sexuality Since*

1800 (London, 1981), is especially good at discussing the discovery and denigration of the figure of the effete homosexual.

There is a plethora of work on the development of social policy designed to marshal a healthier imperial race before, during and after World War I. Anna Davin's 'Imperialism and Motherhood', *History Workshop Journal*, 5/1 (1978), 9–66, and Jane Lewis's *The Politics of Motherhood: Child and Maternal Welfare in England, 1900–1939* (London, 1980), generated much fine work on the politics of 'maternalism', including the excellent comparative essay by Seth Koven and Sonya Michel, 'Womanly Duties: Maternalist Politics and the Origins of Welfare States in France, Germany, Great Britain and the United States, 1880–1920', *American Historical Review*, 95/4 (1990), 1076–1108. Matthew Thompson's *The Problem of Mental Deficiency: Eugenics, Democracy and Social Policy in Britain, 1870–1959* (Oxford, 1998) reminds us that those deemed mentally 'feeble' were also a target of social policies designed to improve racial health. The still classic works on social insurance and unemployment are E.P. Hennock, *British Social Reform and German Precedents: The Case for Social Insurance 1880–1914* (Oxford, 1987), and Susan Pedersen, *Family, Dependence, and the Origins of the Welfare State: Britain and France, 1914–1945* (Cambridge, 1993).

On the shattering experience of the Great War for many men, see Paul Fussell, *The Great War and Modern Memory* (Oxford, 1975); Joanna Bourke, *Dismembering the Male: Men's Bodies, Britain and the Great War* (London, 1996); Michael Roper, *The Secret Battle: Emotional Survival in the Great War* (Manchester, 2009); and Fiona Reid, *Broken Men: Shell Shock, Treatment and Recovery in Britain, 1914–1930* (London, 2010).

9   The Rise of the Mass

Introduction

In 1937 a new organization called **Mass Observation** set out to study the responses of 'the mass' to the coronation of King Edward VIII. They believed that scientifically observing the behaviour of the mass would facilitate a better understanding of the political culture that had developed in Britain since the Great War. As we saw in Chapter 6, the foundations of a liberal system of political representation had been laid by 1885, but it was not until 1918 and 1928 that all men and women were able to vote. Just as politics was finally made democratic, culture was increasingly experienced in new mass forms. If **rational recreation** had helped create an understanding of the individual as the subject of politics in the Victorian era, so mass culture became seen as synonymous with the nature of democratic politics. Increasingly commercialized, the forms of mass culture deepened long-held fears of the demos as an unthinking, easily manipulated and indistinguishable entity. As soon as Britain became a democracy, many across the political spectrum argued that its mass political culture was degraded and set about trying to create a better-informed and more critical citizenry. Hence the formation of Mass Observation. The task of this chapter is to show how the liberal political culture that in the nineteenth century had afforded the vote to very few propertied men as individuals was transformed into a mass democracy.

The work of many hands, this transformation was nested into other historical processes. As the electorate steadily increased before the Great War, political parties assiduously sought to build mass memberships and craft distinct cultures of sociability that reflected their political programmes. Just as the **Great Depression** helped galvanize colonial nationalist movements in Ireland and India, so in Britain it catalysed the mobilization of a labour politics. Although women were involved in the political parties and trade unions of the labour movement, they were, as the gathering momentum of the women's suffrage campaigns made manifest, still denied the right to vote. These political movements, like colonial nationalism, exposed the ways in which the liberal political system was fatally compromised by its own contradictions. Imbricated in the institutional and social forms of the **ancien regime** it had sought to displace, it had failed to deliver on its promises. In return for the denial of their citizenship, colonial subjects were promised civility and the rule of law, women were promised the protection of **separate spheres**, and the industrious were promised, if not prosperity, at least employment. The responsibility for that failure was then turned back onto those very groups as a justification for their continuing exclusion from citizenship. In turn, this language of difference was taken up by those in political movements. Just as colonial subjects advocated for the nation they imagined would one day be free, so the British labour movement increasingly spoke on behalf of a working class, and the women suffragists evoked the interests of their sex. These arguments and political movements were vital in ensuring that all men and women in Britain finally became citizens of their own country after the Great War.

A strategy of cautious containment, not a ready embrace of demos, characterized the reforms of 1918 and 1928 that finally made Britain a democracy. The long-held condescension of the governing elite to those they perceived as the lower classes did not lessen as a consequence of the Great War. If anything it deepened as the critique of mass culture and mass politics accelerated, drawing on theories of the collective psyche of 'the crowd' that were developed by French and Italian social scientists before the war. Condescension turned to fear in the wake of the Russian Revolution of 1917, the wave of revolts across the Empire in 1919, and Britain's **General Strike** in 1926. The question then became how best to incorporate previously excluded men and women into the political system without destabilizing it. Even those who had long argued for a democratic franchise were fearful that commercialized mass culture had corroded the critical capacities of Britain's new citizens. A new culture of democracy had to be created during the 1920s. Those who had only recently viewed democracy with terror began to celebrate it as an innately English achievement gifted to the **British world**. Democracy came to represent continuity and stability, in marked contrast to the alien systems of bolshevism, socialism and fascism spreading across Europe, to which it stood in opposition.

TIMELINE

1867	National Union of Conservative Associations
1869	Municipal Franchise Act
1870	Education Act Married Women's Property Act
1871	Factory and Bank Holiday Acts
1872	Secret Ballot Act
1877	National Liberal Federation
1883	Corrupt Practices Act Primrose League

1884	Third Reform Act Social Democratic Federation Fabian Society
1886	Women's Liberal Federation Liberal Unionist Association
1888	Match girls strikes
1893	Independent Labour Party
1894	Local Government Act
1896	Gustave Le Bon, *The Crowd*
1897	National Union of Women's Suffrage Societies
1899	London Government Act
1900	Labour Representation Committee
1903	Women's Social and Political Union
1905	First hunger march by unemployed
1906	WSPU hunger strikes
1907	Women's Freedom League Men's League for Women's Suffrage
1908	Women's National Anti-Suffrage League
1911–12	Great Transport Strike
1918	Representation of the People Act
1920	National Union of Societies for Equal Citizenship
1926	General Strike
1928	Equal Franchise Act
1929	Great Depression
1931	National Government
1937	Mass Observation

The Emergence of Mass Culture

In the late nineteenth century a new type of commercialized mass culture developed in Britain that would be recognizable to us today. This was the age that gave us, for instance, variety theatre, the cinema and many of the organized spectator sports that still predominate in the **British world**. Commercialized popular culture did not just seek to engage consumers en masse; it made it possible to imagine the mass audience as nationally homogeneous. At three o'clock on a Saturday afternoon, for example, it was not just working men in Oldham who went to watch a football match, it was working men across the country. While these men talked in different dialects, they had all just got paid, they largely dressed alike, and they all had wives who were busy trying to stretch the family's meagre resources by buying provisions for the week at the local market. Nothing typifies the idea of the working classes as an undifferentiated mass better than images of a football crowd (see Figure 9.1). It was this sea of humanity, and their seemingly common or coordinated responses to the game, that typified the mass society that **Mass Observation** sought to comprehend in the late 1930s.

The emergence of this commercialized mass culture displaced neither the customary culture discussed in Chapter 2 nor the self-improving **rational recreation** examined in Chapter 4. Instead, it grew around and sometimes even incorporated elements of them. In part this was made possible by the creation of new times and spaces for leisure that clearly separated it from the world of work. Not all of this process was driven by commercial or industrial imperatives. The introduction of mass 'elementary' education for children after the Education Acts of 1870 (1872 in Scotland) and 1880 introduced children between the ages of five and thirteen to new time disciplines. The school day, which was regimented by a new and strict 'timetable' of classes and activities, began at 9am and ended at 3pm, stretched over a week that ran from Monday to Friday, and over a school year with three terms punctuated by 'holidays' over Christmas, Easter and the summer. By 1900 the rhythm of the school day, week and year was well established in over 5,691 Board schools across England and Wales, as well as those in Scotland and Ireland. Many worried that mass education would flatten out the rich linguistic and cultural differences in Britain, especially in Wales, Ireland and the Scottish Highlands, where Welsh and Gaelic were steadily being eroded as languages of advancement.

Similarly, the rhythm of the working day and week had been largely set by a series of **Factory Acts** and the Bank Holiday Act of 1871 (that prescribed uniform national holidays when banks were not allowed to open). The ten-and-a-half-hour working day started at 6am and ended at 5:30pm and stretched from Monday morning to Saturday lunchtime. A new industrial time discipline was slowly instantiated by employers. In an age before alarm clocks, mills and factories would hire a 'knocker-up' to wake their employees each morning by knocking on their doors (or windows with a long

Figure 9.1 110,000 in Selhurst Park for the FA Cup final, 1901

THE CROWD.

pole) – a practice that endured in some mill-towns into the 1950s. Once begun, the day was punctuated by bells, whistles and horns. When payday arrived at the end of the week on Saturday, men invariably headed to the pub and then to play or watch a sport, while their wives took what they were given of their husbands' wages to shop for cheap food at the local market. Sunday became the day of rest and recreation, ideally (but rarely for most working men) involving both worship and family. Workers were usually allowed one week of unpaid holiday a year that (in a sign of the continuing hold of customary culture) was invariably taken during the local **wakes week**. Only salaried white-collar workers received paid holidays, as so-called 'brain work' was considered more exhausting than manual work. It was not until 1911 that the trade union movement began to campaign for paid holidays, a battle that was finally won for 11 million workers in 1938, by which time twenty-four other countries had introduced them. By then, the social right to paid holidays also came with the obligation to indulge in forms of leisure and recreation that would make one an informed and responsible citizen.

Mass culture also manifested itself in the creation of new spaces for recreation. The seaside resort of Blackpool became a popular holiday destination for the textile workers of Lancashire and Yorkshire during their local wakes week in the late nineteenth century. It grew from hosting a million visitors in 1883 to four times that number by 1914 and reached 7 million during the 1930s. The development of London's West End, centred around the reconstruction of Shaftesbury Avenue, Regent Street and Oxford

Street between the 1880s and 1910s, was designed to attract fashionable and well-to-do ladies to its theatres and department stores. It also acted as a magnet for prostitutes, pick-pockets, chancers and those content to window-shop. But it was the music hall and football stadium that became the axiomatic new spaces of commercialized mass culture. **Music halls** and football stadiums proliferated in cities across the country in the four decades before the Great War. Both emerged out of cultural forms – pub music and football – that had long existed, and came to inhabit new purpose-built buildings, forms of ownership and regimes of labour. They also both increasingly made the audience spectators and consumers of entertainment as a commodity.

The Music Hall

Music halls were not new. They had grown out of pub saloon theatres in the 1850s. By 1870 there were already 31 large halls in London and a further 382 scattered across the country's other towns and cities. These halls offered a huge variety of entertainment on stage – from songs (often comic or romantic), dance, acrobatics, mime and even animal performance – as well as a good amount of alcohol and conviviality off stage. Such was their growing popularity that a new golden age of building ever larger and more grandiose halls began in the 1880s (see Textbox 9.1 and Figure 9.2). This was made possible by a concentration of ownership and the development of provincial and national chains. The largest of these was the Moss, Stoll and Thornton; it was formed by amalgamating ten separate companies and was worth £1.5 million when it was publicly floated in 1900. London's 35 largest halls drew an estimated audience of 45,000 every night in the 1890s. Moss, Stoll and Thornton built even grander theatres in London in the following decade. They opened the Hippodrome in 1900 with a retracting stage and a giant water tank for aquatic spectacles, the Hackney Empire in 1901, and the Coliseum in 1904 that had an audience capacity of 2,500 (500 more than the Empire Theatre which opened on Leicester Square in 1884).

   With increased capacity came more amenities, larger programmes with even greater variety, and the development of a star system for the entertainers. Star artists – like Charlie Chaplin, who had learned his trade as part of a troupe of dancing boys at the turn of the century before becoming a star comic a decade later – were rotated through several halls in a single night. Accommodating these stars ensured that programmes were more tightly directed. The same was true for the audiences. Regimented seating facing the stage was introduced from the 1870s, and the grand new halls instilled new disciplines into the audiences. Food and drink were no longer allowed in the auditorium (and by 1909 the London County Council had banned all liquor from twenty-one of the Moss Empire's twenty-nine halls), the audience was set back further from the stage to prevent them from disrupting the performance, and the differential pricing of seats segregated the audience by social class. Although performers continued to

9.1 Place: Britannia Music Hall, Glasgow

The Britannia Music Hall in Glasgow, which opened in 1859, was one of the earliest and most successful music halls in Scotland. The Britannia sat 1,500 people squeezed onto parallel wooden benches. One journalist who visited the Britannia in 1860 wrote of seeing **Jacobite** songs, blackface minstrelsy, a satirical election address and erotic female dancing all in the same evening. The venue's increasing association with the prostitution trade led to the appointment of police inspectors who made spot visits, leading performers to hastily (and temporarily) tone down their material. As the century wore on, the Britannia became subject to more and more intensive forms of policing, and eventually all women were banned unless accompanied by a man. In 1896 the Britannia became one of the first buildings in Glasgow to be electrified, enabling it to project some early 'Animated Pictures'. Long a venue that attracted the leading star turns of the day, in 1906 Stan Laurel (of Laurel and Hardy) made his first stage appearance there. Forced to compete with picture houses in the early twentieth century, the Britannia's shows became increasingly outlandish. Renamed the Britannia Panopticon by a new owner in 1906, it became the site of a freak show, a waxworks display and even had its basement converted into a zoo. Even this was not enough to compete with the new forms of electrified mass culture emerging in Glasgow, and the Britannia finally closed in 1938. (S.W.)

Figure 9.2 Britannia Music Hall, Glasgow

A MUSIC HALL GALLERY.

Figure 9.3 The upper gallery and the gods of a London music hall, 1900

interact with their audience, they were increasingly expected to provide a spectacle and to get on with the show. The cheapest seats (where there was standing room only), and the unruliest members of the audience, were the highest and furthest removed from the stage in 'the gods' (see Figure 9.3). There remained a demotic spirit in the gods – an insistence that all were equal in the kingdom of leisure and equally subject to their praise and abuse – that lasted until after the Great War. Even so, by 1912 the music hall had become respectable enough to earn a Royal Command performance in front of King George V at the Palace Theatre.

Football

Some version of football, known as soccer in the United States, had long been played in Britain. How and when it was played varied enormously between regions and by social group. During the nineteenth century football was not only organized by specific national institutions which codified the rules of the game, but was also increasingly commercialized as a spectator sport. Like much organized sport in Britain, the modern version of the game was first developed in private schools as part of their mission to train muscular, Christian young men. Thus a new set of common rules was first developed at the University of Cambridge in 1848 to allow those who came from different private schools to play the same game. Even though the Football Association (formed in 1863; its Scottish equivalent was founded a decade later) largely adopted the Cambridge rules, alternatives, like the 'Sheffield rules' developed by privately educated men from that city, continued to operate elsewhere. Propagated by upper-class men, these versions of the game were extended to working people from the 1870s and 1880s through clubs that were invariably started by local notables (like Ipswich Town), churches (like Southampton and Celtic), chapels (like Everton and Aston Villa), employers (like Arsenal and Manchester City), pubs (like Millwall and Bolton Wanderers) and clubs (like Rangers and Queen's Park). Friendly games between these clubs were slowly supplemented by the creation of competitive matches, first for the Football Association's Cup, which began in 1873, and then by the Football League (formed in 1888, with its Scottish counterpart following two years later).

Unlike other games that developed into organized sports – rugby union, cricket and tennis – with standardized rules and national organizations from the 1870s and 1880s, by the 1890s football had become both professionalized and commercialized. The FA Cup and leagues further consolidated the rules, enclosed the game within grounds and stadiums where there was a price of admission to watch, and paid the best players more to lure them from other teams or regions. By the 1890s it is estimated that over 12,000 people were paying to watch teams in the FA Cup and leagues. Some clubs, like Preston North End and Manchester United, became limited companies and sought more capital from shareholders to build bigger stadiums and pay higher wages for better players. Construction of new purpose-built stadiums like Chelsea's Stamford Bridge (1905) and Manchester United's Old Trafford (1908) that could accommodate larger crowds and generate more revenue accelerated, many of them (like Bramhall Lane, Ibrox, Anfield and Highbury, to name but a few) designed by the Scottish architect Archie Leitch. With Ibrox, Hampden Park and Parkhead, Glasgow alone boasted three of the largest stadiums in the world. With tickets ranging between 3 and 6 pence, easily within reach of many, attendance quickly rose. Special 'football' trains were run on Saturdays to enable supporters to watch their teams play away at other stadiums. On the eve of the First World War, the average attendance at First Division (now called the Premier League) matches was over 23,000. By this time as many as 14 per cent of adult males attended football games in Scotland and it was possible, as we saw in Figure 9.1, for 110,000 to watch Tottenham play Sheffield United in the 1901 FA Cup final.

Only mass political meetings came close to generating these numbers. While music-hall audiences were usually disaggregated into types (like 'roughs' and 'swells'), those attending football matches quickly became pejoratively called a 'crowd'. The so-called respectable classes had their usual crop of fears. Some complained that the times of the games on a Saturday afternoon encouraged alcohol consumption (men going from work, to the pub, to the game). Others disapproved of the gambling that quickly developed around the game, with the football pools allowing even those who did not attend to place a pool bet and guess the sequence of scores across the league. As many as 2 million played the 'pools' by 1914 and by the 1930s pools companies were collecting an estimated £20 million a year. Most of all there was a concern about 'the mass' of people who appeared gripped by what the press described as the 'mania' and 'madness' for football. It did not help that 'the crowd' was overwhelmingly male and failed to behave as those who had started the game to inculcate Christian manliness had hoped. Although the new stadiums removed fans from the pitch-side into 'stands', they failed to render the crowd passive spectators. They remained extremely vocal in support of their team and in the abuse of rivals, prone to throw things at each other or at players who earned their displeasure, and likely to invade the pitch and stop the game at key moments. Violence, or what the press reported as 'disturbances', between fans was not uncommon, especially those of local teams when the rivalry acquired a sectarian edge. Despite the best efforts of the new stadiums and increased policing on match days, the football crowd remained a sometimes unruly mass.

The new mass culture, and a concern with the seemingly irrational, instinctive and unruly responses of its spectators, encouraged academic theories of 'the crowd'. In Britain these were most evident in the critique of the **jingoism** whipped up by the popular press and **music halls** during the **South African War**, in Hobson's *Imperialism* (1901). But across Europe intellectuals were grappling with the rise of the mass. The German philosopher Friedrich Nietzsche provided an early and influential critique of how commercialized culture produced a homogeneous, irrational and herd-like mass. Gustave Le Bon's *The Crowd* (1896), often seen as the foundational text of the new study of crowd psychology, was the product of several decades of French intellectual efforts to come to terms with the demotic elements of the Third Republic. Much of this work stood in contempt of 'the crowd' and hoped, like Le Bon, that strong leaders capable of directing – not following – its irrational patterns would emerge.

The Rise of the Mass Political Party

This uncertainty about mass culture and the fear of the crowd informed the development of mass politics. We have already seen in Chapter 6 how the extension of the electorate between 1867 and 1884 triggered the growth of centralized party machines to organize and mobilize the new voters. The development of these party organizations, and their growing influence in constituencies across the country, helped transform how politics was conducted, with elections being fought on an increasingly national scale. As the electorate continued to grow in the decades before the Great War, political parties sought to build mass memberships around party cultures that forged new bonds of solidarity and loyalty between electors, their families and the party.

Why did the size of the electorate increase after 1884 although the next act of reform did not come until 1918? The system of electoral registration established by the **Reform Act** of 1867 was designed to service a limited electorate and was ill equipped to deal with the rapid expansion of urban populations after 1870. Changes in the law, as well as the efforts of parties to maximize the numbers of electors who registered to vote, made it increasingly difficult for registration courts to accurately police who was disqualified as an alien, as a lodger (not a tenant or householder) or by the year-long residency clause. The result was a quite dramatic growth of what one historian has termed the 'slum vote'. Whereas the electorate stood at 5,600,000 after the **Reform Act** of 1884, it included over 8 million (6.7 million in England and Wales) voters by 1914, of whom around 500,000 were plural voters who could vote twice. This still meant that at least 40 per cent of adult men in England and Wales, and a yet higher proportion in Scotland and Ireland, could not vote.

As the size of the electorate grew, the old forms of campaigning became less effective. In 1880, when the median borough electorate was under 4,000, it remained just about possible for candidates to make personal, face-to-face appeals to voters. That was beyond even the most dedicated candidate five years later when the median borough had doubled in size. Moreover, the **Corrupt Practices Act** of 1883 made the job of canvassing and organizing these voters even harder for parties by preventing them from paying election workers. This job now fell upon those prepared to volunteer for the party, and whose work was overseen by the burgeoning ranks of professional party agents.

The Party Machine

Building a mass membership on whose voluntary labour they could draw became a priority for parties. As it was not until the formation of the Labour Party in 1900 that members had to pay a fee for joining a party, members provided support by their labour rather than from their pockets. As a consequence, the Labour Party excepted, we have no reliable estimates of the size of party membership until World War II. Nonetheless, it is clear that parties quickly found local volunteers. Founded in 1867, the National Union of Conservative Associations had a remarkable 400 local branches before the National Liberal Federation (NLF) was even created in 1877 (Scotland had its own versions of these organizations). Three years later, the NLF had 77 local associations and their number had grown to 200 by 1900 despite the breakaway of the Liberal Unionist

Association in 1886, which itself had 155 affiliates two years later. Annual conferences were to energize activists, not to pass resolutions that reflected grassroots sentiments. Heaven forbid that parties should leave their members and activists to their own devices. Instead, paid agents working in coordination with the parties' central offices in London channelled their enthusiasm and labour. As their numbers proliferated, they professionalized, establishing their own exams, journals, benevolent funds and publishing manuals on how to register electors and run campaigns. By 1900 the Conservative Party had 400 agents on their pay roll, with the Liberal Party close behind with 321. As the national party's 'fixers' on the ground, the influence of these agents was often resented by local supporters.

This new organizational structure was frequently put to the test. The decades between 1884 and the Great War saw unparalleled levels of electoral activity as political parties sought to win the hearts and minds of the growing electorate. Whereas 140 constituencies had no contest at the general election of 1868, that number fell to an all-time low of 39 by 1885. Thereafter, the number of uncontested constituencies rose again even during the fiercely competitive elections of 1906 and January 1910. Yet on those occasions, most of the 111 and 72 constituencies that avoided a contest were based in Ireland (80 and 64 respectively). On mainland Britain, the voters in fewer than forty constituencies were denied the opportunity to exercise their right. Those who were given the chance took it. Turnout at elections reached levels that would never again be consistently matched, routinely reaching 80 per cent of those registered to vote after 1886 and peaking at a remarkable 87.7 per cent in January 1910. Compared to that of the mid-Victorian period, this was a mass electoral system.

The increasing size of the electorate and the growing number of contests meant that parties worked ever harder to make sure that their appeals reached voters. The number of mass public meetings during elections proliferated. Before its abolition with the advent of the **secret ballot** in 1872, the old nomination ceremony had obliged all candidates to speak at the same time, to voters and non-voters alike. After 1872, parties had to organize large outdoor election rallies so that their candidates could present themselves to the **constituency** as a whole. In the large urban boroughs, this could mean making speeches to tens of thousands of people. Although parties sought to protect their candidates, these meetings were often gruelling events for them as they strained to be heard without amplification and dealt with heckling from the unconvinced or hostile. When Winston Churchill stood in the Dundee by-election of 1908, an outdoor meeting turned to farce when a suffragette rang a large bell that drowned out his voice. In large dispersed constituencies, like the rural counties, candidates were compelled to hold lots of smaller meetings in villages and towns. As disruption and a little disorder were often a feature of these public meetings, parties also organized indoor meetings where they could better control attendance by issuing

Figure 9.4 Gladstone speaking on Blackheath Common, 1874

tickets and even staging novelties like magic lantern shows (which became quite a craze in the 1890s) or live music. This may have been a good technique for rallying supporters, but not for reaching the undecided voter. Here the door-to-door canvass, and the legwork of those supporters, remained essential. Although it was no longer required that candidates give voters their personal attention, it remained imperative that the party did.

As electioneering slowly adapted to reach the mass electorate, print became an ever more indispensable weapon. Very few would have heard the speeches given at mass outdoor meetings but they were quickly reproduced in the press. As we can see from Figure 9.4, journalists were always afforded pride of place near the candidate's platform and sometimes even received advance copies of the speech so it could run the next day.

For politicians with a national reputation like Gladstone, those reports could be relayed by telegraph to newspapers across the country by the 1870s. The provincial press, which as we saw in Chapter 6 had exploded in size by the late nineteenth century, was especially diligent in reporting on all types of election meeting for those who did not attend them. Political parties were acutely aware of how important print was as a way of communicating with the mass electorate. From the 1880s they began developing their own national propaganda machines to supply local constituencies with leaflets and posters. Created in 1887, the Liberal Publication Department produced 10 million leaflets for the 1892 election, a frenzy of activity matched by the Conservative Party's Central Office. For the election in January 1910, both parties distributed a remarkable 86 million leaflets – more than six leaflets for every voter. While fly-posting of cheaply and locally produced handbills had long been a common feature of elections, centrally produced posters also became ubiquitous following the breakaway success of the Pears Soap advertising campaign in the late 1880s. In 1910 the Liberal and Conservative Parties produced 5 million colour posters between them for the two elections of that year.

The Culture of Mass Party Politics

Building mass political parties required more than inundating voters with attention during elections. If this mode of electioneering were to work, it required an army of volunteers to help organize meetings, to knock on doors to canvass voters, and to distribute materials. Parties captured the loyalties and efforts of their volunteers by the social worlds they created as much as by the appeals they generated. Each party developed its own culture of association that presented voters and non-voters alike a distinct vision of a whole way of life. These cultures were propagated in local party clubs that were often aimed at working men and became the centre of social life for many. In the four decades before the Great War, their numbers proliferated. The construction and use of these clubs reflected the distinct cultures of each party.

The small town of Keighley in Yorkshire, just north of Bradford, had no less than 13 Conservative Clubs serving a population of less than 42,000 people in 1907. The first Conservative Club in Keighley was built in 1876. Before that, the party's headquarters had, not unusually, been a pub. The new club replicated something of the atmosphere of the pub: it contained a billiard room, a bar, a card and smoking room, a newsroom, a room for the party secretary and a multi-purpose room that was used to stage political debates, to hold glee singing three nights of the week and for large dinners. The cost of membership of the club was on a sliding scale from a guinea to just 6 shillings (paid by instalment if necessary), and soon after its opening some 600 members joined. Conservative Clubs like this were infused with what one historian has described as a culture of beer, Britannia and bonhomie that facilitated the mixing of different social groups. Not to be left behind, the Liberal Party in Keighley also built its first club in 1876 with funds provided by the Duke of Devonshire. There was no bar in this club, which, despite its billiard room, emphasized a culture of self-improvement with rooms for reading, conversation, debating and music. Three years after its construction, it claimed between 300 and 400 members. As the number of clubs proliferated, they became more modest in design, usually containing just two or three rooms – typically one for reading, one for games and possibly a bar.

When it emerged in the 1890s, the labour movement also propagated its own distinctive political culture. In its heartland of the Yorkshire textile district, small Labour Clubs and Labour Churches were established to allow working people to discuss socialism without fear or rebuke (see Textbox 9.2). Bradford alone had 23 Labour Clubs with some 3,000 members, as well as a Labour Church, by 1892. It was there that Keir Hardie convened a conference to establish the Independent Labour Party in 1893, when 5,000 people attended a service at the Labour Church. By 1895 the ILP boasted 35,000 members and local clubs across most of the country's industrial districts, where songs were sung, music played by voluntary orchestras and speeches evoked the new society its members wished to build. The various Clarion Clubs associated with the country's first socialist newspaper, *The Clarion* (launched in 1891 by Robert Blatchford and selling 40,000 copies in its first year), supplemented this work. Its readers soon established a range of associational activities, from cycling clubs with their own 'clubhouses', to handicraft clubs, vocal unions, drama clubs, rambling clubs and cafés, and their activities were then reported by the newspaper. These cheap and non-commercial activities

9.2 Source: The Socialist Commandments

After their creation in the 1780s, Sunday schools became one of the primary institutions for promoting literacy and education, as well as Christianity, amongst the working classes. Socialist Sunday schools began to develop in the 1890s as alternatives that would allow children to learn about Christian as well as secular forms of socialism. This distinction was an arbitrary one, for Christian socialists believed that socialism was the secular expression of Christianity. The Socialist Ten Commandments were widely disseminated within Socialist Sunday school prayer books, in the magazine *Young Socialist* and on posters. This version (Figure 9.5) was found

on a poster in the cupboard of the office of Bolton's Socialist Party and is thought to date from 1912 when the Socialist Sunday school was run by a suffragette, Sara Reddish. The Commandments illustrate the collectivist and ethical streak in turn-of-the-century British socialism. The source shows how the labour movement adapted to pre-existing forms of working-class life and association to get its messages across. This rendition of the Socialist Commandments – with its addition of women – was, however, specific to Bolton and reflects the influence of Reddish and the women's suffrage movement within the town's socialist circles. (S.W.)

SOCIALIST

Ten Commandments

Used in all the Socialist Sunday Schools, and
committed to memory by the Children.

I. **Love your School Companions**, who will be your
co-workers in life.

II —**Love Learning** which is the food of the mind, be
as grateful to your teachers as to your parents.

III.—**Make every day Holy** by good and useful deeds,
and, kindly actions.

IV.—**Honour good Men and Women**, be courteous to
all ; bow down to none.

V.—**Do not Hate** or speak evil of any one ; do not
be revengeful, but stand up for your rights and
resist oppression.

VI.—**Do not be Cowardly**. Be a friend to the weak,
and love justice.

VII. **Remember that all Good Things** of the earth are
produced by labour. Whoever enjoys them
without working for them is stealing the bread of
the workers.

VIII.—**Observe and Think** in order to discover the truth.
Do not believe what is contrary to reason, and
never deceive yourself or others.

IX.—**Do not think that they who love their own Country**
must hate and despise other nations, or wish for
war, which is a remnant of barbarism.

X.—**Look forward to the day** when all men and women
will be free citizens of one community, and live
together as equals in peace and righteousness.

Socialists' Party, 16, Wood-st., Bolton. (Reproduced from original postcard c1912)

Figure 9.5 The Socialist Commandments, c.1912

were designed to build fellowship and to model the anti-materialist and uncompetitive
'new life' that socialism would inaugurate. Socialist Sunday schools that provided education and introductions to the Christian principles of socialism also proliferated (see
Textbox 9.2 and Figure 9.5). When the National Council of British Socialist Sunday
Schools was established in 1909, it boasted over 200 affiliated Sunday schools and

its own monthly publication *The Young Socialist*. Whereas the political culture of the Conservative Party took people as they were, both the Liberal Party and the labour movement sought to create an associational culture that would transform them.

For these political cultures to become mass parties, it was imperative that women be included. All political parties sought to harness the organizing capacities and voluntary labour of women without threatening the primacy of men as voters or as party members. The Conservative Party established the **Primrose League** in 1883 to rally men, women and (from 1889) children to the cause around largely recreational and ceremonial events. By 1891 there were over a million members across the country, half of whom were women, with some local branches established exclusively for women. The Primrose League pioneered the use of women to arrange and staff social events that attracted voters and a broader membership to the party. Women's active role in the life of the party no doubt influenced the vote by its conference to support the enfranchisement of women householders in 1887. When women householders finally did get the vote, in 1918, the party was well placed to attract their support: it claimed over 4,000 local branches just for women by 1922. The Liberal Party created its own separate organization for women in the form of the Women's Liberal Federation in 1887, a council of 500 women delegates elected by local associations. When the Women's Liberal Federation voted to support the campaign for women's suffrage in 1892, the organization was bitterly divided and around 10,000 of its 70,000 members formed a rival, anti-suffrage, Women's National Liberal Federation in protest. The labour movement also courted women as supporters and volunteers. *The Clarion* had a column intended for its women readers, and even though women – like the future suffragette Christabel Pankhurst – joined its cycling and rambling clubs, they were disproportionately involved in more 'feminine' handcraft and drama clubs. A Women's Labour League was established in 1906 to push for so-called women's issues and the increased representation of women as voters and elected officials. When the Labour Party revised its constitution in 1918, it also established separate sections for women that by 1922 included some 100,000 members. Where political parties had initially depended on women's voluntary labour to engage the mass electorate, they increasingly had to compete for the support and votes of women as they were enfranchised.

Feminism and the Suffrage Question

Women were not just part of mass politics in their capacity as party workers. At the local level, women were increasingly part of the mass electorate. The Municipal Franchise Act of 1869 briefly allowed women householders to vote and stand for office in local elections. Despite the passage of the **Married Women's Property Act** in 1870, the courts first restricted the right to vote to unmarried women householders in 1872 and then disbarred women from standing for election in 1880. In Scotland even unmarried women householders were not able to vote at local burgh elections until 1882. Despite these restrictions, 685,000 women were voting in local elections by 1890. To complicate things still further, different rules applied to the school board elections inaugurated by the Education Acts of 1870 and 1872. As education was seen as an issue in which women as mothers had a particular interest, all women householders, regardless of their marital status, were able to vote and stand for office. Around 370 women had been elected to school boards in England and Wales by the time of their abolition in 1903, while a further 76 had been elected in Scotland (where school boards continued until 1918). The Local Government Act of 1894 allowed some married women householders to vote, but only those who did not qualify to vote by residence at the same property as their husband. By 1900 a million women were voting and they formed just under 14 per cent of the local electorate. More significantly, the Act removed the property qualification for both men and women to be elected as school board members, Poor Law guardians, or **parish**, municipal and district councillors. By 1900 there were around a 1,000 women serving as Poor Law guardians, close to 450 on school boards, another 200 on **parish** councils and some 160 as district and municipal councillors. The story was a little different in Ireland, where women remained excluded from municipal franchises (with the single exception of Belfast) until 1898 and were not allowed to stand as Poor Law guardians until 1896. While women in England, Wales and Scotland were allowed to stand for election to county councils from 1908, women in Ireland were not.

Women's Suffrage as a Mass Movement

Ultimately, however, the case for women's suffrage was fought around parliamentary representation. As we saw in Chapter 6, women's largely successful agitation for legal equality and access to education and the professions from the 1850s did not translate into support for their inclusion in the **Reform Acts** of 1867 (1868 in Scotland) and 1884. Opponents of women's suffrage argued that women were not suited for the masculine world of politics because their opinions should remain subordinate to those of their fathers, husbands and brothers. The exclusion of women from electoral representation in 1867 and 1884 catalysed the formation of as many as seventeen groups advocating the enfranchisement of women, the largest of which were the Women's Suffrage Societies based in London, Manchester and Edinburgh. Many of these groups organized meetings, lobbied MPs and published tracts to advance the case for women's suffrage. In 1897 an umbrella organization, the **National Union of Women's Suffrage Societies** (NUWSS), was established under the leadership of Lydia Becker and Millicent Fawcett to demand that propertied women be given the vote on the same terms as men. The movement did not gather momentum until the **South African War** (when Fawcett

Figure 9.6 Mrs Fawcett and the NUWSS in Hyde Park, *c.*1913

headed the government inquiry into the use of concentration camps) had ended. By 1905 the NUWSS had almost 50,000 members spread across 305 affiliated branches (see Figure 9.6).

Ironically, the growing support for the NUWSS owed much to the more radical arguments and tactics of the **Women's Social and Political Union** (WSPU) established in 1903. Formed by Emmeline and Christabel Pankhurst, the widow and daughter of an ILP stalwart in Manchester, the WSPU broke away from the NUWSS. Predominantly, if not exclusively, white and well-heeled, they were frustrated not by its refusal to embrace the enfranchisement of all women other than propertied ladies, but by its continuing fidelity to the Liberal Party and the moderation of its tone and tactics (see Textbox 9.3 and Figure 9.7). The WSPU adopted a more confrontational style, heckling MPs at election meetings, occupying space by chaining themselves to railings, and organizing mass rallies like the one at Hyde Park in July 1908 that attracted between 300,000 and 500,000 people. Although many of its protests focused upon London, the WSPU had branches in cities across Britain, though not in Ireland where the Irish Women's Freedom League, established in 1908, remained the radical wing of the suffrage movement. Believing that these supposedly radical forms of protest demonstrated that women were too unstable to be ready for the vote, the *Daily Mail* quickly branded the WSPU as 'suffragettes'. Whereas the NUWSS sought the accommodation of women as equals within the liberal polity on the same terms as men, the WSPU increasingly argued that women should be enfranchised precisely because they had different qualities from men. These arguments, and their confrontational tactics, scared many, including those sympathetic to women's suffrage. Some of these people flocked to the 'law abiding' NUWSS or the **Women's Freedom League** (WFL) which broke from the WSPU in 1907 to promote non-violent resistance and published its own paper *The Vote*. At the height of its popularity, the WSPU's paper *The Suffragette* sold 20,000 copies, and by 1914 its membership stood at just 2,000; half the size of the WFL and dwarfed by the 100,000 members of the NUWSS.

Frustrated by the refusal of the newly elected Liberal government of 1906 to entertain a bill in support of women's suffrage, despite the support for one by the majority of their MPs, the WSPU escalated its protests. Like colonial nationalists, they sought to demonstrate the fundamental contradiction of a political system that not only refused citizenship to those who were deemed unfit for it on the basis of their race, sex or class, but also used state violence to enforce their subjugation. The arrest and imprisonment of 'suffragettes' served to illustrate how the continuing subjugation of women rested not on rational argument but illiberal and masculine force. By 1914 over a thousand had served time in prison. In 1909 some of those imprisoned went on hunger strike to protest the criminalization of their protest. When the government resorted to forcible feeding, the WSPU quickly branded it torture and compared it to the persecution experienced under the Spanish Inquisition or tsarist Russia (see Figure 9.8). The forced penetration of women's bodies by male doctors disgusted many and touched a nerve with those who had opposed compulsory vaccination and the vaginal inspection of prostitutes authorized by the Contagious Diseases Acts. By 1912 even the NUWSS had abandoned its loyalty to the Liberal Party and formed an alliance with the labour movement.

Increasingly, the WSPU began to embrace its own use of violence and physical force, attacking public property and leading members of the government. By 1913 Christabel Pankhurst, safely ensconced in Parisian exile to avoid arrest, was arguing that the WSPU was justified in the use of what she described as 'terrorist' actions: setting fire to buildings, cutting telephone lines and slashing paintings in art galleries. If these tactics mimicked the masculine force of the illiberal state, Christabel Pankhurst continued to insist that women needed the vote to protect themselves from men. In *The Great Scourge and How To End it* (1913) she argued that far from being protected by men in the private sphere, women's moral purity and health were threatened by the rapacious sexuality and double standards of their unfaithful husbands. Estimating that at least 75 per cent of British men were infected with sexually transmitted diseases before marriage, she insisted that only the enfranchisement of women would protect them, maintain social purity and ensure the future health of the imperial race. 'Votes for Women, Chastity for Men' became her new rallying cry.

Some men were active in their support for women's suffrage. Although the NUWSS, WSPU and WFL all had male members and activists, a distinct Men's League for Women's Suffrage

9.3 Person: Sophia Duleep Singh (1876–1948)

Sophia Duleep Singh was born in Suffolk. Her father, the Maharaja of Lahore, had been defeated by Britain in the annexation of the Punjab and made to surrender his lands and property, including the famous Kohinoor diamond, to Queen Victoria, in return for a pension of £25,000. Sophia was the sixth of seven children he had with his part German, part Ethiopian wife. Educated at home as an Indian princess, she was raised among the British aristocracy. Queen Victoria was her godmother, and granted her an apartment in London in which she lived for most of her life. When her father died in 1893, she inherited £23,000 and became a philanthropic supporter of South Asians in Britain. After a turbulent period in which she tried and failed to break the travel ban imposed on her family and return to India, Singh became a suffragette in 1909. While Singh was a prominent member of the **Women's Social and Political Union** and worked with the Pankhurst sisters, it was with the Women's Tax Resistance League that

she was most active. The League called on suffragettes to withhold their taxes, arguing that there should be no taxation without representation. Singh's conspicuous wealth and aristocratic lifestyle drew a storm of publicity to the organization. In 1911 her refusal to pay for licences for her five dogs, carriage and manservant led to a small fine of £3. In the coming years she continued not to pay for dog and servant licences, as well as various other taxes. This resulted in the impounding of many of her possessions by bailiffs, including a seven-stone diamond ring and a 131-pearl necklace. These items were repurchased by members of the League, who turned their public auctioning into large political rallies. Like many in the suffrage movement, she threw herself into supporting the war effort, promoting the importance of women's work and raising funds for the troops. After the war she withdrew from public life and died at her home in Hilden Hall near Wycombe in Buckinghamshire. (S.W.)

(MLWS) was established in 1907. Both Bertrand Russell, the liberal-left intellectual, and George Lansbury, the ILP MP who with his leader Keir Hardie led the campaign for women's suffrage in the **House of Commons**, fought by-elections solely on the issue. In 1909 the MLWS published a letter listing the support of prominent men, including eighty-six academics, eighty-three former government ministers, fofty-nine church leaders, twenty-four military officers and leading novelists like Thomas Hardy, H.G. Wells and E.M. Forster. Yet most men remained deeply hostile to women's suffrage. The old misogyny that insisted women were too irrational, emotional and bound by the biological rhythms of their bodies was endlessly repeated. Men were not alone in arguing against the enfranchisement of women. A Women's National Anti-Suffrage League was founded in 1908 by prominent social and literary figures like the Countess of Jersey and the novelist known by her husband's name, Mrs Humphrey Ward. The 'Antis', as they became known, emphasized that women had a naturally different role

Figure 9.7 Princess Sophia Singh (fourth from left) raising money for troops from across the British Empire on 'Our Day', 19 October 1916

oriented around the household, perhaps extending to charity work, social work and even involvement in local government.

'Winning' the Vote

The outbreak of the First World War took the wind from the sails of the women's suffrage movement. Almost all the suffrage organizations suspended their campaigns in August 1914 and patriotically embraced the war. Even the WSPU renamed its *Suffragette* newspaper *Britannia* in October 1915. Emmeline and Christabel Pankhurst supported the **Order of the White Feather** created by the arch 'Anti' Mrs Humphrey Ward to pressure men to volunteer and to call for universal male conscription. The Pankhursts called upon all women to demonstrate their fitness for the franchise by supporting the war effort in whatever capacity they could: as Voluntary Aid Detachments, as munitions workers or even by embracing food economy on the kitchen front. Only the **Women's Freedom League**, and a few who broke ranks with the NUWSS and WSPU, joined the pacifist movement and dismissed the war as a product of masculine imperialism.

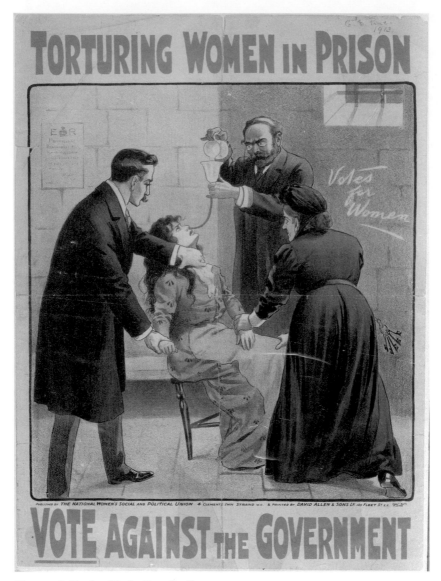

Figure 9.8 The forcible feeding of suffragettes

It was war and the arrival of the suffrage for most men in 1918 that finally won some women the right to vote in parliamentary elections (see Figure 9.9). The **Representation of the People Act** did not concede the central demand of the pre-war women's suffrage movement that women be given the vote on the same terms as men. Instead, it created new principles for the exclusion of both some men and many more women. Like earlier Reform Acts discussed in Chapter 6, the Representation of the People Act in 1918 was partial and grudging in its expansion of the electorate. Although the initial bill's

Figure 9.9 Christabel Pankhurst at the polling booth, 1918

attempt to exclude men in receipt of poor relief was removed by the time it became law, in the wake of the Russian Revolution and the increasing strength of the labour movement in Britain, the Act was designed to temper demos, not to finally make Britain a democracy.

In the absence of mass campaigns for either manhood or women's suffrage during the Great War, working-class men, unlike colonial subjects, were enfranchised in 1918 for helping to defend the nation and Empire. The privileging of military service was clear by the way the Act not only enfranchised returning veterans under twenty-one years of age (the normal age of adulthood and citizenship), but disenfranchised for five years those who, as conscientious objectors, had refused to serve. Some women were also given the vote in return for their contribution to the war effort, working for organizations like the Auxiliary Army Corps and the Red Cross. Because military service was defined in precise and restrictive ways for women, only 3,372 of them received the vote that way. Working-class women who had worked as munitionettes and in other forms of industrial labour to support the war effort were pointedly not included. Instead, the women's franchise was limited to three other very specific groups of 'ladies': those who qualified under the university franchise, those who were householders in their own right, and those married to a householder as long as they were over thirty years of age. Restricting the vote in these ways ensured that there were more men than women in an electorate that still excluded 25 per cent of adults. When women were finally given the vote on the same terms as men with the **Equal Franchise Act** of 1928, an additional 5,240,000 people joined an electorate in which women outnumbered men by some 2 million.

Like the Representation of the People Act of 1918, the Equal Franchise Act of 1928 was not the result of a mass mobilization. The NUWSS reconstituted itself in March 1919 as the National Union of Societies for Equal Citizenship (NUSEC) to fight for the equalization of the franchise, under the leadership of Eleanor Rathbone, and disbanded when this was achieved in 1928. It never attracted anywhere near the amount of support the NUWSS had before the war. Moreover, in conceiving of citizenship far more broadly than the suffrage question, its six-point programme laid out the terms of a '**New Feminism**' that included equal pay, equality before the law within marriage and as parents, the opening of the legal profession and magistracy to women, as well as pensions for civilian women and their dependent children. By 1929 Rathbone had joined the handful of women MPs who followed the election of Constance Markiewicz and Nancy Astor in 1918. Like many feminists after 1928, her attentions turned to the politics of difference as much as equality, emphasizing 'social' issues especially pertinent to women: such as birth control, child welfare and family allowances paid to mothers as wages for housework in Britain; and an end to child marriage and female circumcision in the colonies. Now that they had the vote, feminists like Rathbone hoped they could make the polity end the forms of economic and sexual subjugation that continued to render women dependent upon men.

The Politics of Labour

Labour, like the women's movement, was vital in generating a new era of mass politics. Just as the women's movement articulated a new politics of sexual difference, so those representing the labour interest gave voice to a politics of class difference that was structured primarily around the working man. It was a politics that first emerged in the wake of the **Great Depression** around new forms of trade unionism, but found expression through the range of political parties that competed to represent the interests of labour. Critically, this politics, which combined a radicalized 'social' **liberalism** with strains of socialism, shifted attention away from the suffrage question to the failed promises of liberal political economy to reward the industrious with peace and prosperity.

The Labour Movement

We have already seen in Chapter 6 how by the late 1860s unions of skilled workers had slowly coalesced under the Trades Union Congress and the Labour Representation Committee to advance the interests of 'labour'. By 1886 they had succeeded in getting no less than six trade unionists elected as Liberal MPs. Many of the largest trade unions, like the Amalgamated Society of Carpenters and Joiners and the Miners Federation of Great Britain, remained affiliated with the Liberal Party. They were ardent supporters of **free trade** and largely accepted the wage-fund theory, which insisted higher wages for some meant lower wages for others, even after it was renounced by J.S. Mill in 1869. For the most part, trade unions of organized skilled workers believed their members deserved higher wages and accepted this would come at the cost of others. Not surprisingly, then, it was semi-skilled and unskilled workers who were most vulnerable to the wage cuts and unemployment experienced by many during the lowest point of the **Great Depression** in the mid 1880s.

Radicalized by this experience, a new generation of trade union leaders, with more socialist than liberal affinities, sought to organize these workers, and in 1888 and 1889 successfully orchestrated a series of strikes in London. What was termed '**New Unionism**' began in the most unlikely of places and among the most marginalized of workers: the match girl workers at the Bryant and May factory in London, who worked long hours for low wages that were docked by fines. Annie Besant – a freethinking advocate of birth control, a Fabian socialist and member of the Social Democratic Federation – helped organize the strike against what she described as the conditions of 'white slavery'. The following year Ben Tillett, a young Christian socialist, managed to organize 10,000 dock workers who endured notoriously casualized labour conditions in which they were hired and fired by the hour. With the help of other union leaders, like Tom Mann of the Amalgamated Society of Engineers and Will Thorne of the Gasworkers' Union, Tillett organized a strike-relief fund so the dock workers would not be starved out. Funds poured in from across London and Britain as well as from trade unionists in Australia. Five weeks and 450,000 food tickets later, the dock workers' demands for a minimum of four hours labour and 6 pence an hour were met. The dockers then formed a General Labourers' Union, elected Tillett as their leader, and quickly got 20,000 members. Inspired by these tactics and successes, trade unionism flourished and could boast a membership of 2 million by 1900, although less than 15 per cent of them belonged to the new unions.

The competition between political parties to speak for and represent the labour interest intensified during the 1880s and 1890s. We have already seen that during these decades a range of socialist-inspired groups and political parties – from the Fabians, Labour Churches and Clarion Clubs to the Social Democratic Federation and the Independent Labour Party – began to compete with the Liberal Party for the loyalties of trade unionists. By 1900 many of these groups, with the help of forty-one trade unions, formed a new Labour Representation Committee (LRC) to increase the number of MPs speaking for labour independently of the Liberal Party. These efforts were aided by the counter-offensive conducted by employers against unions. That offensive began with the formation of the National Free Labour Association in 1890 to supply 'scab' labour to help break strikes. The defeat of the Amalgamated Society of Engineers by the Engineering Employers' Federation in a lockout that lasted almost half of 1897, and the House of Lords ruling in the Taff Vale case (1901) that the Amalgamated Society of Railway Servants was liable for the damages caused during a strike the year before, seemed to put in question the very future of trade unionism. When the Liberal Party condoned these actions, a growing number of trade unions, a further 120, shifted their affiliation to the new LRC.

By 1903 the LRC boasted the support of over 50 per cent of unions affiliated with the Trades Union Congress. An electoral pact with the Liberal Party quickly followed. The Liberal Party would not put up candidates against those of the LRC in return for their support of Liberal MPs in the next parliament. This enabled the LRC to return twenty-nine MPs at the 1906 election, after which it became known as the Labour Party, with Keir Hardie as its leader. The presence of Labour MPs and the Liberal Party's need to maintain its union support ensured that the Taff Vale ruling was quickly overturned by the Trades Disputes Act of 1906. There was no breakthrough for the Labour Party. At the elections of 1910 it won just forty and forty-two MPs. Although the labouring classes constituted the majority of the mass electorate after 1884, the Labour Party failed to dislodge the electoral hegemony of the Liberal Party. Indeed, before the Great War it remained primarily a local party with its MPs returned from those regions – namely Clydeside, the West Riding, South Wales and East London – where the Liberal Party was at its weakest.

This was all the more surprising because, alongside the struggles of women's suffrage and colonial nationalists in Ireland and India, the decade before the Great War was marked by a new wave of industrial unrest. As with the match girls in 1889, it began with the mobilization of those long reviled by trade unions – the unemployed. Between 1905 and 1908 groups of unemployed men scattered across the country invented a new form of protest, the **hunger march**. Fittingly, the origins of the hunger march lay with unemployed boot-workers. In May 1905, 150 of them determined to march around 80 miles from Raund in Northamptonshire to London to petition the War Office against undercutting the prices recommended by the National Union of Boot and Shoe Operatives (see Figure 9.10). A week later, 400 of Leicester's 1,000 unemployed men followed suit. On 5 June Keir Hardie informed the **House of Commons** that marches had now left Glasgow, Newcastle, Leeds, Liverpool, Manchester, Birmingham and Leicester, to speed the passage of an Unemployment Bill as 'it is only force which carries measures of this kind through the House'. However, it was a march from Manchester in 1908 which never actually reached London that coined the term 'hunger march'. These hunger marches were full of veterans of the **South African War** who, having risked their lives in the Transvaal for the British state, now insisted upon their 'right to work'. The marches sought to demonstrate that those out of work were not unemployable; they were industrious

Figure 9.10 The invention of the hunger march

and manly victims of economic processes over which they had no control. Ramsay MacDonald (who was elected as a Labour MP in Leicester in 1906) and Keir Hardie were vocal in support and sought to wed the cause of the unemployed to that of the new Labour Party. The hunger marches made 'unemployment', a term first coined by J.A. Hobson in 1895, politically visible at a time when there was no way of officially measuring its extent. They helped create the conditions for the introduction of labour exchanges in 1909 and unemployment benefits to those included in the system of National Insurance in 1911, which also enabled the recording of unemployment statistics.

Nonetheless, the plight of the unemployed was soon upstaged by what became known as 'the **Great Labour Unrest**', the largest wave of industrial militancy Britain had ever experienced. It was caused by the convergence of more aggressive forms of management and a growing confidence in the collective power of the trade union movement. Many employers met the contraction of overseas markets and declining profits by creating larger combines, introducing 'efficiencies' through **scientific management**, and keeping wages low (at a time when prices were rising). These developments had already caused major strikes by the railway union in 1907 and the shipbuilders' and miners' unions in 1908, but they were dwarfed by those that unfolded between 1910 and 1912. In 1909 2,690,000 working days were lost to strikes, but by 1910 this jumped to 9,870,000 and then reached a remarkable 40,890,000 in 1912. One of the distinguishing features of the Great Labour Unrest was that the strikes were not just long and bitter but took place in sectors like mining, railways and docks that were vital to the economy as a whole. New gigantic 'amalgamated' unions – like the National Union of

Figure 9.11 The military occupation of Liverpool during the Dock Strike, 1912

Railwaymen, the National Transport Workers' Federation and the Irish Transport and General Workers' Union – were formed to bring whole sectors to a standstill. Despite the serious consequences of these strikes for other workers (up to 80 per cent of workers in the potteries were laid off during the five-week-long miners' strike early in 1912), there was an unprecedented wave of sympathy strikes.

Asquith's Liberal government responded with a combination of attempts to mediate and resolve disputes – through a newly created Industrial Council (1911) and the creation of regional wage boards for miners (1912) – and increasingly violent and militarized policing. The Home Secretary Winston Churchill dispatched troops to South Wales during the bitter mine and transport disputes of 1910 and 1911, resulting in the death of one striker in November 1910 and the shooting of two others in August 1911. That same month, a warship and over 2,000 troops occupied Liverpool during the dock workers' strike (see Figure 9.11), while in London troops killed several striking railwaymen. Keir Hardie declared they were 'murdered by the Government in the interests of the capitalist system'. The Liberal Party and its government, which had already lost the support of the Miners' Federation of Great Britain in 1909, had deeply alienated many trade unionists. And despite these bitter conflicts, their ranks swelled, climbing from 2.5 million in 1910 to over 4.1 million in 1914. It was at this moment, in the midst of a counter-offensive by both employers and the state against organized labour, that the labour movement became the voice of the working class.

A Language of Class

Neither industrialization nor the valorization of the market by liberal political economy created a working class. That was the work of politics. As Karl Marx and Fredrich Engels did in the mid nineteenth century, we would now identify both the skilled and unskilled manual labourers who made textiles, mined coal, loaded, unloaded and built ships, constructed buildings and so on, as working-class. Yet, while Marx and Engels saw Britain as the birthplace of a new form of industrial capitalism that begot a new industrial working class, they were serially disappointed that it generally shunned socialism and supported the Liberal and Conservative Parties. Although some Chartists had spoken on behalf of the working classes, **Chartism** had generally focused its ire on the unrepresentative nature of the state, not the exploitation of workers by employers. Class for most Chartists was about an alliance of the productive classes, those who worked for a living, against those who lived off rents from land and monopolized the state. And, as we saw in Chapter 6, the six points of the Charter sought to democratize the state rather than to transform capitalism or market relations. The attachment of many working men to **free trade** eased the transition of many Chartists, as well as of the fidelity of the early trade unions, to the 'advanced' or radical wings of the Liberal Party in the 1850s and 1860s.

It has often been suggested that the **Great Depression**, the formation of the Social Democratic Federation and the Fabians in 1884, and the formation of the Independent Labour Party in 1893 marked the birth of a British socialism that spoke to and for the working class. Certainly, the influence of Marx, and his critique of capitalism as exploitative of wage labour for profit, was apparent in the SDF and ILP. Both parties advocated the fundamental reform of capitalism through the common ownership of the means of production and distribution and exchange by the state. As they believed this could only be achieved by constitutional process, much of the rest of their platform had a distinctly familiar feel to it. The SDF's primary demands – adult suffrage (which eventually included women), **annual parliaments**, proportional representation, payment of MPs, abolition of the House of Lords and disestablishment of the **Anglican Church** – echoed a radicalized version of **Chartism**. In addition, the ILP called for free non-sectarian education; an eight-hour day; welfare provision for the unemployed, sick and old; and the collective ownership of land and the taxation-to-extinction of unearned income. These latter points drew on a long-standing radical critique of the aristocratic monopoly of land. The contrast between the productive classes and the 'idle rich' living off rents was reactivated by the Fabians in their *True Radical Programme* (1887). Perhaps befitting a movement dominated by liberal-left intellectuals like the Webbs and George Bernard Shaw, the Fabians sought not to replace capitalism but to save it from itself through better social policies. Even for the SDF and ILP, the battle between capital and labour was understood in moral and political, as much as economic, terms. They tended to see common ownership as a means of removing obstacles in the way of working men rather than an end in itself. The task of the state was to restore the dignity of labour by allowing industrious working men to reclaim their independence and look after themselves and their families.

In many ways, the politics of labour that emerged after the 1880s represented the last flowering of Victorian radicalism. That is why the Liberal Party was able to electorally contain its influence for so long. Yet the Labour Party was increasingly effective at articulating politics as a conflict between parties that represented distinct classes. They gained when the Liberal Party was not just unable to quell the industrial unrest between 1910 and 1914, but was widely seen as having sided with employers over organized labour. By 1914, the membership of all but three of the 63 unions had voted to create a political fund that would support the Labour Party. Whereas the outbreak of the Great War momentarily quieted the campaigns of women suffragists and colonial nationalists, it did not still the labour movement. The ILP, and key figures like Ramsay MacDonald and Keir Hardie, remained staunchly hostile to the war, which they saw as an outcome of imperial competition for capitalist gain. Radicalized by the revolution in Russia in 1917, they called for the independence of Ireland, India and Egypt. While the Labour Party and the War Emergency National Workers Committee (formed by the unions, the cooperative movement and the Fabians in August 1914) supported the war, a good many within their ranks remained critical of it. Many of them joined their counterparts in the Liberal Party to create the Union of Democratic Control in November 1914 to push for greater parliamentary influence over foreign policy and the creation of a new international organization to avoid future conflicts and avoid a punitive peace settlement. Although both the ILP and UDC were subject to intensely hostile attacks from the press, the latter claimed a remarkable 300,000 members a year after its formation.

Yet the politics of class were most evident in the increasing importance of organized labour to the war effort. Trade unions that had been targets of state violence before the war were suddenly invited to negotiate a no-strike deal with government ministers who were fearful that continuing unrest would disrupt the war economy. Their anxiety was not baseless. The war's disruption of trade created an immediate surge of unemployment among 4.2 per cent of insured workers. As men enlisted to fight (almost 30 per cent of industrial workers had joined up by February 1916) unemployment quickly gave way to a labour shortage. The government, now the largest employer, sought to address this shortage in a variety of ways. It introduced the 'dilution' and 'substitution' of skilled labour by semi-skilled (and often female) workers, and sought to increase productivity through new scientific forms of management, including limiting overtime to 10 hours for men and 7.5 hours for women. None of this was welcome to skilled workers, who experienced the gradual erosion of their hard-won and fiercely-protected working conditions and wage differentials.

Worse still, as wartime inflation drove up the price of food and rent (the two biggest demands on working-class budgets), the real wages of most skilled workers declined (in engineering, railways and construction) or remained static (in textiles and mining). Despite the no-strike deal, short 'flash' strikes did occur throughout the war and intensified in 1917–18 when over 11 million working days were lost. By 1918 women transport workers in London were radicalized enough to demand and win the same war bonus pay rise as men. In these conditions trade union membership soared: between 1914 and 1919 it grew 90 per cent and reached 7,837,000 workers or about 40 per cent of the total workforce. For the War Emergency National Workers' Committee, wages and working practices took second place to the escalating price of rent and food. These items accounted for the vast majority of manual workers' household budgets and it was widely believed that 'profiteers' as much as shortages were driving the inflation. A rent strike in Glasgow – where up to 20,000 tenants withheld payments to landlords, who had pushed up rents by 25 per cent as workers flocked to the city's shipyards – spread to other cities and forced the government to introduce rent controls. The eventual introduction of food rationing in 1918, long advocated by the War Emergency National Workers' Committee, was also designed to quell the growing unrest around food shortages and prices as well as class-based hostility to profiteers.

Despite the enfranchisement of working-class men in 1918, demobilization and the dismantling of the war economy heightened class tensions. As we saw in Chapter 7, the attempt to return to the central pillars of the pre-war liberal political economy was a disaster. It left many working people, veterans included, either unemployed or facing cuts to their wages as the state reduced public expenditure and employers sought to maintain their profits despite the collapse of trade. Between 1919 and 1923, an average of 36 million working days were lost to strikes, many of which were organized by the big miners', dockers' and railway workers' unions. Mine owners were once again at the forefront of the counter-offensive. They had already cut wages in 1921, having defeated a strike aimed at securing a national pay settlement that would end regional disparities. When the return to the **gold standard** made their coal even less competitive in export markets, they again cut pay and extended hours. Despite a brief period in which miners' wages were maintained by state subsidies, the Conservative government backed the mine owners. On 1 May 1926 the mine owners locked out those miners unprepared to accept the new terms and the Trades Union Congress declared a **General Strike**. Over 2 million workers joined the strike in support of the miners (who themselves were a million strong). Although the strike lasted ten days it ended in ignominious defeat for the TUC. Refusing to negotiate, the government argued the strike was unconstitutional and deployed troops, recruited volunteers and the newly formed BBC radio service to keep essential services running. In the battle between capital and labour, the state once again showed its colours. Those on strike were portrayed as irresponsible in their demands and unpatriotic in their allegiance to the alien creed of bolshevism. The miners held out on strike for a further nine months before they too were defeated and returned to work on the owners' terms. Britain had never been so divided by class antagonism. The defeat of the **General Strike**, quickly followed by the mass unemployment caused by the Great Depression of 1929, led to the haemorrhaging of organized labour. Trade union membership almost halved, falling to just 4.35 million in 1931 or less than a quarter of the total workforce.

It was left to the Labour Party to argue that it alone could represent the working classes. A new constitution, freshly minted in 1918, pledged it to the common ownership of the means of production and established a new organization designed to build support beyond that of the trade unions. Over the following decade it became a national party with a mass membership that effectively replaced the Liberal Party as the alternative to Conservative rule. At the 1922 election Labour became the largest party in Scotland, winning 32 per cent of the votes and returning twenty-nine MPs (even if ten of them represented Glasgow!). The following year another election saw Labour secure 191 MPs and become the second largest party in the **House of Commons** (the Liberals had just 158 MPs). It was enough to allow Ramsay MacDonald to form the Labour Party's first ever minority government. At the 1929 election it won 288 MPs, more seats than any other party, and reduced the Liberals to just 59 MPs, although failing to win an outright majority. It was not good timing to form another minority government. As we saw in Chapters 7 and 8, the new Labour government immediately faced the Great Depression without a majority of votes in the Commons or the political will to embrace systematic change. Ramsay MacDonald was left to form a National Government with Conservative support that finally abandoned **free trade** and the **gold standard** but at the price of austerity measures and welfare cuts that harmed those working-class families Labour had come to power to represent. Many in the labour movement saw the participation of MacDonald and three other Labour members of the National Government in pushing through cuts to unemployment benefit as a betrayal, and they were promptly expelled from the Party. The enfranchisement of all men and women in 1918 and 1928 may have finally created a mass democracy, but the increasing awareness that class structured British politics was a product of the labour movement. Although by 1931 three quarters of the electorate were manual workers who were enduring historically unprecedented levels of unemployment during the world's deepest Great Depression, the labour movement lay largely in ruins.

A Culture for Democracy?

After the Great War, politicians who had long believed that 'democracy' was a terror best avoided increasingly began to proclaim 'democracy' as quintessentially 'English'. No one was more adept at this than the leader of the Conservative Party, Stanley Baldwin, who became the dominant political figure of his generation. He held office as prime minister from 1923–4, 1924–9 and 1935–7; and as deputy prime minister in the National Government from 1931–5. Baldwin's embrace of the rhetoric of democracy allowed him to reinvent the Conservative Party – which had long refused the vote to most men and women – so that it could appeal to the new mass democratic electorate. As with other politicians across the political spectrum, championing democracy and its Englishness also became a way of branding bolshevism, socialism and later fascism as alien and unsuited to Britain. It was a theme he elaborated during the **General Strike**, when he implored people to defend the constitution against the dictatorship of organized labour, and one he frequently returned to. 'True to our traditions', he declared after winning the 1935 election, 'we have avoided all extremes. We have steered clear of fascism, communism, dictatorship, and we have shown the world that democratic government, constitutional methods and ordered liberty are not inconsistent with progress and prosperity.'

The Problem of Mass Culture

Those less eager to win votes were less sanguine about the arrival of democracy. No sooner had suffrage been granted to all men and women than a growing number of cultural critics and politicians from all parties gave voice to their concerns about the apathetic, uninformed and irrational nature of demos. William Inge, a professor of Divinity at Cambridge and the Dean of St Paul's Cathedral, was representative of many when he wrote in his column for London's *Evening Standard* that the 'democratic man is a species of ape … the art of success in democracy is to know how to play upon the ape in humanity'. Much of this remarkably commonly held contempt concerned the corrosive nature of mass culture on humanity and civil society. Commercialized mass culture was accused of dumbing down its audience by appealing to their lowest common denominator and addressing them as an undifferentiated mass. The mass, these critics argued, was rendered passive and uncritical by escapist entertainments that manipulated their emotions. While much of this mass culture was blamed on America, its threat to Britain's new democracy was palpable given what many viewed as the menace of bolshevism and fascism on the continent. If this critique resonated with those fearful of the democratic will or the dilution of 'English' culture, many on the left were also afraid that democracy would not work if the culture industry kept the mass uninformed. And both the right and left were concerned that the huge new media empires that provided mass culture concentrated power in the hands of a few.

Certainly, mass culture truly arrived in Britain after the Great War. Not only did the popularity of older cultural forms, like the press, increase exponentially during the 1920s and 1930s, but new cultural forms like the cinema, radio, popular music and dance halls also became hugely popular. A truly popular press only developed after the Great War. In 1900, when literacy was almost universal and newspapers were less likely to be read aloud, just 1.5 million Britons bought a daily newspaper and 1.75 million on Sundays. By 1930 those figures had risen to 8.5 and 13 million respectively, and by 1945 had doubled again to 15 and 29 million. In 1939 it was estimated that a phenomenal 69 per cent of those over sixteen years of age read a daily newspaper, and 82 per cent a Sunday paper. Similarly, cinema came to dominate the post-war world of entertainment as the **music hall** had before it. Initially, films were often shown in music halls or other buildings, but purpose-built cinemas quickly proliferated, reaching around 3,000 by 1914 (Birmingham alone had 57!). As audiences grew during the 1920s and 1930s, especially with the introduction of 'talkies' in 1927, so the number of cinemas reached 5,000 by 1934. By the end of that decade they were selling 23 million admission tickets a week, equivalent to 40 per cent of the population. As 43 per cent of those tickets cost less than 6 pence, the demographics of cinema audiences were predominantly the urban working class – especially its women, children and the unemployed – of whom 70 per cent went once a week. Mass culture had truly arrived.

As the popularity of the press and cinema grew, so their critics became more vocal. While the growing circulation of newspapers would have delighted the Victorian pioneers of **rational recreation**, the critics of mass culture pointed to what they considered the degraded quality of journalism. News was no longer reported, they claimed, but sold in more digestible packages with banner headlines, photographs, scandalous human-interest stories and sections devoted to trivial things like sport, fashion, houses and gardens that helped generate advertising revenue. *The Daily Mail*, sold by its proprietors Alfred and Harold Harmsworth as the 'busy man's paper', pioneered many of these developments and within six years of its launch in 1896 had become the first newspaper in the world with a circulation of a million. On the back of this success, the Harmsworths became the original press barons (they were made baronets Northcliffe and Rothermere before the war and viscounts after it), building an empire that by 1908 included *The Daily Mirror*, *The Times*, *The Observer* and *The Sunday Times*. It was an influence only matched by their rival Max Aitken, also ennobled as Lord Beaverbrook and made the Minister of Information in 1918, whose media empire grew to include the *The Daily Express, The Sunday Express, The Evening Standard* and *The Glasgow Evening Citizen*. Beaverbrook and Rothermere used their newspapers to advance their own political agendas, even going so far as forming their own organizations (like the Anti-Waste League, the Empire Free Trade Crusade and the United Empire Party). Rothermere infamously used a *Daily Mail* editorial to declare his support for Oswald Mosley's British Union of Fascists in 1934. Even Stanley Baldwin, a

Figure 9.12 Brixton's Astoria Cinema, 1929

persistent target of Beaverbrook and Rothermere, publicly attacked their influence in 1931, accusing them of exercising 'power without responsibility'. Those on the liberal-left were no less concerned and struggled to find newspapers that maintained an independent voice reflecting their own views. By 1929 the Trades Union Congress was forced to buy *The Daily Herald*, which was the second-largest-selling newspaper behind *The Daily Express*, to be sure it continued to support the Labour Party. *The Manchester Guardian*, which had long supported the Liberal Party, established the Scott Trust in 1935 to ensure the paper did not have to bend to the will of a sole proprietor.

The increasing popularity of movies was met with the development of palatial cinemas with much larger capacities. With names like 'Empire' and 'Palace', they were often extravagantly themed as Egyptian temples, Spanish haciendas or, in the case of the Brixton Astoria (which opened in 1929 and could seat 4,000) in Figure 9.12, an Italian Renaissance villa. Built with luxurious materials like marble staircases, pillars and chandeliers, and staffed by uniformed employees, these cinemas were designed to transport their customers to other worlds even before the show started. The huge capital investment required to build these cinemas encouraged the development of 'chains' like the Gaumont formed in 1927, Associated British

Cinema (ABC) in 1928 and Odeon in 1933. By 1939 these chains were operating over a thousand cinemas across the country, about 20 per cent of the total. A further 15 per cent of cinemas were owned by smaller chains, like that operated by the Brixton Astoria's owner Arthur Segal, who built five other equally lavish Astorias in London. Cultural critics abhorred not just the escapist glamour of these cinemas but the predominance of American movies on show. By 1926 only 5 per cent of the films released in Britain were not imports. There was little interest among the working classes in British films, which were often adaptations of canonical novels and plays. The majority, 63 per cent as **Mass Observation** discovered in Bolton, preferred watching American westerns, gangster movies, comedies and romances. The appeal of these movies infuriated many cultural critics who believed they encouraged violence, materialism and escapism. As the left-wing writer George Orwell put it in *The Road to Wigan Pier* (1937): 'You may have 3 halfpence in your pocket and not a prospect in the world … but [that doesn't stop] you indulging in a private daydream of yourself as Clark Gable or Greta Garbo, which compensates you for a great deal.' If mass culture was understood to provide an escapist and alien culture of compensation, the prospects for democracy, and an informed and engaged public, were not good.

The man of letters and cultural critic J.B. Priestley was particularly scathing about the 'new post-war England' that he believed was the product of this Americanized mass culture. In *An English Journey* (1934) he decried the way in which mass culture had turned much of the country into 'a large-scale, mass production job, with cut prices'. Characterizing mass culture as trivial, materialist and escapist, he associated it above all with femininity and 'factory girls that look like actresses'. Yet it was the homogeneity and 'cheapness' of a culture in which 'everything was given away with cigarette coupons' that truly appalled him. 'Too much of this life', he wrote, 'is being stamped on from outside, probably by astute financial gentlemen, backed by the Press and their publicity services. You feel that too many of the people in this new England are doing not what they like but what they have been told they would like. (Here is the American influence at work).' While Priestley recognized that culture had been democratized and made readily accessible to all, he, like so many other intellectuals, feared it was not a culture fit for democracy. It neither enabled the mass to properly practise their new democratic responsibilities, nor informed their leaders about the opinions of the mass.

Countering Mass Culture

Many of the critics of mass culture thus sought to provide counter-cultural alternatives that would address this democratic deficit. Some were unabashedly elitist. At the University of Cambridge two literary scholars on the fringes of the English faculty,

F.R. and Q.D. Leavis, were especially influential. In 1930, a year after their marriage, F.R. Leavis published *Mass Civilization and Minority Culture*, a searing critique of the way commercialized mass culture had corroded the country's aesthetic and critical standards. In it he argued that only a highly educated minority could now uphold English culture. To form this cultural vanguard they established the literary magazine *Scrutiny* two years later as Q.D. 'Queenie' Leavis published her own *Fiction and the Reading Public*. Despite only having a thousand subscribers, *Scrutiny*, and the students who studied with the Leavises, had enormous influence. It spread the Leavis creed and the aesthetic values of their minority culture against the mass-culture barbarians at the gate across large parts of the British world. Literature was also the vehicle for the publisher Victor Gollancz's attempt to reanimate the critical skills of citizens. In 1936 he established the Left Book Club to publish books cheaply that would educate and inform readers of the pressing problems of the day, especially the spread of fascism and the necessity of socialism. George Orwell's *The Road to Wigan Pier* and Arthur Koestler's *Spanish Testament* about the Spanish Civil War were both published in 1937. Like the proliferation of film clubs that showed non-commercial movies, Gollancz deliberately avoided commercial forms of distribution. Instead readers paid a subscription to belong to the Left Book Club and received their monthly book through the post. They were also encouraged to form local discussion groups with other members to discuss that month's reading, in order to develop the skills of reading critically so essential to being a good citizen. By 1939 the Left Book Club had 57,000 subscribers and 1,200 discussion groups. Gollancz and his authors believed that their job was to educate those left ignorant of the condition of Britain by the commercial mass media; otherwise they feared, the spectre of fascism would soon take grip of the country.

The biggest and boldest interventions to create a non-commercial yet mass culture fit for democracy were taken by the state. The less successful of these was the introduction of a quota system to protect the British film industry in 1927. As the year before, just 5 per cent of the films shown in British cinemas were made in Britain or the British Empire; the quota system sought to increase that to 25 per cent by 1936. Although the policy did encourage a significant rise in the number of production companies, many of them were short-lived and were set up, sometimes as subsidiaries to American companies, to produce 'quota quickies' that fulfilled the requirement but were cheap to make and invariably of poor quality. Nonetheless, the protectionist policy, introduced before the abandonment of **free trade** in 1931, did nurture the remarkable talent of Alfred Hitchcock, responsible for the first British 'talkie', *Blackmail*, in 1929. It also encouraged figures like J.B. Priestley to write screenplays like *Sing as We Go* (1934) that sought to portray the realities of life in Britain.

Without doubt the the creation of the British Broadcasting Corporation (BBC) in 1922 was far more successful. Widespread concerns about the poor quality of commercial radio stations in Europe and the United States informed the decision to afford the BBC monopoly rights to broadcasting, as well as public funding, in return for strict standards of quality control. Developing those standards was left to its autocratic first Director-General John Reith, whose *Broadcast Over Britain* (1924) set out his vision of how public service broadcasting should educate and not simply entertain. Where commercial radio had to attract listeners and advertisers by pandering to their demands, the BBC, he insisted, would lead, not follow, the public. Recruiting his staff from an Oxbridge-educated elite, the BBC duly delivered a diet of classical music, religion, news, drama, and announcers with crystal-glass pronunciation of the King's English. As listeners paid a licence fee that funded the service, it was also kept free of advertising. Informing the citizenry was part of the BBC's brief, and impartiality was its watchword. Each of the main political parties was afforded equal time during elections to present their manifestos. Yet the objectivity of the BBC was always in question by those whose culture, activities or politics were not represented in its broadcasts. Slowly, however, the BBC's unbending cultural elitism began to waver. The development of regional services and programmes loosened Reith's control of programming, as did market research which unsurprisingly found listeners wanted more variety shows. These shows, with their heady mix of comedy and dance music, had more than a passing resemblance to music hall programmes. In 1933 only four variety shows were aired a week and invariably only after 10pm; by 1936 that number had increased to twenty-five. This greater responsiveness to listeners, together with cheaper radio sets, meant that listening to the wireless went from being a minority pursuit of 125,000 licence-paying households in 1923, to something close to a national pastime with 3 million licence payers in 1933 and 9 million by 1939. Despite its concessions to the listening public, the BBC sought to provide a model of a non-commercial mass culture for democracy.

Conclusion

In 1914 the English translation of *The Sociology of Political Parties in Modern Democracy* by the German sociologist Robert Michels was published. It made for gloomy reading. Michels argued that political parties had tamed the demotic spirit of mass politics by creating organizational structures that produced an 'iron law of oligarchy'. Michels was not alone in recognizing that a new era of mass democracy had begun across Europe or in lamenting the forms it was taking. This pessimism about mass democracy only deepened with the rise of fascism and was increasingly echoed in critiques of mass culture. New forms of commercialized mass culture had developed alongside mass politics from the 1880s. To its many critics, mass culture reduced its audience to passive and uncritical spectators of entertainments that they consumed en masse in ways that proved they were unfit to be citizens. Given the prevalent fear of the mass among those who were already part of the polity, and the widespread concern that women and the working classes were not equipped for citizenship, it is not surprising that Britain did not become a democracy until 1928. Those in the women's suffrage and labour movements, who fought so hard for the vote from the 1880s, passionately believed that citizenship would transform the lives of those they represented. Yet when the vote had finally, and grudgingly, been given to everyone, little changed. Politics remained dominated by men and their concerns. While the Labour Party now claimed to speak on behalf of the working class, it served only to displace the Liberal Party, not to make the state more representative of the interests of organized labour. Across the political spectrum there were those who argued that commercialized mass culture had generated such an irrational, ill-informed and uncritical citizenry that the mass was subverting democracy itself to the alien forces of bolshevism, fascism and American culture. The mass may have had the vote, but many continued to see them as unfit to exercise it. It was the hope of better understanding mass culture and its democratic potential that led to the formation of **Mass Observation** in 1937.

FURTHER READING

Many historians have explored the rise of mass culture in the late nineteenth and early twentieth centuries. A key concern of much of the early work was the effect of mass culture on the working class. Eric Hobsbawm argued that the homogeneity of mass culture was a key component in 'The Making of the Working Class, 1870–1914' in his *Worlds of Labour* (London, 1984). Other scholars – like Ross McKibbin, 'Why was there No Marxism in Britain', in his *Ideologies of Class: Social Relations in Britain, 1880–1950* (Oxford, 1990), and Gareth Stedman Jones, 'Working-Class Culture and Working-Class Politics in London, 1870–1900', in his *Languages of Class: Studies in English Working Class History, 1832–1982* (Cambridge, 1983) – assumed that the working class was already 'made' and suggested that commercialized mass culture depoliticized working people and kept them from the politics of class struggle. That argument echoes the critique of mass culture by some early socialists, explored by Chris Waters, *British Socialists and the Politics of Popular Culture, 1884–1914* (Manchester, 1990).

In contrast, Patrick Joyce's *Visions of the People: Industrial England and the Question of Class, 1848–1914* (Cambridge, 1991) and Peter Bailey's *Popular Culture and Performance in the Victorian City* (Cambridge, 1998) argue that even the most commercialized mass forms of leisure like **music hall** enabled working people to have fun and express themselves. For general surveys of the gendered nature of commercialized leisure, see Catriona Parrat, *More than Mere Amusement: Working-Class Women's Leisure in England, 1750–1914* (Boston, Mass.,

2001), and Brad Beaven, *Leisure, Citizenship and Working Class Men in Britain, 1850–1945* (Manchester, 2005).

The best account of the development and culture of the music hall is Peter Bailey's *Music Hall: The Business of Pleasure* (Milton Keynes, 1986). The history of football has received much more attention: see Tony Mason, *Association Football and English Society, 1863–1915* (Brighton, 1980), Dave Russell, *Football and the English: A Social History of Association Football in England, 1863–1995* (Preston, 1997), and Matthew McDowell, *A Cultural History of Association Football in Scotland, 1865–1902* (Lewiston, NY, 2013).

The literature on the development of mass politics in Britain has long been overshadowed by debates about how and when the Liberal Party was displaced by the Labour Party. George Dangerfield's *The Strange Death of Liberal England* (London, 1936) classically argued that this happened in the decade before the Great War as even **New Liberalism** failed to meet the challenges of Irish nationalism, women's suffrage and industrial unrest. This view has been challenged by those who have emphasized the electoral hold of the Liberal Party in much of the country and the localized nature of labour politics down to the 1920s. Peter Clarke, *Lancashire and the New Liberalism* (Cambridge, 1971), was the first to make this argument but his work was extended by Duncan Danner, *Political Change and the Labour Party, 1900–1918* (Cambridge, 1990). The appeal of the Conservative Party is well addressed from different angles by Ewen Green's *The Crisis of Conservatism: The Politics, Economics and Ideology of the Conservative Party, 1880–1914* (London, 1995) and Jon Lawrence, *Speaking for the People: Party, Language and Popular Politics in England, 1867–1914* (Cambridge, 1998).

Lawrence also provides a particularly good account of the local culture of mass party politics, a subject addressed in Patrick Joyce's *Work, Society and Politics: The Culture of the Factory in Later Victorian Britain* (Brighton, 1980). Yet still the best account of how parties operated locally, and the different flavour of their clubs and associational life, is that provided by Moisey Ostrogorsky's contemporary study *Democracy and the Organization of Political Parties* (London, 1902).

The politics of the women's suffrage movement has a particularly rich historiography. The two most useful recent surveys are those by Jane Lewis, *Before the Vote was Won: Arguments For and Against Women's Suffrage* (New York, 1987), and Susan Kent, *Sex and Suffrage in Britain, 1860–1914* (London, 1987). The fullest account of the movement across Britain and Ireland is Elizabeth Crawford, *The Women's Suffrage Movement in Britain and Ireland: A Regional Survey* (London, 2006). Laura Mayhall's *The Militant Suffrage Movement: Citizenship and Resistance in Britain, 1860–1930* (Oxford, 2003) importantly focuses on the influence and tactics of the WSPU. Nicoletta Gullace provides an important reassessment of how women became enfranchised in 1918 in her *The Blood of Our Sons: Men, Women, and the Renegotiation of Citizenship During the Great War* (New York, 2002). Cheryl Law's *Suffrage and Power: The Women's Movement, 1918–1928* (London 1997) and Martin Pugh's *Women and the Women's Movement in Britain, 1914–1959* (Basingstoke, 1992) track the changing directions of feminism after 1918, as does Susan Pedersen's *Eleanor Rathbone and the Politics of Conscience* (New Haven, 2004).

The formation and character of the labour movement have been much debated. There is no better survey of the history of trade unionism than Alastair Reid's *United We Stand: A History of Britain's Trade Unions* (London, 2004). Reid has revised Henry Pelling's *A Short History of the Labour Party*, 12th edn (Basingstoke, 2005), which remains the best general account of the labour movement's formation. It needs to be supplemented by studies of its constituent parts, such as David Howell, *British Workers and the Independent Labour Party, 1888–1906* (Manchester, 1983), Karen Hunt, *Equivocal Feminists: The Social Democratic Federation and the Woman Question* (Cambridge, 1996), and Mark Bevir, *The Making of British Socialism* (Princeton, 2011). The centenary history of the Labour Party – D. Tanner, P. Thane and N. Tiratsoo (eds.), *Labour's First Century* (Cambridge, 2000) – also offers important insights.

IV

1931–1976: Society Triumphant

10 Late Imperialism and Social Democracy

Introduction

At this stage, with less than a century left to cover before we reach the present, it is worth recalling that we are perhaps only half way through the story of the rise, demise and reinvention of liberal political economy. The last three chapters have shown how a variety of economic and political crises from the late nineteenth century provided fundamental challenges to the central tenets of liberal political economy. The first Great Depression punctured faith in the efficiency of free markets, and the Great War accelerated the erosion of cheap government and *laissez-faire*. Yet it was the second Great Depression, and the final abandonment of **free trade** and the **gold standard** in 1931, that marked the decisive moment of transition to a new system of government and economic management. The next three chapters will outline the development of a new social democratic system of government that sought to actively manage markets so as to secure the rights to work, health, housing and education for all members of society. Rather than allowing markets to determine the fate of individuals, governments would now manage the economy in the interests of society as a whole.

This system had three chief characteristics. First, the development of new forms of economic management and planning by the state that stretched across, and depended on Britain's imperial economic system. Britain did not introduce anything approaching the 'New Deal' President Roosevelt developed in the United States to combat the Great Depression that unfolded after the financial crash of 1929. Yet the new importance attached to developing colonial economies, the introduction of protectionist tariffs and a new **Sterling Area** to bolster the value of the pound, as well as the designation of 'Distressed Areas' with the highest rates of unemployment at home that required assistance, all signalled a new approach to state planned economic management. The experience of mass unemployment during the Great Depression was vital to the Labour Party's success at the end of the Second World War in arguing that the state should nationalize and publicly own key industries to secure 'full employment'.

Economic management enabled the second important feature of social democratic government, namely a system of welfare that would provide social security for all. The welfare systems developed either side of the Great War had been limited to specific demographics and proved deeply inadequate for the challenges of the Great Depression. The imperatives of war and the election of the Labour Party in 1945 enabled a new type of **welfare state** to be built. Thereafter the state took responsibility for delivering the most vulnerable – children, the poor, the sick, the old – from the insecurity and contempt that had blighted their lives. It also invested in all members of society by providing free health care and education, as well as housing for those who needed it. Needless to say, the universality of welfare did not extend to Britain's colonial subjects. Labour unrest, and the growing force of anti-colonial movements, ensured that rudimentary forms of welfare were coupled to development schemes in many British colonies from the 1940s but they were always deeply inadequate. Migrants from across Britain's unravelling Empire increasingly fled these poor social and economic conditions. As they arrived in 'the mother country' in the decades after the Second World War, the question of who constituted a British citizen and had access to the expanding services of the welfare state was keenly debated. Britain's welfare state was no less an imperial formation than its planned economy.

The third and final characteristic of **social democracy** in Britain was its dependence upon this imperial system and the influences of broader global processes. The first age of the British Empire had relied upon the monopoly forms of chartered companies, and the second upon the imperialism of free trade and overseas investment. The third age – characterized by imperial tariffs, the **Sterling Area** and **colonial development** schemes – helped sustain the new priorities of social democratic Britain. If the so-called 'Third British Empire' emerged in response to the economic challenges of the Great Depression, its continuing survival, and the violent suppression of anti-colonial movements, depended on upholding American Cold War concerns with restricting the global spread of communism. Similarly, social democracy in Britain may have had indigenous roots but it was nourished by American loans and, at least ostensibly, protected from Soviet attack by American military bases and nuclear missiles on British soil.

When I was born in 1965, just a few miles from an American military base, Britain's Empire had been largely 'lost' but social democracy seemed secure. It had delivered unprecedented levels of employment, health, wealth, education and housing. And yet we now know that social democracy had a remarkably brief life. By the time I had become an adult and voted for the first time, a reinvented form of **liberalism** was ascendant. It proclaimed that markets were most effective at generating wealth and organizing social life and began to dismantle social democratic Britain. To understand why the life of social democracy was so brief, we must grapple with the conditions of its formation, its frailties and its fall at the hands of those neoliberals who championed the virtues of the market as the principle of government. That is the task of the next three chapters.

TIMELINE

1931	National Government, imperial tariffs, Sterling Area Political and Economic Planning
1934	Special 'Distressed' Areas Act
1935	Restriction of Ribbon Development Act
1936	Jarrow Crusade Keynes, *The General Theory*

1937	Orwell, *The Road to Wigan Pier* Mass Observation
1938	Paid Holidays Act
1939	Declaration of War (September)
1940	Dunkirk (June)
1940–1	The Blitz (August to May)
1941	Cabinet Committee on Post-war Reconstruction (February) Lend-Lease (March) Atlantic Charter (August)
1942	Beveridge Report
1943	Bengal Famine County of London Plan
1944	Education Act Bretton Woods conference (July)
1945	VE Day (8 May) Labour election victory (July) Family Allowances Act
1946	National Insurance Act Bank of England nationalized National Health Services Act
1947	Marshall Plan Town and Country Planning Act Nationalization of coal and railways
1951	Nationalization of steel industry John Bowlby, *Maternal Care and Health* The Festival of Britain Conservative Party returns to power
1953	Coronation of Queen Elizabeth II
1954	End of food rationing Independent Television Network (ITV)
1955	Priestley, *The Age of Ad-Mass*
1957	Consumer Association

1959	Labour Party's Television and Radio Room David Butler's 'Swingometer'
1962	Advertising Standards Agency
1963	Consumer Council
1968	Trades Descriptions Act

The End of Liberal Political Economy?

As we saw in Chapter 7, the foundations of liberal political economy – cheap government, **free trade** and the **gold standard** – that had endured for over a century were demolished amidst a global crisis by an emergency National Government in 1931. It was far from clear what they were to be replaced with, although the imperial foundations of the British economy were left thoroughly exposed. After 1931 the value of the pound was fixed and maintained by the creation of a new '**Sterling area**' that bound together the Dominions (minus Canada), the colonies and economies closely entwined with Britain's (like Denmark) into a single currency system whose reserves were managed by the **Bank of England**. Effectively this was a devaluation, reducing the value of the pound in relation to the dollar from $4.86 to $3.40. It made exports across the British Empire more competitive while ensuring that trade within the Sterling Area remained at 1931 currency prices. At the Imperial Conference held in Ottawa in 1932, Neville Chamberlain tried hard to establish a system of imperial tariff preferences that would realize his father's dream of a trans-colonial trading system with Britain at its centre. Instead, the eventual agreement demonstrated the diminished reality of Britain's imperial economy, for neither the Dominions nor the colonies were prepared to disadvantage their own manufacturers for the benefit of those in Britain. Over the next decade British exports to the Dominions gradually declined, while imports from the Dominions increased. It was to the so-called dependent colonial economies that Britain increasingly looked to for salvation. The Colonial Development Act of 1929 sought to provide new sources of raw materials and fresh export markets for Britain's struggling manufacturers. In the ten years of its operation, £21.5 million was provided for colonial infrastructure projects like the Zambesi Bridge, and 35 per cent of those funds were spent in Britain purchasing equipment and goods from British manufacturers. By 1934 Britain exported and imported £41 and £58 million to and from the colonial economies as opposed to £88 and £157 million to and from the Dominions. Neither was sufficient to reanimate British export industries. By 1938, cotton goods, which had accounted for 40 per cent of the value of British exports and two thirds of world trade in 1914, had shrunk to just a quarter of the world share, less cotton than was exported in 1851. Exports of coal and ships were sinking fast too. The indexed volume of exports sank from 141 in 1929 to just a 100 in 1938.

New Industries and the Domestic Market

If the Empire could again prop up the British economy – and some companies, like Imperial Chemical Industries and Unilever, did thrive in the imperial market – it would not offer salvation. Instead, Britain's manufacturers slowly began to reorient themselves to the domestic market. A series of 'new industries' based around semi-skilled light engineering produced a wave of new products that spanned the exotic and the everyday – from cars to vacuums, washing machines to toasters, radios to irons. Produced in factories on assembly lines powered by electricity, many of these goods were aimed at British consumers whose homes were also on the new 'National Grid' of electrical power created in 1926. In 1920 just 730,000 households had access to electricity but by 1938 no fewer than 9 million did. Although some new, electrically powered, 'Industrial Parks' were created in the north of England, like Manchester's Trafford Park, the vast majority of the new industries were based in the more affluent Midlands and southeast. If the north had been the symbol of industrial modernity in the nineteenth century, the south inherited that mantle between the wars. Where men had been associated with the work of heavy industry, probably around half of the workforce in the new industries – between 500,000 and 750,000 – were women. Paid less than men, the vast majority of these women, over 70 per cent in 1931, were under thirty-four and single. They produced goods that were aimed at women like themselves as consumers: lipstick, cigarettes, tampons, canned foods as well as consumer durables for the more affluent.

In 1934 the left-leaning writer J.B. Priestley bemoaned the proliferation of these 'factories that look like exhibition buildings' with their 'factory girls looking like actresses'. He associated them with a new post-war, suburban England in the thrall of Americanized mass culture, and bemoaned how the industrial north and its working men were falling into ruins. It was certainly true that while much of Britain was on the breadline, some were doing very nicely indeed. The deflation of the interwar years did mean that the indexed cost of living steadily declined, from 216 in 1918 to 175 in 1928 and 166 in 1938 (having bottomed out in 1933 at 148). For the middle classes whose salaries largely stayed consistent or rose, the lower cost of living meant a higher disposable income. In 1914 a bank clerk and a doctor respectively earned £142 and £395 per annum but by 1938 their annual salaries had risen to £368 and £1,094. The number of middle classes drawing a monthly salary, rather than a weekly wage, grew steadily from 9 to 13 million between 1921 and 1951. As the size of middle-class families continued to contract, their disposable incomes rose and they began to join the hitherto exclusive set of those who owned cars and houses. By 1938 there were 2 million car owners in Britain and, as is evident from Map 10.1, their distribution was tellingly concentrated in the Midlands and south of England.

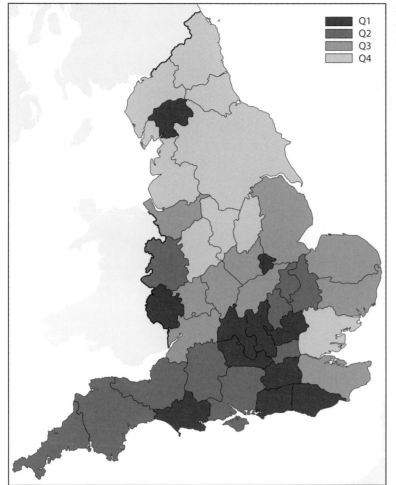

Map 10.1 Number of cars per capita in England and Wales, 1931

Q1
Q2
Q3
Q4

Similarly, over 80 per cent of the 4 million new houses built between 1914 and 1938 were for middle-class owner-occupiers who flooded into what quickly became a new type of property market (with property developers, mortgages, agents, brochures and advertising). Indeed, the number of private houses built accelerated greatly after 1929, peaking at 300,000 a year in 1934. Many of them were built by very large property-developing construction firms like Costain, Wimpey and Ideal Homestead. Their estates of semi-detached homes, with bay windows and gardens, were laid out around gently bending roads. Exhibitions of 'Ideal Homes' for sale, as well as all the labour-saving devices they could be filled with, proliferated across the country. My wife's grandparents bought their first and only house, a bungalow on the new Richings Park Estate in Iver, shown in Figure 10.1, at the Ideal Homes Exhibition in London's Earls Court in the mid 1920s. Built on the grounds of an old landed estate sold after the war, Richings Park was designed by an architect who had authored *Ideal Homes for the People* (1900)

RICHINGS PARK. IVER. BUCKS.   Buckinghamshire Advertiser.

Figure 10.1 Ideal Homes in Richings Park, Iver

and helped develop garden suburbs at Letchworth and Wembley. In 1914 just 10 per cent of Britain's housing stock was owner-occupied but by 1938 32 per cent was. It was in these new private houses that the consumer durables produced by the new industries primarily found a home.

The Rediscovery of Poverty

Deflation and the declining cost of living were little compensation for those whose wages and benefits were cut. In conditions of mass unemployment and underemployment, when employers always have recourse to a large surplus pool of labour, working-class wages rarely climb. At a time when half a million miners lost their jobs, the wages of those still employed fell from £180 to £149 per annum. In 1931 the 7 million Britons supported by social welfare payments within the households of those out of work not only took a 10 per cent cut to their benefits but had the time they could draw 'the dole' reduced from 62 weeks to just 41. Workhouses were not closed when Poor Law Unions were abolished in 1929 and the principle of less eligibility enshrined in the **New Poor Law** continued to inform the calculation of unemployment relief a century later. That 'relief' was always so meagre, and the process of claiming it sufficiently punitive, it served as a deterrent to all but the most desperate. Most hated of all was the introduction of the household 'Means Test' in 1932. This calculated relief not by an individual's loss of earnings but the total income of all members of the household.

Even though the official figures recorded that one in four were out of work in 1932, this only recorded unemployment among the 12 million workers with social security insurance. The national figures also belie profound regional and local variations that made unemployment an almost universal experience in some areas. Single-industry towns could be devastated when the local works closed. When Palmer's shipyard in Jarrow was closed in 1933, 80 per cent of the town were unemployed. Jarrow's Labour MP Ellen Wilkinson described it as *The Town That was Murdered* (1939) in the book she published with the Left Book Club. So profound where the regional differences that the government designated the old industrial heartlands of South Wales, the northwest and northeast of England, as well as Clydeside in Scotland as particularly 'distressed areas' in 1934.

Nothing did more to make unemployment visible in those parts of the country less affected by it than the **hunger marches** organized by the communist-led National Unemployed Workers Movement (NUWM). In 1922, 1929, 1930, 1932, 1934 and 1936 the NUWM brought together the unemployed from across the nation to march to London and demonstrate their fitness for, and claim their right to, 'Work or Full Maintenance'. 'The trickle of these little streams from all parts of the country', declared the leader of the men from South Wales on the first national hunger march in 1922, 'will awaken the public to the fact that we are not a newspaper paragraph, or a recorded statistic, but men who wear boots and clothes, who eat, drink, sleep, love and laugh and cry like themselves.' It was a form of protest that by 1932 had spread around the globe as hunger marches took place in the United States and Canada, as well as France, Jamaica and Trinidad the following year. In Britain it was the march from Jarrow in 1936, known as the Jarrow Crusade, led by Ellen Wilkinson and the town's council, not the NUWM, that finally got the public's attention down south.

As the unemployed headed south to remind the more affluent of their existence, so metropolitan intellectuals headed north to once again rediscover poverty and document the condition of England. What became known as the 'hungry thirties' generated a profusion of documentary films, photographs and writing, almost all of which focused on the poverty of the industrial north. Filmmakers led the way. At the Empire Marketing Board (see Textbox 7.3) the documentary filmmaker John Grierson attracted a cadre of talented directors who shared his passion for making films about the lives and labour of ordinary people. When the Empire Marketing Board was disbanded in 1933, Grierson established a Film Unit for the **General Post Office** and enabled those directors to produce a remarkable series of films. Their titles alone reveal the commitment to teaching affluent Britons how the other more-than-half lived: *Coal Face* (1935), *Housing Problems* (1935), *Enough to Eat* (1936), *Spare Time* (1939) and, probably the most famous, with its script by the poet W.H. Auden and musical score by the composer Benjamin Britten, *Night Mail* (1936).

No less than filmmakers, writers headed north to document the conditions of the industrial working class. Fenner Brockway, the pacifist and socialist, led the way for the men of letters after he lost his seat as an MP for the Independent Labour Party in 1931. In 1932 his *Hungry England* was a tour of what would become a well-travelled path around the wasted industrial regions of England, Wales and Scotland. J.B. Priestley largely followed in his footsteps for his *English Journey* (1934), comparing his 'factory girls looking like actresses' in the south with the haunted faces of unemployed men in the north. George Orwell's *The Road to Wigan Pier* (1937) forsook the grand tour, focusing instead on working-class life in impoverished Wigan, which stood proxy for the industrial north. When the journalist Charles Madge, the ornithologist Tom Harrison and the documentary filmmaker Humphrey Jennings established **Mass Observation** that same year, they set up shop in the industrial, northern, town of Bolton, which they then tellingly labelled 'Worktown'. Not all those involved in this documentary movement were men. Grierson's sister Ruby played an important role in many documentary films; while Olive Shapely and Joan Littlewood at BBC Manchester pioneered hard-hitting documentary radio features about life during the Depression. Some of these highly educated men and women compared their journeys to the industrial north to earlier colonial encounters with different landscapes and people. Their work manifested both an awe for the industrial working class, especially its men, as well as a sense of them as a race apart. They were responsible for creating many of our most haunting images of the Great Depression of the 1930s and dramatizing its human cost.

Planning and the Science of Government

As across much of the world, the Great Depression was both a political and economic crisis in Britain. It convinced many that markets were not effective in generating wealth or ensuring that it was sufficiently widely distributed to secure social and political stability. Unemployment could no longer be viewed as cyclical, as J.A. Hobson, who first coined the term in 1895, had thought. The creation of a system of National Insurance designed to protect workers from temporary unemployment only provided evidence that unemployment had become a structural problem. The failure to solve that problem in turn highlighted that the existing political parties, and the new democratic system they operated within, had not addressed the broader malaise of Britain's imperial economy.

In this context there was both a good deal of sympathy for and alarm at the growing popularity of the Communist Party of Great Britain (CPGB) and the British Union of Fascists (BUF). The CPGB was established in 1920, fuelled by the rise of industrial militancy after demobilization and the injunction to spread global communism at the Third International. Although it had remarkably few members – at its height in 1931 there were just 7,500 – its influence was great. The communist-led NUWM was one manifestation of this, and local pockets of strength in Glasgow, the East End of London and South Wales also belied the involvement of middle-class fellow travellers in cultural projects like Unity Theatre and the Left Book Club that had a broad influence after their creation in 1936. Many more looked with a certain degree of envy and admiration at the Soviet Union whose command economy and five-year plans they believed had enabled it to avoid global capitalism's Great Depression.

Similarly, for some Britons, fascism seemed a sound alternative to the deepening political and economic crisis. In protest at their failure to address the problem of unemployment, Oswald Mosley resigned from the Labour Party in 1929. In 1931 he formed the New Party to advance the policies of corporatist economic management that he had unsuccessfully advocated within the Labour government. Having been impressed by a tour of fascist Europe in 1931, he established the British Union of Fascists in 1932. Two years later the BUF was boasting that it had 40,000 members and had also attracted the support of the press baron Viscount Rothermere whose papers the *Daily Mail* and *Daily Mirror* reached millions. The wind was only taken from the sails of the movement in 1936 when Mosley declared his support for Adolf Hitler and the violent anti-Semitism of his black-shirted supporters became apparent at the infamous Battle of Cable Street in London's East End.

To escape the economic crisis, the ineffectiveness of party politics and the threat of fascism and communism, many turned to planning. The idea of planning, with its insistence that trained experts skilled in the arts of **scientific management** were best equipped to organize an activity, was not new. We have already seen it in the **garden city** movement and the kinds of social scientific administration that informed New Liberal reforms before the Great War, as well the state's management of the war economy itself. Yet during the 1920s and 1930s, faith in experts and their scientific forms of management became more pervasive as Britons recognized that economic, social and political stability – to say nothing of the quality of cultural life – should no longer be left to the whim of markets.

Planning as a Domestic Science

The genre of science fiction, pioneered by H.G. Wells in *The Time Machine* (1895) and *War of the Worlds* (1897), certainly helped increase familiarity, if not always comfort, with what Aldous Huxley's 1932 novel described as the *Brave New World* of organizing society scientifically. Wells and Huxley offered dystopian views of the dehumanizing effect of a world organized around science and technology, one that was brilliantly rendered comic by Charlie Chaplin's film *Modern Times* (1936). In contrast, scientific socialists like J.D. Bernal and J.B.S. Haldane believed that socialism was a science and could use technology to unleash the world's resources and distribute them fairly to all.

The idea that scientific planning offered a potential liberation from the failings of capitalism and democracy, or at least could improve life, was not confined to intellectuals.

Scientific management and the vogue for planning began to pervade even the most intimate recesses of the home – the kitchen and the bedroom. The arts of household management were rendered a domestic science by the proliferation of academic courses like the one in Household and Social Science started at King's College London in 1915. By 1930 there were around 3,000 graduates of these courses and most were teaching so-called 'Domestic Subjects' to girls in elementary schools, although some went to the colonies to do public health work as part of **colonial development** schemes. While working-class girls in elementary schools were taught how to run households they were unlikely to ever inhabit, privately educated middle-class girls could imagine owning an ideal home. As the new suburban middle-class 'house-wife' had to make do with no domestic servants other than occasional visits of a 'maid' or 'home-help', ideal homes came with an efficient kitchen designed to minimize time and motion within it, as well as a host of labour-saving devices like electric toasters, cookers and washing machines. A plethora of magazines like *Good Housekeeping* (1922), *Women and Home* (1926), *Woman's Journal* (1927), *Women's Own* (1932), *Women's Illustrated* (1936) and

Figure 10.2 Marie Stopes, *c.*1920

Woman (1937) were launched to provide constant advice and encouragement to middle-class women about how best to run their homes without servants but in the service of husband and children. If domestic science reinscribed the idea of separate spheres, it did so by elevating middle-class women's domestic work into a science of planning and efficient management.

The idea that expert advice could provide scientific solutions to better organize domestic life also extended to emotional and sexual life, as the work of Marie Stopes demonstrates (see Textbox 10.1 and Figure 10.2). Alongside the sex manuals and birth

10.1 Person: Marie Stopes (1880–1958)

Born in Edinburgh, Marie Stopes went to University College London where she studied botany and geology. She was the first woman to complete a PhD in palaeobotany at Munich's prestigious Botanical Institute and the first to be appointed at the University of Manchester as an Assistant Lecturer in 1904. A keen supporter of women's suffrage, Stopes unusually kept her name when she was briefly and unhappily married to a Canadian botanist between 1911 and 1916. Shortly after the marriage was annulled, Stopes started to write *Married Love* (1918). It imagined marriage as a union between equals who would enjoy a relationship based on emotional and sexual reciprocity. Women, she argued, should not lie back and think of England as they satisfied their husband's sexual appetites. Instead she championed women's sexual fulfilment, through foreplay and the use of birth control to rid sex of the fear of pregnancy. Ultimately, for Stopes, the mutual orgasm represented the climax of a marriage based on reciprocity and equality. The book was hugely popular. By 1931 it had sold 750,000 copies, gone through 19 editions and been translated into 10 languages. The sex manual as a genre had been born, and its successors, like Theodore van de Velde's *Ideal*

Marriage (1926) and Helen Wright's *The Sex Factor in Marriage* (1930), were just as popular and much more explicit. Stopes's advocacy of birth control soon surpassed the notoriety of her views on marriage and sex. Nothing spoke of the new recognition of the need for planning than birth control. Its primarily Anglo-American advocates argued that women must be able to liberate themselves from unplanned pregnancies that reduced many to grinding work and poverty. Stopes opened Britain's first birth control centre, called a 'Mothers' Clinic', in 1921. That same year she founded the Society for Constructive Birth Control and Racial Progress and joined the Eugenics Society. While Stopes believed all married women should have free access to birth control, she was particularly invested in spreading advice on contraception to poor women. Planned parenthood for the poor meant not just less poverty and better social conditions but less risk of Britain's racial degeneration. Indeed, Stopes favoured forced sterilization of the most 'unfit' and 'feeble-minded'. Other birth control campaigners did not embrace the **eugenics** movement, but Stopes's work illustrated that planning sex in the bedroom was, for some, intricately related to planning a better society.

control clinics pioneered by Stopes, the advice column, where readers detailed their problems in letters that were published alongside the expert advice offered, became features of popular newspapers like the *Daily Mirror* and women's magazines in the 1930s. The best known of these agony aunts was Leonora Eyles in *Woman's Own*. She was a socialist whose popular advice manual on household management, *Women's Problems of Today* (1926), enabled her column to be billed as 'the woman who understands'. Above all Eyles offered advice to women about love, happiness and how to survive marriage. Some, like the Presbyterian minister Herbert Gray, feared that rising divorce rates showed that the pressures of the Great Depression and the Americanization of British culture threatened the institution of marriage and with it the future of the British race. In 1938 Gray established the Marriage Guidance Council to offer expert advice and guidance not just for troubled relationships but also for couples contemplating union. Marriage and relationships, it seemed, now needed experts to help plan their survival and health.

Planning a New Deal?

In the turmoil of the interwar years, many increasingly looked to the social sciences for solutions. Before the Great War it was possible to count the number of social surveys conducted on one hand, but in the seventeen years following it there were a remarkable 156. Some addressed a specific social problem – like housing, health or unemployment – while others focused on a particular locality or region, but all insisted that expert knowledge was required to understand the condition of Britain and plan a better future for it. Whereas social surveys before the Great War never quite escaped blaming the poor for their poverty, those of the interwar years consistently highlighted that many social problems were caused by the failure of markets and governments. Where capitalism and democracy had brought chaos and despair, threatening Britain with fascism and communism, social scientists offered to plan for a better future.

At the height of the political and economic crisis of 1931, an ambitious 'National Plan for Britain' was published in *The Weekend Review* by its Assistant Editor, an ornithologist by training, Max Nicholson. The article inspired the creation of a new think tank called Political and Economic Planning (PEP) that was expressly unaffiliated with any political movement and had a decidedly imperial and internationalist outlook. The Scottish Development Council, with similar aims but a less effective organization, was established in the same year. PEP was privately funded by many of its founding members, an eclectic group that included Max Nicholson and Gerald Barry (the editor of *The Weekend Review*), Israel Sieff (chairman of the giant retailer Marks & Spencer), Leonard Elmhirst (who had returned from working as secretary to the Indian nationalist and social reformer Rabindranath Tagore to found Dartington Hall, the experimental centre for educational and rural development), Basil Blackett (a onetime civil servant in Britain and India, expert on international finance and advocate of a **Sterling Area**), the biologist Julian Huxley (who was later the first director of UNESCO and, alongside Max Nicholson, helped establish the World Wildlife Fund) and Mischa Zvegintzov (a Russian émigré and research chemist at ICI). Throughout the 1930 and 1940s, PEP published a fortnightly journal *Planning* and convened groups of experts to develop plans for addressing what they considered the pressing economic, social and political problems of the age. Their work shared two central ideas. First, that experts could scientifically understand problems and identify solutions in ways that transcended politics. And, second, that this scientific approach to government required the agencies of the state, as well as the voluntary sector, to be actively engaged in implementing these plans.

In this way PEP echoed the arguments of the most brilliant economist of his generation, John Maynard Keynes. During the 1920s Keynes was a forceful critic of the **Treasury**'s belief that a return to cheap government and the **gold standard** would stimulate trade. The return to gold in 1925 made British exports less competitive, and because it was impossible to reduce costs by systematically cutting wages, persistent high levels of unemployment followed, causing a structural disequilibrium in the economy. The only way to restore the economy's balance was to create employment by government investment in public infrastructure projects that would, in turn, reduce welfare payments and stimulate demand. Whereas the advocates of liberal political economy sought to restore the value of the pound by balancing the budget, Keynes proposed that governments spend when in deficit to generate jobs and demand. As demand could only be managed within the domestic market, Keynes's approach required a retreat from Britain's reliance on exports to its imperial economy. In his *General Theory of Employment, Interest and Money* (1936) Keynes offered his ideas as a middle path between socialism and capitalism. His aim was not to replace a market economy but to manage it to ensure its survival; not to eradicate inequality, only to lessen it so that social cohesion and stability were secured.

Keynes's ideas had little traction politically. For the Conservatives, they smacked of too much intervention of the wrong kind, and for the Labour Party they had too little to say about public ownership and the abolition of poverty. Only Lloyd George's Liberal Party embraced Keynes, in its 1929 election manifesto *We Can Conquer Unemployment*, written by Seebohm Rowntree. Consequently, there was no British 'New Deal' of public infrastructure projects to provide jobs for the unemployed. The Special Areas Act of 1934, which identified 'distressed areas' in need of greater investment, was an anaemic version. Initially a total of just £2 million was made available, with a further £3 million following in 1936, and these funds were channelled through local authorities to ensure there was not too much direction from central government. The result was a meagre hotchpotch of initiatives that ranged from the creation of new 'Trading Estates' to attract businesses to these areas, land settlement schemes to encourage the unemployed to establish small agricultural holdings, and funding for voluntary groups like churches and youth groups to organize activities for those out of work. While Italy opened its first motorway in 1924, and Germany and the United States began to develop their Autobahn and interstate freeways during the 1930s, the British government did little. The government only assumed responsibility for the maintenance and development of 'A' (arterial or 'trunk') roads in 1936. Although the Ministry of Transport developed a five-year plan of investing £73 million, it was never fully implemented. Despite the growing number of cars on the network, less than 300 miles of new road were built between 1931 and 1938.

 ## States of Warfare and Welfare

It was the demands of World War II, and the determination of many that Britain would never again endure the multiple crises of the 1930s, that made planning central to the science of government. With the declaration of war, the British state immediately took command of almost all areas of economic, social, political and cultural life. Thus, unlike World War I, it was a war fought from the outset with a conscript army, food rationing and a new Ministry of Information. As Britons were mobilized for another total war, they embraced the idea that only planning for a post-war world could ensure that the failed promises of a new social contract in 1918 were not repeated.

The World at War

Britain's declaration of war with Germany in 1939 had little to do with anti-fascism. Despite the growing numbers of German Jewish refugees from 1933, most Britons remained oblivious to the rabid anti-Semitism of Nazi Germany. The British government was concerned to limit the number of Jewish refugees arriving, and in 1940 even interned 40,000 as enemy aliens. As in 1914, it was Britain's fear of Germany's growing military machine and imperial ambitions in Europe – as it annexed Austria and Czechoslovakia in 1938 then Poland the following year – that triggered the war. While Germany quickly forged the Axis alliance with Italy and Japan, after the German invasion of France and the Netherlands Britain remained isolated. By May 1940 what was left of the British, French and Belgian forces that Germany had not captured had retreated to the northern coast of France at Dunkirk. Under attack from the Luftwaffe, the German Airforce, it took 8 days and over 800 vessels, a quarter of which had been requisitioned from private owners along England's south coast, to rescue 338,000 troops. Having won the Battle of France, Germany turned their attentions to an aerial battle for Britain. They began with a sustained and intense aerial bombardment, known as 'the Blitz', that lasted from August 1940 to May 1941 and included fifty-seven consecutive days of bombing. Britain, the unrivalled superpower of the world a generation earlier, was on the brink of invasion and defeat.

Once again the Empire came to Britain's rescue. All the white Dominions but Ireland, which remained neutral throughout, almost immediately declared their support for Britain's declaration of war in 1939. Canadian troops arrived in Britain in 1940, shortly followed by more logistical and financial support (including loans totalling almost £2 billion). By the end of the war a million Canadians and a million Australians had seen military service. The Colonial Office promoted a new language of partnership among a Commonwealth of nations, and successfully had the military colour bar lifted (although all colonial troops remained under British officers) to elicit support among the dependent colonies. A staggering 2.5 million Indians volunteered to defend Britain, fighting in Europe as well as North Africa and South East Asia. While many other colonies raised troops – there were regiments from Africa (with over 150,000 recruits), Hong Kong, Malaya, Palestine, the West Indies and even Fiji – most were regionally engaged fighting the Axis powers in North Africa, the Middle East or South East Asia. Many colonies sent donations to British war charities or even provided loans to the British government. Those in West Africa donated £1.5 million to charities and provided a further £1 million in interest-free loans.

None of this was enough to save Britain from imminent defeat. Once Britain had raided its sterling reserves and sold off its overseas investments, it was forced to send Keynes to Washington in March 1941 to negotiate a $21 billion line of credit for American military supplies. So tough were the terms, including the relinquishing of all remaining British assets in the United States, that Keynes accused America of seeking to 'pick out the eyes of the British Empire'. Only when Germany turned its attentions to an invasion of the Soviet Union, and their Japanese allies attacked the United States in Hawaii at Pearl Harbor, in June and December of 1941, could Britons breathe again. When American troops finally arrived on British soil at the start of 1942, they built their own military bases and maintained sovereignty within them, including the operation of the colour bar. In effect, Britain had traded a hostile occupation by the Germans for a friendly occupation by Americans.

Britain had long waged its wars overseas with colonial troops but now it was fighting for survival at home with the help of its colonies and foreign imperial powers. The fear of chemical warfare, and the reality of strangled supply lines and aerial bombardment campaigns, turned civilians into military targets. This blurring of the distinction between civilian and military targets was not entirely new but its scale was unprecedented. In September 1939 as war was declared, 38 million gas masks were distributed to Britons in preparation for possible chemical attacks. Invasion scares, and talk of a German fifth column already at work in Britain, were endemic from the summer of 1940 through 1941. Civil defence fortifications were constructed along the southern and eastern coasts of Britain, while ARP (Air Raid Precaution) Units were established across the country to distribute gas masks, maintain shelters and police the 'blackout' at night. British cities like London, Plymouth, Belfast, Glasgow and Coventry, associated with supply chains, naval bases or munitions work, were relentlessly bombed during the Blitz. In every sense war had come home to the British. And yet they suffered remarkably few casualties in what was the deadliest conflict ever. Germany and the Soviet Union alone suffered 5.5 and 10 million military casualties, while two thirds of the war's estimated total of 50–70 million dead were civilians. Britain's casualties accounted for a tiny percentage of these, with 382,000 military and 67,000 civilian deaths. The British Dominions and colonies lost a further 200,000 soldiers and had half a million civilian injuries.

The People's War

As the Home Front become the Front Line, the entire population had to be mobilized in support of the war effort. During the Great War the issue had been maintaining the morale of troops; now the morale of all Britons was seen as no less vital. The Ministry of Information, with John Reith from the BBC as its head, used opinion polling, social survey techniques and market research to measure and improve morale. **Mass Observation** and the British Institute of Public Opinion, formed in 1937 as an affiliate of the Gallup organization in the United States established the previous year, were enlisted to help. The government also created its own Wartime Social Survey. Between 1941 and 1944, alone the Wartime Social Survey completed no less than thirty-six surveys on issues ranging from attitudes to food and clothes rationing, vaccination and public health campaigns, concerns about heating and lighting, and even the effectiveness of the Ministry of Information's propaganda work. The ministry also retooled the GPO Film Unit and used many of its documentary directors, like Humphrey Jennings, to produce short propaganda pieces. In films like *The Heart of Britain* (1941), *Listen to Britain* (1941), *Fires Were Started* (1943) and *A Diary for Timothy* (1945), Jennings pooled the talents of Britain's leading writers, actors and musicians (E.M. Forster, Laurence Olivier, Michael Redgrave, Benjamin Britten) to capture the everyday experience and reality of war. His films portrayed the heroism of ordinary people doing ordinary things to survive in extraordinary circumstances. In the hands of the Ministry of Information, this was to be a 'People's War'.

George Orwell and J.B. Priestley, once equally suspicious of patriotism and the mass cultural passivity of the working classes, now celebrated the role of 'the people' as active defenders of British liberty and democracy against fascism. They saw Dunkirk as crucial in creating a new spirit of collective endeavour that could now be turned to imagining a better future. In a series of hugely popular 'Postscripts' broadcast on the BBC after the Sunday evening news at 9pm between June and October of 1940, Priestley urged Britons to extend the fight against fascism into one for a socially just post-war world. Orwell's *The Lion and the Unicorn* (1941) similarly suggested that Dunkirk had started an 'English revolution'. The people had mobilized for war, he insisted, to deliver a people's peace with a new socially democratic contract between the state and its citizens.

This was not such a big leap given the wartime government's recognition that to maintain the morale of the people they had to create a new sense of social community in which the privations of war were equally and fairly shared. Nothing illustrated this idea of community better than the evacuation from London of almost 3 million working-class children thought most at risk from aerial bombardment between September 1939 and May 1941. Sent to stay with strangers in rural households or less dangerous regions, evacuation posited the nation as an interchangeable family in which everyone had each other's welfare at heart. The welfare of all, like the war effort, was increasingly understood as a collective responsibility. The businessman Lord Woolton, bought in by the Conservative government to be Minister of Food, immediately insisted that the system of rationing would ensure 'fair shares for all'. Implementing the new ethos of fair shares and equality of sacrifice, however, depended upon planning by experts. Nutritionists, for instance, planned food rationing. They calculated the calorific levels and food stuffs necessary for different groups of people to remain healthy. Their work also structured the recipe books and radio broadcasts that demonstrated how unusual foods (like powdered egg and tapioca) could be incorporated in a family's diet on the 'Kitchen Front'. Domestic science came of age as women were urged not just to 'Keep Calm and Carry On' but to maximize their resources: 'Make Do and Mend', 'Dig for Victory', 'Turn That Gas Down' and so on. As even the royal family reputedly had ration cards, and the grounds of Buckingham Palace were conspicuously 'dug up for victory' to grow foods, it seemed as though the experts had indeed designed a system of rationing that all had to endure. Moreover, despite shortages of food the nutritional health of the population actually rose during the war. Expert planning had triumphed.

Of course, the reality behind the rhetoric of fair shares and equality of sacrifice was compromised. In the post-war years a certain mythology sprang up around the 'spirit of the Blitz' as a halcyon moment in which aristocrat and pleb happily brushed shoulders in the tube station, waiting out an air raid by singing songs of hope and defiance together. In reality many middle-class families preferred to build 'Andersen' shelters in their gardens rather than visit communal sites, just as they could afford to buy additional rations on the black market or eat unrationed luxury foods in restaurants. Those in the countryside were less at risk of bombs and were more likely to be able to grow crops or harvest wild foods. Even the experience of evacuation was deeply varied. Middle-class parents sent their children to friends and relatives, not to strangers. And while many of those who took in evacuees were shocked by their poverty and cared for them well, others viewed their ration cards with more affection than the children.

Planning the People's Peace

Nonetheless, to find Orwell's English revolution we need look no further than the plans for post-war reconstruction that proliferated from 1940. Winston Churchill, who became prime minister of the wartime coalition government formed at the depth of the crisis on May 1940, initially shunned talk of post-war reconstruction. The reconstruction agenda was, however, so important to the government's Labour members that two months later one of them, Arthur Greenwood, was allowed to establish a new cabinet Committee on Reconstruction. In doing so, the government was playing catch-up. Political and Economic Planning had immediately set up a Post-War Aims Group that within a week of the war's declaration had drafted a set of war aims. *Picture Post*, an influential documentary magazine, had a series of experts contribute to its 'Plan for Britain' in January 1941. The following month Nuffield College, Oxford, began a Social Reconstruction Survey. In June, Greenwood appointed William Beveridge, once Lloyd George's muse and director of the LSE between the wars, to chair an Interdepartmental Committee on Social Insurance. In Scotland the Secretary of State Thomas Johnston took matters into his own hands and appointed a Council of Industry in 1942 that partially fulfilled the vision of a centralized economic agency imagined by the Keynesian James Bowie's *The Future of Scotland* in 1939.

Published in November 1942, the 'Beveridge Report' became the foundation of a new post-war social democratic settlement. It outlined a system of social insurance for all Britons that would protect them 'from the cradle to the grave' against what it described as the five great evils of 'want', 'squalor', 'ignorance', 'idleness' and 'disease'. Beveridge was still a New Liberal at heart. He certainly believed that social security should be extended to all, but also that doing so required a delicate balancing act between the responsibilities of the state and the individual. The taint of moral opprobrium hung over his description of unemployment as idleness, or his use of the terms squalor, ignorance and disease to describe the need for housing, education and health. Yet so keenly anticipated was Beveridge's report that 92 per cent of Britons had heard of it the day after its release. Unusually for a dry and technical government report, it sold 650,000 copies in total (including 50,000 in the United States). Churchill warned that its publication had created dangerous optimism and false hopes but the widespread support for it ensured that by 1943 a new Ministry for Reconstruction was created with Lord Woolton at its head. In 1944 both the government and Beveridge published plans for achieving the 'full employment' (which Beveridge defined as no more than 3 per cent unemployed) that was seen as inseparable from the system of universal social security. If high rates of unemployment had become normalized in the first half of the twentieth century, the war economy made full employment seem possible not just in Britain but also in Australia and the USA, where similar measures were taken in 1945 and 1946. The influence of the Beveridge Report also spread across the Dominions where it helped to generate similar proposals like Canada's Marsh Report. For the dependent colonies demanding independence, social security and full employment remained distant dreams, as was painfully apparent when the Bengal Famine killed 3 million people in India.

Building Social Democracy and the Welfare State

Although **Mass Observation** predicted it, few expected the Labour Party to win the election in 1945, let alone with a massive majority of 145 seats with 48 per cent of the popular vote. Although the Conservative Party had committed itself, albeit cautiously, to implementing the Beveridge Report and delivering 'high and stable' levels of employment, many of its candidates believed the war had been fought to defend the British Empire, not to build a New Jerusalem. Some even equated the planning of social democracy with totalitarianism and, as Churchill infamously declared on radio in 1945, the Gestapo. In contrast, the Labour Party's election manifesto *Let Us Face the Future* outlined a new type of social democratic welfare state. Shedding the pejorative language of the Beveridge Report, it argued that employment, education, housing and health were basic social rights that all Britons wanted and should enjoy. To deliver its commitment to 'full employment', the Labour Party argued would require a mixed economy that balanced public and private ownership. The manifesto promised to nationalize not just the energy, transport, iron and steel industries but also the **Bank of England**. This stopped some way short of its 1918 constitution's promise to implement the 'common ownership of the means of production, distribution and exchange' but it was a radical departure even from Keynesian principles.

Despite the enormity of Labour's victory, the British people did not necessarily embrace socialism in 1945. If everyone who later claimed to have voted Labour in 1945 had actually done so, turnout would have been considerably larger than the actual 66 per cent. Moreover, the armed forces vote, supposedly radicalized by the educational work of the Army Bureau of Current Affairs, had an even lower turnout of 40 per cent. If the electorate remained hesitant about embracing Labour's vision of the future, it certainly did not want a return to the crises of the 1920s and 1930s. Although some of Labour's senior figures – like Aneurin Bevan, who became Minister for Housing and Health – spoke the language of socialism and class struggle, *Let Us Face the Future* appealed to 'all men and women of a progressive outlook' who did not want a return to Tory government. Above all, Labour argued that veterans should never again endure the broken promises of the Great War, and children, like those in Figures 10.3, should face the future in confidence and not be left to the mercy of the market. What they offered was not socialism but a social democratic system where capitalism would be managed by experts to provide the welfare of all. In so far as this was the revolution Orwell hoped for, it was a technocratic, not a demotic, one. The experts charged with developing and

Figure 10.3 Facing the Future, 1945

managing the mixed economy and welfare state may have had a democratic mandate, but the task of making social democracy work was largely delegated to them.

It is difficult now to appreciate the magnitude of public ownership ushered in by the Labour government. The programme of nationalization began with the **Bank of England**

and the coal industry in 1946, and continued through the transport sector (railways, ports, air and road haulage) in 1947, the gas and electricity industries in 1948 as well as, finally in 1951, iron and steel. The costs were no less high than the political stakes: £2.6 billion was paid to the former owners of these industries in compensation. By 1951 over 2 million people, 10 per cent of the total workforce, worked in these nationalized industries. The new institutions of the welfare state also required a huge influx of employees, such as teachers, nurses and social workers, as well as civil servants responsible for their management. In 1945 the number of these public sector workers exceeded 400,000, three times more than in 1939. In addition, government contracts ensured that many more – some 423,000 by 1957 – were kept hard at work in the defence industries. And, of course, the construction of the new public infrastructure – of houses, roads, schools and hospitals – also generated employment. Despite demobilization, the public sector and state investment delivered full employment by 1948. It lasted until the 1970s and was one of the most remarkable achievements of post-war social democracy.

If full employment now seems a distant memory, Britons remain firmly attached to the system of free and universal health care that was created by the National Health Service Act of 1946. Previously they either had to pay for health care privately, receive it through an insurance scheme, rely upon charity or, as a last resort, the medical services of the workhouse. Such was the uneven quality and sometimes iniquitous nature of care that both the British Medical Association and PEP devised nationally organized health plans during the 1930s. Yet the National Health Service (NHS) did not just provide a national system of coordination; it made health a social right. Everyone enjoyed free and full access to dentists, optometrists and local doctors with a general practice. While community health services were established to carry out preventive medicine (like health visiting and vaccination programmes), hospitals were the sites of emergency, chronic or longer-term care. At the NHS's foundation in 1948, some 2,800 hospitals provided half a million patient beds around the country. All who worked within the National Health Service were placed on salary scales and similarly remunerated wherever they worked.

Several British cities – especially London, Plymouth, Coventry, Cardiff, Swansea, Belfast and Glasgow – had been badly damaged by wartime bombing, with a million homes of Britain's already inadequate housing stock destroyed in the process. Calls for better urban planning were hardly new and they had proliferated between the wars with the largely unregulated growth of suburbia. At the end of 1940 the new Minister of Works, Lord Reith, hired the chief advocate of an integrated national vision of town planning, Patrick Abercrombie, to develop plans for the reconstruction of London and Plymouth. By 1943, Abercrombie, a founding member of the Council for the Protection of Rural England in 1926 and a professor of town planning at University College London, had drawn up innovative plans for the reconstruction of Plymouth and London. A central feature of these plans was their remodelling of the anonymous and socially segregated city into a series of socially mixed, urban-village communities, all enjoying easy access to open spaces. Bevan, the minister for both health and housing, embraced the vision, having condemned the social segregation of unplanned urban development as 'a monstrous affliction upon the essential psychological and biological oneness of the community'. The Town and Country Planning Act of 1948 gave the state sweeping new powers – with compulsory purchases of land for new developments, large subsidies to local councils for the construction of new public housing, and the authority to preserve historic buildings and woodlands – to realize the vision. Between 1947 and 1951, 150,000–200,000 new 'council' houses were built each year, representing almost three quarters of all the new housing stock constructed in those years.

Compromises and Limitations

The achievements of Clement Attlee's post-war Labour government were all the more substantial given that the price of wartime victory was peacetime bankruptcy. Keynes described the situation Labour inherited as Britain's 'financial Dunkirk'. In 1945 Britain's war debts amounted to £22 billion and by 1947 its **national debt** had risen to 238 per cent of GDP (it had been 125 per cent in 1939). The only other time in Britain's history that national debt as a proportion of GDP had been a little higher was after the **Napoleonic Wars** when austerity measures and the rule of cheap government were introduced to prepare Britain for the **gold standard**. Instead of cutting in the name of 'sound finance', the Labour government spent to build a new social infrastructure. Repaying war debts and financing reconstruction required more loans and these came, to reaffirm Britain's new position of dependence, from the USA. In 1945 Keynes was dispatched to Washington to secure a loan of £750 million, but it came at a heavy price. The USA insisted that trade preferences within the **Sterling Area** be dismantled and that holders of sterling could exchange it for dollars. No European country received more American aid or loans through the **Marshall Plan** that began in 1948 than Britain (£154 million and £1.84 billion respectively). Yet by 1950 Keynes was again back in Washington begging for further loans of £145 million (as well as a line of credit worth £930 million) to be paid back at 2 per cent interest over 50 years. The last of these loans was only paid off in 2006.

In these straitened circumstances, corners had to be cut. It was left to the Festival of Britain in 1951 to produce a vision of what the New Jerusalem could look like if it were fully realized (see Textbox 10.2 and Figure 10.4). Instead the new welfare state was hewn from those old Victorian buildings that had stigmatized their inhabitants. The majority of NHS hospitals were repurposed voluntary hospitals or workhouse infirmaries; 45 per cent of them were built before 1891, and 21 per cent before 1861. Despite the 536 new schools built between 1945 and 1956 to accommodate the increased numbers of pupils after the 1944 Education Act, the vast majority of schools, over 5,000 of them,

Figure 10.4 The Festival of Britain on London's South Bank, 1951

10.2 Place: The Festival of Britain's South Bank, London

The Festival of Britain was held to mark the centenary of the **Great Exhibition** in 1951. If the Great Exhibition celebrated the achievements of liberal political economy, the Festival of Britain was used by the Labour government in an election year as 'a tonic to the nation' amidst continuing wartime austerity measures to demonstrate the future potential of social democracy. The Festival was held in towns and cities across Britain in 1951 but its focal point was a set of attractions on the South Bank of the River Thames in London. They included the Skylon, a sleek steel tower suspended in mid-air with no visible means of support, and the Royal Festival Hall, a concert hall designed by the modernist architect Robert Matthew. The South Bank also featured a Dome of Discovery, an attraction that showcased Britain's scientific endeavours, encouraging its visitors to imagine an optimistic future of leisure and abundance made possible by state-directed technocratic planning. Another popular exhibition was the Telekinema, a state-of-the-art 400-seat cinema with the capacity to show 3D films. With its concrete modernism and faith in technological progress, the South Bank anticipated the built environment of the post-war welfare state – particularly the construction of new towns and mass housing estates in the 1950s and 1960s. Many of these nascent urban forms were displayed at the festival's Town Planning pavilion. While the Great Exhibition displayed goods produced around the Empire, the Festival was a more parochial affair, one where the empire was seldom mentioned and vendors selling foreign food were explicitly banned. During the five months in which it was open the South Bank was visited by more than 8 million people. The new Conservative government elected in September 1951 hastily demolished many of the buildings and attractions. Only the Festival Hall still stands. (S.W.)

remained Victorian, mainly the board schools built from the 1870s. Even the new estates of council housing lacked many of the resources that were initially imagined to be so central to building a sense of community upon them. In 1952 a survey of 100 of these estates found that only in 1 out of 46 had the planned nursery school materialized, 6 out of 24 infant welfare clinics, 2 out of 22 playgrounds and 4 out of 50 community centres. The beacons of social democracy were illuminated dimly by Victorian gaslight, and for many the pall of liberal condescension hung over them.

Examples of the compromised nature of social democracy abound. School meals were made universally available in 1944 and it was hoped that they would forge a sense of community among pupils and improve their nutritional health. Yet, as limited funds meant that those who received school lunches were means-tested to see who could afford them, the stigma of poverty remained. Only 48 per cent of schoolchildren signed up to be fed. By 1951 the escalating cost of supporting the United States' war in Korea necessitated the introduction of a shilling charge on prescription drugs and a £1 charge for visits to the dentist – leading to the resignation of Aneurin Bevan and Harold Wilson (who would become Labour's next prime minister in 1964). Most unpopular of all was the persistence of wartime rationing. Many already resented that food supplies were shared with the British zone of occupied Germany (which was costing £100 million a year to maintain), but when rations of petrol and food were reduced in 1947, as the government introduced new austerity measures to stop a run on the pound, the anger was palpable. Few now remember that the rationing of food lasted until 1954 and that clothing, coal and furniture remained rationed as late as 1958. Few at the time could forget it.

Rationing highlighted the technocratic, not democratic, nature of post-war social democracy. The hopes of convincing 'the people' to continue their collective mobilization during the war into post-war reconstruction were rarely realized. The programme of nationalization was coupled with an attempt to encourage workers' participation in the management of industry, even in the private sector, through the creation of Joint Production Committees (JPCs) or works councils. This attempt to institute industrial democracy had some success in larger firms (75 per cent of those with more than a thousand employees had them) and in particular sectors like engineering (where 63 per cent of factories had JPCs in 1950). Yet, unlike in Germany and France, where worker consultation was made compulsory, JPCs remained conspicuously absent in many sectors, and in smaller firms, where they were often ridiculed by management and unions alike as addressing trivial issues like 'tea and toilets'. Similarly, although social surveys, films and exhibitions sought to involve residents in the plans for reconstructing cities like Plymouth and London, they had little success. Community associations were formed on many new council estates to allow residents to discuss issues and forge a new sense of collective belonging; instead of activating a new democratic spirit of community, they often became dominated by middle-class 'busy-bodies'.

Finally, for all its talk of universality, the construction of post-war social democracy remained structured by differences of gender, class and race. Full employment, social security and the new forms of welfare were all predicated upon the idea of a male breadwinner supporting a wife and family. Even though the proportion of married women in the labour market doubled to 22 per cent of all married women between 1931 and 1951, working women still earned only two thirds of a man's wage. Married women were encouraged to stay at home, for motherhood was seen as an important social responsibility. Social workers were particularly influenced by the work of the psychologist John Bowlby who, following his studies of children evacuated during the war, argued in *Maternal Care and Health* (1951) that absent working mothers produced anti-social children at risk of becoming juvenile delinquents. The universal Family Allowance introduced in 1945 was paid to the mother for each child she had – not, as some feminists had hoped, in return for their household and affective labour. It was a pro-natalist policy designed to check the falling birth rate, reverse the ageing of the population, and even protect marriage as divorce rates spiked at 60,300 in 1947 (up from 4,100 in 1935). Widows were supported by their husband's pensions.

Nowhere were the continuing divisions of class more evident than in schools. The Education Act provided a secondary education for all but enshrined class difference. While those who could afford it, a small elite of 5 per cent, were allowed to privately educate their children, those in state schools were streamed, aged eleven, into a tripartite system. That system was informed by educational psychologists like Cyril Burt who believed a child's innate intelligence could be tested aged eleven when classified into three basic types, abstract, mechanical and concrete. The eleven-plus exam was used to stream children into three types of school specifically designed to develop whichever of these 'aptitudes' they possessed. Grammar schools (most of which had been fee paying before 1944) catered to the 15 per cent of pupils deemed capable of 'abstract' thought, while a smaller number of technical schools were established to educate the 7 per cent of children with 'mechanical' minds. The rest, 78 per cent of schoolchildren, were sent to secondary modern schools to be prepared for a life of manual labour. At the age of eleven, one's life opportunities were essentially determined by an education system that socially reproduced the inequities and hierarchies of class. Higher education was an elite affair. Unlike the United States, where the GI Bill led to the expansion and social democratization of universities, the war changed little in Britain. In 1939 just 50,000, or 2 per cent of school leavers, went to university, and a further 19,000 received some type of further vocational or teacher training. By 1954 those numbers had increased to 82,000 university students (3 per cent of school leavers) and a further 40,000 in further education. Only the Workers' Education Association, founded in

1903, provided any opportunity for most to continue their education through evening classes, taken by 20,000 people across 800 local branches in 1945. As late as 1963, fewer than one in a hundred working-class children made it to university through grammar schools.

Even these compromised forms of social democracy were far superior to very patchy and limited welfare measures offered to colonial subjects through the Colonial Development and Welfare Act of 1945. As we'll see in the following chapter, '**colonial development** and welfare' was intended to help resuscitate Britain's ailing economy and prevent the growth of labour unrest and nationalist movements. As the Dominions, especially Canada, sought to define the terms of their own national citizenship independently of Britain, the **British Nationality Act** of 1948 afforded British citizenship to all colonial subjects. Thereafter, colonial subjects who passed through or migrated to Britain – unlike those 345,000 'Displaced Persons' from eastern Europe and the Baltic States recruited as 'European Voluntary Workers' to fill the post-war labour shortage – were afforded full access to welfare services. After 1948, as growing numbers of people either fled the carnage of partition in India and Pakistan or were actively recruited from depressed colonial economies in the Caribbean, government departments and local voluntary groups worked hard to ensure these new Commonwealth citizens knew how to make the most of the welfare state's jobs, schools and medical services. Indeed, many men and women from the Caribbean were hired to provide those welfare services, working on the buses or in hospitals as doctors, nurses and auxiliary workers. By 1965 there were as many as 5,000 Jamaican nurses working in the NHS and by 1960 up to 40 per cent of junior doctors in the NHS were from Britain's former colonies in South Asia.

 Managing Affluence and Consensus

The greatest achievement of the post-war Labour government was that it firmly established social democracy, for all its imperfect manifestations, as the new common sense. For at least three decades, all three political parties were committed to delivering full employment and maintaining the welfare state through a mixed economy. The principle task of government, they agreed, was to ensure the welfare of the population and generate rising standards of living for all. The only question, and the primary source of debate and disagreement between the parties, was how these goals were best achieved: what the precise role of the state, and the balance between public and private ownership, should be. Indeed, the Conservative Party, the party still most attached to the idea of private enterprise, was elected in 1951 and remained in power for all but eight of the following twenty-five years. During that time social democracy delivered unparalleled wealth and welfare for Britons. Politics, and the measure of success for rival parties, became about which party could best manage the economy and improve the standard of living for voters. At the same time opinion polling, advertising and television transformed the conduct of politics. In a new age of prosperity, where the measure of politics was material improvement, politics increasingly became a type of commodity that was sold to voters as consumers.

The Stately Homes of England

In 1938 Noel Coward, Britain's most popular artist, had a hit song that comically chronicled the plight of the aristocracy struggling to maintain 'The Stately Homes of England'. Coward wittily satirized the lengths the upper classes would go to, mortgaged to the hilt, despite infusions of money and glamour from American heiresses, to prove they still had the upper hand. Ironically, after the war the aristocracy and the monarchy enjoyed new prestige. Like their stately homes, which were increasingly opened to visitors to generate revenue, the sporting and cultural events of the aristocratic 'season' between April and August – like Henley Royal Regatta, Wimbledon, Royal Ascot, the Chelsea Flower Show and the Proms – became public spectacles. Many were even televised in the 1950s. Debutante balls, where daughters who had come of age were 'presented' to join the marriage market, and 'High Society' weddings were reported in the 'society' and 'fashion' pages of the press. If the aristocracy became more culturally visible, they lost little of their political prominence. The Conservative Party remained a deeply aristocratic party. In 1951, 25 per cent of its MPs had attended Eton, its leaders remained aristocrats until they elected Edward Heath in 1965, and 95 per cent of its MPs belonged to one or more of London's exclusive gentleman's clubs as late as 1974. When the journalist Antony Sampson published an *Anatomy of Britain* in 1962, he found that the 'old privileged values of aristocracy, public schools and Oxbridge ... still dominate government today'.

The prestige and visibility of the monarchy also increased following the coronation of Queen Elizabeth II in 1953. The monarchy's reputation had been dealt a severe blow in 1936 when Edward VIII abdicated over his inability, as head of the **Anglican Church**, to marry the American divorcee Mrs Simpson. Elizabeth's coronation was the first to be televised and 20 million Britons eagerly watched its pomp and ceremony, which included European royalty and guests from around the Empire. If some hoped for a new Elizabethan age that could restore Britain's greatness, others were content that the Queen's youthful and growing family had restored faith in an ancient institution. Her annual Christmas broadcasts on television, which began in 1957, became staple watching for many and demonstrated just how the monarchy had modernized. To some it seemed that the Conservative Party, elected in 1951 and in power for the next thirteen years, had successfully re-established the **ancien regime**.

Figure 10.5 London's Great Smog, 1952

'You've Never Had It So Good'

It was certainly not the case that Conservative rule was made possible by Britons' continuing fascination with the aristocracy and monarchy. Just as the Conservative Party had reinvented itself by adopting the rhetoric of democracy during the 1920s, so after the war they became the champions of social democracy. What distinguished them from the Labour Party was their embrace of the rhetoric of choice and consumption.

10.3 Source: Monte Fresco's Photograph of London's Great Smog, 1952

This photograph (Figure 10.5) was taken by Monte Fresco (1936–2013) in London during the 'Great Smog' of December 1952. Son of a tailor in the East End of London, Fresco left school at fourteen and, encouraged by his uncle who was a photographer for the *Daily Mail*, began work as a darkroom printer and took his own photos. He took this photograph when just sixteen years old. Fresco went on to become a celebrated news and sports photographer at the *Daily Mirror* for over thirty years when photographs were occupying an increasingly important place in the selling of news and newspapers. In December 1952 Fresco was navigating the 'Great Smog'. Heavy fogs, known affectionately as 'pea soupers', had been a common part of life in London since the late nineteenth century, when Arthur Conan Doyle made them a key part of his Sherlock Holmes stories. The Great Smog was, however, the worst the city had ever seen. A bitterly cold spell caused millions of Londoners to light coal fires, the primary source of indoor heat at the time. The sulphuric smoke emitted by these fires, combined with the smog produced by numerous coal-burning power stations in the city, created a dense fog lasting for almost a week. Many Londoners wore masks outside and described having to shuffle along streets to avoid colliding with other pedestrians. The smog even seeped into houses and public buildings, and some concerts and film screenings were cancelled due to lack of visibility. In the weeks after, medical investigators estimated that 4,000 people died as a result of respiratory problems exacerbated by the smog (some claimed as many as 12,000 died). The image shows a bus conductor, usually charged with collecting tickets from passengers, who has left his bus in a desperate attempt to guide it through the smog. Eventually all above-ground public transport was suspended as visibility had been reduced to just a few feet. The event initiated a major debate about the environmental state of British cities. In the following decade a number of clean energy acts were introduced by Parliament, prohibiting the burning of certain fuels, relocating power stations away from cities and incentivizing the use of gas- or electric-powered central heating in homes. (S.W.)

In 1951 their election slogan declared they wished to 'Set the People Free' from the overbearing and still persistent grip of the wartime and welfare state. In doing so they captured the animus against the persistence of rationing. Formed in 1945, the British Housewives' League was at the forefront of the campaigns to end rationing. Their petition against bread rationing in 1946 collected half a million signatures. Rationing, their manifesto declared, demonstrated 'that over-control by the State is not in the interests of a free and happy home life and the development of personality in accord with Christian tradition'. This antipathy to 'the State', and the planning of its experts, was also evident in the campaign of the Road Haulage Association against the nationalization of freight transport. The Conservative Party supported these positions but advocated a resetting of the balance between the state and the market. Rather than a return to the idea of setting markets free, they sought to liberate businesses and consumers from the strictures of technocratic state planning.

On their return to government in 1951 the Conservatives found it harder than they had imagined to lift the gloom of austerity, symbolized by London's 'Great Smog' (see Textbox 10.3 and Figure 10.5), and to dismantle state controls. Road haulage, like the iron and steel industry, was only slowly and partially denationalized and hardly changed the balance of the mixed economy. Rationing did not end when the last food controls were lifted in 1954, for clothes and furniture remained rationed until 1958. Yet, as Europe and the world's economy slowly recovered from the disruption of war, the tide began to turn and Britain's economy emerged from its indebted state of austerity. Where the Labour government had, by necessity, focused on the construction of public housing, the Conservatives promised to build not just a 100,000 more houses a year, but to give citizens the chance to join a 'property-owning democracy'. Home ownership in England and Wales had fallen to 27 per cent in 1947 but steadily grew to 43 per cent by 1961. With full employment achieved, wages began to steadily climb and even to outstrip the cost of living. The average wage rose from £7 10s in 1950 to £18 by 1964, while real wages (adjusted for inflation) rose over 3 per cent between 1951 and 1973. This recovery ensured that in the decade after 1948 more than 3,000 additional families became subject to income tax. This allowed the Conservatives to gradually scale back the basic rate of income tax from 47.5 per cent in 1947 to 38.75 per cent in 1959; the top rate remained around 90 per cent. In these conditions, consumer expenditure rose 45 per cent between 1952 and 1964 and inequalities of wealth continued to decline. Although the Paid Holidays Act of 1938 finally allowed manual workers two weeks' paid holiday, it was only after 1945 that the working class were able to enjoy them as consumers. By 1951, 25 million people went on holiday in Britain and huge seaside holiday camps, like those developed by Billy Butlin, catered for this new market. Two million people fled the crowds and went on holiday overseas. No wonder that in 1957, the Conservative prime minister Harold Macmillan insisted 'Most of our people have never had it so good. Go around the country … and you will see a state of prosperity such as we have never had in my lifetime – nor indeed in the history of this country.'

Macmillan was mostly right, although his attempt to claim that the Conservatives were responsible for the economic recovery was mostly wrong. So similar was the Conservative Chancellor 'Rab' Butler's economic strategy to that of his Labour predecessor, Hugh Gaitskell, that in 1954 *The Economist* coined the term 'Butskellism' to describe it. Indeed, the central tenets of Keynesian demand management within a mixed economy remained in place whatever party was in power through to the 1970s. These were the boom years in Britain. Between 1951 and 1973 Britain's gross domestic product grew each year on average 2.4 per cent, unemployment remained below 2 per cent, infant mortality fell from 31 to 17 per 1,000. Twenty-nine 'new' towns (the most iconic, Milton Keynes, was one of the last in 1967) were built, home ownership rose from around 30 per cent to over 50 per cent, and public sector house rentals rose to 30 per cent (and over 50 per cent in Scotland) as the private sector fell from 58 to 14 per cent. Many more households possessed consumer durables like washing machines (from 7.5 to 67 per cent), fridges (from 3.2 to 68 per cent) and televisions (from 2 to 90 per cent). And whereas less than 5 per cent of Britons owned cars in 1950, by 1973 almost 25 per cent did and they were able to drive on 1,000 miles of new motorway network constructed since 1958. By 1976, 80 per cent of Britons had four weeks' paid holiday (up from 4 per cent in 1971) and increasing numbers – 7 million of them – went abroad for them, while a further 34 million stayed in Britain.

The post-war economic boom was not unique to Britain; it was shared across much of the world. The British economy actually grew less rapidly than the United States and many of its European rivals. We know this because a plethora of new forms of internationally comparable economic data – from GDP (gross domestic product) to shares of world trade, productivity rates and standards of living – were developed by institutions like the United Nations, the World Bank and **International Monetary Fund**, tasked with rebuilding and managing the world economy from the United States. As we shall see in the next Chapter, the delivery of growth and prosperity in the West was very much part of the United States' **Cold War** battle with the Soviet Union and it needed to measure the effectiveness of those governments it was investing in. With the lowest rates of growth of total and per capita GDP in Europe, a shrinking percentage of world trade, considerably reduced overseas investments driving invisible earnings, and rising wages that fuelled both demand for imports and inflation, Britain's balance of payments was constantly in deficit and placed huge pressure on the value of the pound and the integrity of the **Sterling Area**. While the Conservatives championed their success at improving living standards and unleashing a new consumer culture, the Labour Party insisted that Britain's economy was falling behind its international competitors and had to be modernized to avoid 'decline'. It was Harold Wilson's promise to modernize the British economy with 'the white heat of technology' that finally led to the re-election of the Labour Party in 1964.

The Rise of the Consumer

The debate about how best to manage social democracy's mixed economy and deliver increasing affluence to Britons made the consumer a subject of growing political import. Although market research and advertising had become increasingly prominent between the wars (the head of Britain's largest advertising agency was appointed to run the Empire Marketing Board's 'Buy British' campaign in 1931), they came of age in the post-war period. The proponents of advertising viewed it as the private sector's own form of demand management. They argued that alongside government planning, advertising was an engine of economic growth. If social scientists had often followed

Rowntree's insistence that consumers must first make rational choices to meet their minimum needs, market researchers and advertisers sought to understand their seemingly irrational desires and choices. The growing influence of the psy-sciences generated new theories of consumer behaviour and new techniques – from discussion groups to personal consultations and personality testing – to discover how best to mobilize their desires. The Tavistock Institute for Medical Psychology, a key conduit for the spread of psychoanalysis in Britain, advised large corporations like Shell, Guinness and Birds Eye Foods how to market their products as well as how to manage their 'human relations' on the shop floor. While social scientists classified the population by income and class, the psy-sciences helped market researchers create new categories of people – like 'housewives', and 'youth' – to target as consumers.

The biggest boon for the advertising industry in Britain was the launch of commercial television. The Conservative government created Independent Television (ITV) in 1954 to break the BBC's monopoly of broadcasting and showcase how commerce could be a force for cultural innovation. Like commercial television elsewhere in the world, ITV was funded entirely by its advertising revenue. Six minutes of every hour of broadcasting was given over to adverts. As manufacturers rushed to advertise their products in the homes of those affluent enough to have a television, competition between brands became so intense that concerns mounted about the veracity of many adverts. The Advertising Standards Association was established in 1962 to ensure that adverts were 'legal, decent, honest and truthful', although they received a remarkably modest 8,000 complaints a year. The proliferation of commodities, higher-pressure sales techniques, and the growth of credit arrangements (like hire purchase and mail order instalment plans) which 20 per cent of the population were using by 1969, caused widespread concern. NGOs, like the Consumer Advisory Council (1955), the Consumer Association (1957) and the Consumer Council (1963), were established to protect and advise consumers, as well as to lobby government on their behalf. New magazines, like *Shopper's Guide* (1955) and the Consumer Association's *Which?* (1957) tested products so consumers could make informed decisions. It was not until the Trades Descriptions Act of 1968 and the Consumer Safety Act a decade later, informed by consumer activism in the USA, that British governments began to regulate consumer culture. Until then consumers had to take responsibility for their own choices.

Politics in the Age of Ad-Mass

Twenty-one years after his *English Journey* lamented the spread of an Americanized consumer culture across the country, J.B. Priestley published an excoriating account of the new *Age of Ad-Mass* (1955) that had sprung up in the post-war social democracy he had once held such high hopes for. Ad-Mass was a phrase of his invention used to describe 'a whole system of increasing productivity, plus inflation, plus a rising standard

of material living, plus high pressure advertising and salesmanship, plus mass communication, plus cultural democracy and the creation of a mass mind'. It was hardly
a novel critique of how social democracy's welfare capitalism had spawned a corrosive, commercialized mass culture which valorized materialism over all else. Its analysis
echoed others on the left across Europe, most notably the German Frankfurt School of
critical theorists who, a decade earlier, had argued that the 'culture industry' propagated
'mass deception' to obscure the inequities of capitalism. Priestley feared that politics in
post-war Britain had become so enmeshed in the techniques of market research and
commercial advertising that it had been reduced to the status of a commodity and sold
to citizens en masse as consumers rather than as critically informed individuals.

In fact, party membership and the activities of all those clubs established in the
late nineteenth and early twentieth centuries, reached its zenith in the early 1950s.
The membership of both parties more than doubled between 1943 and 1953, when
the Conservative Party boasted 2.8 million members, almost three times the size of the
Labour Party's membership of a million – although that was a fraction of those whose
union dues supported the party. The Conservative Party thereafter lost members as dramatically as they had once gained them. By the mid 1970s they claimed about 1.1 million
members, still half a million more than the Labour Party – and these levels were only
a little higher a decade earlier. Certainly during the 1950s the conduct of politics was
changing fast as the old forms of electoral campaigning – staging public meetings and
canvassing one and all – were no longer working. The advent of television and opinion
polling had changed the game. The initial hopes that television would boost attendance
at election meetings quickly subsided. While 30 per cent of voters attended an election meeting in 1951, fewer than 10 per cent did fifteen years later. Attention gradually
shifted away from local campaigning to the national level where parties could control
their messaging. Some politicians bemoaned the changes and sought new ways of connecting with voters by holding 'surgeries' in their constituency offices and conducting
'walkabouts' or personal canvasses. Elections now bore little resemblance to the world
summoned up by Hogarth's prints in the 1750s, or even to those a century later.

Politics and television had become inseparable by the end of the 1950s. In 1945 just
15,000 households had a television, yet fifteen years later 10 million did, 70 per cent of
households. It was impossible for politicians to ignore a medium with that reach, and
the party political broadcast – where party leaders made their pitch to voters during
elections – pioneered for radio during the 1930s, was quickly transferred to television.
Still in 1955 two thirds of the electorate listened to those broadcasts on radio and just a
third watched them on television. At the 1959 election those proportions were reversed.
By then both parties were staging morning press conferences and coordinating the
speeches of their leaders to capture the news agenda on television. The Labour Party
even created a Television and Radio Room under one of its most innovative campaigners, a youthful Tony Benn. At the 1964 election, 85 per cent of the electorate watched a

party political broadcast on television. Television created not just new forms of electoral campaigning but a new style of politician. Those who excelled as orators at public meetings rarely adapted well to television, where politicians had to be seated, refrain from gesticulation, and speak straight to camera. Harold Macmillan, who as Conservative prime minister in the 1950s and early 1960s, lived through this transition, admitted 'almost everything that one has learnt for public speaking has to be forgotten for a television performance. One has to remind oneself … that the audience … consists of two or three persons sitting quietly in a room, not subject to any of the emotions which can be stirred in a great public gathering.'

It was not just the presentational demands of television that transformed British politics. The increasing use of market research, public relations and opinion polling by the political parties fundamentally altered how campaigns were conducted and how politics itself was conceived. Fittingly, the Conservative Party in the run-up to the 1959 election hired an advertising agency to shape their campaign. Outspending the Labour Party twenty times in the process, the campaign culminated with the defining message 'Life's better with the Conservatives. Don't let Labour ruin it' (see Figure 10.6) and a commanding Conservative victory. By the 1964 election the Labour Party had also hired an advertising agency. Its coordinated 'Let's Go with Labour!' campaign (see Figure 10.7), complete with balloon races, car stickers and badges, modernized the image of the party and forefronted its dynamic and television-savvy young leader Harold Wilson, who regularly chaired the Party's morning press conferences. Thereafter, advertising agencies played a key role in the crafting the image and appeal of political parties. With dwindling membership available to canvass support, and party budgets focused on the national campaign, local campaigns became such a sideshow that by 1969 the party affiliations of each candidate had to be put on the ballot card so that voters knew who to vote for.

No less than advertising, opinion polling also transformed British politics. The wartime work of Mass Observation and the British Institute of Public Opinion at the Ministry of Information paved the way for the formation of new professional societies like the British Market Research Society (1946) and the American Association for Public Opinion Research (1947). Where once politicians and journalists alone claimed the expertise to read the winds of public opinion, the growing prestige and authority of opinion polling made the Labour Party commission its first private poll in 1956. By 1959 four of the nine national daily newspapers were publishing weekly polls tracking the fortunes of the parties in the month before the election. By 1966 opinion polls had correctly called the results of all but one election.

Quantitative and seemingly scientific approaches to measuring public opinion had gained ascendancy and with it came a different understanding of the politics. Intuitive understandings of how to push public opinion gave way to one where parties were pulled by polling, while complex issues and debates were reduced to a numerical

Figure 10.6 'Life's better with the Conservatives', 1959

representation of those for and against simple statements and questions. Where once political scientists had focused on institutions and history, a new breed of psephologist emerged that pioneered quantitative analyses of electoral behaviour. David Butler, an Australian who trained as a political scientist in the United States, popularized this

Figure 10.7 'Let's Go with Labour', 1964

method on television as a pundit for the BBC election night coverage between 1950 and 1979. As poll results were declared across the country, his 'swingometer' captured the percentage of votes required to 'swing' from one party to another for a victory to be secured. It was a classic demonstration of how the new quantitative understanding of politics compressed all local variations into an aggregate national trend and portrayed elections as a two-horse race. The new techniques and forms of post-war politics – market research, opinion polling, advertising and television – were closely entwined. Under their spell, politicians were able to plan and centrally manage campaigns much as they hoped to orchestrate the social democratic state. Yet they also tended to assume citizens were consumers and politics had to be sold to them as a commodity that could improve their standard of living.

Conclusion

Already struggling to recover from the costs of World War I, Britain was rocked by the experience of the Great Depression. Such was the depth of the economic and political crisis that Britain finally abandoned the liberal political economy that many felt had made it Great. In its place came a reconfiguration of its imperial political economy around protectionist tariffs and the Sterling Area and a growing interest in planning to avoid the blights of poverty and unemployment. If British governments forsook the Keynesian economics that informed America's New Deal during the 1930s, the outbreak of World War II made planning the war effort and surviving on the Home Front a necessity. Britons mobilized not just to fight fascism but to secure a people's peace that would ensure there could be no return to the dole queues and **hunger marches** of the 1930s. The Labour Party's promise of a better future around a mixed economy and a welfare state propelled them to victory at the 1945 election. Inheriting a country crippled by war debts, they built a new social democratic system that, despite its limitations, ensured Britons were protected from the vicissitudes of the market. Despite differing emphases with regard to the extent of state planning, all political parties embraced social democracy and within a generation it made Britons more affluent than ever before. The success of governments came to be measured by their ability to improve standards of living and the rights of the consumer came to have a new political prominence. Post-war affluence and social democracy were not just a British story. It was made possible by the development of colonial economies, American loans in the context of an escalating **Cold War** between Britain's wartime allies the United States and the Soviet Union, and the construction of new transnational systems of economic management in Euro-America. It is that context, as well as the contradictions and political movements it generated, that helped unravel the social democratic settlement that we turn to in the next two chapters.

FURTHER READING

Historians conventionally date the advent of social democracy in Britain between the publication of the Beveridge Report of 1942 and the election of the Labour government in 1945. Much of the debate is less about timing than about the degree to which the British people were radicalized by the war and what they were voting for in 1945. A long-held view, which was a product of the post-war social democratic consensus itself, was that the 'people's war' did indeed usher in Orwell's English revolution and led seamlessly to the 'people's peace' and the electorate's embrace of social democracy if not socialism itself. If this was most eloquently expressed in the very last paragraph of A.J.P. Taylor's *English History, 1914–1945* (Oxford, 1965), it was widely rehearsed in a host of other books like Paul Addison, *The Road to 1945: British Politics in the Second World War* (London, 1975); Arthur Marwick (ed.), *Total War and Social Change* (Basingstoke, 1988); Kenneth Morgan, *The People's Peace: Britain Since 1945* (Oxford, 1988); and most recently Ross McKibbin, *Parties and People: England, 1914–1951* (Oxford, 2010).

As the social democratic settlement was increasingly called into question from the 1970s, that account was challenged. Angus Calder's still terrific *The People's War* (London, 1969) and Harold Pelling's *Britain and the Second World War* (London, 1970) argued, as I have, that the war was not a dramatic sea change but an acceleration and development of trends that were set in motion during the 1930s. By the 1980s the revisionist unpicking of the 'myth of the

Blitz' was in full swing. Corelli Barnett's *The Audit of War: The Illusion and Reality of Britain as a Great Nation* (London, 1986) echoed the arguments of those on the right that the war had not radicalized the British people and that they were duped into voting Labour by left-wing intellectuals working at the BBC and Ministry of Information. For Barnett, the period from 1945 until the election of Margaret Thatcher in 1979 was an abhorrent abandonment of economic liberalism.

During the 1990s a number of historians explored the complexities and continuing divisions within British society during the war. While Stephen Brooke's *Labour's War* (Oxford, 1992) uncovered important ideological rifts within the Labour Party, Steven Fielding, Nick Tiratsoo and Nick Thompson's *England Arise! The Labour Party and Popular Politics in 1940s Britain* (Manchester, 1995) suggested the British people were radicalized neither by war nor by Labour politics. Penny Summerfield's *Reconstructing Women's Wartime Lives* (Manchester, 1998) and Sonya Rose's *Which People's War? National Identity and Citizenship in Wartime Britain 1939–1945* (Oxford, 2003) importantly recaptured the ways in which gender, race and class continued to structure different experiences of war for 'the people'. The most recent and readable introductory surveys are those by Mark Donelly, *Britain in the Second World War* (London, 1999), and Juliet Gardner, *Wartime: Britain 1939–1945* (London, 2004).

Historians now increasingly look back to the 1930s for some of the origins of post-war Britain. The halting advent of Keynesian economics is well covered by W.R. Garside, *British Unemployment 1919–1939: A Study in Public Policy* (Cambridge, 1990), and by Peter Clarke, a biographer of Keynes, whose survey of Britain's twentieth century in *Hope and Glory: Britain 1900–2000* (London, 2004) has good chapters on Keynes's growing influence on economic policy. Jed Esty's *A Shrinking Island: Modernism and National Culture* (Princeton, 2004) smartly locates Keynes as part of the introspective turn in British culture explored by Alison Light's *Forever England: Femininity, Literature and Conservatism Between the Wars* (London, 1991). The growing interest in planning more generally is the subject of Daniel Ritschel's *The Politics of Planning: The Debate on Economic Planning in Britain in the 1930s* (Oxford, 1997). David Edgerton's *Warfare State: Britain, 1920–1970* (Cambridge, 2006) reminds us of the increasing prevalence of experts and technology in the work of the state.

Historians remain divided about whether standards of living generally improved during the 1930s, yet agree that great contrasts of want and plenty characterized the decade. While Andrew Thorpe's *Britain in the 1930s: The Deceptive Decade* (Oxford, 1992) provides a good introduction, Steven Thompson's *Unemployment, Poverty and Health in Interwar South Wales* (Cardiff, 2006) reminds us just how bad that decade was in the 'distressed areas'. The central place of women in producing and consuming the goods that transformed not just middle-class suburban homes but the lives and imaginations of many women are explored in Miriam Glucksmann, *Women Assemble: Women Workers in the New Industries in Inter-War Britain* (London, 1990), Sally Alexander, *Becoming a Woman and Other Essays in 19th and 20th Century Feminist History* (London, 1994), and Judy Giles, *The Parlour and the Suburb: Domestic Identities, Class, Femininity and Modernity* (2004).

The character of the post-war world is receiving more and more attention from historians. Ironically, the nature of the mixed economy and the new tools of macro-economic management have received less attention, but are excellently discussed in J.C.R. Dow, *The Management of the British Economy 1945–60* (Cambridge, 1964), Catherine Schenk's *Britain and the Sterling Area:*

From Devaluation to Convertibility in the 1950s (London, 1994) and Jim Tomlinson's seminal essay 'Managing the Economy, Managing the People: Britain, 1931–1970', *Economic History Review*, 58/3 (2005), 555–85. Glen O'Hara's *Governing Post-War Britain: The Paradoxes of Progress, 1951–1973* (Basingstoke, 2012) examines the breadth of ideas and their transnational contexts that informed debates about economic policy.

Historians have become increasingly interested in the politics of consumption that surrounded growing affluence. Ina Zweiniger-Bargielowska's *Austerity in Britain: Rationing, Controls and Consumption, 1939–1955* (Oxford, 2000) importantly established how thoroughly the Conservative Party benefited from the particular dissatisfaction of women with rationing. The impact of affluence and consumerism on British politics is discussed in Matthew Hilton's *Consumerism in Twentieth-Century Britain: The Search for a Historical Movement* (Cambridge, 2003) and Lawrence Black's *Redefining British Politics: Culture, Consumerism and Participation, 1954–70* (Basingstoke, 2010). The changing nature of British politics in the era of television and opinion polling is covered in Jon Lawrence's *Electing Our Masters: The Hustings in British Politics from Hogarth to Blair* (Oxford, 2009) and Laura Beer's *Your Britain: Media and the Making of the Labour Party* (Cambridge, Mass., 2010).

11 Social Democracy and the Cold War

Introduction

In 1931 Britain only just remained the world's pre-eminent superpower. The United States of America may have eclipsed her industrial output and become her creditor during the Great War, and the dollar may have displaced the pound as the global currency in 1931, yet territorially the sun still never set on the vast British Empire. Even in 1953, Britons could still imagine themselves as living in one of the world's most powerful countries. They had again emerged from the Second World War victorious, with an Empire that still claimed a fifth of the globe, and able to attract most of the world's leaders for the coronation of Queen Elizabeth II. As Elizabeth ascended the throne, Edmund Hillary and Tenzing Norgay reached the summit of Mount Everest, the world's tallest mountain. Few cared that Hillary was from New Zealand and Tenzing from Nepal, for the expedition was British-led. The following year Roger Bannister became the first man to run a four-minute mile. By 1976, though, Britons could no longer be under any illusions about their country's diminished status. Some condescendingly joked, forgetting Britain had once been part of the Roman Empire, that it had been reduced to the status of Italy with rockets. That is to say, its Empire had been reduced to just Hong Kong, Gibraltar and the Falklands – and its economy ranked alongside Italy's in size. All that appeared to be left of Britain's former global influence was one of five seats on the United Nations Security Council and a formidable nuclear arsenal. How and why this seemingly dramatic reversal of fortune happened, and what it meant for Britain's place in the world, is the story of this chapter.

It is a story most often told as one of decline and fall, or of Britons wilfully abandoning the conceits of empire to focus on building their own social democracy. Neither is quite right. Social democracy remained embedded in broader imperial and global structures. It relied upon the reconfigured forms of imperialism that gave rise to what is sometimes described as the Third British Empire. Moreover, Britain's social democracy, like its new global role, was shaped and constrained by the **Cold War** that broke out between the United States and the Soviet Union after World War II. Social democracy in Britain would have been impossible without American loans or the new structures and institutions of global economic management created in the United States after the war. The British Empire would have collapsed even faster had it not been strategically useful to the United States in constraining the global spread of communism. The spread of anti-colonial movements across the British Empire during the 1930s only escalated after World War II. Far from being met by Britain's peaceable and pragmatic withdrawal, they faced violence and persecution, as well as divide-and-rule strategies that sowed the seeds for bloody postcolonial civil wars. Colonial nationalists played no lesser role than the strategists of American foreign policy, or the expert planners of the welfare state and mixed economy, in forging the global history of Britain's social democracy.

The end of the British Empire enabled Britons to carve out new forms of global influence. Post-colonies found that the structures of colonial power were considerably harder to rid themselves of than the Union Jacks lowered at their independence ceremonies. British corporations, military hardware and experience, like cultural institutions and brokers, remained powerful and enduring influences in many former colonies. If imperial structures had influenced the formation of internationalist agendas between the wars, so decolonization helped make possible new forms of global citizenship. Anti-colonial movements and Cold War politics forged a new globally minded politics through organizations like the Movement for Colonial Freedom (1954), the Campaign for Nuclear Disarmament (1958), the Anti-Apartheid Movement (1959) and Amnesty International (1961). Alongside new humanitarian and environmental organizations – like Oxfam (1943) and the World Wide Fund for Nature (1961) – they urged Britons to assume moral leadership of the world. For all its good intentions, the imperialism of this internationalism, with its implicit understanding that postcolonial countries needed the help of Britons to protect their populations and environments, was hard to shake off.

Even before the British Empire fell apart, it was clear that Britain's imperial economy, fortified as it had been by the **Sterling Area** and policies of **colonial development**, could not prevent the continuing collapse of British exports. From the 1950s the growing affluence of Britons fuelled more imports and worsened Britain's deteriorating balance of payments problems, which in turn placed the pound and the entire Sterling Area under increasing pressure. Some Conservative and Labour MPs saw Europe as the answer. Europe's economies, increasingly fused together by the **Marshall Plan's** Organization for European Economic Co-operation (1948), the formation of the **European Coal and Steel Community** (1951) and the **European Economic Community** (1957), had grown faster than Britain's. As trade with Europe began to outstrip that within the Sterling Area in the early 1960s, British governments, both Conservative and Labour, prepared unsuccessful applications to join the EEC. It was only in 1973, when the Sterling Area, like the **Bretton Woods** system itself, had collapsed and all currencies floated freely, that Britain was finally allowed to join the EEC. Yet, with the Oil Crisis ushering in a period of so-called stagflation (stagnant growth and rising inflation), Europe alone could not stop Britain's economy from reaching uncomfortable new heights: a balance of payments deficit of £3 billion, a million people unemployed, and inflation at 10 per cent. Two years later, a Labour government turned to the **International Monetary Fund** to help prevent another run on the pound. In return for a loan of $3.9 billion, it was forced to implement 20 per cent cuts in public expenditure. For many in the Labour Party, the echoes of 1931 were too loud. This was effectively a **structural adjustment** of the British economy by an American-backed IMF, and it heralded the beginning of the end of social democracy in Britain. Between 1931 and 1976 the brief life of social democracy was always structured and often determined by global forces beyond Britain.

TIMELINE

1922	Lugard, *Dual Mandate in British Tropical Africa*
1929	Gandhi's Salt March protest Colonial Development Act
1931	Sterling Area created Statute of Westminster Roundtable Conference on government of India League of Coloured People
1932	Imperial Economic Conference at Ottawa BBC British Empire Service
1938	British Council Hailey, *African Survey*
1941	Lend-Lease and Atlantic Charter
1942	Fall of Singapore US military bases in UK
1945	Bretton Woods and devaluation of pound
1946	Assisted Passages Scheme
1947	Independence of India and Pakistan Arrival of *Empire Windrush* Marshall Plan
1948	British Nationality Act American nuclear weapons at RAF Lakenheath
1949	NATO Devaluation of the pound Colonial Development and Welfare Act
1951	European Coal and Steel Community
1954	Movement for Colonial Freedom
1957	Treaty of Rome
1958	Campaign for Nuclear Disarmament
1959	Anti-Apartheid Movement

1960	Macmillan's 'Winds of Change' speech in South Africa
1961	The World Wide Fund for Nature Amnesty International
1962	Commonwealth Immigration Act
1963	Application to join EEC
1967	Devaluation of the pound (again)
1971	Friends of the Earth
1973	Oil Crisis Admission to EEC
1976	*Wall Street Journal*'s 'Goodbye Britain'
1977	Greenpeace

 The Third British Empire

Although the British Empire reached its zenith in 1919 with the extension of its imperial rule over the Mandate territories, a third phase of British imperialism developed during the 1930s in response to the global economic crisis and the spread of nationalism across its colonies. There were three aspects of this Third British Empire – economic, political and cultural – and each provided ways in which Britain sought to tighten or maintain its faltering hold upon its colonial world.

Maintaining the British World

By the 1920s the talk of imperial federation had given way to the growing demands of the white settler colonies of the **British world** for increasing independence from London. This was achieved at the Imperial Conferences of 1926 and 1930 that together defined the terms of the **Statute of Westminster** (1931), in which the British Parliament finally waived its jurisdiction over Australia, Canada, New Zealand, Newfoundland, South Africa and the Irish Free State (which believed that it already possessed such independence). This de facto political independence belied the continuing hold of Britain over what effectively remained colonial economies. Just months before the Statute of Westminster was passed, Britain had left the **gold standard** and created the **Sterling Area**. This certainly eased the flow of trade within the currency bloc, to the benefit of all.

The benefits came at a cost. As the **Bank of England** became the holder of all sterling reserves, national governments were unable to spend down their reserves when they saw fit to do so. Moreover, when those reserves came under pressure, as they did with increasing frequency after the pound was pegged to the dollar in the 1940s, the British government would alone have the power to decide whether to devalue the currency.

Yet Britain's control of its imperial economy was loosening. Britain came out on the wrong side of the agreement struck at the Imperial Economic Conference held at Ottawa in 1932 to work out a new system of preferential imperial tariffs. The deal distinctly favoured the new Dominions and India, who not only protected their industries by insisting British exports would be subjected to tariffs (albeit at preferential rates), but also ensured their manufacturers gained access to the British market. Between 1931 and 1936 the Dominions' share of imports to Britain rose from 28.7 per cent to 39.2 per cent, while their share of exports from Britain rose by just 5.5 per cent. In 1929 Britain had a healthy balance of trade surplus with the Empire, exporting more than it imported. By 1936 the tables had turned and it had a surplus of imports worth £126 million. Not surprisingly, in 1931 the Empire Marketing Board (see Textbox 7.3) switched its efforts from encouraging Britons to 'Buy Empire' goods to a 'Buy British' campaign.

The growing political and economic independence of the Dominions meant that Britain had to work harder to ensure the Britishness of the **British world**. Traditionally the flow of migrants from Britain to the white settler colonies that were now Dominions had ensured this. Yet as population growth in Britain stagnated, the number of those emigrating dropped dramatically. British governments sought to counter this trend by subsidizing emigration through the Empire Settlement Acts of 1922 and 1937. Both Australia and Canada were keen to recruit skilled labour from Britain's ailing agricultural sector to help settle and farm their vast territories. 200,000 Britons left for Australia under this scheme between 1922 and 1933. As unemployment rose across the British world during the 1930s, the Dominions no longer saw themselves as 'colonies' for Britain's surplus workers. Even so, with the exception of Canada, which banned emigration of children under fourteen in 1925, they continued to receive orphaned and pauper children shipped out by organizations like Dr Barnado's, the Salvation Army, the Child Emigration Society and the Church of England Advisory Council on Empire Settlement.

Keeping the British world suitably British also became the work of culture. What we now know as the BBC World Service was first launched as the British Empire Service in December 1932, the very same month as the Imperial Economic Conference at Ottawa. Its aim was to promote British culture to an imagined audience of the white Anglo diaspora spread across the Dominions to ensure they remained culturally bound to Britain. By the end of the decade, as Europe and the world descended into war, the Empire Service was rebranded as an Overseas Service and quickly began broadcasting first in Arabic and German and then in all European languages by 1942. This projection of British culture overseas by the state was also reinforced from 1934 by the formation of the British Council. More expressly than the BBC, its aim was to promote British culture abroad through lectures, musical concerts, theatre and the teaching of English. Significantly, as British influence in the Middle East was waning in the face of anti-colonial movements across the **Mandates**, it was in Egypt that the first overseas office was opened in 1938. Yet during the 1930s the British Council also took its cultural diplomacy to parts of the world, like Latin America and southern Europe, where British influence was considerably more attenuated.

Representation and Rebellion in the Colonies

With the Dominions gaining greater political and economic autonomy from Britain, the future of the British Empire rested increasingly on India and Africa. This was hardly a firm foundation, for India had been wracked by a fresh wave of nationalist protest. In 1929 the Hindustani Socialist Republican Association bombed the Central Legislative Assembly (created just a decade earlier) in New Delhi. Just months after the Viceroy had vaguely promised eventual 'Dominion' status for India, Jawaharlal Nehru, the new leader of the **Indian National Congress** (INC), committed it to seeking nothing but complete independence and asked his followers to raise the Indian flag across the country on 26 January. In March Gandhi began a 240-mile 'Salt March' from his Ashram to India's western coast in Gujarat to protest against the government of India's taxes upon a commodity whose production it monopolized. The march captured the national imagination, and the sympathy of many across the world, and culminated with the arrest of 100,000 Indians as well as a boycott of British goods.

The flames of protest were momentarily doused when Gandhi and the INC agreed to attend a Roundtable conference in London during the winter of 1931 to discuss the future of India's representative structures of self-government. Arriving in Britain as unemployment reached unprecedented levels, Gandhi, dressed in his homespun clothing, visited textile workers in Lancashire to explain his support of the boycott of British goods and advocacy for native industry (see Figure 11.1). This public relations battle, and Gandhi's insistence that the INC spoke for all India, could not obscure deep divisions among the Indian delegates. After all, the conference delegates had been invited by the British to represent distinct communities (Muslims, untouchables, women, Anglo-Indians, Sikhs) under the assumption that they had different and competing interests. It took several years, as well as many more protests and arrests, before the Government of India Act in 1935 further enshrined these communal divisions. Although it expanded the powers of provincial government and increased its electorate to include 30 million people, a sixth of the adult male population, it did so in part by separate electorates and reserved seats for particular 'minority' communities.

Figure 11.1 Gandhi in Lancashire, 1931

In the name of balancing diverse interests, the British fostered divisions that punctured the momentum of nationalist protest and enabled colonial rule to persist.

A similar pattern of bolstering imperial rule through the modest devolution of powers to colonial subjects was also evident in Africa. In 1922 Sir Frederick Lugard, recently retired as governor of Nigeria and just appointed as Britain's representative on the League of Nations Permanent Mandates Commission, published the *Dual Mandate in British Tropical Africa*. It quickly became the bible of colonial administrators in Africa. Lugard was an archetypal man of the British Empire. Born in India to missionaries, Lugard joined the British East Africa Company and Royal Niger Company before being appointed as a governor of Hong Kong and then Nigeria. The task of British colonial rule in Africa, Lugard argued, was to both enrich Britain and elevate the condition of Africans. This was Britain's dual mandate in Africa. Although tropical Africa was a treasure trove of natural resources for British industry and a future market for its goods, Lugard believed that much of it was inaccessible to and uninhabitable for white settlers. Thus the dual mandate would need to be delivered by a system of 'indirect rule'. Indigenous rulers, mainly local chiefs installed to represent different 'tribes', were afforded jurisdiction over 'customary' matters. In contrast, new representative structures would be developed to give voice to white settlers while consolidating the authority of the governor.

Lugard retired as governor of Nigeria in 1919 but his ideas were substantiated in its first constitution three years later. The Nigerian Constitution of 1922 established a pattern of partial and limited representative government that was eventually adopted by many of Britain's other dependent colonies. It created a Council whose members were either elected (by a tiny electorate consisting of male British subjects and the very few 'natives' with an income of more than £100 per annum) or selected by the governor to represent different 'interests' and 'communities' within the colony. By 1924 a similar regime was operating in Kenya, where an elaborate system of separate communal electorates was designed to provide suitably balanced representation of white settlers, Arabs, Indians and a limited number of Africans on the Legislative Council. The exceptions were Northern and Southern Rhodesia, which specifically excluded all but propertied British subjects (women as well as men) from electing their representative councils and only allowed native authorities and selection to provincial councils in the late 1930s and early 1940s. In South Africa, where women and poor whites had been given the vote in 1930, 'native' voters (who were largely confined to the Cape) were disenfranchised by the Representation of the Natives Act of 1936. Instead they were confined to a separate electorate to vote for a very few communal representatives.

These hesitant steps to develop partial and highly racialized systems of representative government did not convince many Africans that British rule had a dual mandate. Instead they encouraged nascent nationalist movements. The Nigerian National Democrat Party was formed in 1923 to represent those excluded from the new representative structures. Its cautious calls for self-government were eclipsed after 1936 by the more radical energies of the Nigerian Youth Movement, whose leaders Benjamin Azikiwe and H.O. Davies had just returned from studying in the USA and at the London School of Economics. Azikiwe would go on to be the last Governor-General and the first president of Nigeria. Just a year after the formation of Kenya as a colony, a young Kenyan civil servant named Harry Thuku formed the Young Kikuyu Association in opposition to the land-grab policies of white settlers. His arrest and deportation in 1922 led to the emergence of the Kikuyu Central Association and a new generation of nationalist leaders, including the man who would become the first president of an independent Kenya, Jomo Kenyatta. The growing claims of Africans to political representation and economic justice helped reconfigure colonial rule, rhetorically at least, to address the dual mandate and serve native as well as British interests.

Colonial Development

There was no better articulation of that ambition than the idea of **colonial development**. Lugard's belief – that Britain could enrich itself and enhance the lives of Africans by developing its colonial economies and societies – resonated. It was especially appealing to Britain's first majority Labour government seeking any way possible to revive a deeply depressed domestic economy. As we saw in the last chapter, the aim of the Colonial Development Act of 1929 was precisely to improve colonial infrastructure like roads, railways and bridges that would enable the cheaper extraction of natural resources and the deeper penetration of British goods. Africa became a veritable laboratory for a host of British academics who hoped to advance knowledge in fields like agricultural science, medicine and anthropology by planning how best to develop colonial Africa. The exhaustive *African Survey*, conducted under the direction of Lord Hailey between 1933 and 1938, testified to that ambition. A former governor of the Punjab and the United Provinces, Hailey's three-volume study reflected the reorientation of British imperial hopes away from unruly India to the continent of Africa. Drawing upon the expertise of many scholars and administrators, the *African Survey* criticized the practice of 'indirect rule' for having failed to deliver. It had failed on all fronts, these experts agreed, having neither addressed the continent's socioeconomic problems, developed its resources nor properly represented its people. In the spirit of planning that gripped 1930s Britain, Hailey's *African Survey* called for the coupling of social with economic development through investments in the infrastructure of public health and education. Further still, he insisted, the development of Africa would entail granting Africans political representation.

The *African Survey*'s modest critique of colonial rule was echoed in the Moyne Commission of Inquiry into the labour unrest that engulfed the Caribbean during the 1930s. As the Great Depression hit, wages fell, unemployment grew, and migration routes were cut off, a series of sustained strikes, **hunger marches** and riots broke out in 1934–5 and 1937–8. These were confined neither to any one island (British Honduras, Guyana, Jamaica, Trinidad, Barbados, St Kitts and St Lucia were all involved) nor to the sugar and banana plantations, for coal, oil and dock workers also mobilized. In Jamaica a general strike during 1938 was so violently repressed that 46 were killed, 429 injured and thousands detained or prosecuted. Radicalized by these events, a new generation of labour and nationalist leaders – like Alexander Bustamante and Norman Manley in Jamaica – displaced the influence of Marcus Garvey's Universal Negro Improvement Association. They called not just for better working conditions but universal suffrage and even the end of colonialism. So damning was the Moyne Commission study of the social, economic and political conditions of Britain's colonies in the Caribbean that only a preliminary report was issued in 1939.

It was only after the outbreak of World War II, when the loyalty of the dependent colonies to the mother country was paramount, that the recommendations of Hailey and Moyne resulted in the Colonial Development and Welfare Act of 1940. This coupling of welfare with economic development represented a significant acknowledgement of the failures of colonial rule and the seriousness of anti-colonial movements. The Act was nonetheless a palliative gesture that committed just £5 million a year for the next decade on initiatives across the British Empire, even if 40 per cent of it went to the

Caribbean. In committing a further £500,000 for research, it cemented the belief that experts were central to the new science of colonial government. Colonial rule was now to be justified in part by its promise of welfare and its design by scientific experts.

The 1940 Act set the pattern for the succession of Colonial Development and Welfare Acts that were passed after the war in 1945, 1949, 1950 and 1959. While considerably more resources were committed to these measures – £120 million was allocated for **colonial development** in 1945, and while that fell to £52 million in 1952–3, it had risen again to £150 million by 1960–1 – their aim was increasingly to fortify the pound by encouraging trade within the **Sterling Area** as much as to defuse anti-colonial movements. They were not successful at either. In 1938 the dependent colonies accounted for 6.9 per cent of Britain's imports and received 10 per cent of her exports. While these proportions rose to 14.3 and 16.4 per cent by 1952, they sank back down to 10.9 and 11.5 per cent by 1965, at which point trade with the EEC accounted for a larger share of British overseas trade. The poor results of development programmes fuelled the scepticism of Britons who felt that colonial development only entailed further austerity at home. The **groundnut scheme** in Tanganyika, designed to grow peanuts that could produce much-needed cooking oil in Britain, was an infamous disaster. The project collapsed five years after its inception in 1946, at a total cost of just under £50 million, thanks to a shortage of equipment, labour and rain. It left a rail line to an area of over 50,000 acres that had been reduced to a dust bowl.

Diasporas and Imperial Citizenship

One measure of the failure of colonial development schemes was the scale of migration across the British Empire. It was not that large-scale migration was anything new for an Empire that had relied first on slavery and then indentured labour. While indentured labour finally come to an end under the eye of the **League of Nations** in 1922, workers continued to migrate in search of work. During the 1920s the contraction of British shipping and overseas trade meant that seamen from across the Empire often found themselves ashore in the 'coloured' quarters of British ports like London, Cardiff and Liverpool, looking for work or return voyages. About 3,000 'coloureds' from the Caribbean, North, West and East Africa, India, Malaya, Singapore and Hong Kong lived in Cardiff's Tiger Bay during the 1930s. These multi-racial communities were subjected to increasing racial hostility, discrimination by trade unions and regulation by the state. The Aliens Orders of 1920 and 1925 compelled all those looking for work to register with the local police or face deportation. The white British women they sometimes married were denied citizenship even if their husbands were subjects of the British Empire. Their 'half-caste' children were objects of concerned fascination by eugenically minded social scientists and charities, as in Muriel Fletcher's *Report on the Colour Problem in Liverpool and Other Ports* (1930) for the Liverpool Association for the Welfare of Half-Caste Children. The League of Coloured People was established in 1931 to protect the civil rights and employment prospects of these multi-racial communities. Their newspaper *Keys* was a particularly important way of connecting the struggles of often isolated communities and forging a sense of a common identity as 'Coloured People', who included those from the Pacific Islands, South and East Asia, the Middle East, Africa and the Caribbean. They critically argued that people of colour from across the British Empire should be considered no less British than those from the white **British world** of the Dominions, who were automatically granted the legal rights of citizenship on arrival in Britain.

The significance of this claim only grew during World War II. Then Britain called upon all its colonial subjects as part of a 'Commonwealth', or family of nations, to defend the motherland, and actively recruited 'coloured' or colonial labour to man merchant ships and work in coalmines. Anti-colonial movements gathered force after 1945. The Pan-African Congress was held in Manchester that year, with George Padmore from Trinidad, Kwame Nkrumah (see Textbox 11.1) from the Gold Coast, Kenyatta from Kenya, and W.E.B. Du Bois from the United States all present. On 18 February 1947 the British government announced its withdrawal from Mandate Palestine, where it had succeeded only in becoming a target of both Palestinian and Jewish attacks. Two days later came the announcement that India would finally become independent. The following February, a protest by ex-servicemen in Accra, protesting their poor treatment since demobilization, was violently stopped when the British head of police shot dead three of the veterans. Five days of rioting followed, as well as the declaration of a state of emergency and the arrest of six leaders of the nationalist party, the United Gold Coast Convention, including Nkrumah. The resulting Watson Commission proposed that an all-African committee draw up a constitution and pave the way for elections with universal suffrage. Britain's repackaging of the Empire as a new 'Commonwealth' in which all nations, independent or not, belonged, hardly helped quell the tide. But by 1948, following the example of the fourth French Republic in 1946, the **British Nationality Act** granted all who lived within that Commonwealth the status of citizens with the right to live, work and vote in Britain.

This Act would quickly serve to demonstrate the abject failures of Britain's colonial rule rather than the cohesion of the Commonwealth. **Colonial development** funds and the political reforms envisaged by the Moyne Commission had done little to revive the Caribbean economy. In Jamaica, where 50,000 men were unemployed, some 500 people boarded the *Empire Windrush* in Kingston on 24 May 1948, Empire Day, to seek work in the mother country. By the mid 1950s, 20,000 people were making this voyage from the Caribbean each year, so that by 1958 125,000 West Indians had made their homes in Britain. Similarly, when the divide-and-rule strategy of communal representation in British India culminated in partition at independence, 21 million Muslims and Hindus were left displaced on the wrong side of the new national border between Pakistan

11.1 **Person: Kwame Nkrumah (1909–1972)**

Kwame Nkrumah was an anti-colonial activist and intellectual who became the first prime minister of Ghana and then, after its independence from Britain in 1957, its first president. Nkrumah was born in a small village in southwest Ghana (then the British Gold Coast colony). The son of a goldsmith and a trader, he was baptised and educated as a Catholic. Like many anti-colonial leaders, Nkrumah studied abroad from 1935, first at Lincoln University near Philadelphia, then the University of Pennsylvania and from 1945 at the London School of Economics. During this time Nkrumah became involved in radical black politics in both the USA and the UK, drafting *Towards Colonial Freedom* (eventually published in 1947) and assisting the veteran West Indian activist George Padmore to organize the Pan-African Congress in Manchester in 1945. In 1947 Nkrumah returned to Ghana to become General Secretary of the newly formed nationalist party, United Gold Coast Convention. Nkrumah was instrumental in building support for the UGCC across the country and both he and the party became increasingly popular after protests and riots convulsed Accra in 1948. The declaration of a state of emergency led to the arrest of Nkrumah and another five leaders of the UGCC. Although the Watson Commission recommended the introduction of constitutional changes including universal

suffrage, Nkrumah broke from the UGCC in 1949 to form his own more radical Convention People's Party that demanded 'self-government NOW'. Two years later, despite being imprisoned for leading a general strike, Nkrumah and the CPP swept to victory in the nation's first democratic election. As prime minister from 1952, Nkrumah oversaw the largely peaceful transition to independence five years later, winning two further elections against his rivals, who saw his socialist politics as undermining their regional and traditional forms of authority. A critic of what he disparagingly called the 'tribalism' that prevented Africans from uniting against colonial powers, once Nkrumah became president in 1957 he made such parties illegal and arrested those he considered to threaten the security of independent Ghana. As both prime minister and president Nkrumah championed a socialist programme of state-directed modernization and economic planning, following the lead of other postcolonial leaders such as Jawaharlal Nehru in India. While Nkrumah's life struggle was securing independence for the Gold Coast, he was a pan-Africanist who thought beyond the limits of the nation-state. Throughout his career he was in dialogue with black activists such as C.L.R. James, W.E.B. Du Bois and Marcus Garvey. In 1958, as the first independent nation in Africa, Ghana hosted the All-African People's Convention. (S.W.)

and India. The ensuing violence and dispossession of land forced some to emigrate: by 1951, 110,000 Indians and 11,000 Pakistanis had arrived in Britain, and a decade later there were 275,000 Indians and 119,000 Pakistanis. Under the terms of the British Nationality Act these subjects of the Commonwealth automatically became British citizens, unlike the 345,000 immigrants displaced by war and by the redrawing of Europe's

Figure 11.2 Kwame Nkrumah

political geography in 1945. Whereas people of colour in Britain had previously been confined to multi-racial neighbourhoods of port towns, they now settled in London, the Midlands and the northwest of England, working in the transport, engineering and textile sectors. Even so, in 1966 just 1.2 per cent of England's population had been born in the Commonwealth. The figure for Britain was even less, at just 0.2 per cent – Scotland and Wales, outside of Cardiff, remained homogeneously white.

As the pace of decolonization accelerated and campaigns to 'Stop the Coloured Invasion' gathered momentum in Britain during the late 1950s and early 1960s, the British government restricted the rights of Commonwealth citizens. The Commonwealth Immigration Act of 1962 revoked the right of all colonial subjects to British citizenship and restricted entry only to those who had a voucher to work, either in a sector where labour was short or when they had been specifically recruited. Although this did reduce the number of migrants from 30,130 a year in 1963 to 22,900 in 1972, it could not rid Britain of the legacies of British colonialism.

Newly independent nations like Tanganyika, Kenya and Uganda also sought to rid themselves of the legacies of colonialism. Two years before independence, only 7 of Tanganyika's 299 senior civil servants were black Africans. By the early 1960s, Britain's former African colonies began programmes of 'Africanizing' government posts. It was not just white Africans who were the targets of these programmes but the sizeable

Figure 11.3 Kenyan Asians at Nairobi Airport, Kenya, trying to get to Britain before the Immigration Act of 1968

population of South Asians encouraged to settle in East Africa. Instead of renouncing their British passports to become African, Kenyan Asians migrated to Britain between 1964 and 1968 (see Figure 11.3). Fearful that this trickle of human misery squeezed out by the collapse of colonialism would lead to a torrent, Britain's immigration laws were further tightened in 1968 to only allow entry to those with a parent or grandparent already resident. However, after the former colonial soldier Idi Amin led a military coup to become president of Uganda in 1971, he accelerated the Africanization policy his predecessor had begun in 1968 by giving the remaining 80,000 Ugandan Asians ninety days to leave the country. While some of these refugees scattered across the Commonwealth (to Canada, India, Australia and Kenya), the vast majority went to Britain, and overwhelmingly to England. Over 150,000 people of South Asian descent – mainly Gujaratis, Sikhs and Muslims – fled East Africa for Britain between 1964 and 1972. As we shall see in the following chapter, their presence aggravated a white racist politics in Britain that disavowed the obligations incurred by imperial rule as it collapsed. Despite this disavowal, the deep, enduring and damaging legacies of British imperialism were made most apparent during decolonization.

For all the heat and hatred that surrounded the migration of Commonwealth citizens, Britons were still encouraged to emigrate to the white Dominions. Indeed, from 1947 the Assisted Passages Scheme provided British migrants with heavily subsidized 'passage' to the Dominions, temporary accommodation on arrival and in some cases generous loans. It was designed to serve the interests of both Britain and the Dominions, enabling the former to strengthen its cultural ties to the British world, and allowing the latter to safeguard the 'whiteness' of their populations while recruiting skilled labour for their rapidly developing economies. Although the largest number of emigrants left Britain for Australia, where they were known as 'ten pound poms', this last wave of white settlement extended across the British world to New Zealand, Canada, Kenya, South Africa and Rhodesia and lasted until 1972. In the first five years of the scheme a million Britons made use of it to emigrate, and even in its final phase between 1964 and 1972, 2 million emigrants left Britain for better lives in the Dominions. Alongside those who chose to emigrate were the children who were given no choice. Although the numbers are disputed, between 4,000 and 10,000 children, usually orphans or those under the care of social services, were dispatched to Australia, New Zealand and Rhodesia from 1945 until the practice was discontinued in 1967. Thus even some Britons endured the costs of the forced migrations of British imperialism. Characteristically, it is only they who received a formal apology for the British government's role in these schemes, from prime minister Gordon Brown in 2010. As we can see from Graph 11.1, the number of emigrants from Britain exceeded the number of immigrants for at least four decades after 1945. Indeed, in that period the total number of immigrants remained smaller than those who emigrated in just the first decade of the twentieth century.

Hot and Cold Wars

Britain's efforts to reinvent its Empire from the 1930s were shaped by geopolitical considerations as much as by anti-colonial movements. The imperial internationalism of the **League of Nations** certainly informed the elaboration of representative political structures and **colonial development** schemes in the 1920s and 1930s. Britain's growing dependence upon the United States – first financially and then militarily – deepened in the era of the world wars. Churchill may have sat alongside Joseph Stalin

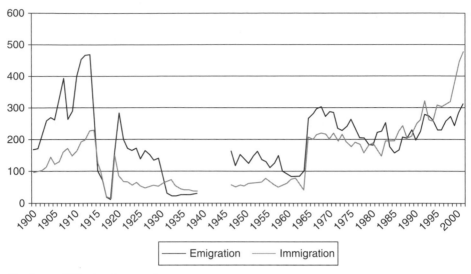

Graph 11.1 UK migration trends, 1900–2000

and Harry Truman at the Potsdam Peace Conference of 1945, and Britain may have secured a place alongside the Soviet Union, the United States, China and France on the United Nations Security Council, but her role as a global superpower was effectively over. Indeed, Britain was gradually reduced to a client state of the newly hegemonic American Empire. The new structures of world governance and economic management – the United Nations, the World Bank, the **International Monetary Fund** and the International Bank for Reconstruction and Development that supported the **Bretton Woods** system – were all located in New York. Britain's new social democracy and even the survival of its Empire relied upon American support. In return Britain would support the United States' political and military ambitions across the globe as it fought both a Cold War against the Soviet Union and frequently hot wars to prevent the spread of communism elsewhere.

A Special Relationship?

The **Cold War** between the United States and the Soviet Union began almost immediately peace had been declared after World War II. It was first evident in Greece's civil war, where Britain sought to maintain a monarchy against a popular communist movement to ensure that Greece, the only non-Soviet-influenced country in the Balkans, remained so. By 1946 Churchill was warning an American audience in Fulton, Missouri, that Britain was already fighting a **Cold War** against the Soviet Union in the Balkans to prevent the spread of their 'iron curtain' of control across central, eastern and southern Europe. It was only when Britain withdrew from supporting the Greek monarchy in 1947 that the United States developed the 'Truman doctrine' and stepped in as the self-declared 'leader of the free world' to contain the spread of global communism. With the protagonists and their ideological battle-lines now clearly drawn, Germany, and Berlin in particular, once more became the battlefield in 1948. Although Berlin, like all Germany, had been divided into four occupied zones by the wartime Allies, Britain, France, the United States and the Soviet Union, the city itself was an island in the Soviet-controlled zone of Germany. When the Soviet Union sought to gain control of the entire city by placing its three rival sectors under a blockade, the Western Allies organized an airlift of supplies. Britain was at the centre of this conflict. The US Air Force operated out of the bases it had established there in 1942, while the air forces of the Dominions all supported Britain's Royal Air Force. The airlift went on for a year and led to the formation of the **North Atlantic Treaty Organization (NATO)** which institutionalized the military alliance between the United States, Canada, Britain and the other western European countries and facilitated the expansion of American military bases in Britain. At the same time Britain, France and the United States combined their zones to assist in the reconstruction of what would become the West German Democratic Republic.

The United States' investment of $14 billion in the reconstruction of western Europe between 1948 and 1952 under the **Marshall Plan** was part of its Cold War with the Soviet Union. Post-war devastation and austerity fuelled the growth of communist parties across western Europe, especially in France and Italy, while socialist or social democratic governments were elected in Britain and Sweden. For the United States, European reconstruction was critical to containing socialism and communism. The aim was to demonstrate the American claim that capitalism, not communism, could best deliver affluence and social security. The Marshall Plan's Organization for European Economic Co-operation, together with the new institutions of global economic governance rooted in the United States – the **Bretton Woods** system, the **International Monetary Fund**, and the World Bank, as well as the United Nations Food and Agriculture Organization sited in Rome – created new ways of assessing the ability of governments to deliver economic growth and prosperity. Only ten countries had national income measures in 1939, but by 1948 46 did and by 1955, when the United Nations standardized these measures to enable international comparisons, 78 were publishing this data. It was also in the early 1950s that statistics for measuring shares of world trade were developed. Above all, it was the calculation of gross domestic product (GDP), invented in 1942, which became the key international index for managing and measuring economic growth. And this data illustrated just how successful American reconstruction and the management of welfare capitalism in Europe were. The annual average growth rate of GDP in western Europe was 4.7 per cent between 1950 and 1973. This was more than double the 2.1 per cent that rapid industrialization in Europe between 1870 and 1913 delivered, and triple that of the 1.4 per cent during the dismal era of the two world wars between 1913 and 1950. Apart from Britain, whose GDP in this period was 2.5 per cent, every western European economy had annual average growth rates of over 3 per cent, while Italy and Germany reached 5 per cent, and France, Finland and Austria exceeded 4 per cent. By any standard this was a spectacular success and for the most part – in Germany, France, Italy, Spain and Britain – it helped ensure that parties of the right had more electoral success than those of the left.

If America's strategy of containing communism in western Europe was largely peaceful and economic, it expected Britain's support when it felt compelled to go to war elsewhere. The United States only agreed to granting Britain's Labour government a further round of loans in 1950 in return for Britain's support of its United Nations-sanctioned war against communist North Korea. Similarly, when in 1964 Britain's next Labour government asked Washington for loans to prevent a further devaluation of the pound, the price was a declaration of support for America's increasingly unpopular war against communism in Vietnam. Britain only devalued the pound in 1967 because the Labour prime minister Harold Wilson refused the American terms for another loan – direct military support in Vietnam – knowing it would split his party. For all the talk of a 'special relationship' between Britain and its former colony, the asymmetries of power were striking. While the United States did not condone the survival of the British Empire, during the 1950s it silently supported violent counter-insurgency measures to suppress anti-colonial movements in Malaya, Kenya and Cyprus for fear that independence would usher in communism.

The **Suez Crisis** of 1956 proved the turning point. Britain's influence in Egypt had endured long after formal independence in 1922, thanks to the installation of a pro-British royal family, considerable investment in the private company that operated the Suez Canal, and the continuing British military occupation of the Suez Canal (81,000 troops were stationed there). In 1952 the popular nationalist leader Gamal Abdel Nasser unseated King Farouk and by 1954 had forced the withdrawal of all British troops from Egypt. As the West insisted it would not sell arms to Egypt, Nasser turned to the Soviets and broke the trade embargo. Fearful of the growing Soviet threat to the security of their oil supplies, Britain and the United States cancelled their funding of Nasser's prize development project, a hydroelectric dam at Aswan on the River Nile. In retaliation Nasser nationalized the Suez Canal prompting Britain and France to ally with Israel in a military offensive aimed at taking control of the Suez Canal and toppling Nasser's government. The success of the military operation met a chorus of condemnation at home and abroad, even from the Commonwealth (see Textbox 11.2). Critically the United States insisted it would no longer back the pound unless Britain and its allies immediately withdrew and allowed United Nations peacekeeping troops to take their place. Within a week they had, and within two months the British prime minister Anthony Eden had resigned. Britain not only lost strategic control of the Suez Canal, the very lifeline of its Empire, but international prestige. When Iraq's Soviet-backed

11.2 Source: Bevan's speech to the House of Commons on the Suez crisis, December 1956

After Britain failed to regain control of the Suez Canal from the Egyptian government, Aneurin Bevan delivered a famous anti-war speech to Parliament on 6 December 1956. A month earlier, his speech condemning the invasion of Suez was the highlight of the largest anti-war rally in Trafalgar Square. Famed for his brilliant oratory, and for not mincing his words, the power of this speech by Bevan lay in its satirizing of the government's misleading claim that it had intended all along to withdraw its troops once a UN force had been established. Once he had made the Conservative Foreign Secretary Selwyn Lloyd look a fool, he turned to his point of principle. Bevan's speech was an argument against military intervention and a tacit support of the claims of national self-determination made by anti-colonial leaders such as Nasser. Bevan argued that

the 'social furniture of modern society is so complicated and fragile that it cannot support the jackboot', and that centuries of British imperial and military dominance had been replaced by a multi-polar constellation of different national interests. The speech can be read as a vision for Britain's changing relationship with the world during this crucial period. It can also be read as testifying to the important if diminishing role of oratory in British politics and its Parliament. The rhythm of the speech, and Bevan's use of the laughter and interruptions of other MPs, is important to its effect. At this time many MPs would have spoken, like Bevan, in regional accents. As with all great speeches, this one is better heard than read. It runs for forty-nine minutes and a recording of it can be accessed on the website supporting this book. (S.W.)

revolution displaced yet another British-backed monarch in 1958, Britain's supply of oil and military presence in the Middle East rested entirely on the colonial port town of Aden. The Suez Crisis dramatically exposed what had been evident in Whitehall since at least 1942 – that Britain could no longer act militarily, or survive financially, without American support. It also marked the moment when the United States realized that Britain's colonial relationships in the Middle East might threaten its own supply of oil and its hopes of containing Soviet influence in the region.

Going Nuclear

By 1950 American support for Britain's post-war welfare state came with an insistence that its imperial warfare state not be neglected so that it could assist the United States in containing global communism. The loss of the Indian army, which had so long played a vital role in the expansion of the British Empire, was a massive blow to Britain's military and strategic presence in the world. Making good this loss required serious investment in Britain's military capacity and the industries that armed its post-colonies and allies. As we can see from Graph 11.2 defence expenditure increased so significantly between

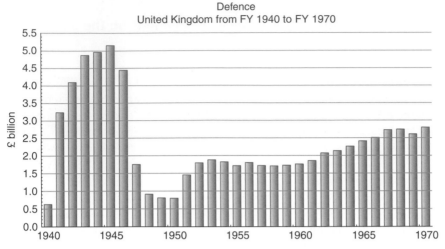

Graph 11.2 Defence expenditure, 1940–1970

1950 and 1953 that it amounted to the largest ever peacetime rearmament, before level-ling off and then rising again throughout the 1960s. These were the decades when the state-sponsored British arms industry grew substantially. This was not simply a product of the growth of the Royal Ordnance or the nationalization of those industries that produced planes, engines, tanks, submarines and ships. A host of private companies – which fed off the state's provision of education, research, expertise and contracts – grew large. Nine of Britain's largest fifty employers in 1955 were defence contractors employ-ing between 21,000 and 75,000 workers. It has been estimated that by the late 1950s the arms industry accounted for £1 billion of assets and employed 1.6 million work-ers. Land Rover, General Electric Company (GEC), Harland and Wolff, Ferranti, Rolls Royce, Vickers and Marconi became household names and their products had a global reach. Such was their importance to the British economy and its overseas trade by the 1970s that many of these companies were themselves nationalized, like the iconic Rolls Royce in 1971 and the creation of British Aerospace in 1977.

It was tragically evident with the bombings of Hiroshima and Nagasaki in August 1945 that nuclear technology would transform warfare. As Britain had led the way in this technology, the United States were content to sign an agreement in 1943 that both countries would share their expertise and have the right to veto each other's use of nuclear weapons against a third party. By 1946 the United States effectively ended that agreement and two years later deployed their B-29 nuclear bombers on their Lakenheath air base (see Textbox 11.3 and Figure 11.4) – a decade before a formal agreement let the British public know of their existence. Even though a good deal of ambiguity surrounded whether the British government possessed a veto over their use, many rightly feared that these B-29 bombers made Britain a target of a pre-emptive

11.3 Place: RAF Lakenheath

RAF Lakenheath is a Royal Air Force base in Suffolk that has been used as an American military base since 1942. Although a makeshift air base had existed at Lakenheath since the First World War, the site was fully developed in 1940, when it was turned into a fully functioning decoy airbase to lure Luftwaffe bombers away from nearby RAF Mildenhall. Although the base was occasionally used during the Second World War, it was during the **Cold War** that Lakenheath came into its own. In 1948, as the Soviet blockade of Berlin accelerated tensions between East and West, President Harry Truman stepped up America's military presence in Europe, creating a permanent, combat-ready fleet of planes and nuclear warheads that were primarily stationed at Lakenheath.

Throughout the 1950s the base acted as a razor-wire-separated American enclave on British soil that even included a high school for children of service personnel. In 1956 a nuclear disaster was narrowly avoided after a B-47 Bomber crashed into a storage depot where three nuclear weapons were stored. Fortunately, the bombs did not yet have their fissile cores installed. Since 1960 the base has been continually operated by the 48th Liberty Wing of the US Air Force and currently houses 4,500 American service personnel supported by 2,500 British civilians. The base has provided planes and personnel for a number of conflicts in recent decades, including the 1986 bombing of Libya, the 2001 invasion of Afghanistan and the 2003 invasion of Iraq. (S.W.)

Figure 11.4 RAF Lakenheath, 1958

nuclear strike by the Soviet Union. This made the development of Britain's own independent nuclear arsenal an urgent priority. While some hoped that the nuclear weapons programme would extend Britain's global influence and triangulate the nuclear race between the USA and USSR, it was justified as the only plausible way of defending Britain in an atomic age. This was the doctrine of deterrence: no one would dare launch a nuclear attack on Britain because it could retaliate in kind. Protection and deterrence for Britain's colonial subjects was not considered when these weapons were tested. The first successful detonation, 'Operation Hurricane', occurred in 1952 on Montebello Islands off Australia's northwest coast, and over the next five years other tests were held in the Australian outback as well as Malden and Christmas (now Kiritimati) Islands in the South Pacific.

The dominant influence of the United States and Britain's nuclear programme were highly controversial. As early as 1947, a small group of young MPs on the left of the Labour Party – Michael Foot, Richard Crossman and Ian Mikardo – published a pamphlet called *Keep Left* urging the Labour government to remain non-aligned in the Cold War. They argued that Britain should act as a democratic socialist 'third force' in world affairs to offset the equally flawed politics of the USSR and USA. Others in the Labour Party, like the hugely influential Aneurin Bevan and the rising star Harold Wilson, grew increasingly disenchanted by the way defence expenditure – and the expensive nuclear programme – became a drain on the welfare state. Both resigned in protest when the terms of American loans in 1950 included the redirection of funds from the welfare to the warfare state. Tirades against the influence of American mass culture and its corrosive effect on the working class, so common between the wars, were reanimated. At a conference on 'The American Threat to British Culture' in 1951, the socialist historian E.P. Thompson decried how 'In place of the great proletarian values revealed in class-solidarity and militancy, we now have, even among sections of our own working-class movement, the values of private living growing up – the private fears and neuroses, the self-interest and timid individualism fostered by pulp magazines and Hollywood films.'

It was the development of Britain's nuclear arsenal that most attracted the ire of the British public. Although the Peace Pledge Union had campaigned against Britain's rearmament and its embrace of nuclear weapons since 1948, it was the launch of the **Campaign for Nuclear Disarmament (CND)** a decade later that captured the public imagination. CND brought together a diverse range of people – pacifists, socialists, religious organizations, women's groups – around a platform of unilateral disarmament. Much like the *Keep Left* pamphlet, they argued that Britain had a moral duty to lead the world, in this case out of Cold War nuclear madness by unilaterally renouncing and decommissioning its nuclear weapons. Such was the success of the campaign that its march from London's Trafalgar Square to the Atomic Weapons Research Station in Aldermaston on Easter weekend grew from 10,000 in 1958 to 100,000 two years later.

CND also attracted the support of a new breed of cultural celebrities cultivated by television and radio, such as the philosopher Bertrand Russell, the historian A.J.P. Taylor, the novelist Doris Lessing, the conductor Benjamin Britten and the sculptor Henry Moore. By 1960, when opinion polls were indicating that 61 per cent of the public supported unilateral disarmament, the Labour Party formally adopted it as a policy.

Decolonization

In the two decades after 1947 the Third British Empire collapsed. Although, as we have already seen, anti-colonial nationalism had prospered across the British Empire in the 1920s and 1930s, few expected that the end would come so fast. The speed of the collapse hardly supports the contention that Britain planned and executed a peaceful and pragmatic withdrawal from its Empire. Quite the opposite was the case: the pressure of nationalist revolt drove decolonization. It was resisted – often with violent repression – by Britain, and unfolded at such a pace that the scars of imperialism continued to generate conflict in newly independent countries. Without an empire, Britons reinvented their old imperial networks and organizations to articulate a new vision of Britain's international leadership through the humanitarian work of non-governmental organizations (NGOs). Economically they were forced to turn to Europe for salvation. Belatedly, and decidedly ambivalently, Britain joined the **European Economic Community** in 1973.

The Empire may have come to Britain's rescue during the Second World War but the conflict also highlighted its fragility and catalysed anti-colonial movements. Even in Britain, Scottish and Welsh nationalists refused to support the war effort and were imprisoned as conscientious objectors. Ireland remained pointedly neutral. In Australia eyebrows were raised at Britain's failure to defend the country from Japan after the fall of Singapore in February 1942. That loss decisively challenged the notion, held by many colonial subjects, that it was impossible to defeat the mighty British Empire. Subhas Chandra Bose, the ex-leader of the **Indian National Congress** (INC), who had embraced armed rebellion, elicited German and Japanese support to establish an Indian National Army that attracted 30,000 volunteers to rid 'Free India' (*Azad Hind*) of British rule.

If the INC still embraced non-violence, it was nonetheless outraged that the British Viceroy declared war on India's behalf without consulting their representatives elected under the Government of India Act passed just four years earlier. Despite its promise to deliver independence for India when the war was won, the British government failed to win the support of the INC during World War II. This promise only prompted the Muslim League to insist on the creation of a separate Muslim homeland, Pakistan. Meanwhile the INC enumerated how the defence of Britain came at India's cost. It was not just the cost of the lives of Indian soldiers but the expense of their deployment and the debts incurred by Britain in importing vital supplies from India for which it refused to pay. In 1945 Britain acknowledged that its debt to India in Sterling reserves was £1.5 billion, but J.C. Kumarapa, the Indian nationalist economist, calculated that the total costs were actually 5,700 million rupees.

Six months after the fall of Singapore, the INC escalated its protests with the 'Quit India' campaign and was promptly outlawed and its leaders arrested. As attacks – both violent and non-violent – on government property (railway stations, post offices and police stations were the favoured targets) broke out across India, the colonial state made a staggering 60,000 arrests. The arch-imperialist Churchill was unwavering and declared: 'I have not become the King's First Minister in order to preside over the liquidation of the British Empire.' As INC leaders remained incarcerated for the rest of the war, it was the Bengal Famine of 1943 that provided the final nail in the coffin of colonial rule. The Japanese invasion of Burma after the fall of Singapore disrupted the supply chains of rice for India, and when the colonial government failed to provide adequate relief or transport sufficient food reserves, 3 million people were killed in one of the worst famines of the twentieth century. It was inconceivable that the British government would have presided over a famine that killed even a fraction of its own citizens.

When independence came to India in 1947, it came violently and quickly. As the INC and the Muslim League both cemented their rival positions in the provincial elections of 1945 and 1946, the colonial government was unable to broker an agreement between them over the nature of an independent state. 'Communal' tensions escalated between Hindus, Sikhs and Muslims and culminated in widespread violence in August 1946. A year later the British government and the INC accepted a solution that both had refused to countenance just months earlier: the partition of the country, and of the two northern provinces of Punjab and Bengal, to create two independent states of India and Pakistan. When the Union Jack was finally lowered – with the British Viceroy Lord Mountbatten, Queen Victoria's great grandson, watching – the borders of the two countries were still ill-defined. At least 15 million people were stuck with little warning on the wrong side of fuzzy borders. With no apparatus really available to the new countries to police partition, Hindus, Sikhs and Muslims attacked each other, killing an estimated 500,000 people.

In the scramble of decolonization, partition, first used in Ireland in 1922, was significantly not used in Palestine. In Palestine violence between Arabs and Jews escalated after 1945 as Zionists, emboldened by the demands of Jewish refugees in Europe for a homeland, and a United Nations resolution for a two-state solution, escalated their military campaign. Unable to suppress Zionism, keep the peace or reconcile the competing demands of Arabs and Jews, Britain simply resigned its mandate and withdrew from Palestine – just a month after the hasty retreat from the carnage of India and Pakistan.

The ensuing battle between Jews and Arabs culminated in a Zionist victory and the declaration of the state of Israel in Palestine in May 1948. Similarly, in both Nigeria and Cyprus, Britain's inability to resolve 'communal' tensions that they had often helped to propagate as a strategy of colonial rule, resulted in deadly civil wars.

Where Britain felt that its presence was worth defending, and when it had the military capacity and American backing to succeed, it did so to a startling degree. Between 1945 and 1967 the British government embarked on at least ten counter-insurgency campaigns. In recent decades, as the United States has been engaged in wars in Iraq and Afghanistan, its strategists have looked back to the methods of counter-insurgency developed by Britain in these years as a model. The idea of a British model probably endows greater coherence to what were often ad hoc methods that were developed pragmatically according to the forces available on the ground and understandings of racial difference (Zionists were thus treated very differently to the Malay Chinese). Yet there were common features to some of these campaigns: after a declaration of a state of emergency, appeals to the 'hearts and minds' of local populations were balanced with extreme military violence and the forced detention of civilians and combatants, invariably on racial or ethnic lines, in camps where they could be tortured for 'intelligence' and 're-educated'. These camps, the records of which the British government has spent decades hiding, have been compared to Stalin's Soviet gulag. Some elements of these tactics, especially those concerning 're-education' programmes, had been trialled in the 'denazification' of German prisoners of war and those living in the British zone of occupied Germany between 1945 and 1948.

Malaya and Kenya were the sites of the two largest and deadliest of these campaigns. In Malaya, the clumsy restoration of British rule following the defeat of Japan, and the decline of commodity prices for rubber and tin, only served to exacerbate poverty, labour unrest and growing support for the Malayan Communist Party (MCP). When a sustained series of strikes (300 in 1947 alone) were met with violence, arrests and deportations, the conflict quickly escalated and culminated in the murder of three European plantation managers in June 1948. The resulting 'Emergency' pitted the guerrilla tactics of the Malayan Races Liberation Army (MRLA) based in inaccessible 'jungle' bases against the full force of the imperial state. While the MRLA made targets of colonial resource extraction, attacking transport infrastructure as well as rubber plantations and tin mines, the imperial state made targets of the ethnic Chinese, whom they held largely responsible for supporting the MRLA's communist-inspired 'Anti-British War of National Liberation'. The tactics were ugly and quickly blurred the lines between civilians and combatants. Food supplies to rural areas were cut off or booby-trapped, violence and torture were used to gain intelligence, the bodies of killed insurgents were mutilated and publicly displayed, aerial bombardment and 'jungle' patrols on foot wiped out whole villages, and (in a nod to the concentration camps of the **South African War**) a million civilians (all ethnic Chinese) were forcibly relocated into 'New Villages'. Such was the scale of operations that Britain called on the support of troops from Australia, Rhodesia and Fiji. Although the Federation of Malaya received independence in 1957, the war continued until 1960 when the MRLA was finally defeated. It cost 20,000 people their lives, and $1.2 billion, much of which was charged to Malaya itself.

In post-war Kenya British corporations such as Unilever, Imperial Chemical Industries and Shell, white settlers who often owned huge estates of fertile land, and British servicemen offered loans and land to emigrate, had all benefited from the investment of colonial development funds. In marked contrast, black Kenyans, 100,000 of whom had fought to defend the British Empire during World War II, were impoverished and radicalized. This was especially the case for those Kikuyu who had been increasingly displaced from their land during the 1920s and 1930s and either forced to work as contract labour on British plantations or migrate to Nairobi. Although the Kenyan African Union, led by Kenyatta from 1947, accelerated their non-violent campaign for independence, it was the **Mau Mau**, or Land and Freedom Army, who began attacking and killing white settlers. In 1952 the colonial government declared a state of emergency, arrested nationalist leaders like Kenyatta, and developed a hugely violent counter-insurgency campaign to defeat what they thought was a primitive and irrational enemy under the influence of global communism. The centre-piece of this campaign, which lasted until 1960, was less the military tactics that killed 20,000 people suspected to be Mau Mau than the 800 concentration camps where an estimated 160,000–320,000 Kikuyu civilians were detained without trial as potential insurgents (see Figure 11.5). Subjected to torture, rape, forced labour, starvation rations and re-education programmes, tens of thousands died in these camps.

Despite the deliberate suppression of information about these counter-insurgency campaigns, some news of them filtered back to Britain. Fenner Brockway, the pacifist, socialist and long-time anti-colonial campaigner, established the Movement for Colonial Freedom (MCF) in 1954 to provide a counter-weight to the Labour Party's refusal to support independence movements. MCF immediately attracted the support of young MPs on the left of the party – like Tony Benn, Barbara Castle and Harold Wilson – eager to distance Britain both from the violence of colonialism and from both sides in the Cold War. Brockway was first to protest about the conduct of war in Malaya in 1956 when he received pictures of Royal Marines displaying the decapitated heads of Malayan Chinese. That same year, MCF published *The Truth About Kenya: An Eyewitness Report* by a former camp officer exposing conditions in the camps. Two years later, when news broke that eleven detainees had been beaten to death in the infamous Hola Camp, Barbara Castle demanded explanations in the House of Commons. The government's defence, that a violent revolt required violent responses, did not even convince some of its own supporters. One of them, **Enoch Powell**, argued that it was no longer possible to say 'We will have African standards in Africa, Asian standards

Figure 11.5 Detaining Kikuyu as insurgents, *c.*1954

in Asia and perhaps British standards here at home.' 'The Tory party', Powell insisted, 'must be cured of the British Empire.'

It was a Conservative prime minister, Harold Macmillan (who had succeeded Anthony Eden after the Suez debacle), who in 1960 first signalled Britain's hasty retreat from Africa. Twelve months after France and Belgium had announced that they planned to withdraw from some of their African colonies, Macmillan pointedly ended a month-long tour of British Africa with a speech to the Parliament of apartheid South Africa. 'The wind of change is blowing through this continent', he told them, 'and whether we like it or not, this growth of national consciousness is a political fact. We must all accept it.' The political and financial cost of defending colonial rule was now a price the British government was no longer willing or able to pay. Even then, however, it was unimaginable that five years later Rhodesia, a British colony governed by white settlers, would declare independence from Britain over the refusal of Harold Wilson's Labour government to condone white minority rule. Despite maintaining still lucrative relations with apartheid South Africa, it was no longer possible for the British government to support white rule in Africa while seeking to incorporate newly independent African states into the Commonwealth. When yet another 'Emergency', this time in Aden, escalated out of control after the Six Days' War between Israel and the Arab states, Wilson resolved that his government would end its counter-insurgency campaign to maintain Britain's military presence there. There was no one decisive moment when the British Empire came to an end but the pace of decolonization unquestionably accelerated in the decade or so after Suez, as we can see from Map 11.1. Ghana and Malaya became independent in 1957, Nigeria and Cyprus in 1960, Sierra Leone, Kuwait and Tanganyika in 1961, Jamaica, Trinidad and Uganda in 1962, Kenya and Singapore in 1963, Malawi and Zambia in 1964, Gambia and the Maldives in 1965, Barbados, Botswana, Guyana and Lesotho in 1966, Yemen in 1967, Mauritius and Swaziland in 1968. Decolonization continued over the next three decades but it remained largely confined to smaller territories and island states in the Caribbean, Pacific and Middle East.

Imperial Internationalism Reborn

European decolonization in the shadow of the **Cold War** was, then, a hurried, messy and violent business. Certainly, violence and war was as endemic to the ending of British imperialism as it was to the French Empire in Vietnam and Algeria. Yet as Britons lost an Empire, they carved out new ways of acting in the world as its moral guardian – even when their claims to do so rested on old imperial experience and expertise. During the 1950s both the Movement for Colonial Freedom and the Campaign for Nuclear Disarmament articulated a new understanding of Britain's place in the world based around ethics not self-interest. Both organizations saw it as Britain's duty to provide moral leadership that would set an example by refusing the polarization of the world according to the politics of the **Cold War**. By the late 1950s and early 1960s they were joined by other newly established organizations, like the Anti-Apartheid Movement (1959), the World Wide Fund for Nature (1961) and Amnesty International(1961), concerned to mobilize Britons in the interests of a broader set of international issues that often ironically arose from the legacies of British or European colonialism.

The Anti-Apartheid Movement began encouraging Britons to help end apartheid by boycotting South African goods, then quickly moved to organize internationally. By 1961 it had succeeded in securing South Africa's exclusion from the Commonwealth (1961), had an anti-apartheid resolution passed at the United Nations (1962) and ensured the country's exclusion from the Olympic Games (1964). As the pace of decolonization quickened, some feared that Africa's unique flora and fauna would be at greater risk under African governments with supposedly less incentive or knowledge of how to preserve them than their former colonial masters. Max Nicholson and Julian Huxley, founding members of Political and Economic Planning back in the 1930s, came back together to help launch a World Wide Fund for Nature to help conserve endangered species. Its manifesto proclaimed itself to be 'An International Declaration' and assumed that the preservation of Africa's wildlife was a global trust, for it was far too important to be left to Africans. At times the rhetoric even appeared to value the

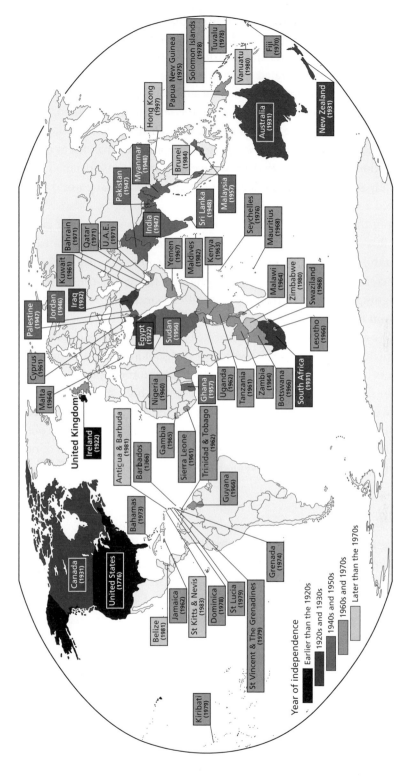

Map 11.1 Map of decolonization, 1776–1983

Papua New Guinea (1975)
Solomon Islands (1978)
Tuvalu (1978)
Vanuatu (1980)
Fiji (1970)
Hong Kong (1997)
Australia (1931)
New Zealand (1931)
Myanmar (1948)
Brunei (1984)
Pakistan (1947)
Malaysia (1957)
India (1947)
Sri Lanka (1948)
Bahrain (1971)
Qatar (1971)
U.A.E. (1971)
Yemen (1967)
Maldives (1982)
Kenya (1963)
Seychelles (1976)
Mauritius (1968)
Kuwait (1961)
Jordan (1946)
Iraq (1932)
Palestine (1947)
Malawi (1964)
Zimbabwe (1980)
Swaziland (1968)
Cyprus (1961)
Egypt (1922)
Sudan (1956)
Lesotho (1966)
Malta (1964)
Uganda (1962)
Tanzania (1961)
Zambia (1964)
Botswana (1966)
South Africa (1931)
United Kingdom
Ireland (1922)
Nigeria (1960)
Ghana (1957)
Anticua & Barbuda (1981)
Barbados (1366)
Gambia (1965)
Sierra Leone (1961)
Trinidad & Tobago (1962)
Bahamas (1973)
Guyana (1966)
Canada (1931)
United States (1776)
Grenada (1974)
Belize (1981)
Jamaica (1962)
St Kitts & Nevis (1983)
Dominica (1978)
St Lucia (1979)
St Vincent & The Grenadines (1979)
Kiribati (1979)

Year of independence

Earlier than the 1920s
1920s and 1930s
1940s and 1950s
1960s and 1970s
Later than the 1970s

welfare of African wildlife over Africans. What would later come to be called human rights were central to the project of Amnesty International. In 1961 a London lawyer, Peter Benenson, wrote a newspaper article called 'The Forgotten Prisoners' outlining the plight of those incarcerated for their political or religious views This was, he was at pains to point out, a global phenomenon. In his book *Persecution*, published later that year, his cases were drawn from Europe, the United States, China, the Soviet Union, the Philippines, Portugese Angola and South Africa. Benenson, like those who began to organize Amnesty's local network of groups, pointedly refused to include nationalist leaders who had advocated the use of violence among those deemed prisoners of conscience. By 1969 Amnesty claimed 15,000 members across the world and a decade later it reached 200,000.

Each of these groups incited Britons to embrace a new form of global citizenship. In part this was because they addressed issues that they believed transcended national borders and for which a national political mobilization was insufficient. Indeed, Britons were increasingly informed about the plight of those suffering overseas by a host of campaigning non-governmental organizations operating internationally to provide relief from famines and other disasters. Some of these, like Save the Children, Oxfam and War on Want, had been established earlier but became more visible in the 1960s. Often hiring ex-colonial officers with knowledge of local conditions, a new generation of leaders became both more active in the field and more present in Britain, not least by establishing their own charity stores on British high streets. From the 1970s international environmental groups like Friends of the Earth (1971) and Greenpeace (1977) began to establish offices in Britain. Britain may have lost its Empire but some Britons continued to believe that they could and should influence the lives of others overseas. The civilizing mission was reinvented as the task of a new type of global citizen.

Towards Europe

In 1943 **Jan Smuts**, the elder statesman and architect of the idea of a British Commonwealth, laid out his vision of Britain's place in the post-war international order to the Empire Parliamentary Association in London. To take its place alongside the United States and the Soviet Union as a global superpower, he suggested, Britain would need to build the 'the next world-wide British system'. To do so, he thought they would need to draw not just on the Commonwealth but on a closer union with the democracies of western Europe. At the end of the war, this vision of Britain as part of a united Europe became increasingly influential. It informed the project of European reconstruction, which in Europe was widely seen as essential to building the prosperity and supranational solidarity that would make war impossible. In 1946 even Winston Churchill declared that only 'a United States of Europe' could rebuild prosperity on the continent. Indeed, Britain, or rather Attlee's Foreign Secretary, Ernest Bevin, helped persuade the United States of the need to invest in Europe's reconstruction and prosperity to arrest the spread of communism. The **Marshall Plan** was predicated on building integration by only providing funds to those countries who joined its Organization for European Economic Cooperation. Britain negotiated an exception to this rule, insisting that the Sterling Area and its continuing imperial influence made it, in the words of Bevin, 'not simply a Luxembourg'. Thus while both post-war Labour and Conservative governments hoped a united Europe would serve as a bulwark against the increasingly bipolar Cold War world, they determined to remain aloof from it.

Instead, it was the French who took the lead in developing the **European Coal and Steel Community** (ECSC) in 1951. The six countries that joined the ECSC (France, West Germany, Italy, the Netherlands, Belgium and Luxembourg) handed over control of these industries to a new supranational body that would both manage their growth and ensure that no nation could use their supplies for military purposes. The success of this venture seeded further plans for integration among 'the Six' that resulted in the Treaty of Rome establishing the **European Economic Community** in 1957. Britain, which became loosely 'associated' with the ECSC in 1955, had initially joined these negotiations but promptly withdrew when faced with ceding sovereignty to a body that would damage its trading relationships within the **Sterling Area**. Instead, Britain scrambled to get all those countries that had received Marshall aid but were not part of 'the Six' – Austria, Britain, Denmark, Ireland, Norway, Portugal and Sweden – to form a European Free Trade Area in 1959. By this time, as the pace of decolonization quickened, the political and economic calculations began to change. Britain's GDP per capita fell to the lowest in Europe between 1952 and 1965, its balance of payments worsened, and, as we can see from Table 11.1, its trade with Europe began to exceed that with the Commonwealth by the early 1960s.

Table 11.1 UK trade by area, 1950–1979 (percentage)

Area	1950	1960	1970	1979
Imports				
Europe	25	30	34	62
United States	8	12	13	10
Commonwealth	40	31	23	11
Exports				
Europe	25	29	41	56
United States	5	9	12	10
Commonwealth	38	34	20	12

Just two years after the creation of the European Free Trade Area, and against the wishes of the vast majority of his own party as well as the leadership of the Labour Party, the Conservative prime minister Harold Macmillan opened negotiations in preparation for Britain's application to join the EEC in 1963. Although most Britons assumed that the application would be successful (surely the EEC could not spurn a country of Britain's still considerable economic might), it was not. Four years later, this time under the Labour government of Harold Wilson, Britain applied again and was once more humiliatingly denied membership. Although the French president Charles de Gaulle was the leading sceptic, the issue was not French Anglophobia. Two things deeply concerned Europeans. The first was the United States' growing influence over Britain, for quite apart from its nuclear presence, American investment in the UK doubled from $542 million to $1.6 billion during the 1950s. The second was the continuing strength of Britain's economic ties to its Commonwealth through the Sterling Area, not least the debt it owed in Sterling balances. It was after the collapse of the Sterling Area, between the devaluation of the pound in 1967 and the floating of Sterling in 1972 amidst the reconfiguration of the global economy ushered in by the Oil Crisis, that Britain finally secured entry to the EEC in 1973. Economically this accelerated the growth of British trade with the continent. Arguably decimalization of the currency, the introduction of metric weights and measures alongside the old imperial scales, and even an aborted attempt to construct a Channel tunnel, signalled a larger cultural shift in Britain's view of its place in the world. The politics of this shift were tortuous, for both political parties were deeply divided. When, in order to avoid a split in his party and government, Harold Wilson held Britain's first ever referendum on whether Britain should stay within the EEC in 1975, more than two thirds of the electorate voted in favour. Britons may have only become Europeans reluctantly, but they were Europeans nonetheless.

'Goodbye Britain'

It was, however, quickly apparent that being part of the EEC was not a sufficient replacement for the two props – American loans and the Sterling Area – that had helped sustain the value of the pound and Britain's social democratic economy in the post-war period. The decisive turning point was 1967. As Britain's balance of payments steadily worsened during the 1960s, the pound came under increasing pressure, forcing Wilson's Labour government to repeatedly – in 1964 and 1967 – ask the United States for loans to help shore up its reserves. In 1967, when Wilson was no longer willing or able to pay the price of the loan – Britain's military support for the Vietnam War – he was forced to devalue the pound by 14 per cent to $2.40. This effectively split the Sterling Area. For the first time many governments within it, outraged they were not consulted about devaluation, simply refused to follow suit and devalue their currency. Although the Basel Agreement of 1968 sought to patch up these differences, the central banks of the Dominions and newly independent members of the Commonwealth increasingly held US dollars and other currencies rather than sterling as their reserves. With the USA struggling to cut its own growing trade deficit, and with the costs of the Vietnam War escalating, the dollar was under increasing pressure as gold reserves flocked to the increasingly stronger currencies of the Japanese yen and German Deutschmark. Gradually between 1971 and 1973, as the dollar was taken off the **gold standard**, the key mechanism for managing exchange rates within the **Bretton Woods** system collapsed.

As oil, like many commodities, was priced in dollars, its devaluation had major implications for the Organization of Petroleum Exporting Countries (OPEC) in the Middle East. Yet, while other commodities rose steeply in the early 1970s, it was only when America supported Israel in the Yom Kippur War against Syria and Egypt during the summer of 1973, that the Arab member states of OPEC imposed an embargo of exports to the USA and a 70 per cent rise in the price of oil. The ensuing 'Oil Crisis' had a dramatic effect on the world economy. Inflation soared, stock markets crashed, and as governments adopted deflationary measures and sought to protect the values of their now floating currencies, unemployment rose to levels unprecedented in the post-war period. The curse of 'stagflation' (stagnant growth and rising inflation) hit almost all industrialized countries. In Britain, Edward Heath's Conservative government unsuccessfully sought to contain the crisis by introducing an 'incomes policy' that capped wages in an effort to contain inflation and reduce labour costs to make British exports more competitive. The resulting tide of industrial unrest culminated with the National Union of Miners declaring a three-day week that ran down coal supplies and caused widespread power blackouts. This economic crisis quickly became a political crisis as Heath called an election asking voters to decide 'Who runs the country?' – the trade unions or the elected government. He lost. Once again, a new Labour government faced an economic blizzard. Despite deflationary policies, inflation, unemployment, and the budget deficit failed to fall. That pleased neither the trade unions nor the financial markets and the value of the pound continued to fall. In April 1976 the *Wall Street Journal*'s headline was 'Goodbye Britain'. In November the Labour government turned to the **International Monetary Fund** to help restore international confidence and stop the collapse of the pound. It was handed the bitter pill of a **structural adjustment** programme. In return for a loan of £2.3 billion, it was forced to make £2.5 billion worth of cuts to public expenditure (amounting to 20 per cent), as well as to sell off £500 million of shares in British Petroleum. This almost split the Labour Party, as Macdonald's austerity measures had in 1931. It marked a decisive turning point and painfully illustrated just how dependent Britain's social democracy had been on its changing economic position in the world and global forces that were often beyond its control.

Conclusion

British social democracy was neither solely made nor solely sustained in Britain. It was forged in moments of global crisis. First, during the Great Depression of the 1930s, liberal political economy was finally abandoned in favour of an imperial system of protection, the **Sterling Area** and the cautious use of economic planning and development. Second, during World War II, the British government needed to mobilize its colonial allies and became reliant upon America's financial and military resources. And finally, during the **Cold War**, America helped bankroll Britain's reconstruction and permitted its economic dependence upon the Sterling Area in return for the utilization of its Empire in containing the spread of global communism. Most of all, the post-war institutions of global economic management located in the United States undergirded the entire system of Western welfare capitalism and ensured that governments came to be judged by their ability to manage economic growth and provide social security. When colonial nationalists forced Britain to decolonize, she turned to Europe. Yet it was only in 1973, when the entire international system of managing Western welfare capitalism had begun to fall apart, that Britain became part of the **European Economic Community**. The global economic turmoil that followed the Oil Crisis proved the final undoing of Britain's social democratic political economy and in 1976 the **International Monetary Fund** effectively helped usher in new systems of economic management. Britain's social democracy had a global history it could not escape.

FURTHER READING

Traditionally, histories of social democracy and of Britain's changing place in the world have been told separately. Indeed, very often histories of the late British Empire and decolonization have also been kept apart from accounts of the **Cold War** and European integration. The task of the reader, then, is to think across disparate literatures.

Only recently have historians become interested in the final stages of the British Empire. A good overview of the changing political economy of British imperialism after 1931 is P.J. Cain and A.G. Hopkins, *British Imperialism: Crisis and Deconstruction 1914–1990* (London, 1993). Philippa Levine's *The British Empire: Sunrise to Sunset* (Harlow, 2007) and John Darwin's *The Empire Project: The Rise and Fall of the British World System, 1830–1970* (Cambridge, 2009) usefully complement each other as general overviews with different foci and interests. *The Oxford History of the British Empire*, vol. IV: *The Twentieth Century* (Oxford, 1999), edited by Judith M. Brown and William Roger Louis, is also a useful resource. For the economics of late imperialism it is necessary to consult Stephen Constantine, *The Making of British Colonial Development Policy 1914–1940* (London, 1984), Joseph Hodge, *Triumph of the Expert: Agrarian Doctrines of Development and the Legacies of British Colonialism* (Athens, Ohio, 2007), and Catherine Schenk, *The Decline of Sterling: Managing the Retreat of an International Currency 1945–1992* (Cambridge, 2010). For helpful discussions of the reconfiguration of

British Empire under the influence of the League of Nations and imperial internationalism, see Mark Mazower, *No Enchanted Place: The End of Empire and the Ideological Origins of the United Nations* (Princeton, 2009), Susan Pedersen, *The Guardians. The League of Nations and the Crisis of Empire* (New York, 2015); Mrinalini Sinha, *Specters of Mother India: The Global Restructuring of an Empire* (Durham, NC, 2006). Like Sinha, Mark Matera's *Black London. The Imperial Metropolis and Decolonization in the Twentieth Century* (Berkeley, 2015) recovers anti-colonial uses of internationalism.

On migrations, voluntary and forced, across the predominantly white British world, see Marjory Harper and Stephen Constantine, *Migration and Empire* (Oxford, 2010) and Ellen Boucher, *Empire's Children: Child Emigration, Welfare and the Decline of the British World, 1869–1967* (Cambridge, 2014). For the migrations generated by imperial divisions of labour, communalism and partition, see Laura Tabili, *'We Ask for British Justice': Workers and Racial Difference in Late Imperial Britain* (Ithaca, NY, 1994), Mike and Trevor Phillips, *Windrush: The Irresistible Rise of Multicultural Britain* (London, 1998), Jacqueline Nassy Brown, *Dropping Anchor, Setting Sail: Geographies of Race in Black Liverpool* (Princeton, 2005), Sanya Aiyar, *Indians in Kenya: The Politics of Diaspora* (Cambridge, Mass., 2015), and Spencer Mawby, *Ordering Independence: The End of Empire in the Anglophone Caribbean, 1947–1969* (New York, 2013).

Too much of the literature on decolonization continues to be written from a British perspective. The best of this work acknowledges both the frailty of British rule and its continuing traction. For good examples, see W.R. Louis and R. Robinson, 'The Imperialism of Decolonization', *Journal of Imperial and Commonwealth History*, 24/3 (1996), 345–63, David French, *The British Way in Counter-Insurgency, 1945–1967* (Oxford, 2011), and Sarah Stockwell, *The Business of Decolonization: British Business Strategies in the Gold Coast* (Oxford, 2000). The violence of late colonial rule and decolonization is evident in Bridget Brereton and Kevin Yelvington, *The Colonial Caribbean in Transition* (Kingston, 1999), and Gyan Pandey, *Remembering Partition: Violence, Nationalism and History in India* (Cambridge, 2001), and has been movingly captured by Caroline Elkins in *Imperial Reckoning: The Untold Story of Britain's Gulag in Kenya* (New York, 2005). For a rare comparative treatment of decolonization, see Martin Shipway, *Decolonization and Its Impact: A Comparative Approach to the End of Colonial Empires* (Oxford, 2008).

The shadow of the **Cold War** upon Britain and the late British Empire has received little attention. Alan Milward's *The Reconstruction of Western Europe, 1945–51* (London, 1984) remains the best guide to the United States' role in the reconstruction of the European economy. Victoria de Grazia's *Irresistible Empire: America's Advance Through Twentieth-Century Europe* (Cambridge, Mass., 2005) addresses the beguiling hold of American-fuelled prosperity on the European mind. The resistance to American military presence, and Britain's nuclear arms race, are chronicled in Holger Nehring's *Politics of Security: The British and West German Protests Against Nuclear Weapons and the Early Cold War, 1945–1970* (Oxford, 2013).

Alan Milward's *The Rise and Fall of a National Strategy, 1945–1963* (London, 2012) charts Britain's slow reorientation towards Europe. Matthew Hilton et al., *The Politics of Expertise: How NGOs Shaped Modern Britain* (Oxford, 2013), is the most comprehensive account of the proliferation of NGOs and their increasingly international orientation. The political and economic 'crises' of the 1970s in its global and British manifestations are usefully explored in Niall Ferguson et al. (eds.), *The Shock of the Global: The 1970s in Perspective* (Cambridge, Mass., 2010), and Andy Beckett, *When the Lights Went Out: Britain in the Seventies* (London, 2009).

12 The Ends of Social Democracy

Introduction

Those Britons born in 1945 who came of age in the political upheavals that engulfed much of Europe and the Americas in 1968 would have been forgiven for thinking that social democracy was here to stay. They lived in a country that had never been as prosperous, where affluence was more evenly spread and where people were healthier, better housed and better educated than ever before. My parents' generation, born in the 1930s, could raise a family on a single breadwinner's wage in a job that lasted a lifetime and provided a generous pension that sustained a lengthy retirement. They were able to send their children to school and even university, not to mention doctors and dentists, for free. In short, like the collapse of the Soviet Union, everything seemed forever, until it was no more. Unlike the Soviet Union, the end of social democracy in Britain did not come suddenly with the **International Monetary Fund**'s **structural adjustment** programme in 1976. Instead, like coastlines, it was gradually eroded. In some places, that erosion was rapid, but in other areas, as with rocky headlands, it took longer. In exploring when and how social democracy came to an end, this chapter will also seek to explain why, despite its substantial achievements, its life was so brief.

Parts of the answer to that question lie in the previous chapters. We have already seen how social democracy was always compromised by a series of internal and external constraints. It grew around rather than eradicated the influence and persistent wealth of Britain's **ancien regime**. A system developed to generate economic growth and to spread its benefits more equitably among the population was designed and managed by a technocratic class of experts who increasingly became a target for criticism. The plans of these experts were rarely realized, for fighting two world wars had left Britain dependent on American loans and American **Cold War** ambitions. Rather than the bright, modernist, future envisioned in the Festival of Britain, much of the social democratic infrastructure of schools, hospitals and housing stock remained Victorian. This type of social democracy by gaslight would have sufficed for those colonial subjects struggling for independence, having exposed the empty promises of late imperialism to deliver colonial development and welfare. Even in Britain, a system that promised social security for all privileged the labour of white men over those of married women who were expected to raise children and care for men at home without pay. Indeed, the welfare state sought to substantiate a white, heterosexual norm.

These limitations and contradictions were increasingly criticised during the 1950s and 1960s. Different groups complained either that social democracy had not gone far enough and was not socially democratic enough, or had gone too far and strayed from the liberal political economy that had made Britain Great. Those who felt ignored, marginalized or reviled by social democracy – people of colour, Catholics in Northern Ireland, second wave feminists, as well as gays and lesbians – began to organize and to challenge the silent assumptions of its claim to universality. Young people were often a key element of these movements. As advertisers sought to tap the disposable income of young unmarried people in work, new forms of pop music, comedy, novels and theatre were aimed at the 'youth' market. These new cultural forms provided outlets for the anger of 'youth' at institutions – from the family to universities and the **Church of England** – that claimed the right to govern their actions. For some, these political and cultural revolts were symptomatic of a broader national decline as Britain lost its Empire, slipped down the list of the largest economies, faced a moral crisis as Britons stopped going to church, and confronted the potential break-up of the Union as Scotland, Wales and Catholics in Northern Ireland all sought devolution. Out of this critique emerged both a racist English nationalism and a 'new right' determined to restore authority, protect the Union, and correct the balance between the state and the market.

TIMELINE

1925	Plaid Cymru
1934	Scottish National Party
1938	National Marriage Guidance Council
1947	The Clapham Commission Kenneth Little, *Negroes in Britain*
1949	Simone de Beauvoir, *The Second Sex*
1956	John Osborne, *Look Back in Anger*
1957	Wolfenden Report
1958	Indian Workers' Association 'Race Riots' in Notting Hill and Nottingham West Indian Standing Committee
1960	Legalization of gambling Birmingham Immigration Control Association The Beatles
1961	The Pill for married women *Private Eye* Ferdynand Zweig, *The Worker in an Affluent Society* Committee Against Racial Discrimination
1962	Commonwealth Immigration Act
1963	Chatterley trial Robbins Report Minorities Research Group

1964	Mary Whitehouse Clean Up TV campaign Martin Luther King visit
1965	Child Poverty Action Group Abolition of death penalty Race Relations Act
1966	Playboy Club opens in Soho Shelter and *Cathy Come Home*
1967	Decriminalization of abortion The Pill for unmarried women Decriminalization of homosexuality (over age of twenty-one) Student sit-in at LSE Welsh Language Act BBC launches Radio 1
1968	Northern Ireland Civil Rights Association Immigration Act Race Relations Act Powell's 'Rivers of Blood' speech Black People's Alliance
1969	Divorce reform Monty Python Women's Liberation Conference Battle of Bogside
1970	Gay Liberation Front Equal Pay Act Glastonbury
1972	Bloody Sunday and direct rule in Northern Ireland *The Joy of Sex*
1973	Brixton Black Women's Group
1974	Centre for Policy Studies
1975	Margaret Thatcher becomes leader of Conservative Party
1976	IMF loan and structural adjustment Commission for Racial Equality Sex Pistols' Anarchy in the UK Rock Against Racism
1979	Referendum on devolution

Affluence and its Limits

Little more than a decade after the creation of social democracy, commentators began discussing the disappearance of the 'traditional' working class. They pointed to a diverse set of developments, from the growing affluence of many working-class households, to the destruction of the classic slums and the relocation of many in new towns and suburbs, the shrinking proportion of unskilled manual workers, and the loss of the working classes' apparently tribal loyalty to the Labour Party after its three successive electoral defeats in the 1950s. As the forms of middle-class life also changed, distinguishing between classes became harder despite the amazing resilience of privilege, influence and wealth among what became known as 'the Establishment'. What did become increasingly clear was that not all had been lifted out of poverty. The persistence of poverty and the unevenness of social services for specific groups like children, the elderly and people of colour became a central concern for a new generation of increasingly politicized NGOs.

The Reformation of Class

The understanding that Britain's economy, society and political order were structured by divisions between the upper, middle and working classes had been first articulated by the labour movement in the late nineteenth century. If those differences were entrenched during the Great Depression between the wars, they appeared to flatten out during the long boom of the social democratic economy from the 1950s to the 1970s. Inequalities between classes lessened as the benefits of economic growth were broadly shared through progressive tax policies that redistributed wealth. The top rate of tax had been reduced from 47.5 to 38.75 per cent between 1945 and 1959 but it had climbed to 83 per cent by 1974. Thus whereas in 1940 the richest 10 per cent in Britain possessed around 80 per cent of the country's total wealth, by 1970 it owned little more than 60 per cent of it. The same trend was evident in respect of income as well. In 1949 those in the top 10 per cent income bracket accounted for 33 per cent of all personal income before tax and 27 per cent after it. By 1975 those figures had fallen to 25 and 22 per cent respectively. The chief beneficiaries of this redistribution of income were the property-owning and salaried middle classes. In 1946 only a quarter of national income was in the form of monthly salaries rather than weekly wages, but by 1968 that had risen to a third. Those in the bottom 50 per cent income bracket barely saw any rise in their portion of total income.

The reformation of class in post-war Britain was not just about the redistribution of wealth and income. It also entailed the restructuring of work as well as changes to the ways in which people thought about and experienced class. The traditional view of a working-class man as a manual worker, a football fan with a flat cap and a fancy for beer and a flutter, had always been a cliché, but that figure became increasingly hard to find in post-war Britain. As Britain's economy adapted to its new global conditions, the nature of work itself changed quite dramatically between 1951 and 1971. The agricultural sector, which employed 1.2 million people in 1951, 6.4 per cent of the total workforce, had just 680,000 workers, or 3.2 per cent of all workers, twenty years later. Although the proportion of the workforce employed in the manufacturing sector stayed level at around 34 per cent in these decades, there were significant shifts within it. As Britain's share of world manufacturing exports shrank from 25.4 to 10.8 per cent, some industries like coal and textiles, that had once propelled Britain's industrialization, fared badly. Coal output decreased from a post-war peak of 224 million tons in 1954 to 17 million tons by 1970, making the numbers of miners fall from 517,000 in 1963 to 281,500 by 1970. The textile industry was also a shadow of its former self. Its post-war peak of production was in 1962 when its total output was 2,612 million yards of woven cloth, less than a third of the 8,050 million yards it had produced in 1913. The proportion of textile workers within the workforce fell from 7.1 per cent in 1951 to 4.5 by 1971. In contrast, other manufacturing industries either held their ground until the 1970s – like shipbuilding – or increased their output and number of employees – like the car and chemical industries. One consequence of these shifts was that the proportion of unskilled manual workers fell from 70 per cent of the workforce in 1931 to 47 per cent by 1974.

It was the service sector that grew most rapidly. The numbers employed in services rose from 10.5 milliion to 12.6 million between 1951 and 1971, accounting for 49 and 53.5 per cent of the total workforce. While workers in transport, communication and distribution made up almost half of the total, their numbers remained relatively flat. The real growth came in education and health services, as well as finance and business. In 1951 education and health services employed just 3.2 per cent of the workforce but twenty years later they accounted for 9.5 per cent of it.

Women became an increasingly central part of this service economy. Almost all the growth in women's employment between 1951 and 1971, during which time their share of the total workforce increased from 31 to 35 per cent, came in the service sector. An ever-larger share of women workers were married, 46 per cent of them by 1971, double the proportion in 1951. If women predominated as workers in health and education services, they dominated white-collar clerical work: 70 per cent of clerical workers were women in 1970. Women's work was far from equal. It was rarely seen as a career, more likely to be part-time, less protected by trade unions, and came on top of the unpaid domestic work. It also always paid less. In 1970 women's weekly earnings, whether in manual or non-manual work, were half those of men. Even a decade later, after the **Equal Pay Act** of 1970, and the attempt to make equal pay for equivalent work compulsory five years later, women were still paid on average only 70 per cent of the male wage. Despite their second-class status as workers, the increasing presence of women in the workforce began to undermine the traditional, if always misplaced, view of the working-class labourer as male.

As the number of women in paid employment rose, so did the proportion of women who belonged to trade unions. In 1945 women represented 20 per cent of Britain's 8 million trade unionists, but by 1979 they accounted for 30 per cent of the 13 million who belonged to a trade union. Much of the growth in membership in this period came in the so-called white-collar sector of the service industries, especially those under government control. Between 1951 and 1968 white-collar union members increased by 30 per cent and a decade later 44 per cent of all white-collar workers were members of a union. Nonetheless, the trade union movement was slow to recognize that the restructuring of the British economy required reaching out beyond its traditional constituency of white, working-class men. Even when its membership began to include more women and people of colour, its leadership continued to give the impression that the working class was homogeneously white and male.

Indeed, some were concerned that the new-found affluence of the white male worker had changed the experience and politics of class. Certainly the experience of the working class had never before been so intensely studied. Sociology as an academic discipline only came of age in Britain after the Clapham Commission (1947) gave universities a generous funding stream of £400,000 a year for social research that they hoped would measure the progress of the welfare state's investments. It quickly produced a whole range of sociological inquiry that drew upon the traditions of empirical research for measuring social change pioneered by Booth and Rowntree, as well as ethnographic approaches to understanding 'community' grounded in anthropological research in the colonies, and some forms of American sociology.

Fittingly, it was Rowntree who first investigated the success of the welfare state in eradicating poverty. Fifty years after his first study of poverty in 1901, he returned to York to complete a third and final survey. Poverty, he concluded, had effectively disappeared, with just 3 per cent of the town, mainly the elderly, living below the poverty line. Ten years later, Ferdynand Zweig's *The Worker in an Affluent Society* suggested that affluence not poverty was now the problem, for workers had become more middle-class in their orientation around family and consumer goods. That same year a group of sociologists, led by John Goldthorpe, began a study of this new type of 'Affluent Worker', focusing on car workers in the prosperous southeastern towns of Luton and Cambridge. Goldthorpe's team found that these workers shunned the clubs, pubs and streets that were the traditional sites of working-class sociability. Instead they stayed at home where they could maximize their income and privately enjoy their higher standard of living. Yet the study, which was eventually published as *The Affluent Worker* in 1967, insisted they still saw themselves as workers and supported the Labour Party.

Figure 12.1 L.S. Lowry, 'Going to Work', 1943

This sense of the loss of traditional working-class communities drove much of the work that became known as 'community studies'. Despite the diversity of this field, it was often associated with the work of Michael Young and Peter Willmott, who established an **Institute for Community Studies** in 1954, and three years later published *Family and Kinship in East London*. As slum clearance schemes accelerated in the mid 1950s, the book highlighted the displacement of working-class families who had been relocated from Bethnal Green to a new housing estate in semi-rural Essex. As the agricultural sector collapsed, traditional industries shrank, and slum clearance schemes destroyed 1.3 million homes and replaced them with 4 million council homes (40 per cent of which were blocks of flats of three stories or more), 'community studies' registered the growing pains of social democracy as it transformed the experience of the working class, and investigated the new ties that would bind it together again.

Paradoxically the more people wrote about the disappearance of the traditional working class, the more they became culturally visible. The work of the artist L.S. Lowry, portraying working-class Britons as stick figures dwarfed by oppressive industrial landscapes, became hugely popular in the 1950s as the mills in his native northwest of England began to close. Figure 12.1 captures factory workers walking through snow to work at the Mather & Platt engineering firm in Manchester's Newton Heath in

Figure 12.2 Shirley Baker, 'Cycling Along a Terraced Street', Salford, 1962

1943. A decade later the factory was closed and Mather & Platt established new factories in India. A series of photographers, such as Roger Mayne and Shirley Baker, also sought to capture the changing texture of working-class communities in the 1950s (see Figure 12.2). Many of the back-to-back, terraced streets they photographed in London and Manchester had literally disappeared in slum clearance schemes by the early 1970s when these photographs attracted the praise of critics. The figure of the Conservative-voting, traditional, working class family was brilliantly evoked in the popular television sitcom *Till Death Do Us Part* from 1965. The main character, Alf Garnett, venerated Winston Churchill and the Queen – portraits of both hung in pride of place on his wall. It was his rage against the transformations he witnessed in his native East End of London, and his irrational outbursts in which he blamed them variously on 'socialism', coloured immigrants and the young, that gave the show its satirical edge.

Laments for lost traditional working-class community also proliferated in memoirs. Richard Hoggart's *The Uses of Literacy* (1957) bemoaned how mass culture had corroded the working-class community he had grown up in between the wars. Worse still, his own educational success had left him 'anxious and uprooted' in his new sense of classlessness. In the 1960s oral history, community publishing, community theatre and new forms of 'history from below' were pioneered to recuperate the experience of working-class lives before they were lost. When creative writing at school became compulsory from 1967, children were taught to write about what they knew from their own experience. In 1969 Valerie Avery's account of her East London childhood, written in her English class during the 1950s when she was fifteen years old, became an assigned text for pupils studying English. Much of this work was ambivalent about the world that had been lost. It recognized that some of the old sense of community and fellowship, now viewed nostalgically, was the product of grinding poverty that was now gladly absent. Yet in the hands of some, like the historian E.P. Thompson, whose *The Making of the English Working Class* (1963) became hugely influential, the recuperation of this history was an attempt to energize the politics of the working class in the present.

The Rediscovery of Poverty and Privilege

By the 1960s the concern that affluence had transformed the working class was coupled with the recognition that it had not yet reached all the population. There was increasing criticism of the way in which poverty, far from being abolished by the welfare state, had just taken new forms. In his 1951 study of York, Rowntree continued to define poverty in absolute terms as existing below a line determined by whether individual or household income met their minimum physiological needs. Researchers at the London School of Economics, influenced by the work of its professor of social administration Richard Titmuss, began to challenge this approach. When two of his students, Peter Abel-Smith and Peter Townsend, published *The Poor and the Poorest* in 1965, they changed the understanding of poverty by defining it in relative, not absolute, terms. Poverty, they argued, should not be conceived in terms of basic physical necessities but in relation to people's capacity to enjoy goods and services that made them feel a full participant in social life. Calculating that this would require 140 per cent of full welfare benefits to achieve, their research showed that the number of households living in poverty had actually risen from 4 million to 7.5 million, or 10.1 to 17.9 per cent of all households, between 1953 and 1960. Worse still, they discovered clusters of poverty among the elderly and children because it was at its worst in one-person households and those with more than six inhabitants. It was a sobering check to those who believed that abundance had swept the land and the welfare state had provided a safety net for all.

Abel-Smith and Townsend helped launch the Child Poverty Action Group in 1965. Their research also helped redirect the work of Help the Aged, originally established in 1961 to aid elderly refugees from Yugoslavia, to focus on the poverty of pensioners. Like Shelter, launched in 1966 to address the problem of homelessness, these NGOs politicized charitable work and emphasized campaigning, lobbying and consciousness, as much as fundraising. Shelter is a good example. It grabbed public attention when *Cathy Come Home* was broadcast on BBC One and watched by 12 million viewers. The fictional film, shot in documentary style, portrayed a young woman who lived her dream and moved to London, married and had three children. A victim of London's chronic housing shortage and the inadequacy of welfare services, she quickly lost her husband, home and eventually her children. Shelter argued that Cathy's plight was not an unusual one. They calculated there were 3 million other homeless families in Britain, victims of the end of private rent control in 1957 and the still inadequate supply of public housing. The film's young director, Ken Loach, was himself part of a new generation of activist filmmakers and documentary photographers determined to expose the lingering inequities and injustices of social democracy. Between 1965 and 1967 he made other films about the inadequacies of the welfare system, focusing on a young woman forced to have an illegal abortion, and a schizophrenic navigating mental health services. In 1970 his naturalistic film *Kes*, a moving account of a young boy's attempt to escape the realities of working-class life in a northern mining town, became a cult classic. Those who came of age after the mid 1950s did not measure the progress of social democracy, as their parents did, from the perspective of the 1930s. They were appalled that 96 per cent of households in Britain with annual incomes below £20 still used an open fireplace for their heating and hot water. As late as 1971, over 10 per cent of households had no indoor toilet, 9 per cent no bath and 34 per cent no washing machine.

To these critics, class difference was no less persistent than poverty and continued to determine the course of people's lives. This was the premise of the documentary television investigation *Seven Up* that in 1964 interviewed fourteen seven-year old children who represented an apparent cross-section of British society. The programme, which every seven years revisited its subjects, sought to demonstrate that accidents of birth in a class system still set the parameters of their lives. Nowhere was the persistence of this class system, and its distribution of wealth and opportunity, more apparent than in the sphere of education. We have already seen in Chapter 10 how the 1944 Education Act produced a tripartite class structure with state schools, but it also left the world of elite education untouched. Private education remained the preserve of a privileged 7 per cent of schoolchildren, while only 3 per cent of school leavers went on to universities; 40 per cent of the 118,000 students at university in the 1960s had been privately schooled. During the 1950s and 1960s commentators coined new terms like 'the Establishment' or the 'intellectual aristocracy' to capture the deeply embedded personal networks that bound together the 'public' (the most elite private) schools, universities (especially Oxbridge), the City of London, the BBC, the elite cadre of civil servants, the plethora of 'gentleman's clubs' in London and the world of private business.

When the Labour Party returned to power in 1964, it did so with the promise, largely borrowed from Anthony Crosland's *The Future of Socialism* (1956), to restore social democracy to purpose. The task was to eradicate poverty and ensure that while not all Britons would be afforded the same education, they would at least enjoy equality of educational opportunity. The prime minister Harold Wilson appointed Crosland as Minister of Education to oversee this transformation. Yet while the privately educated Crosland got rid of the eleven plus test and replaced the tripartite system of public education with a new type of 'comprehensive school', he ducked the abolition of private schools that many in his party believed was essential to achieve equality of opportunity. By 1980, 88 per cent of schoolchildren were educated in comprehensive schools while 6 per cent were afforded the privilege of private school. Britain had never come closer to a universal and socially democratic model of education but it came at the price of allowing the elite to continue to buy their privilege.

In 1963 the **Robbins Report**, following the lead of public universities in the USA, recommended a dramatic expansion of higher education to increase social mobility as well as the competitiveness of the British economy. Supporting the call for a doubling of student numbers in twenty years, Crosland introduced a system of universal grants that effectively made university free for all. By 1970 Robbins's target of 219,000 undergraduates had already been reached and university funding had increased proportionately. New university campuses – like those at Sussex, East Anglia, York, Essex, Warwick and Lancaster – sprang up around the country and pioneered new forms of academic study and curricula. Crosland also created a new type of 'polytechnic' to facilitate the expansion of higher education. The new polytechnics were less prestigious and cheaper than universities, for they focused on teaching, not research, and were oriented around the 'practical' not the 'liberal' arts. Ironically, they resembled a secondary modern type of higher education. Very quickly around 30 polytechnics soon boasted a student population that matched those of the universities, with 215,000 undergraduates by 1970. By then, some 14 per cent of school leavers were receiving a higher education, 10 per cent more than a decade earlier. And whereas in 1962 women were half as likely as men to be full-time students at universities, eight years later they represented 48 per cent of those in higher education. However limited the expansion of higher education was, universities became more accessible to women and the working class. As we shall see shortly, universities became key sites of protest during the late 1960s and 1970s.

Commonwealth Citizens and the Colour of Class

The reformation of class and the questioning of the welfare state's universal reach were also deeply racialized. As we saw in Chapter 11, the **British Nationality Act** of 1948 extended 'Commonwealth citizenship' to all colonial subjects, allowing them the right to migrate to Britain and enjoy equal access to jobs and welfare services there. Even though relatively small numbers of migrants moved to Britain as Commonwealth citizens, they faced increasing levels of hostility from white Britons. The presence of what became known as the 'immigrant problem' catalysed discussion about how Commonwealth citizens could best be integrated into British society and its welfare services. Much of that discussion about 'community' and 'race relations' was led by those considered to have imperial expertise in the study of racial difference and the management of 'communal' groups.

Figure 12.3 *Picture Post*: 'Is there a British Colour Bar?'

Racism and Race Relations

Tellingly, it was anthropologists, long charged with studying the dynamics of racial difference across the Empire, who produced the first investigations of British communities of colour. Kenneth Little began his doctoral research in anthropology at the LSE exploring the dynamics of the mixed-race community of Cardiff's port area, Tiger Bay, during the war. Outraged by his discovery of the colour bars and racism that segregated the community, he eventually published *Negroes in Britain* (1947), warning that racial tension and conflict would persist unless its causes were better understood and addressed. Two years later the popular magazine *Picture Post* provocatively asked its readers 'Is there a British Colour Bar?' Having sent the photographer Bert Hardy to document conditions in Tiger Bay, London's East End and Liverpool's South End, it answered unequivocally yes (see Figure 12.3). Employment, housing and even pubs and clubs were invariably divided by race. By the mid 1950s, as the so-called immigrant problem grew, a plethora of other studies of emergent black British communities were published, like Anthony Richard's *Colour Prejudice in Britain* (1954) on Liverpool, Michael Banton's *The Coloured Quarter* (1955) on Stepney and Sheila Patterson's *Dark Strangers* (1963) on Brixton. Banton and Patterson were Little's students at the University of Edinburgh, and while they sought to understand the cultures of specific communities, they did so to discover how Commonwealth citizens could better become British.

The warnings of growing racial tension and conflict in these communities appeared prophetic in 1958. In that year unrest broke out in Nottingham and London's Notting

Figure 12.4 'Stop the Coloured Invasion', Trafalgar Square, May 1959

Hill as an increasingly hostile white working class attacked those they branded 'coloured' and accused of taking their jobs, houses and women. Widely reported and quickly designated as 'race riots', as were subsequent events in Middlesbrough and Dudley near Birmingham in 1961 and 1962, they made manifest the intensification of white racism. A fluid set of fascist groups – like Oswald Mosley's Union Movement (1948), the White Defence League (1957) and the British National Party (1960) – with overlapping leaders and membership, sought to mobilize racism against Commonwealth citizens. Gangs of 'Teddy Boys' were often at the forefront of violent attacks against black Britons. Smartly dressed, young, working-class, men with a penchant for rock and roll, Teddy Boys were Britain's first self-identified 'youth' subculture forged in rebellion from the austerity and dreams of their parents' lives. Despite the strong influences of African American music and dress upon their style, they went on 'nigger hunts' in immigrant communities, and helped swell the numbers at fascists rallies like the 'Stop the Coloured Invasion' meeting at Trafalgar Square in 1959 organized by the White Defence League (see Figure 12.4).

Eschewing the violence of these groups, the Birmingham Immigration Control Association was formed in 1960 to campaign against Conservative MPs in the city who did not publicly support their demand for a five-year moratorium on immigration.

This emboldened Conservative MPs like Cyril Osborne who had long campaigned on this issue but had been a marginal, even embarrassing, voice in the party. This type of pressure, and the rising tide of white racism it reflected, shifted the politics of the Conservative Party so that by 1962 it passed the Commonwealth Immigration Act. The Act ended the extension of British citizenship to all colonial subjects and restricted immigration only to those who had successfully applied for employment vouchers. The new scale of racial animosity now authorized by the Conservative Party was such that in 1964 Peter Griffith, its candidate at a by-election in the Birmingham suburb of Smethwick, successfully ran his campaign on the slogan 'If you want a nigger for a neighbour, vote Labour.' White racism was not just a product of those pockets of poverty that persisted amidst Britain's newfound prosperity. If the white working class had traditionally conceived of their whiteness in relation to a distant imperial other, the presence of a black British working class made that whiteness a defining feature of their class difference.

Black Politics

White racism in turn helped generate new forms of black politics. In some ways these also emerged out of the endeavours of local authorities and voluntary groups, including black British associations and clubs, organizing Community Relations Councils to address the so-called immigrant problem. These councils sought to better integrate Commonwealth citizens into their communities by ensuring they could claim the jobs and social services they were entitled to. By 1960 nine of these councils were clustered in north London and the Midlands. Black Britons, many of whom had initially been recruited as labourers by the British government or private companies, increasingly refused to accept that they were the problem and began to assert their rights as Commonwealth citizens.

The creation of the Indian Workers' Association (IWA) and the West Indian Standing Conference (WISC) in 1958 was animated as much by the politics of India and the Caribbean as the racial conflicts in Britain. Local groups of the IWA had initially formed in the 1930s to advance the cause of Indian independence, mainly among students from the subcontinent, but they had fallen largely dormant after 1947. It was Nehru's visit to Britain in 1957 that prompted the formation of the new national organization. With many of its leaders, like Piara Khabra from Southall (who became Britain's first Sikh MP in 1992), strongly influenced by communism on the subcontinent, the IWA initially focused on organizing among Indian workers. Indian workers felt their interests were not represented by trade unions and remained excluded from certain types of work by employers and foremen. The West Indian Standing Conference was created after the Notting Hill riots, with strong support from the West Indian High Commission, to coordinate local groups whose membership was confined to specific islands. WISC sought to forge a common West Indian identity and promote better race relations, especially around the issue of policing. In 1961 IWA and WISC came together as the Coordinating Committee Against Racial Discrimination (CARD) to oppose the Commonwealth Immigration Bill and to highlight how racism prevented Commonwealth citizens from enjoying their rights to employment and social services. As a consequence of their work, when the Bill was passed as law the following year it created a National Advisory Committee for Commonwealth Immigrants to produce reports detailing what social services were available for Commonwealth citizens.

The influence of the civil rights movement in the United States was only apparent in 1964. That November, on his return from Africa, Malcolm X arrived in Britain and participated in an Oxford Union debate broadcast on television. The following month, Martin Luther King visited Britain on his way to Oslo to pick up a Nobel Prize for Peace. As well as preaching at St Paul's Cathedral, he met with the leaders of CARD. CARD had a broad base of support among black Britons and included representatives from the IWA, WISC, West Indian Students' Union, the National Federation of Pakistani Associations and the Council of African Organizations, as well as anti-racist organizations like the Anti-Apartheid Movement and the Campaign for Nuclear Disarmament. It campaigned for legislation against racial discrimination and duly supported the passage of the **Race Relations Act** passed by the new Labour government in 1965. The Act provided state funding for Community Relations Councils (five years later eighty-one were scattered across England and South Wales), outlawed racial discrimination in public places, and established a Race Relations Board (on which the anthropologist Kenneth Little sat) to hear cases. Pushed by CARD, a new Race Relations Act was passed just three years later that addressed their chief complaints about the 1965 Act. Discrimination was made a criminal offence and its prosecution was extended to the critical areas of housing, employment and credit. Many looked to figures like Malcom X, who returned to Britain shortly before his assassination and visited Smethwick to highlight the white racism of Griffith's election campaign, and the Black Power leader Stokely Carmichael, to radicalize black politics in Britain. Ironically, following his first visit to Britain in 1967 Carmichael was banned from re-entering the country under the terms of the Race Relations Act of 1965 – on the grounds that his speeches would incite racial hatred. Increasingly, the Black Power movement in the USA, and its influence on the uprisings in Jamaica (1968) and Trinidad and Tobago (1970), began to inspire a new generation of black politics.

Powellism

The emergence and radicalization of black politics was also a response to an increasingly racist English nationalism. In 1968 the **Race Relations Act** was coupled with a still more restrictive Commonwealth Immigrants Act that only allowed entry to those

Commonwealth subjects with immediate family (spouses, parents or grandparents) who had been born in the UK. It was what he perceived as the inadequacies of these measures that inspired the Conservative MP **Enoch Powell** to deliver his infamous 'Rivers of Blood' speech in 1968. Powell was not a marginal figure in the Conservative Party like Cyril Osborne or Peter Griffith. He was a rising star in the party whom many tipped to be its future leader. A classicist by training and a powerful orator, he was equally as critical of Keynesian welfare capitalism as he was of Britain's continuing imperial conceits (as was evident in his criticism of the treatment of **Mau Mau** at the Hola camp). He had been promoted fast, serving as a junior minister at the **Treasury** and as Minister of Health. As Parliament was debating the Race Relations Bill in 1968, he travelled to Birmingham, that powder-keg of racial tension, and delivered a speech claiming Britain was being 'swamped' by Commonwealth immigrants and predicting disaster: he felt like a Roman observing the fall of his Empire and imagining the River Tiber 'running with much blood'. For Powell the Empire had been a folly and Britain had no obligations to its former colonial subjects. Distancing himself from fascist groups, he insisted people of colour were not biologically inferior, they were just culturally different and, as a consequence, could never be properly integrated into British society. He feared that the Race Relations Bill would turn Britons into aliens in their own land, penalizing those who felt their national culture, their jobs, their houses, their schools, their hospitals and their communities were being stolen from them. If the bill passed, he warned, perversely evoking the memory of slavery, in 'fifteen or twenty years the black man will have the whip hand over the white man'.

Powell's speech did not depart from Conservative Party policy of tighter immigration restrictions and a voluntary repatriation scheme, but its tone was so inflammatory he was immediately sacked from his position as Shadow Secretary for Defence. While few Conservative MPs publicly backed Powell, there was an outpouring of support from trade unionists and the general public. London dock workers went on strike and marched to Westminster with banners declaring 'Back Britain, not Black Britain'. Sympathy strikes in support of Powell quickly spread across London, including 600 meat packers from Smithfield market. A week later an opinion poll reported that 74 per cent of Britons agreed with Powell and 69 per cent thought he should not have been sacked. White racism was effectively unbound by what became known as 'Powellism'.

It was no surprise, then, that the year after the Conservative Party returned to power in 1970 they passed a new Immigration Act that replaced the employment voucher scheme with work permits that only allowed temporary residence and provided assistance for voluntary repatriation. Yet when Idi Amin expelled Asians from Uganda, the government created a Ugandan Resettlement Board that effectively overruled the 1971 Immigration Act and allowed entry to 27,000. Powell was the figurehead of opposition to this policy and opinion polls reported he had become Britain's most popular politician. Powell and his supporters were further outraged when the Labour government's

Race Relations Act of 1976 extended the criminalization of discrimination and established a Commission for Racial Equality to actively promote racial equality.

A Generation in Revolt

People try to put us down (Talkin' 'bout my generation)
Just because we get around (Talkin' 'bout my generation)
Things they do look awful cold (Talkin' 'bout my generation)
I hope I die before I get old (Talkin' 'bout my generation)

'The Who', a band renowned for smashing their equipment at the end of their performances, released a song called 'My Generation' in 1965. It was an instant hit and its lyrics became an anthem for the post-war baby boom generation that came of age in the late 1950s and 1960s. A million more fifteen to twenty-four year olds were alive in 1960 than a decade earlier. Given that their wages had grown faster than the national average, these young people had an increasingly large disposable income. Across the Western world, market researchers and social scientists alike identified a new category of 'youth' to describe this demographic. Fuelled by a consumer culture that often commodified rebellion, as well as the expansion of higher education, it gave rise to new forms of writing, music, comedy and politics that eventually exploded in the revolts of 1968 across much of the world. Yet this new generation, less prepared than their parents to take the past as a guide to the future, took particular forms in Britain. 'Youth' represented a bundle of new attitudes that was equally hostile to the remnants of the **ancien regime**, the Victorian moral code and the paternalism of the social democratic state. It was not until the late 1960s and early 1970s that new forms of feminist, black, as well as gay and lesbian politics highlighted just how dominated by white heterosexual men this revolt had been.

Angry Young Men and the End of Deference

In the mid 1950s, as Teddy Boys were strutting the streets of London, and James Dean played the disaffected teenager Jim Stark in *Rebel Without a Cause* (1955), the world of British high culture was catching up. A new figure, 'the angry young man', emerged from the work of a cadre of young, male, writers who appeared to capture the spirit of their generation. The angry young man was a composite figure that expressed the frustrations of a generation either stuck in the white working class or dislocated by upward social mobility. They were either angered by the confines imposed upon them by their traditional working-class parents, families and communities, or resentful that while affluence or education had helped them escape those communities, they remained excluded from the social world of the privileged. Socially disaffected, they felt alienated from a political system that did not appear to speak to them: as Jimmy Porter put it in John Osborne's play *Look Back in Anger* (1956), there were 'no good, brave, causes left'. If Jimmy Porter was Britain's first angry, young, white, man he was quickly followed by a host of others as the publishing world fell over itself to find him companions. It found them in the first novels of a series of twenty-something authors: Clive Wilson's *The Outsider* (1956), John Braine's *Room at the Top* (1957), Kingsley Amis's *Lucky Jim* (1957) and Alan Sillitoe's *Saturday Night, Sunday Morning* (1958). Each of these were quickly made into films that launched the careers of actors like Albert Finney and Richard Burton who in turn became the masculine face of this new generation. It was left to Shelagh Delaney's play *A Taste of Honey* (1958) and Lynne Reid Banks's novel *The L-Shaped Room* (1960), both of which were adapted to film in 1962, to articulate the voice of young women grappling with the risk and reality of pregnancy. Typically, these became known as 'kitchen-sink' dramas.

While the literary and cinematic worlds were discovering angry young men and women, radio and television were producing a new generation of just as white and clever young men whose satirical comedy challenged the paternalism and conservatism of their elders. *The Goon Show*, which ran from 1951 to 1960, started it all. Written by Spike Milligan, and starring Peter Sellers and Harry Secombe, the show's surreal and satirical comedy was hugely popular and influential. It helped inspire the satire boom of the 1960s that began with the stage show *Beyond the Fringe* (1960) and continued with the magazine *Private Eye* (1961–), the TV programme *That Was the Week that Was* (1962–3) and *Monty Python's Flying Circus* (1969–74). Progressively more daring and vicious in their lampooning of public figures, these comics, invariably educated at private schools and Oxbridge, were very much products of the Establishment they mocked. The BBC would surely not have commissioned their shows had they not come from this connected and privileged world. Paradoxically, it was Britain's intellectual aristocracy that made British comedy associated with a satirical, anti-Establishment, irreverence.

So-called 'pop music' also epitomized this growing youth culture of rebellion and its commodification. Inspired by the growing popularity of the Billboard Charts in the USA, the newly launched magazine *New Musical Express* began publishing charts of record sales in Britain from 1952. *NME*, as it later became known, fed the growing interest of young people in new styles of music but remained a cultish affair with a circulation of just 200,000 by the end of the decade. Such was the shortage of recordings and vinyl in the early 1950s that their first chart included just fifteen songs. When vinyl records became more freely available by the late 1950s, the size and number of rival charts grew, as did the numbers of record shops. These shops became important gathering places for young people, especially those who began forming bands during the 'skiffle' craze. Skiffle, which did not require expensive instruments, was immensely popular and generated a thriving club scene where bands – like John Lennon's skiffle band 'The Quarrymen' (1957) – could perform in cities like Liverpool, London and Manchester. Initially, American artists dominated the British charts, but the growing number of British bands meant that the BBC and ITV launched their own 'chart' shows *Six Five Special* (1957), *Oh Boy!* (1958) and *Top of the Pops* (1964). As cheaper portable record players allowed many young people to listen to music in their bedrooms without their parents listening, the volume of record sales increased dramatically. In 1950 expenditure on records was £100 million but by the mid 1970s it reached its peak at £8,000 million (in 2010 values). This huge market was dominated by a small number of major record companies who agreed in 1969 to have the top fifty chart sales independently measured by the British Market Research Bureau.

The commercialized music industry was relentlessly male. Record companies created artists like Tommy Steele (1957) and Cliff Richard (1959) as domesticated rock and roll artists who would appeal to young women consumers. Neither was it an accident that the Beatles (1960), the Rolling Stones (1962), the Kinks (1963) and The Who (1964), like almost all other British bands, were exclusively white and male. It was not until the mid 1960s, when artists like Cilla Black and Sandy Shaw emerged, that women began to challenge the masculinity of pop music. Although African American artists had long been part of Britain's music scene, and despite the growing influence of soul and reggae, it took another decade for mixed-race and black British bands (like The Specials and Steel Pulse) to break through.

Alternative and less domesticated musical cultures rose alongside commercial pop music. Teddy Boys had long been associated with unruliness but by 1964 they had been displaced by the spectre of a violent and drug-fuelled style war between 'Mods' and 'Rockers'. Where Rockers listened to rock and roll, dressed in leather, styled their hair in elaborate quiffs and rode motorbikes, Mods listened to soul, ska and beat music, dressed neatly underneath large parka jackets, wore their hair short and rode often customized Vespa scooters. When these groups gathered at seaside towns along the south coast over the bank holiday weekends of the spring of 1964, there were small but violent clashes between them. The press quickly portrayed these skirmishes as representing a new type of uncontrolled and rebellious youth. Many of those arrested were found with 'purple heart' amphetamines, prompting the government to criminalize the possession of non-prescription drugs for the first time with the Drugs (Prevention of Use) Act of that year.

1964 was also the year that new pirate radio stations like Radio Caroline and Radio London were created. Unlike the BBC's Light Programme, these stations continuously broadcast pop music from ships in the North Sea and English Channel beyond the government's licensing jurisdiction. Within two years they boasted an estimated 15 million listeners and were attracting £2 million in advertising revenue. The BBC responded by launching its own pop music channel in 1967, Radio 1, and aggressively recruited many of pirate radio's star DJs like Kenny Everett, Tony Blackburn and John Peel to win back this audience. As the number of new independent record labels grew in the

1970s, John Peel became the voice of the alternative 'indie scene'. Privately educated, this anti-Establishment figure ironically insisted on paternalistically educating rather than following the tastes of his listeners in a late-night show that by the late 1970s had canonical status. It was not until 1981 that Britain's first black pirate radio station, Dread Broadcasting Corporation, was launched in west London.

The increasing commercialization of pop music, even in its apparently counter-cultural forms, was also evident in the promotion of music festivals. Created a year earlier, the Isle of Wight Festival attracted hundreds of thousands in 1969 when Bob Dylan played the week after the Woodstock Festival in the USA. The Glastonbury Festival began in 1970 but was dwarfed in size by the estimated 600,000 people that gathered at the Isle of Wight that year, making it bigger than Woodstock. As with Woodstock, filmmakers – like Nicolas Roeg and David Puttnam who released *Glastonbury Fayre* in 1971 – flocked to film these festivals and record what they represented as a youthful, drug-fuelled counter-culture promoting peace and love. Partly inspired by them, and partly in response to their commercialism, a vibrant Free Festival movement took off in the early 1970s that eschewed mainline acts and admission charges. Popping up on open fields across the country, these free festivals aimed to create utopian and experimental spaces for the performance of new forms of life and music.

This sense that music could help change the world extended beyond these counter-culture spaces. In 1971 the ex-Beatle George Harrison and his collaborator Ravi Shankar organized the world's first charity concert and album in aid of those in Bangladesh displaced by its war against, and partition from, Pakistan. The formation of Rock Against Racism in 1976 marked a new type of rock activism. Initially formed in protest against Eric Clapton declaring his support for **Enoch Powell** and shouting 'Keep Britain White' at a concert in Birmingham, it became a platform for those musicians distressed by the continuing rise of white racism in Britain. Its largest event was staged in 1978 when 100,000 people marched from Trafalgar Square to Hackney's Victoria Park for a concert that featured the Clash, Buzzcocks, Tom Robinson Band and Steel Pulse, the black reggae band from Handsworth in Birmingham.

The politicization of British youth culture owed much to the expansion of higher education in the 1960s. Even in the late 1950s and early 1960s students had been active in the Campaign for Nuclear Disarmament and the Anti-Apartheid Movement, but a student movement emerged during the 1960s. Frequently in conversation with students elsewhere, especially Europe and the United States, students criticized the undemocratic nature of the government and curriculum of universities, the continuing hold of racism and imperialism, as well as the limits and contradictions of social democratic welfare capitalism. Always a minority of students, activists coalesced around a variety of issues on different campuses between the mid 1960s and early 1970s. As around the globe, student protests in Britain reached their height in 1968 when the Vietnam Solidarity Committee organized a mass demonstration against the war in London that drew at least 100,000 people from across the country.

Anti-imperialism was particularly important to the student movement in Britain. The Anti-Apartheid Movement had a strong presence on many campuses and the introduction of fees for overseas (predominantly Commonwealth) students in 1967 prompted a National Day of Action by the Radical Student Alliance that reputedly involved 100,000 students across the country. The first sit-in at the LSE, a centre of student activism, was prompted by the appointment of the Rhodesian Walter Adams as its new director in 1967, two years after he had supported white minority rule and Rhodesia's Unilateral Declaration of Independence from Britain. Commonwealth citizens played leading roles in student activism. Born and raised in Lahore, Tariq Ali went to the University of Oxford where he became head of the Student Union in 1965 and hosted Malcolm X. By 1968 he was playing a leading role in the International Marxist Group and the anti-Vietnam protests, and was also an editor of the socialist magazine *Black Dwarf* that took its name from the unstamped radical paper founded in 1817 (see Figure 12.5). Basker Vashee, who

Figure 12.5 *Black Dwarf*, 1968

as General Secretary of the Rhodesian Students' Union had been deported for protesting against the Unilateral Declaration of Independence, led the campaign against the appointment of Walter Adams at the LSE. Students did not lament the loss of Britain's Empire; they were more concerned with the continuing hold of racism and imperialism in Britain and the world at large.

The End of Christian Britain

Those alarmed by the younger generation's lack of deference and enjoyment of sex, drugs and rock and roll, lamented the declining moral authority of the **Anglican Church** and the apparent erosion of Christian family values. Concern over the increasingly empty pews of the Anglican Church was nothing new. Commentators in the nineteenth century, as we have seen, were deeply worried by the rapid growth of Dissenting congregations and the absence of the urban poor from Anglican Sunday services. In fact, both Anglican and Catholic church attendance in England actually rose during the first three decades of the twentieth century. Even so, some felt the Christian family itself was in peril. A spike in divorce rates during the 1930s, rising from around 300,000 a year to 450,000 by the end of the decade, so alarmed the Presbyterian minister Dr Herbert Gray that he established the National Marriage Guidance Council to help shore up the institution of marriage in 1938. The following year the Registrar General recorded for the first time rates of illegitimacy and discovered that 30 per cent of first children were born out of wedlock. That the arrival of these children was invariably a trigger for marriage, and that less than 5 per cent of births were illegitimate, was of little consolation when the illegitimacy rates doubled during the war. After the war things did not seem so bad. The decline of church attendance almost levelled out while rates of divorce and illegitimacy actually fell.

It was when all these trends changed during the early 1960s that the talk of a crisis of the family began to resonate more widely. Church attendance fell by almost a third between 1960 and 1977; by 1977 just 3.5 per cent of Britons regularly went to church. The Church of Scotland had the most rapid fall: having had a record 1.32 million attending services in 1956, it lost 65 per cent of them within 20 years. Fewer people, also, were using the Church to mark life's passage. In 1956, 60 per cent of Britons were baptised, but by 1970 that had fallen to 46 per cent and a decade later reached 36 per cent. The same was true of marriage. As late as 1962, 70 per cent of people in England and Wales married in church, yet by the late 1970s just 50 per cent did. Although marriage rates were higher in Scotland and Northern Ireland, the trend was the same. The divorce rate in Scotland increased by 400 per cent between 1960 and 1974, while the proportion of illegitimate births doubled between 1960 and 1980. Clearly, the established churches finally lost their grip upon most Britons during the 1960s.

The Victorian moral code that had underpinned Christian Britain and its understanding of the social order also collapsed in the 1960s. Although the Anglican Church opposed the Obscenity Act of 1960 for what it considered a relaxation of laws, Penguin Books immediately challenged the Act by publishing a full edition of D.H. Lawrence's last major novel, *Lady Chatterley's Lover*. The novel, which had been banned since 1928, depicted the sexual awakening of the aristocratic Constance Chatterley at the hands of her working-class gamekeeper. During the resulting trial, the chief prosecutor disastrously asked the court whether this was a book 'you would wish your wife or servants to read'. Penguin's lawyers ensured it was a line that was not forgotten, repeatedly using it to illustrate just how out of the touch the government, and the 'Establishment' more broadly, were. The jury, of three women and nine men, agreed and Penguin won the case. Many in both the Anglican Church and Church of Scotland also set themselves against the legalization of gambling in 1960 and 1968, the abolition of the death penalty in 1965 (see Textbox 12.1 and Figure 12.6), the decriminalization of abortion and homosexuality in 1967, the end of censorship of the theatre in 1968, and the reform of the divorce laws in 1969 (1964 and 1976 in Scotland). Such was the erosion of the moral authority of the churches that all of these so-called 'permissive' measures were passed into law by Parliament – although homosexuality was not decriminalized in Scotland until 1980, and abortion remains illegal in Northern Ireland.

Some railed against what they viewed as the new 'permissive' culture that they thought undermined both family values and a sense of personal responsibility. They pointed to the rise of drug culture among young people, as well as a series of high-profile violent crimes like the Great Train Robbery of 1963 and the Moors Murders in 1965, as symptomatic of a society that was losing its moral compass. Television, and in particular the BBC, was accused of propagating 'permissiveness'. In 1964, Mary Whitehouse, an Anglican schoolteacher, and Norah Buckland, the wife of a vicar, founded the Clean Up TV campaign, which the following year became the National Viewers' and Listeners' Association. Their manifesto declared that as Christian women they abhorred what they saw as 'the propaganda of disbelief, doubt, and dirt ... promiscuity, infidelity and drinking' broadcast on the BBC. They called upon the BBC to instead 'encourage and sustain faith in God and bring Him back to the heart of our family and national life'. Although by June 1965 they had collected just 385,000 signatures on a petition, Whitehouse denied she was a voice in the wilderness and frequently cited the letters she was sent to show she had the support of the public. Her message certainly resonated with Christians concerned by what the Catholic journalist Malcolm Muggeridge described as 'the moral breakdown of our society'. Muggeridge was speaking alongside Mary Whitehouse

12.1 Person: Albert Pierrepoint (1905–1992)

Albert Pierrepoint was one of the last executioners in Britain, a hangman who executed more than 400 people between 1940 and 1955. Pierrepoint was widely regarded as the nation's 'Official Executioner' during this period, even though no such post existed. For most of his career Pierrepoint worked on a freelance basis. He began his other working life in a cotton mill, before becoming a grocer in Bradford, and finally ran a pub in Oldham called 'Help the Poor Struggler'. Hanging was a Pierrepoint family trade; his father and uncle had both been high-profile executioners. As his father, whose daytime job was as a clogger, died when Albert was seventeen, it was his uncle who taught him the trade of executions, chiefly at Pentonville Prison. Pierrepoint was involved in executions all over Britain as well as in Gibraltar, the Suez Canal Zone, Ireland, Egypt, Austria and the British zone of Germany after the Second World War, where he executed over 200 Nazi war criminals. For each execution he was paid a small fee (equivalent to about £100 today). His executions followed a set routine. Pierrepoint would arrive at the prison the night before and interview the prisoner to find out their age, weight and height, after which a dummy execution would be performed, followed by the real thing early the next morning. In 1950 Pierrepoint hanged an acquaintance of his who had frequently visited his local pub, an experience that led him to doubt the efficacy of capital punishment. Pierrepoint retired in 1956, after which he came out against the practice. The last execution in Britain took place in Liverpool in 1964, and in 1965 capital punishment for murder was abolished. Although never enforced, capital punishment remained in effect for treason, espionage, mutiny, piracy and arson in a naval dockyard. The death penalty was fully abolished in 1998. (S.W.)

and Cliff Richard at the Festival of Light, a nationwide series of protests against the demoralization of the country that culminated with a rally of an estimated 35,000 people in Trafalgar Square. This, the largest mobilization of those who claimed to represent the 'silent majority' of Christian Britons, in effect served to demonstrate their increasing marginality.

A Sexual Revolution?

Sexual intercourse began
In nineteen sixty-three
(Which was rather late for me)
Between the end of the 'Chatterley' ban
and the Beatles' first LP.

So ran the opening verse of Philip Larkin's poem 'Annus Mirabilis' in 1967. The cultural shift Larkin sought to capture, of imagining sex outside of marriage, or acknowledging sex in the public domain at all, was real if overplayed. Sex before and outside of

Figure 12.6 Albert Pierrepoint writes his memoir, 1973

marriage was not an invention of the 1960s, but it was previously accompanied by varying levels of knowledge and a good deal of secrecy. Men were expected to be curious and sexually adventurous whereas a woman's respectability rested in large measure upon her assumed innocence. There was no greater shame or fear for a woman than pregnancy before marriage; an illegitimate child could mean three months' 'confinement' to punitive hostels for unmarried mothers. As late as 1968 there were over 170 of these 'mother and baby homes', the vast majority privately run by the Anglican Church, the Salvation Army, the Church of Scotland and other religious groups, although some were state-funded social services. As unmarried women were generally thought to be neurotic, some even languished in mental asylums. So while there was undoubtedly sex before 1963, it was undoubtedly coded in very different ways that made women especially vulnerable.

The introduction of oral contraceptives, known simply as 'the Pill', promised to free women from the fear of unwanted pregnancy. The Pill was made available to married women by the state through the NHS in 1961, but it was commercially marketed from 1963 (hence Larkin's date), and only made available by doctors upon prescription to unmarried women in 1967. The vast majority of sexually active women continued to practise traditional techniques of birth control – abstinence or withdrawal – or used condoms or a diaphragm. Just 50,000 women took the Pill in 1962, and even though that number reached a million by 1969, it still only meant that less than a fifth of sexually active British women had used it. The biggest change came in 1974 when Family Planning Clinics were allowed to prescribe the Pill to women without the knowledge of their family doctor. Within five years 36 per cent of women were taking the Pill. The Pill did free a growing number of women from the fear of pregnancy, but it certainly did not revolutionize sexual relations. In 1969 a survey found that 63 per cent of women were virgins when they married, as opposed to 26 per cent of men, and 40 per cent did not use any form of birth control. In most families, and in all schools, sex remained a dirty and unspoken word. Alex Comfort's immensely popular sex manual, *The Joy of Sex* (1972), which sold over 12 million copies and portrayed sex between a heterosexual couple, prospered in this world.

It was the growth of a sex industry that continued to cater to male heterosexual pleasure, as much as a revolution in attitudes, that made sex less of a dirty word. London's Soho had always been a centre of prostitution but a growing number of sex shops and members-only clubs offering shows with full frontal nudity and 'hostess services', like Raymond's Revuebar (1958), began to open under the frequently corrupt patronage of the Metropolitan Police. This once illicit and seedy world gained newfound respectability during the 1960s with the relaxation of the laws regarding obscenity and theatrical censorship. When the American pornographer Hugh Heffner opened the Playboy Club in 1966, it attracted stars like Peter Sellers, Joan Collins and Rudolf Nureyev (see Figure 12.7). As striptease shows and venues proliferated across Soho, a new generation of pornographic magazines like *King* (1964), *Penthouse* (1965) and *Mayfair* (1966) were launched that combined sexually explicit stories with naked pictures of real women. By 1970 there were over forty shops in Soho selling 'erotic' materials – including 'under the counter' hard-core porn. While hard-core pornographic films went mainstream and became immensely profitable in 1970s America, early films like *Behind the Green Door* (1971) and *Deep Throat* (1972) remained banned from public release in Britain, so were instead shown in professedly 'private' Tatler Cinema Clubs that proliferated across British cities at this time. Such was the prevalence of porn that its exploitation of children and women became a target of the Festival of Light campaign and its offshoot the self-funded *Longford Report on Pornography* (1972), as well as the women's liberation movement.

Figure 12.7 Hugh Heffner and his 'bunnies' at the Playboy Club, 1966

The Rise of Identity Politics

As the limitations of social democracy became increasingly evident during the 1960s, different groups of young people began to reject those forms of politics organized around classes that were always assumed to be white, male, heterosexual and English. Instead they developed a new set of politics around their experiences as women, gay men and lesbian women, as well as people of colour, and of different nations and religions. In doing so they pioneered new forms of political engagement and sought to recall social democracy to its radical promise of security for all by recognizing the importance of difference.

Women's Liberation

The reanimation of feminist politics in Britain was anticipated by the work of French and American feminists in the 1950s and 1960s. Simone de Beauvoir's *The Second Sex* (1949) and Betty Friedan's *Feminine Mystique* (1963) were powerful condemnations of the ways in which women's hopes and expectations were always subordinated to the men they were supposed to serve. Welfare capitalism, they argued, confined women to a patriarchal domestic life and sexualized them as the objects of male desire. Haunted by the ways the revolts of 1968 had ignored and even aggravated women's oppression, feminists called for women's liberation from sexism and patriarchy.

For British feminists this meant breaking from a socialist politics that saw class relations as solely a consequence of capitalism. Fresh from her work as a member of the International Marxist Group and from editing *Black Dwarf*, Sheila Rowbotham published *Women's Liberation and the New Politics* in 1969. It insisted that women's oppression by patriarchy and sexism was a product of culture as much as economics. That same year Rowbotham attended a conference of the **History Workshop** movement and, like her colleagues Anna Davin and Sally Alexander, was appalled at the men's lack of interest in, and even contempt for, women's history. They resolved to hold a Women's Liberation Movement conference – like the one held in Chicago in 1968 – the following February at Ruskin College, Oxford. Five hundred women attended and they articulated four key demands: equal pay, equal education and job opportunities, free contraception and abortion on demand, and free twenty-four-hour nurseries for childcare. Later that year a group of activists took these demands to the Miss World competition at London's Albert Hall. Protesting outside the hugely popular televised show, they carried placards reading 'Miss-fortune demands equal pay for women', 'Miss-conception demands free abortion for all women', 'Miss-placed demands a place outside the home' and shouted the slogan 'We're not beautiful, we're not ugly, we're angry'. Once they had gained admission they disrupted the show by heckling and throwing flower bombs that forced its misogynist compeer, the American comedian Bob Hope, off the stage. The protest, broadcast live on primetime television, announced the arrival of the women's liberation movement in Britain.

The work of the women's liberation movement in Britain concerned raising the consciousness of the women involved as much as that of the public. Activists began to organize 'consciousness-raising' groups to provide supportive environments in which women could share their experiences of oppression, learn from each other, and be themselves. The first of these groups was organized in London and Leeds during 1969 but within two years there were 70 in the metropolis alone, by the mid 1970s 1,500 were scattered around the country. In these groups many women realized how patriarchy extended into all areas of their life so that 'the personal is political'. They also provided a therapeutic group context in which women could explore themselves and seek to express their hopes, fears and desires. The engagement with psychoanalysis, whether in the critical form of the widely publicized *Female Eunuch* (1970) by the Australian contributor to *Private Eye* Germaine Greer, or the New Zealander Juliet Mitchell's attempt to rescue it in *Psychoanalysis and Feminism* (1974), was a central thread of women's liberation. Understanding women's oppression in the present also required recuperating the historical experience of women in the past. Sheila Rowbotham's *Hidden from History: 300 years of Women's Oppression and the Fight against It* (1973), like her fellow feminist historians in **History Workshop**, pioneered this work. Given the antipathy of men, feminists had to find new ways of publishing their work. Feminist magazines like *Shrew* (1970) and *Spare Rib* (1972, see Figure 12.8) laid the foundation for the creation of Virago, Britain's first feminist publishing company, in 1973. Dominated as they sometimes were by white, middle-class and heterosexual women, these forms of consciousness-raising were criticized by radical feminists who championed lesbian separatism, as well as by black British feminists. Forming their own groups like the Brixton Black Women's Group (1973) and the Southall Black Sisters (1979), black feminists argued that consciousness-raising did not speak to the different issues facing black British women such as access to housing, education, and childcare for single parents. Black feminist groups also played a critical role in raising awareness of domestic violence and sexual abuse, freedom from which became the last demand of the women's liberation movement at its final conference in 1978.

Gay and Lesbian Politics

At the same time, homosexual men and women developed new analyses of their oppression as well as new forms of activism to contest it. As the social democratic state constructed its welfare services around heterosexual families with a male breadwinner, homosexual men and women remained pathologized. Homosexual men were subjected to humiliating forms of policing and prosecution for their 'immoral' and 'indecent' acts. Like lesbian women, they were also made the objects of medical study and experimentation in the quest to 'cure' their same-sex desires. Ironically, the decriminalization of same-sex relations between men began from an attempt to make the policing of homosexuality more effective. Established in 1954, the Wolfenden Committee spent three years investigating why the Metropolitan Police had failed to stamp out the soliciting or 'cottaging' of homosexual men in London's public spaces. Acknowledging the ubiquity of

Figure 12.8 *Spare Rib*, 1972

male homosexuality, they finally concluded that the only hope of taking it off the streets was to decriminalize same-sex relations between men in private. Their recommendations only became law in England and Wales a decade later (and in Scotland not until 1980). To reassure the public that 'predatory' homosexuals would not encourage youthful sexual experimentation, the Sexual Offences Act fixed the age of consent for homosexual men at twenty-one (as opposed to sixteen for heterosexuals). The inequity of this difference led to the formation of the Committee for Homosexual Equality in 1967, the first organization committed to representing and advancing the rights of homosexual men in Britain. As sexual relations between women had never been criminalized, lesbian women were less the object of unwelcome police attention than of medical study. In 1963 those lesbians being studied by sexologists established the Lesbian Minorities Research Group, launching their journal *Arena Three* the following year, to help end the sense of isolation engendered by the medicalization of their sexuality.

As homosexual men contemplated the very partial nature of decriminalization, and the intensified policing of sex between men in public spaces that tripled the number of prosecutions for 'indecency' between 1967 and 1972, they were influenced by events in the United States. Outraged by an aggressive police raid in June 1969 on the Stonewall Inn, a bar in New York's Greenwich Village frequented by homosexual men, transgender people and lesbian women, a new, more activist and confrontational form of politics developed that claimed the identity of 'gay'. The Gay Liberation Front was formed in the immediate aftermath of Stonewall, and the first Gay Pride march was organized on the anniversary of that raid. A few months later, in October 1970, a group of students at the LSE formed a Gay Liberation Front in Britain and slowly gathered support as consciousness-raising groups spread. Published the following year, its *Manifesto* challenged gay men and women to 'come out of the closet' and liberate themselves from 'the oppression which lies in the head of every one of us' and 'to rid society of the gender-role system which is at the root of our oppression'. Echoing the women's liberation movement to which it allied itself, the *Manifesto* insisted gay men and women had to make themselves visible and their demands heard.

Figure 12.9 First Gay Pride rally in London, 1972

It was a tactic on display in September 1971 when gay and lesbian activists disrupted the Festival of Light rally at Trafalgar Square by releasing mice, sounding horns and kissing on stage. Six months later they held the first Gay Pride rally through central London with an estimated 2,000 people shouting 'out and proud' (see Figure 12.9). *Gay News* was also launched in 1972 and two years later the London Lesbian and Gay Switchboard, a telephone service to provide support to the community and those coming out, was established. In 1977 Jeffrey Weeks, who had joined the first GLF group at the LSE in 1970, published the first gay history, *Coming Out: Homosexual Politics in Britain from the Nineteenth Century to the Present*. Yet, it was the Tom Robinson Band's anthem 'Glad to be Gay', first performed at the Gay Pride march of 1976 and eventually released in 1978, that had the greatest mainstream success. Banned from being played on Radio 1, let alone performed on BBC's *Top of the Pops*, it climbed to 18 in the charts and reached number 1 on the listener-voted charts of London's largest commercial station, Capital Radio.

Black Power and Multiculturalism

In many ways the Black Power movement anticipated the politics of the women's liberation movement and the Gay Liberation Front. In November 1967, months after Stokely Carmichael's visit to Britain, Obi Egbuna, the Nigerian-born novelist recently returned from the USA, published *Black Power in Britain*. It called for black men to liberate themselves from the racist oppression that made them feel inferior and taught them that they had to assimilate. Many embraced the new radical black politics. The Black People's Alliance, formed in 1968, drew together around fifty organizations to form 'a militant front for black consciousness against racism'. When the Black Panthers movement was established in 1969, the **Home Office** believed there were more than 2,000 Black Power activists across Britain. A plethora of publications – such as *Black Power Speaks*, *The Black Eagle* and *Freedom News* – appeared, debating the forms and meanings of Black Power. Inspired by the Black Power movement in the United States and the uprisings in Jamaica (1968) and Trinidad (1970), radical black politics in Britain was both resolutely internationalist and committed to local struggles.

A key rallying point came after a series of police raids on the Mangrove, a West Indian restaurant that was a popular meeting place for Black Power activists. The raid resulted in a demonstration against police harassment in 1970 that quickly turned violent. The arrest and trial of nine protestors became a *cause célèbre* of black politics and its analysis of the institutional racism of British society and the police force (see Textbox 12.2 and Figure 12.10). Campaigns against the violent racism of the police were a consistent feature of black political organizations and culminated with the protests against the policing of the Notting Hill Carnival in 1976. Groups like the Brixton Black

12.2 Place: The Mangrove, Notting Hill, London

The Mangrove was a Caribbean restaurant that opened in Notting Hill, West London, in 1968. It was owned by Frank Crichlow, a Trinidadian and black British activist, Roy Hemmings and Jean Cabussel. The restaurant became an iconic meeting place for black intellectuals, artists and activists in the 1960s and 1970s. Famous customers included Bob Marley, Jimi Hendrix, Nina Simone and C.L.R. James. The Mangrove served as a makeshift community centre for London's West Indian community, a place where people went to seek legal aid, talk about politics or eat Caribbean food. The restaurant also served as the informal HQ for the Notting Hill Carnival, and acted as an editorial base for *The Hustler*, a community newspaper. The restaurant was subject to repeated instances of police harassment and intimidation by a group of renegade police officers that *The Hustler* referred to as 'The Heavy Mob'. Although it was raided twelve times between January 1969 and July 1970, police never found evidence of any illegal activity. Meanwhile Frank Crichlow was forced to defend the restaurant against a host of spurious licensing charges, including permitting dancing and allowing his friends to eat sweetcorn and drink tea after 11pm. On 9 August 1970, as a result of these events, Crichlow, along with fellow activist Darcus Howe, led a demonstration that ended in the arrest of Crichlow, Howe and seven other protestors. The protestors became known as the 'Mangrove 9', and were eventually acquitted in a trial that drew national attention to the problem of police racism. (S.W.)

Figure 12.10 The Mangrove owners after a court appearance, 15 August 1970

Panthers also got involved in squatting to find black families housing, while those involved in the Black Education Movement protested, in the words of Bernard Coard's book of 1971, *How the West Indian Child is Made Educationally Subnormal in the British School System* and established their own alternative, 'supplementary', schools. By the early 1970s the formation of black women's groups emerged as much in critique of the masculinity of the Black Power movement as the whiteness of the women's liberation movement.

Nationalisms and 'the Troubles'

Scottish and Welsh nationalism also gathered force in the late 1960s. Politically the nationalist movements in these countries had been represented by **Plaid Cymru** in Wales since 1925, and the Scottish National Party (SNP) from 1934. Emboldened by the internationalist rhetoric of self-determination enshrined in the **League of Nations**, as well as the growing force of nationalist movements across the British Empire, especially the increasing independence of the white Dominions, both parties were no longer content with the low priority given to supporting home rule in Wales and Scotland by the Labour and Liberal parties despite their electoral dependence upon voters in these countries. While Plaid Cymru was chiefly concerned about the decline of the Welsh-speaking population, both political parties followed Ireland by adopting a policy of neutrality during the Second World War. During the 1940s and 1950s the electoral campaigns of Plaid Cymru and the SNP together attracted little more than 5 per cent of the votes.

That began to change in the late 1960s. Voters in Scotland and Wales returned a record number of Labour MPs in 1964 but were disappointed by the failure of the Labour government to arrest the decline of the coal and shipbuilding industries so vital to their economies. If Scots had ultimately embraced Union as a way of advancing their own economic ambitions at home and abroad, it was not clear how these could be furthered given the accelerating pace of decolonization and deindustrialization. Plaid Cymru's first MP was elected in 1966, and the following year the SNP also had an MP elected. As electoral support for these parties grew, the Labour government passed the ameliorative Welsh Language Act in 1967 (which gave Welsh equal status in legal proceedings) and established the Kilbrandon Commission in 1969 to explore models of devolving power to Scotland and Wales. This did not arrest the electoral momentum of both parties, especially in Scotland, where the discovery of North Sea Oil off the Scottish coast and Britain's entry into the European Union provided new ways of imagining Scotland's economic future without England. At the election of October 1974 the SNP attracted 30 per cent of the votes in Scotland and had seven MPs elected, while Plaid Cymru won the support of 11 per cent of Welsh voters and returned three MPs to Westminster. This success became crucial in 1976 when the Labour government lost its parliamentary majority and offered Plaid Cymru and the SNP a referendum on the devolution of powers to Welsh and Scottish Parliaments in return for the support of their MPs. The referendum, which created a huge platform for the nationalist movements in both countries, was held in 1979 but just 12 per cent of electors in Wales, and 33 per cent in Scotland, voted for devolution. The SNP immediately withdrew its MPs' support for the minority Labour government, triggering the election which returned Margaret Thatcher's Conservative government. For the first time since the Jacobite rebellion of 1745, the threat of the break-up of Britain on the mainland had arisen and been adverted. Yet the genie of Welsh and Scottish nationalism, released by the perceived failures of social democracy in those countries, could not be returned to its bottle.

In Ireland, Britain had already begun to break apart in 1922. Since then the Union with Ireland had stubbornly lived on through the partition of the predominantly Protestant population of Northern Ireland from the Irish Free State. The **Irish Republican Army** continued its military operation to reunite the island of Ireland but in 1962 they declared a formal cessation of their armed struggle and sold much of their armoury to the new paramilitary Free Wales Army formed in 1963. The IRA had done little to challenge the discrimination and impoverishment endured by Northern Ireland's Catholic minority. That discrimination intensified after the Second World War when the Protestant-dominated government of Northern Ireland became responsible for the provision of housing and employment. Disproportionately excluded from local elections that only enfranchised propertied ratepayers, the gerrymandering of electoral boundaries ensured that Catholics were also systematically under-represented at both the Stormont and Westminster Parliaments. Even though Catholics accounted for 39 per cent of the population, eleven of Northern Ireland's twelve MPs at Westminster in 1966 belonged to the Protestant Ulster Unionist Party. Three years later Protestants accounted for 75 per cent of the elected representatives in Stormont. Catholics not only found it difficult to secure jobs and public housing, they were confined to living in designated areas by perimeter fencing that enforced a sectarian divide, and frequently faced harassment from a police force that was almost 90 per cent Protestant.

The Campaign for Social Justice was established in 1964 to make visible the systematic discrimination against Catholics. Eschewing the language of anti-colonial nationalism for that of the civil rights movements sweeping the United States, its work was subsumed by the Northern Ireland Civil Rights Association (NICRA) in 1967, an organization that began organizing non-violent marches through Protestant neighbourhoods. In October 1968 NICRA planned a march through the Unionist-controlled town of Derry, where Catholics outnumbered Protestants two to one but were confined to insufficient public housing in designated areas. When the march was first banned, and then violently broken up by the Royal

Ulster Constabulary, the civil rights movement in Northern Ireland became world news. Television footage of police beating unarmed protestors, including a Labour MP, caused outrage across much of the world and a peaceful demonstration of 15,000 in the city a few weeks later. In response to these events, the prime minister of Northern Ireland, Terence O'Neill, introduced a conciliatory but remarkably modest reform programme. It was enough to split his own Unionist Party, with a new group of 'Unofficial Unionists' echoing the hard-line 'loyalism' of the firebrand Presbyterian preacher Ian Paisley. In the spring of 1969 loyalist paramilitary groups, like the Ulster Volunteer Force and Ulster Protestant Volunteers, began a bombing campaign designed to cut off electricity and water supplies to Catholic Belfast. NICRA's continuing protests were met by such violent repression from the RUC that two men were beaten to death with police batons. The escalating conflict came to a head in August 1969 when Protestant marchers in Derry threw pennies over the barricades at the junction marking the Catholic area of Bogside. Despite the widespread use of CS gas and the deployment of armed police, the 'Battle of Bogside' lasted three days. British troops were deployed to separate the police from the Catholic population at Bogside, and riots spread to Belfast where six people were killed. Within a month the British troops had constructed 'Peace Lines' that divided Catholic and Protestant neighbourhoods in Derry and Belfast. 'The Troubles', a deadly civil war between Catholic nationalists and Protestant Unionists that lasted a generation, had begun.

Following the defeat of the revolts of 1968, many radical groups across Europe – like ETA (1968) in Spain, Baader-Meinhof (1968) in West Germany and the Red Brigade in Italy (1970) – turned to violence to achieve their political objectives. In Northern Ireland the violent suppression of the civil rights movement led a group of 'Provisionals' to break from the IRA to reactivate a military campaign against Britain in December 1969. The year before, 'IRA=I Ran Away' had been written on a wall in Catholic West Belfast, but during 1970 and 1971 the Provisional IRA successfully regained the support of many by defending Catholic communities from the loyalist paramilitaries and the RUC. The British military increasingly became seen as enforcers propping up Unionist rule. Nowhere was this more evident than in the infamous events of 'Bloody Sunday' in Derry on 30 January 1972 when the British military shot twenty-six unarmed protestors at a civil rights march, killing fourteen. The British government only took responsibility for this massacre in 2010.

The militarization of the conflict was complete when Edward Heath's Conservative government declared a state of emergency, dissolved Northern Ireland's Stormont Parliament and imposed direct, military, rule from London. The IRA now targeted Britain's military as an occupying force. By the end of 1972, the deadliest year of the conflict, 496 people had been killed and there had been over 2,000 bomb attacks. Fresh attempts to find a political solution began in 1973 by establishing a new 'power-sharing' government in the North and an all-island 'Council of Ireland', but this agreement collapsed by March as elections returned a majority of Unionists opposed to it and the loyalist Ulster Workers' Council declared a general strike. **Enoch Powell** lent his support to this loyalist rebellion and the following October was returned to Westminster as an Ulster Unionist MP. During that general election the IRA extended its campaign to the mainland, killing twenty-six people by bombing pubs in Birmingham and Guildford. The new Labour government promptly introduced the Prevention of Terrorism Act that gave the British state substantial new security powers to arrest and detain those suspected of supporting terrorism, and censored broadcasters from mentioning organizations like the IRA now deemed illegal. If the British Union did not break up during the 1970s, it was held together by the thinnest of threads.

Conclusion

In December 1976, as the Labour Government was announcing that the **International Monetary Fund** had demanded the structural adjustment of the British economy, a new punk band called the Sex Pistols released their debut single 'Anarchy in the UK'. The song expressed the alienation of a punk movement that revolted against social democracy's promises of emancipation and the revolutionary hopes of 1968. Where a decade earlier youth had embraced radical dreams of liberation, punk captured the despair and rage of a new generation's experience of deindustrialization, rising unemployment, cuts to welfare programmes, increasing racial conflict, police violence and the growth of the security state. As the Sex Pistols sang in their next single 'God Save the Queen', 'There is no future / And England's dreaming' (see Textbox 12.3 and Figure 12.11).

A year before the release of 'Anarchy in the UK', the Conservative Party elected Margaret Thatcher as its leader. Like her predecessor Edward Heath, Thatcher was neither an aristocrat nor had been privately educated. She was also the first woman to lead a political party in Britain. Within the Conservative Party Thatcher became a vehicle for those who believed a new form of political economy was required to restore order and make Britain Great once again. Within a decade this new form of political economy had been named 'Thatcherism'. Thatcherism did not just emerge at the same time as the Sex Pistols' version of punk; it shared many features. It evoked a sense that the country was in an increasingly anarchic 'crisis'. It was just as critical of what it viewed as the failures of social democracy to generate prosperity as it was of the permissive culture and radical politics that emerged from the 1960s. It championed a form of English nationalism that mobilized white racism and it enthused a DIY individualism that put its faith in the free market (not the corporate monopolies of what the Sex Pistols called 'the great rock n' roll swindle'). The Sex Pistols may not

12.3 Source: The Sex Pistols, 'God Save the Queen'

In 1977, as Britain prepared to celebrate the twenty-fifth anniversary of the Queen's ascension to the throne, the Sex Pistols released one of the most controversial songs of the post-war era. 'God Save the Queen' openly mocked the monarchy and its 'fascist regime'. The record cover had a Union Jack emblazoned with a crude and defaced silhouette of the Queen, whom the lyrics insisted 'ain't no human being'. Although the song suggested that the 'mad parade' of monarchy only continued 'Cause tourists are money', for her subjects, 'the flowers in the dustbin', 'There is no future / And England's dreaming'. 'God Save The Queen' attracted widespread controversy among politicians and journalists. The BBC and the Independent Broadcasting Authority refused to play the song. Despite this, the song came second in the charts (although some claimed that the charts were rigged against the band).

Figure 12.11 Poster for 'God Save the Queen', 1977

have had a vision of the future, but like Thatcherism they believed that social democracy was not working and needed to be destroyed.

Although this politics came to be named after Thatcher, it was not her creation. In Britain, **Enoch Powell** anticipated much of it. Since the 1950s Powell had developed a critique of welfare capitalism and advocated a return to economic **liberalism** around the reduction of public expenditure, tighter monetary controls and the deregulation of currency and labour markets. He even resigned as Chief Secretary of the **Treasury** in 1958 in protest at the refusal of the

Macmillan government to reduce public expenditure sufficiently. During the 1960s, when he served as both Minister for Health and Shadow Defence Secretary, and was widely viewed as a potential leader of the party, Powell frequently lamented the way in which welfare capitalism and permissiveness had eroded personal responsibility and respect for the rule of law, and even threatened British culture. In some ways Powell's analysis drew on the work of economist Friedrich Hayek who worked at the LSE during the 1940s and whose critique of Keynesian welfare capitalism, *The Road to Serfdom* (1945), was widely influential. Powell was involved with both the internationally oriented Mont Perelin Society that Hayek founded in 1947 to propagate ideas of economic liberalism, as well as the Institute of Economic Affairs, whose creation in Britain during the mid 1950s was inspired by Hayek.

By the time Powell left the Conservative Party in 1974 in opposition to Britain's entry into the **European Economic Community**, the ideas of economic **liberalism** he had helped espouse were growing in popularity across the world. That year, Hayek won the Nobel Prize for Economics and in Britain Keith Joseph established the Centre for Policy Studies to 'convert the Tory Party' to economic liberalism. Joseph appointed Margaret Thatcher as his deputy chairman. The following year, as Conservative MPs elected Thatcher as their new leader, Milton Friedman, an admirer of Hayek and Powell, was appointed by the new Chilean dictator Pinochet to introduce liberalizing shock therapy to that country's economy through austerity measures, tight monetary controls and deregulation. The **International Monetary Fund's structural adjustment** programme for Britain, which began in the year Friedman was awarded a Nobel Prize, bore the mark of shock therapy.

The year 1976 did not mark the end of social democracy in Britain. It proved much harder to destroy than its critics on both the left and right imagined. Yet just as the political and economic crisis of 1931 ushered out the classical liberal economics of **free trade**, cheap government and the **gold standard**, so various pressures culminated in a Labour government accepting the savage cuts demanded by an IMF loan in 1976, which proved a decisive moment. As we have seen, social democracy was weakened by the compromised national, imperial and global conditions in which it was constructed within Britain. Increasingly a new generation of Britons born immediately after the war, as well as Commonwealth citizens fleeing the ruins of Britain's late Empire, forged new forms of politics that were frequently transnational in formation and cosmopolitan in orientation. These politics sought to expose the limits and contradictions of a social democracy built around the primacy of the white, heterosexual, industrial working-class man. These politics in turn generated a reaction by the very white working class whose communities were being broken up by slum clearance schemes and the collapse of industries that had once supported them. The genius of Thatcherism was to wed their sense of dispossession to a new political economy of liberalization from which they had nothing to gain.

FURTHER READING

Historians have only turned their attention to the history of post-war Britain in the past generation. Consequently, there is a good deal less canonical reading than for earlier periods and much new work is constantly being published that addresses many of the areas discussed in this chapter. A useful and empirically rich starting point remains A.H. Halsey and Josephine Webb, *Twentieth-Century British Social Trends* (Basingstoke, 2000). Changing employment patterns, including the abiding disparities between men's and women's pay, are well covered in Nicholas Crafts et al. (eds.), *Work and Pay in Twentieth-Century Britain* (Oxford, 2007).

Selina Todd's *The People: The Rise and Fall of the Working Class 1910–2010* (London, 2015) provides a good overview of the changing forms of work and working-class life in the post-war period. It should be read in conjunction with Mike Savage's *Identities and Social Change in Britain Since 1940: The Politics of Method* (Oxford, 2010) which is our best account of the proliferation of attempts to understand how to define class and study its changing forms. The gendered nature of the experience of class can be explored in Elizabeth Roberts, *Women and Families: An Oral History, 1940–1970* (Oxford, 1995), and Stephanie Spencer, *Gender, Work and Education in Britain in the 1950s* (Basingstoke, 2005). Kathleen Paul's *Whitewashing Britain: Race and Citizenship in the Postwar Era* (Ithaca, NY, 1997) remains the best introduction to the racism experienced by Commonwealth citizens and their changing status with regard to immigration laws. Camilla Schofield's *Enoch Powell and the Making of Postcolonial Britain* (Cambridge, 2013) grapples with the formation of Powellism and the history of white racism.

The political debates that surrounded the changing nature of society amidst the apparent affluence of post war-Britain are well detailed in Lawrence Black and Neil Pemberton (eds.), *An Affluent Society? Britain's Post-War 'Golden Age' Revisited* (Aldershot, 2004), and Lawrence Black, *The Political Culture of the Left in Affluent Britain, 1951–64: Old Labour, New Britain?* (Basingstoke, 2003). In contrast, the rediscovery of poverty and the formation of new NGOs to address the inadequacies of the welfare state are addressed in David Vincent, *Poor Citizens: The State and the Poor in Twentieth-Century Britain* (London, 1991), and Matthew Hilton et al., *The Politics of Expertise: How NGOs Shaped Modern Britain* (Oxford, 2013).

The emergence of post-war youth culture is set in a longer context by David Fowler, *Youth Culture in Modern Britain, 1920–1970: From Ivory Tower to Global Movement – A New History* (Basingstoke, 2008). The still essential starting point remains Stuart Hall and Tony Jefferson (eds.), *Resistance Through Rituals: Youth Subcultures in Post-War Britain* (London, 1976). Good overviews of the music scene in the 1960s and 1970s are provided by Keith Gildart, *Images of England through Popular Music: Class, Youth and Rock 'n' Roll, 1955–1976* (New York, 2013), and David Simonelli, *Working Class Heroes: Rock Music and British Society in the 1960s and 1970s* (Lanham, 2013).

The declining authority of the established churches in the 1960s is the central thesis of Callum Brown's *The Death of Christian Britain: Understanding Secularisation, 1800–2000* (London, 2001). It is an argument that remains controversial, as is evident from John Wolffe (ed.), *Religion in History: Conflict, Conversion and Coexistence* (2004). There is a similarly lively debate between historians about when the new 'permissiveness' emerged and how transformative it was. Frank Mort's *Capital Affairs: London and the Making of Permissive Society* (2010) urges us to consider the 1950s as the beginning of those changes. Despite the title of Hera Cook's *The Long Sexual Revolution: British Women, Sex and Contraception in the Twentieth Century* (Oxford, 2004), she still sees the 1960s as a transformative moment, as does Jeffrey Weeks in *Sex, Politics and Society: The Regulation of Sexuality Since 1800* (London, 1981). That account is questioned from different perspectives by Kate Fisher and Simon Szreter, *Sex Before the Sexual Revolution: Intimate Life in England 1918–1963* (Cambridge, 2010), Pat Thane and Tanya Evans, *Sinners? Scroungers? Saints? Unmarried Motherhood in Twentieth-Century England* (Oxford, 2011), and Rebecca Jennings, *Tomboys and Bachelor Girls: A Lesbian History of Post-war Britain, 1945–71* (Manchester, 2007). Matt Cook's *Queer Domesticities: Homosexualities and Home Life in Twentieth Century London* (London, 2014) and Claire Langhamer's *The English in Love: The Intimate Story of an Emotional Revolution* (Oxford, 2013) chart the reconfiguration of affective life in the home.

The new forms of politics that emerged in Britain around the revolts of 1968 have yet to be the subject of a single book. A useful comparative treatment that is alive to the transnational nature of these movements is Martin Klimke and Joachim Scharloth (eds.), *1968 in Europe: A History of Protest and Activism, 1956–1977* (Basingstoke, 2008). Jodi Burkett's *Constructing Post-Imperial Britain: Britishness, 'Race' and the Radical Left in the 1960s* (Basingstoke, 2013) helpfully includes chapters on the anti-Apartheid movement, students and civil rights in Northern Ireland and can be read alongside Celia Hughes, *Young Lives on the Left: Sixties Activism and the Liberation of the Self* (London, 2015). Elizabeth Nelson's *The British Counter-Culture, 1966–73: A Study of the Underground Press* (Basingstoke, 1989) and Jonathon Green's *Days in the Life: Voices from the English Underground, 1961–1971* (London, 1988) provide sources from the underground press. Dennis Dworkin's *Cultural Marxism in Post-war Britain: History, the New Left and the Origins of Cultural Studies* (Durham, NC, 1997) is an indispensable intellectual history of the New Left. David Bouchier's *The Feminist Challenge: The Movement for Women's Liberation in Britain and the USA* (London, 1983) does a good job of outlining the Anglo-American formation of second wave feminism while Natalie Thomlinson's *Race and Ethnicity in the Women's Movement in England, 1968–1993* (London, 2016) explores its fraught racial politics. The politics of the Gay Liberation Front is addressed in Lucy Robinson, *Gay Men and the Left in Post-War Britain: How the Personal Got Political* (Manchester, 2007).

Only recently have we begun to see accounts of the formation of black politics in Britain that are written by those who were not activists. Paul Gilroy's *There Ain't No Black in the Union Jack: The Cultural Politics of Race and Nation* (London, 1987) was inspirational for many but remained alone in the field for too long. It can now be supplemented by Marc Matera, *Black London, The Imperial Metropolis and Decolonization in the Twentieth Century* (Berkeley, 2015), Kenetta Hammond Perry, London is the Place for Me: Black Britons, Citizenship and the Politics of Race (Oxford, 2016) and Anandi Ramamurthy's *Black Star: Britain's Asian Youth Movements* (London, 2013) gets us out of London and addresses the different politics of Asian youth during the 1970s and 1980s.

Histories of the civil rights and nationalist movements in Northern Ireland, Wales and Scotland are also in short supply. The earliest attempt to see them in the round was Tom Nairn, *The Break-Up of Britain: Crisis and Neo-Nationalism*, 2nd edn (London, 1981). Simon Prince locates the civil rights movement in a much needed broader context in his excellent *Northern Ireland's '68: Civil Rights, Global Revolt and the Origins of the Troubles* (Dublin, 2007), while Richard English's *Armed Struggle: The History of the IRA* (London, 2003) is the definitive account of the IRA during the Troubles. Christopher Harvie's *Scotland and Nationalism: Scottish Society and Politics, 1707 to the Present*, 4th edn (London, 2004) and T.M. Devine's *The Scottish Nation: A Modern History* (London, 2012) provide a deep history of Scottish nationalism, while Jim Phillips's *The Industrial Politics of Devolution: Scotland in the 1960s and 1970s* (Manchester, 2008) focuses on its recent connection to deindustrialization.

V

1976–: A New Liberalism?

13 The Neoliberal Revolution and the Making of *Homo Economicus*

Introduction

The **International Monetary Fund** loan and structural adjustment programme accepted by the Labour government in December 1976 stabilized the plummeting value of the now free-floating pound, and by the summer of 1978 inflation had fallen from 23 to 8 per cent while the number of unemployed had levelled out at 1.4 million or 5 per cent of the workforce. To keep inflation in check the government insisted that public sector wages should continue to be set below the rate of inflation, in part to offset the wage inflation in the private sector. In 1978, with inflation hovering between 8 and 10 per cent, it sought to impose a 5 per cent pay deal upon public sector workers who were represented by two of the largest unions with 1.4 million members. The resulting strikes and disruption to public services – from rubbish collection to grave-digging – became known as 'the Winter of Discontent'. During it, the leftist social theorist Stuart Hall took stock of what he called Britain's 'Great Moving Right Show'. After all, a Labour government had ceded sovereignty over economic policy to the IMF, cut public services, partly privatized BP, and taken on the powerful public sector unions. These policies had a striking resemblance to those of the Conservative Party under its new leader Margaret Thatcher. Describing these for the first time as 'Thatcherism', Hall suggested they had been remarkably successful at forging a new 'populist common sense'. The new creed combined a belief that only the competitive pressures of free markets could end welfare dependency and restore personal responsibility, with an insistence upon respect for the rule of law and the primacy of the Christian family. Three months after Hall published this article, Margaret Thatcher's Conservative Party was elected to form a new government.

In the decades that followed, Conservative and Labour governments continued 'The Great Moving Right Show'. Within a generation the central pillars of Britain's post-war social democracy had been largely dismantled. The aspiration of government was no longer to manage a mixed economy to provide prosperity and social security for all. Instead its priority was to allow markets to transform government as well as economic and social life. In the nineteenth century, liberal political economy had posited that, once markets had been set free from the mercantilist shackles of the **ancien regime**, the work of government was to leave the economy alone and focus instead on social problems and the civil rights of those deemed able to possess them. In contrast, the new form of economic liberalism that gradually took hold of Britain from the 1970s believed that the discipline and logic of free markets were not confined to the economic domain but should extend to all areas of social and political life. Where once the state had collectively ensured the welfare of society as a whole, this 'neo' form of **liberalism** now considered that it was the responsibility of individuals to secure their own prosperity and security from a market economy that provided cheaper and more efficient services. As these neoliberal principles eventually took hold, they created a new type of person – *homo economicus* – who understood themselves and the world in purely economistic terms. As Margaret Thatcher declared in 1981: 'Economics are the method, the object is to change the heart and soul.'

Over thirty years after he published 'The Great Moving Right Show', Stuart Hall reflected upon the remarkable success and resilience of this 'neoliberal revolution'. **Neoliberalism**, he argued, was now the common sense of the age, embracing much of the world and even surviving the global financial crisis of 2008 that plunged the global economy into recession. This chapter will explore how this revolution swept Britain. In doing so it completes our history of the rise, fall and reinvention of liberal political economy. Yet just as liberalism and social democracy emerged in critique of the systems they sought to displace, and yet remained haunted by their continuing presence, so the neoliberal revolution was shaped around the sometimes surprisingly enduring forms of social democracy. Indeed, one of the ironies is that, at least initially, much of the neoliberal revolution in Britain was enacted from the top down by a state that social democracy had given unprecedented power. Even so, this neoliberal revolution was not the product of any one set of ideas or social or political group. Neither did it happen overnight. It unfolded fitfully amidst a good deal of protest and contention. It was also importantly embedded in broader global political and economic processes that shaped how it unfolded in Britain.

TIMELINE

1976	International Monetary Fund loan
1978–9	'Winter of Discontent'
1979	Election of Thatcher
1980	Employment Act Right to Buy scheme Assisted Places scheme
1981	Howe budget
1982	Employment Act Neighbourhood Watch
1983	Falklands War and Thatcher's second term Kinnock becomes leader of Labour

1984	Miners' strike
	Crimewatch on TV
1986	Body Shop goes public
1986	Big Bang deregulation of financial markets
	Privatization of British Telecom and British Airways
	Abolition of Greater London Council
1987	Debtors Anonymous and National Debt Line
1988	Section 28
	Education Act
1991	Citizen's Charter
1992	Private Finance Initiative
1994	Privatization of coal and rail
1995	Blair and repeal of clause 4
1998	*Who Wants to Be a Millionaire*
2000	Millennium Dome Experience
2001	Decriminalization of cannabis
2002	Countryside Alliance protest against foxhunting ban
2005	Gay marriage

Making Markets and Structural Adjustment

The **International Monetary Fund structural adjustment** package of 1976 was a Trojan horse that ushered in new forms of economic liberalism. **Neoliberalism** did not arrive in Britain fully formed; it cohered slowly over several decades as different ideas and policies developed in response to particular events or predicaments. The stagflation of the 1970s helped promote a 'monetarist' emphasis on reducing inflation by controlling the money supply. This entailed reducing public expenditure and the borrowing required to sustain it, trying to balance the books by selling off nationalized industries, and breaking the power of the trade union movement, which was blamed for pushing up wages and making British business uncompetitive. Increasingly this approach was complemented by supply-side policies that 'incentivized' work by cutting benefits, encouraged 'entrepreneurial' culture by reducing corporate and personal taxation rates, and privatized once public goods and services to make them more efficient. The principle of competition was also introduced to services that remained public – like health and education – to improve their delivery to citizens as consumers. It was hoped that the new market for services, both public and private, would end dependency upon 'the nanny state' and force citizens to take responsibility for investing in and securing their own futures.

Privatization

The IMF loan led the Labour Party to begin selling off public assets with its part privatization of BP, but the policy accelerated under Margaret Thatcher's Conservative governments. Although many in the Conservative Party had long advocated denationalization, privatization was at first driven less by ideology than a pragmatic need to raise revenue. It was the most profitable nationalized industries that were privatized first: further tranches of BP (1979 and 1983), British Aerospace, British Sugar, as well as Cable and Wireless (1981), Ferranti and BritOil (1982). The former Conservative prime minister Harold Macmillan equated the policy to selling off the family silver. In addition, as the state reduced its grants to local governments, they were encouraged to sell off their own assets, such as council houses and school playing fields, to replace lost revenues. Only after 1983, when Thatcher's Conservative Party was re-elected to a second term in office, was the policy extended to ensure that so-called 'lame duck' industries, that drained the public purse, were sold off. The aim was to reduce expenditure and make these industries competitive by exposing them to the discipline of the market. In this phase of privatization, major companies with significant numbers of employees – like Associated British Ports (1983), British Telecom and Jaguar (1984), British Airways (1986), Rolls Royce (1987), British Steel (1988) and British Coal (1990) – were sold off. Thereafter, Conservative governments turned their attention to the public utilities and transport infrastructures, privatizing water (1989), gas (1990), electricity (1994) and the nuclear industry British Energy (1986), as well as British Rail (1996), airports, bus and freight services. The growing hostility to the privatization of these services, and to their replacement with large private monopoly providers, was most evident when plans to sell the Royal Mail postal service were dropped in 1994.

Between 1979 and 1997, over eighty public companies were privatized, raising an estimated total of £86 billion. In addition to this revenue, the amount of public borrowing required to sustain nationalized industries and their employees was dramatically reduced. In 1981 subsidies to industries in the public sector ran to £2.7 billion, but a decade later they had been slashed to just over £1 billion (at 1988/9 prices). In 1975 nationalized industries boasted 1,816,000 employees; by 1997 they had just 242,000 workers. Indeed, with cuts to welfare services too, the percentage of the workforce

13.1 Place: Millennium Dome, Greenwich, London

Towards the end of the twentieth century, former industrial neighbourhoods played host to a number of fantastical regeneration projects, usually conceived of as partnerships between the state and the private sector. Perhaps the most spectacular of these projects was the Millennium Dome in Greenwich, first conceived by John Major's Conservative government but ambitiously expanded by the newly elected Labour government under Tony Blair in the late 1990s. The Dome was a vast exhibition space built to herald the new millennium, a conscious allusion to the monumental spaces of the 1851 **Great Exhibition** and the 1951 Festival of Britain. The dome was also billed as a triumph of New Labour's dedication to public-private infrastructure projects, where state contracts were funded and implemented by private businesses and developers. A significant amount of the capital for the dome was raised through the introduction of a weekly National Lottery in 1994. The dome consisted of seven pavilions designed to reflect life in contemporary Britain at the millennium. Its 'Spirit Level' hosted an exhibition on the human mind, sponsored by the British arms manufacturer BAE Systems, while the 'Learning Curve' pavilion on education and learning as a life-long process for a flexible workforce was sponsored by the supermarket chain Tesco. With only 6.5 million visitors in 2000, the Dome failed to become commercially viable and fell into disuse, becoming a source of ridicule. One *Guardian* article suggested alternative uses for the dome, including turning it upside down to create a giant satellite dish. In recent years the dome has become a concert venue sponsored by the British telecoms company O2. (S.W.)

employed by the public sector, excluding the National Health Service, shrank from 28 to 8 per cent in the same period.

Privatization may have slowed down but it did not stop when a Labour government finally returned to power in 1997 for the first time since 1979 (see Textbox 13.1 and Figure 13.1). The very first act of the newly elected government was to return the **Bank of England** to the private sector. Two years later, parts of the portfolio of the government-owned Student Loans Company, created when tuition fees were first introduced in 1998, were sold off to raise £2 billion. A number of municipal airports were also sold (from Bristol in 1997 to Leeds in 2007), as were the London Underground (2003) and British Nuclear Fuels (2007). Yet the real development was the proliferation of so-called public/private initiatives through the **Private Finance Initiative (PFI)**. First developed by Australian governments in the 1980s and adopted by the Conservative government in the mid 1990s, PFI became the principal way that the Labour government sought to improve Britain's ageing public infrastructures after 1997. PFI used public funds to raise private capital to fund the construction and maintenance of new hospitals, roads and schools for a designated period. It was effectively a credit mechanism that ensured that government borrowing would be confined to servicing the annual cost of the contract,

Figure 13.1 The Millennium Dome Experience PLC

effectively the debt on loans, not the considerably larger capital costs required to build and maintain infrastructure. Controversially, the cost of servicing PFI contracts not only deferred payments upon future generations, they were often vast. In 2007 the total capital value of PFI contracts was £68 billion, while to service these contracts the exchequer was committed to an additional £251 billion. If privatization had initially been designed to reduce government borrowing, by the late 1990s it was being used to leverage loans. Although during the financial crisis of 2008–9 the Labour government was forced to nationalize some of Britain's failing banks, they were privatized again, along with the Royal Mail, after the Conservatives returned to power in 2009.

Privatization dismantled the state built around managing the mixed economy since the 1930s. The work of privatization was not just to reorient the responsibilities of the state; it was also used to sell the idea of 'popular capitalism'. Increasing the number of those who owned property and owned shares was a key strategy of Thatcher's Conservative government, one that was presented as a democratizing move. It was first laid out when the Housing Act of 1980 allowed tenants the **right to buy** the council houses they inhabited. The minister responsible, Michael Heseltine, proudly proclaimed that the government wanted to foster the 'deeply ingrained desire for home ownership' for it 'enables parents to accrue wealth for their children and stimulates the attitudes of independence and self-reliance that are the bedrock of a free society'. With council houses offered for sale at bedrock rates, 30–50 per cent below their market value according to the amount of rent paid by their tenants, the politics of the Act transcended its economics as a way of raising revenue. Not surprisingly, at these prices, it was a hugely popular measure. A million council houses were sold by 1987 and a further million by 1999. Between 1979 and 2009, the number of households in public housing fell from 5.5 to 3.8 million (just 18 per cent of all households). While the proportion of households who owned their own property rose from 55 per cent in 1979 to 70 per cent by 2001, this did not accelerate a trend evident since the 1950s (see Graph 13.1). Even so, the long-held Conservative dream of a property-owning democracy had edged a little closer.

Just as **right to buy** was portrayed as a way of democratizing the property market, so privatization was increasingly presented as a way of propagating a broader culture of share ownership. The privatization of British Telecom in 1984 was the first to be accompanied by a huge 'Tell Sid' advertising campaign aimed at the general public. The minimum share price was set at a relatively modest £250 and applications were heavily oversubscribed, with more than 2 million applicants. So successful was the campaign that 'Tell Sid' became a recurring motif in future privatizations like that for British Gas. With the minimum share price set at just £150, applications for British Gas shares were oversubscribed by four times. A rash of books that aimed to demystify trading in shares began to be published, with titles such as *The Shares Game: How to Buy and Sell Stocks and Shares* (1987) and *How to Make a Killing in the Share Jungle* (1989). The money pages of newspapers followed suit as a growing number of people became interested in buying and trading shares on the stock market.

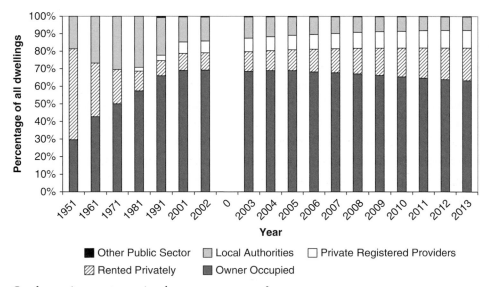

Graph 13.1 A property-owning democracy, 1951–2013?

Figure 13.2 The flotation of shares in British steel, London Stock Market, 1987

There was little mystery about the success of these share issues of newly privatized companies. As with council houses, the initial share prices were grossly undervalued. Thus for BT and British Gas the unit price of a share was set at 50 pence but on the opening day of trading the price reached 93 and 62.5 pence, an 86 and 25 per cent gain respectively (see figure 13.2). So eager were some to profit that, like the Conservative MP Keith Best, they made fraudulent applications under false names. The enormous profits made on these shares helped Britons overlook the fact that they were being asked to buy shares in a company they had already owned when it was nationalized. The so-called 'Big Bang' deregulation of the stock market in October 1986 was also presented as a way of making it more accessible to the general public. The government's portrayal of the City of London as an elitist institution, dominated by a privately educated 'old boy' network and restrictive practices, struck a chord. In one stroke, the Financial Services Act removed fixed minimum commissions, the distinction between brokers who dealt with clients and jobbers who traded on the floor, and the exclusion of foreigners as members of the stock market. The traditional ways of conducting business in what some proclaimed as 'the finest gentleman's club in the world' had been eradicated.

Yet for all the rhetoric, popular capitalism remained a chimera. In some areas the right to buy scheme, which was not confined to tenants, was used as a way of securing second 'rental' homes in the property market. By 2013, 36 per cent of the council houses sold in London were being let back to councils by private landlords at much higher 'market' rents, which were then subsidized by government-funded Housing Benefit. A shortage of new public housing stock pushed up rents and property prices. In 1976 half of all the 324,840 houses built in Britain were publicly owned, but by 1980 just 88,530 of a total 242,000 were publicly owned, and by 2004 that figure had shrunk to just 130 of the 203,490 new houses built. The sustained boom in property prices in Britain since the 1990s has in fact priced many first-time buyers out of the market. Indeed, the proportion of owner-occupiers has actually contracted since 2003 (see Graph 13.1).

Similarly, the Thatcherite dream of broadening share ownership remained illusory. The number of individuals who owned shares did increase from around 4 million to 11 million between 1983 and 1990, but thereafter it fell back down to a plateau of around 10 million, or 20 per cent of households (half of which held only privatized shares in a median of three companies). Rather than democratizing capital, privatization and the Big Bang deregulation of financial services opened up the City of London to overseas,

Table 13.1 Ownership of UK shares

Sector	1957	1963	1969	1975	1981	1990	2000	2010
Individuals	65.8	54.0	47.4	37.5	28.2	20.3	16.0	11.5
Insurance companies	8.8	10.0	12.2	15.9	20.5	20.4	21.0	8.6
Pension funds	3.4	6.4	9.0	16.8	26.7	31.7	17.7	5.1
Investment trusts	5.2	7.4	,,	,,	,,	1.6	1.3	2.1
Unit trusts	0.5	1.3	2.9	4.1	3.6	6.1	1.1	6.7
Banks	0.9	1.3	1.7	0.7	0.3	0.7	1.4	2.5
Other financial institutions[1]	2.8	3.9	10.1	10.5	6.8	0.7	2.8	16.0
Charities	1.9	2.1	2.1	2.3	2.2	1.9	1.4	0.9
Private non-financial companies	2.7	5.1	5.4	3.0	5.1	2.8	1.5	2.3
Public sector[2]	3.9	1.5	2.6	3.6	3.0	2.0	-	3.1
Foreign	4.4	7.0	6.6	5.6	3.6	11.8	35.7	41.2
Total	100.0	100.0	100.0	100.0	100.0	100.0	100.0	100.0

[1]Includes Stock Exchange for 1957 and 1963 and Invesment trusts for 1969, 1975 and 1981.
[2]Public sector comprises local and central government and public corporations.

Sources: ONS 'Ownership of UK Quoted Shares 2010'; Moyle (1971).

primarily American, finance. Individual investors owned the greatest proportion, 65.8 per cent, of shares in 1957. As Table 13.1 illustrates, that proportion steadily shrank in the following decades, reaching just 11.5 per cent by 2010. In contrast, the percentage of shares owned by foreign companies rose dramatically, from just 3.6 to 41.2 per cent between 1981 and 2010. For all the rhetorical claims of popular capitalism, privatization and deregulation actually helped concentrate wealth and open British companies up to a wave of overseas takeovers.

Deindustrialization

Privatization signalled the refusal to allow the state to subsidize industries in order to sustain employment. It replaced the social democratic priority of full employment with reducing government expenditure and maximizing profits or share value. As a consequence it ushered in the collapse of Britain's manufacturing sector and the massive growth of unemployment. Whereas manufacturing sustained the long boom of the post-war years with an annual rate of growth of 3.1 per cent, between 1973 and 2007 manufacturing growth fell to a paltry 0.4 per cent (almost 2 per cent lower than Japan, Italy, France and the United States). As companies were sold, their workforce was quickly 'downsized' to make them more productive and to increase dividends for shareholders. When that failed, they simply closed. In 1979 over 7 million workers were employed in the manufacturing sector, yet by the mid 1990s that had fallen to just 4.5 million and continued to fall to 4.25 million by 2010. Employment in manufacturing accounted for 34 per cent of the total workforce in 1971, but by 2000 it had fallen to just 15.7 per cent. Factories, mills and shipyards closed with devastating effect across the former industrial heartlands of Britain. Unemployment quickly rose to levels not seen since the 1930s. In 1979, unemployment stood at an unprecedented post-war height of 1.3 million, 5.7 per cent of the workforce. Four years later, at the end of Margaret Thatcher's first term of government, it reached 3.2 million, 14 per cent of the workforce. Although it fell briefly to 1.5 million in 1990, it reached 3 million again three years later and has never since fallen back to below 1.5 million. It has since become routine for more than 2 million people to be out of work, something still unimaginable in the mid 1970s.

The return of mass unemployment set the scene for the deregulation of the labour market and an assault upon the trade union movement. The Conservative Party had long blamed trade unions for making British business uncompetitive and the country ungovernable. Following the Winter of Discontent, the Employment Acts of 1980 and 1982 sought to curtail the powers of unions. They made secondary picketing and closed shops (where employment required joining a specific union) illegal, and required that elections be held to elect union officials, to hold a strike, or to allow use of political funds to support the Labour Party. Trade unions had never before had as many members as the 13 million they had in 1979, but the collapse of manufacturing industry had already helped reduce their membership to 11 million by 1983 and by 2002 it had fallen to just over 7 million.

The defeat of the **miners' strike** in 1984 was decisive. Although the National Union of Mineworkers had helped bring down the Heath government in 1974, their power and numbers were already in decline with the discovery of North Sea Oil and the increasing use of nuclear power. A union that had boasted 1.25 million members in 1920, had shrunk to 450,000 by 1950, and to just 240,000 in 1983 when there remained just 170 working mines. When the National Coal Board announced the closure of the twenty most unprofitable of these mines in 1984, the NUM's leader, Arthur Scargill, called a national strike without having held the now legally required national vote of his members. The dispute was a bitter, violent and deeply divisive one that lasted almost a year. Despite widespread support for the miners – opinion polls indicated that at least 30 per cent of the country supported the strike – many were critical of Scargill's refusal to hold a ballot. In Nottinghamshire, unaffected by the potential closures, many miners continued to work and even voted out their local NUM officials who had supported the strike. With large stockpiles of coal, the use of informants and police violence, as well as a largely hostile media, the striking miners were eventually forced to return to work having achieved only a temporary reprieve for the closure of five mines. It was a devastating defeat. By 1992, when British Coal closed 32 of its remaining 50 deep mines and laid off a further 30,000 miners, it employed just 20,000 miners. When British Coal was privatized in 1994 there were just 10,000 miners left, and by 2004 there were only 6 mines left employing fewer than 3,000 miners. The communities that had been built around coal-mining over the previous two hundred years fell into ruin like the NUM, once the most powerful union in the country.

The attack on trade unions was not just to ensure they could never again bring down governments; it was also essential to the deregulation of the labour market. Making labour cheaper and less secure was seen by Conservative governments as necessary to attract investment from abroad, as well as to increase the competitiveness of British business and the efficiency of public services. The explicit aim was to make Britain a magnet to foreign companies looking for a foothold in European markets but wary of the strong labour laws and higher corporate tax rates on the continent. Mass unemployment helped drive down employment standards, so that accepting lower wages and casual or part-time jobs became a necessity for many. Despite the growing disparity between those in work and those unemployed or underemployed, the annual growth rate of real wages fell from 3.16 per cent between 1951 and 1973 to 1.23 per cent between 1973 and 2001. The days in which a single male breadwinner's wage could support a household, and job security meant many had one employer throughout their working life and were supported in retirement by generous state and company pensions, were gone. As early as 1986 it was estimated that a third of those employed were part of the new 'flexible' workforce. The dramatic growth of short-term contracts and part-time work significantly reduced labour costs. By the 1990s two thirds of those in part-time jobs worked less than sixteen hours a week and could thus claim no maternity or redundancy pay unless they improbably had five years of continuous employment.

Lower wages, shorter contracts and less security at work accelerated the growth of women's employment to supplement household income. Women's participation in the labour force rose from 52 to 71 per cent between 1975 and 1997 (in 2014 it was 74 per cent). The greatest area of growth was among women with children, especially those with children under the age of five: by 1992, 43 per cent of these women were working, compared to 25 per cent in 1973. The vast majority of women with children were employed in part-time jobs, indeed over 90 per cent of the increase in women's employment between 1971 and 1993 was in part-time work. By 1993 almost half of women employees were working part-time. And, of course, much of this growth occurred in lower-paid work in the service sector, especially in health, education, clerical, retail and the growing personal 'care' services. Even those women in full-time work continued to earn around 75 per cent of what their male colleagues did. Needless to say, the growth of women's employment did not ease their double shift at home. In 1988 women working part-time remained responsible for housework in 88 per cent of households, and even when both partners were working full-time that figure fell to just 72 per cent.

The growth of the service sector was as dramatic as the collapse of manufacturing. In 1971 the service sector already employed over 50 per cent of the workforce, but by 1999 that figure had risen to 75 per cent. The two largest areas of growth were financial and business services (which employed 18.6 per cent of the labour force in 1999, up from 6.2 per cent in 1971), and the health industries (whose share of the workforce rose from 4.1 to 10.2 per cent between 1971 and 1999). The expansion of financial and business services was a consequence of both the outsourcing of work – like catering, cleaning, customer service and accountancy – that many companies had traditionally conducted in-house, and the growth of computing which enabled the decentralization of services related to the delivery and analysis of information. The export value of these business and financial services almost doubled between 1980 and 2000, helping to offset some of the growing trade deficit that accompanied the collapse of manufacturing.

It is impossible to consider deindustrialization and the rise of the service economy in Britain outside of the global context. It is true that Britain's deindustrialization occurred faster and went further than that of any other OECD country, but like the rise of its service sector (where it was second only to the USA), the process was evident in all countries that had industrialized early. The 'globalization' of the world economy through ever faster telecommunication, information technology and transportation systems meant that manufacturing was outsourced overseas and 'back-office' business services were 'offshored' to reduce labour costs. This book was typeset in India. During the 1990s the manufacturing of most things – from soft toys and clothes to cars and computers – increasingly took place not in the Midlands but in Asia. Similarly, 'customer service' operations were first outsourced to call centres in South Asia, and then handled remotely through the internet. In the new global division of labour, Britain was a consumer of goods made overseas and an exporter of financial services, luxury or legacy brands and technology. Combining many of these features, the arms industry, which benefited from a combination of early privatization and continued public investment in the 1980s as the **Cold War** intensified, was a beneficiary. In 1980 the export of arms made in Britain was valued at £580 million, a decade later the total value reached £2.4 billion, and at the turn of the twenty-first century Britain was the second largest exporter of arms in the world.

Marketization of Public Services

Three important areas of public service – health care, education and policing – were not privatized. Although there were some who advocated privatizing them, they remained politically the final frontier and illustrated the stubborn hold of social democratic values among the electorate. Nonetheless, both Conservative and Labour governments came to believe that even here the competitive discipline of markets was required to make the public sector cheaper and more efficient in delivering services. This entailed transforming both the providers and users of these services. Doctors, teachers and police officers were stripped of the professional autonomy and elevated social status they had possessed within the welfare state to make them more accountable and efficient. Citizens were, in turn, 'empowered' as consumers to demand higher-quality service and greater choice, even if that entailed them having to take responsibility for finding out what choices and services they could expect. Much of this was made possible by the development of an 'audit culture' that sought to measure the performance of public services and rank them in league tables so that citizens could make informed choices as consumers.

The first element of this programme was cutting funding levels of these services, a process that, as we have seen, began in 1976. In 1975 public expenditure peaked at 48 per cent of GDP, but by 1989 it had been reduced to 34 per cent (it did not again rise over 40 per cent until 2008 and three years later was only 3 per cent shy of its level in 1975). As we can see from Graph 13.2, after 1976 education and health, like housing, took the biggest hits within welfare budgets. The education budget peaked at 6.5 per cent of GDP in 1975 but by 1989 it had fallen to 4.25 per cent. Health expenditure hovered around 5 per cent of GDP in the late 1970s and early 1980s but fell to 4.3 per cent by the end of the decade. These cuts would prove to be short-lived, for expenditure on

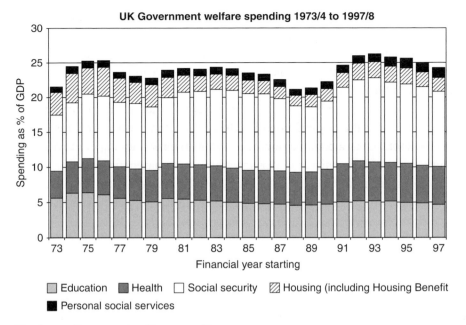

Graph 13.2 Government welfare expenditure, 1973–1997

health and education, as for social services generally, began to grow again in the 1990s and into the twenty-first century. In fact, levels of public expenditure actually increased from £210 billion to £270 billion between 1979 and 1997 when Conservatives were in power advocating the virtues of small government.

Indeed, cuts to public services during the 1980s served as a prelude to greater levels of state intervention in the 1990s. Their purpose was to wring efficiencies out of welfare professionals, who were portrayed as having unfairly privileged conditions of work. In the sphere of education, the salaries of teachers stagnated in real terms, the number of students they taught remained the same (or, as in universities, increased dramatically), and the tenured security of their jobs was removed. The Education Act of 1988 signalled the radicalization of efforts to transform public services. Schools and teachers were no longer trusted to teach children as they saw fit; instead the Education Act of 1988 introduced the first National Curriculum that had to be taught to every pupil. Standardized testing was introduced to measure the performance of teachers and schools, so the state could identify those that were failing, and parents could seek out those ranked highest in the league tables of published results. Parent choice became the new watchword of policy. While the Assisted Places Scheme had since 1980 provided public funds to allow a very few parents access to private schools, the 1988 Education Act broke the model of a universal comprehensive school system by creating new types of self-governing Grant Maintained Schools and City Technology Colleges that could set their own competitive admissions policies. Although by 1997 these schools educated 20 per cent of schoolchildren, a new Labour government created an additional type of 'independent state school' in 2000 with the Academies, which, like the then-defunct City Technology Colleges, could be partially privately funded. By 2010, 45 per cent of state-maintained secondary schools were Academies and increasing numbers were also established and run by 'not for profit' private providers. Education may not have been privatized, but a combination of audit culture, competition between different types of school for resources and pupils, as well as the outsourcing of provision to private companies, had created a new market within which parents now had to decide how to educate their children.

Education was by no means alone. The National Health Service was subject to a range of similar reforms. Private health care was promoted by the deregulation of providers, the encouragement of consultants to build private practices, and the provision of tax relief to employers and individuals. The big change came with the creation of an internal market in 1991 that made hospitals compete for funding from both regional health authorities and local general practices who referred patients whom they in turn competed to attract. In 2000 the Labour government introduced a massive new funding programme that increased health care expenditure to 7.8 per cent of GDP, generating 42,000 more doctors and 90,000 more nurses. Yet it retained the competition for resources within an internal market, while introducing performance targets to secure uniform standards of care. No less than internal markets, the auditing of performance by newly established state agencies created a new entrepreneurial-minded management culture across the public services. The numbers of increasingly highly paid managers, and the use of management consultants, proliferated across the public sector. By 1991 audit culture had so gripped all areas of the public sector that the Conservative government of John Major launched the 'Citizen's Charter' to stipulate what level and speed of service people could expect, whether they were reporting a crime to the police or attending their local hospital.

Deregulation also forced parts of the public sector to compete with the private sector. Take the prison service, which first had the transportation of prisoners outsourced, and then saw a profusion of private prisons built and managed through **Private Finance Initiative** after 1992. There are now sixteen such prisons in the UK responsible for 12 per cent of the prison population. Similarly, the BBC was first given a fresh competitor in the form of the new television Channel Four in 1982 (which, as its name implies, increased the choice of television channels to four). By 1990 the Broadcasting Act not only made the BBC subcontract most of its work to independent production companies, but opened up the world of broadcasting to non-terrestrial (satellite) providers who signed lucrative contracts with the government. Viewers were afforded the luxury of choice: instead of just four channels, they could now search to find something decent to watch from over a hundred channels.

Wealth, Debt and Poverty

The sale of public assets, the deregulation of markets, and the attempts to make markets out of public services, restructured the relationship between the citizen and the state. Social democracy had been constructed around the imperative of securing prosperity for all by generating economic growth, taxing individuals and companies to redistribute wealth where necessary, and providing a safety net of welfare for those in need. In contrast, neoliberalism saw taxation as a burden that discouraged individuals from generating wealth and taking responsibility for their own financial future. If Thatcherism at first preached fiscal responsibility and living within ones means, by the mid 1980s the deregulation of banking, mortgage and credit markets fuelled the inflation of property prices and a massive consumer boom. As Britons were taxed less, they became deeply indebted, while those involved in financial services grew immensely rich. The gap between the rich and the poor, north and south, grew to levels not seen since the nineteenth century. As a new underclass became stuck in a cycle of poverty, so governments attacked the so-called 'dependency culture' but could not contain the escalating bill for social benefits.

The Tax Revolt

Since World War II the standard rate of income tax had steadily declined from a peak of 50 per cent to 30 per cent by 1979 (the same level as it had reached after the Great War). During the 1950s and 1960s some in the Conservative party, like **Enoch Powell**, argued that the income taxes used to sustain the welfare state were reducing the 'incentive' to generate wealth. It was a view that gained greater resonance when the Labour Party introduced capital gains tax and a corporate tax rate of 40 per cent in 1965. By 1971 Edward Heath's Conservative government reduced the top rate of tax from around 90 to 75 per cent in 1971 and, two years later, had to introduce a sales tax, VAT, at 10 per cent of purchases, to offset the loss of revenue. When Labour returned to power in 1974 it promptly increased the top rate of tax to 83 per cent for the 750,000 people who earned over £20,000 (or £186,150 in today's figures). Taxation had become increasingly politicized as rising inflation meant that more people, no longer just the middle classes, fell into the standard tax band rate for the first time during the 1970s. The Thatcher government successfully mobilized these disaffected new taxpayers against the very redistributive system that had improved their living standards. Thus while the basic rate of tax was lowered from 33 to 30 per cent in 1979, the top rate was slashed to 60 per cent, and VAT, which disproportionately hit the poor, was increased to 15 per cent. Tax revenues as a percentage of GDP actually rose from 35 to 38 per cent between 1975 and 1985. More significantly, the balance of who paid them had begun to shift fundamentally.

Taxation soon became a bad word and no politician, of either political party, was prepared to use it unless they were reducing taxes. Between 1986 and 1997 Conservative governments reduced the basic rate of tax from 29 to 23 per cent, while the top rate of tax was limited to 40 per cent in 1988 – an announcement met with such derision by Labour MPs in the **House of Commons** that proceedings were halted for ten minutes – and VAT rose to 17.5 per cent in 1991. Corporate taxation was also progressively reduced to between 35 and 25 per cent depending on the size of the company. Whereas in 1985 Britain had the highest tax revenue as a percentage of GDP in Europe and the OECD, by 1995 it had the lowest. It was hoped that making Britain the lowest tax centre in Europe would attract overseas investment and foreign companies. Soon Britain itself, and not just its offshore ex-colonial islands, from the Isle of Man to Barbados, became a tax haven, attracting the super-rich by making all income earned outside the UK tax exempt. The Labour Party did not fundamentally reverse this trend, although it sought to introduce some backdoor redistribution by creating tax credits for lower-income families. The basic rate of tax was reduced to 20 per cent in 2007, and only after the financial crash of 2008 had unleashed the Great Recession was the top rate of tax increased to 50 per cent on income over £150,000 (this was subsequently cut back to 45 per cent in 2013).

Ironically, the greatest tax revolt came against the very Community Charge that the Conservative government, inspired by the rejection of local property taxes in the USA during the 1970s, introduced in 1989. Local government had traditionally collected tax from property owners according to the rateable value of each property. The Community Charge sought to redirect the cost of paying for local services away from property owners to all adult residents on the Electoral Register who theoretically benefited from them (including students and the unemployed, albeit at a reduced rate of 20 per cent). Quickly dubbed 'the poll tax', it sparked protests, campaigns of non-payment, and riots around the country. The largest protest, which attracted a demonstration of 250,000 in central London on 31 March 1990, ended in a large-scale riot when police sought to block access to Whitehall and then led mounted horseback charges to disperse the protestors. The unpopularity of the measure was a decisive blow to the authority of Margaret Thatcher (who had championed the idea since the early 1970s), and little more than six months later she resigned. A year after the protest in London, the Poll Tax was replaced by a Council Tax charged by household and based upon the rateable value of property. The principle of redistributive taxation may have crumbled, but the idea of a fair system that did not target those who could least afford it remained alive and kicking.

Debt-Financed Boom and Bust

For many Britons, tax cuts made little difference given their experience of increasingly insecure forms of employment and largely stagnant wages. Of far greater importance for them was the deregulation of the credit industry which fuelled a boom in both the property market and retail industry. Rising house prices allowed some to secure lines of credit that were in turn used to 'make over' their principal asset or to access private services like health, education and pensions whose public provision by the state they no longer trusted. As forms of credit also became available to those who did not own property, personal and social identity were increasingly understood, and publicly performed, through the world of goods and their brands.

The deregulation of credit markets began in the early 1970s. Even though pawnshops, hire-purchase and mail-order payment by instalment had long offered unsecured forms of credit, only 20 per cent of consumers used them. The Consumer Credit Act of 1974 sought to make credit more freely available to consumers but created a strong regulatory framework to protect them. Although Barclays had issued the country's first credit card as early as 1966, the number of credit and charge cards issued by Britain's banks doubled from over 6 to 12 million (a quarter of the adult population) between 1976 and 1981. When the regulatory framework of the 1974 Act was dismantled in 1982, the effects were dramatic. By 1988 the number of credit cards had doubled again to 22 million, meaning 40 per cent of households now used one, and 13 per cent had two or more. A decade later 50 per cent of adults held a credit card and by 2014 59 million cards were in use. In 1976 credit cards accounted for less than 20 per cent of consumer spending, but by 1990 that figure had risen to 50 per cent and by 2013 to 75 per cent. For banks, who made no money from cash transactions, this was a hugely profitable business. Credit card holders were charged membership fees as well as 20 per cent interest on the unpaid 'revolving balance' of credit, while retailers were charged transaction fees for every purchase. From the mid 1980s, as electronic terminals were increasingly installed in shops to facilitate credit and charge card transactions, new networked cashpoint machines also began to spread across the country, introducing new charges to many of their users. Consumer debt rapidly rose. In 1993 the outstanding debt of unpaid credit card balances was just over £10 billion; by 2013 it had mushroomed to £56.9 billion.

Alarmingly, the scale of debt incurred through mortgages and home equity loans dwarfed the size of unsecured loans through credit cards. As part of the effort to expand home-ownership, the mortgage market was also deregulated between 1979 and 1986. Banks, and not just mutually owned building societies, were allowed to offer mortgages for the first time, and to do so without large cash reserves to back their loans. As mortgage lenders competed for customers, they became less demanding. Before 1982, loans would average 80 per cent of the house's value and would tend to be for at most two and a half times the borrower's income. By 1988, mortgages were issued for 90–100 per cent of the value of the home, and extended to four times the size of the borrower's salary. In short, more people were buying more houses that were getting more expensive and they did so by borrowing more money. Worse still, many began to use the equity of their houses to borrow still more. By 1988 home equity loans reached a total of £19.2 billion or 4 per cent of GDP.

It was not long before this house of cards came crashing down. Twice. The first time came between 1988 and 1990 when a sharp rise of interest rates was used to combat the inflation caused by the consumer and property boom caught out many people who were too leveraged in debt. So insignificant had the problem been before that we have no data on mortgage repossessions until 1979, when just 2,503 households lost their homes. Contrast this to 1992 when 75,000 houses were repossessed, almost more than in the preceding two decades put together, and 3.5 per cent of mortgagees were more than six months behind in payments. A further 20,000 people went bankrupt or declared themselves insolvent in 1993. New organizations offering counselling to those in debt quickly proliferated. Debtors Anonymous and the National Debt Line were both established in 1987. They were followed by the Consumer Credit Counselling Service in 1993.

As consumer confidence returned, credit card lending tripled between 1993 and 2003 and the property market bounced back, primed by low interest rates, with real house prices doubling in the decade after 1996. With house process rising so far and so fast, the ballooning size of mortgages propelled total household debt in Britain to unprecedented heights: between 1990 and 2013, it rose 314 per cent from £347 billion to £1,437 billion, with mortgage debt consistently accounting for over 85 per cent of that. Levels of household debt relative to income in Britain were considerably higher than in the USA or across Europe, peaking at over 160 per cent in 2007 as opposed to under 140 per cent in the USA and under 100 per cent in Europe. As banks provided the credit, loans and mortgages that allowed household debt to rise so far, they themselves became seriously over-leveraged, lacking the cash reserves to cover the loans they had made. Banks became increasingly dependent upon effectively selling on the future risk of their debts on derivatives markets that had been deregulated in 1986. Between 1986 and 2005, the trade on UK bank assets on London's stock market rose from 762 billion to 5,526 billion. This enabled British banks to increase their leverage ratio (the level of their debt as a proportion of total assets) from 20 to almost 50 per cent between 1990 and 2007. With consumers and banks so dangerously over-leveraged, Britain was hit especially hard by the global financial crisis of 2007–8. Once again it was plunged into recession. Almost 50,000 houses were repossessed in 2009, 35,000 individuals in England and Wales alone declared themselves insolvent, and a further 20,000 were declared bankrupt by courts.

Rich and Poor

This low-tax, debt-financed world of boom and bust made fortunes for some but deepened the debt and dependency of many. CEOs of newly privatized industries saw their salaries inflate as they learnt the measure of value was not the numbers of employees a company could support but its share price and dividends to share-holders. When British Telecom was privatized in 1984, the salary of its CEO doubled to £172,206, but by 1991 his successor was earning a base salary of £450,000 and was afforded a bonus of £225,000. Before privatization, the CEO of British Gas was paid £50,000; a decade later his successor was receiving a salary of £475,00 as well as a £600,000 incentive bonus, a £1 million share option and a promised pension of £180,000. Yet it was not just those CEOs in privatized industries who were paid grossly inflated salaries. In 1980 the CEO of Barclays Bank was paid £87,323, which was 13 times more than the average wage of £6,474; by 2011 the Barclays CEO received £4,365,636 a year, 169 times more than the average wage of £25,900. In 1980 the CEOs of six of Britain's largest companies were paid between 13 and 44 times more than their average employee, but by 1999 the bosses of FTSE 100 companies received on average 47 times more than their employees and by 2009 that figure had risen to 128. In just three days they earned more than their employees did in a year.

It was not just CEOs who got filthy rich in these decades. As we can see in Graph 13.3, the share of income of the top 10 per cent rose considerably from the 1970s to 2010. In the 1970s their earnings were almost in step with the second-highest-earning decile at just over 5 per cent higher, and equivalent to that of the bottom 40 per cent. By 2009 they were double the size of those in the highest 80–90 per cent of earners and equal to the amount earned by the bottom 50 per cent. Even those figures obscure how much of the increasing share of income of the top 10 per cent was driven by the richest 1 per cent. Their share rose from its historically lowest point in 1976, at 6 per cent, to 18 per cent in 2009. Within that 1 per cent, there was a top group of the super-rich whose earnings rose to even more stratospheric heights. Under the

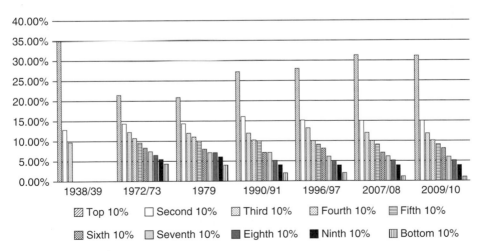

Graph 13.3 Share of income, 1972–2009

Labour governments of 1997 to 2010, the top 1 per cent initially earned an average of £200,000 a year, and the top 0.1 per cent an average of £600,000; by 2010 those figures had increased to £350,000 and £1.4 million respectively. Graph 13.3 also illustrates how the share of income of the bottom 40 per cent gradually declined, with the greatest drop being the lowest 10 per cent. In 2009, 13.4 million Britons were living on less than 60 per cent of the average salary of £25,000 – the definition of relative poverty.

Just like wealth, poverty was unevenly spread. Poverty was concentrated in urban environments and was disproportionately present in northern and southwestern England, Scotland's Clyde Valley and Islands, northern and mid Wales, and Belfast and the northern coast of Northern Ireland. The southeast of England, increasingly stretching up to the Midlands, became progressively wealthier. Those living in the poorest areas of Britain were also those areas with the highest mortality rates and levels of malnutrition. In the twenty-first century, the map of poverty in Britain bore an uncanny resemblance to that of the 1930s. Perhaps the greatest difference was that, with a growing number of children born outside of marriage, and divorce rates having peaked in 1982, the rising level of single-parent families ensured women and children bore the greatest brunt of the poverty. In 1975 under 8 per cent of British families had single parents but by 1991 that had risen to 18 per cent and rose still further to 24 per cent by 2005, while the proportion of men as lone parents stayed much the same. By 2010 half of all single-parent families were low-income, living on less than 60 per cent of the average wage.

As ever in Britain, wealth and poverty were not just about numbers; they were also about privilege and the experience of class difference. While private schools represented only 7 per cent of schoolchildren, in 2009 their alumni accounted for 26 per cent of BBC executives, 33 per cent of MPs in the House of Commons, 44 per cent of the *Sunday Times* Rich List, 56 per cent of all lawyers, 62 per cent of senior officers in the armed forces, 70 per cent of finance directors, and 71 per cent of judges. Those leaving private schools were five times more likely to attend Oxford or Cambridge University than those educated in publicly funded state schools. Privately educated students still represent around 40 per cent of students at Oxbridge. Alumni from Oxbridge made up 75 per cent of judges, 59 per cent of the **Cabinet**, 55 per cent of diplomats and 38 per cent of the House of Lords. When sociologists teamed up with the BBC to launch the 'Great British Class Survey' in 2013, they found that many thought class was best defined not solely by wealth but by access to the networks that helped secure upward social mobility. The Survey proposed the nature of class could best be understood within seven, rather than the traditional three, categories: the elite, the established middle class, the technical middle class, newly affluent workers, emergent service workers, traditional working class and the precariat. The precariat are the burgeoning underclass, representing some 15 per cent of the population, who are unemployed or underemployed and supported by welfare payments. Despite all the attempts to attack so-called 'dependency culture' by cutting welfare programmes, expenditure in these areas continued to grow significantly from the 1970s. Government spending on social welfare stood at 6 per cent of GDP in 1974, but rose to 8.24 per cent in 1993, and 7.8 per cent in the recession of 2010. Inequality and poverty may have been lessened in Britain's post-war social democracy, but both increased sharply after 1976 under the neoliberal consensus.

The Security State

The emphasis on developing one's financial assets (particularly property), together with the spectacular rise of poverty and unemployment, created a new concern with security among Britons. This was mirrored by the state's own development of a new security apparatus designed to police the rising tide of social unrest and political protest, as well as to protect Britain from external 'threats', whether those be illegal immigration or terrorist attacks. Unprecedented numbers of Britons were incarcerated in prison while the proliferation of cameras sought to deter or help detect crime on the road and high street alike. Terror also became a constant feature of everyday life as Britain's policies abroad, in Northern Ireland and in the former territories of its colonies in the Middle East, helped foment fear of attack. Taken together, these developments generated a security state of unparalleled power that belied the claim that the rule of markets would keep government small.

Enemies Within

The surge in unemployment, crime and political protest that accompanied deindustrialization created a new politics of security. New techniques of covert and militarized policing, often developed as part of counter-insurgency tactics in Northern Ireland, became increasingly widely used to combat football hooliganism from the mid 1970s, as well as strikes and political protests during the 1980s. Closed-circuit television cameras (CCTV), first used to monitor football hooligans around stadiums on match days during the 1970s, were widely deployed during the miners' strike. Britain's security service, MI5, which operated undercover agents in Northern Ireland, also sought to infiltrate groups thought 'subversive'. During the 1980s the use of phone-tapping, informers and discrediting 'dirty tricks' were all deployed against those considered by Margaret Thatcher as 'the enemies within' – a list that included the **Campaign for**

Nuclear Disarmament, anti-nuclear women peace activists at Greenham Common, and the NUM. Stella Rimington, who became the first publicly declared Director General of MI5 in 1992, had a career that connected work on Northern Ireland, internal subversion and counter-terrorism, before becoming M. Indeed, from 1992 MI5 were given primary responsibility over the police for counter-terrorism in Britain and slowly acquired new powers of surveillance via CCTV, phones and internet traffic, not least through the Government Communications Headquarters (GCHQ) at Cheltenham.

The new forms of militarized policing that had been developed in Northern Ireland during the 1970s migrated to mainland Britain after riots swept across British cities in the summer of 1981. The use of riot gear and military convoys and formations, including charges by police on horseback, was especially visible during the miners' strike. At the 'Battle of Orgreave' in June 1984, when the NUM organized a mass picket of 6,000 men to prevent the operation of a steel plant there, they were met by a larger police force in full riot gear who 'kettled' and flanked the pickets (see Figure 13.3). The ensuing violence, which was caught on camera and film, saw many injuries on both sides. Although ninety-three arrests were made, the trials of the few who were prosecuted collapsed and the South Yorkshire Police Force later paid over £500,000 in compensation to thirty-nine picketers. Two years later the same

Figure 13.3 Police line at the Battle of Orgreave

techniques were used to break the pickets of newspaper workers at the new News International printing plant at Wapping which left 6,000 workers redundant. By the time of the Poll Tax riots of 1990, these police tactics had become routine, and they have remained so ever since.

Police racism also became more manifest. As the violence of white racism intensified during the 1970s, black Britons became increasingly vocal in complaining that they were not sufficiently protected by the police. Instead they felt targeted by police under the stop-and-search laws. These laws gave the police the power to stop and search any Britons suspected of criminal activity, but young black men were disproportionately affected. A searing critique of the police state as experienced by many on a daily basis was developed by black women's groups, culminating in the Scrap SUS Campaign launched in Lewisham by the lawyer Mavis Best in 1978. When the government commissioned a report on the riots of 1981 by Lord Scarman, racist policing emerged as a key ingredient and the 'SUS' laws were promptly repealed. Scarman blamed police racism on a few 'rotten apples' but the failure to convict those responsible for the racially motivated murder of Stephen Lawrence in 1993 showed it was institutionally entrenched. Indeed, this was the conclusion of the official MacPherson report on the case in 1999. Lawrence's murderers were eventually convicted in 2012. Following accusations of undercover efforts to discredit the victim's family and their campaign for justice, a new inquiry into the case was established in 2015.

For Conservative governments, the security state promised to restore law and order to a permissive society that had lost its moral compass. Despite this, Britain's prison population only grew modestly between 1979, when it stood at 41,000, and 1989, when it almost reached 50,000. Even so, overcrowding and mistreatment, especially in decaying prisons built in the Victorian era, led to a series of riots in twenty-five British prisons in the spring of 1990 that began with a rooftop protest at Strangeways Prison in Manchester. Afterwards some prisons were refurbished and the demeaning practice of slopping out for those in cells without a toilet was abolished in 1996. The dramatic growth of the prison population only began in the mid 1990s. Already by the time Tony Blair's Labour government had been elected, with the promise of being 'tough on crime and tough on the causes of crime', over 60,000 were imprisoned, but by 2015 that figure had risen to 86,000. Despite the construction of a number of new prisons, the prison system is at least 10 per cent over capacity. 2016 saw a fresh wave of prison riots across the country.

Not surprisingly, given the history of racist policing, there was a disproportionately large number of black Britons, and those now designated as ethnic minorities, in prison. Although ethnic minorities constituted only 11 per cent of Britons, they represented almost a third of the prison population in 2014. In the past decade, following the London bombings of July 2005, the number of incarcerated Muslims doubled;

14 per cent of those in prison are Muslims, although Muslims represent just 4.5 per cent of Britons. It was not only convicts who were incarcerated by Britain's security state. With increasingly restrictive immigration laws, there was a dramatic rise in the number of those claiming asylum as refugees. There were around 4,000 asylum seekers a year in the 1980s but during the 1990s that figure climbed to over 20,000 a year, reaching a peak of 84,000 a year in 2002 (at the height of the Balkan war), before falling back to around 20,000 a year over the next decade. This prompted a series of laws in 1996, 1999, 2002 and 2006 that sought to tighten the eligibility for asylum. Just 188 people were detained under immigration and asylum laws in 1975, as opposed to 28,000 people in 2010. Since 1991 the majority of asylum seekers are refused entrance and held in one of the fifteen privately operated detention centres scattered across the country until their case is processed and they can be deported. In 2010 over 57,000 people were deported or took part in a 'voluntary return' programme.

Securing Ourselves: Watchful Britain

The new politics of security quickly insinuated themselves into the everyday lives of Britons who were asked to help police their own communities. From the early 1980s homeowners were encouraged to start Neighbourhood Watch schemes. First developed in the United States during the 1970s, Neighbourhood Watch was introduced to Britain in 1982 and quickly spread as homeowners were keen to protect their chief financial asset and even enhance its value by improving the safety of their community. Citizens were encouraged to be watchful and become 'the eyes and ears' of the police to help secure their own homes and communities. The signs posted on houses and street lampposts to deter crime and demarcate the communities that had begun Neighbourhood Watch schemes quickly became a familiar sight. By 1985, 4,000 communities had started these schemes, and a decade later there were 130,000. The idea of citizen policing was also propagated by the launch of television programmes like **Crimewatch** on BBC1 in 1984. A hugely popular programme, CrimeWatch created a new genre, the 'reality TV' crime show. It made the British public both more aware and more fearful of crime by asking that it provide information that could help 'solve' a crime and secure a prosecution. The following year, the business speculator Michael Ashcroft (whose fundraising services as Treasurer and Deputy Chairman of the Conservative Party would later make him a lord) put up reward money for information that would lead to an arrest for the murder of a policeman on the Broadwater Farm Estate in north London. This began a series of 'Community Action' adverts on television asking for anonymous information about specific crimes, culminating in the creation of the national organization CrimeStoppers in 1988. By then, the prevention of crime and the prosecution of criminals had become the responsibility of everyone.

This vigilante model of citizen policing quickly became incorporated into the work of government. By 1989 the CrimeStopper model of anonymous reporting through a 'hotline' was adopted by the Department of Social Security to prosecute benefit fraud. It was also made part of the prosecution and restriction of what was defined as 'anti-social' rather than criminal behaviour by the new Labour government's Crime and Disorder Act in 1998. This legislation enabled members of the public to seek 'Anti-Social Behaviour Orders' (ASBOs) from magistrates that would prevent individuals (aged ten or over) from behaving in ways that were harmful or upsetting to one or more people. As defying an ASBO was made a criminal offence, a whole range of new behaviours – such as noise pollution, begging, urinating in public, spitting, verbal abuse, not picking up dog excrement – could effectively be criminalized by the reports and objections of a single individual. Over 4,000 ASBOs were issued in 2005 alone.

While Britons policed each other, their behaviour was frequently caught on CCTV. First used to police football grounds and strikes, by 1984 CCTV began to be adopted by city councils to deter crime. A decade later seventy-nine local authorities had installed CCTV systems to secure housing estates, as well as high streets and shopping malls so they would become safe spaces of consumption. Wary of the growing number of cameras, Britons became reconciled to them in 1993 when the abduction of two-year-old Jamie Bulger from a shopping mall in Liverpool was caught on camera and led to the arrest of his murderers. By the mid 1990s, 300,000 CCTV cameras were sold every year and the police invested £300 million in surveillance systems. Speed cameras were introduced in 1992, and by 2000 600,000 motorists in England and Wales had been caught speeding by 1,600 cameras. In the following decade speed cameras became ubiquitous and 4,737 of them filmed 1.75 million drivers speeding. The cameras not only halved the number of road accidents between 1992 and 2007 but they also generated significant revenue – more than £114 million in 2007 alone. It was not just on the road that Britons were monitored on camera: by 2015 there were almost 6 million CCTV cameras across the country, with 750,000 in facilities like schools, hospitals and care homes, and at least 500,000 in London alone. So endemic has CCTV become that it has been estimated that Londoners are filmed 300 times every day. Libertarians complain that CCTV has created a surveillance society that infringes the privacy of citizens, while a group called Motorists Against Detection (MAD) claimed to have destroyed or damaged 700 speed cameras in 2003 alone. Most Britons appear to just accept that they now live in a surveillance society. In 2008 Westminster City Council in central London painted over a mural by Banksy (Figure 13.4) that portrayed a graffiti artist at work on a wall with a CCTV camera and a security guard filming him. Britain was indeed now, like the Banksy mural, 'One Nation Under CCTV'.

Figure 13.4 Banksy, 'One Nation Under CCTV', 2008

Governing Ourselves: Heart and Soul

The valorization of the market, and the insistence that people become responsible for their own futures and security, was by no means just the work of the state. Margaret Thatcher may have hoped to change 'the heart and soul' of Britons, but she was by no means solely responsible for the creation of *homo economicus*. It was the diffusion of an entrepreneurial culture as much as the dismantling of social democratic structures that increasingly made people understand their lives as a series of economic calculations about their futures as individuals, rather than as someone with a collective set of social rights and responsibilities. This DIY logic extended also to the world of politics, where the age of the mass party gave way to more flexible and constantly changing forms of political mobilization.

The Economization of Everyday Life

The idea that the logic of the market was fair, that it rewarded hard work and talent with wealth, became embedded within a new entrepreneurially minded popular culture. During the 1980s a new cult of personality built up around exemplary entrepreneurs, who became a new type of business celebrity. Figures in finance and management who represented the logic of deindustrialization, like the asset-strippers James Hanson and James Goldsmith, as well as those in the new 'creative industries' like Alan 'Amstrad' Sugar, Richard 'Virgin' Branson, Anita 'Body Shop' Roddick, were the subject of endless newspaper profiles and biographies. There were four biographies of James Goldsmith alone between 1982 and 1991, with titles such as 'Tycoon' and 'Billionaire'. The success of these business celebrities in helping to propagate the idea that making money was good in and of itself was brilliantly pilloried by the comedian Harry Enfield's character 'Loadsamoney' in 1987. Loadsamoney was a brash East End plasterer who boasted about how much money he had, and always conspicuously held a large 'wad' of cash in his hand. Ironically, even the world of alternative comedy that produced Loadsamoney depended on the deregulation of television and reproduced market models (see Textbox 13.2 and Figure 13.5). That same year, Oliver Stone's film *Wall Street* was released, with Michael Douglas playing the lead character, a stockbroker called Gordon Gekko, declaring 'greed is good'.

While Loadsamoney and Gordon Gekko were satirical characters who mocked the greed they celebrated, a decade later TV shows were produced that simply valorized money and measured success in terms of business. Nowhere was the lust for and worship of wealth more evident than in the huge popularity of the TV game show *Who Wants to Be a Millionaire* that began in 1998 and ran until 2014. *Who Wants to Be a Millionaire* was a traditional game show where contestants answered multiple-choice questions whose value increased to a maximum of £1 million. Its staggering success spread across the world, even featuring in the film *Slumdog Millionaire* (2008) set in India's Mumbai. Business acumen, not just wealth, was exalted in a new breed of reality TV show: *The Dragon's Den* and *The Apprentice* with Alan Sugar (the latter modelled after Donald Trump's *Apprentice* in the USA), both of which began in 2005. In these shows, contestants competed against each other by presenting their business plans and engaging in entrepreneurial tasks set for them by the exemplary business

13.2 Person: Jennifer Saunders (1958–)

Jennifer Saunders is a comedian, actor and screenwriter, and was an early pioneer of the alternative comedy scene in 1980s Britain. Her father was a senior officer in the Royal Air Force and as a child she frequently moved to different parts of the country as her father changed bases. After leaving school, Saunders attended the prestigious Central London School of Speech and Drama where she met her future comedy partner Dawn French, who had once lived on the same RAF base (although they had never met). The two comedians lived together in London in the late 1970s, where they performed improvised comedy shows, including a show called 'The Menopause Sisters' in which they wore tampons in their ears. The two comedians rose to fame for their work with 'The Comic Strip', a group of alternative comedians associated with The Comedy Store, a club in Soho which opened in 1979, the same year that Margaret Thatcher was elected. The Comedy Store styled itself as a site for counter-cultural, left-wing comedy, with audiences encouraged to boo off anyone who made racist or sexist jokes. The Comic Strip's breakthrough on television came on the first night of Channel 4 broadcasting in 1982, but their biggest success was *The Young Ones* (1982–4), a TV series that mocked Thatcherism and student culture alike. Although Saunders was part of the all-women television show *Girls On Top* in 1985, it was the sketch show she wrote with Dawn French, *French And Saunders*, which ran for twenty years from 1987, that cemented her fame. During that time she also wrote and starred in *Absolutely Fabulous* (1992–2005), a television show that explored relationships between mothers and daughters and became an international success. *Absolutely Fabulous* was produced by their own Saunders & French Productions company. Given the overwhelmingly male environment of the alternative comedy scene, Saunders's success was remarkable. Her career also illustrated how quickly alternative comedy prospered as it became mainstream, and how dependent it was on the deregulation of television production and the proliferation of production and management companies like Paul Jackson Productions and Avalon Entertainment. Some alternative comics were concerned about the way in which television had commodified and depoliticized the genre. Comedian Tony Allen, for example, called the medium 'the greatest breakthrough in aesthetics since chloroform'. (S.W.)

celebrities who picked the winner. Competition and success were understood only in the narrowest economistic terms of a business culture that now subsumed primetime television.

Television was also a good barometer to the growing importance of spending as well as making money. Deregulation and the proliferation of satellite broadcasting facilitated the arrival of the American-inspired home shopping channel *QVC* (*Quality, Value, Convenience*) in 1993 and *Ideal World* (2000). In the property boom of the late 1990s and 2000s, when the value of people's homes was so closely tied to the lines of credit they could secure, a number of home improvement shows like *Changing Rooms* (1996) and *House Doctor* (1998) came on air. Shows about improving your home in turn

Figure 13.5 Jennifer Saunders, October 1985

gave way to programmes like *Property Ladder* (2001), *Escape to the Country* (2002) and *A Place in the Sun* (2004) that encouraged people to realize the value of their homes or speculate on the property market. Similarly, the personal 'make-over', where contestants had fashion experts restyle their clothing wardrobe, became popular with *What Not to Wear* (2001) and the American imports *Extreme Makeover* (2002) and *Queer Eye* (2003). Dressed up in the language of personal empowerment, these programmes preached that enhancing the appearance of yourself and your home increased the value of your assets and your self-esteem.

Consumption also became a way of demonstrating one's personal virtue by spending ethically and responsibly. The spread of charity stores to raise income for organizations like Oxfam, first pioneered in the 1950s, proceeded apace during the 1970s. They helped produce a new type of ethical consumer who sought to buy goods, often at a higher price, that conspicuously promoted their own identification with issues such as fair trade and environmentalism that had once been rooted in counter-culture. The Body Shop is a good example of this phenomenon. Its founder, Anita Roddick, ruthlessly presented herself and her commitments as the human face of capitalism, with huge success. Awarded an OBE in 1988, she was Britain's first exemplary businesswoman. Roddick had the idea of selling cosmetics that used 'natural' ingredients and so did not require animal testing, and that came in recycled containers, on a visit to Telegraph Avenue in Berkeley, California, headquarters of the counter-cultural revolution. The products were supposed to regenerate the consumer's body both spiritually and physically. The rise of the Body Shop was meteoric. By 1991, within fifteen years of opening the first shop in Brighton, and just seven years after being floated on the stock market, there were 700 branches around the country. When L'Oreal purchased the company in

2006, there were over 2,000 stores scattered across the world. The Body Shop helped pave the way for the massive expansion of the markets not just for 'alternative therapies' but for products that were perceived as enhancing the health and fitness of consumers. As the growth of poverty helped propel an obesity epidemic in Britain, the display and use of health and fitness products, or even employing a personal trainer, became a sign of affluence and the virtuous exercise of personal responsibility.

However remarkable the sight of Britons jogging on the street would be to someone from the 1970s, it pales in comparison to the commodification of gay and lesbian culture. For all the work of the Gay Liberation Front in the 1970s, homophobia and discrimination against those in same-sex relationships remained rife and if anything deepened in the 1980s as HIV/AIDS decimated gay communities. Yet by the 1990s the club scene and disposable cash of these communities was actively courted by city governments, as 'the pink pound', valued at £70 billion in 2006, became a vehicle for reviving inner-city areas as well as a target of businesses and advertisers. It was inconceivable in 1986, when Manchester's Chief Constable of Policing, a Methodist lay preacher, described those suffering from HIV/AIDS as 'swirling in a human cesspit of their own making', that gays and lesbians would win the right to legal recognition as civil partners in 2005 or be able to get married in 2014. Yet even this enormous step forward for civil rights was quickly commodified (see Textbox 13.3 and Figure 13.6).

13.3 Source: The Gay Wedding Guide (http://thegayweddingguide.co.uk)

The gay and lesbian wedding business is a remarkable achievement. Gay men and lesbian women had long been pathologized and persecuted in Britain for threatening the model of the Christian family. In the 1970s the Gay Liberation Front was especially critical of the sexist and gendered nature of family life. If fresh waves of homophobia were generated by the HIV/AIDs pandemic in the 1980s, by the 1990s what was now termed the lesbian, gay, bisexual and transsexual (LGBT) community returned to the the fight for equal civil rights. The equalization of the age of consent was finally achieved in 2000, following a ruling by the European Court of Human Rights. The legal recognition of same-sex relationships followed in 2005 with the creation of a new category of 'civil partners'. The campaign for the right of gay men and lesbian women to be formally married began with Equal Marriage in Scotland (2008) and, south of the border, Equal Love (2010). That right was finally secured in 2014. Since then, the gay and lesbian wedding business has thrived, with many businesses, like the Gay Wedding Guide, being formed to cater for this new market, offering anything from cards to cakes, clothes, venues and legal advice on pre-nuptial agreements. The gay wedding business is now estimated to be worth £18.2 billion over the next fifteen years.

Figure 13.6 Gay wedding cards

The 'Me' Decades

The self-help industry became very big business in Britain even if, again, much of it was imported from the United States. In 1976 Tom Wolfe wrote a powerful essay in *New York Magazine* describing the 1970s as the 'ME decade' where the 'new alchemical dream is: changing one's personality – remaking, remodelling, elevating, and polishing one's very *self* … and observing, studying, and doting on it. (Me!).' In some ways the new attention to remaking oneself emerged from the consciousness-raising groups of the 'liberation' movements of that decade. Feminists especially developed an interest in psychoanalysis as a mode of analysing the ways in which repressive patriarchal structures had rendered the personal political and of achieving emancipation from them as individuals. Although self-help programmes like Alcoholics Anonymous (AA) and Weightwatchers came to the UK from America in 1947 and 1965 respectively, they grew most rapidly only after the 1970s. Although AA already had 480 groups around the country in 1972, that number had doubled five years later and by the end of the century had reached over 3,000. Fifty years after its foundation in Britain, the fee-paying Weightwatchers claimed to have over 6,000 meetings across the country. Common to all these groups was the centrality of sharing experience as a mode of self-realization in the context of a small, autonomous and supportive group. In these worlds the self was neither atomized nor seen as a work of art where there were no limits to self-empowerment. Indeed, the point was to use groups to help support individuals to push against their sense of powerlessness against patriarchy, addiction and their metabolism.

That type of collective work of self-realization was quite different from the **self-help** manuals that proliferated from the 1980s. Self-help manuals were hardly new – Samuel

Smiles had coined the phrase and formed the genre back in the 1850s. The self-help industry of the late twentieth century was both more prolific and different in character. Although it still provided guides to everyday life and self-improvement, it no longer focused on the development of 'character' but on transforming particular elements of the self: how to become wealthy, survive families, be a good parent, quit smoking, be assertive, lose weight, exercise properly, succeed at work, make friends, be good in bed, find a life-partner and so on. Britons were increasingly compelled to work harder at just about everything they did – in the words of a Radiohead song from 1997, 'to live fitter, happier and more productive lives'. This type of advice was also increasingly found in women's magazines, as well as those that were produced for men from the 1980s, and the new 'lifestyle' sections of newspapers. It was joined on those pages in the 1990s by a new genre of confessional journalism where the author's life, and even their death, became news and was shared with readers to inform and guide them. Ruth Picardie started it all writing about her struggle against cancer in 1996 in the *Guardian*, while John Diamond also chronicled his death in the *Times* and Kathryn Flett detailed the break-up of her marriage in the *Observer* during 1997. This confessional sharing of experience in the public domain became a televisual phenomenon a few years later with the advent of reality TV shows like *Big Brother* (2000). And, of course, five years later, when online social media companies like MySpace and Facebook began, almost everyone was able to connect and share personal experience, and too much information, with friends and strangers alike. This may have democratized intimate life but it has also elevated the individual, and the projection of one's self-image, to the centre of social life.

The combination of increasingly precarious forms of employment, the demands of experiencing happiness, and the new culture of confessional sharing, helped foster a therapeutic revolution. A country once renowned for its stiff upper lip and talent for small talk began to flock to therapists. Already by 2004, 67 per cent of Britons considered it acceptable to see a therapist or counsellor, and by 2010 94 per cent did, and it was estimated one in five was in some type of therapy – a figure that increased to one in four by 2015. Although there is no central register of data, it appears that the number of therapists doubled from 30,000 to 70,000 between 1993 and 2012, the vast majority of whom were women. It is not hard to see why therapy became so quickly normalized for individuals were now expected to reach an almost impossible measure of happiness. Once it had been an achievement to sustain a stable marriage and a job that supported a household; now both are expected to be emotionally fulfilling and a means to personal 'growth'. Happiness and well-being even became a concern for government. Just as the Labour government appointed a 'happiness Tsar' in 2003, so in 2011 the Conservative government announced its own 'happiness agenda'. At the heart of both these interventions was the idea that unhappiness was unproductive and cost the country in lost revenue. In this calculation, the well-being and happiness of the population was a sound investment in future economic prosperity.

The End of Politics?

For the most part, Britons have adapted themselves to these extraordinary transformations. After all, they were presided over by elected governments that represented all three major political parties. If Harold Wilson's Labour government had taken the **International Monetary Fund** loan that first began the **structural adjustment** of Britain's political economy, the Conservative governments of Thatcher and her successor John Major in the 1980s and 1990s radicalized that project. By the time Tony Blair was elected as leader of the Labour Party in 1994, Labour spoke the language of social cohesion but not only accepted the privatization programme and labour laws but believed that market rationales and private capital were essential to modernize the public services that remained. After 2010, when the Liberal Democrat Party joined the Conservative Party in a governing coalition, all three political parties had helped engineer the neoliberal revolution.

Strikingly, they had done so with fewer and fewer people voting for them and even fewer belonging to them as members. The proportion of Britons who turned out to vote in general elections hovered between 70 and 80 per cent between the 1950s and the 1980s, then fell precipitously during the 1990s to a nadir of 60 per cent in 2001 before rallying slightly to 66 per cent in 2015. By the late 1990s the turnout of voters at local elections fell below 30 per cent for the first time. And while the Conservative and Labour parties won their greatest victories in 1979 and 1997 with around 43 per cent of the votes cast, no party won an election with more that 35 per cent of the vote in the three elections held between 2005 and 2015. Britons, who had fought so hard to gain the right to vote at elections, found casting that vote less and less significant. Similarly, political parties also ceased to have a mass membership. By the late 1970s the Conservative and Labour parties boasted little more than 2 million members, but in retrospect this still seems like a golden age, for during the twenty-first century their joint membership has hardly come to half a million. There are two exceptions to this trend. The Scottish National Party's campaign for independence in the 2014 referendum saw their membership increase by 60,000 to 85,000 in a month and generated a turnout of 85 per cent. Since the election of Jeremy Corbyn as its leader in 2015, representing a new anti-austerity politics, membership of the Labour Party has grown to over 500,000, making it now the largest political party in Europe.

If voting and belonging to a political party became increasingly rare, politics was increasingly conducted by other means. In the first place, the number of NGOs grew dramatically. In the first two decades of the twenty-first century the number of NGOs with charitable status rose from 100,000 to 170,000; they boasted 600,000 employees and probably twice as many volunteers. The greatest growth area of all was among the campaigning NGOs, such as those concerned with environmental issues. In the mid 1970s there were about 40 environmentally focused NGOs in Britain with around 0.5 million members; by 2008 there were over 160 'green' NGOs with a combined membership of 2.5 million people – five times more than the Conservative and Labour parties combined. Volunteering for NGOs, whether working in a charity shop to help raise money or writing letters for Amnesty International, became a common part of life for many. During 1991, 76 per cent of the population claimed to have done some voluntary work, although it is important to recognize that this included all of the charitable sector and not just those engaged in political campaigns.

In some ways politics was also reshaped by the appearance of more transitory organizations and what we might called 'pop-up' or 'DIY' protests. Occupations became a key part of this form of politics. In September 1981 a group from Wales called 'Women for Life on Earth' set up a camp outside RAF Greenham Common in Berkshire to protest against the decision to site American nuclear cruise missiles there. Despite many attempts to evict them, what soon became known as the Women's Peace Camp occupied the perimeter of the nuclear base without electricity, running water or basic amenities. The continuing presence of the women-only camp attracted global media attention, but in 1982 and 1983 they also organized larger protests in which tens of thousands of women held hands and encircled the site of the nuclear base. The camp remained in place even after the cruise missiles returned to the United States in 1991. It existed for nineteen years and arguably provided the model for the proliferation of protests against road construction projects in the 1990s.

In 1992 protestors set up camp on the historic Twyford Down to try to prevent its excavation for the extension of the M3 near Winchester. Like the Greenham women, they were met with eviction notices and violence from police and the privately owned Group 4 security company hired to protect the site. When construction started in 1993, protestors chained themselves to trees and construction equipment. The protest provided a model that quickly spread. Anti-road protestors occupied trees to try to escape eviction at Jesmond Dene near Newcastle in 1993, a tactic that was copied at the protests against the clearance of 120 acres of historic woodland to build the Newbury bypass from 1994 (see Figure 13.7). Within two years there were twenty camps set up along the route of the bypass, including in trees and underground tunnels. Heavy policing and private security firms ensured that the road was completed by 1998, with much of the aggregate used for its construction having come from the recently demolished airstrip at nearby RAF Greenham Common. Occupations also became a central feature of the protests against the government's austerity cuts introduced following the global financial crisis of 2008 and 2009. When in October 2011 the anti-austerity organizations UK Uncut and Occupy London were barred from occupying the Stock Market, as Occupy Wall Street had done in New York, they set up camp outside nearby St Paul's Cathedral where they remained until evicted three months later.

Strikingly, the past thirty years have seen some of the largest political demonstrations ever held in Britain. We have already seen that the protests against the Poll Tax were nationwide and generated a march across London in March 1990 that included, even by police estimates, 200,000 people. The size of that protest was dwarfed by those

Figure 13.7 Road protestors at Newbury

in 2002 and 2003 against the ban on fox-hunting and the Iraq War. The **Countryside Alliance** was formed in 1997 to highlight the plight of rural Britain and to defend its traditional sports like shooting and fox-hunting. In 2002 it organized a 'Liberty and Livelihood' demonstration in London, especially focused on opposing the proposed ban on fox-hunting, that attracted 500,000 people. At the time this was the largest demonstration ever seen in Britain. Six months later the globally coordinated protests against the Iraq War attracted the support of over a million people in London. It was not only twice the size of the largest protest in Britain's history, it was also the largest of all the protests in sixty countries across the world. It was a protest that, like the Live Aid concert in 1985 to raise funds for victims of the famine in Ethiopia and the Occupy protests of 2011, marked the new capacity to coordinate protests around the globe. Of course, as we have seen in previous chapters, Britons had long been engaged in the politics and humanitarian crises generated by the British Empire. But from the 1980s, new media technologies and the porous nature of national borders in the face of environmental or economic crises meant that Britons increasingly saw themselves as part of a broader global public.

Indeed, the nation as a political unit came under increasing strain in the twenty-first century. As plans for European political and economic integration proceeded apace at the Maastricht Treaty conference in 1991, Britain remained a begrudging participant, refusing either to sign up to its 'Social Chapter' guaranteeing minimal social rights (although the Labour government eventually did in 1997) or to join the monetary union created by the lunch of the Eurozone in 1999. Hostility to European integration, especially the freedom of workers to move across borders, fuelled a nationalism that was reflected in growing support for the UK Independence Party. First formed in 1993, its increasing share of the vote at elections eventually culminated in the election of its first MP in the general election of 2015 when it won 12.5 per cent of the national vote.

Nationalist sentiment also gathered steam in Scotland and Wales. During the 1980s and 1990s, both nations effectively felt disenfranchised as they endured policies that devastated their industries and communities, introduced by Conservative governments that few had voted for. In 1979 the Conservative Party won a little more than 30 per cent of the vote in both Scotland and Wales and by 1997 their proportion had fallen to under 20 per cent (when it no longer had a single MP returned from Scotland). The promise of a referendum on devolution for Scotland and Wales helped propel Labour to victory in 1997. Those referendums created a new Scottish Parliament (with power over most areas other than energy, finance and security) and a National Assembly for Wales (which did not get similar powers until 2011) in 1998. That same year, the 'Good Friday' Belfast Agreement secured a peace deal for Northern Ireland through a power-sharing Assembly. The Agreement gradually ended decades of civil war by ensuring both Britain and Ireland revoked their claims to sovereignty over the province and allowed the people of Northern Ireland to decide its future. As the Catholic population will soon outnumber Protestants, many Unionists are concerned that a referendum will be used to pull the province out of the United Kingdom. Indeed, in Scotland, in less than a decade after devolution the Scottish National Party became the largest party within the Scottish Parliament, and in 2011 it formed its first majority government. Within three years a referendum was held for Scotland to become independent, and although this was narrowly lost by 55 to 45 per cent, at the general election six months later the SNP returned all but three of Scotland's MPs. Britain may not have broken up yet but the future of the Union looks very uncertain.

As I finished writing this book in June 2016, Britain voted to leave the European Union in what became known as **Brexit**. They voted in a referendum that the Conservative Party had promised during the 2015 election campaign to ensure their supporters did not switch their allegiances to the UK Independence Party and to settle a long-standing dispute among their own MPs between the pro- and anti-Europeans. The vote was close: 51.9 per cent of the 72.2 per cent of Britons who turned out voted leave, and 48.1 per cent voted to remain in the European Union. Yet the country was by no means just split in two. While in England and Wales 53.4 and 52.5 per cent voted to leave, in Scotland and Northern Ireland 62 and 55.8 per cent voted to remain. This has prompted renewed calls for Scottish independence by the leader of the SNP and Scottish First Minister Nicola Sturgeon, while Northern Ireland's Deputy First Minister and Sinn Fein leader Martin McGuinness suggested a border poll on a united Ireland. Rural areas of England and Wales were more likely to vote leave than more affluent urban areas, while voters under 44 were more in favour of remaining in Europe than voters over 44. The vote has sent a seismic shock through Britain, the rest of Europe and the world. The prime minister David Cameron, who led the remain campaign, resigned and Conservative MPs quickly replaced him with Theresa May. The political and economic uncertainty in Britain and in Europe is great and was quickly reflected on the world's financial markets. It remains unclear when the British government will actually invoke the treaty clause that will open negotiations with the European Union.

As the leaders of Britain's chief political parties all campaigned to remain in Europe, the Brexit vote has commonly been understood as a revolt against what was termed the political Establishment. It has much in common with revolts by other electorates across the world against the political parties and leaders that have traditionally held power – from the Occupy movement to the remarkable election of Donald Trump as President of the USA. We can think of these revolts, taken together with the spread of new forms of allegiance and political action like those represented by Islamic terrorist groups, as part of a global insurgency. There is little question that in Britain, as elsewhere, this revolt has been fertilized by the sense of many that politics as usual is not working for them. That sense of disenfranchisement is hardly surprising after decades of cuts to welfare services, ever more insecure and poorly paid forms of employment for those in work, growing levels of personal debt, as well as rising and increasingly visible levels of inequality. Consequently, the issue of immigration was at the ugly heart of Brexit debates. A racist (and not always white) English, but also Welsh and Cornish, nationalism was quickly inflamed. It targeted not just those eastern Europeans able to work in Britain as a consequence of freedom of movement within the European Union but also those people of colour (often Muslims) seeking refuge in Europe from civil wars (sometimes caused by British and NATO military interventions) in Africa and the Middle East. The line between immigrant and potential terrorist was thinly drawn, prompting a rise in 'hate crimes' during and after the vote, including the murder of a Labour MP renowned for her work with immigrants and refugees.

The Brexit debate staged a bastard history of Britain that erased its imperial past. That Britons had long enjoyed freedom of movement within their Empire, emigrating in vast numbers to 'settle' its colonies at the expense of indigenous populations, was conveniently forgotten (still in 2008 around 200,000 British citizens emigrated abroad, the vast majority across the former British world). Colonial subjects also migrated to Britain as Commonwealth citizens after the British Nationality Act in 1948, even if that right to belong was applied increasingly restrictively after 1962 and eventually revoked in 1981. To paraphrase Stuart Hall: they were over here because we were over there. The Brexit vote also mobilized a different type of racialized nostalgia for a Britain that would regain its 'independence' and sovereignty even though it remains a Union of different nations and is a member of other political groupings like NATO and the Commonwealth. It is the forgetting of Britain's imperial history that is most striking. Britons, as we have learnt in these pages, only turned to Europe as its former colonial subjects claimed their own long-denied independence. Quite how a multiracial, post-imperial, post-European Britain will reimagine itself is hard to predict even if the United Kingdom survives. What does seem clear is that Brexit is part of a seismic shift that is transforming the world and its politics, the like of which we have not seen since the late 1960s and early 1970s.

Conclusion

In the past forty years Britain has experienced a revolution no less transformative of its political, economic, social and cultural fabric than any it is history. For much of the twentieth century, Britons believed that markets had to be disciplined and planned to secure prosperity for society as a whole. Yet as a succession of global challenges to the political and economic systems that helped manage welfare capitalism in the West intensified after 1968, an evangelical faith that only unregulated markets could revive the faltering economic growth of Euro-American economies slowly grew. The **International Monetary Fund** that in 1976 first insisted that Britain's social democratic political economy had to be structurally adjusted. Within a decade, 'Thatcherism' succeeded in privatizing Britain's nationalized industries and introduced new markets to what was left of the public sector. As factories closed and urban deprivation deepened, towers of glass and steel were constructed in the City of London to house the increasingly prominent and deregulated world of financial services. The distance between rich and poor, north and south, deepened, and with them new security systems and forms of policing were developed to maintain law and order, as well as to protect the assets of the wealthy. While most Britons internalized the new priorities of looking out for themselves, there were many who insisted that collective organization was necessary to protect the rights, resources and values they held in common. If many forms of political organization and protest developed in the nineteenth century were criminalized, they were not entirely eradicated. Increasingly politics, and the articulation of alternatives to the rule of markets, took new forms and shapes on both the global and local stage.

This, then, is the history of our neoliberal present. In these pages I have proposed that only a global history of modern Britain can account for the rise, demise and reinvention of a liberal political economy that reified the market as the organizing principle of government. It is a history that is inseparable from the growth and collapse of the British Empire, as well as the continuing, if precarious, global hegemony of the American Empire which replaced it. The liberal political economy that germinated within the British Empire may have had a world system built around it, but events, processes and peoples far beyond the British world shaped the history of its rise, demise and reinvention. In that sense, the history of Britain has to be told as a global story, not because of the old imperial conceit that Britain made the world, but because the world often made Britain. This global history of the rise, fall and reinvention of liberal political economy in Britain reminds us that markets, like 'British' values and their professed **liberalism**, are neither timeless nor progressive. It is a history that reminds us that even those shibboleths that appear to be a permanent and indisputable part of the world are products of history that can be made history. In that sense, history is not just about learning what happened in the past, it is about imagining possible futures, it is about making history.

FURTHER READING

Historians have only recently begun to turn their attentions to the transformation of Britain in the past four decades. Brian Harrison's *Finding a Role? The United Kingdom, 1970–1999* (Oxford, 2010) and Peter Clarke's *Hope and Glory: Britain 1900–1990* (London, 1996) provide useful overviews of the closing decades of the twentieth century, albeit ones oriented around political developments. The earliest and most influential accounts of 'Thatcherism' were those by Stuart Hall and Martin Jacques (eds.), *The Politics of Thatcherism* (London, 1983), Stuart Hall, *The Hard Road to Renewal: Thatcherism and the Crisis of the Left* (London, 1988), and Andrew Gamble, *The Free Economy and the Strong State: The Politics of Thatcherism* (Basingstoke, 1988). More recent efforts to place Thatcherism in a longer historical frame include Eric Evans, *Thatcher and Thatcherism* (London, 1997), Ewen Green, *Thatcher* (London, 2006), and Richard Vinen, *Thatcher's Britain: The Politics and Social Upheaval of the Thatcher Era* (London, 2009). A new generation of historians, well represented in Ben Jackson and Robert Saunders (eds.), *Making Thatcher's Britain* (Cambridge, 2012), have recently entered the fray and sought to challenge the idea that Thatcherism was transformative and represented a radical break. The particular Scottish story is told in David Torrance, *We in Scotland: Thatcherism in a Cold Climate* (Edinburgh, 2009), and David Stewart, *The Path to Devolution and Change: A Political History of Scotland Under Margaret Thatcher* (London, 2009). The best account of events in Northern Ireland in the run-up to the peace process is David McKittrick and David McVea, *Making Sense of the Troubles: The Story of the Conflict in Northern Ireland* (Lanham, 2002).

Intellectual historians have importantly reminded us that 'Thatcherism' was part of a broader constellation of 'neoliberal' ideas that rejected the social democratic forms of welfare capitalism and took particular root in Anglo-America. Daniel Rodgers, *Age of Fracture* (Cambridge, Mass., 2011), and Daniel Stedman Jones, *Masters of the Universe: Hayek, Friedman, and the Birth of Neoliberal Politics* (Princeton, 2012), provide fine accounts of this intellectual shift. Shifting from the realm of theory, David Harvey's *A Brief History of Neoliberalism* (Oxford, 2005) and Monica Prasad, *The Politics of Free Markets: The Rise of Neoliberal Economic Policies in Britain, France, Germany, and the United States* (Chicago, 2006), are equally impressive comparative treatments of the spread of neoliberal policies. Thomas Piketty's *Capital in the Twenty-First Century* (Cambridge, Mass., 2014) helped refocus scholars on the growing levels of inequality in wealth in Britain, France and the United States since the 1970s.

The 'New' Labour governments of Tony Blair and Gordon Brown have not yet received much attention from historians. The first effort was made by Steven Fielding, *The Labour Party: Continuity and Change in the Making of New Labour* (Basingstoke, 2003). A growing literature exploring the neoliberal forms of New Labour's policies has emerged in other disciplines. John Clarke, *Changing Welfare, Changing States: New Directions in Social Policy* (London, 2004), and Patrick Diamond and Michael Kenny (eds.), *Reassessing New Labour: Market, State and Society Under Blair and Brown* (Oxford, 2011), are important points of departure.

While much of this work focuses on political and intellectual elites, it is considerably harder to find accounts that dwell on the changing experience of Britons at this time. Some of the best work in this vein comes from popular histories that focus on particular decades, like Andy Beckett, *When The Lights Went Out: Britain in the Seventies* (London, 2009), Alywyn Turner, *Rejoice! Rejoice! Britain in the 1980s* (London, 2010), and Andy McSmith's *No Such Thing As Society: A History of Britain in the 1980s* (London, 2010).

Paul Gilroy's *There Ain't No Black in the Union Jack: The Cultural Politics of Race and Nation* (London, 1987) remains the best account of race, policing and the framing of law and order in the 1970s and 1980s. Barbara Harford and Sarah Hopkins edited an important collection, *Greenham Common: Women at the Wire* (London, 1984), to capture the experience of the women protesting at Greenham. There are several books that do a similar job for those communities involved in the miners' strike, like *An Oral History of the Miner's Strike in a South Yorkshire Pit Village* (1986) and Hywel Francis, *History on Our Side: Wales and the 1984–1985 Miners' Strike* (Ferryside, 2009). George McKay (ed.), *DIY Culture: Party and Protest in Nineties Britain* (London, 1998), explores the pop-up political culture of the 1990s, focusing especially on the anti-road protests. The best access we have to the anti-austerity movements that followed 2008 are in David Graeber's *The Democracy Project: A History, a Crisis, a Movement* (London, 2012), Tania Palmieri and Clare Solomon (eds.), *Springtime: The New Student Rebellions* (London, 2011), and Joshua Clover, *Riot, Strike, Riot: The New Era of Uprisings* (London, 2016).

Glossary

Acts of Union Acts that unified Scotland and Ireland with England and Wales under the same political authority, thus creating the United Kingdom. The Act of Union with Scotland was in 1707 and the Act of Union with Ireland was in 1800.

Agricultural Labourers' Union Reform movement established in 1872 by Joseph Arch. It demanded higher wages, emigration schemes and the enfranchisement of rural workers. A strike in 1874 ended in collapse of membership.

air control Means of pacifying revolts or troublesome nomadic tribes across the British Empire by aerial bombardment first developed in the Middle East in 1919.

Aliens Act (1905) Britain's first official legislative measure to control immigration, particularly Jewish immigration from eastern Europe. Set up immigration controls, registration and a mechanism for deportation.

Aliens Registration Act (1914) Required foreign residents to register their presence in Britain with the police.

American War of Independence (1776–83) War fought to secure the independence of some of Britain's North American colonies. With the aid of France, the colonists won and created the United States of America. Known in Britain as the American Revolution.

Amritsar Massacre (1919) Non-violent protestors against the Rowlatt Act were shot by troops of the British Indian army, led by Brigadier-General Reginald Dyer, in a closed square in the Punjab region. The massacre fuelled the non-cooperation movement and exposed the illiberal nature of the British Raj.

ancien regime Originally a term used to describe France before the Revolution of 1989, it is now used by historians to refer to eighteenth-century Britain. Generally the term refers to a confessional state dominated by a monarch.

Anglican Church The Anglican Church, a Protestant denomination created by Henry VIII in 1534, is the official state church of England and Wales. To this day the British monarch remains head of the Church.

Anglo-Irish War (1919–1921) Also known as the Irish War of Independence, it began after Sinn Fein's won the election of 1919 and declared Ireland to be an independent republic. Fought between the Irish Republican Army on one side and the British army and Royal Irish Constabulary (including the notorious Black and Tans), it resulted in an independent, though partitioned, Irish Free State.

annual parliaments The idea that a new House of Commons would be elected each year, by an annual general election. The idea was popular among many agitating for parliamentary reform, and became one of the six demands of the **Chartists**.

Anti-Corn Law League A movement for the repeal of the **Corn Laws**, it was founded in Manchester by Richard Cobden and John Bright in 1838. The League's advocacy of free trade appealed to manufacturers as well as to the labouring classes in need of cheap bread, and identified the Corn Laws as only furthering the interests of the landowning aristocracy.

Anzac Day The commemoration of the disastrous World War I Gallipoli campaign against the Ottoman Empire in 1915, and a national holiday in Australia and New Zealand.

Ascendancy (Anglo-Irish) The term used to describe the elite that ruled Ireland from the seventeenth to the twentieth century. The Ascendancy mostly comprised English Protestant settlers, who were landowners and clergymen.

Assize Court Assize Courts were held locally twice a year as High Court judges toured the country in six circuits. The courts, which existed until 1971, usually dealt with serious crimes such as murder or treason.

Balfour Declaration (1926) Declared the Dominions and Britain to be 'autonomous communities within the British Empire, of equal status', accepting the growing drive towards political independence in the Dominions. It is often confused with another declaration made by the Foreign Secretary Arthur Balfour in 1927, committing Britain to support the creation of 'a national home for the Jewish people' in Mandate Palestine as long as it did not 'prejudice the civil and religious rights of existing non-Jewish communities' there.

Bank of England England's (and eventually Britain's) central bank, created in 1694 as part of the financial revolution. The bank was initially a mechanism for allowing private citizens to invest in Britain's national debt, allowing the state to raise money for an unprecedented military build-up in the eighteenth century. As time passed the bank became responsible for all monetary policy in Britain.

Bank Holiday Act (1871) Established uniform nationwide holidays when banks were not allowed to open.

Berlin Conference (1884–5) The major European powers convened to self-regulate colonization, particularly in Africa. They resolved to end slavery in Africa and assigned 'spheres of influence' to European powers, exacerbating the **New Imperialism** of the late nineteenth century.

Board of Trade Beginning in 1620 as a temporary committee managing trade with British colonies in North America and India, it became a permanent government body in 1786.

Bretton Woods Agreement A 1944 international agreement that established the architecture of the post-war international economy. The agreement pegged all currencies to the US dollar and established the **International Monetary Fund** and the World Bank.

Brexit   A referendum vote on the future of Britain's membership of the European Union held in June 2016.

British Nationality Act   A law passed in 1948 extending 'Commonwealth citizenship' to all colonial subjects, allowing them the right to migrate to Britain and enjoy equal access to jobs and welfare services there.

British world   A term used to describe not just the formal British Empire, but also the parts of the world that were influenced by British economic and cultural exchanges.

Cabinet   A group of members of Parliament who serve official ministerial roles in government. The body emerged out of the Privy Council of royal advisors in the eighteenth century, during which time a 'prime minister' emerged to lead the cabinet and take on many of the powers of an official head of state.

Campaign for Nuclear Disarmament (CND)   A pressure group formed in 1948 to campaign against nuclear weapons. The group mobilized a coalition of pacifists, socialists, religious organizations and women's groups with particular success between 1957 and 1963 as well as during the early 1980s when Cold War tensions reached their height.

'Captain Swing' disturbances   Widespread riots in which agricultural labourers destroyed threshing machines and invoked the mythical figure 'Captain Swing' in threatening, anonymous letters, mostly between August 1830 and December 1831.

Catholic emancipation   This was the process of removing civil restrictions imposed on Catholics in Britain. The biggest development was the Catholic Relief Act of 1829 that permitted Roman Catholics to sit in Parliament following a decade of unrest in Ireland led by Daniel O'Connell.

Chadwick, Edwin   (1800–1890) A social reformer, researcher and acolyte of Jeremy Bentham, he was secretary of the Royal Commission responsible for the New Poor Law of 1834. His research on public sanitation resulted in the *Report on the Sanitary Condition of the Labouring Population* (1842) and inspired sanitation reform.

Charity Organization Society   Established in 1869 by Octavia Hill and Helen Bosanquet, it was characterized by a 'scientific' approach to philanthropy that included detailed case work and using charity to encourage self-help rather than dependence.

Chartism   A national movement, begun in 1838, comprised largely of working men, whose Charter for political reform had six demands: universal male suffrage, annual elections, a **secret ballot**, constituencies of equal size and the abolition of all property qualifications for, and payment of, MPs.

Cheap government   The belief that government should be run cheaply, with as little National Debt or tax burden on the population as possible.

Church of England   See **Anglican Church**.

Church of Scotland   The national church in Scotland, which, like the Anglican Church, was a product of the Protestant reformation. During the seventeenth century it was established on a more radical, Presbytarian basis that included the refusal of the Anglican Book of Common Prayer and the abolition of bishops. Disputes over the boundaries between civil and ecclesiastical law after the Act of Union in 1707 led eventually to the Disruption of 1843 with the formation of the breakaway Free Church of Scotland.

City of London   Originally demarcated the walled boundaries of the medieval city but from the early eighteenth century it was used to refer to the nation's chief financial institutions which operated there.

Civil War in England   A devastating war between 1642 and 1651 that pitted supporters of Charles I against supporters of the English Parliament. Charles I was eventually defeated and executed, although monarchical governance was restored in 1660. The war was a major turning point in the constitutional development England and Wales, limiting the power of the monarchy and elevating the political status of Parliament.

clergy   The collective name for those who held offices and were responsible for the institutional practice of religion within the national churches.

Cobbett, William   A one-time farmer, military officer and **loyalist** who became a radical journalist and politician and was eventually elected as MP for Oldham in 1832. Cobbett was best known for campaigning in favour of political reform and **Catholic emancipation** and against the **Corn Laws**.

Cobden–Chevalier Treaty   A trade agreement signed in 1860 between the French and British governments to reduce the number of tariffs on traded goods between the two countries.

Cold War   A geopolitical conflict between the nations aligned with the United States (including Britain) and those aligned with the Soviet Union, lasting from 1947 until 1989. Although there was never any outright military conflict between the two superpowers, a series of proxy battles was fought in Korea, Vietnam and Afghanistan, among other places.

colonial development   The idea that economic development, through building infrastructure and promoting trade, would enrich Britain and tie colonial subjects to the Empire. A series of Colonial Development Acts were passed between 1929 and 1959.

Combination Acts   (1800) Legislation that prevented the unionization or collective mobilization of labourers. Although it was repealed in 1824, trade unions were not formally recognized by the state until 1871, when picketing remained illegal.

Committee of Reconstruction   Government committee formed in 1916 to consider post-war social and economic policies, especially in relation to issues like slums, rents and housing.

Companies Act   (1844) Made it easier for businesses to incorporate as joint-stock companies by no longer requiring royal or parliamentary approval. The limited liability of shareholders to creditors when companies made large losses or went bankrupt was not introduced until 1855.

Congo Free State   King Leopold II of Belgium's personal reign over a large area of central Africa from 1885–1908. Ostensibly justified on humanitarian and philanthropic principles, in reality it was enormously exploitative and violent.

Congress of Vienna   A meeting of European leaders and diplomats in 1814–15 after the Napoleonic War. The meeting was an attempt to solve long-standing political and territorial disputes between European powers to ensure lasting peace. The Congress is credited with ushering in a century of European political stability, while consolidating the powers of major European monarchies.

constituency   A fixed space – such as a town and its hinterland, part of a city or a rural area – that elects **a member of Parliament** (or, in some cases before 1948, multiple MPs).

Contagious Diseases Acts   Introduced in Britain in 1864, 1866 and 1868 to try and reduce the spread of sexual diseases among soldiers following the discovery that one in three had venereal disease. The Acts allowed the state to regulate prostitution in garrison towns, forcibly inspecting and confining those prostitutes with sexual diseases to a 'lock' hospital for three months.

Corn Laws   Introduced in 1815, the Corn Laws raised a tax on foreign wheat imports. Identifying them as a key element of the ancien regime's mercantilist system, proponents of free trade and liberal political economy agitated successfully for their repeal in 1846. See also **Anti-Corn Law League**.

Corrupt Practices Act   (1854, 1883) These Acts served to define what was thereafter viewed as corrupt electoral practice. They introduced official election-auditing and fines for bribery, 'treating' and intimidation of voters. The 1883 Act further outlawed the employment of election workers and placed limits on campaign expenses.

Cotton Famine   (1861–5) When supply lines of cotton imported from the American South were interrupted by the American Civil War, it caused a 'famine' of cotton for British textile mills, forcing many in Lancashire out of work or on to short-time.

Countryside Alliance   A pressure group founded in 1997 principally to oppose the banning of fox-hunting by the Labour government.

Crimewatch   A popular and long-running TV series founded in 1984. Featuring re-enactments and footage from CCTV, the show made the British public both more aware, and more fearful, of crime while asking for its help in policing it by providing information that could help 'solve' a crime and secure a prosecution.

Criminal Law Amendment Act   (1885) Raised the age of sexual consent to sixteen, enabled the prosecution of brothel keepers, and further criminalized same-sex relations between men.

Crown colony   Colonies that were governed by direct rule from London.

customs duties   Taxes charged on imported goods.

Declaration of Independence A document drawn up by 1776 by rebels in Britain's North American colonies, declaring that they would secede from British control.

Defence of the Realm Act (DORA) Passed at the outbreak of World War I in 1914, DORA gave the British government unprecedented and wide-ranging powers over social, economic and political life in Britain.

Dissenters The term used to describe Protestants who refused to accept state interference in their religious practice and thus did not recognize the authority of the established Anglican Church. By the late eighteenth century, Dissenters were also referred to as non-conformists, a category that also included those, like Methodists, who broke from the Anglican Church on other grounds.

District Officer The British government's local 'man on the spot' across its Empire. As District Officers possessed a high degree of autonomy and were often geographically isolated, much of the governance of the Empire depended upon their individual discretion.

East India Company A corporation chartered by the British Crown in 1600 that was given the monopoly of all trade with India. As the East India Company's economic, political and military control of India increased during the eighteenth century, its powers and privileges were curtailed by Parliament, culminating with its abolition in 1858 after the Great Revolt.

Easter Rising (1916) An insurrection organized by the Irish Republican Brotherhood and other republican groups that ultimately led to the capture of Dublin's General Post Office. The brutality of its defeat by British forces, including the execution of its leaders, became a defining moment for the Irish republican movement.

Electoral Register Introduced in 1832, it required electors to demonstrate in court their eligibility to vote in elections, rather than in public on the hustings as they voted.

Empire Windrush A former German cruise ship repurposed after the war by the British navy as a troopship but best known for transporting 492 immigrants from Jamaica to London in 1948.

enclosure The result of thousands of parliamentary acts between the sixteenth and the nineteenth centuries that 'enclosed' commonly owned grazing land or wilderness into privately owned property.

Enlightenment Term used to describe a diverse set of beliefs and cultural practices that emerged mainly during the long eighteenth century. Common to many of these beliefs and practices was the assumption that the world could be progressively improved once the natural laws that governed its operation had been discovered by scientific observation and rational debate.

Equal Franchise Act (1928) Gave women over twenty-one the right to vote on the same terms as men.

Equal Pay Act Passed in 1970, when women were paid on average half the salary of men, to try to reduce the discrepancy between male and female wages.

eugenics The belief that it was possible and necessary to scientifically improve the racial health of particular groups – both physically and psychologically – through good breeding, at the expense of others whose reproduction had to be limited.

European Coal and Steel Community The earliest forebear of the European Union. The ECSC was created in 1951 between six European countries to create a common market for coal and steel. Britain was not a member.

European Economic Community A 1957 treaty between six different European countries that established a customs union and common market. Britain's applications to join the union, having failed in 1963 and 1967, finally succeeded in 1973.

excise tax/duty The equivalent of a contemporary sales tax targeted at particular commodities like beer, wine, spirits, soap, coal, coffee and tobacco, but collected from merchants rather than consumers.

Factory Acts A series of laws regulating the conditions of industrial employment in the nineteenth century. They placed limits especially on the number of hours women and children of a certain age could work in factories, though these were not evenly or effectively enforced.

factory reform A political movement in the early nineteenth century targeted at improving working conditions in factories. Factory reformers wanted independent inspections, shorter working hours and the prohibition of child labour.

'First' British Empire Term for the British Empire up until the American Revolution, broadly defined as a period of mercantilist trade and territorial settlement within the Atlantic world. See also **'Third' British Empire**.

First Opium War (1839–42) A militarized conflict between Britain and China over trade. The war began when Britain refused to accept China's prohibition on imports of opium from the East India Company. The resulting Treaty of Nanking established Britain's colonial presence in the ports of Hong Kong, Canton and Shanghai.

fiscal-military state A term used to describe the development of a new type of state after 1688 whose military ambitions were financed by loans facilitated by the Bank of England and serviced by taxation revenue.

flying shuttle A device invented by John Kay in 1733 that allowed a single weaver to weave cotton thread into fabric at a faster rate. The invention was the first of a series of machines and devices invented to speed up the processing of cotton, stimulating a boom in Britain's domestic textile production in the eighteenth and nineteenth centuries.

Foreign Office The government department responsible for managing Britain's non-imperial overseas interests. It was formed in 1782, and in 1968 was merged with the Commonwealth Office and the Colonial Office, which had previously been responsible for managing Britain's imperial concerns.

four nations England, Scotland, Wales and Ireland.

free trade   The minimizing of duties, tariffs and legal barriers on trade between nations. Free trade became a popular political cause after the Napoleonic Wars, as exemplified by the movement to repeal the **Corn Laws**.

friendly societies   Mutual aid organizations that, in return for subscriptions and contributions, allowed members to help each other in case of accident, sickness, old age or death. Hugely popular in the nineteenth century, they encouraged friendliness by providing a convivial social life for many members.

garden cities   Utopian vision for urban planning devised by Ebenezer Howard in 1898, combining the order of cities with the peaceful and moralizing elements of nature and the countryside.

Geddes Axe   An attempt by the post-war coalition to reduce government spending, especially on military and welfare programmes, from 1922. It was named after Eric Geddes, a former businessman who chaired a newly created Committee of National Expenditure.

General Post Office   Britain's postal service, founded in 1660 and initially given a monopoly on the transfer of items from specific senders to receivers. This monopoly was extended to telegraph in 1869 and telephones in 1912. The Post Office's services were eventually split up and privatized from 1969.

General Registrar's Office   The state office responsible for collecting vital statistics – births, deaths and marriages – created in 1836.

General Strike   (1926) Triggered by wage cuts experienced by minors, the Trades Union Congress declared a general strike, which brought out over 2 million workers. It lasted for ten days and ended in defeat for the TUC.

Glorious Revolution   The overthrow of the Catholic James II in 1688 after the invasion of England by the Protestant William of Orange from the Netherlands at the invitation of Whig parliamentarians. William was married to James's Protestant daughter Mary. The Revolution confirmed Britain's status as a Protestant country, establishing a constitutional monarchy and renewing the authority of Parliament.

gold standard   Fixed the value of the pound to gold reserves held by the Bank of England. Established in 1821, suspended at the outbreak of World War I and resumed in 1924, it was finally abandoned in 1931.

Gordon Riots   A series of large anti-Catholic riots in London in 1780.

Great Depression   The first Great Depression (1873–96) began when a global financial crisis was triggered on the Vienna Stock Exchange, caused by over-investment in railway. The resulting collapse of commodity prices around the world inaugurated a global economic depression. The second Great Depression (1929–1939) began with a stock market crash on Wall Street that led to a collapse of commodity prices and consumer demand, as well as a steep decline in world trade and widespread unemployment.

Great Exhibition   (1851) The world's first trade fair, held in a building called the Crystal Palace, constructed for the event.

Great Famine (Ireland) (1845–52) Also known as the Potato Famine, its immediate cause was a blight on potato fields; potatoes were the staple of the Irish diet. The famine was also blamed on the long-term subjugation of Ireland to the interests of mainland Britain's economy. Over a million people died, and over 2 million emigrated.

Great Labour Unrest Wave of industrial militancy between 1910 and 1912, characterized by long strikes in vital industries, supported by large amalgamated unions.

groundnut scheme A failed **colonial development** scheme in Tanganyika in the 1950s. Thousands of acres of land were cultivated with the intention of turning the colony into a major exporter of peanuts. The project ran into environmental problems and was eventually abandoned after flooding, the discovery of poor soil conditions and a scorpion infestation.

habeas corpus A writ to ensure that only a court can decide whether someone has been legally arrested, imprisoned or detained.

History Workshop A movement founded in 1976 that encouraged 'ordinary people' to tell their own histories. It was associated with similar movements encouraging community-run publishing houses, oral history projects and community arts movements.

Home Charges The administrative fees imposed on British colonies, particularly India, for the maintenance of British rule. This included interest on loans, military charges and payments to civil servants.

Home Office Created in 1782, this is the ministerial department charged with maintaining domestic law and order.

House of Commons The lower chamber of Britain's Parliament. Unlike the House of Lords, members of the Commons are elected by specific constituencies for fixed terms.

House of Lords An unelected second chamber that traditionally consisted of peers with hereditary titles, bishops (Lords Spiritual) and leading jurists (Law Lords). Women were not allowed to sit in the Lords until 1958 and it was only in 1997 that hereditary peers lost their automatic right to sit in the Lords. Despite several subsequent attempts at reform, it remains an unelected chamber.

hunger marches Protests conducted by unemployed men to publicize their plight and demonstrate their determination to work by marching considerable distances.

hustings A raised platform purpose-built for an election contest in a central location of the constituency. On this platform candidates for election as MPs addressed their constituency and electors voted. All votes were publicly declared on the hustings in front of those assembled beneath. To reduce the often unruly crowds that gathered below them, a constituency might have many hustings, for they had to be built for every 600 electors. After the introduction of the **secret ballot** in 1872, hustings ceased to exist.

Imperial War Graves Commission Founded in 1917 to direct the task of burying those who had died across the Empire during the First World War. It has continued to do this work, and to help maintain war cemeteries across the former British Empire, ever since. In 1960 it became known as the Commonwealth War Graves Commission.

Imperial Weights and Measures Act (1824) Standardized units of measurement that designated three types: yards, pounds and gallons.

indentured labour/indentured servitude The practice of transporting labourers from one area of the Empire to another, by varying degrees of coercion, often giving passage in exchange for labour to work off the 'debt' of transport. Common in seventeenth-century England as well as the North American colonies, it became widely practised across the British Empire after the abolition of slavery in 1833. It was not abolished until 1922.

Indian National Congress (INC) A nationalist organization formed in 1885 to work towards Indian independence. Initially an elite group of Western-educated Indians, Congress was radicalized in the early twentieth century under the influence of figures such as Bal Gangadhar Tilak and Mohandas Gandhi.

Industrial Revolution Traditionally understood to entail a series of dramatic innovations in manufacturing production between 1764 and 1834 that allowed the growth of the British economy to 'take off' and far exceed its global competitors.

Institute for Community Studies Established by sociologists Michael Young and Peter Willmott in 1954. The ICS's most prominent work concerned the social effects of slum clearance in East London.

Inter-Departmental Committee on Physical Deterioration Established in 1904 to explore the problem of racial degeneration and national health.

International Monetary Fund (IMF) An organization formed in 1944 as part of the Bretton Woods Agreement to help stabilize and rebuild the international economy after the war.

Irish Land League A political movement in Ireland concerned with the land question and the plight of tenant farmers. Established in 1879 and led by Michael Davitt, it called for fair rents, fixed tenure and free sale for tenants. Its tactics of boycotting landlords and rent strikes provoked the Coercion Act and Irish Land Act of 1881.

Irish Republican Army (IRA) A paramilitary group formed in 1917 during Ireland's anti-colonial struggle. The group retained its arms after the creation of the Irish Free State in 1922, principally campaigning for northern and southern Ireland to be reunited. In the 1970s and 1980s during the northern Irish Troubles the IRA was the principal body fighting for and organizing the republican movement.

Jacobites Supporters of the deposed James II and his heirs. Jacobites led failed rebellions in 1715 and 1745 and tended to be Catholics or high church Anglicans.

jingoism Extreme, populist nationalism or patriotism, identified as an issue in Britain during the **South African War**.

joint-stock companies Companies whose stock is publically traded and can be bought and sold by private citizens. Until the **Companies Act** of 1844, these were only formed by royal charter or parliamentary legislation.

Justice of the Peace A local official, usually a member of the gentry, appointed to maintain law and order and to arrange and oversee trials and judicial hearings.

Lady Chatterley's Lover A sexually explicit 1928 novel by D.H. Lawrence that was banned after its publication for its explicit portrayal of cross-class sexual relations. The novel was re-released in 1960, resulting in a high-profile obscenity trial that the publisher, Penguin, won.

laissez-faire (French: literally, 'leave alone') The term refers to the belief of many classical political economists after Adam Smith that the state should not interfere with the market, as non-interference would produce most wealth. See also **liberal political economy**.

Langham Place Circle An elite group of women who, from the 1850s, campaigned to secure basic legal rights for women, such as property ownership, divorce and access to universities and the medical profession.

League of Nations Created in 1920 as an attempt to use international cooperation, arbitration, disarmament and collective security to perpetuate peace after the First World War.

liberal political economy A set of theories for organizing economic life, associated with Adam Smith and his followers, that championed open or free markets, international free trade, the gold standard and cheap government. The imposition of these policies across the British Empire required a great deal of state intervention despite the common belief that government should leave the economy alone.

liberalism A vision of government based on a faith in liberal political economy, religious and civil liberties, the rule of law, meritocracy and individual self-improvement.

loyalists A term used to describe those who maintained allegiance to the king and to the Church of England during the revolutionary upheavals of the late eighteenth and early nineteenth centuries.

Luddites A small and fiercely mythologized group of textile workers who destroyed spinning machines in Lancashire, primarily between 1811 and 1813.

Lugard, Frederick (Lord Lugard) A British colonial official instrumental in redefining the form and scope of the British Empire in the early twentieth century. Lugard, who served as the governor of Hong Kong and then Nigeria, argued in favor of 'indirect rule', a system whereby indigenous leaders would be ceded limited authority to govern territories under the watch of the British Empire. Lugard also insisted colonial rule had a 'dual mandate' to materially benefit both Britain and its colonies. Lugard became Britain's representative on the **League of Nations** Mandates Commission.

Magna Carta   A document signed in 1215 promising Englishmen freedom from political persecution. Although the document was never legally enforced, it was frequently invoked by those seeking political reform in the eighteenth and nineteenth centuries, as well as by politicians seeking to assert the longevity of English liberties and democracy during the twentieth century.

Malthus, Thomas   An Anglican priest whose *Essay on the Principle of Population*, published in 1798, argued that sustained population growth in Britain was impossible because food supplies could never increase at a fast enough rate. Malthus's work became a central reference in the development of classical political economy and, later, the study of demography.

Manchester school   A term used to describe advocates of liberal political economy in the nineteenth century. As a city of merchants and manufacturers and the headquarters of the **Anti-Corn Law League**, Manchester was closely associated with the politics of **free trade**.

Mandates   The former Ottoman territories in the Middle East and German colonies in Africa delegated to British and French colonial control by the Treaty of Versailles and the League of Nations.

Married Women's Property Acts   (1879 and 1882) Allowed women to inherit and own property, as well as to earn income from it, establishing a separate legal personality from their husbands.

Marshall Plan   Also known as the European Recovery Programme. The USA invested $13 billion in rebuilding the infrastructure and economies of war-torn Europe in 1948 so as to prevent the spread of communism.

martial races   Specific castes or tribes in India identified by ethnographers as particularly loyal and militaristic, and thus over-represented in the British Indian army.

Mass Observation   A social research organization established in 1937 to investigate the culture and politics of the mass society, using ethnography and anthropological methods of inquiry.

Matrimonial Causes Act   (1857) Ensured that divorce cases no longer had to be held in Parliament.

Mau Mau   Kikuyu-dominated groups that staged an anti-colonial rebellion in Kenya, resulting in a brutal military counter-insurgency campaign between 1952 and 1960. During the conflict British forces interred hundreds of thousands of Kikuyu Kenyans in a network of concentration camps with high mortality rates.

members of Parliament (MPs)   Those elected to represent constituencies and sit in the House of Commons, Britain's lower chamber of Parliament.

mercantilism   The belief that as bullion, land and labour were the source of all wealth, and there was a finite supply of each in the world, governments would best enrich themselves through the imperial conquest of territories and their resources. Mercantilists favoured monopolistic companies to conduct trade overseas and high tariff barriers to protect domestic markets. It remained dominant across much of Europe into the nineteenth century.

Middle Passage   The weeks-long sea voyage from West Africa to the Caribbean or North America that was endured by millions of slaves in the seventeenth, eighteenth and nineteenth centuries. The voyage was a horrific experience, one that resulted in the deaths of 15 per cent of those who experienced it.

miners' strike   (1984) A strike that became a high-profile showdown between the National Union of Mineworkers and Margaret Thatcher's government. The strike, which began after the announcement that twenty pits would be closed, lasted almost a year and was eventually defeated by the government.

Ministry of Munitions   Established with Lloyd George at its head, the new ministry directed the wartime economy towards the massive production of ammunition and other war-necessitated products.

Mitchel, John   Nineteenth-century Protestant Irish nationalist, who connected the Great Famine to the English imposition of liberal political economy in Ireland, and called for an 'Irish' political economy.

Municipal Corporations Act   (1835) A reform of local government that insisted 178 incorporated towns (with a corporation charged with governing the town's affairs) create elected town councils. It also allowed unincorporated towns to become incorporated, and enabled incorporated towns to establish police forces.

music halls   Growing out of saloon theatres in the 1850s, these offered entertainment on stage as well as alcohol and sociability off stage. They were largely attended by working-class people.

nabob   Originally a Mughal term for a political official, the term came to refer to Europeans who made a fortune in India by corrupt means.

Napoleonic Wars   (1803–15) A war between Napoleon's France and various different European states and coalitions. The war saw Napoleon conquer vast swathes of Europe, although he was eventually defeated and overthrown.

national debt   The money borrowed by the state from private citizens and interests. Created during the 1690s, it enabled the British state to fund its military campaigns. Interest on the loans was paid from taxation revenue and provided lenders a stable rate of return on their investment.

national efficiency   A term used in the late nineteenth and early twentieth centuries, as international competition intensified, to refer to efforts to increase the productive potential of a nation-state, whether economically, socially or culturally.

National Government   A government formed in 1931 when no single party, following the split within the previously elected government of the Labour Party, had enough MPs to form a majority in the House of Commons. Coalition governments, consisting of ministers from all parties, were also formed during World War One and World War Two.

National Union of Women's Suffrage Societies (NUWSS)   Established in 1897 by Lydia Becker and Millicent Fawcett as an umbrella organization for advocates of women's right to vote, it demanded propertied women receive the vote on the same terms as men.

National Union of Working Classes and Others   A reform and suffrage movement, founded in 1831, that was oriented more explicitly around working men than Political Unions were.

Navigation Acts   A series of laws that effectively granted British merchants a monopoly on all imperial trade. Lasting from 1661 until they were abolished in 1849, the Acts made it illegal for non-British ships to carry goods and to trade within the British Empire. This ensured that North American or Indian producers were forced to carry their trade through Britain's ports rather than trade directly with her rival European powers.

neoliberalism   The term used to describe a loose set of economic and political ideas that reify the free market as a principle of government. Associated with the deregulation of trade, capital and labour markets, the privatization of public services and the increasing ubiquity of finance capital, neoliberalism has been broadly dominant in Euro-America since the 1980s.

New Feminism   A feminist programme that went beyond the question of the suffrage and equality before the law by including social issues like equal pay, contraception and the need for the state to support women's work as mothers.

New Imperialism   The acceleration of imperial expansion, and the increased rate of territorial claims, across the world in the late nineteenth and early twentieth centuries.

New Journalism   Developed from a new style of journalism that emphasized the importance of making rather than simply reporting news, with investigative reporting that was sometimes sensationalist in tone in order to sell papers and spur public debate.

New Liberalism   While adhering to certain core attributes of liberalism, like individualism, free trade, free press and civil rights, the liberalism of the early twentieth century featured a more activist state focused on providing state-sponsored solutions to social problems like poverty and unemployment.

New Poor Law   A reform of the poor law introduced in 1834. It established a centralized Poor Law Commission which issued directives to new local Poor Law Unions that relief should be minimal and only afforded to those incarcerated in workhouses where families were separated.

New Unionism   Developing from the 1880s, New Unionism organized across divisions of skill and craft within particular sectors (like transport workers) in ways that generated higher membership among semi-skilled and unskilled workers. New Unionism was also characterized by more explicitly socialist aims and tactics.

Nine Years' War   A Europe-wide war in the late seventeenth century that saw King Louis XIV of France engage in conflict with various other states and coalitions.

North Atlantic Treaty Organization (NATO)   A Cold War treaty signed in 1949 that created a military alliance between twelve countries, including the USA, Britain, Canada, France and Italy, that pledged them to mutual defence of each other – ostensibly against the Soviet Union.

Northcote-Trevelyan Report   Written by Charles Trevelyan and Stafford Northcote in 1854, as the state's administrative functions were rapidly growing, to argue that appointments should no longer be driven by politics or patronage. Instead they proposed a new 'civil service' structured by competitive recruiting, meritocratic promotions and an elite group of generalists to oversee expert specialists.

Old Corruption   A term used by parliamentary reformers in the late eighteenth century to describe a political system that enabled the aristocratic elite to advance their own interests and enrich themselves through 'rotten' parliamentary constituencies, bribes and sinecures.

Opium Wars   See First Opium War.

Order of the White Feather   A women's group that pressured men to volunteer to fight during the First World War and called for universal male conscription.

Ordnance Survey   Large-scale mapping of the entirety of Great Britain, begun in England and Wales in 1791 and extended to Ireland in 1824 and Scotland in 1843.

organically powered economy   An economy whose primary source of energy comes from wood and plants rather than fossil fuels. This was the case in Britain before the **Industrial Revolution**.

Panopticon   A template for institutional buildings (prisons, asylums, factories, schools and so forth) developed by Jeremy Bentham, and designed to allow observation of inmates from a central point.

parish   The geographical area of ecclesiastical governance surrounding a church. Before the early nineteenth century, these were important political units responsible for the administration of the poor law, policing and local roads.

party whips   Parliamentary party officers responsible for making sure MPs vote according to the instruction of party leaders.

'pauper press'   Most often referred to newspapers that were cheaper because they refused to pay stamp duties and taxes. These were widely read by the working classes.

Penny Post   Introduced in 1840, it created a single, cheap and universal rate for letters to be delivered across the entire country.

People's Budget   Introduced by David Lloyd George while serving as Chancellor of the Exchequer in 1909, it raised taxes (including income tax for higher income brackets and estate tax) to fund new welfare measures, including Old Age Pensions and National Insurance.

Permanent Settlement   A reform of land ownership in late eighteenth-century Bengal. The system called for 'zamindars' (landholders) to pay a fixed rent to the British East India Company, in return for permanent hereditary ownership of their land.

Peterloo Massacre   The name coined to describe an occasion when cavalry charged into a demonstration for reform on St Peter's Fields, Manchester, in 1819, killing fifteen.

Petty Sessions   A small local magistrate court without a jury.

Plaid Cymru   A Welsh nationalist party founded in 1925.

Police Act   (1856) Made a police force compulsory for all towns and counties.

Political Unions   Reform movement founded in Birmingham in 1829. Its members generally called for the vote for all adult men, annual elections and a **secret ballot**.

Powell, Enoch   A Conservative MP best known for his 'Rivers of Blood' speech in 1968 that condemned non-white immigration to the UK. Powell was also an early advocate of neoliberal policies.

prime minister   The head of the British government. At first appointed by the monarch from his cabinet of advisors, the prime minister today still cannot form a government without the monarch's approval. However, from the early nineteenth century, monarchs increasingly selected the leader of the largest political party in the House of Commons, and members of Parliament became responsible for selecting their own party leaders. It was not until the late twentieth century that regular members of some political parties were allowed to vote in elections for their leaders.

Prime Minister's Questions   The conventional practice of the prime minister answering questions from MPs in the House of Commons.

Primrose League   Established by the Conservative Party in 1883 to rally men, women and children around recreational and ceremonial events, creating a party culture that was only tangentially related to high party politics. This was exemplified by the disproportionate involvement of women, who could not vote.

Private Finance Initiative (PFI)   A mechanism for using public funds to raise capital loans to construct and maintain new hospitals, roads and schools for a designated period. PFIs were first developed by Australian governments in the 1980s and were taken up in Britain by the Conservative and Labour government of the 1990s.

protectorate   A means of 'indirect rule' over colonies in which local princes, sheikhs, etc. retained considerable political and legislative power.

Public Health Act   (1848) An effort to promote sanitary measures by enabling towns to establish local boards of health on an adoptive basis (and mandated such for towns whose mortality rate exceeded 23 per 1,000). Local boards of health were made mandatory for all localities in 1875.

putting-out system   A system of production that preceded and, later, worked alongside the factory system. In this system tasks, such as textile weaving, were outsourced to individual households.

Quarter Sessions   Courts held four times a year at county level.

Race Relations Act   A 1965 law that outlawed racial discrimination in public places and established a Race Relations Board to adjudicate cases.

rational recreation   The idea that leisure time should be spent engaging in the pursuit of self-improvement, rather than pleasure or pastimes considered immoral.

Reform Act of 1832   The first major reform of the electoral system, it sought to remove customary but irregular voting rights. It made voting contingent on a property qualification: in boroughs, men renting or owning property worth £10 per year could vote; the qualification in the counties was 40 shillings per year on freehold property. A number of 'rotten boroughs' were abolished and some parliamentary seats were redistributed.

Reform Act of 1867   The second major reform of the electoral system, it extended the franchise by reducing the property thresholds put in place in 1832. Borough franchise was extended to all male ratepayers and lodgers paying at least £10 per year in rent, and to those in the counties occupying property rated at £12 per year or those owning land worth £5 a year.

Reform Act of 1884   The third major reform of the electoral system, it removed the county/borough divide in property qualifications, giving the vote to male ratepayers and lodgers occupying properties worth £10 a year.

Reform League   Reform group founded in 1865 that led the agitation for the Second Reform Act of 1867.

Representation of the People Act   (1918) Granted the vote to returning male veterans over twenty-one; women over thirty who were either members of or married to a member of the Local Government Register, property owners, or graduates with a university constituency vote; and some women who had served in the Auxiliary Corps or the Red Cross during the First World War. It disenfranchised men who had refused military service during the war.

'revolution in government'   A series of reforms in the nineteenth century that transformed the British government along the lines of an Enlightened science of government around liberal principles.

Right to Buy   A scheme introduced in 1980 to allow the residents of public council housing to cheaply purchase their homes below market rates.

Robbins Report   A 1963 government report that recommended a dramatic expansion of higher education to ensure greater social mobility as well as the growth and competitiveness of the British economy.

'rotten' or 'pocket' borough   A symbol of the 'unreformed' electoral system, these boroughs were either sparsely populated with electors or had a landowner as the only elector, but were able to send an MP to Parliament.

Rowlatt Act   Passed in 1919, this Act extended emergency measures of the First World War's Defence of India Act (1915), stifling the press, popular political action and sedition. A focal point of anti-colonial reformers, it was the subject of the protests at **Amritsar** that were infamously repressed.

Royal Statistical Society   A charity and learned society for the promotion of statistics, established in 1834.

scientific management   A way of organizing workers and workplaces for maximum efficiency and output. It refers to a host of practices, from the data-driven analysis of workflows to the provision of better light, ventilation and nutrition to improve workers' productivity.

Scottish Highlands   The mountainous northern reaches of Scotland. This region has historically remained distinct, both from England and from 'lowland' Scotland. Until the eighteenth century the area was ruled by a handful of Gaelic-speaking clans, who supported and aided the **Jacobite** Risings of 1715 and 1745.

Scottish National Party (SNP)   The principal political party calling for Scotland's independence as a nation. The SNP was founded in 1934 but was a relatively minor political force until the 1970s.

Scramble for Africa   Following the **Berlin Conference**, the European powers aggressively laid claim to African territories in the era of the **New Imperialism**.

secret ballot   The practice of casting a vote in secret, usually behind a screen on a ballot paper upon which the names of the candidates were printed. Introduced for parliamentary elections in 1872, the secret ballot was ostensibly a means of countering corruption and outside influence.

self-governing colonies   Allowed a degree of political independence within the British Empire that was afforded almost exclusively to the white settler colonies that became known as Dominions.

self-help   The practice of self-improvement that also became the title of the influential 1859 book by Samuel Smiles encouraging men to develop their industry, fiscal responsibility and sober morality.

Separate spheres   The idea that men and women were best suited to different and separate spheres of life. Men's capacity for reason allowed them to operate in the sinful public world; while women, as innocent and irrational creatures of biology, should stay at home and care for their husbands and children.

Settlement Houses   Associated with the new philanthropy of the late nineteenth and early twentieth centuries, these were dwellings situated in impoverished urban areas where students or middle-class reformers could live among the poor whom they helped.

Seven Years' War   A war principally fought between Britain, France and Spain that spanned Europe, North and South America, India and Africa between 1756 and 1763. Britain's victory laid the territorial groundwork for its future empires in India and North America, with Britain gaining control of a central stripe of the North American continent, a number of Caribbean sugar islands and parts of Bengal.

shell-shock   A term coined in 1915 to describe the mental breakdowns experienced by soldiers at the Front during the First World War. Its treatment eventually became an important inroad for psychoanalytic practice in Britain.

Six Acts   A suite of repressive legislation introduced in 1819, following the Peterloo Massacre, that effectively banned mass meetings, imposed stamp duties and new definitions of sedition to restrict the 'freedom' of the radical press, and allowed the inspection of any property for arms.

Smith, Adam   The author of *The Wealth of Nations* in 1776, Smith was an early advocate of free trade and a critic of mercantilism.

Smuts, Jan   Military leader, politician and eventually prime minister of South Africa. As a member of the British Imperial War Cabinet during the Great War, Smuts was one of the founders of the idea of the British Commonwealth. He argued that Britain could rival the superpowers of the United States and the Soviet Union by forming a closer union with the commonwealth. As an advocate of racial segregation in South Africa, his view of the British Commonwealth was highly racialized.

Social democracy   The system of government developed after World War Two to deliver social security for all through a mixed economy of public and private ownership as well as the state provision of universal rights to welfare services.

The social question   The prevailing concern with the social condition of Britain during industrialization and urbanization. Social issues like poverty and sanitation were seen as separate from, and unconnected to, Britain's economic transformation.

South African (Boer) War   Fought between Britain and the Transvaal Republic and Orange Free State from 1899 to 1902. It resulted in the consolidation of the British Empire in South Africa, and was characterized by guerilla warfare and the British use of concentration camps to hold civilian populations. Over half of the war's 75,000 dead were civilians.

South Sea Bubble   The first collapse of London's stock market in 1720. It was caused by speculative over-investment in the stock of the South Sea Company, created in 1711 to facilitate imperial trade and colonization in the Pacific.

Spare Rib   A feminist magazine founded in 1972 that became one of the mouthpieces for the women's liberation movement in Britain.

Statute of Westminster   (1931) Established the legislative independence of the Empire's self-governing Dominions.

Sterling Area   A group of countries, primarily from the British Empire, whose currencies were pegged to the value of the British pound, beginning in the 1930s.

structural adjustment   Loans by the IMF or the World Bank to countries facing economic difficulties, in return for a set of reforms (usually privatization of infrastructure, lowering of trade barriers and deregulation of the economy).

Sturges Bourne Act   (1818) Introduced a sliding scale of voting at **parish** meetings: the more property one owned, the more votes one had.

Suez Crisis   A military and diplomatic crisis initiated by the nationalization of the Suez Canal by the Egyptian president Gamal Abdel Nasser in 1956. Britain, France and Israel launched a brief military incursion to regain control of the canal but were forced to cease the operation by the United States.

Swadeshi movement A phase of the Indian nationalist movement, developed in the early twentieth century, most famously by Mohandas Gandhi after 1918, that called for economic self-determination and criticized British-led industrialization in India. It included boycotts of British cotton in favour of handmade Indian textiles, among other things.

tariff A tax on goods that are imported into or exported from a given state. Tariffs are usually imposed to stimulate or protect domestic industries.

Teddy Boys A subculture of smartly dressed young working-class men in the 1950s, often associated with the new music of rock and roll, who were frequently responsible for violent attacks on black Britons.

temperance movement A broad social movement against the consumption of alcohol that began in the early nineteenth century. Temperance reformers pushed for tighter licensing laws and built temperance halls as alternatives to pubs, for sober **rational recreation**.

Test and Corporation Acts Series of laws dating back to 1673 that imposed numerous civil disabilities on non-Anglicans. Its repeal in 1828, along with the Catholic Emancipation Act in 1829, allowed non-Anglicans to hold public office. See also **Catholic emancipation**.

'Third' British Empire Term to describe the last stage of British imperialism, organized around protective tariffs, the Sterling Area and colonial development policies in service of Britain's economy.

Tory A member of Parliament who championed the authority of the monarch over Parliament, the supremacy of the established Anglican Church, mercantilist economic policies that saw land (not trade) as the source of wealth, and imperial expansion. Although liberal Tories began moving away from these policies in the 1810s and 1820s, they were finally abandoned during the 1840s, when the Tories were rebranded as the Conservative Party.

Trades Union Congress An alliance of trade unions formed in 1868 to pressure Parliament to address the interests of labour more generally.

transportation A punishment for crimes in the seventeenth, eighteenth and nineteenth centuries. Transportation involved being forcibly deported to British colonies to carry out hard labour. British colonies in North America and later Australia were common destinations.

Treasury The ministerial body in charge of the state's finances.

Tull, Jethro An agricultural reformer who invented the horse-drawn seed drill in 1701. The invention allowed seeds to be planted in neat rows, initiating a sustained period of improved agricultural efficiency.

turnpike roads Toll roads. Turnpikes were created by individual Acts of Parliament that granted an individual or a corporation the right to charge tolls in order to fund the construction and maintance of a road.

universal male suffrage The right of every man (usually above a certain age) to vote. This was a key demand of the Chartists and other electoral reformers. Universal male suffrage (above the age of twenty-one) was granted in 1918.

urbanization The rapid growth of British towns and cities in the eighteenth and nineteenth centuries.

vestry A committee of ratepayers that would assemble to govern the affairs of a **parish**.

wakes week A week-long holiday held in a local **parish** every year at the time of the saint's day after which the parish church was named.

War of the Spanish Succession (1702–13) A major European war prompted by an uncertain line of succession to the Spanish Empire. As a result of the conflict, Britain expanded its territorial holdings in Canada.

welfare state The provision of universal welfare services – especially health, education, family allowance, unemployment benefit and pensions – by the state to its population.

Whigs Members of Parliament who championed the rights of Parliament over the monarch, the toleration of Dissent, the military defeat of Catholic rivals on the continent of Europe and, increasingly, the promotion of trade and commerce, cheap government and electoral reform. Although most Whigs became part of the new Liberal Party in the 1860s, those who remained hostile to electoral reform and home rule for Ireland broke away to become Conservatives in the 1880s.

The White Man's Burden The title of an 1899 Rudyard Kipling poem, and shorthand for the justification of Anglo-American imperialism as a duty to bring 'backwards' people into civilization, industry and health.

Women's Freedom League Broke away from the **Women's Social and Political Union** in 1907 to promote non-violent resistance.

Women's Social and Political Union Founded in 1903 by Emmeline and Christabel Pankhurst, this was the more radical and confrontational wing of the women's suffrage movement, known for civil disobedience and large rallies. It argued that women should receive the vote *because* of their differences from men.

Workmen's Compensation Act (1897) Made industrial accidents and injuries on the job the liability of the employer rather than the employee.

Wilson, Woodrow President of the United States of America from 1913 to 1921.

Index